FOURTH EDITION

Contemporary Management Theory

Controlling and Analyzing Costs in Foodservice Operations

James Keiser
Pennsylvania State University, Retired

Frederick J. DeMicco
Pennsylvania State University

with Robert N. Grimes
Cyntergy Corporation

Prentice Hall
Upper Saddle River, New Jersey   *Columbus, Ohio*

Library of Congress Cataloging-in-Publication Data
Keiser, James
    Contemporary management theory : controlling and analyzing costs
in foodservice operations / James Keiser, Frederick J. DeMicco, with
Robert N. Grimes. — 4th ed.
        p.   cm.
    Previous eds. published under title: Controlling and analyzing
costs in foodservice operations.
    ISBN 0–13–083908–6
    1. Food service—Cost control.   2. Food service—Cost
effectiveness.   I. DeMicco, Frederick.   II. Grimes, Robert N.
III. Keiser, James   Controlling and analyzing costs in
foodservice operations.   IV. Title.
TX911.3.C65K43 2000
647.95'068'1—dc21   99–23913
                                                                    CIP

Cover photo: © Super Stock
Editor: Neil W. Marquardt
Editorial Assistant: Susan Kegler
Production Editor: Linda Hillis Bayma
Production Coordination: Carlisle Publishers Services
Design Coordinator: Diane C. Lorenzo
Illustrations: Carlisle Communications, Ltd.
Cover Designer: Dan Eckel
Production Manager: Laura Messerly
Marketing Manager: Shannon M. Simonsen
Marketing Assistant: Adam Kloza

This book was set in Garamond Light by Carlisle Communications, Ltd. and was printed and bound
by R.R. Donnelley & Sons Company. The cover was printed by Phoenix Color Corp.

Printed in the United States of America

10 9 8 7 6 5 4 3 2 1

ISBN: 0-13-083908-6

Prentice-Hall International (UK) Limited, London
Prentice-Hall of Australia Pty. Limited, Sydney
Prentice-Hall of Canada, Inc., Toronto
Prentice-Hall Hispanoamericana, S.A., Mexico
Prentice-Hall of India Private Limited, New Delhi
Prentice-Hall of Japan, Inc., Tokyo
Prentice-Hall (Singapore) Pte. Ltd., Singapore
Editora Prentice-Hall do Brasil, Ltda., Rio de Janeiro

About the Authors

James Keiser is a graduate of Cornell School of Hotel Administration and Wharton School of the University of Pennsylvania. He is a retired professor of hotel and institution management at the Pennsylvania State University. Mr. Keiser has also been employed as a hospitality consultant, hotel manager, hospital foodservice director, food cost accountant, and hospital administration officer in the U.S. Air Force. He is the author of *Principles and Practices of Management in the Hospitality Industry,* published by Van Nostrand Reinhold, 1989.

Frederick J. DeMicco is associate director and associate professor in the School of Hotel, Restaurant, and Recreation Management at Pennsylvania State University, where he is professor-in-charge of the HR&IM undergraduate program. Dr. DeMicco teaches courses in international management, foodservice management, and leadership, with research in the areas of cost control, total quality management, gerontology, and managed services. His research in the hospitality industry spans the life cycle from children to older employees and mature customers. Dr. DeMicco serves on the editorial board of the *Hospitality Research Journal,* as well as several other research journal editorial boards.

Robert N. Grimes is Chairman and CEO of CynterCorp, located in Gaithersburg, Maryland. Mr. Grimes founded Cyntergy in 1988, which focused on providing computer support services to the hotel, foodservice, and retail industries. Under his guidance, Cyntergy has been expanded and repositioned within CynterCorp to offer these industries a range of technology-related solutions and products. In 1996, Mr. Grimes co-founded, with *Nation's Restaurant News,* an international foodservice technology tradeshow and conference known as FS/TEC. Mr. Grimes has received many industry awards, including the Greater Washington 1994 Entrepreneur of the Year award sponsored by *Inc.,* Ernst & Young, and Merrill Lynch.

Preface

The first edition of this book appeared in 1974 and the third edition in 1993. Earlier editions concentrated on the management function of cost control. This was based on the assumption that profit was the difference between sales and costs and usually more could be accomplished in controlling costs than increasing sales in an individual operation. (In non-profit operations, the control of costs could provide more benefits to clients.) Even with the intended stress on cost control, some academic programs thought of the book as more of a food accounting book and others as a food management text.

Foodservice operation has changed greatly from the first edition and even the third. Today operators and educators, although very concerned with costs, are also concerned with other management roles. The computer, with its data processing and management information systems, can be usefully integrated into almost every area of foodservice operation and has radically affected concepts and mechanics of foodservice operation. This change has been so dramatic that we were very happy when Rob Grimes, an international authority on computerization in food service, agreed to contribute his knowledge in this area.

In addition to computer developments, there have been developments in various areas of management that can be applied to food service. To better address the needs of students interested in the contemporary world of food management, we have changed the focus of the book from control in food operations to the broader area of modern food management. There are now added chapters on management theory and organization (chapter 1), total quality management (chapter 3), systems approach (chapter 4), and marketing (chapter 7). Another new chapter (chapter 5) discusses a feasibility study with a business plan and financing. This chapter should be helpful to those who plan to start a new operation or change a present one. The chapter on management information systems (chapter 6) has been greatly expanded and other chapters integrated with it. Other existing chapters have been updated. An unusual addition is the Industry Insights feature, where industry experts share their wisdom independent of the authors.

To better reflect the new focus of the book, the title has been changed to *Contemporary Management Theory: Controlling and Analyzing Costs in Foodservice Operations*. It is the belief of the authors that although changes in this edition are very substantial and will enhance and change the book, the essential material from earlier editions remains.

ACKNOWLEDGMENTS

A book such as this requires expertise in a number of areas, and we are fortunate that a number of experts in various fields were willing to share their knowledge with us.

Although many were involved, we would especially like to thank some colleagues in the Penn State Hotel, Restaurant and Institutional Management program. They include Dr. Arun Upneja, Dr. John Williams, Mr. Peter Yersin, Dr. David Cranage, Ms. Patricia Silfies, Mr. Jim Poffley, and Mr. Marc Lubetkin. We can't thank Christina Breda of CynterPubs too much. Christina was invaluable in securing industry examples and illustrations as well as in assisting Rob with his work.

A work such as this also requires support from one's family. Appreciation must go to our wives, Josephine Keiser, Kristen Cyphers DeMicco, and Beth Grimes. Fred's daughters, Courtney, Kyleigh, Lauren, and Kendra, and Rob's daughters, Lauren and Melissa, were also patient and supporting.

Bonnie Henninger deserves much credit in typing and preparing the manuscript.

Finally, we would like to thank the following people who reviewed this edition: Carl P. Borchgrevink, Michigan State University; Janet W. Gloeckner, James Madison University; Rebecca Gould, Kansas State University; James R. McClain, California State University, Fullerton; Lawrence E. Ross, Florida Southern College; and Hubert B. Van Hoof, Northern Arizona University. We also thank the reviewers of the previous edition: John R. Dienhart, Kansas State University; Janet W. Gloeckner, James Madison University; and Cheri Suttle, University of South Carolina, Columbia.

James Keiser
Fred J. DeMicco
Robert N. Grimes

Brief Contents

Contents

Management and Organization in the Foodservice Industry

Throughout this text management is approached and utilized in many different ways. In this chapter, we consider some of the different theories of management which may later arise in specific applications. This chapter also discusses the management function of organization which is necessary for any operation.

After completing this chapter you should be able to:

1. Provide a definition of management.
2. Describe the characteristics of management.
3. Appreciate the goals of management.
4. Utilize principles of classical and behavioral approaches to management.
5. Describe the types of organizations.
6. Appreciate how the informal organization interacts with the formal organization.
7. Define the culture of an organization.
8. Understand how management can change in a cybernetic age.
9. Appreciate the roles of status, power, and politics in an organization.
10. Apply principles of re-engineering.

To be successful, a food service organization (or any other organization) must have management. The organization may have the prime goal of producing a profit for its owners. The manager of a nonprofit operation tries to produce the best products or services that available resources permit. In either situation the better the management the better the results. Despite its importance, no single accepted definition of management exists. Different approaches have been and will be successful in different times and circumstances.

Many notable individuals have made contributions to food service management. A few that come to mind are Auguste Escoffier, the king of chefs and chef of kings who made important contributions in kitchen organization, equipment, respect for employees, recipe formulation, and product merchandising. Elsworth Statler, a leading hotelier of his time, introduced food cost accounting, uniform restaurants in his various hotels, and standard recipes. The Stouffer family stressed standards in production and service, training of employees, and functioning with cooks, rather than chefs, to produce quality food at reasonable prices in their many restaurants. Howard Johnson introduced commissionary production for his chain. Ray Kroc of McDonalds and Colonel Sanders of Kentucky Fried Chicken provided (perhaps unwittingly) a systems operating concept, financing through franchising, and mass marketing techniques. The Marriott organization has made many management contributions in such areas as employee compensation, total quality management, and general management techniques. In this chapter we will begin with theoretical management concepts and then proceed to specific management applications in food service operations and special types of management, such as financial or marketing management. A great deal of emphasis will be on the management function of control.

MANAGEMENT DEFINED

Here is a sampling of definitions of management one might find in textbooks, business journals, and academic studies. Management is:

- *Getting things done through others.* This behavioristic definition of management assumes that because management can be accomplished only through people, the consideration of how to motivate these people and satisfy their needs should precede all other considerations.

- *Effectively utilizing resources to achieve personal and organization goals.* According to this definition, the manager has a number of resources at his disposal, and his job is to coordinate them for the best benefit of the organization. The usual resources are typically referred to as the six Ms of management: men (personnel), materials, methods, machines, money, and markets. These are what the manager and the organization have to work with. If there is no management, the goals of the operation may not be achieved, despite an abundant supply of each M.

- *Making decisions.* This definition assumes that the primary job of the manager is to make the decisions that assure the organization's continuation and success. The operations-research approach to management is heavily oriented toward decision making.

- *Working cooperatively as a group toward a common goal.* Here management is seen as a process. Common goals are assumed to have been formulated, and the cooperation or group effort to achieve these goals is emphasized.

- *Establishing and achieving objectives.* This definition accents the goal-oriented nature of management in which the success of management is determined by how well it achieves its goals.

- *Planning, organizing, controlling, staffing, directing, representing, and innovating.* Though not really a definition, this list of the functions of management is usually included under the management-science approach. If a manager can perform these functions, she should theoretically be able to run any operation. The list of management functions varies among management theorists, but planning, organizing, and controlling almost always appear.

- *Guiding human and physical resources into dynamic and viable organization units that obtain objectives to the satisfaction of those served with a high degree of morale and sense of attainment on the part of those providing the service.* This long-winded definition includes both the idea of optimum utilization of the management resources and a behavioral consideration for both the customers of the operation and its personnel.

- *Serving as a factor of production.* This definition dates back to Adam Smith (1723–90), who considered management along with land, labor, and capital to be parts of the production process. There can be no doubt that, as intangible as management may be, it is also a very definite resource. Developing countries may find their development helped or hindered by the amount of management talent available. Thus, management has also been considered as a class or an elite that can help fellow members of society toward a better life through more effective utilization of the resources available to them.

CHARACTERISTICS OF MANAGEMENT

The preceding definitions suggest a number of different approaches to the study of management. In analyzing these various definitions, it may be easier to think of management's general characteristics. First, it is *goal oriented.* Good management must know where it is going and what it is trying to accomplish. Therefore, it must have goals. The planning and decision-making functions become critical in formulating these goals, and the success of management can, in fact, be measured by how well it achieves its goals. Of course, this measurement assumes the goals are realistic and obtainable. If not, it may be necessary to change the goals for the best interests of the organization. The function of control, in particular, may indicate how well goals are being met. Food service managers should know what they want to achieve in terms of service, quality, new business, and profit. Without goals managers flow with the tide, which may mean out to sea. How well managers achieve realistic goals is the measure of their success.

Associated closely with goal orientation are *responsibility and accountability.* Managers must work both toward organizational goals and toward completing the specific tasks at hand properly. In other words, management is responsible for its own goals and for those of subordinates. One problem goals present is that they compete for the operation's resources. Thus, management must establish goal priorities, which forces managers and/or owners to become resource allocators, deciding which individual or unit gets priority in the distribution of available resources.

Particularly in enterprises in which the product is service and tends to be handcrafted, *management concerns itself with people.* Quite often managerial success is measured by how well managers can motivate and stimulate the people they direct. Successful managers not centered on people work in the food service field, but they usually have exceptional strengths in other areas and work with somebody who can deal effectively with people problems. Even though they experience success, these managers would be even more successful with a people orientation. The food service industry is a people industry. In a factory, managers need to deal only with the employees as people. In a retail establishment, dealing with the individual customers becomes the main focus. In the hospitality industry, however, managers must deal with employees and customers at the same time. An interest in people is therefore a prime reason for joining the hospitality profession.

Management usually requires a *coordination of effort,* a number of people working together rather than people working individually. Effort coordination is crucial because, despite individual motivation, uncoordinated businesses tend to be weak and unfocused. Their approach tends to be hit-or-miss, and their successes tend to be a matter of luck.

The need for coordination, in fact, bespeaks a need for management. Such complicated service establishments as restaurants require more coordination than many simpler nonservice businesses.

Management is not passive. An organization, along with its resources and its environment, constantly changes. If it is to survive and prosper, management must both change and influence change. A common fault among managers (with all of us, in fact) is that they prefer to do those things that interest them, ignoring other equally important tasks. Managers of foodservice operations may be fascinated by food production. But if they spend all their time with this one function, the operation is in for a hard time. One solution would be for managers to delegate appropriate authority and responsibility for other concerns to someone qualified in those other areas. Fast-food operations took over from more traditional restaurants because they better responded to demographic and societal changes.

ENVIRONMENTS OF MANAGEMENT

Management cannot be passive because no food service or other management operates in a vacuum. Management feels forces and stresses from both within and outside the organization. Effective managers must therefore understand these forces and adapt to them and, in some cases, adapt them to their purposes. The forces arising from outside the operation are called the *external environment.* Forces within the operation are part of the *internal environment,* as Figure 1.1 illustrates.

External forces include the general economic level, political conditions, and cultural and social changes. The external environment may quite specifically affect customers, supplies, and competition. For example, if the economic climate deteriorates, management may not be able to proceed with its plan and may have to accommodate to the external changes. Many social/cultural changes in the last few years have led to widespread revisions in food service management. The aging of the baby boomers, a growing interest in healthy foods and ironic lack of interest in others, growth in the population of different minority groups, a second baby boom, poverty of time, and increased disposable income are only a few of these changes. Internal environmental factors include the time available, costs, geographical distances to travel, and effort required to achieve some purpose. The type of employee, the organization's culture, structure, power, and politics, and interpersonal relationships are part of the internal environment.

Figure 1.1
Environments of Management

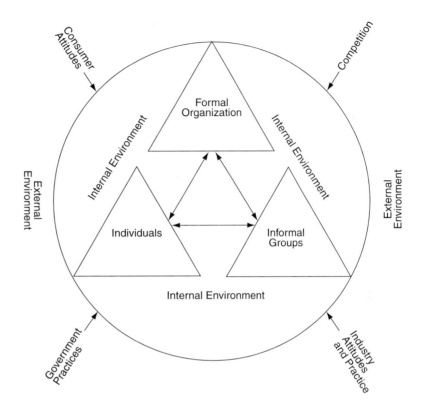

Internal and external environmental factors can easily complicate the role of management. Managers may want to accomplish a definite project, but the external or internal environments determine the probabilities for success. Effective managers must be alert to their environments and the changes possible within them. Thus, the most well-informed managers are usually the effective managers.

GOALS OF MANAGEMENT

What are the overall goals of management in an organization? For a profit-making operation, the goal is usually the highest profit, the maximum increase of the owner's equity, or both. For a nonprofit operation, an overall goal might be to provide the highest level of service given the resources available. A nonprofit hospital dietary department, for example, would seek to provide the best food and service to its patients with the resources it can command. Subgoals achieved collectively pave the way to achieving the major goals. A chef's subgoal may be to maintain a certain food cost percentage or create certain culinary standards. A headwaiter may strive to provide faster dining room service. These subgoals ideally should complement the economic self-interest of the organization. Indeed, the job of management can be described as the consolidation and continuation of all subgoals.

Although the traditional job of the manager is to ensure that the firm prospers, changes in the internal and external environment tend to interfere with this goal. For example, some analysts now suggest that any operation must be responsible to certain other constituencies along with merely providing the owners with a profit. One of these constituencies or stakeholders is the operation's employees. The operation has a responsibility to the people it employs to provide not only satisfactory wages but also pleasant working conditions and should attempt to accommodate an employee's personal situations, such the flexible scheduling needs of a single parent employee.

The enterprise is also responsible to the local community. It must try to be a good citizen and neighbor, active in good works, paying its fair share of expenses, and making every effort to keep its neighborhood free from clutter and pollution.

A third responsibility is, of course, to the customers of the enterprise. They should receive honest value and courteous service. An operation should feel a responsibility to accommodate its customers, not just collect money from them. Obviously this social approach to management has yet to be universally accepted. But it is a worthy goal toward which all management can strive. Indeed, with the current changes in the external environment—the pressures of government and other forces—the social approach may soon become a major consideration.

But first, some trade-offs between these various responsibilities must take place. A food service organization may feel a strong responsibility for its employees, but if its actual need for them decreases, it cannot continue to pad the payroll. If a company encounters excess costs by trying to provide benefits it cannot afford, it will be forced to discontinue these excess benefits and may also be forced out of business, putting others out of work as well.

Some believe that the goal of an enterprise should be its own long-term survival. A problem can arise in the enterprise when management opts for short-run profits with little concern for the long-term consequences.

Service to the community may also present certain problems. For instance, chain operations with standard building designs commonly find that their structures are praised in some communities and banned in others as aesthetically undesirable. A manager must meet these issues with wisdom. Will acceptance of a community's suggestions create goodwill? Or will it waste money? Remember, the best of public relations cannot save a financially failing enterprise.

WHAT MANAGERS DO

We have considered how important management is to a food service or any enterprise, but what is it that managers actually do? The answer varies with the organization and the hierarchy level of the manager. One theory of management (the management process approach or **classical administration** usually identified with Henry Fayol) theorizes that common threads or management principles can be applied to any endeavor. In other words, if managers are competent in these principles, they can manage any type business with some technical information about the business and can manage businesses in different enterprises. Many individuals have shown they can be successful in different fields because they have basic or universal management skills.

Classical administration theorists are especially interested in two areas: (1) the basic principles that guide the design, creation, and maintenance of the organizational structure of the enterprise and (2) the basic functions of management within the organization. In the first area management must determine what is to be accomplished, the best way to accomplish the goals, and who is responsible for what. Advocates of classical administration believe organizational structure is the heart of management and certain principles should be utilized to achieve success.

The list of basic management functions may vary with the theorist but almost always includes planning, organizing, and controlling. Management functions may be described as:

- *Planning*. Planning is deciding what has to be done. It involves short-range (tactical) and long-range (strategic) objectives, or goals. An example of a short-range objective might be deciding production quantities for the day. A long-range objective might be deciding what types of businesses the organization should compete in. Planning involves forecasting the environment, determining objectives compatible with that forecast, and coordinating the available resources with the desired objectives in mind.

- *Organizing*. Organizing is determining what tasks and skills are required to achieve the chosen objectives, then allocating the human resources to achieve these goals. From a traditional management standpoint, organizing structures an enterprise; it creates the framework of jobs and activities. However, to a management behaviorist, organizing constitutes the sum of human relationships in any group activity.

- *Directing*. For management to succeed, the personnel must understand the results expected of them. Directing (sometimes expressed as "leading") requires a manager to explain to others what needs to be done, then to help them do it. Training new employees, helping them improve their skills, and motivating them are all tasks involved in directing. Without adequate direction, staff members tend to work at cross-purposes, inefficiently, and perhaps against the operation's interests. Direction includes supervision, and it is highly personnel-related because it directly involves the staff. Competent, considerate managers can usually achieve a higher level of production from their staff and have happier personnel than managers who direct curtly or callously. Some hard-nosed managers are also effective, however, getting results even though disliked but perhaps respected or feared by subordinates.

- *Controlling*. From a traditional management standpoint, controlling means evaluating how well the work is being done. This requires that actual results be compared to desired or anticipated results (standards of performance). Food cost percentages and labor budgets are typical standards of control. Management behaviorists, however, argue that rigid control can be self-defeating. They hold that it forms a barrier between the employees and their organization.

These theorists would prefer to base control on the assumption that employees are eager to do their best for the operation and require little evaluation. Chapter 2 covers the function of control in detail.

Table 1.1
Schematic Diagram of Classical Management Theory

External Environment				
Social-Political-Legal-Economic-Religious-International				
Internal Environment				
Resources of Management	**through**	**Management Functions**	**produce**	**Organizational Goals**
Men (personnel)		Planning		Return to investors (if a commercial organization)
Machines Money		Organizing Controlling		Decent livelihood for employees
Methods		Directing		Good product or service for patrons
Markets		Staffing		
Materials		Representing		Good neighbor in the community

Functional Management

Management may also be on a function basis, such as financial management, sales management, personnel management, or production management. Since the main function of a food service operation is the production and service of food, other functions are staff or supportive in nature.

THE BEHAVIORAL APPROACH (HAWTHORNE EXPERIMENTS)

Beginning in the late 1930s, a new approach to management developed that might be called the *human relations approach*. This approach focuses on the employees themselves. As such it is largely behavioristic. Using this approach, we recognize that an organization really consists of the people working in it and that management should be primarily concerned with working with these people.

Forerunners of the human relations approach were the famous **Hawthorne experiments** conducted at the Hawthorne Plant of the Western Electric Company in Chicago between 1927 and 1932. There were a number of these experiments, some of which involved changes in production due to changes in lighting and other environmental alterations. The researchers were eager to learn if production could be increased by changes in these factors to enable the company to promote the sales of lighting equipment.

In one Hawthorne experiment, five workers who assembled telephone relays by hand were taken from the general assembly floor. Their production was not paced by a machine but depended instead on the speed of the operators. One unit per minute was considered very satisfactory. In addition, a group financial incentive with extra pay was given to the better groups. Unknown to the chosen five workers, careful records had been kept of their previous production, a standard to which future production could be compared.

The five workers were moved to a room by themselves with the same general environmental conditions as those on the main assembly floor. Changes were made in their routine. Rest periods were introduced. Production rose. Rest periods were increased. Production rose again. A coffee break was inaugurated. Production continued to rise. Hours were lopped off the working day. Still production increased. Saturday work was eliminated, and production continued to increase. At first these results suggested that the increases were due to the rest periods, the shorter hours, and the coffee breaks. To prove this hypothesis, all the new benefits were taken away to see if production would fall back to the original standards. Even without these special benefits, the production of the five workers continued to increase. Benefits were reintroduced, and production rose higher than ever. Not only did production increase, but the workers experienced only a fraction of the illness of those on the regular assembly line. They also appeared happy and eager to go to work.

Why were workers producing at a very high rate and working in the best interests of the company? What was the motivation? It could not be economic: They were receiving no more money incentive than the other workers. This tended to disprove the then prevalent **rabble hypothesis** that industrial workers are a disorganized rabble of individuals acting only in their self-interest.

Although the results and conclusions of the Hawthorne experiments have been interpreted differently by different people, it seemed certain that some psychological factors could cause higher production. One was the existence of an "informal work group," which might decide for itself whether to go "all out" for the enterprise on the one hand or to sabotage it on the other. In the Hawthorne experiments, the five workers considered themselves a select group and believed they were expected to produce. Thus, they were eager to do so, and their production continued to rise. This higher production was not a response to management but seemed to be due to a decision they had made among themselves.

Two other conclusions might be drawn from the Hawthorne experiments. One is the importance of a sense of belonging, the desire to feel a part of something, especially the job. The five employees had developed a group feeling among themselves. The importance of first-line supervision was also evident. No longer could just anybody be made a supervisor. A title by itself could not be expected to motivate workers to produce. Perhaps the "Bull of the Woods," or authoritative supervisor, could be effective when people were worried about jobs and accepted more dominance. But even in the 1930s this style of supervision was being questioned. With the workforce today having even higher aspirations, the authoritarian supervisor may be questioned even more. Perhaps most of all, the Hawthorne experiments showed that contributions could be made by acquiring an understanding of the dynamics of human behavior. It opened the way for psychologists, socialists, and other behaviorists who began to contribute to the science of management.

CLASSICAL PRINCIPLES OF ORGANIZATION

The more basic principles of classical organization appear in the following paragraphs. Although they are sometimes stated as laws, keep in mind that they are not always effective and often are modified or abandoned. The elements of organization—the work to be done, personnel, environment, and relationship between the personnel—all have their effect on the usefulness of these principles, so think of them as useful guides to follow but not as inviolate laws to be strictly construed.

Objectives

Every enterprise, and every segment of an enterprise, should have carefully defined objectives. For example, the objectives of a hospital might include caring for the sick and wounded, promoting public health, training medical personnel, and investigating medical problems. The dietary department of the hospital could have its own objectives: serving patients and staff food of the highest quality or providing the finest service that resources permit. Other objectives might include providing dietary instructions and training personnel. In addition, subsections of the dietary department, like the kitchen or the therapeutic section, would have their own objectives.

Not only should every section of the hospital have its objectives, but every individual position in the hospital should also have its own job specifications and job description. If every individual segment of an organization meets its objectives or goals, the overall goals of the enterprise should be well on the way to being accomplished. But problems may arise in setting individual objectives. If, for example, objectives are too demanding, employees may grow discouraged. If they are too easy, employees may feel unchallenged, grow bored, and reduce their production. Objectives that are less quantitative than qualitative, such as providing a high level of service rather than any specific number of meals, produce results that are hard to measure.

Specialization

There are two types of specialization. One involves having an employee perform only related jobs instead of working in different areas, which is called **homogeneous assignment**. The other type of specialization, called **departmentation**, involves having a segment of the enterprise specialize its activities. The purposes of specialization are to increase productivity, make supervision easier, and produce better control. Contrarily it can be argued that over specialization makes workers feel like drones and jobs should be as broad and creative as possible.

Homogeneous Assignment

Specialization of the individual dates back at least to Adam Smith who in the 1770s found that workers could produce more when they worked only on a few specialized tasks rather than trying to produce a complete product. He saw that when workers alternated tasks, they required extra setup and cleanup time. Psychological adjustments may also be required. Different tasks may have to be completed in different areas, which can also cause delays.

Although specialization of the individual can increase production and may make a worker particularly adept at performing a certain task, it can cause problems. Repetition produces boredom, and when work becomes routine, the worker gains little feeling of expertise, achievement, or pride. The food service field is fortunate that most of its positions usually require several duties and interaction with other workers. This is not true of a strict assembly line, where special efforts may be made to make the work enjoyable. These efforts include shifting workers to new and different jobs or having workers make more complete items. The hospitality manager should be aware of the advantages of specialization and should try to keep personnel working at one job as much as possible rather than assign them a number of jobs. However, personnel should not be idle when their regular work is finished but should do other work.

Authority

Every organization should have a top authority and a clear line of authority from the top to every person in the organization . Everyone should know whom he or she is responsible to and whom he or she is responsible for. This is called a **chain of command**. Also known as the *scalar principle* or *hierarchy of authority,* the chain of command dictates that those of a lower position in the hierarchy are responsible to those in higher positions.

Efficient management uses as short a chain of command as possible. The fewer supervisors that instructions must pass through until they reach the person who performs the work, the better the chain of command. A short chain of command, though, may conflict with another principle, *span of control,* which concerns the number of subordinates one person can effectively supervise. Also involved with the authority principle are two other principles, **delegation** and **unity of command**. A crucial ramification of authority is responsibility. If you have the authority to do something, you should be responsible for the results. Problems arise when you are made responsible for a certain area but lack the authority to obtain the desired results.

Span of Control

Span of control refers to the number of people who can effectively work under one supervisor. Early authorities suggested, rather arbitrarily, that supervisors should have no more than six immediate subordinates. Figure 1.2 shows the direct relationship of one supervisor and three subordinates.

There are different types of relationships between a supervisor and subordinate(s). One type is a direct relationship between the supervisor and subordinates, such as supervisor X and subordinate A, or X > A. When another subordinate (B) is added, there is both another direct relationship X > B and a group relationship of X > A + B. There is

Figure 1.2
Delegation Diagram. There are 7 direct relationships; adding indirect relationships gives a total of 18 relationships.

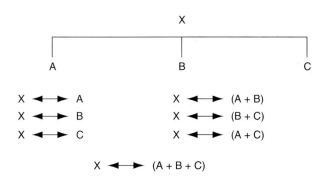

also a sub or indirect relationship of A + B. While direct relationships increase arithmetically, indirect relationships can increase geometrically. One early theorist (V. A. Graicunas) calculated that supervising a group of 12 involved 2,000 relationships, which he considered an impossible burden on the supervisor.

More modern theorists have been trying to discover the factors that determine how many subordinates one supervisor can handle. Some of these factors include the amount of contact required, the level of the subordinate's education and training, the supervisor's communication ability, similarity of function among employees, geographical proximity, the complexity of the work, and the amount of time a supervisor can spend with the subordinates. It is also obvious that the supervisor's own ability and energy will affect the number of subordinates that can be handled. If the subordinates are doing routine work with only casual contact necessary, the original suggestion of six may be far too low a number. If, on the other hand, very involved work requiring much help is performed, the supervisor may be better off supervising fewer employees.

The food service industry as a whole has been noted for its wide span of control. Part of this may be due to one person being responsible for a section and supervisor of all workers in it. In a smaller kitchen the chef may be the one supervisor and all kitchen help report to her, or the headwaiter is the one supervisor in the dining room and all must report to him.

Even though there are more people than can be optimally supervised, it may not be feasible to try to fit in another supervisor. Eight people may be working in a kitchen, and the ideal number may be six to one supervisor. But do you hire another supervisor for two extra employees?

Some authorities believe that the span of control should be replaced by **span of information**. In this approach, the number of subordinates is not as important as the amount of information that is generated and must be acted upon. As long as supervisors can handle the information that is generated, it does not matter how many report to them.

Delegation

Delegation is the process by which authority gets distributed downward through an organization. In theory, delegation is quite logical; in practice, it may become garbled. Some managers find it difficult to delegate authority to others; either they feel that they can do the job better themselves, or they may unconsciously rebel at distributing any authority. Rivalries can result from a struggle for the authority being delegated. This struggling often occurs in an institutional environment where the nature of the institution does not incorporate such direct measures of achievement as profits made or quotas filled. In such a situation, advancement can be tied to politics, or sometimes to winning the fight for delegated authority. Examples of this problem readily appear in governmental agencies, which routinely fight for authority delegated by Congress. Congress itself is rife with this problem, with different committees fighting over areas of particular personal interest to the members of the committees.

At what level should authority be delegated? A pat answer might be at the lowest competent level to handle the situation. The lowest competent level may be further defined as the lowest level where the person making the decision can anticipate all ramifications of the decision. The head waiter of a restaurant might like to change menu pricing, but he probably would not appreciate all the ramifications of this decision. Thus it should be made at a higher level.

The idea of delegation often includes the **exception principle**, which dictates that recurring decisions are handled in a routine manner, but unusual ones are referred upward for appropriate action. To use the exception principle effectively, you must institute policies and standard operating procedures. Instead of having to go to supervisors for a decision each time an event occurs, the subordinate can confidently proceed if the policies of the organization or supervisor are posted. Problems may arise when it is not clear whether a particular complication should be handled under the policy or referred upward for a higher decision. The exception principle can reduce considerably the workload of busy executives and also save subordinates time. In delegation, it is understood that even though authority and responsibility have been delegated, the higher level of authority is ultimately responsible for the acts of subordinates. Thus, it is impossible for a supervisor to say he is absolved of blame just because one of his subordinates made a bad decision. Practical problems may arise, though, when managers have comparatively little say over the choice of subordinates yet are responsible for their actions (see Figure 1.3).

Unity of Command

Unity of command requires that every person be accountable to a single superior and that a superior must not bypass a lower superior in dealing with a subordinate. The unity of command rule appears in the Bible: "No man can serve two masters: either he will hate the one and love the other; or else he will hold to the one and despise the other" (Matthew 6:24). Many managers have a tendency to correct mistakes of lower-level subordinates themselves rather than going through the immediate supervisor. This practice leaves the employees confused about who the real supervisor is and certainly detracts from the authority of the immediate supervisor. Hearing complaints about the food in her hotel, the manager should not directly approach the chef. Instead she should proceed through the catering manager or whoever the chef's immediate supervisor happens to be.

CENTRALIZATION AND DECENTRALIZATION

Related to both balance and authority is the role of centralization, or how much power and authority should be retained by headquarters or individual supervisors, and decentralization, or how much power and authority individual units or subordinate supervisors should have. Fayol believed that in every business situation there is an optimal balance between centralization and decentralization. This optimal balance depends on the capabilities of the managers involved in various departments. Fayol thought managers must always decide to what extent they want to centralize or decentralize the segments under their authority. Some argue that centralization provides better control and possibly better management, because the top people can be more informed and involved. The very advantages of centralization, however, can turn into disadvantages in some circumstances. Having to clear all decisions through a top, and perhaps somewhat distant, authority may be cumbersome. It can stifle initiative among employees. Also, top-heavy authority may not be truly aware of the individual facts and circumstances and thus may not make the best decisions about them. Examples of the centralization/decentralization issue in the hospitality industry might center on whether a hotel should maintain one central kitchen or maintain decentralized kitchens for some of the preparation or how much authority (and responsibility) a local manager should have in a chain.

Whether food production decisions should be made in the kitchen or at a higher level is another question. Fast-food operations, with their standard procedures and centralized control, have proven to be very successful. Even though these operations have a standard format that may not vary with the locale, they have universal appeal and can compete with the varying conditions in different locales. One factor that must not be overlooked in a decentralized organization is that the people in charge of the segment are receiving excellent management training and probably are more advanced in this area than if they were in a more specialized position in a centralized organization. This management training must also be balanced in that it may take away time that should be spent on the immediate goals of the enterprise.

THE ORGANIZATION CHART

An **organization chart** shows in graphic form the relationship between jobs along with the lines of authority, responsibility, and communication. It is relatively easy to prepare, and every operation should have one. In fact, each department can draw up a suborganization chart of its personnel. The armed forces frequently prepare organization charts that include photographs of the people above their names, their titles, and their responsibilities. This practice allows new employees to learn the identity of personnel more easily. In preparing the organization chart, management frequently gains a better understanding of its own operation, which can in turn suggest areas of improvement.

One potential problem is that some employees who are content as long as their status is not formally spelled out may object to the introduction of an organization chart. These employees may readily take directions from another but resent the other if he is placed on a higher level in the chart. Age and seniority may aggravate this situation.

Figure 1.3, a typical organization chart, depicts the various components of a restaurant. The ownership has given the manager the responsibility and authority to run the operation. Under her are three major divisions: the dining room, the kitchen with its supporting units, and the cost controller.

The dining room is subdivided into four categories: hosts/hostesses, banquet, waiters/waitresses, and beverage. In this restaurant, the hosts and hostesses do not direct the waiters and waitresses. In case of difficulty between a hostess and a waiter, the chief host or hostess asks the dining room manager or the assistant (depending upon who is on duty) to settle the dispute. (Some operations would prefer to give more authority or empowerment to lower ranking employees.) The bus persons work under the waiters and waitresses, with one bus person assigned to every two servers. The banquet manager makes banquet arrangements and also directly supervises the banquet waiters and waitresses, most of whom are called in only when needed. Bartenders are under the direction of the head bartender, who is responsible to the dining room manager.

The kitchen manager and the assistant kitchen manager are responsible for all food production. The head cook works with the other cooks, including the banquet cooks (who also maintain a line of communication to the banquet manager). The other kitchen production units do not report to the head cook but to the kitchen manager or the assistant. A steward is responsible for the dishroom, the potwashers, the storeroom, and the various cleaning and housekeeping functions.

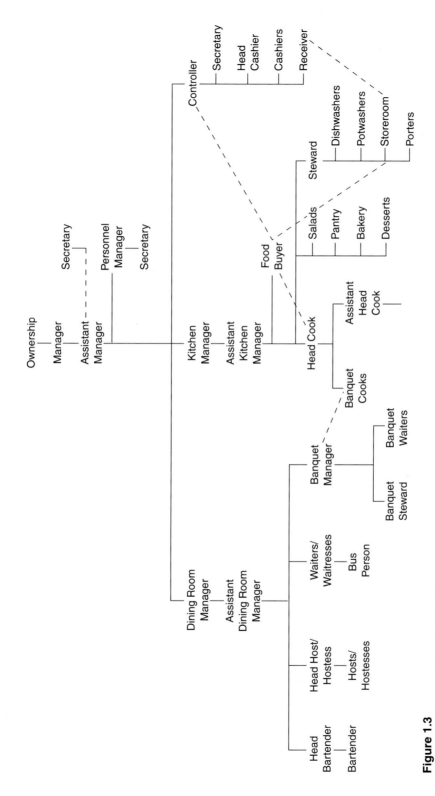

Figure 1.3
Typical Restaurant Organization Chart

The food buyer works directly under the kitchen manager. No one reports directly to the food buyer, although he does have lines of communication with the food cost controller, the head cook, the storeroom, and the receivers. In this particular restaurant, the food buyer sometimes relieves the kitchen manager or the assistant.

In many operations, the cost controller is primarily a staff position with little direction over employees. The restaurant depicted in Figure 1.3, however, assigns certain positions under the cost controller's direction for control purposes. The cashiers and receiving clerks report to the cost controller, along with her own clerical assistance. (Many operations require these people to report directly to the manager.) The personnel manager appears directly under the manager and assists all sections in the screening of applicants, the training of employees, and the maintenance of employee records.

If the manager sees something wrong in the receiving department, she should not approach the receiver directly but should contact the cost controller. Conversely, the receiver should not go directly to the manager but should go through the appropriate supervisor, the cost controller.

TYPES OF FORMAL ORGANIZATION

The traditional mode of organization requires a definite arrangement of positions within the hierarchy of the organization's management. The arrangement of the positions in a relative place in the hierarchy can be shown on an organization chart. Personnel in an organization chart are usually shown as one of four types of organization: line, staff, functional, and matrix.

Line Organization

In line organization, the personnel are primarily directed to carry out the functions needed to achieve the organization's goals. In a restaurant, for example, these areas would be the kitchen, dining room, and sanitation, where personnel are all engaged in carrying out the goal of producing and serving food for the customers. Each level of the hierarchy has authority over the level beneath it. Line organization is the simplest and most direct type of organization. It resembles the military, where sergeants are in charge of squads; above them, lieutenants are in charge of platoons; above them captains are in charge of companies; above them majors are in charge of battalions; and so forth to the president, who is commander in chief of the armed forces.

Staff Organization

In a staff organization, employees perform work which contributes indirectly to goal achievement by performing whatever services the line personnel do not encounter in their regular duties. A bookkeeper or secretary, for example, may not be involved with the direct food production goal of a restaurant. These would then be staff positions. Positions that provide advice and counsel are almost always staff positions.

Functional Organization

The third type of organization is of a functional nature. In this category people are organized by the functional nature of their work. This can lead to miniline (and staff) organizations with each function being so organized. In such a situation a high-level manager in one function would have little authority over those in other functions. A restaurant, for example, may have an accounting department under a chief accountant, whose responsibilities include cash control and to whom all cashiers report. (This is actually a miniline organization.) Accounting is a function that supports the primary mission of the restaurant.

In the traditional theory of organization, the work to be done to meet the organization's goals is determined and then broken down into various segments, components, or compartments. Each receives responsibilities that, together, accomplish the organization work. To make these individual components or departments as effective as possible is a goal of management. Functional organization or departmentalization may be helpful. This involves grouping personnel and activities according to the functions they perform. Typical groups in a foodservice operation might include administration, production, sanitation, and dining room service.

The functional arrangement is probably the most commonly used type of organization. People performing similar tasks are organized together. Thus, the kitchen or dining room are organized in separate functions, each with its own line of organization and necessary staff assistance. A problem can arise in functional organization when employees see only their own goals and their own interests. If this happens, the overall organizational goals may be sacrificed for departmental or self-interest goals. The systems approach to management would try to break down these departmental barriers.

Integrating Staff, Line, and Functional Organization

One organization chart can represent the first three types of organization. The employees and supervisors primarily interested in the productive thrusts of the enterprise would be line. Those primarily involved in giving advice and providing related support are staff. Functional personnel work for the organization in incidental capacities. Matrix organization is normally used for special projects and is not on the regular organization chart.

Line organization is the simplest form. Decisions from the top can be directly transmitted and acted upon more readily and speedily than if they were coming from a staff or functional position. If staff support is absent, the line management must contend with nonproduction problems. Without staff support, for instance, a chef might be forced to do a considerable amount of paperwork rather than concentrate his efforts on food production. Few line managers have all the knowledge they need to handle different or complex problems at their fingertips. For example, the typical manager cannot keep up with all the new environmental or safety legislation in the country and in her locality. It would be better to call on staff specialists for this information rather than attempt independent and hasty or limited research in these areas.

The staff organization, of course, allows specialized experts to handle the problems in their fields of expertise, thus freeing the line management from such work. In addition to having broader knowledge of the field, a staff person can spend more time on the problem than the line executive who is primarily concerned with the production of his unit. Yet a manager must know where to draw the line between staff, line, and functional authority. Because the staff personnel do not have authority over line personnel, their decisions or recommendations can be thwarted by line management. A tendency also exists for the staff personnel to approach the line personnel directly, bypassing line management and creating confusion in the minds of the line personnel. With strong staff support, there is a tendency toward strong centralization, because the experts can usually be found at the central headquarters. This can have its advantages, though, if the enterprise needs strong centralization, as do fast-food operations or some chains.

Functional organization, like staff organization, can relieve the line executives of routine specialized decisions, because functional managers handle the decisions for their functions. However, functional people may make organizational relationships more complex. They may pose a coordination problem over who has the authority to make decisions. Also, as with staff organization, functional organization tends to encourage centralization.

In planning organization, a manager can improve his understanding of the work by considering carefully the relationships between staff, line, and functional positions. Not only must they be thought out, but they must be communicated to eliminate confusion about responsibility. Problems arise when staff personnel enter areas that are the responsibility of line personnel or when functional personnel go beyond their functional responsibilities.

MODERN ORGANIZATIONAL THEORY

The traditional or classical theory of organization, which stresses specialization, well-defined jobs, and narrow responsibility, has come under attack from management theorists with behavioristic backgrounds. These theorists originally relied on the famous Hawthorne experiments.

The behavioral theorists cite a number of weaknesses in the classical approach. For example, the traditional theory stresses the **economic person concept**, in which money is the prime motivation. It also emphasizes exact rules on the assumption that employees will automatically conform to these exact rules. Behaviorists point out that the idea that employees (or any other people) act in a rational manner at all times is doubtful. Yet, the classical theory works on the assumption that people are rational and will respond to rational incentives or directions.

The classical theory often infers that employees will function independently of their environment. In other words, they will do what management requires without regard to outside events that might influence their performance. Behaviorists also feel that the strict lines of authority and responsibility stipulated by the classical theory are self-defeating. Strict reminders of exactly who is superior and who is inferior can lead to resentment and poor job performance. Modern theory adherents would, however, agree with the classical people on a definition of management: the accomplishment of an organization's goals through people. The all-important aspect of this definition for both groups would be the various human relationships between the people in the organization. The two groups would probably also agree that the worker's environment has changed considerably since Fayol developed his principles of organization. Few managers can now operate completely in the authoritarian and unilateral style once available to them. This style has gone the way of monarchies and rule by divine right.

PRECEPTS OF MODERN ORGANIZATION THEORY

No one approach has emerged from **modern organization theory**. There are, however, some general precepts that can be applied and are widely used.

- *Participation.* Whenever possible, all members of an enterprise should partici-pate in the affairs of the enterprise. Participation can include both decision making and being informed about the enterprise. In decision making, members of the enterprise can help define their own goals, working conditions, and orga-nizational goals. (In some European countries this type of participation is achieved by having worker representation on boards of directors.) If employees are to feel close to an organization, they must know a lot about the organization and what is going on in it. Thus, management should report both to stock-holders and to rank-and-file employees about the affairs of the enterprise.

- *Sociability.* A sense of belonging for all members of an enterprise should be stressed. An adversarial relationship between management and nonmanagement staff or supervisory and nonsupervisory employees should be eliminated as much as possible. If individuals feel they belong, they have a tendency to do everything they can to accomplish the organization's goals—a real improvement on the classical approach of assigning very narrow specialized goals.

- *Upward authority.* In the traditional organization arrangement, authority flows from the top down; orders and instructions are passed by superiors to subordi-nates. Management assumes that the instructions will be accepted without dispute. The modern theory assumes that authority really has no meaning unless employees accept it. Thus, in the modern theory, authority travels both downward and upward—and laterally and diagonally, too. In any case, the authoritarian one-way line of authority is no longer inviolable.

- *Personal consideration.* Modern theory stresses the person over the job or goal she is to accomplish. Employees are not robots programmed to carry out tasks decreed from on high.

- *Group recognition.* People naturally form groups. Some of these groups are difficult or impossible to place on an organization chart, and they may change or vary with the composition of the employees. Nevertheless, modern theory recognizes these groups and considers how they may help accomplish the orga-nization's goals.

- *Self-fulfillment.* An employee's individual goals and problems should be consid-ered. This precept can lead to such practices as job enrichment, in which managers try to encourage job satisfaction. A job should not be just an income source. It should also provide satisfaction and feelings of accomplishment and camaraderie. The food service field is particularly fortunate in that many of its jobs are creative and thus allow a feeling of satisfaction. A cook, for example, can derive pride from her culinary creations. A waiter can be very proud if he provides conscientious service. This satisfaction is often missing in very special-ized assembly line jobs.

- *Flat hierarchy.* Flat hierarchy or flat organization refers to having few levels or hierarchies between lower-level employees and top management. Many different ranks can engender feelings of inferiority. They do not stimulate the feeling that "we're all in this together." The more ranks or levels of hierarchy, the more remote top people are from the lower-level people. Thus, modern theory encourages a blurring or elimination of the middle levels of the typical hierarchy. Technology providing ready access to information in various levels of management can eliminate the need of a level of management to process and pass information along.

- *Loose span of control.* Few behaviorists approve of a tight span of control or a supervisor who constantly checks subordinates. With a loose span of control, subordinates feel freer to achieve the goals in their own way without somebody constantly looking over their shoulder. The tightness or looseness of control depends on the nature of the work involved. From the behavioristic standpoint, an individual employee should be allowed as much self-determination or freedom as possible.

INFORMAL ORGANIZATION

When two or more people casually join together in an enterprise, there may be an organization, but there is also an informal organization. The formal organization is preplanned to encourage employees to work toward the goals of the enterprise, while the informal organization develops without definite planning or effort. Management can encourage goal setting, but the drift is always toward informality. In some lower-level employee groups, informal organization may actually take over the formal one. The workers may look for work cues from one of their own (who thereby becomes an informal leader) rather than from the assigned supervisor. An extreme but dramatic case of informal organization is a prison riot.

CULTURE OF AN ORGANIZATION

The culture of an organization can be described as a collective personality created by stakeholders such as management, employees, owners, and customers at a given point in an organization's history. This culture, including its various subcultures, helps determine the way people think, feel, and act within the organization. Of course, not all the stakeholders have equal influence, and different situations may change the amount of influence of the various stakeholders.

Examples of the effect of the organization's culture include employees working hard or goofing off when possible, striving for quality or just getting the food out, welcoming new employees or giving them a hard time, being friendly or cool, showing concern for customers' feelings or ignoring them, favoring regimentation or individualism, displaying respect for the organization's traditions or lacking traditions, emphasizing profit and long-term employment or assuming the job-for-the-moment orientation.

Obviously, an organization's culture affects its operation, and management should be aware of the aspects of the culture even though they may be contrary to mission statements or policy manuals. Because a positive culture can be very beneficial, management should do all it can to encourage positive aspects.

Changing aspects of the culture can be difficult and take time. Sudden developments such as layoffs or threat of closing can have immediate effects, both good and bad. Management by example sets a certain tone that other stakeholders pick up. Policies and insistence on adhering to those policies can have an effect. In thinking of changing the culture, management should be very aware of the present culture, how it wants to change it, and how to keep positive aspects. A culture in a foodservice operation of wanting to serve good food and accommodate patrons is a valuable asset.

CHARACTERISTICS OF INFORMAL ORGANIZATIONS

Informal organizations have several important characteristics to consider. First, they are an agency of social control and have a culture that requires conformity of all their members. This culture may be considerably more rigid than the supposed culture of the business executive. Although the culture may start out in rebellion against the strictness or supposed limitations of more orthodox culture, the informal organization may itself be more restrictive. For example, the culture may call for decidedly anticonservative dress, which means that everybody in the informal group will dress in an "anti" way. Even though the culture may be a rebellion, it normally tolerates little dissension within the group.

The informal group may also have a status system all its own, though the status symbols may be opposed to that within a traditional group. For example, a person with the worst criminal record may have the highest status. A person who goofs off constantly may achieve higher status than the faithful worker. Official status may have relatively little effect in the informal group compared to the unofficial or informal status. The informal leader, rather than the formal manager, is the one who counts.

The informal group may also have a communication system of its own. Information travels rapidly through the grapevine. Management studies have shown that grapevines tend to be accurate. Many managers are interested in knowing what is being communicated along the grapevine, because its messages may be considerably different from formal announcements and interpretations may differ from those intended.

Informal organizations also have a tendency to resist change. The informal organization must have a certain stability to survive. Often during a change in environment, the informal organization dissolves because it cannot adapt to the change, and another informal organization usually rises in its stead. Changes in the informal group also affect the stability of informal relationships. If management wants to break up a negative informal group, it transfers group members.

LEADERSHIP IN INFORMAL ORGANIZATIONS

Although its leadership is seldom planned, the informal organization inevitably produces that leadership. Those leaders may enjoy little effective position, authority, or status on the formal organization chart, but in actual practice they have a great deal of status, authority, and clout. Reasons for gaining informal leadership vary widely and may be unrelated to the work itself. For example, an informal leader may be a bully, an especially good bowler, or an old-timer on the job. Dealing with informal leaders can be one of the most difficult aspects of management. Ignored, they can make a great deal of mischief. On the other hand, catering to them only expands their power and undercuts formal authority.

INDUSTRY INSIGHTS   by Herman Cain

Herman Cain is the Chief Executive Officer and President of the National Restaurant Association. He is a dynamic speaker who is highly sought after for speaking engagements. His leadership made Godfather's Pizza an extremely successful business.

I have been "accused" of being a leader ever since I ran for student body president in the seventh grade. At that time I had barely learned how to spell leadership, so I certainly had little understanding of what leadership was or what makes a leader.

Most of my career I have been encouraged to take leadership positions without consciously pausing to reflect upon why I was encouraged to lead or what I was supposed to be as the leader.

After graduating from Morehouse College in 1967 and starting my professional career, I realized that businesses paid "mo money" to people who could really lead and get results ("leadership") ver-

sus someone who just occupied a position, which a colleague of mine calls "positionship."

"Mo money" was a motivator for me early in life because my family did not have a lot of money when I was growing up. As my career progressed, I became more and more motivated by increased responsibility, challenging objectives, and the thrill of victory when I achieved goals beyond expectations. I was even more motivated when I achieved results that were not expected to be achieved at all.

I have held a wide range and variety of leadership positions. This does not make me an expert, but it does give me enough battle scars to have an experiential perspective on what causes people to respond positively and effectively to a leader. People always want to feel that you genuinely listen to what they say, even if you decide not to pursue their idea. People want to feel they contribute to something successful and that you as a leader appreciate their contribution even if no one else understood their impact. People want to be led by leaders they admire and trust, and most people want to respect their

An interesting situation sometimes occurs when management makes informal leaders part of the formal management or supervisory setup. The new formal leaders may suddenly change from "one of us" to "one of them" and may lose clout they had as an informal leader.

Management should be aware of the leadership in its informal groups. It should try to get the leaders to direct their groups to activities that work toward the goals of the organization as much as possible. These informal leaders are a natural development; if one leaves the scene, another informal leader will take his place.

BENEFITS AND DRAWBACKS OF INFORMAL ORGANIZATIONS

Benefits

Informal organization may be inevitable, but it can also be necessary and desirable. The informal organization can be very helpful in accomplishing the work of the group. It is impossible for the formal organization to plan or direct every activity. Even when there is a void in planning an assignment or direction, the informal organization can take over and accomplish the work.

leaders even if they do not like them. If people do like their leader, then it's a bonus.

I believe *great leaders are born* and *good leaders are made*. What better example of a born great leader than one of the most admired and respected presidents in our history, Abraham Lincoln. I do not recall ever reading that Lincoln took a leadership seminar.

I believe that all of us possess some leadership and that we can become good leaders. Just as some of us must work harder to learn how to sing, some of us have to work harder at becoming a good leader.

Despite all the books and articles written and published on the subject of leadership, there still appears to be a severe deficiency of good leadership in many organizations and institutions. Just examine the number of failed businesses annually, a staggering waste of human capital.

My career represents "success against many odds," achieved with a person-to-person leadership style. Leadership is dynamic and continuous, rather than static and discrete. If you wait for a "leadership moment" to lead, then it could be too late. There are "three plus three" critical components of leadership, which are easy to remember and easy to apply every day. Eventually, three plus three becomes common sense.

Three plus three refers to the three critical qualities a leader must possess and the three critical things a leader must do.

Three critical qualities a leader must possess

D-Factor (Peter Drucker)	Ability to recognize that people must motivate themselves
E-Factor (Entrepreneurial)	Ability to take risks and make the tough decisions
F-Factor (Focus)	Ability to block out the unnecessary and concentrate on the necessary

Plus

Three critical things a leader must do

REMOVE	the barriers which prevent people from being self-motivated
LEAD	the actions required to achieve desired results
INSPIRE	the passion within people to perform better than expected

—"The Hermanator"

The informal organization can lead to a longer span of control. Individuals and groups learn to interact more effectively. This allows the manager to spend less time on coordination and integration and more time supervising people.

The informal organization can help minimize problems with formal organization procedures, such as excessive red tape or unclear procedures. Organizational goals can be accomplished through favors and friendship. "You scratch my back and I'll scratch yours" might prevail. In the armed forces, the supply department or foodservice department is in a unique position to do favors for other departments and, consequently, to get things it wants. A mess sergeant or foodservice officer has a great deal he can trade when he needs resources from other areas. Problems arise when individuals use this particular power or resource for personal gain. When they use it to advance organizational goals, it can make the wheels turn more smoothly.

Drawbacks

Although the informal organization is almost inevitable and can be a positive force for organizational goals, it can also have a negative effect. If the informal organization is against the enterprise, it may actually try to sabotage the work. Because it is a group, management may find it difficult to pinpoint and punish individuals. The informal organization is made up of human elements, and human elements are difficult to predict. No one may ever be quite sure what individuals in an informal group really want or what they will do. Certainly informal groups cannot be expected to follow automatically the orders of a supervisor.

One of the advantages of an informal group is that it provides employees with a means of social satisfaction. The sociability aspects of the informal group can also cause a loss of productive time. Such informal group activity as gossiping, coffee breaks, and betting pools, to name only a few, drain productive time. For example, from a strict efficiency standpoint, it makes sense to have two chambermaids clean a hotel room together, especially in making the beds. Despite the theoretical efficiency of a team approach to hotel cleaning, however, often in practice it is more efficient to use one person because coworkers tend to talk, take breaks together, and waste time.

INFORMAL RELATIONSHIPS

In a formal operation, the relationships between individuals in the organization are spelled out in terms of authority, appropriate responsibilities, and accountability. In the informal organization, the leadership is not formally spelled out or planned. It is usually evident, and the power centers within it are usually known. Informal relationships affect both the formal organization and the informal organization. They are influenced by such factors as status, power, and politics. The status of any one individual employee may be quite different from that indicated on an organizational chart, and the power of that individual may also vary considerably. These informal relationships may well rise above and be apart from those suggested by either the formal or informal organization.

USES OF STATUS

Status is your position in the pecking order of the group. Formal status can be conferred by management, and informal status can flow from the regard accorded an employee by his or her peers. Status is probably inevitable in any organization; in even the most egalitarian groups, a sense of status arises. Some people, as the saying goes, seem to be more equal than others. Management confers formal status according to the nature of the position filled. A manager has more status than a dishwasher in a foodservice establishment. In older, traditional kitchens, the status of cooks is reflected in the height of their white caps. The highest cap is worn by the chef; the lower hats are worn by successive underlings. Escoffier, the king of chefs and the chef of kings, is credited with formulating this symbol of status.

Because status is very important to individual employees, it makes good sense for a manager to provide each job with as much status as possible. Status can appear in a job title: Instead of being called dishwasher, the employee might be referred to as a scrub steward, a machine operator, or a sanitation specialist. A clerk in the storeroom can become an inventory specialist. Uniforms can also affect status. The military has long recognized this principle and has provided different uniforms for different ranks. In the hospitality field, a trim uniform may provide its wearer with more status (at least to himself) than normal work clothes. One hospital had difficulty maintaining an esprit de corps among the floor food-serving leaders because their uniforms made them look like servants with aprons. A change to more professional garb resulted in a distinct improvement in the morale of the group. Even a name tag may provide status in the eyes of the wearer.

Awards can also provide status. Pins for long periods of service may give the wearer a feeling of status. In one military hospital, status was used to motivate the hospital corpsmen to prepare for the weekly inspection. All that was required was a plaque saying "Honor Ward" with appropriate insignia that looked very impressive. This plaque was awarded to the group that in the opinion of the inspecting officer was best prepared for the inspection. The award implied a certain degree of status among the personnel in all the wards, and they competed vigorously to obtain it.

Occupations can by themselves connote status. Status is sometimes assumed by implication. Dietary aids occasionally call themselves dietitians when away from the hospital because dietitians have more status. Many people who might earn far more money doing something else consider the high status of the position equal to greater monetary rewards.

STATUS SYMBOLS

Status symbols can take many forms. In some organizations, access to the executive rest room is a high status symbol. In some organizations, you can tell the status of the employee by the size and design of his desk. Top executives sit behind fancy desks; lower-echelon executives have more utilitarian desks. Perhaps you have heard the old water fountain analogy: Top executives have their own silver water carafes, vice presidents drink from ordinary carafes, and the rank-and-file employees use the water fountain. In some operations, status can be determined according to where people eat. Top managers may eat together, and to be admitted to their table is a mark of status. The status here may be either formal or informal. It may be formal in the sense that only people of a certain rank are permitted to eat together or that certain tables are reserved for higher executives. It may be informal, as when the invitation from the group rather than the location of the table confers the status.

Many operations use an induction ceremony to provide status. Nurses, for example, have their capping ceremonies to designate a certain educational attainment. A hospitality operation can utilize the same concept with its employees by supplying some sort of acknowledgement when they have achieved a certain proficiency. One hospital developed a training program for its tray handlers. It consisted of about six hours of instruction. At the end of the instruction, a tangible symbol of recognition—a certificate—was presented at a graduation ceremony. Besides making the tray handlers generally more proficient in their jobs, the fact that they had achieved a certain professional accomplishment proved to be important to them. The certificate was invariably framed and placed in a position of honor in their homes.

Status is not only inevitable, but it also has certain functions and uses. To begin with, it is obviously a motivational device. To achieve a certain status, employees often strive conscientiously to improve their work. The status is the carrot they strive to reach. Status can soothe one's ego and may even compensate for lower salaries. It can also make employees happier in their jobs and provide them with more of a sense of fulfillment.

A study of status among dining room and kitchen personnel revealed how much status means to hospitality employees. In the operation studied, the waitresses could give the orders to the chefs, who considered themselves "higher" than the waitresses. Thus, a condition arose in which higher-status people appeared to be serving and taking orders from lower-status employees. The conflict was resolved by installing a buffer device, whereby the orders came to the cooks indirectly on a rotating spindle.

POWER

Power is the ability to get someone else to do your bidding. Power is inherent in formal organizations where it takes the form of the authority needed to accomplish the organizational tasks. The informal organization, however, has the power to affect the formal organization, and informal leaders have the power to affect their informal organization.

The desire for power is quite natural. Some psychologists feel it rivals sex as a human motivator. Proponents of this theory believe people with feelings of inferiority compensate with a drive to wield power over others. As with status, power is inevitable in an organization. If misdirected, its effects can work against the goals of the organization. A position may have power simply because it carries the responsibility for achieving certain goals. This could be called **legitimate power**, or power of authority. It usually appears on a formal organizational chart. Thus, in a line organization, a direct line of power can be shown from the top down to the lowest-level member in the organization. Just because a position, or an individual in a position, is supposed to have power, does not necessarily make that power effective. Informal leaders or groups may contravene legitimate power. Many a new college graduate in her first job in a position with some power finds she has a problem with subordinates who may be older and more experienced. They are often reluctant to accept her and effectively block her power even while paying it lip service.

Power may be based on an ability to provide rewards, punishment, or forms of coercion. Someone in a position to bestow salary raises or promotions or provide other tangible benefits has a definite power. People will obey in hopes of receiving the reward.

An individual may have power because of his particular expertise or knowledge. A cook's power may flow from his skill in producing fine dishes. If a person is the only one capable of a certain skill in an organization, he may have a certain power even over his nominal superiors.

The nature of one's position may also carry a certain type of power. In the armed forces, the supply sergeant wields more power than his rank might suggest because of his access to and control over resources. Moreover, a person may have power because of her personal qualities. If others want to identify with her, she will naturally have a certain amount of power over them. This phenomenon is sometimes called "basking in reflected glory." It is most evident in the retinues surrounding certain celebrities.

It must be stressed again that a superior position in a formal organization does not by itself convey power. Other factors contribute. If a person has to use punishment or coercion to maintain power, the impression on employees will be negative. However, there may be no alternative.

Every organization of any size has power centers, and in analyzing the organization's effectiveness, you must locate these centers. Sometimes very direct means must be employed to dilute some of the power in these centers when they work against the goals of the organization. Personal power struggles that contravene the goals of the organization must be stifled. It may unfortunately be necessary to remove both sides from power and install a new power figure if neither of the original sides can accept the other. As the English historian Lord Acton said, "Power corrupts and absolute power corrupts absolutely." Some people who gain a measure of power become obsessed with obtaining more. Sometimes they become unscrupulous in their methods. Individuals who want to obtain power for power's sake can be harmful to the organization and, at the very least, make others in the organization uncomfortable. Yet in all fairness, some people who are eager to acquire power for themselves also pull their organization along with them.

POLITICS

Probably the most overlooked subject in management textbooks is politics. Like status and power, politics are inherent in an organization. The you-scratch-my-back-and-I'll-scratch-yours philosophy is natural to practically all environments. Politics are beneficial when they allow an organization to work toward its goals. Tit for tat helps lubricate the organizational machine. If it were possible to write a book of standard operating procedures to cover every eventuality, and everyone followed them to the absolute letter, there might be no need for politics. In the real world, however, trading favors can be helpful. As it is with power, when politics are exercised for their own sake rather than for the goals of the operation, trouble begins. The same occurs in our larger society when politicians work for their own political ends rather than for the goals of the country. Although politics are an important function of an organization, the informal political process is very difficult to teach. This is probably why it remains so widely overlooked. We do not propose to discuss business politics exhaustively, but here are some techniques you might consider:

1. *Acquisition of favors that must be repaid.* People who do favors for others normally expect them to do things for them in return when the occasion arises.

2. *Alliances.* Politicians like to effect appropriate alliances. If somebody supports you with the understanding that you will support him, both of you have increased your political power.

3. *Conviviality.* Friendliness can help politicians. People who are well liked frequently gather political strength because people like them and want to help them.

4. *Constituency building.* Politicians often try to weld different blocs or groups together to provide a larger political base. People who can get several different sections of an organization to unite behind them increase their influence.

5. *Currying favor.* Enjoying the approval of superiors can bring political advantages. Politicians sometimes play up to others or at least act as accommodating as they can. Of course, these people risk the disapproval of other employees.

The art of politics can facilitate the operation of an enterprise. Once the decisions have been made on the basis of office politics alone, the organization's goals may suffer. When an organization is rife with politics, people who do not like political games grow uncomfortable. They may be forced into political activity for their own protection if advancement and recognition stem more from politics than from achievement, and favoritism always discourages those who are not favored.

MANAGEMENT AND ORGANIZATION IN A CYBERNETIC AGE

Although the foodservice industry has been somewhat belated in entering the computer era compared to other industries, the effect of new technology has been dramatic. It is said that information is power, and computers offer much more access to information. Junior executives and functionaries who previously filtered information to higher levels may not be necessary if top executives can get the information directly on their computer screen. Faulty decision making can be caused by late, incomplete, or faulty information. Computers can provide more information faster than any previous medium. This technology can allow for more centralized management or organization since information can be sent easily to a central headquarters as it becomes available at the unit level. Or, since information that was once only available to higher management is now available through computers to lower levels of management, they may be able to make decisions at their own level. Regional or area managers of large chains may themselves be less important or see their responsibilities changed.

The operating systems for foodservice operations may have to be based on a management information system (see Chapter 6). Computers change forecasting, ordering, inventory, and production systems among others. With computers processing information, fewer employees may be needed. Staff such as servers may become more productive using handheld computers. With computers doing much of their previous paperwork, supervisory and management personnel theoretically have more time to spend with patrons or in production areas.

SYSTEMS MANAGEMENT

Systems management theory, although it is usually dated to 1968, has been around much longer. We defer our systems management discussion to Chapter 4 but briefly, systems management is a way of looking at the total enterprise, planning its organization, and providing the means for solving its problem.

TOTAL QUALITY MANAGEMENT

An approach to management sometimes called **TQM** (total quality management) or **TQC** (total quality control) or CWQC (company-wide quality control) became increasingly popular in the late 1980s. TQM is covered in Chapter 3.

RE-ENGINEERING

To some, re-engineering is finding a more efficient way of operation, but it is far more than this. Re-engineering is a radically new process for an organization that stresses commitment to customer service. It focuses on making improvement in all dimensions of a food service organization—the human dimension, work process dimension, and the technological dimension. Re-engineering helps food service organizations overcome the barriers in achieving better customer satisfaction.

Re-engineering is not easy. It can be a long, hard process requiring extensive participation but it can lead to a dramatic improvement in responding to customer needs and satisfactions.

Today the customer is all important. Whatever a food service operation can do to help customers perceive the operation in fulfilling their needs is most important for market success. Re-engineering is both internal and external. It involves new approaches in recruiting, training, and developing staff, using newest technology, and perhaps revamping marketing approaches.

Re-engineering in a food service operation must consider three thrusts:

1. *The customer must be the starting point of change.* Identify your customers (or who you want to be your customers) and what they really want. Is it cheap prices, speedy service, gourmet food, luxurious surroundings, a new dining experience, take out, etc.? Too often, management provides what they only think their customers want or, worse yet, what they want to provide. A restaurant owner might like to specialize in certain foods, but are they what the customer desires? Success in food service is satisfying customers' needs and expectations. You also have to find your market niche and differentiate your operation from your competitors'.

2. *Design work processes in light of organizational goals.* Although not as much as in most industries, the industrial model was in vogue and stressed change for efficiency or lower cost with less than total regard about how a customer might react. Paper table service might be cost efficient for many food service operations but what is the customer reaction in your food service operation? One big aspect of change in work processes is the empowerment of employees. Lower level employees are empowered to make decisions on the spot when there is customer dissatisfaction. For example, if something is wrong with a food item, a server can make an appropriate adjustment without bringing in higher authority. Of course, there may be limits as to how much an employee is empowered to offer.

3. *The technological dimension.* Technologies are rapidly changing and improving. They should be considered not because they are advanced but by how they allow the food service operation to achieve higher levels of customer satisfaction. Technology should not only be considered in reducing personnel needs but more importantly to allow personnel to better satisfy customer needs. A hand held terminal system to record customer orders at the table should not just be used for reducing serving personnel but also to provide better service by the same server.

The re-engineering process is sometimes described as the three R's—rethink, redesign, and retool.

Rethink. This involves looking at your current objectives and underlying assumptions and considering how well they fit into the commitment of increased customer satisfaction.

Redesign. How does the food service operation produce its food items and services? How are jobs structured? Who does what and what are the results and what could they be? There is no best way but always a better way. Redesign and examine how workers can better satisfy customers. Is any work irrelevant or redundant? Can jobs be redesigned to make them more satisfying to employees and also more customer focused? Is there feedback so management and employees know about performance and customer satisfaction? Is the feedback immediate and direct?

Retool. What new technologies such as systems, equipment, or automation are available to increase service quality and customer satisfaction?

Re-engineering, if properly performed, can provide the general benefits of better customer satisfaction and profits, if a profit making organization, or better utilize resources for a non-profit organization.

Benefits leading up to this include a new thinking about the operation, more involved employees, emphasis on individuals, a flatter organizational structure, more "whole" jobs for employees, more employee participation, and more emphasis on team work.

In a real way re-engineering incorporates many concepts discussed elsewhere in this book such as a systems approach, total quality management, information systems, business planning, and marketing concepts.

SUMMARY

To be successful, any organization needs management. There are many definitions of management but they all share certain characteristics: goal orientation, responsibility, and accountability, and concern with people. Management cannot be passive and must respond to forces and stresses from its outside environment. Goals of management include producing a return to owners (if profit-making), providing a quality product to customers and a decent livelihood to employees, and being a good neighbor in the community.

There are different streams of management theory. Classical administration theorists believe management is the successful accomplishment of such management functions as planning, organizing, contributing, and directing. Behaviorists believe that management is the completion of goals through people, and management should be concerned with motivating people.

Organization is crucial in management. Again, operations can take different approaches. Classical organization theory is more concerned about the structure and arranging jobs to fulfill organizational objectives. Modern organization advocates are more concerned with the people in an organization and believe tightly defined jobs and narrow responsibility can be self-defeating.

With any organization there is also an informal organization. A manager should understand its characteristics and try to have the group work for the organization's objectives instead of fighting them. Inherent in an organization are power, politics, and status. The manager must be aware of these at work in the organization and deal with them.

Management has changed in this computer era. Information is power, and more people have access to information. Management information systems, total quality management, and a systems approach to management are becoming more important. Later chapters cover these concepts.

The corporate culture of the operation affects both customers and employees. Thus, the culture and factors influencing it should be identified.

KEY TERMS

behavioral approach

chain of command

classical administration

classical principles of organization

CWQC

decision making

delegation

directing

economic person concept

exception principle

Hawthorne experiments

homogeneous assignment

internal environment

legitimate power

modern organization theory

objectives

organizing

rabble hypothesis

re-engineering

social approaches to management

span of information

TQC

TQM

unity of command

REVIEW QUESTIONS

1–1 Briefly discuss five ways work can be divided for organizational purposes.

1–2 Define *span of control.*

1–3 Define *unity of command.*

1–4 How does span of control differ from span of information?

1–5 Define an organizational chart.

1–6 Differentiate among line, staff, and functional organizations.

1–7 Behaviorists are often critical of the classical approach to organization. What are some of their criticisms?

1–8 When is modern management generally thought to have started?

1–9 Identify characteristics of management.

1–10 Explain six resources of management.

1–11 How must a manager be a politician?

1–12 Define *organizing* in management terms.

1–13 Define *directing* in management terms.

1–14 Define *external environment.*

1–15 List the four goals of management.

1–16 Why is corporate culture important?

1–17 What are the three thrusts of re-engineering?

1–18 What is the culture of an organization?

The Function of Control and Cost Control

This chapter provides an introductory view of control and costs from a management perspective. It also provides a framework for the many cost-control procedures covered in subsequent chapters.

After completing this chapter, you should be able to:

1. Describe five types of managerial control.
2. Discuss the importance of cost control to a foodservice operation.
3. Explain the importance of the contribution margin and cost-volume-profit relationships.
4. Outline a seven-point management process to achieve control.
5. Explain how control interacts with other management functions.
6. Compare the traditional and behavioristic approaches to control.
7. Discuss total quality management.
8. Explain why cost control is often lacking in foodservice.
9. Explain why cost percentages may not be the best control procedure.

This book is especially concerned with cost control in foodservice operations. **Control** is one of the basic management functions. The others include planning, organizing, directing, and coordinating. But control differs from other basic management functions in that whereas all management functions rely on each other, a need for control does not arise until the other functions are employed. You do not need control over planning, for example, until planning has been accomplished.

The word *control* derives from a Latin word meaning register. Used as a verb, it could mean regulate, verify, or hold in restraint. As a noun, it could be defined as a standard of comparison. But we use *control* here to mean "helping to ensure performance conforming to plans, objectives, and goals." (Notice that this definition assumes the existence of plans, objectives, and goals.)

TYPES OF CONTROL

One can name a number of different types of control, although cost control probably overlaps most of them. For example, one could exert control over an organization's goals. In today's complex, competitive, and ever-changing world, if an organization does not plan, which implies forming goals, it probably will encounter trouble.

One could exert control over quality. A foodservice operation quickly finds difficulty if it serves food of poor or erratic quality. Any cost-cutting effort must be concerned first with the effects on product quality. (See Chapter 3 for Total Quality Management.)

Control over personnel can take many directions. In this book, we specifically concern ourselves with control over personnel costs, but other personnel controls include performance appraisals, organizational development, and employee relations. Employee attitudes toward an employer are vitally important in the behavioral approach to control, and many organizations stress time management, or control over time.

Control over physical assets, or property management, is also important. Control over funds is as important in foodservice as in any other type of organization, and food management must also involve control over sales. A restaurant might establish sales goals for such categories as dining room sales, beverage sales, or banquet sales, among others. This work involves determining what level of sales is feasible, determining how to accomplish these levels, comparing actual sales to budgeted sales, and taking corrective actions if necessary.

IMPORTANCE OF COST CONTROL

For a commercial or profit-making operation, costs are the difference between sales and profits. Here is the equation:

$$\text{Sales} - \text{Cost} = \text{Profit}$$

Savings in costs have a major effect on profit. Let us assume that a foodservice operation has sales of $500,000 (100 percent), a food cost of $150,000 (30 percent), other expenses of $325,000 (65 percent), and a profit of $25,000 (5 percent). These facts can be expressed this way:

Sales	$500,000	100%
− Food Cost	150,000	30%
− Other Costs	325,000	65%
= Profit	$ 25,000	5%

Let us assume that better cost control can reduce food costs by 3 percent of the $150,000, or $4,500, which provides a new food-cost percentage of 29.1 percent ($145,500/$500,000). Profit increases by nearly 20 percent to $29,500. These facts can be expressed this way:

Sales	$500,000	100%
− Food Cost	145,500	29.1%
− Other Costs	325,000	65%
= Profit	$ 29,500	5.9%

To achieve this same profit increase by increasing sales would require a $90,000, or 18 percent, sales increase (assuming other expense percentages remained constant). Another way of expressing these figures is that a less than 1 percent decrease in total expenses increased profit by 18 percent.

Increases in costs have the opposite effect. If food costs had increased by 3 percent, or $4,500 (less than 1 percent of sales), the profit would have been reduced by 18 percent to $20,500. The figures would now be as follows:

Sales	$500,000	100%
− Food Cost	154,500	30.9%
− Other Costs	325,000	65%
= Profit	$ 20,500	4.1%

A hospital or school foodservice operation may not be concerned with making a profit; however, every reduction in costs means more resources available to serve patrons or clients or perhaps provide better employee benefits. Financial compensation for rank-and-file foodservice employees is generally low compared to manufacturing or other industries. With competition limiting the opportunities to pass on higher costs to the customers or users, cost control may be the only way to provide better individual benefits for employees.

COST CONTROL AS A MANAGEMENT FUNCTION

Control is intertwined with other basic management functions: planning, organizing, directing, and coordinating. These basic functions interact: to have proper control it is necessary to have planning to provide short- and long-term goals, organization to provide the human and other resources necessary to achieve them, and directing and coordinating to delegate appropriate tasks to appropriate personnel. According to one scheme of management, to secure control an organization must

1. define its objectives,
2. prepare the plans and programs to achieve these objectives,
3. provide suitable organization to implement the plans or programs,
4. set policies and procedures to provide direction,
5. provide the necessary funds,
6. provide the necessary personnel, and
7. inspect, regulate, verify, and compare performance goals or objectives.

The term for forming long- and short-range objectives and goals is, of course, planning. If an organization really wants to accomplish something, it must know what that something is, and control is vital to the actual movement toward that planned goal. Without control, planning would be merely an academic exercise; plans would have no validity and there would be no way to measure progress toward a goal. Many pie-in-the-sky ideas issue forth as plans unsupported by control.

Plans get accomplished within organizations. An organization determines what has to be done and assigns responsibility to personnel or sections to accomplish this work. This is called organizing. Control sees to it that personnel sections pursue individual goals that collectively approach the organization's overall goals.

Establishing policy procedures is largely a function of direction. Direction, too, must submit to some control. Lord Acton's observation that "power corrupts and absolute power corrupts absolutely" is as true in the field of management as in politics. There must be control over the authority to direct, not only to keep individuals from abusing power but also to keep the goals of the enterprise paramount.

An organization can accomplish very little without funds; to achieve its goals or plans, an organization must have financial resources. Control over funds is thus a vital aspect of overall control. An organization's cash and other fiscal assets must be jealously controlled.

Employees are also necessary to practically every endeavor, and their activities must be directed, motivated, and controlled. In the traditional view, controlling personnel involves both keeping an eye on everyone and comparing their activities. The more modern concepts about control emphasize motivation and the idea that if people are oriented toward an enterprise, they will work on its behalf and need comparatively little on-the-spot supervision.

Still, some comparison is necessary. In addition to being tools of planning and direction, policies and procedures are also tools of control. With definite policies and procedures, a manager can determine whether performance matches them and can take appropriate action when it does not. Along with policies and procedures, periodic and special reports may be required to let management evaluate its overall progress.

Some control obviously is essential to both the largest and the smallest hospitality organizations. It becomes increasingly important as the organization grows and involves more personnel. A small refreshment stand operated by its owner requires comparatively little control since its owner is present and, therefore, needs fewer formal reports and fewer policies, except those required by outside authority. The owner may also be highly motivated to achieve success since the rewards are more direct. But as an organization gets larger, its personnel acquire vested interests of their own. Moreover, this larger size brings more difficulties in communication, and the overall picture gets cloudier. When the goals of the enterprise are not necessarily intertwined with an employee's goals, the need for control becomes much greater.

Constant checking, rechecking, verifying, regulating, and comparing are the very essence of control. **PPBSE**—planning, programming, budgeting, staffing, and evaluating—are the letters to remember. An enterprise must *plan* its goals. It must *program* how they can be accomplished, *budget* the necessary funds and personnel, and provide the personnel, or *staff*, to accomplish them. The results must be *evaluated* to see how they compare with the planned objectives or goals. Evaluation is central to the control process.

Control also involves communication. Managers must know what is going on. It has been said that almost all faulty decisions can be attributed to unreliable or insufficient information. Thus, proper control implies the necessary interchange of information for planning and decision making, and management information systems (MISs) provide increasingly important links in this communication chain.

Every foodservice manager knows the consequences of a lack of control: the operation may still function, but it seems to have a life of its own. The personnel "do their own thing," which may not serve the best interests of the operation. There may be little basis for decision making since hard data on which to base decisions cannot be found. Costs may skyrocket while the manager looks in vain for ways to bring them back to realistic levels.

Thus, the process of control is directly related to the process of planning. To exercise adequate control, an operation must know where it is going or what its objectives are, which of course means planning. Control becomes the comparison of actual performance with the planned goals and objectives and an appraisal of any discrepancies.

As in many other areas of management, one can use different approaches to the process of control. The most traditional approach is the measurement of actual performance against planned performance, or what you planned to do compared with what you actually accomplished. Those approaching control from a behavioristic slant believe management is the accomplishment of stated goals through the personnel involved. If these personnel do their best work and are highly motivated, there is little need for the formal or traditional approach to control. In fact, the traditional approach may be self-defeating insofar as it may cause conflicts and difficulties within the group. Both approaches have elements to recommend them to the foodservice operator, and we will consider them both in some detail. The traditional approach, however, is by far the most widely utilized; thus, it will be emphasized throughout this book.

COST-VOLUME-PROFIT RELATIONSHIP

To control costs and enhance profit or service, managers must understand the relationship between cost, volume, and profit. Volume for these purposes can be considered in dollars, sales, or income. Profit is the difference between sales and costs.

In this book we are especially interested in costs. Costs can in one sense be considered a reduction in the value of an asset to produce gain. Once food is purchased, it becomes food inventory and an asset. When the food is sold, the inventory food asset is appropriately reduced, and the amount used is considered a cost. A building is purchased for $1 million for restaurant use. It is assumed for accounting purposes that the building has a business life of 25 years. The depreciation on the building (straight line) for accounting purposes would be 4 percent (100 percent/25 years), or $40,000 a year. We can consider this yearly accounting reduction in the value of the building asset as a cost. However, not all outgoes of funds are costs in an accounting sense. We hire and pay labor, which does not appear as an asset but as an expense. For our purposes, expenses and costs will be used interchangeably.

Costs can be classified in a number of ways. Variable costs are in close relationship with volume (i.e., they vary closely with the volume or sales of the business). If 500 meals are served, about five times the amount of food would be used than if 100 meals were served. Fixed costs do not change, regardless of changes in volume. Rent, depreciation, or a manager's salary, which are the same regardless of changes in volume or dollar sales, are considered fixed costs. Many costs have elements of both fixed and variable costs and are considered semivariable (or semifixed) costs. An example would be a restaurant that has a regular staff but hires extra help when volume increases above a minimum amount. The regular staff would be a fixed cost and the extra help a variable cost. Together, total labor cost would be considered a semivariable cost (or expense).

CONTRIBUTION MARGIN

Important to both costs and profits is the **contribution margin**, or that portion of sales that is available for overhead (which may be considered fixed costs) and profit. It may be expressed as a percentage or

$$CM = \frac{\text{Profit and Fixed Costs}}{\text{Sales}}$$

The equation

$$\text{Sales} - \text{Costs} = \text{Profit}$$

can now be expanded to

$$\text{Sales} = \text{Variable costs} + \text{Fixed costs} + \text{Profit (or} - \text{Loss)}$$

The contribution margin can also be illustrated by contrasting traditional and contributional approaches in the format of an income statement. The traditional approach would be

Sales	$500,000	100%
− Cost of Goods Sold (Food Cost)	150,000	30%
= Gross Profit	350,000	70%
− Other Costs	325,000	65%
= Profit	$ 25,000	5%

The contributional approach would be

Sales	$500,000	100%
− Cost of Goods Sold (food, variable labor, supplies, etc.)	275,000	55%
= Contribution Margin	225,000	45%
− Fixed Costs	200,000	40%
= Profit	$ 25,000	5%

The contribution margin can also be defined as what is left over from sales or income after variable costs are subtracted.

$$\text{Sales} - \text{Variable costs} = \text{Contribution margin}$$

VARIABLE RATE

Variable costs can be expressed in the **variable rate**, which is found by dividing variable costs by sales.

$$\text{Variable Rate} = \frac{\text{Variable Costs}}{\text{Sales}}$$

Using the figures from the contributional approach,

$$\text{Variable Rate} = \frac{\$275,000}{\$500,000}, \text{ or } 0.55$$

That is, 55 percent of dollar sales is needed to cover variable costs, so 45 percent is left over for the contribution margin or rate to cover fixed costs and profit.

These relationships can be expressed in a formula.

$$\text{Sales} = \frac{\text{Fixed Costs} + \text{Profits}}{\text{Contribution Rate}}$$

$$\$500,000 = \frac{\$200,000 + \$25,000}{0.45}$$

$$\$500,000 = \$500,000$$

If profit or loss is the difference between sales and costs, the break-even point is found when costs, both fixed and variable, equal income or sales. If sales increase above the break-even point, the operation should be more profitable since the fixed costs have already been covered and only variable costs must be subtracted from the additional income.

The sales revenue necessary to break even can be found using this formula:

$$\frac{\text{Fixed Costs}}{\text{Contribution Margin}} = \frac{\$200,000}{0.45} = \$444,444$$

The operation needs sales of $444,444 before it meets fixed costs. Up to sales of $444,444, the operation is running at a loss; after $444,444, 45 cents of every sales dollar is profit.

We can also calculate the number of meals that must be sold to break even. Assume the average sales price per meal is $12. If the contribution margin is 0.45, or $5.40 per meal, we can use the formula

$$\frac{\text{Fixed Expenses}}{\text{Contribution Margin per Meal}} = \frac{\$200,000}{\$5.40} = 37,037$$

to find that 37,037 meals must be sold to break even.

Another use of the contribution margin is to determine the dollar sales necessary to produce a desired profit. Instead of a profit of $25,000, the operation desires a profit of $50,000.

$$\frac{\text{Fixed Costs} + \text{Desired Profit}}{\text{Contribution Margin Expressed as a Percentage of Sales Revenue}} = \frac{\$200,000 + \$50,000}{0.45} = \$555,556$$

Assuming the contribution margin remained the same, the operation would need $555,556 in sales to produce $50,000 profit.

Management should consider the contribution margin in a number of areas of decision making. A common situation arises in menu pricing. Ensuring that an appropriate contribution margin is in the menu price is crucial and is covered in more detail in Chapter 9. A question can arise: Should management reduce selling prices to increase the number of unit sales? A related question, then, is whether the higher unit volume at a lower unit profit increases the total contribution margin amount to overhead and profit more than fewer unit sales will at a higher unit profit. Chapter 24, which discusses cost-volume-profit analysis and break-even analysis, can be helpful in making these decisions.

Management may decide that a particular meal (say, breakfast) is not profitable and should be dropped. However, when the contribution to overall fixed costs is considered, it may well be best to continue serving breakfast if more than variable costs are recovered. The same analysis may be required about staying open on a slow day of the week, or a seasonal operation's closing down in the off season. The decision whether to expand operations may hinge on the effect on the contribution margin. Chapter 24 shows how this data can be expressed in a graphic break-even chart form.

TRADITIONAL CONTROL THEORY

Traditional control theory depends upon someone's having the responsibility and authority for achieving the goals of his or her part of the enterprise. It is a "boss-subordinate" relationship. The boss (or supervisor) is responsible for the activities of subordinates and must take necessary action when results do not meet the standards. The traditional theory of control usually includes two aspects. One is the direction of personnel and their activities, known as "keeping an eye on things," sometimes called **MBWA** (management by walking around). If employees believe a supervisor is constantly on the scene, they tend to stay busy and are less inclined to be careless, negligent, or disruptive. In this context, other means of formal or elaborate control systems become a substitute for absentee ownership or management. If the manager is constantly on the scene, knows completely what is going on, and is interested in the goals of the operation, there is less chance that resources will be used ineffectively and inefficiently. If the manager is not on the scene, there should be some way to know what is going on and when corrective action is necessary.

The other aspect of traditional control is measurement, or the comparison of actual performance with planned performance and the consideration of any discrepancy. This aspect of control is sometimes presented in these four steps:

1. *Establishment of standards (or goals).* The standards may be of a financial nature, like budgeted costs. They may be of a time nature, like the amount of time necessary to perform a certain task (which is often expressed in production quantities, or number of covers per workday or work hour, or food cost per patient-day). They may specify quality. For example, in manufacturing, quality control inspectors develop quality tolerances and analyze rejects. Defining quality in the hospitality foodservice field can be challenging because it is inherently difficult to define the quality of food items and because the personal aspects of service such as pleasantness, cooperation, and helpfulness are hard to measure on quantitative scales. Standards can also specify quantities, which in a foodservice operation could involve portion control in the food served or receiving control over purchases.

2. *The measurement of performance.* Once your standards have been set, you can measure what is actually being performed. But sometimes the costs of the measurement must be balanced against the advantages it can deliver. Although control reports generally are desirable, the time and effort to prepare the reports can outweigh the loss at-

tributable to the lessened control that might occur without them. The time spent by a supervisor's keeping track of certain subordinate activities may be more than the loss from unobserved poor performance. Supervisors have a natural tendency to spend more time on what interests them and less time on other activities. For example, a supervisor can spend 80 percent of the time implementing food-cost control to the neglect of labor costs, even though the latter may amount to more of the total expenses in the operation.

3. *Comparison and analysis.* Once the actual performance has been measured, it can be compared with the standards set previously, and any discrepancies can be noted. Questions often arise about when or how often this should be done. Operations that utilize control systems tend not to have control problems since the systems act as preventive control measures. Without control, parts of the operation begin to act independently and can run wild. Thus, managers must decide on the best balance between too much control and too little control for their particular operation. It is helpful to remember that comparison and analysis are facilitated when both the planned goals and the actual measurements are made in the same units, whether they be dollars, man-hours, or some other unit of measure. Managers must decide how much tolerance to allow before taking corrective action. This obviously calls for individual decisions for each operation. For example, a manager may decide that for every cook-day of work, between 100 and 120 meals should be produced, or that a food-cost percentage of between 28 and 30 percent is desirable.

The measurement function can be shown graphically as

Standard	*Actual*	*Difference*
Amount of predetermined resources for result desired	Amount of actual resources used to obtain results	Between resource use planned and actual amount used; an excessive difference should be investigated.

4. *Corrective action.* Managers must reduce or eliminate the discrepancies between the predetermined standards and measurements of actual performance, as shown in their comparison and analysis. They must determine what types of preplanning, reorganizing, or new controls can correct these deficiencies. This may mean a change in personnel, different job assignments, more observation by management, or many other approaches. It often involves difficult choices but is one of the responsibilities of management (as opposed to nonmanagement) personnel. Managers must act, however unpleasant the consequences. Another problem in the corrective action phase is that managers may overreact and take drastic action to correct relatively insignificant problems that might have resolved themselves and caused far less trouble than the managers' action.

PRIME COSTS

Foodservice operation control usually involves two main costs: food and labor. They are often referred to as **prime costs** and usually contribute the bulk of costs in foodservice operations. However, other costs are also important. A number of control techniques are applicable to these two costs, and they are all complemented by cost accounting techniques. In employing cost-control techniques and cost accounting techniques, a manager should remember that the purpose is to find out what the costs are, whether they are out of line, and (if so) where they are out of line. Corrective action can then be taken.

BEHAVIORISTIC APPROACH TO CONTROL

Behaviorists have attacked the traditional theory of control. They often believe that the authority-responsibility or superior-subordinate relationship limits and demeans employees. Management, after all, means the accomplishment of the organization's goals through people, who should be eager to do their best. Behaviorists argue that the control ought to be a desirable goal formulated by the group itself. When the group achieves these goals, they reason, effective control exists, and the need for the external procedures of traditional control systems disappears. Since the controls are, in effect, the individuals themselves, there should be a greater degree of harmony, better coordination among the participants, and a resolution of conflict.

This approach does not involve merely providing control; it also seeks to make the work more meaningful and important. An early example of the effectiveness of this type of control arose from the Hawthorne experiments conducted during the late 1920s and early 1930s. Some of these experiments encouraged workers to pace themselves. Production soared without the usual controls or strong supervision, possibly because the workers had aligned themselves in an informal group and were determined to produce to their utmost without the usual formal controls or motivations.

Of course, aspects of the behavioral approach can be combined with aspects of the traditional approach. Certainly the individual employees should be aware of their importance to the enterprise. People like to have pride in their work, and being part of a service-producing institution can be a matter of pride. As much as possible, they should be included in the formulation of goals. Communication should travel not just from the top down, but also from the bottom up. The rank-and-file employees should be aware of how efficiently the overall operation is proceeding toward its goals.

Management can implement the **behavioristic approach to control** in a number of ways. Much of the behavioristic approach involves motivation and morale. If people feel favorably toward the organization they work for, they need little control. Obviously the personnel selection process is important. If employees have a personal need to produce quality goods, the need for quality control is to a large extent eliminated. The cook who will not serve something of inferior quality is certainly an asset to a fine foodservice operation. In fact, problems can arise when an employee has high standards but the operation just wants to push out ordinary food rather than desirable and creative items. In this case, the employee may well become unhappy. The hospitality field has unusual advantages in that it should stress product and service quality. Many manufacturers are more concerned with quantity and provide their employees with little incentive to produce quality work. A hotel, by contrast, must maintain clean rooms; thus, the maid has an incentive to do a good job of cleaning. A maid should therefore be a person who derives satisfaction from doing a competent job, and the operation should reinforce these goals and values. If it does, the maid will need less supervision on the job. Socialization among employees can also reduce the need for control. If employees feel they are part of a group, they will be reluctant to let the group down by doing less than their best or by producing inferior work. In some of the food operations of yesteryear, food returned to the kitchen was an insult to the whole kitchen staff, not just the person who produced it.

Peer pressure may be the most effective of all controls if it supports the goals of the organization. But if it contravenes the goals (if, for example, there is pressure to hold production down, or not to do more than you have to), the results can be disastrous.

In hiring, orienting, training, and supervising new employees, management should strive to see that they fit in with the group. Federal laws must also be considered. An employee who is a misfit probably will be unhappy, the overall quality of work will suffer, and the need for control will increase. Management development itself can have an effect on behavioristic control. Managers adept at behavioristic techniques should have to rely less on traditional authoritarian methods.

Control may also be achieved through the use of symbols of prestige or importance. Everyone has a need for prestige, recognition, and acceptance. By fulfilling these needs, management can help produce a happy, willing employee who is motivated toward the goals of the organization and requires little control. These needs may be fulfilled by using euphemistic titles (scrub steward or machine operator instead of dishwasher), by giving awards like "employee of the week," and by stimulating the acceptance of all employees with meetings, gatherings, and social events.

Top management should exert as little pressure or formal control as possible. Some behaviorists feel that when control comes from the top, workers become more apathetic and require even more control, which in turn may require another layer of supervision and cause the top to become more remote. Positive results can be realized by encouraging employees' participation in establishing their own objectives and then asking how they expect to accomplish them. Of course, the supervisor should also participate in such interviews. Employees may then be rated on how well they achieve their own objectives.

COSTS

So far we have considered more of the theoretical aspects of control in cost control. Let us also consider some cost aspects. Throughout most of the text we will be dealing primarily with costs under the conceptual area of control.

Cost control is often lacking in the foodservice industry, a situation attributable to many factors. Most foodservice operations are relatively small, and in many cases the management is relatively unsophisticated. Or the management may be more concerned with such other aspects as creating culinary masterpieces or marketing their operations. In many cases the quantity (span of control) or quality of supervision may be lacking. For example, a cook may be a supervisor simply because she can cook food, not because of any supervisory talents or control capabilities. The changing varieties of foods produced by a foodservice operation are harder to control than the long production runs of the relatively few items most factories produce. Fast-food operations, with their unchanging and relatively limited menus, have given new insights into foodservice control (and, incidentally, rather resemble factory production runs).

Most operations are either retail (such as retail stores) or manufacturing (such as factories) in nature. A foodservice operation is both, which adds to the problem of cost control.

The nature of the product or food complicates control. A menu item is different from most retail sales, and the large element of amorphous personal service and atmosphere in the product makes it more difficult to control.

ABSENTEE OWNERSHIP OR MANAGEMENT

The further removed an owner or manager is from some aspect of an operation, the more need for control. Those who operate their own one-person hot dog stands may need some accounting information for control but relatively little else because they do everything themselves. When they bring in employees, more control is necessary since they now must control others. One aspect of the traditional control theory is keeping an eye on things. The more "things" that are going on, the more necessary control becomes. In many ways, then, control procedures are a substitute for owners or managers. A problem in some foodservice establishments is that in the beginning the founder was there and on top of things. As the operation prospered and grew, control procedures did not keep pace since the founder could no longer give the same attention to the larger operation.

A contribution of the large multiunit chain operations is that because of their size and numbers, they have been forced to develop and utilize cost-control procedures that are gradually trickling down into other types of operations.

RELATIONSHIP WITH QUALITY CONTROL

With every cost-control effort there should be a quality-control effort. It is easy to cut costs by cutting quality or portion sizes. One national fast-food service chain got into trouble by cutting portion sizes and quality. It experienced a quick and direct reaction and a drop in sales. It took several years to recover, even after portions and quality returned to former levels. Cost control and quality control are not mutually exclusive and often complement each other. Standard recipes, for example, are a cost-control procedure but also can be a quality-control procedure. Determining what preferred costs should be also requires that the desired quality levels be determined. Without defined cost-control procedures, defined quality levels may not be spelled out.

Cost controls can also provide information on quality-control problems. Too low a labor-cost percentage can be an indication of less-than-optimum service or quality. Total quality management, as discussed in Chapter 3, can be very important in control.

COST-BENEFIT RELATIONSHIPS

The effort, time, and expense of cost control must be evaluated against its benefits. To save on what it thought was excessive use of pencils and perhaps some pilferage, a hospital required its employees to turn in a used pencil stub to get a new pencil. The inconvenience, time, and effort devoted to administering the procedure far outweighed any savings it produced. Throughout this text you will find many cost approaches and procedures discussed. But no one operation will want to use all of them. Different operations have different needs and levels of needs, and just because there is a procedure for a certain cost area does not necessarily mean it should be adopted.

Deciding what procedures to use includes evaluating the need for control, which may be contending with an actual or potential loss, appraising the culture of the operation, and evaluating the sophistication of the staff.

The culture includes the attitudes of employees. For example, at first, the introduction of precheck registers and automated beverage systems caused many waitresses and bartenders to resign. That lesson suggests that management must decide how to introduce innovations and how much dissonance it is willing to take. Many good control procedures have been overtly or covertly sabotaged by employees.

Some operations have found that despite a desire to cooperate, some employees have difficulty using cost-control approaches. Old-time cooks may find standardized recipes bothersome. Some waitresses have problems with computerized ordering. Fortunately, the wider adoption of these new procedures produces more acceptance, and after an initial period of fear, most can adapt to their complexity.

Some operations with cost procedures in such areas as purchasing, receiving, storing, and production experience little loss. The question then arises: Are the procedures necessary? The other real question is, What would the losses be without the control? The increased use of computers makes many control procedures far less costly to employ. At a relatively small expense, an operation can now stop many of its losses or at least alert management to them.

The advent of computerized systems can bring an overabundance of cost procedures and makes much more management information available. But management must decide how much and what kind of information it needs to avoid information overkill. (Chapter 6 discusses management information systems.)

UNCONTROLLABLE COSTS

Management may have little or no control over certain costs. Union agreements or local wage rates may determine salary levels, for example. Rent agreements and some types of insurance may be fixed costs that present management with little opportunity for reductions at an operations level. (The negotiating level is a different story.) One generally has little say over certain financing costs. But sometimes costs thought to be uncontrollable can be affected by cost controls. Even if wage rates are set by negotiation, making employees more productive can reduce labor costs.

MANAGERIAL CONCERN

A major factor in the effectiveness of any cost-control procedure is the concern or perceived concern of management. Many cost-control procedures have failed because management did not enforce them. Employees are quick to notice how much importance their supervisors place on cost control. Operations may institute such cost-control procedures as weighing incoming foods, writing out standard recipes, or formulating work-production standards. But if management does not insist that they be followed, these controls are useless. Effective cost control requires a strong commitment from management. If employees believe management does not care, why should they? At the extreme, if employees observe managers themselves "ripping off" the operation, the employees will consider it a license for their own rip-offs.

PERCENTAGE SYSTEMS

Cost percentages such as a food-cost percentage (food cost per sales) or a labor-cost percentage (labor cost per sales) are widely used in the foodservice field to provide cost analyses and control. Although these percentages can be helpful, an overreliance on them may be misleading. These percentages assume, for example, that selling prices are correct. If the selling prices are higher or lower than they should be, the resulting percentages will be distorted. Assume a foodservice operation has labor costs of $3,000 and sales of $10,000, providing a labor-cost percentage of 30 percent. If selling prices were raised 10 percent and the number of items sold remained the same, sales would be $11,000. The labor-cost percentage would now be 27.3 percent ($3,000/$11,000), indicating an improvement, whereas in actuality productivity has remained the same.

The percentages might better be used as a pricing device rather than a cost-control device. It has been said that you bank dollars, not percentages. Let us assume that your menu offers a steak for $15.00 with a 50 percent food cost. Another item is a chicken dinner at $10.00 with a 40 percent food cost. On a percentage basis, the chicken would be a more profitable item for the operation; however, on a gross profit basis, the steak is more profitable.

	Selling Price	Food Cost	Gross Profit
Steak	$15.00	$7.50 (50%)	$7.50
Chicken	$10.00	$4.00 (40%)	$6.00

There is also a problem in determining the desired percentage and comparing the percentages between different operations. Layouts, menus, and the type of personnel can affect percentages considerably. A 30 percent food cost for one operation is not necessarily appropriate for a different operation.

FINANCIAL CONTROL

Aspects of financial control are discussed throughout this book, especially in the chapters on food-cost accounting, budgeting, and financial statements. Financial control should be a major part of cost control. Financial control is attained through analysis of dollar amounts and figures. Larger operations may have a food (and beverage) controller to specifically deal with these figures. People dealing with this financial data in a foodservice operation are sometimes called "bean counters," "figures people," or "the pencil nerds."

Financial control often involves management accounting, which produces numerical information to help management conduct the enterprise. Financial accounting, on the other hand, is primarily concerned with the financial resources and profits (or losses) of the enterprise. Some aspects of financial control in a foodservice operation include budgets that project sales and costs. Actual sales and cost figures are then compared to the projected figures, and the variances and differences are analyzed.

Food-cost accounting systems are another area of financial control. The systems may be primarily concerned with percentages that show expenses and profit as a percentage of sales, or standard cost systems that determine what costs should be and then compare actual costs to them, a process that provides a variance to be analyzed.

Ratio analyses use ratios and percentages to help analyze an operation. Inventory turnover (cost of goods sold divided by average inventory) might be a ratio used. The food controller may also produce regular operating reports, perhaps on a daily basis, that show such detailed information as labor costs, menu tracking, labor-cost percentages, work-production standards, comparison of turnover rates, overtime and overtime percentages, and any costly accidents. Computers and data processing can make more information available more rapidly. It is now possible to produce daily income statements or even a statement for each meal (showing profit or losses), whereas with strictly manual methods, such information might not be available for weeks, and then only on a weekly or monthly basis.

Special studies may also be part of the controller's work. Whether it is better financially to make a food item from scratch or buy it in prepared form, or how long it would take for a proposed piece of equipment to pay for itself are two typical examples of questions such studies can answer.

SUMMARY

Control, one of the basic management functions, is vital in any endeavor and can be exercised in different ways and different areas. This text is concerned with the area of cost control for foodservice operations. Cost control is important in profit-making operations since costs are the difference between sales and profit, and lower costs provide a higher profit. In nonprofit operations, cost control allows a manager to provide better service to clients with resources available.

One management approach to control includes:

- defining objectives,
- preparing plans and programs to achieve objectives,
- providing a suitable organization to implement the plans and programs,
- setting policies and procedures to provide direction,

- providing the necessary funding,
- providing the necessary personnel, and
- comparing performance with goals or objectives.

In considering control, one should also consider cost-volume-profit relationships. Important to both costs and profits is the contribution margin, or that portion of sales that is available for overhead and profit. Many management decisions should be based on their effect on the contribution margin.

The variable rate is found by dividing variable costs by sales. It and its partner, the contribution rate, can be used for such calculations as sales revenue needed to break even, number of meals necessary to break even, or sales necessary to produce a certain profit. Control can also be approached from a traditional or a behavioristic standpoint. The traditional theory includes two aspects. One is direction, or keeping an eye on things; the other is measurement and comparison of actual performance with planned performance followed by an investigation of any discrepancy. This process involves:

- establishing standards and goals,
- measuring performance,
- comparing and analyzing, and
- taking corrective action.

The behavioristic approach to control emphasizes the individuals who are doing the work instead of the use of supervision and quantified measurement to achieve control. It stresses that if workers feel positively toward an organization, they will do their best and need little control. Strict controls can also be self-defeating since their rigidness can alienate the workers. Cost control is a substitute for an absent manager or owner. If that individual could do all the work, there would be little need for control. However, when others do the work away from the supervision of the owner or manager, a need for control arises.

For every cost control there also should be quality control. It is easy to cut costs by cutting portion sizes or quality, but in the long run (or short run) there may be a real disadvantage to the establishment. The concept of total quality management has important control applications.

There is a cost-benefit relationship regarding costs. Some cost-control procedures may cost too much in relation to benefits gained. A manager should be aware that it is necessary to concentrate on major costs regardless of interest. A food-centered manager should not neglect labor costs.

Many of the cost-control procedures in foodservice establishments involve food- or labor-cost percentages. Although such percentages are helpful, total reliance on them can cause problems.

KEY TERMS

behavioristic approach to control
contribution margin
control
cost-benefit analysis
MBWA

PPBSE
prime costs
total quality control
traditional control theory
variable rate

REVIEW QUESTIONS

2–1 Briefly discuss three areas of control in foodservice establishments.

2–2 Why is cost control so important to a commercial (profit-making) foodservice establishment?

2–3 List the steps necessary to provide control.

2–4 What happens to a foodservice establishment when control is lacking?

2–5 What is a contribution margin and why is it important?

2–6 What is the difference between an income statement prepared on a traditional basis and one prepared on a contribution-margin basis?

2–7 What is the variable rate?

2–8 An operation finds that income does not total expenses on certain days. Explain from a contribution standpoint why it should or should not close on those days.

2–9 How does traditional control theory differ from behavioral control theory?

2–10 What are the elements of traditional control theory?

2–11 How can a foodservice operation implement the behavioristic approach to control?

2–12 Why is cost control often lacking in the foodservice industry?

2–13 Why is control a substitute for absentee ownership or management?

2–14 Why should a foodservice operation not rely primarily on percentages for control?

2–15 How does total quality management affect control?

PROBLEM

2–1 The following information is given for a restaurant:

Sales	$1,000,000
Food cost	$ 300,000
Nonfood variable costs	$ 350,000
Fixed costs	$ 250,000
Average selling price per meal	$ 20

a. What is the profit?

b. What is the contribution ratio?

c. What is the variable rate?

d. What is the break-even figure in dollars?

e. How many meals have to be served for the operation to break even?

f. The owners would like to increase profits by 50 percent. What new sales volume and number-of-meals-sold volume are now necessary?

3

Total Quality Management (TQM)

Food service operations are becoming more and more competitive. Keys in the competition fight are satisfied customers, lower costs, and better employee performance. TQM is a management concept that has been adopted by many operations to achieve these.

After completing this chapter, you should be able to:

1. Discuss the TQM process.
2. Appreciate the real costs of poor service and poor quality.
3. Utilize the TQM process.
4. Evaluate such TQM tools as empowerment, benchmarking, outsourcing.
5. Understand the concept of service blueprinting.

QUALITY CONTROL

Quality control as a management approach is getting more and more attention, largely because of the success of Japanese industry, which is based on the teachings of an American consultant, **W. Edwards Deming**. Now American companies, including hospitality businesses, are considering and teaching methods that are embodied in his **14 points of management** (Figure 3.1). The approach is sometimes referred to as *total quality management* (TQM), *total quality control* (TQC), or *company-wide quality control* (CWQC). Originally Deming developed a statistically oriented approach for manufacturing enterprises. It has since been adapted by many hospitality organizations, including the Ritz-Carlton Hotel chain (which has won the coveted Malcolm Baldridge Award), the Marriott organization, and Taco Bell fast-food chain.

When this theory is put into practice, three elements must function together like a three-legged stool (if one element is missing, the result is disaster):

1. Create a constancy of purpose for improvement of products and services.
2. Adopt a new philosophy: poor quality is unacceptable.
3. Cease dependence on mass inspection.
4. End the practice of awarding business on price tag alone.
5. Constantly and forever improve the system of production and service.
6. Institute modern methods of training on the job.
7. Institute modern methods of supervising.
8. Drive out fear.
9. Break down barriers between departments.
10. Eliminate numerical goals for the work force.
11. Eliminate work standards and numerical quotas.
12. Remove barriers that hinder hourly workers.
13. Institute a vigorous program of education and training.
14. Create a structure in top management that will push every day on the above 13 points.

Figure 3.1
Deming's 14 Points

1. *Quality as defined by the client.* This refers not to what management necessarily likes to produce, but what the customer really wants.

2. *Systematic or database approach to the studying process.* Dr. Deming believed that 85 percent of quality lapses are caused by the processes, procedures, or equipment used and that only 15 percent are caused solely by employees. For example, could production errors in the kitchen be decreased by better training, different foodstuffs, different equipment, or better standard procedures? Dr. Deming also contended that top management is responsible for 96 percent of the quality of a system's products and services; thus the worker is tied to only 4 percent of the problems associated with poor quality.

3. *Employees and associates working together.* The operation functions together as a team (this involves the behavioristic approach to control).

Dr. Deming offered 14 points of guidance to managers (Figure 3.1). Whether an operation adopts a formal TQM program or not, these points can be very useful.

Deming believed that with each improvement, processes and systems run better. Productivity increases as waste decreases. Clients get better products, which ultimately increase market share and provide better return on investments. This is illustrated in the Deming chain reaction (Figure 3.2).

For the chain reaction to occur, principles of total quality management must be followed. They include:

1. *Client focus.* The focus should not be on profit, loss, or return on investment, but on the customer. If you meet and exceed client wants and expectations, profits will follow.

2. *Obsession with quality.* Obsession with quality must permeate the whole organization. This will delight the customers and provide better control and procedures.

Figure 3.2
Total Quality Management
(TQM) Deming Chain
Reaction

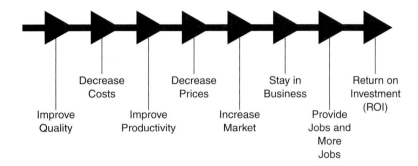

3. *Recognizing the structure in work.* Let workers monitor themselves as much as possible. If they are motivated, they will provide better services and create less waste.

4. *Freedom through control.* Have standard procedures. Variation in output can be reduced by reducing variation in the way work is performed.

5. *Unity of purpose.* Foster an environment where all employees work toward a clear vision of what is to be accomplished. Slogans such as "We are family" or "We are the best" are believed.

6. *Looking for faults in systems.* There is no one best way. There is always a better way. Any system can be improved. Operations should be constantly improving the way they operate. Too often SOW (the same old way) predominates.

7. *Continued education and training.* In a quality organization, everyone at every level is constantly training to improve his or her performance.

THE REAL COSTS OF POOR SERVICE AND QUALITY

The costs of waste and rework are more easily seen and understood by management and translated to "bottom line" outcomes (e.g., food cost, excess labor costs, etc.). However, another cost also translates to the bottom line, the cost of losing a guest (customer). This could be thought of in financial management terms as the opportunity cost of lost customers (and future value). Financially speaking, it could also be viewed long term as the future value of a guest to be projected over the life of a guest. The bottom line is if you lose a guest due to poor service or quality, you cannot bank on these future dollars, which represents an opportunity cost to you.

Let's look at some examples. One would think that customers cheated out of their service would complain. According to the U.S. Office of Consumer Affairs, between 37 and 45 percent of consumers who are unhappy with service do not complain. They go elsewhere. They may go elsewhere, but they never forget. And when they remember you, it's always with the kind of word of mouth that causes you to die a thousand deaths: once from embarrassment and 999 times at the cash register as would-be guests get the message. They join the one dissatisfied guest as they vote with their feet and cross the street.

INDUSTRY INSIGHTS Managing for Quality   by Patrick Mene

Patrick Mene is Vice President, Quality, The Ritz-Carlton Hotel Company and a graduate of Penn State's Hotel, Restaurant and Institutional Management program. Patrick was involved in Ritz-Carlton winning the 1992 National Quality Award, the Malcolm Baldridge Award. To date, the Ritz-Carlton Hotel Company is the only hospitality firm to win the coveted Baldridge Award.

The cost to identify and correct any defective work is high and embedded everywhere in any enterprise. This defective work, known as the cost of poor quality, not only impacts costs but prevents the enterprise from maximizing revenues and damages employee morale. Some broad examples of defective work are: (1) hiring the wrong employee, (2) employees not conforming to standards, (3) managers blaming workers for management-controlled problems, (4) buying the wrong equipment, (5) not resolving a customer's problem immediately and completely, (6) issuing an illegible invoice.

A well-documented example of the cost of poor quality occurred in a Ritz-Carlton resort hotel in the United States. This property featured a magnificent outdoor pool and sunbathing area accommodating several hundred guests. Among the most popular products served there was the frozen yogurt and the yogurt-based cream drinks made by a machine at the poolside area. A chronic problem was the unreliability of the yogurt machine. The failures were frequent, causing lost sales, rework, added steps, accidents, employee fatigue, turnover, and customer dissatisfaction. Management of the property decided the purchase of a new yogurt machine would remedy the trouble. The choice of a $12,000 unit was influenced by a $5,000 discount on the purchase price.

Management was surprised when workers at the pool area complained about the new equipment. Some managers resented the protest, even claiming the workforce was "insatiable." An investigation by the hotel purchasing agent uncovered the following facts:

1. The capacity of the new machine was inadequate for production needs.
2. The workforce was not trained in an important particular: to store the yogurt mix between 30°F and 45°F. The use of improperly stored mix rendered the unit inoperable.
3. The workers were substituting expensive ingredients.
4. Procuring the substitute ingredients caused extra work paid at the overtime rate.
5. Customers of the pool bar were dissatisfied with the sporadic unavailability of yogurt during the summer.

In the words of one worker, "Seven thousand dollars was spent. Things are worse. Yet management thinks they saved $5,000." Management for quality was a vital missing element in the original planning and in the replanning of yogurt production.

These costs of identifying and correcting defective work cannot be readily accounted for or allocated to a specific department (by traditional accounting methods)*. These costs of quality are built into the operating standards, built into the overhead, and built into the budget. In fact, meeting budget is a further limitation to reduce these costs.

CONVENTIONAL MANAGEMENT EFFORTS DON'T ADDRESS POOR QUALITY

The underlying causes of poor quality remain unaddressed when we focus our efforts on:

- delegating goals to each division head (and subsequently to their subordinates)
- encouraging everyone to reach these goals by counseling, establishing blame, and motivating
- Poor quality costs can only be reduced on a project-by-project basis with the personal involvement of upper management.

*Where would you charge the costs of the machine case?

1. To the pool bar where the defective work in the yogurt occurred.
2. To purchasing to make the transaction.
3. To administration and general because the general manager authorized its purchase.

Table 3.1
The Future Value of a Guest

Restaurant Segment	Check Average	Meals per Year	Revenue Future Value		
			1 Year	5 Years	25 Years
Quick service restaurant	$ 4.75	24	$114	$ 570	$ 2,850[1]
Casual theme restaurant	$14.00	18	$252	$1,260	$ 6,300[1]
Fine dining	$45.00	9	$405	$2,025	$10,125[1]

[1]The future value would be higher if you build in the interest yield from a bank, for example.

CUSTOMER VALUATION

The value of guests is obvious in that businesses fail without them. The fact is that few service businesses can survive long without a substantial number of repeat guests. Therefore, retention is critical.

What is the value of a long-term customer? One way of answering this question is to think of the present value of the same guest as the revenue potential from that guest over a lifetime. Table 3.1 shows the monthly, one-year, and five-year revenue potential of a dinner guest for three different restaurant segments. When guests do business, they bring with them the potential for a sizable future revenue stream.

Table 3.1 actually undervalues the worth of a guest. The revenue potential of a repeat guest also includes any business brought to the property through positive word-of-mouth referrals. In addition, recent research into service-related businesses suggests that revenue and profitability are higher for purchases made by repeat customers than for purchases made by first-time or one-time customers.

The flip side is the cost of a dissatisfied customer. When dissatisfied guests walk out the door, they take with them future business. It is reported that the average dissatisfied customer tells 8 to 10 people about his or her problems with a business, and that 1 out of every 5 dissatisfied customers tells 20 people.

Using the information in Table 3.1, if an unhappy guest tells 10 other potential guests of the casual theme restaurant the potential future cost is $63,000 over 25 years. And their guests are likely to dine with others in their party, therefore inflating the figure further. A service survey found the following information on why guests quit coming to a retail business:

- 3 percent of guests move
- 14 percent leave for competitive reasons
- 14 percent are dissatisfied with the product
- 68 percent quit because of a poor service attitude of the business

SERVICE QUALITY: WHY, WHAT, HOW

Service quality is essential for industry survival. Therefore, the basics of service quality and the popular total quality management (TQM) can be distilled down to two fundamentals:

1. Meeting or positively exceeding customer expectation through quality products (food) and service ("doing the right thing[s]").

2. "Doing things right" to insure profitability through process engineering and guarding against defects or deficiencies (Figure 3.3).

In reality, the first fundamental is an outcome or effect of the second. That is, if you do things right (to meet/exceed customer expectations), the product or service generally will satisfy quality needs of guests. In sum, service quality is a combination of doing the right things for guests and doing things right (the process, defect free, including standard operation procedures [SOPs], guest policies, etc.).

Let's look at doing things right, or continuously improving process efforts. TQM implies that you continuously fine-tune the process or activities, work flow, or steps involved in a process such as preparing a menu item or taking a food order from a guest because there is always room for improvement or a better way.

It is said, "If you wait until something is broken to fix it, there may not be anything left to fix." All customer interactions can be broken down to a systems model of activities and processes. TQM recommends that an operation gets the process right, rather than correcting problems in a poorly designed process.

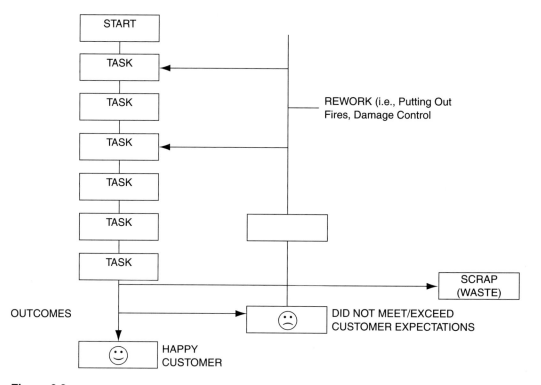

Figure 3.3
A Typical Process

THE PROCESS

TQM is not something that is finished and accomplished but is a continual improving process accomplished through three- to five-person teams utilizing executives, supervisors, and lowest-ranking employees. Special quality improvement teams may be assembled to work on problems or situations brought to light by individual employees or others. Standing problem-solving teams concentrate on any problem they perceive. A comprehensive performance evaluation process empowers people who are performing a job to develop better job procedures and performance standards. Although the process function of continual improvement is constant, when one problem is resolved, another problem is addressed by the team and the process starts over again. Since improvement is continual, problems may be readdressed over time perhaps using more sophistication, new technology, or a different approach.

Process teams have the goals of

1. aligning the entire organization around common objectives and the general mission of the operation.
2. encouraging all to think beyond the status quo and consider new ways to accomplish daily activities.
3. increasing and helping communication among the various segments of the operation.
4. integrating problem solving. (A change in the dining areas, for example, could have ramifications in the kitchen.)

The general process is directed by a steering committee of top executives. They assist the other committees in setting objectives and preparing action plans. A designated quality leader, either from the organization or an outside consultant, may help teams develop their plans. Figure 3.4 illustrates the Ritz-Carlton quality model.

ESTABLISHING A TQM PROCESS

Establishing a TQM program and making it work is not easy and requires the enthusiastic support of top management along with the entire staff. The program system may be divided between tactical (day-to-day operations) and strategic (or long-range planning) aspects.

DATA COLLECTION SYSTEMS

TQM programs require management information systems to provide information on

1. *On-line patron preferences.* What do your patrons want in menu items, service levels, pricing, decor, etc.? TQM is based on what your patrons want, and you need an information system to provide this input.

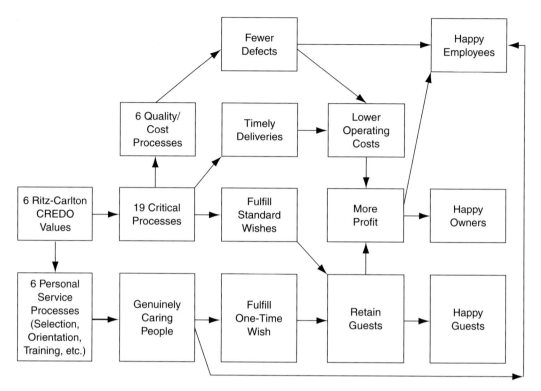

Figure 3.4
Ritz-Carlton Quality Model
Courtesy: Ritz-Carlton Hotel Corp.

2. *Quantity of error-free products.* When were food items overproduced, wasted, or returned by customers? When were problems with employee performance reported? TQM considers improved quality necessary to decrease costs and increase production, which in turn decreases prices and increases market share.

3. *Opportunities for quality improvement.* The goal of a food service TQM system is to become more integrated, more proactive, and more preventive. There must be constant concern to determine that the operation is providing what patrons want most in an appropriate time period, every time.

Data collection in service industries is more difficult than in manufacturing where information, such as production units and rejects, or lack of quality can be measured quantitatively. Sources of data collection in food service can be from POS registers, back office computers, comment cards, employee termination reports, informal conversations with customers, visual inspections, and financial data. If customer comment cards are utilized, they should be well thought out. Instead of just asking patrons to rate the service, they could also respond about what they liked about the restaurant or how it might be improved.

In considering financial data, remember that costs are not the only crucial component. The concern also is with providing quality and guest satisfaction. According to TQM theory, if this is done, costs will be lower and resulting profits will increase.

STANDARDS

Data collection by itself is a fruitless exercise without measures, standards, and past performance data for comparison. Originally, TQM was statistically oriented. The statistical approach may work better in industries other than foodservice. Some measures of quality, such as employee friendliness, are difficult to measure quantitatively. However, many aspects in a foodservice operation can be measured, including costs, returns, employee turnover, time required to serve, and volume changes.

Without some type of measurement it is difficult to see if you are matching goals, improving, or just standing still. One of the problems in utilizing TQM is determining which standards or measurements are significant.

EMPOWERMENT

In TQM, **empowerment** means giving employees the responsibility and authority to solve patron problems. Ideally the employee can immediately devote time to resolve the problem. This can be hard, say, for a waitperson who is serving others at the same time. In TQM theory, the first person who detects a problem is empowered to break away from routine duties, investigate, correct the problem immediately, document the incident, and then return to regular duties. The employee should be empowered to make adjustments (up to a predetermined dollar limit) without having to go to a higher authority. Thus, if a patron is unhappy with a menu item, the server can say it is on the house.

Empowerment is important in TQM. Originally the program was more focused on management and could be defined as management actions designed to share power and decision making with employees. However, empowerment is becoming more employee-focused and directs more concern to the motivational states of employees and the processes that shape them. Crucial to this notion is the culture of the organization or shared behavioral expectations.

A constructive culture fosters self-perception, interaction, self-actualization (or feeling of achievement), affiliation, and encouragement of persons. This in turn should foster a sense of meaningfulness, impact, and choice. The result may be better relationships with supervisors, less turnover, promotion satisfaction, and more cooperation within the organization.

HUMAN RESOURCES

Quality is achieved through people, and the human resource and operations functions should be integrated. Before someone is hired, the job requirements should be determined and written down as job specifications. A prospective employee should be considered in light of these specifications. The duties of the job should also be well thought out and detailed in a job description. Some operations use various tests to determine the suitability of applicants. Both human resources and operations people together should decide on hiring decisions. TQM requires employee involvement. This can lead to greater employee satisfaction and in many cases lower employee turnover.

Inherent in TQM is the assumption that even the lowest-level employee is vital to the operation. All employees should be aware of what is happening in the operation, and supervisors should use modern methods of supervision with a team approach.

BENCHMARKING

Benchmarking is a relatively new term that has become a management buzzword in recent years. It also is an element of TQM. **Benchmarking** can be defined as a process that identifies best practices and approaches by comparing a company's functional productivity with other companies both within and outside its industry (which is also called **extra-industry benchmarking**). It considers not only how well you may be doing but also how other operations function. A simple type of benchmarking is visiting a competitor and observing specific aspects of that operation. TQM practitioners are especially interested in how other operations treat their customers and their levels of customer satisfaction.

Strategic benchmarking is a term used to compare financial performance measures such as return on investment, return on assets managed, or operating ratio. It compares one operation's performance with other leading companies or industry statistics. Operational benchmarking, which compares costs and industry statistics, can be very useful. Organizational benchmarking is concerned with the staffing efficiency such as personnel productivity measures.

Benchmarking can utilize other industries' methods. A restaurant that at times has a large number of people waiting for tables may study how a theater or an amusement park handles its crowds. Benchmarking provides three main benefits. First, benchmarking provides numeric (and sometimes qualitative) goals to measure performance. Second, benchmarking provides insights into other organizations' innovations or approaches. Third, benchmarking takes organizations beyond their own four walls. It forces managers and others to consider perspectives other than those they are familiar and comfortable with.

OUTSOURCING

In TQM, a restaurant or other operation strives to find the best process to achieve customer satisfaction. In many situations, the best process idea might be having an outside organization provide the product or services. **Outsourcing** the function, especially if those outside organizations are specialists in the area, may produce an item or service better or cheaper. Outsourcing can involve the factory technique of having long, efficient production runs of items. At one time, large kitchens had their own butcher shops, but most now find it easier to purchase their meat items from specialists. If a limited quantity of bread or pastry items is needed, why not purchase them from a specialist?

Manufacturing enterprises try to tie in outsourcing with another concept called *just-in-time delivery*. This eliminates tying up money in inventory and storage space. Outsourcing can be used by food service operations to a lesser extent. An extreme example in outsourcing is the kitchenless kitchen described in Chapter 17.

Possible advantages of outsourcing to a foodservice operation include:

- more consistent quality from specialists
- perhaps a lower cost (even with a profit for the producer)

- less space and specialized equipment required
- no need to have inventories of raw materials for the products and consequently less investment in inventory and space
- potential reduction in the need for hard-to-find skilled employees
- simplified production supervision
- provision of a wider variety than the operation can supply itself

In the future it is likely that more and more foodservice operations will try to eliminate or cut down on their manufacturing or production function by utilizing outsourcing.

SERVICE DESIGN BLUEPRINTING

Dr. Deming stressed in TQM theory that mistakes and problems in an organization delivering a service (or product) are most likely caused by a faulty process or processes used in preparing that service or product and not by the employees. Process development is a management responsibility with employee impact.

Service system blueprints can help to eliminate process problems. The simplest definition of a service system blueprint is "the picture of a service system." Service system blueprints are flowcharts that systemize the description, documentation, and analysis of a service process. Although service blueprints are flowcharts, there is some difference from the standard flowchart technique. Usual flowcharts have on-off or yes-no rules (when something happens or doesn't happen, do this or that). Service blueprints show the pattern of a service and steps involved. This may not present yes-no decision points.

Service system blueprints can:

- depict interactions between the process and the customer
- more easily identify critical process points where customer service can be affected
- be more precise than verbal definitions and less subject to misinterpretations by allowing the testing of assumptions on paper and facilitating elimination of bugs
- communicate details of a service in ways that are useful to managers and employees
- reveal systems or interactions that might not be apparent if not plotted
- help encourage creativity and problem solving
- cut down the time and inefficiency of random service development that might not visualize the whole picture
- identify key service elements contributing to consumer satisfaction
- provide a benchmark to measure execution, analyze proposals, compare competitors, and develop promotional plans
- be very helpful in training
- be useful in developing or purchasing new software
- help in decision-making activities such as strategy setting, allocation of resources, integration of service functions, and evaluation of overall performance

CONSTRUCTING AND READING A SERVICE BLUEPRINT

It is beyond the scope of this text to delve into detailed construction of service blueprints, but a familiarity with the nomenclature and steps in the process of reading them can be helpful. A concept blueprint is a macro-level or broad-picture blueprint (Figure 3.5). It provides a view of the service at an overview level and demonstrates how various jobs and sections or departments function in a relationship to the service as a whole. A detailed blueprint is a micro-level blueprint. It shows details of an element of the service system that might be identified but not described on the concept blueprint. Service blueprints analyze performance that is defined as the series of actions, or tasks, undertaken in rendering a service understood to be an instrumental interaction.

A service is considered instrumental if it is a means or pathway to a definite end or outcome. Service interaction differs from social or other types of interaction by being pur-

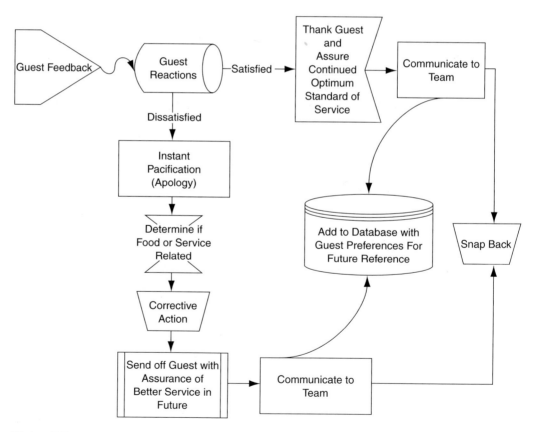

Figure 3.5
24-hour Coffee Shop Service Blueprint

poseful and goal-directed, designed to achieve specified outcomes. The interaction refers to reciprocal or mutual actions taken by both the patron and service contact person. Having the patron or user involved in the creation and service process differentiates service industries from the manufacturing sector.

We have considered service as a process but it is also a structure. The structure can involve the physical setting, organizational structure, management system, and organizational culture, along with many other factors.

A crucial element in a foodservice business is the customer. Since customer satisfaction or desire is the goal of the process, the customer is the most important part of the process. A service blueprint depicts process and structure by employing the horizontal and vertical dimensions of a flat surface. Process is depicted from the left to right on the horizontal axis as a series of actions (rectangles) plotted chronologically along the horizontal axis of the service system blueprints. A flow line marks the service path by connecting discrete actions chronologically.

Service structure is depicted on the vertical axis as organizational strata, or structural layers. Three primary structural strata are common to all services: consumer interaction, support functions, and management. Within these three primary strata, finer distinctions can be made. In essence, a service system blueprint turns the traditional organization chart upside down and adds action to it.

In the consumer stratum, a line of interaction demarcates actions performed by the consumer from actions performed by contact personnel. Consumer actions are placed above the line. Actions performed by contact people are located below the line. As noted earlier, these actions are charted on the service path proceeding from left to right.

The actions of contact personnel are further classified by a line of visibility which separates onstage from backstage actions. Onstage actions refer to the public performance of the service, or actions visible to the consumer. Not surprisingly, onstage actions often represent the tip of the service iceberg. Contact people do not normally work in a vacuum. Other departments contribute services or materials (facilitating goods) used in rendering the service.

Lines of internal interaction separate support functions from the backstage, contact stratum. Lines of internal interaction delineate the service firm's internal customer, whether across departmental lines or from one work station or professional specialty to another within the same department. It is this characteristic that makes the concept blueprint useful as a communications tool for conveying the service "big picture" to all service employees. Such a device builds awareness of how an individual's job contributes to creation of the service overall.

Finally, the concept blueprint demonstrates management's role in facilitating the operation of the service system. A line of implementation separates the planning and organizing functions from "doing" activities. By documenting process and structure, both concept and detailed blueprints support management's task as decision-maker.

HOW TO READ A SERVICE SYSTEM BLUEPRINT

Learning to read a service system blueprint is similar to learning to read a map. It is necessary to learn the conventions—north is up, south is down. The conventions are few in service blueprinting, but it is important to understand them (Figure 3.6).

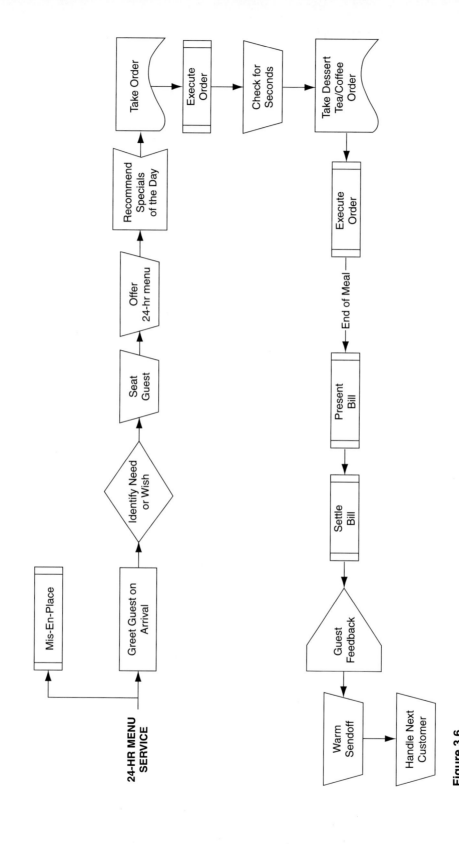

Figure 3.6
24-hour Coffee Shop Service Blueprint at the Micro Level–Mid-Day/Evening/Late-Night/Early Morning 24-hour Menu Service

A service system blueprint answers the question: Who does what, to whom, how often, under what conditions? On a service blueprint, the process symbol (rectangle) describes "who does what, to whom," the flow of lines denotes "how often," and the decision symbol (diamond) describes "under what conditions."

The basic operations paradigm—Input → Processing → Output—is a second framework for reading service blueprints: *input* refers to the action, event, or condition that initiates the services; *processing* refers to changes made to the input during the service process; and *output* refers to the final outcome or result.

A service blueprint scanned with these frameworks in mind conveys to the reader a sense of basic contours and dynamics. To gain a sense of the basic service path and interaction, scan the blueprint horizontally along the line of visibility. To gain a sense of the backstage and support functions, scan the blueprint vertically.

To read a service blueprint in detail, begin at the line of interaction. Who does what to initiate the service? First, trace the service process by following the service path from the consumer's point of view.

Second, trace the contact person's path. Note setup and follow-up activities in the backstage area.

Third, trace the path of support functions, noting points of initiation and termination and noting how and when handoffs occur.

Finally, examine the management stratum, paying special attention to management information reports. What is included? What is left out? What do these reports tell you about management values and priorities?

Reading a service system blueprint from the right gives a sense of its horizontal integration, the rationality of the service from the consumer's point of view. Reading a service blueprint from top to bottom gives a measure of the vertical integration, the rationality and economy of handoffs between departments and/or work stations.

The design of a service blueprint should meet two criteria: economy and symmetry. Economy in a service blueprint is achieved when two points are linked by the shortest possible distance and when the service system blueprint is free of redundancy. Symmetry in a service blueprint is achieved by identifying the decisions (branching) or procedural sequences that are of equal weight and by placing them in the blueprint at the same line or row. The communications power of a service blueprint is enhanced when these criteria are met.

A TQM APPLICATION

The food service industry has been slower than many to adopt TQM. A notable success in using its principles came in the 1990s with a fast-food chain. Previously the chain's development was based on good location sites, advertising, and new products. The key to productivity was based on tight supervision and control over employees.

Extensive consumer studies show that customers did not care that much about new products. What they really wanted was expressed in the acronym FACT: Fast service, Accurate orders served in a Clean restaurant at the right Temperature. The chain decided it was not fulfilling these expectations as well as possible. To improve its performance, a number of changes were made. These included:

- redesigning the layout of stores
- revamping the POS technology
- more efficiently allocating its labor forces
- preparing more food items off-site (outsourcing)
- using automation and different equipment to provide more food items
- restructuring management procedures completely

The supervisor's role changed to being more of a coach than police officer. The manager's role changed from just monitoring employees to include developing their talents so they could contribute more to the team effort. A customer toll-free number along with other feedback devices to keep track of customer desires was also implemented.

FAILURES IN TQM

Although TQM has been enthusiastically adopted by many and even considered the Holy Grail by some, not everyone is convinced and there have been notable failures by companies utilizing it. One survey of 531 companies found that 68 percent of them had tried some sort of quality initiative but only 41 percent found it very effective. A new field of consultants has sprung up to advise organizations how to extract themselves from TQM programs. Reasons given for the failure of TQM include:

- *Lack of short-term results.* TQM was expected to be an immediate panacea but conversely requires a long-term commitment (some say 10 years) to pay off.
- *Unwillingness to share power with subordinates.* Regrettably, in some operations, this is an understandable feeling.
- *The cost in money, time, and effort involved in installing a TQM system.* Installing TQM is not cheap.
- *Employees' fears that more efficient operations will eliminate their jobs.*
- *Excessive red tape in using procedures, charts, and rules.*
- *Top officials who talked about TQM but could not change to adapt to a TQM situation.*

In summary, TQM has shown itself to be an effective management approach. However, it is not easy to install and requires a great deal of money, time, and effort. It must have total commitment from the organization, especially top management. Managers also must realize that it can take time for TQM to become part of the organization's culture and for results to accrue.

SUMMARY

TQM, although developed by an American, W. Edwards Deming, was first used successfully by the Japanese. It has now been adopted as an approach throughout the world. For the theory to work, three elements must function together:

1. quality as defined by the client
2. systematic or database approach for the studying process
3. employees and/or associates working together

Deming believed that with each improvement, processes and systems get better, production gets better, and market share increases. To achieve this, Deming specified 14 points that must be followed.

The opposite of quality is poor products and service, which not only turns off the customer but the customer often spreads his opinions or experiences to others. The basics of TQM can be distilled in two statements:

1. Meet or exceed customer expectations.

2. Do things right to ensure profitability.

TQM is not done once and finished but is a continuing and ever-improving process accomplished through three- to five-person teams. It is heavily dependent on employees who have the responsibility and authority (empowerment) to solve patron problems.

To determine how well an operation is doing, benchmarking, or comparing with the best others offer, is employed. Sometimes the best quality can be achieved by outsourcing or having others who can do a better job supply it.

The TQM approach may be helped by using service design blueprinting to provide the picture of a service system.

KEY TERMS

benchmarking
CWQC
Deming, W. Edwards
empowerment

extra-industry benchmarking
fourteen points
line of implementation
outsourcing

REVIEW QUESTIONS

3–1 Discuss what you think is good and bad about the TQM approach.
3–2 What are the three elements that must function together in TQM?
3–3 How are employees involved in TQM?
3–4 Explain customer valuation.
3–5 What are the goals of process teams in the TQM process?

3–6 Explain the management information systems used in TQM.
3–7 How can empowerment be utilized in the foodservice industry?
3–8 Why may outsourcing be a good idea?
3–9 Briefly explain service system blueprinting.

PROJECT

3–1 Briefly describe a foodservice operation with which you are familiar.
    a. What do you view as operational problems or difficulties it is encountering?

    b. How might TQM help with these problems?
    c. Make specific recommendations that utilize TQM principles or philosophy.

Systems Approach
to Foodservice Management

The systems approach to management had its beginnings in applied mathematics and computer science. Some managers use the systems approach by instinct, but all managers should be aware of its benefits, applicability, and usefulness.

After completing this chapter, you should be able to:

1. Define the systems approach to management.
2. Understand the basics of general systems theory.
3. Discuss the benefits of this approach as set forth in this chapter.
4. State the elements and draw a basic diagram of a system.
5. Explain how to implement the systems approach to management in a hospitality establishment.
6. Explain how a systems approach might be applied to both a dietary operation and a fast-food restaurant.

AN INTRODUCTION TO THE SYSTEMS APPROACH

At one time, if someone wanted to open a foodservice business, she would start by finding a suitable location. Then she would plan a structure, allowing space for dining, food preparation, and dishwashing. If the structure were already standing, she would designate space for these functions, and storage would probably fill any leftover crannies. Next, this hopeful operator would secure furnishings for the dining area that she considered both appropriate for the guests she expected and within her budget. Whereas she would arrange for general preparation equipment in the kitchen, she would usually give more thought to dining room decor than to kitchen planning. Then she would hire personnel, write a menu, purchase food, and—possibly after some sales promotion—swing open her doors. With luck, the quality of her food and service, the location of her business, and perhaps her own personality would be a successful combination.

The restaurant owner gave little consideration to the interaction of the various individual foodservice components or to whether they would work together smoothly. Similarly, the chef concentrated on food production and thought little of the dining room. The headwaiter, in his turn, served patrons with little thought about kitchen problems unless they interfered with customer satisfaction.

Eventually this owner might realize that the menu was crucial to the success of her operation instead of being almost an afterthought in the planning process. She might discover that customer acceptance, profitability, personnel morale, space, and equipment were all affected—and in large part determined—by the items on the menu. Thus, foodservice planning gradually came to start with the proposed menu. Instead of installing general kitchen equipment and hiring a general kitchen staff, an operator secured equipment and personnel appropriate for the specific type of menu she intended to serve. Because her goal was now to serve a predetermined menu rather than to run a general foodservice, she began to look seriously at a new management idea called the *systems approach* that particularly suited her menu orientation.

Today's foodservice operators face many problems: high labor costs, a skilled labor shortage, intense competition, and decreasing profit margins, to name just four. To overcome these problems, they must become as efficient as possible. This need for efficiency has led straight to the systems approach in which all foodservice components—ordering, storing, sanitation, and so forth—are coordinated to achieve the goals of the restaurant.

This systems approach requires operators to determine in advance how each change in their facilities will affect the whole business and its goals. The systems approach also requires the various subsystems to be integrated efficiently. The goals of a restaurant may be the highest profit consistent with patron satisfaction, whereas an institution might have the goal of providing the best foodservice that resources permit. Balanced nutrition, friendly service, thorough sanitation, and ample food variety might be some of the subgoals.

Modern foodservice operators no longer consider preparation and serving separately; rather, they treat these elements as integrated subsystems of the operation. They must anticipate how, together with the other subsystems, these two elements can best accomplish the objectives of the entire business.

Technological progress has supplemented the systems approach. For example, convenience foods can provide more variety and better quality. Better methods for storing, holding, and reconstituting these foods have also been developed. Data processing has lent new dimensions to food management. More efficient equipment and even some automation have been introduced. Products such as disposable utensils often streamline the foodservice system.

In its most basic form, a system meshes men, machines, material, methods, markets, and money to achieve the goals of an operation efficiently. In addition to these traditional six Ms of management, a system includes a variety of subsystems that should be both interdependent and interrelated. For example, the dining room and kitchen should not be autonomous areas but should instead complement and support every other area in the restaurant. Owners may consider cutting costs in the dishroom by using more disposables, but they must also consider the subsequent effects of that decision in the dining room, in the kitchen, on the goal or profit maximization, and on patron satisfaction. Put more simply, the change to disposables will affect the dishroom, the kitchen, and the profits. Managers had better know in advance what the effect will be.

The Systems Approach in Perspective

The systems approach is not unique to the foodservice industry. It has not only been heralded as an answer to the knottier problems of business management, but also been advanced as virtually the only approach to such complex problems facing society as transportation, housing, education, and health care. Nevertheless, the systems approach is not really new. Plato, St. Thomas Aquinas, and Machiavelli advanced various forms of the systems approach. In fact, at one time or another, most of us—whether or not we are philosophers or business managers—think systematically. All the systems approach does is to take systematic thinking and formalize it into a step-by-step procedure that a manager or restaurant owner can use easily and to good advantage.

The word **system** means different things to different people, so it is usually easier to discuss than define it. To some people, system denotes a way of thinking about an organization. To others, it is a problem-solving tool. Someone interested in the organizational aspects of management may visualize a system as a set of components (or parts) to be coordinated and set in motion toward certain goals. We can, however, offer you this formal definition of a system: a grouping of separate components that work together toward a goal in the most efficient way possible. As you can see, an automobile, the human body, and a restaurant can all be grouped under this definition.

We have some trouble pinning down what we mean when we talk about systems because they have such broad applications. In management, a complete system encompasses all of the aspects of a business: its goals and objectives, resources, various interrelationships, and processes. And all of these aspects, in turn, are affected by the environment in which the system functions.

It may be easier to talk, for the moment, about systems negatively—to ask what happens when a system is missing. Frankly, nothing at all may happen. It's possible that your restaurant has fallen into such a comfortable routine that it can "run itself." More likely, however, a business that runs itself has its various components working against each other toward narrow, self-serving goals. Rarely do such goals correspond to the overall goals of the restaurant. For example, your chef may want to express himself with some fancy gourmet dish. But his need for self-expression may conflict with your need to cut expenses. Here's another example: If the personnel in a certain area suddenly ask to have their jobs enlarged and made more important, meeting their request could erode the importance of other sections and employees elsewhere—to the detriment of everyone.

THE BASICS OF GENERAL SYSTEMS THEORY

A system can be defined as an organized, interacting, interdependent, and integrated set of components and variables. This definition describes what is sometimes called the *general systems theory*. Some generally accepted basic characteristics (which have been refined for a management information system [MIS] that will be discussed in Chapter 6) of the general systems theory follow.

1. The components of a system are interrelated and interdependent. The dining room cannot work independent of the kitchen or vice versa.

2. The system (or operation) must be viewed as a whole so that a manager can predict what effect on the whole system the actions of the various components will have. Cost-cutting moves, for example, may be desirable for short-term profits but may produce long-range problems in customers' perceptions of value.

3. Systems have defined goals or outputs. In an MIS the goals are to provide the necessary information at the right time and in the right place.

4. Systems must have input; in an MIS, this input is data.

5. Systems transform input into output. In an MIS, this involves collecting, selecting, storing, processing, and disseminating the data.

6. Systems can atrophy or undergo entropy. This means that a lack of useful input can either solidify a system or cause it to run down. An MIS must constantly have new relevant data to be effective.

7. Systems must have controls in the form of **feedback** detailing how well the system accomplishes its goals and what adjustments or what new or different information it needs.

8. Systems usually contain smaller subsystems. Most systems are hierarchies of major systems and subordinate systems.

9. Systems are differentiated. Despite the fact that systems are interrelated and interconnected and that smaller systems fit into larger systems, specialization occurs. The chef of a restaurant needs entirely different information than that needed by the maitre d' manager or the catering manager. On the other hand, all managers share a need for such information as predictors of future activity.

10. Systems generally exhibit **equifinality**. This is a fancy way of saying that there is no single way to achieve the desired output or goals of a system. The MIS analyst usually has different ways that can be used to design a system to meet organizational goals.

The Systems Approach and the Hospitality Manager

The systems approach can help hospitality managers in several ways:

1. It helps hospitality managers examine their operation, its goals, and its resources.

2. It helps organize the personnel and the work in an operation. It helps coordinate these people and their work to achieve the goals of the operation.

3. It suggests ways to solve problems or at least puts problems in a perspective. It reveals the importance of such problems and, therefore, the effort that should be devoted to their solution.

4. It provides the manager with an approach to develop an MIS.

Let us discuss these advantages to the systems approach more thoroughly.

Goals and Resources.   As we have already pointed out, every system has its subsystems, and every system is itself a subsystem of some larger system. The food production system, for example, is quite obviously a subsystem of the entire restaurant. Thus, the goals of the food production system must coincide with those of the restaurant.

Just as the food production system is a subsystem of the entire operation, so it has its own subsystems—the bakery, the salad tables, or vegetable prep, for example—that must also help accomplish the operation's goals. Anyone who has the slightest doubt about the roles of these various subsystems can use the systems approach to put them all into perspective and see what they contribute to the restaurant's overall goals.

Organization and Coordination.   A manager or an owner can get too close to the operation to see the faults a more objective person might notice immediately. But the systems approach can help provide the objectivity that is lacking. Are the subsystems pursuing complementary goals? Can some of these subsystems be combined? Has the right kind of equipment been installed? To answer questions like these, managers must consider all the goals of the overall system. Then they can pinpoint the subsystems that are essential to reach these goals.

Organizing includes determining the exact labor skills required to achieve goals. By tailoring the input of a system to the desired output, managers use the systems approach and, at the same time, accomplish a great deal of organizing. Breaking the overall operation down into its subsystems, they can easily see what has to be done and assign employees to do it. By designing a system, in other words, managers also design their operation. The only difference is that each job in a system must help achieve the goals of the operation. Therefore, its relationship to every other job is clearly established rather than being more or less separate.

Solutions and Perspectives.   Consider an example of the use of the systems approach to solve a hospitality feeding problem. The 747 jets were both faster and larger than any previous commercial airliner. They provided more passenger space, but they allowed much less time for meal service. The procedures that had fed passengers on the smaller airplanes were therefore inappropriate on the 747s. Moreover, the 747 engineers had allotted no more food preparation space than smaller jets had. Despite these constraints, the airlines wanted to maintain their dining standards in the 747s.

How did they solve their problem? They resorted to the systems approach. It allowed engineers to view airline foodservice as a system working with the other airline systems. Management listed the goals it wanted its foodservice to attain, and it prepared menus it thought appropriate. Meeting the menu goals required specific new equipment and the development of certain new feeding processes, which were devised as subsystems.

The new equipment included high-speed ovens, pressurized coffee makers, an elevator lift service, redesigned galley carts, aesthetically pleasing disposables, and special trash compactors. The new galley carts ensured straight-through service with no time-consuming backtracking, and they sacrificed none of the old efficiency.

Further analysis of the production objectives led to an alteration in the feeding procedures—specifically, changes in the ground commissary and the on-board preparation mix. In other words, the systems approach helped the airlines' analysts solve the problem of more meals in less time. Merely installing new equipment and urging the personnel to hustle would not have done it. The new procedures and the new equipment had to be integrated into an overall system.

Today's fast-changing internal and external environments require managers to have an MIS for planning, controlling, and decision making. An MIS is a specialized subsystem of the general system (usually feedback). Not only is the systems approach the best way to develop this specialized subsystem, but it is easier to develop an MIS for an organization that uses a systems approach in its organization.

The systems approach can be used in tandem with the reengineering approach discussed in Chapter 1.

Elements of a System

Analysts have traditionally diagrammed systems as three boxes (*input, process,* and *output*), connected by a backward running arrow (*feedback*), all surrounded by space labeled *environment*. As this is a useful way to describe a system, both the diagram (see Figure 4.1) and a discussion of each of these five elements follows.

Output.   If you were asked what you were trying to accomplish with your restaurant, you might answer, "I'm trying to provide the best food I can with what I've got to work with." That statement is, of course, a *goal*; it is also the output you want from your system. However, you've stated your goal far too vaguely. You must be more specific, perhaps this way: "I want to provide the same number of meals I provide now with fewer skilled employees. I want to improve the food around here. And I want to provide a wider menu choice." This is a more specific description of the "best food service I can," but you can make your goals even more specific.

It's time now for you to decide how many fewer skilled employees you need, how to measure food quality, and how many new menu items you want to incorporate. Moreover, these specifically stated goals must correspond to the overall purpose of your foodservice. Gourmet food, for example, would be out of place and out of the question in a corner luncheonette.

Process.   Process refers to how a system's input is treated to achieve (or not to achieve) its goals or output. Actually, each system usually has more than one process. These processes, in most cases, correspond to the typical restaurant subsystems: administration, production,

Figure 4.1
Systems Format

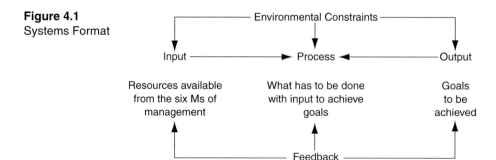

service, and sanitation, to name just four. Another subsystem, usually called *assembling materials* by business analysts, involves purchasing, receiving, storing, and issuing.

By changing processes (or subsystems) restaurant owners can often utilize some of the new technical innovations that appear on the market. For example, the adoption of convenience foods might help operators eliminate a good deal of other activity and some superfluous employees. Another innovation, disposable utensils, could certainly cut down on and simplify the sanitation subsystem.

Input.   The resources available to a system are known collectively as **input**. Input is processed to achieve output of one sort or another. To put it another way, resources are treated in ways that contribute to attaining the goals of the restaurant. Input includes some or all of those six Ms of management: manpower (or personnel), machines (or equipment), materials (largely food and cleaning supplies), markets (the customers), money (an operator's financial resources), and methods (such procedures as personnel policies, standard recipes, and operating instructions).

Once you have established goals for your restaurant, you must determine the best way to approach them. Then you collect the resources (or input) you need. We began with output, moved on to process, and saved input for last because this is the way managers actually proceed—even though input appears in the first position on our diagram. Managers must modify a process or a goal when they lack certain resources. If, for example, they cannot find the skilled personnel they need, they may be forced to change several processes and modify certain goals.

Resources are sometimes divided into two categories: human and material. Human resources, unlike material resources, are not static. People feel and sometimes express needs and desires; machines and food do not. Thus, the human resources—your personnel—require and deserve your consideration, particularly in view of the fact that their satisfaction can help achieve your goals.

One more critical resource is money. In fact, money can help overcome shortages among most of the other resources. It is a rare restaurant that has all the money it needs, but the systems approach to restaurant management can help managers make effective use of whatever money they have available.

Feedback.   **Feedback** is the term systems analysts use to describe the element of a system that signals a need for adjustments or changes in the processing of input. If your food is simply not good enough, or if your expenses exceed your budget, feedback rapidly alerts you to the need for an adjustment or a remedy. Another way to put it is that feedback compares actual output to desired or ideal output.

Feedback can take the form of various business reports. If you are an on-premises restaurant manager, you may not need formal written reports. If you are not directly involved in the running of your establishment, you may need this sort of regular information. In any case, you will constantly need informal reports from your various subsystems, even if you are on the scene. These informal reports may include, for example, charts that show the amount of food prepared, how it was used, the amount of leftovers, and how the leftovers were used. In practically all cases, restaurant owners need information about their costs, and they should devise some way to compare these costs with those that prevail in the area.

INDUSTRY INSIGHTS   Four Seasons Hotel   by Stan Bromley

Stan Bromley is Regional Vice President and General Manager, The Four Seasons Hotel Company, based in Washington, DC. He is a Penn State Walter J. Conti Visiting Professor and a Silver Plate Award winner. Before joining The Four Seasons, Stan was Vice President of Food and Beverage of Hyatt Hotels.

A LEADERSHIP EYE FOR DETAIL: WHAT IS IT? HOW TO GET IT. HOW TO TEACH IT. DO I NEED IT?

My job is to make sure that the food is hot . . . not cold, service is friendly . . . not rude, rooms are clean . . . not dirty, the public areas are painted . . . not chipped, response to any request is fast . . . not slow. My job is to ensure that our employees and guests believe we are caring and sincere. That's it. That's what I do. I'm a hotel General Manager.

Although I enjoy a position and title of Regional Vice President—overseeing five Four Seasons hotels—my basic job is still very simple. It demands an eye for detail that alerts me to those things that interfere with success. Certainly managers at any level and in any business must depend on observations from those with whom they work. Accurate information makes managers' jobs much easier. Unfortunately, the true picture is not always presented, and it is the job of successful managers to get accurate information and to follow through until issues are resolved. Isn't it natural to prefer believing what we are told? Then we can allow ourselves to think of the glass as more than half full, to see the positive (because that's what is usually reported) and avoid the negative (which is usually declared only under duress).

I found that the only way to really know a job is being done well is to follow this Eye for Detail Golden Rule: "I see, taste, smell, and hear things in my own hotel as rigidly as when I visit a competitor. As I identify problems in my own hotel, I will act on them until they are solved to our own satisfaction and our standards."

To be effective as a hotel General Manager, you need to go find the things that prevent the product or service from being rude, slow, dirty, or insincere. Over the years I have found that the word "passion" is the key to the pursuit of an eye for detail. It creates the love or desire to do your job well, actually

---

All this information is feedback. Each operation must decide what sort of feedback is essential for amending its processes and reaching its goals. In addition, the cost of the feedback must be compared to the benefits derived. Elaborate reports that detail every aspect of the business can themselves eat into profits. By contrast, quick, informal reports—even conversations and rumors—can straighten out a faltering process and turn a loss into profit. The idea is to be aware of the need for feedback and to act on feedback you have received.

Our talk about charts, formal business reports, and informal discussions suggests that feedback should be designed to supply the precise information you need to operate your restaurant. Routine financial statements supply some feedback, but their data may not be specific or complete enough to help with an immediate problem. For example, you may be interested in personnel shortages and requirements, food shortages, or food quality information; these are only three of many possible kinds of information often overlooked in routine financial statements.

to be a part of it and to live and breathe it. It's the passion that makes successful managers curious enough to seek out the details of possible short-comings of their own hotel's service or product and to use management and leadership skills to find ways to correct them.

The lessons that come from years of observation and training, a sufficiently inquiring mind, and company operating standards have helped me develop my eye for detail. I've been doing this for 25 years and I still love it. I have represented the brand names of Hilton International, Sonesta, Hyatt, and now Four Seasons. And after all these years, my passion is still evident to me because I am aware before the early morning alarm goes off that I can't wait to get to work.

Detail work is not limited just to the product. As General Managers, our responsibilities include being role models for corporate culture, example setters for appropriate behavior, and father or mother figures to our employees and managers. We recognize the important aspects of personal relationships. We work with a diverse group of people from many backgrounds, nationalities, and age groups. We are expected to know how to make a difference for both employees and guests through leadership and management abilities. Although the 50-year-old General Manager may process things differently than a 22-year-old college graduate, we still must learn the best way to be effective leaders with each individual we encounter.

My passion for the job makes the workday fly by and, although I'm usually exhausted when I get home, I believe both in my heart and in my head that an eye for detail enables me to help employees enjoy their workplace, enable guests to enjoy their stays, and produce a profit for the hotel.

See how it works for you. Install your own instant replay camera on yourself tomorrow. Replay the tape. What do you do? Do you rely entirely on those around you or do you make the necessary effort to go back and check on a certain amount of details yourself? Hot or cold? Taste it. Friendly or rude? Ask and listen. Clean or dirty? Go look yourself. Slow or fast? Ask or watch. It doesn't seem to be such a complex formula. Why don't more people do it?

No manager should assume too much responsibility alone. What I look for are the many eyes and ears and "tasters and smellers" of those who work in our hotel—and many curious employees and managers who have the passion to execute both individually and as a cohesive self-supporting team. Successful managers must use their passion and curiosity to ensure that a portion of everyone's every day is dedicated to honing their eye for detail.

Feedback also should be timely. A report on food spoilage delivered within the hour would obviously be ideal. Delivered much later, the specifics of the report may become hazy; what is much worse, the time for corrective action would have passed. As you have perhaps already guessed, in many situations computerized reporting can provide good, efficient feedback. Computers process large quantities of input easily and rapidly, and their output can both reduce the cost and increase the effectiveness of feedback. Yes, computers are themselves systems and parts of larger systems. Anyone concerned can access information via the computer (see Chapter 6, MIS).

Environment. All the elements of a system we have discussed so far interact with each other and with the environment that surrounds them. The restaurant that cannot adjust to changing conditions will have trouble meeting its goals; that is why you should learn to think of your restaurant system in the context of its environment.

Managers generally think in terms of two kinds of environments, external and internal. The **external environment** is made up of the conditions, circumstances, organizations, and individuals with which the system must interact and to which it must react. The **internal environment** includes such characteristics as employee morale, informal work groups, and working conditions. Although restaurant managers can do little to control the external environment, they can certainly do a great deal to control—and usually to improve—the internal environment.

Many managers, realistically enough, view external environment as a restriction or a constraint. Because of its environment, a particular restaurant may not be able to perform according to its preliminary planning. For example, zoning boards or codes may rule out a certain type of decor or restrict outdoor advertising. Moreover, where a commercial restaurant is concerned, the external environment usually centers on the customers and their needs. These needs are obviously influenced by such external factors as the general state of the economy and the local social mores, sociological attitudes, and cultural traditions. To put it plainly, you can sell more shoofly pie in the Pennsylvania German regions of south central Pennsylvania, where people know and love that dessert, than you can in New York, where most people have never tasted it. Environment and input are often related. A limited supply of money, for example, brings on an environmental constraint in the form of reduced spending. The external environment may include such additional factors as the availability of food, governmental legislation affecting food services, and even international developments such as possibilities of armed conflict.

Thus, you can see that a system is not an entity unto itself. It is part of a larger system that may in turn be part of larger systems. The larger systems affect the external environment of the smaller systems. The smaller systems ultimately support the larger ones.

Processes, you will recall, usually correspond to the subsystems of a main system. Each of these subsystems has its own format, like our diagram in Figure 4.1. Notice that the goals of the subsystems, while contributing to the main goal of the system, become increasingly specific. The goal of the dishwashing subsystem is clean, sanitary plates, but of course clean, sanitary plates contribute to the overall goal of the larger system: the restaurant's desire to please its customers.

THE SYSTEMS APPROACH IN A RESTAURANT

Now that you know the systems approach is

1. a way of thinking about an operation,
2. a way of organizing an operation, and
3. a device for solving management problems,

let's see how you can put this knowledge to work in your restaurant.

First, assume that you are a confident (perhaps even a smug) operator. You can see little room for improvement in your operation. Nevertheless, give the systems approach a try; it might help you provide even better service. It might, for example, help you reduce costs or raise productivity. It might also help you achieve greater employee satisfaction and motivation than you now enjoy. On the other hand, assume you have a problem or two. Perhaps recent changes in your restaurant—new equipment, perhaps, or an addition to your menu—have made some of your methods obsolete. Or perhaps you see a major repair job, alterations, or expansion looming on the horizon. In either case—a smooth operation or troubles around you—the systems approach can help.

You can begin by sitting down and composing a step-by-step analysis. Here is a sample.

1. Define the systems to be investigated: the dishwashing section.
2. List the goals of that system: abundant, clean, sanitized utensils in time for peak service periods.
3. List all the subsystems and their respective goals: the food scraping, the rinsing, the dishwashing machines, their operators, the drying procedures.
4. Suggest to yourself the best ways to accomplish the goals of the subsystem: higher pay? more encouragement? more automation? less automation? redesign the area to eliminate cross-traffic?
5. Put your newly analyzed, streamlined system to work.
6. Evaluate your results. The goals of the main system are not being achieved, are being better achieved, are being completely achieved.

We will discuss this six-step list step by step a little further.

Definition of the System

Defining the system may, at first, seem a little simple-minded to most restaurant owners. But sometimes when managers define a system, they discover underutilized or overlooked elements. We recently heard of a dishwashing operation that used the open air to dry racks of plates but was having trouble getting the plates dry. Finally the manager remembered that his dishwashing machine had come equipped with a hot-air blower his employees had completely ignored. Whatever your operation, a hierarchy of goals exists (see Figure 4.2). Identifying and organizing these goals is the first step in the systems approach.

List of System Goals

The goals of the system can be listed in general terms at first. The goals depend, of course, upon which system you are analyzing. If you are examining your entire operation, you might jot down "a greater variety of food," "more ethnic dishes," "speedier service," or "more cheerful surroundings." If you're looking at a subsystem, you might include the specific goals for that subsystem.

Figure 4.2
The Goal/Objective Hierarchy

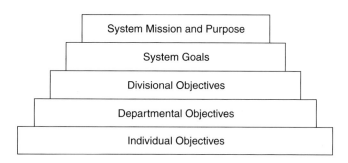

System Mission and Purpose

System Goals

Divisional Objectives

Departmental Objectives

Individual Objectives

In any case, you do not want to maintain the status quo. You want, wherever you can, to improve your operation. Improvement requires that you constantly review your goals. "To serve the best food possible" is not specific enough. You must define what you mean by best food: Flavor? Texture? Aroma? Appearance? Price? Cleanliness? Service? What? Nor is "to provide more employee satisfaction" specific enough. Do you want to work towards an 8-to-5 schedule for more of your employees? Good! That is a specific goal, and the systems approach should help you toward it.

An important goal is energy conservation. Specifically, how can you save energy and energy costs? To achieve the general goal, you should collect a list of lesser goals. For energy conservation this list would include turning off extra lights, using shorter oven warm-ups, turning down the thermostat, insulating the roof, and keeping doors and windows closed. Individually, these steps may not accomplish much. Collectively they can help you reach the goal.

List of Subsystem Goals

You can list all of your subsystems and their respective goals by recalling the various processes that take place in the system or subsystem under examination. Ask yourself why they are present, where they are located, what they accomplish, when they accomplish it, how they accomplish it, and who does the work. Using this systematic approach, you may well formulate an entirely new way of approaching your goals. This systematic approach is sometimes called *brainstorming,* especially when several colleagues participate in it.

Accomplishment of Subsystem Goals

Your list of subsystems and their respective goals (Step 3) leads naturally to Step 4. Suggest to yourself the best ways to accomplish the goals of the subsystems. Having decided, for example, that the goals of your dishwasher subsystem include clean, sanitized plates, you can ask yourself what steps you should take to ensure that you reach this goal. Do you maintain the correct water temperatures? Do you use the right washing and sanitizing chemicals? Can you adopt a different, more reliable, or faster piece of machinery? Are your employees reliable and conscientious? Do they appreciate the essential nature of their work? Do you appreciate their work?

If one of the objectives of your systems approach is to solve a particular problem, the processes (the subsystems) are the places to solve it. In analyzing these subsystems, you may want to think of all the work in your establishment as forming a big pie. Subsystems represent the different slices; each slice stands for some task that contributes to the accomplishment of the restaurant's main goal. Or it may be helpful to prepare a hypothetical, ideal organization chart that illustrates what has to be done and who can do it best. All these ideas—and most particularly the setting of specific goals for each individual subsystem—embody the systems approach to foodservice management.

Installation of a New System

Developing a new or an improved system on paper is not enough. You must put your newly analyzed, streamlined system to work. The installation of a system may, of course, be more difficult than its planning. Many employees are reluctant to accept change. Therefore, you should thoroughly explain the new system before you install it. As you explain the reasons for the change, you should stress how it will make the work go easier, shorten the hours, or bring savings that could result in pay increases. In other words, stress the advantages to your employees. Accentuate the positive.

Your new system may not run perfectly at first. You may need to continue using some elements from your old system during the changeover. Depending on the circumstances, it may be best to make the changes all at once or very gradually. That careful goal analysis you performed should suggest your timing. Those goals should also reassure you that your system probably will work eventually. Don't abandon hope just because of a few preliminary problems. You can expect both employee resentment and some early bugs, but do not be discouraged.

Evaluation of Results

Actually, employee resentment and those bugs are part of the last important step of evaluating the results of your system. Once a new system starts to work, managers should continue to watch it carefully and compare their goals to the output of that new system. This analysis is accomplished with feedback. Remember that feedback can come in many forms: financial reports, machinery breakdowns, missed schedules, employee grumbles, and frequently (for the manager who has followed these six steps conscientiously) praise, happiness, and profit.

Every now and then, however, a new system must be scrapped because its output does not match or surpass that of the previous operation. Obviously this retrenchment can be expensive, particularly if new equipment has been installed. But careful analysis in the preliminary stages should all but rule out these exceptional cases. In fact, the systems approach tends to eliminate extra equipment, because the design of the system specifies exactly what equipment is needed and discourages the introduction of attractive new machinery into an already smooth operation.

This observation leads to one final point in this section. No change should be made simply for its own sake. A change should improve upon past performance. In fact, improvement is the only good excuse for change. The systems approach itself is always and everywhere useful. It costs little for managers to analyze their system constantly, and improvement in that system is routine once the habit of constant, objective analysis is established.

SYSTEMS AND SUBSYSTEMS IN A HOSPITAL FOODSERVICE

A hospital can use the systems concept in a number of interesting and particularly appropriate ways. The goals of a nonprofit teaching hospital would certainly include:

1. general patient care
2. medical research
3. education of medical and paraprofessional personnel
4. public health promotion and disease prevention

Hospitals also subscribe to the more general objectives of providing services, providing a decent living for their employees, and being good neighbors in the community.

Notice that a systems format can be drawn up for each of the four primary objectives mentioned in the first paragraph. Thus, the goal of caring for the patient would have

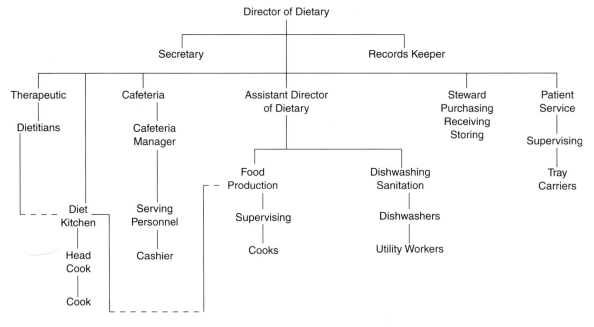

Figure 4.3
Typical Hospital Dietary Organization Chart

its own input, process, and output, together with its own feedback mechanisms. It would be controlled by its own environment. Similarly, the education, research, and public health functions could each be systematized, although in some cases there might be an overlapping of input.

In the area of caring for the patients, for example, medical care, nursing care, foodservice, and housekeeping would appear as subsystems. The hospital foodservice subsystem could itself be broken down further into normal patient foodservice, hospital cafeteria, food production, therapeutic foodservice, and administrative functions that might include purchasing, receiving, storage, and sanitation. Each of these sub-subsystems would have its own input, process, and output. Still, the focus would be on the fact that all subgoals should reflect and complement the overall goals of the hospital rather than merely representing the desires of a particular section.

Analyzing the Dietary Department

Figure 4.3 shows a typical organizational chart for a hospital and Figure 4.4 shows a systems approach. It assumes, logically enough, that the dietary department is one of those components of the hospital that contributes to the care and treatment of patients. Because hospital staff personnel are also served in the hospital cafeteria, it assumes that the dietary department is involved in making the hospital a nicer place to work for its employees.

More specifically, what does the hospital want the dietary department to contribute to the overall goal of patient care and treatment and to employee satisfaction? One contribution would be food that appeals to the patients and contributes to their recovery. How

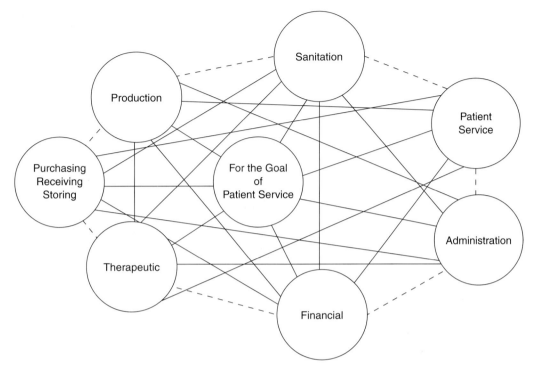

Figure 4.4
Systems Concept for a Hospital Dietary Organization

can this be achieved? Obviously the food should be tasty, should be served at the proper temperatures, and should be attractively arranged and garnished. What else might a patient want? Now is the time to start thinking about selective menus, perhaps an occasional glass of wine, and a systematic study of patient food preferences.

Another goal the hospital expects the dietary department to achieve is to serve enjoyable food to the hospital personnel. How does the dietary department pursue this goal? This question leads to investigations of food preferences among those employees, of food affordability, and of food variety. Perhaps, for example, the employees would appreciate self-service, buffet items, the opportunity to make their own salads, or inexpensive snack foods.

Notice that we have addressed the patient foodservice and hospital cafeteria as though they were separate. It might be well to examine, at this point, the exact place of the hospital cafeteria within the dietary subsystem. Bearing in mind the need for all sub-goals to complement the facility's overall goals, how would you analyze this issue?

It seems that the food for patients has to be not only attractive and palatable, but nutritious as well. The nutritional aspect is crucial. Does the importance of the nutritional aspect set patient foodservice and the cafeteria apart?

Remember, systems analysis should help determine the best way to accomplish work and the best people to accomplish it. Systems analysis should help bring problems into manageable proportions. Using systems analysis to answer the question we have raised, you might ask whether menu planning ought to be a separate subsystem. After all, the major difference in the patient foodservice and the employees' cafeteria lies in the menu planning function.

Other goals unique to the hospital dietary department include therapeutic counseling and nutrition instruction. These goals appear to suggest a separate subsystem, although certainly they must be approached in a way that is harmonious with the other subsystems. Where special diets are required, a special diet kitchen is in order. This special kitchen, too, has all the earmarks of a separate subsystem.

The dietary department is only one system of the hospital working toward the care and treatment goals common to the rest of the units. Therefore, a part of its activity involves cooperation with the other hospital departments: the physicians who order the special diets, the nurses in direct contact with the patients, and typically, the housekeeping department. Notice that care and treatment is only an incidental goal of the employees' cafeteria. Contented, well-fed employees are more likely to work hard toward the major hospital goals, and that is reason enough to provide a top-notch cafeteria. Although both patient foodservice and the cafeteria involve the dietary department, they probably represent distinct subsystems with a good deal of overlapping input.

Dietary Department Input

Its goals established, a system or subsystem must work with the resources necessary and through the processes required to accomplish them. You must determine, for example, whether essential skills are already available in the dietary department. Perhaps some new people are needed; perhaps a position or two can be eliminated. Is the kitchen equipment well suited to the menu already chosen? Should you maintain a generally equipped kitchen that can produce practically any kind of food? Or are you trying to specialize, perhaps by adopting convenience foods?

Once you have determined how your food is to be processed, you will want to examine the utensils essential to the delivery and consumption of that food. What, in other words, is the best way to handle the problems associated with silverware and china? Are disposables the answer? Or do aesthetic considerations outweigh mere practicality? If computer capability is available to you—that is to say, if a computer supplies part of your input—how can you use it in such areas as processing, patient menu selection, cost control, and ordering and inventory maintenance?

When your goal becomes the actual delivery of food to patients, how do you go about it most efficiently and in greatest harmony with the hospital's other systems? Should you, for example, adopt a centralized or a decentralized food delivery system? In some hospitals, the dietary department employees deliver the meals only to the respective floors. Thereafter, the nursing personnel distributes the trays to the rooms. Perhaps this is the most efficient way to handle things; perhaps it is not. In either case, there is need for close contact and mutual consideration between dietary and nursing.

Dietary Goals

Obviously some of our discussion of dietary input has touched upon some of the dietary processes—the use of the input to produce and distribute food, for example. Now let's look a little more closely at the foodservice consumers: those patients on special diets, those patients on regular or "house" diets, and hospital personnel. Take one of these groups, the hospital personnel. Define them precisely. Should your staff-oriented meals appeal mainly to middle-aged people? To people on diets? To hefty appetites? To those in a hurry? Are your patients getting hot food? If not, how can you keep it hot for them? Have you found a foolproof way of making sure the special diets reach those for whom they are intended? The nature and requirements of the foodservice consumers obviously offer certain constraints on the dietary system.

Dietary Department Environment

Most hospitals remain open 24 hours a day. This means the foodservice must provide meals usually for three shifts of employees. Overcoming this environmental constraint, you may choose to install vending machines, improve your food holding techniques, or adjust the actual shift hours.

With the constant change of patient population and the constant change in the conditions of the patients, menu orders also change abruptly. Abrupt changes present constraints for any system. In this case, they make it more difficult to deliver the right food in the right quantity to the right patient.

Hospital layout—part of the general hospital environment—often presents certain difficulties for the dietary system to overcome. Hospitals are typically spread out over quite a wide area. Wide areas to serve automatically result in distribution problems.

In addition, a psychological constraint is imposed by the peculiar environment of a hospital. Patients (and, to a certain extent, personnel) represent a captive clientele. The mere fact that they must eat in the hospital tends to turn them into food critics. Anyone who has been removed from the security of his home and family does not tend to welcome the added insecurity of unfamiliar food. Finally, people tend to focus their general fears and annoyances on something tangible. Patients who are nervous about their doctor, their nurses, an upcoming operation, or their treatment often wind up complaining about the foodservice. It is, after all, one of the few things over which they continue to exercise some control.

In hospital foodservice, money represents both a resource (part of input) and an environmental constraint. All of a hospital's systems have budgetary requirements, and the allotments they receive are rarely enough. The receipt of too little financial input (money) is an obvious constraint. The force of the constraint can be lessened in a hospital—as it could be everywhere—by a little old-fashioned honesty. Budgets should be prepared realistically. Common sense suggests that wasted funds are as big a shortcoming in health care as insufficient funds. It makes as little sense to have too much money as it does to be forced to scrimp.

Feedback in the Dietary Department

Sooner or later, the dietary department must determine whether it has been achieving its goals. Has the food been reaching the right consumers on time? Has it been appetizing? Answers to questions like these can (and often do) come in the form of complaints or gossip. Much better that the dietary department itself undertake to collect the information and make the necessary corrections before the grumbling grows too loud. Regular management inspections serve this purpose, and so do short questionnaire cards. Moreover, regular checks with nurses and doctors—with everyone involved with patient care and comfort—can correct mistakes and head off hard feelings.

Uncomplimentary reports (negative feedback, in managerial jargon) often reflect on the relative efficiency of the employees. These people problems can be analyzed and usually corrected. Personnel efficiency and productivity reports can be developed. Management should also watch its turnover rates and institute regular supervisor evaluations.

Feedback involving hospital costs is particularly essential. Without providing a lengthy analysis of hospital accounting techniques here, we want to point out that a dietary department ought to have some sort of a cost reporting system to be certain that it stays within its budgetary allotment.

MULTIDEPARTMENT MANAGEMENT

Today's workplace competition has grown far more dynamic and multidimensional. A systems approach can utilize a multidepartment management structure to improve efficiency and effectiveness. Because of the prevalence of downsizing, competencies are being spread more widely through organizations to support their new organic designs. Employees are being required to become multiskilled in the various positions within those organizations. Management's leadership in the change effort seems to be the key determinant of whether that change will succeed.

Self-operated and contract management companies are utilizing multidepartment management to an ever-increasing degree. For self-operated organizations, multidepartment managers are being asked to assume leadership demands that require more than meeting standards on current competitive dimensions. The goal is to strengthen competitive position and control costs by accumulating several competencies that interact and augment each other. Contract management companies are developing multidepartment managers and cross-trained employees to attract new accounts and expand services within current client operations.

Marriott has developed a hotel-type model of support services for hospitals and chains that are interested in bringing together departments as "hospitality services." Multidepartment management is not just being integrated into foodservice managers' functions within the health care industry. It is also being introduced into managers' responsibilities in schools and universities, airline feeding, recreational facilities, retirement communities, and hotels. Hospitality managers are rapidly taking on added areas that were not in the scope of foodservice managers just 10 years ago. Multidepartment management will continue to play a key role for organizations well into the next century.

THE SYSTEMS CONCEPT FOR FAST-FOOD OPERATIONS

The systems concept was initiated on a large scale in the foodservice industry in fast-food operations. Significantly, the originators of these operations were not primarily foodservice people but people who came to the industry from the outside with new managerial ideas, including the systems concept. These early developers were primarily interested in making money. They realized that to make money, they would have to attract a well-defined market to serve. One such market, widely ignored by traditional foodservice operations, was the families-with-children group. Cost was very important to this group, but on the other hand they did not need the traditional sit-down service and formality of traditional restaurants. The early developers in the 1950s also realized that mobility provided by automobiles increased the feasibility of bringing family groups to the foodservice operation.

Establishing Goals

The primary goal of making money convinced the operators to offer a cheap snack. The snack might be hamburgers, chicken, pizza, or other types of food that could be eaten with the fingers. In essence, all those choices were what consumers regarded as cheap snack-type meals. The operators also desired minimum labor both in the number of personnel required and the level of skill required. They realized also that meager facilities made for a high turnover of guests. Moreover, this service would have to be speedy enough to satisfy impatient children. For marketing purposes, a standardized image of quality, cleanliness, uniformity, and speedy service was desired. This could best be obtained by having a multiunit organization with each unit contributing to and reinforcing the general image. Economy was also a factor, although some maintain that for value received, economy was only relative.

The need to achieve these goals led to systems analysis. After deciding on the goals (or the desired output), plans were formulated to determine what input to use, what processes would be necessary, and what the desirable choices between the various available alternatives would be. From the first, the traditional approach to food preparation (where the food was prepared and served at the same site) was questioned. Food operations are, of course, one of the few businesses conducted this way. In most industries, products are produced at one site and merchandised at another. Why couldn't the same approach work for food? If the shoe industry operated as foodservice does, every shoe store would have a shoe manufacturing plant attached to it!

Fast-food operators established early that some food preparation labor traditionally done at the restaurant could be accomplished better elsewhere. All possible pre-preparation was performed before the product was delivered to the serving location. Hamburgers were mixed and preformed and, in some cases, even partially cooked before reaching the serving location. French fries were preprocessed up to the point of being blanched.

Refining the System

By concentrating this pre-preparation labor in one spot, new fast-food operations considerably reduced the labor requirements of the individual serving operation. Because a cheap snack was one of their desired outputs, they discarded elaborate menus. The simplified menu provided many ordering and storing economies. Pre-preparation allowed for many of the items to come in frozen form, which simplified storing and handling. With only a few items offered on an unchanging menu, much kitchen equipment could be eliminated. Simpler but specialized equipment could be installed for high production of the few items. The simplified menu and pre-preparation also eliminated the need for skilled chefs on the premises, fulfilling another desired output. The system could be refined for even more efficiency by using conveyor lines and lazy susan devices to bring the products from the preparation equipment to the serving personnel, product color coding, disposables to eliminate dishwashing, and electronic devices that allow one person to take an order and transmit it to the kitchen.

With relatively few items, cost control was enhanced and ordering meant simply the replenishing of the par stock level. Any items purchased by an individual unit had to meet preset standards and specifications, which eliminated complicated decisions on the local manager's part. Because none of the positions (with the possible exception of the manager) required any great skill, personnel could be readily interchanged. When they were not actually waiting on a customer, they could be preparing or wrapping some of the food items or cleaning.

This general approach allowed a local food operation to attain a factory goal of long production runs of relatively few items compared to the traditional restaurant concept of short production runs with many different items. Moreover, with a standardized operation, it was relatively easy to install quality controls involving storage times and leftover usage.

Fast turnover resulted from the ability to provide speedy service with brief intervals between ordering and service. Limited or no seating facilities discouraged customers from dawdling on the premises. High light intensities used in the parking lots encouraged the younger customers to move on.

The success of the fast-food operations is well known. They developed and satisfied a new market; they also accomplished new breakthroughs in operating efficiency. By studying their goals, outputs, and processes, they achieved that definition of a system: An organization of personnel and machines to accomplish a designated purpose. With fewer teenagers and more elderly customers, fast-food operations will have to change their systems to adapt to new groups.

SUMMARY

The bulk of our discussion of the systems concept has focused on the commercial restaurant, but it should be clear that the systems approach is just as applicable in health care foodservice. The systems approach helps refine and streamline the work, provides the best solutions quickest to a variety of dilemmas, and prevents a piecemeal approach to problem solving. A systems approach can be very helpful to the hospitality manager. It can, for example,

- help managers examine their operation, goals, and resources

- help organize the personnel and their work

- coordinate these people and their work to achieve the goals of the operation

- serve as a problem-solving device

The systems diagram consists of *input,* or the various resources available to an operation; *processes,* or the subsystems involved in the system; and *output,* or goals of the system achieved by the input and the processes. *Feedback* refers to the information that tells managers how well the output or goals are being met and whether adjustments or changes must be made. These elements obviously must function within internal and external environments, which can act as constraints on the system.

In foodservice, the systems approach has been supplemented by such technological developments as MIS systems, convenience foods, automation, data processing, disposables, and better methods of storing, holding, and reconstituting foods. Maximum benefits from utilizing these developments can be achieved by employing the systems perspective, which considers how such developments affect the whole operation, not just one segment. The six steps in implementing the systems approach are as follows:

1. Define the system to be investigated.

2. List the goals of that system.

3. List the subsystems and their respective goals.

4. Suggest the best ways to accomplish the goals of the subsystems.

5. Put the newly designed system to work.

6. Evaluate the results.

A system is not an entity in itself; it is always a subsystem of another larger system. Thus, in trying to solve a problem, managers often experience difficulty in that they consider only immediate effects rather than the effects on the whole system.

KEY TERMS

entropy

equifinality

external environment

feedback

input

internal environment

management information system (MIS)

output

subsystem

system

REVIEW QUESTIONS

4–1 How has technological progress supplemented the systems approach?

4–2 Briefly define *system*.

4–3 How can a system be used as a problem-solving tool?

4–4 What is the relationship between systems and MIS?

4–5 Name and discuss the elements of a system.

4–6 Discuss the environment of a system.

4–7 What would be the ideal output of a hospital dietary system?

4–8 Discuss the internal environment of a hospital dietary subsystem.

4–9 Discuss feedback in a hospital dietary subsystem.

4–10 What steps are involved in putting a systems approach into effect?

PROJECT

The systems concept is a way of thinking. It provides an organizational framework for visualizing an operation. It allows recognition of the proper place and functions of subsystems and allows consideration of the internal and external environments. It may be the vehicle of adapting to change and incorporating newer technological concepts. This assignment is intended to give practice in systems thinking and application.

ASSIGNMENT

Develop a systems model for a foodservice operation, identifying the system elements (inputs, outputs, feedback mechanisms, and environments or constraints) for both the general system and appropriate subsystems.

GUIDELINES

1. The operation may be of any type in which you are interested. It may be a fabricated operation or an existing one. If the latter, care should be taken not to simply describe present procedures but to analyze the operation in a systems-concept context and suggest changes for improvements.

2. The subsystems will be those necessary to support the main system. These may include, among others, service, production, administration, sanitation, procurement, storage, and issuing. Even the above may be broken down: Administration may have a separate control subsystem; production may be divided into pre-prep and preparation subsystems; and procurement, storage, and issuing could be separate subsystems. A hospital might also have menu-planning and therapeutic subsystems, while a restaurant might have a beverage subsystem. For most operations, promotion and

feasibility planning will not be subsystems. Personnel is usually not a separate subsystem unless a separate personnel department is requested. If the main system is in itself a distinct subsystem such as the food delivery systems in a hospital, mention should be made of this relationship.

3. The output or goals should be for your operation and not the general goals of return for investors (if profit making), providing a needed product or service, being a good employer, and being a good neighbor. A school lunch program's goals, for example, would include an inexpensive but nutritious meal, fast turnover, nutrition education, and relatively low-skilled help. A fine restaurant might include gourmet food and a dining experience among its goals. Each subsystem will have its specific goals to support the main system. Often, after examination, original or past goals are found to be inappropriate.

4. The processes include what has to be done in the system and subsystems to accomplish the desired output. Ask why, what, when, where, who, and how. Through these questions, an entirely new way of achieving the goals may be developed. Technological developments such as convenience foods, ingredient rooms, automation, and satellite operations should be considered. A system approach can be considered a problem-solving device, and operating problems may be resolved in this phase.

5. Input consists of possible management resources (personnel, money, machines, methods, materials, and markets) that are appropriate. The primary system may not require all of them, and the subsystems will probably require fewer. Markets refer to patrons and not purveyors. Money refers to capital funding or income. Materials include foods and supplies. For personnel, it may be desirable to indicate the level of skill required.

6. The environment, constraints, or limitations show those factors that affect capability. They may be of a time, cost, social, legal, union, or other nature and will vary for the different subsystems. OSHA regulations may be significant constraints.

7. Feedback will consider what should be known to measure the accomplishment of goals and what is feasible to use. For example, the primary system may require a monthly operations report and the production subsystem a daily report of leftovers. It will be necessary to consider the extensiveness and timing of control points.

8. Normally, the goals are determined first, then the processes to attain the goals, and then the resources necessary for the processes. It may be necessary to redefine the goals or other elements of the system if resources, process capability, and other constraints will not permit their attainment.

9. The results of the system analysis will be summarized in a report. Although the nature of the system analyzed will determine the organization content of the paper, possible sections could include:
   - the goals of your operation (and system)
   - a listing of subsystems necessary for your system, which may be similar to the processes in the primary system
   - overall resources needed, along with the feedback and constraints
   - development of each subsystem in a system format

   It may be desirable to include a discussion of why your particular subsystems represent an improvement over existing practices. This is especially true if new concepts are employed.

10. It may be helpful in completing the project to consider the Methodology of Systems:
    - Define the system to be investigated.
    - Define what the system should accomplish.
    - Define the elements or processes (usually subsystems) that make up the system.
    - Consider the resources necessary for the system. It may be necessary to change goals and processes to conform with available resources.
    - Determine what feedback is necessary.
    - Develop subsystems.
    - Consider cost-effectiveness.

5

The Feasibility Study, Business Plan, Financing, and Franchising

Chapter 5 is intended for those who want to establish their own foodservice business. It may also be used by those already in business but who desire a format to objectively look at their operation.

After completing this chapter you should be able to:

1. Determine the feasibility of an enterprise.
2. Prepare a business plan for that enterprise.
3. Discuss financing arrangements.
4. Prepare necessary financial statements.
5. Understand the requirements to receive a loan.
6. Help decide whether franchising should be employed.

A central document that incorporates much of what is discussed in this book is the business plan. This document helps define the business concept, clarifies the goals of the business, evaluates markets and competition, determines costs and capital needs, and enhances chances of success. Some operators do not prepare a formal plan although they may have a plan in their head. It is much more effective to put thoughts down on paper. Although a business plan requires much time and energy, its value is summarized in the saying that businesses don't plan to fail, they just fail to plan. In the foodservice industry with its high rate of failure and turnover, a business plan is especially important.

PURPOSES OF THE FEASIBILITY STUDY/BUSINESS PLAN

1. If the operation has not yet been established, a plan or study can show whether it is feasible both from an operational and financial standpoint.

2. It lays out what will be required in capital, facilities, personnel, legal matters, potential markets, and perhaps the amount that must be secured from investors or financial organizations.

3. It requires the operators to think over the operation in its entirety. They must envision its success and devise an organized step-by-step plan to achieve it.

4. If outside monies are required from investors, the plan or study becomes the basis for the financial proposal.

5. It provides goals and yardsticks by which managers can measure how well they are doing against how well they expect to be doing or should be doing.

DIFFERENCES BETWEEN A BUSINESS PLAN AND FEASIBILITY STUDY

Both terms may be used somewhat interchangeably. Both may be involved in determining if an operation is feasible and will be successful. A business plan and a feasibility study may overlap. A feasibility study gathers basic information such as the market potential and location factors. The business plan defines the strategies to exploit this potential. A feasibility study can determine capital needs while the business plan shows how these capital needs may be attained. A feasibility study may be created by a professional outside the business, or the operation's own starters may want to do it. However, the business plan should be written by the principals themselves. They are the most involved and most informed. They probably have the most to gain or lose. And they are the people who most likely will carry it out. At this point we will divide the subject and discuss a feasibility study and then the business plan.

ANALYSIS OF A FEASIBILITY STUDY

Parts of a feasibility study can usually be accomplished away from the projected site. For example, you can make most of your financial calculations at your desk or computer. On the other hand, you can measure traffic volumes, interview passersby, and consider a building design only at the site.

Part of an actual feasibility study conducted for a commercial foodservice operation appears in Figure 5.1. Much of the information in Figure 5.1 can be applied to noncommercial operations like hospital foodservices.

The format presented is generic in nature. Different operations may require additional information or may not need some of the information used in this format.

Part I: Market Survey

Notice that the pertinent feasibility factors appear in outline form as a kind of shorthand. The outline is divided into two parts: the market for the contemplated operation and on-site considerations. As we look more carefully at this two-part outline, remember that since no single format applies to all operations, Figure 5.1 may overlook some points important

I. Market Survey
   A. Economic factors of the community
      1. Status of neighborhood: progressive, stable, deteriorating
      2. Potential growth of community
      3. Source of community income: number of major industries, stability of income, average income
      4. Demographic factors: families, singles, children, young adults, older persons
      5. Associations that use foodservice facilities: civic, religious, service, fraternal
      6. Food preferences: predominant national, ethnic, religious groups
   B. Competition analysis
      1. Foodservice establishments in area: types, sizes, markets, prices, profitability
      2. Planned additional operations: size, type, location, target market
   C. Proposed operation
      1. Type of operation most feasible
      2. Menu type
      3. Price ranges
      4. Size and capacities
      5. Facilities necessary: banquet, other function, beverage, parking
   D. Projected volume
      1. Expected seat turnovers: by meal, day of week, month of year
      2. Anticipated check averages per meal
      3. Probable beverage volume
      4. Function and other revenue
II. Site Analysis
   A. Location
      1. Area
      2. Frontage
      3. Depth
      4. Topography
      5. Soil conditions
   B. Traffic patterns
      1. Traffic counts
      2. Ease of ingress and egress
      3. Peak traffic periods
      4. Contemplated changes
      5. Traffic destinations
      6. Convenience to main arteries
      7. Parking facilities
   C. Other transportation
      1. Types and amounts
      2. Coverages
   D. Site visibility
      1. Sign regulations
      2. Present and possible future obstructions by other buildings
   E. Legal
      1. Zoning regulations
      2. Required set-backs
      3. Local or state laws of possible concern
      4. Assessments and taxes
   F. Utilities
      1. Availability of water, electricity, gas, waste disposal, sewers, other
      2. Commercial rates
      3. Restrictions

Figure 5.1
Outline for Feasibility Study

for some operations and may include other points that are not pertinent to a specific situation. Nevertheless, it does suggest the scope of a typical feasibility study.

The market survey portion begins at Part A by suggesting that you evaluate the economic conditions of your locality. Its purpose is to define characteristics of an area to help determine what type of operation will serve it best. If income levels are low, the chances for success of an expensive gourmet operation would be slim. Banquet and convention businesses usually depend on nearby organizations that regularly use their services. More specifically, this portion of the study requires that you consider six definite aspects of the locality in this way:

1. You must decide whether the neighborhood is prosperous, stable, or deteriorating.

2. Whatever the present status of the neighborhood, you should look for evidence it will grow, which enhances chances of success.

3. You must decide whether or not the neighborhood enjoys reliable sources of income. You should list these sources. Keep in mind that a stable community enjoys a broad economic base rather than depending on a few dominant industries. You should find out the average income in the area. Statistical data, such as the average income in a specific area, is usually available from the local chamber of commerce, banks, radio and television stations, or newspapers.

4. You must list the basic demographics of the area: the number of families, young children, young adults, and older people. These can be estimates, but the information is helpful when it comes time to decide whether to cater to teenagers, families, or youngsters.

5. You must list the dominant civic, religious, service, and fraternal organizations in the area, especially if you plan to offer banquet or large dining area service.

6. You must consider the predominant national, ethnic, and religious groups in the area when it comes time to plan a menu that will attract large numbers of customers.

Part B of the market survey of our feasibility study suggests that you analyze your competition. It is a good idea, for example, to list the types, sizes, and locations of all restaurants within a predetermined competitive area, perhaps a 10-mile radius. You should list their prices, preferably by visiting the premises and copying the menu. Material in chapter 7 on marketing may be helpful here. The general profitability can often be estimated by observing the amount of business they are doing and by noting the prices they charge. Do not forget to investigate whether any other restaurants are planned for your locality. Local bankers and real estate agents are often aware of these plans. It should be obvious that just because the present operations appear to be succeeding, an automatic need does not exist for more of the same.

Your analysis of the competition will carry you directly to section C of the market survey of your feasibility study. Having determined what sort of operation is presently succeeding in your neighborhood, you will have a pretty good idea about what sort of operation you should establish. You can mark down, for example, the types of service, price ranges, and seating capacities that seem to be successful. The seating capacity is particularly important: No matter how good it is, a facility that is too large for its potential business will suffer excess costs, whereas too small a facility will place a firm ceiling on the amount of business that can be handled and on resulting profits.

Mark down, too, which specific installations—banquet halls, gift shops, tavern rooms—are either abundant or in short supply in the area. Having decided upon an ideal size for your operation, do not fail to make provision for ample parking facilities, particularly if you intend to attract highway travelers.

It is worthwhile to note here that chains and franchises have already developed their type of operation. Thus, they will want to know not what sort of operation will succeed but whether their established operation will prosper.

A feasibility study may show a need for a full-service restaurant with banquet facilities. Despite this need, it would be foolish for a franchised fast-food chain to open a new unit if this demand is already handled by similar operations. It is not unheard of, though, for a group of similar restaurants to operate side by side. Sometimes they generate more business for the entire area than if they were far apart. The idea of choosing brings people into the area.

Section D of the marketing survey involves projected volume. Forecasting the volume you expect is a critical part of a feasibility study and one of the most difficult to accomplish. If you could estimate your volume with some certainty, you could easily project both your expenses and your profit. Unfortunately, there are no certain principles to guide you through that forecast, mainly because so many variables can affect the fortunes of each individual operation. Occasionally textbooks or foodservice magazines publish rules of thumb suggesting that a population of so many thousand will support a particular kind of food service or that x number of hotel rooms are needed for every 1,000 people in town. These rules of thumb are often disproved, for example, by Orlando, Florida, or Las Vegas.

No one can offer really reliable volume forecast guidelines. However, the information in Part I of the feasibility study in Figure 5.1 is as helpful as anything when it comes time to determine whether there is sufficient potential business for the foodservice you have in mind.

Turnover rates typically change during different days of the week, for different meals, and during different periods of the year. A city cafeteria does its biggest volume on business days during the lunch hour. Northern resort restaurants tend to thrive on late spring, summer, and early fall weekends—unless there is skiing nearby. To be accurate, you may want to calculate volume by estimating your turnover ratios for every week of the year and calculating each week's volume separately. All the weeks can then be added to total your forecast. (Remember that holidays and long weekends can alter weekly volumes.) Once you determine an estimate of the number of covers (or customers) for each meal, you can calculate your dollar sales for each meal by multiplying the number of covers by the average anticipated check.

Determining an average check can be a problem. For example, the selling prices for various menu items must be fixed. These selling prices are obviously related to food costs, but other factors can influence them as well—like the amount of service you provide and pressure from your competition. Once you have determined selling prices, you can estimate the number of items the average customer will consume and calculate an average check. Another way to determine the average check is to multiply the selling price of each item by the number of items you expect to sell and then divide this figure by the number of customers you expect.

If you plan to serve liquor, you will want to estimate your probable beverage volume along with your expected turnover and your anticipated check average per meal. There are two easy ways to do this. First, you can assume that beverage sales represent a fixed percentage of food sales. Many foodservice professionals pick a figure in the area of 20 percent, but the actual figure varies from one operation to the next. Assume, then, that your projected food sales are $10,000. You can add $2,000 for beverage sales to that.

Second, you can assume that a certain number of drinks will be served for every meal served. (One figure used is 1.3 drinks.) Now you merely multiply the average price per drink by the number of meals you expect to serve and multiply that result by 1.3. The mixture of beverages sold can complicate this calculation as can a wide price range for items. Beer presents a special problem, being less expensive than cocktails. An assumption of two beers served for every regular drink may be required to account for beer sales.

Part II: Site Analysis

Part II of our demonstration feasibility study in Figure 5.1 concentrates on the actual site on which you plan to build. This site analysis has been broken down further into six general headings, each with its own specific considerations. For example, section A asks you to examine the location you have in mind in terms of its area, frontage, depth of the property, lay of the land, and local soil conditions.

If one of these factors is unsatisfactory, certain types of operations must be ruled out. When several acres of parking space are required, for example, you must have several acres. On the other hand, excess area increases costs and, worse, imparts a deserted look to what might actually be a potentially active operation.

The frontage and depth of the lot must be sufficient to accommodate the planned building. The topography of the land can also affect construction, aesthetics, and visibility. The type of soil on the site can affect building costs or the feasibility of sewage disposal. A rocky soil inevitably raises building excavation costs.

Section B of part II focuses on traffic patterns, which affect the amount of business to expect and, in some cases, what sort of foodservice you can provide. (The roadside establishment obviously requires passing motorists.) The convenience of your site—how easy it is to enter, park, and leave—will determine whether travelers will go out of their way to visit you. Many a restaurant has failed simply because motorists had to turn across a busy, dangerous intersection to reach it.

If peak traffic periods coincide with your busy periods, your operation would have a greater chance of success. The exception would occur if the traffic makes entry or departing very difficult. Before you count on desirable traffic patterns in planning your operation, you would be wise to check on whether those patterns might possibly change. Many a formerly prosperous food operation has been forced to close when new routes bypassed them. The classic example is Colonel Harland Sanders' own Kentucky restaurant. When an interstate route bypassed the Colonel, he was forced to franchise his Kentucky Fried Chicken. For him, things worked out well. However, a future restaurant cannot count on duplicating the Colonel's luck and incredible energy.

Traffic destinations can be important. Clever professionals have an uncanny knack of spotting logical, convenient stopping places. For example, one very busy restaurant is located exactly between two towns 100 miles apart. If it were closer to either town, its clientele would diminish. People in one town would consider it too far, while people in the other might not stop because they were already near home, thus lumping it together with the other restaurants around town and not considering it quite so special.

As part II, section D implies, some operations depend heavily on the visual impact they project to attract business. A familiar building or design can be seen and assimilated before its sign can be read. They are not effective when they are obstructed by trees, hills, or buildings. If you plan to rely on large, gaudy signs, you should determine whether the local advertising ordinances permit them. While you are at it, see if you can find out what the local zoning board has in mind for your site. Look, too, at the taxes you will be paying and at any special local ordinances governing the sale of alcoholic beverages.

Part II, section F indicates that an operation must install an array of utilities, some of which may not be immediately available. Restaurant plans are occasionally abandoned simply because local water and sewer authorities refuse to extend their systems. In short, it is wise to check on the availability of such services as these in advance. Utility costs are no longer insignificant, and foodservice professionals have become increasingly concerned with correlating available fuels and services with their particular locations.

A SALES ESTIMATE IN TABULAR FORM

Table 5.1 should interest anyone investigating a future in the restaurant business. It is a sales estimate for a proposed downtown foodservice operation. Notice that the analyst who prepared this table made a series of projections for each definable meal period. More specifically, she multiplied the projected number of seats by the anticipated rate of turnover per seat. The result of this multiplication is the number of covers for each meal, or 200 for breakfast.

When multiplied by the average check ($3.60 for breakfast), this figure provides an estimated daily sales figure per meal, which turns out to be $720 for breakfast.

The restaurant cited in Table 5.1 will be open 256 days a year, with a projected breakfast sales for the entire year of $184,320. Using the same analysis for the other meals, you can derive a total restaurant food sales of $1,320,960. Adding banquet, special function, and beverage sales produces a total volume of approximately $2 million.

The sales estimate depends a great deal on forecasts of activity, which by their very nature can be difficult to produce. The factors contained in part I of the feasibility study in Figure 5.1 can help determine this forecast of volume. Again, there are no exact rules, because there are so many variables. Instead of multiplying the number of seats by the rate of turnover, you may find it convenient to approach the problem by estimating only the volume. Dividing the planned seating capacity by this estimate yields the rate of turnover. For example, dividing a volume of 200 covers by a seating capacity of 100 yields a turnover of 2. Too high a turnover figure indicates an operation too small for its projected volume. Too low a turnover figure indicates that the planned seating capacity is too high.

Imperfect as our analysis of volume, planned size, and turnover may be, it is still better than deciding the size of an operation by extracting a figure from midair. The physical characteristics of the proposed site, as explored in part II of Figure 5.1, may also help determine the size of the planned operation. Determining the rate of turnover can help you analyze whether the size dictated by the site is feasible.

Table 5.1
Sample Sales Estimate for a Downtown Restaurant

Meal Period	Number of Seats	Rate of Turnover	Number of Covers	Average Check	Estimated Daily Sales	Annual Days	Projected Annual Sales
Breakfast	100	2.0	200	$ 3.60	$ 720	256	$ 184,320
Luncheon	100	4.0	400	5.00	2000	256	512,000
Dinner	100	1.0	100	12.00	1200	256	307,200
Supper	100	0.8	80	11.00	880	256	225,280
Coffee break (a.m.)	100	1.5	150	1.20	180	256	46,080
Coffee break (p.m.)	100	1.5	150	1.20	180	256	46,080

Total restaurant food sales	$1,320,960
Banquet and function sales	279,040
Total food sales	1,600,000
Beverage sales	400,000
TOTAL ESTIMATED SALES	$2,000,000

The projected volume for the planned operation is most important because many of your expenses will be based on it. Food costs, for example, should be directly related to food sales.

A PRO FORMA INCOME STATEMENT

Armed with an annual sales estimate, an analyst can prepare a pro forma income statement (similar to the one in Table 5.2). Pro forma refers to projected or anticipated figures rather than to figures that have been determined from actual operations. (The Latin *pro forma* means "as a matter of or according to form.") A regular income statement shows the income and expenses that were incurred during a past period rather than ones for a projected future period covered in a pro forma statement. The pro forma statement provides our best estimates of what our income should be for a projected period and what our expenses and the resulting profit and loss should be for this same projected income period.

The cost figures on the pro forma statement may be calculated in several ways. One is to consider the particular cost item as a percentage of sales. For example, the food costs should be a certain percentage of food sales, which in this case is 34 percent. To arrive at the 34 percent figure, you can consider what other similar operations are spending for food in relation to their sales. It would be more accurate for operators to determine the food cost in advance of various menu items and divide this cost by the anticipated sales to provide food cost percentages. It is obvious that not all items sold have the same food cost percentage. For example, a certain dessert that costs 50 cents to make may be sold for $1.50 or a 33.3 percent food cost. An entrée item, however, may cost $4.00 and be sold for $8.00 and have a 50 percent food cost. The selling prices the operation offers the public depend on such factors as the ability of the clientele to pay, the amount of service provided, and the luxury of the decor. A luxurious operation may have a relatively low

Table 5.2
Typical Pro Forma Income Statement

INCOME STATEMENT
FOR XXXX

	Amount	Percentage
Sales		
Food	1,600,000	80.0
Beverages	400,000	20.0
Total revenue	$2,000,000	100.0
Cost of Sales		
Food	$ 544,000	34.0
Beverages	120,000	30.0
Total cost of sales	$ 664,000	33.2
Gross Profit		
Food	$1,056,000	66.0
Beverages	280,000	70.0
Total gross profit	$1,336,000	66.8
Expenses		
Salaries and wages	$ 640,000	32.0
Payroll taxes and employee benefits	64,000	3.2
Employee meals	58,000	2.9
China, glassware, silver, and linen	30,000	1.5
Laundry and uniforms	30,000	1.5
Cleaning supplies	26,000	1.3
Energy and utility services	40,000	2.0
Guest and paper supplies	12,000	.6
Music and entertainment	40,000	2.0
Menus and wine lists	10,000	.5
Licenses and fees	2,000	.1
Rubbish removal	4,000	.2
Flowers and decorations	12,000	.6
Administrative and general	70,000	3.5
Marketing	40,000	2.0
Repairs and maintenance	32,000	1.6
Total expenses	$1,110,000	55.5
Profit before occupation costs, depreciation, and income taxes	$ 226,000	11.3

food cost since the patron pays for the "trappings." Meanwhile, an economy cafeteria may have a higher food cost, because the patron is interested primarily in food value. (Menu Pricing and Control are discussed in chapter 9.)

Percentages of the cost of different expense items as compared to sales are available from various sources. The national hospitality accounting firms perform annual studies showing the cost percentages for various types of food operations. Larger restaurant associations often make these figures available.

Some costs should not be determined strictly as a percentage of sales. Advertising and promotion costs, for example, should be determined by deciding what types of promotion to utilize and then costing out this desired promotion. For example, if the promotion is to consist of billboards and newspaper advertising, it is a simple matter to determine how much this advertising will cost and then determine the advertising and promotion figure. This can then be divided by sales if a percentage figure is desired.

Beverage cost determination is similar to food cost determination. Operators determine at what price they will be selling various beverages and the amount of the beverage they will be providing. Once the quantity is determined, the cost to the operator can be determined and cost can be compared to sales to derive a beverage percentage. Again, percentages will differ according to the types of beverages served. The beverage percentage for cocktails will probably differ from the malt beverage percentage. Operators can derive a weighted average to determine their normal beverage figure.

Labor costs can be determined by deciding how much staff will be required for the anticipated volume of service. If the operator decides that one serving person can handle 30 patrons, dividing the number of expected patrons by 30 will produce the number of serving personnel required for the serving period. The salary and fringe benefit costs for these people can then be determined. Then, adding the cost of serving personnel to the cost of other personnel gives total labor costs. Comparing this number to anticipated sales gives the labor cost percentages. In our example, labor costs of $640,000 are compared to sales of $2 million, giving a labor cost percentage of 32 percent. The labor cost percentage varies with different volumes of business. Some employees are necessary whether business is booming or slow. Those employees needed regardless of the business volume are considered to be the fixed-cost employees. Serving personnel and preparation personnel, on the other hand, can usually be increased or decreased depending on the volume of activity and so may be considered variable-cost employees. (Staffing and scheduling are discussed in chapter 12.)

Payroll taxes, like social security and workers' compensation, represent a percentage of payroll and can be calculated rather easily. Other employee benefits can usually be costed out. For example, a two-week vacation is roughly two-fifty-seconds of a yearly salary, or about 4 percent. In calculating the value of an employee's meal, some operations consider this as a certain percentage of total food cost. Other operations determine what the typical employee meal consists of, cost it out, and then multiply it by the number of meals expected to be served.

The amount spent for china, glassware, silver, and linens varies according to the standards of the restaurant. An operation that uses linen tablecloths has much higher linen charges than one that has no tablecloths and uses paper napkins. Glassware quality can differ greatly. Its cost as a percentage of sales from similar operations may be used. Another, and perhaps more accurate, approach is to determine the quantities of these items used and multiply the quantity by the cost of each item to derive a total cost in any one category.

Laundry and uniforms, cleaning supplies, and paper supplies are usually best estimated by using standard percentages for those items compared to sales. Again, more accurate calculations may be made if you determine what the policy for employees' uniforms should be. If they furnish their own and are responsible for washing them, there would be very little expense. On the other hand, if the establishment furnishes employee uniforms, it should determine

1. how many uniforms each employee will require
2. the cost of the uniforms
3. how often they will be cleaned
4. the resulting total expense.

Uniforms deteriorate in time, and a factor should be included for this cost. Because uniforms vary considerably, it is best to get help from a uniform supply house regarding the costs.

Cost of energy and utility service will depend on the geographical area. Cold areas require considerably more heating and warmer areas require air conditioning. Once the nature of the physical structure is known, the local energy companies can usually produce rather accurate estimates of heating or cooling costs.

When considering music or entertainment, operators must determine what and how much they want. If the choice is a combo five nights a week, they can easily determine cost and multiply that amount by the number of days the combo will appear. General percentages are not very helpful here, because the music and entertainment vary so considerably. Piped-in music costs can be readily quoted by suppliers.

Menu supply houses are happy to quote menu and wine list costs. By calculating the number of menus needed and how often they will change, operators can produce an accurate cost for the service.

Licenses and fees can generally be determined accurately in advance. It is necessary only to ask the issuing agency what the costs will be. Rubbish removal charges vary considerably. Some towns provide service in exchange for local taxes. In other places, a flat fee is charged. Still others determine the cost by the number of trash cans or garbage bags handled. In any case, a check with municipal authorities should be sufficient to determine this cost. Floral and decoration costs can vary considerably as well, and operators should determine in advance to what extent they will be used. The costs are available from florists and specialty shops.

The costs of help in the office and office expenses can be readily estimated. Estimates of accounting, legal, and insurance costs are provided in advance by those who want to supply the respective services. Repair and maintenance costs can vary considerably depending on the state of the premises. Building experts (engineers or architects) can help estimate these costs.

As we have noted, proposed costs can be determined in two ways. One is to use standard percentage amounts that, when multiplied by the anticipated sales, yield the amount of the various costs. The other is actually to cost items out, which sometimes requires outside help. Even though items are separately costed to derive a figure, percentage (the calculated cost over anticipated sales) figures can be compared with industry averages to see if they are generally in line. There are good reasons not to depend too much on general industry averages, especially because individual operations may vary considerably from industry averages.

The bottom line on Table 5.2 represents profit before occupational costs, depreciation, and income taxes: $226,000 or 11.3 percent of sales. The occupation costs refer to the costs of maintaining the premises. This can include rent, mortgage payments, real estate taxes, and property insurance. Depreciation is the charge made against assets that deteriorate through use, time, or obsolescence. Income taxes are the taxes on the profit of the enterprise. They vary according to the amount of profit.

PRIMARY PRELIMINARY CAPITAL COST ESTIMATES

The feasibility of a commercial operation is determined largely by economic factors usually expressed as the return on the investment, or how much money its owners have to invest in an operation compared to the amount of money they earn from it. The investment usually consists of two parts: the entrepreneurs' own money invested and the money borrowed or secured from other sources. Before proceeding too far on a proposed operation, entrepreneurs should have some idea of the amount of money they will need. They can then determine how much of their own funds might be available and how much they will need to seek elsewhere. The term *entrepreneur* does not necessarily refer only to an individual; it can refer as well to an investment group or corporation.

Table 5.3 provides preliminary capital cost estimates for an operation. The term *preliminary* is used because this estimate is based on the first stage of a feasibility study. If it

Table 5.3
Preliminary Capital Costs Estimates

Land	$ 100,000	Selling price or preliminary appraisal can give a basis for land cost consideration. Costs of site development and landscaping should be included.
Paved Parking Areas & Driveways	$ 20,000	Cost per square foot is usually available. Multiply this by total footage to determine a projected figure.
Structure Costs	$ 500,000	Architects or builders can usually give an estimated cost based on type of construction and estimated cost per square foot multiplied by total footage.
Furnishings and Fixtures	$ 240,000	An interior designer or supply firm can provide an estimate by multiplying the projected cost per seat by the projected number of seats. Similar operations are usually close enough in cost per seat to allow a general guide figure to be used.
Equipment	$ 160,000	The type of menu and projected volume allows for a projected equipment list. This can then be priced out.
Other Costs	$ 60,000	This figure should include architectural and consultant fees (usually between 7 and 10 percent), office equipment, employee facilities, reserve for contingencies, and cost overruns or increases.
TOTAL	$1,080,000	

appears that capital costs will be too high, the whole project may be abandoned before too much effort is invested in it. If the preliminary estimates, which are ballpark numbers, appear logical, more exact figures can be determined. Table 5.3 depicts some estimates for a particular project. As we already stressed in this chapter, there are no common guidelines for all operations. In Table 5.3, paving for parking and driveways is a relatively minor amount compared to the structure costs of $500,000. Other operations may be able to get by with a comparatively small structure but require a much larger parking lot and driveway. They would have an entirely different ratio on these two costs. Table 5.3 does this sort of analysis for major capital costs and explains ways to determine their specific amounts.

WORKING CAPITAL REQUIREMENTS

In addition to the cost of land, building, furnishings, and equipment, you must keep money on hand to conduct your business. Thus, in planning your restaurant and in planning for the exact amount of money that restaurant will cost you in the beginning, you should include working capital. By definition, **working capital** is the difference between **current assets** (actual cash, or assets readily convertible into cash) and **current liabilities** (debts of all kinds due within one year).

If you have insufficient working capital, you may find it difficult to pay your bills and, consequently, to stay in business. Thus, your feasibility study must show how much working capital you need and what your capital expenditures will be. Cash requirements are usually offset, at least partially, by current liabilities. In other words, if you buy food but do not pay for it until the following month when you are billed, you may not have to have the money on hand at the time of your actual purchase. When you sell the food, it generates cash that should more than pay the bill when it arrives.

The relative difference between the current-asset total and the current-liability total is a measure of your *liquidity,* or how readily you can pay off your current obligations. Liquidity is sometimes expressed as a *current ratio,* which is calculated by dividing current assets by current liabilities. For most businesses, a ratio of about 2:1 is considered adequate, but in the foodservice business, where one typically finds a fast inventory turnover and comparatively few accounts receivable, a ratio of closer to 1.2:1 is more realistic. Another liquidity ratio is the *acid test,* or cash, marketable securities, and accounts receivable divided by current liabilities.

Besides normal working capital requirements, new operations will involve some atypical, one-time expenses. The need for promotion, training, and other preopening expenses should be included in planning, so that once the business is open, it can pay off these initial expenses in addition to usual costs. Figure 5.2 discusses the main items involved in determining working capital. (Financial statements are further discussed in chapter 20)

ANALYSIS AND RETURN ON INVESTMENT

The usual criterion for a commercial endeavor is, once again, the return on the investment. Table 5.4 provides a way to analyze this. This table is a natural progression from previous figures and tables in this chapter.

CURRENT ASSETS *(cash or assets that can be readily turned into cash)*

1. Cash on hand
   Used for cashier banks and petty cash funds.
2. Cash in the bank
   Funds necessary to meet current obligations such as payrolls, purveyors, and utility charges. A beginning operation will need sufficient funds to carry the operation until adequate cash revenue is generated.
3. Accounts receivable
   Funds owed by customers for services rendered. There is a lag between the time charge sales are made and the time they are collected. Funds must be available to compensate for this lag if charge sales are produced. This is no problem if all sales are cash.
4. Inventories
   (a) *Food.* Based on volume of business and number of times the food inventory is turned over during a month. If the cost of sales per month is $100,000, and it is estimated the inventory would turn over four times, the amount of inventory required would be $25,000. Often high-volume operations require less inventory in proportion to sales than lower-volume ones.
   (b) *Supplies.* Varies according to availability, storage capacity, delivery frequency, and types and levels of service provided by the purveyor.
5. Prepaid expenses
   Items such as license fees, insurance premiums, and utilities that are paid in advance.

CURRENT LIABILITIES *(money owed and payable by the operation, usually within one year)*

6. Trade account payable
   Money that is owed to purveyors. This should be about one-twelfth the annual amount of purchases and services secured from purveyors.
7. Accrued expenses
   Expenses that have been incurred by the operation but not yet paid. Usually these are payroll owed to employees and payroll taxes due. Such items as utility bills and other taxes may also be included. One percent of sales is sometimes used as a ballpark figure.
8. Current portions of long-term obligations
   The amount payable within one year of long-term loans.

Note: Items 1 to 8 are required for a going operation. A new operation may have additional costs such as initial promotion costs, grand opening costs, salaries for personnel hired in advance, and training costs. These costs must be able to be carried by cash on deposit or loan sources, until operating revenues catch up.

Figure 5.2
Working Capital Requirements

Table 5.4
Typical Analysis of Return on Investment

	Amount	Percentage
Profit before occupation, depreciation, and income taxes	$226,000	11.3%
Reductions		
Taxes (state and local)	10,000	0.5
Insurance	8,000	0.4
Interest	10,000	0.5
Depreciation		
Building	12,500	1.3
Furniture and fixtures	24,000	1.2
Equipment	12,500	
Other	4,000	0.2
Total reductions	$ 81,000	40.5
Income before debt service	$145,000	72.5
First mortgage	36,000	1.8
Chattel mortgage	24,000	1.2
Total debt service	$ 60,000	3.0
Net income before income taxes	85,000	4.3
Depreciation	49,000	2.5
Cash flow	$134,000	6.7
Cash flow as percentage of equity	33.5	
Profit as percentage of equity (ROI)	21.3	
Profit as percentage of total investment (ROAM)	8.0%	

Figure 5.1 covered possible markets and competition and determined what type of operation would probably be most suitable. We also have discussed the appropriateness of the site for a particular function and other practical considerations necessary to complete the structure on the site.

Table 5.1 provided one approach to determine the number of people served and then the projected sales by considering the rate of turnover for various meal periods.

Table 5.2 took these projected sales and provided the anticipated profit or loss by calculating expenses appropriate for sales and standards of operation, while Figure 5.2 yielded estimates of the amount of capital and operating funds required to bring a project to fruition.

If these preliminary estimates have been favorable, they must still be checked with actual cost prices and bids. All of the previous information is necessary to calculate Table 5.4, an analysis of the return on investment. The profit of $226,000 from Table 5.4 is presented, and after taxes, insurance, interest, depreciation, and other deductions are made, an income for paying off a debt of $145,000 is left. This is the income before debt service or before paying the interest and the principal amount of loans or before any withdrawing of profit. Table 5.4 first shows a mortgage on real estate that has principal and interest payments at $36,000.

The *chattel mortgage* is a mortgage on movable property (as opposed to real estate or real property). This mortgage is sometimes considered as a conditional sales contract, wherein the purchaser acquires the use and possession of the assets but does not actually own them until all of the purchase cost of debts have been paid off. After subtracting the debt service of $60,000, we find we have a net income before taxes of $85,000.

Usually in a new operation, the **cash flow**, or the amount of cash available, is more important than the profit. Cash flow may be defined as profit plus depreciation. Although depreciation is an expense, it is a noncash expense; money need not be put out directly at the time as it must be to pay personnel salaries or buy food. The depreciation in Table 5.4 is $49,000, and adding this back to the net income before income taxes, but including depreciation, produces a cash flow of $134,000. It should be noted that the net income before income taxes is not the same as profit. Principal payments on the first mortgage and on the chattel mortgages are included in the income before taxes, but these are not regular operating business expenses that would be included in the profit figure.

The three ratios employed in Table 5.4 include cash flow as a percentage of equity, profit as a percentage of equity, and profit as a percentage of total investment. If we assume that the owner's equity, or the amount that the owner or owners have invested with their own money, is $400,000, the cash flow as the percentage of equity would be $134,000 divided by $400,000, or 33.5 percent.

Profit as a percentage of total investment in the enterprise is sometimes called the *management proficiency ratio,* or ROAM. (ROAM refers to *return on assets managed* or the total value of the enterprise as expressed by the value of its assets.) ROAM indicates how well management is doing with its assets. In comparing profits of various operations, you should know how the amount of the profit compares to the amount of money invested.

One hundred thousand dollars may be a large profit for an operation that has $500,000 worth of assets, but it would be a very small profit for one with $2 million in assets. The ROAM ratio is not as desirable as the other ratios in considering the feasibility of an operation, because it is concerned more with the money-making proficiency of the management given the available assets than relating profits to needed equity investment. Other methods are preferred to financially analyze a new investment, such as accounting rate of return (ARR) or payback period.

The cash flow may be more important than the profit because it represents the money actually coming in and available. The return on the investment (ROI) is important. When people have money to invest, they naturally want to receive the highest possible return. Thus, investors want to know whether the investment balances the risk they take. Table 5.4 shows a net income before income taxes of $85,000. If this figure is divided by an investment of $400,000 the return on investment would be 21.3 percent. In our example, we have not considered federal income taxes because of the complexities involved. Tax computations, however, would cause the net income before taxes to be reduced by the amount of the taxes.

FINANCING AN ENTERPRISE

For most people desiring to start a foodservice enterprise, the biggest immediate problem is how to finance it. An existing operation that wants to remodel or make extensive equipment changes may also have financing problems.

Debt and Equity

Two areas from which an enterprise can receive funds are equity sources and debt sources. Equity funds involve ownership in the business. Proprietors or sole owners of a business may increase their equity by putting more of their own money into the business or by not withdrawing as much money out of business as it earns in profits. Partners in a business can do the same thing, and they may either bring in additional money or allow earnings to remain in the business to increase their equity. A corporation is owned by the stockholders. The equity in a corporation is increased by selling more stock; if sold to people other than present stockholders, this additional stock dilutes the interest of the present stockholders in the business. Corporations, like other businesses, can allow profits to remain in the enterprise rather than be paid out in dividends. This is internal financing.

Debt financing involves borrowing money from a source that does not acquire an equity interest in the business through loans. Sometimes debt financing can be converted into an equity arrangement, but normally debt financing is the lending of money by nonowners. It is also possible for stockholders to make loans to a corporation. Equity sources can include proprietors, partners, and stockholders. Proprietors and partners simply supply their own money to the enterprise.

DEBT FINANCING

Debt financing involves the use of someone else's money to start, help, or expand an operation that different people own. Using borrowed funds for expansion is sometimes known as *leverage* or *trading on the equity*. If an operation costs $200,000 and the owners put in $50,000 of their own and borrow the balance, they are leveraging 75 percent of the cost and supplying 25 percent. In the unlikely situation that a project was 100 percent leveraged, all the financing would come from borrowed money, and no equity financing is involved. If the business is profitable and the owners can readily pay off interest and debt amortization (or payment of the principal amounts of the loan), a great deal of money can be made by using leverage. This potential exists when borrowed money is used to provide resources that produce more profit than the equity resources alone can. On the other hand, in a highly leveraged project, the debt payments must be made before any return to the owners. Thus, if the cash flow is unsatisfactory, the owners may lose what they have invested in the project.

Sources for the capital financing may be different than sources of funds for short-term or intermediate financing. Capital financing usually involves large amounts of money committed for long periods. Some types of financial institutions avoid this long-term commitment. Capital financing in the foodservice industry is generally of a real property nature that may involve land, buildings, and major pieces of equipment with a relatively long life span. A mortgage, or the pledge of a designated property as security for the loan, is often used to secure capital financing. It is not uncommon for the seller of a hospitality property to give a mortgage loan for the difference between the selling price and the down payment. Or the seller may give a second or "junior" mortgage to make up the difference between the selling price and the down payment and any other financing that may have been secured. Having the seller provide mortgage money may be very helpful to both the seller and the buyer. If the seller does not need the money for other purposes, the mortgage can constitute a worthwhile investment with the property as security. From the buyer's standpoint, it may be the most satisfactory financing available.

APPLYING FOR A LOAN

Unless you are well known to a lending institution, standard steps are typically required before securing a loan. The lending institution will probably want to see a balance sheet that shows capital and possible collateral for the loan. It may also want past income statements that show financial results. It may ask to see pro forma statements (statements that show what you expect to happen in the future of your business). Anticipated inflows and outflows of cash may also be helpful because the money available for the repayment of the loan is not necessarily the same as the anticipated profit. You should indicate any specific collateral available for the loan. You should also specify the exact amount of the loan you want and the exact purposes to which it will be applied. If the income statement and cash budgets do not indicate how the loan can be repaid, calculations should show this. If the business is owned by a proprietor or partnership, financial statements for the proprietor and for each partner may be required. If a business is a corporation with only a few stockholders, financial statements for the major stockholders can be helpful.

A lending institution will probably conduct an investigation of both the company and the principal(s). It may secure information such as a Dun and Bradstreet report. Dun and Bradstreet provides a history of the operation and of the principals or major participants. The report will include known financing transactions, a history of fires or bankruptcies, and the credit experience of firms selling to the company, among many other possible topics. A bank may have the loan application evaluated either by the loan officer or by a loan committee. A reliable business that borrows often from one bank tends to establish a strong bond with that bank. In this case, the bank (or lending institution) may be able to offer valuable financial counsel besides simply lending money.

BASIS FOR LENDING

Loans are usually made on the basis of the four Cs: character, capital, collateral, and the capacity to repay. Normally financial institutions do not lend money to people with a reputation for avoiding payment of their obligations. Thus, lenders often investigate the character of the owners applying for loans. Even a person of perfectly fine character may, because of prior financial difficulties, find it difficult to secure new financing.

Capital refers to the general financial position of the firm, especially the net worth of the enterprise in relation to debt. The more resources the borrower has in relation to debt, the more secure that debt will be. (It could always be at least partially paid off through a sale of the resources.)

Collateral refers to specific assets offered as a pledge or security for the debt. If the debt is not paid, the debtor can use the pledged assets to pay off the loan. A car loan, for example, may be secured by the car itself. Loans that are secured by collateral may often carry a lower interest rate than unsecured loans.

Capacity is the apparent ability to pay. Although lenders may make a loan if it is secured by assets with at least the amount of the loan, normally they would rather see the loan repaid by income generated by the loan itself. If borrowers can demonstrate to lenders that they will earn sufficient income to pay off a loan, it makes the loan more feasible and can reduce capital or collateral requirements.

A fifth C might be *conditions*. Severe economic and money conditions may affect whether a specific loan will or will not be granted at a particular time. If money is tight, a borrower who usually has little trouble securing funds may be unable to so.

Loan approval by a lending institution may sometimes be expressed as the 1-2-3s. The one is the collateral behind the loan. If the loan is based on the value of the collateral, it cannot be more (and is usually less) than the discounted value of this collateral. If the collateral value is $90,000, the loan will be $90,000 or usually less.

The two refers to having a cash flow (net profit plus depreciation less taxes) of at least two times the annual interest and principle payments of the loan. If cash flow is $30,000, the lender might feel secure in providing a loan requiring $15,000 annually in interest and principal costs.

The three assumes that the equity in the business or net worth should be at least one third of the loan. If net worth is $30,000, a $90,000 loan might be considered.

GOVERNMENT PROGRAMS

A number of state and federal programs may be of help to foodservice operations seeking financing. Some of the programs are designed for special purposes such as helping minorities or creating new jobs. Different localities may have programs to help business development in their area.

Federal government loans are usually made through the Small Business Administration (SBA). SBA financing does not compete with private financing. Instead, it facilitates private financing by participating with local banks and lending institutions. If no other financing is available, the SBA may advance all the money. In addition, the SBA can guarantee a percentage of a loan made by a bank to a small firm. The SBA may also promote private financing by advancing part of the funds rather than guaranteeing the bank's loan. Through different programs, the SBA can furnish funds for increased working capital, expansion, or even the inauguration of a new business.

Obtaining an SBA loan requires substantial paperwork and documentation, and there are loan limits. For small businesses and loans up to $100,000, the federal agency offers a simpler "Low-Doc" program.

LEASING

Leasing is yet another means of financing for the hospitality industry. By leasing assets, you gain the use of those assets, but you are not required to lay out substantial immediate money for them. In effect, the leasing company finances the purchase. Some types of leasing have been used by the hospitality industry for years. Linen rentals, for example, have been around for a long time. Today, a wide variety of assets are leased, including furniture, kitchen equipment, linens, and vehicles. The chief advantage in leasing rather than buying equipment is the small cash outlay. The operation can use the funds it saves for other purposes. Or perhaps it cannot borrow enough funds for the equipment it desires.

If the leased equipment requires service, the leasing company often can provide better service than the hospitality organization. There can also be tax advantages in leasing because the costs of leasing are deductible expenses in calculating taxes. If the equipment is purchased, the money comes from earnings on which taxes have already been paid or with money that must be borrowed. The interest charges on borrowed money and the depreciation costs on assets purchased are also tax-deductible items, but leasing the equipment may provide even greater deductions. Although the gross amount of money paid out for leasing may be higher than if you purchased equipment with cash on hand or borrowed money to buy it, the tax considerations may make the net cost lower.

Leasing does pose some disadvantages. Lease costs may still be higher than other means of financing. Also, once a lease is signed, it is hard to change. Thus, you may sacrifice a degree of flexibility. For example, you may desire newer equipment but may have to pay a premium to change the terms on the equipment you presently lease.

FRANCHISING

One approach to start a new business in foodservice (or other areas) is to obtain a franchise. **Franchising** may be defined as a legal agreement in which a franchise or owner agrees to give a franchisee the right or license to sell the franchising products or services under a set of specific conditions. Foodservice franchising goes back at least to the 1920s when the A&W Root Beer Company sold franchises. To a limited degree Howard Johnson's offered franchises in the 1930s.

Foodservice franchising really took off in the mid 1950s, and the success stories of franchises like McDonalds, Kentucky Fried Chicken, and Burger King are well known. Franchising has both advantages and disadvantages.

Advantages and Disadvantages of Franchising

Advantages.   Franchising obviously owes its popularity to the advantages it provides both the franchisor and the franchisee. There are at least eight advantages to franchisees.

1. **Franchisees** buy into an established, successful business. They already know the food is popular and need only determine whether they can sell it at the location they have in mind. Not only is the food popular, but it also involves none of the traditional start-up uncertainty.

2. The typical franchise operation uses a standardized facility that has long since been streamlined and refined to appeal to the target customers and to achieve maximum efficiency. Franchisees need not hire an architect. They may not even need a construction company since franchisors often build, equip, and decorate the franchise outlets.

3. Just as the architectural plans are available to franchisees, so too are the operational plans. Purchasing, storing, cooking, serving, and cleaning procedures have all been thoroughly worked out.

4. Many franchisors provide training programs for new franchisees and their employees. (McDonald's even confers a diploma from its Hamburger University.) Even if they do not provide formal training, almost all franchisors provide at least a detailed training manual. In short, most franchisees are spared all the anguish of opening a new operation and training employees at the same time.

5. Independent restauranteurs earn their reputations slowly and painfully. Franchisees buy a well-known name and, with it, instant recognition and acceptance. They save all the time, effort, and money that building a reputation would normally entail. As a franchisor knows, however, a slovenly franchisee can besmear the name of an entire franchise. Consequently, most franchisors maintain strict control over all the franchises.

6. The franchisor assumes the burden of keeping the operation's name before the public. This helps pay for regional and national advertising that a single franchisee could never afford by itself.

7. In most cases, it is easier to finance a franchise than an independent restaurant. Prospective lenders can observe the results of other franchises in the area and gauge their risk quite realistically. The franchising company itself often helps finance a new unit.

8. To put it bluntly, franchises often earn a lot of money. They often tend to show profits well above those of independent operations doing the same volume of business. A franchise ownership does not guarantee profit, and quite a few franchises have failed or are currently on shaky financial footing. The fast-food concept tends to generate a much higher volume than many conventional restaurants. The carefully arranged procedures they follow (market research having taken much of the guesswork out of attracting customers) increase the likelihood of generous profits.

In addition to the advantages to the franchisee, there are strong incentives for the franchising organization. To begin with, once franchisors formulate the product, design, and system, they can start selling the franchises at little additional cost. The greater the number of franchise operations, the greater the recognition factor; advertising becomes cumulative and self-reinforcing. An independent restaurant cannot normally expand beyond several units. Franchisors, however, spread their units far and wide and reap all the accompanying benefits. Franchising, then, is a way to expand with relatively little in capital funds required on the part of the franchisor.

Disadvantages.   The list of advantages may be impressive, but franchising is not problem-free. Its disadvantages may be summarized as follows:

- Franchisors are obviously in business to make money. They make most of it from initial franchise fees and continuing royalties from franchises. Typically, the initial franchise fee must be paid when the franchise is secured. Depending upon the success and reputation of the franchisor, that fee can be quite steep. The continuing royalty payments are deducted from profits.

- In one sense, a standardized operation provides reassurance. However, enterprising foodservice managers are severely limited in what they can place on the menu, in what they can charge for food, in what cooking procedures to use—in all those areas that imply creativity.

- A disparity of bargaining power often occurs. The franchisor may be financially stronger, which can be a factor in long, expensive legal disputes with individual franchises.

- Disputes can arise over franchisors requiring products be secured from them and the pricing structure of these products.
- The franchisor usually wants to have as many units under its franchise as possible and may oversaturate a geographical area to the detriment of present franchisees. Or the company may favor company-owned stores rather than franchisees.
- There have been disputes over whether a franchisor's termination and renewal clauses are unreasonable and perhaps employed unfairly.
- Franchisees may feel they do not have enough influence in matters of corporate policies, pricing decisions, and marketing policy.
- A franchisor may not be keeping up with current trends. Some even go out of business, leaving their franchises in a bad situation.

These potential hazards show that although a franchise is a legal relationship, there is much opportunity for either success or failure. A thorough investigation should be made before signing up with a franchisor.

THE BUSINESS PLAN

Once its principals decide that a particular operation could be successful at a particular site, a business plan can be developed to show how this can be accomplished. Figure 5.3 provides one outline for a business plan. If the business plan is to be used for outside financing, it would be more formal than one developed by owners of an ongoing business for how they should proceed to operate in the future.

The cover sheet would include the name of the business, address, telephone numbers (if available), and the individual or individuals who prepared the plan. If it needs to be submitted to a bank or other institution, the name of that institution could be included along with the date of submission.

Statement of Purpose

If the business plan is for financing purposes, this section should include the amount and type of outside financing, the amount of financing by the owners themselves, and the intended use of financing. The plan may also have other purposes, such as providing guidance for a future period, planning for an expansion, or planning on how to cope with anticipated new competition. If outside financing is involved, you might include how the funds will be repaid.

The Business

This can be the most important part of the business plan. What is the business? How are you going to run it? Why do you think it will succeed? What is your business philosophy? Some operations may focus on making as much money as possible, becoming an asset to the community, providing specific benefits to employees, or serving the finest quality food. The business philosophy can also be expressed as a mission statement.

Will there be policies and goals to implement the business philosophy? These can be both for customers and employees. Policies could include giving empowerment privileges

A. Front Matter
1. Cover sheet
2. Table of contents
3. Statement of purpose
B. The Business
1. Overview of the business
2. Business philosophy (of owners)
3. Policy and goals
4. Industry analysis
5. Affiliation
6. Operations
7. Timetable
C. Marketing Plan
1. Overview of the market
2. Potential customers
3. Location
4. Competition
5. Marketing strategy
D. Organization of the Enterprise
1. Legal organization
2. Principals
3. Personnel
4. Outside consultants
5. Permits and licenses
E. Financial data
1. Sources and affiliation of funds
2. Capital and equipment needs
3. Real estate
4. Insurance coverage
5. Current balance sheet
6. Current profit and loss statement
7. Personal financial statements
8. Personal income tax returns
F. Pro Forma Statements
1. Income statements
2. Cash flow statements
G. Summary
H. Appendices

Figure 5.3
Outline for a Business Plan

to employees to handle problems in dealing with customers or an explanation of your hiring practices. What are the long-range and short-range goals of the management? Where did they expect the operation to be in one, two, or five years or any other time periods?

The industry segment should zero in on the segment of the foodservice industry that the operation is pursuing. More people may be eating out, which indicates expansion. On the other hand, the fast-food segment in some areas may be saturated, leaving little opportunity.

Perhaps the operation will be a franchise of an organization, part of a chain, or some other affiliation. Benefits and services of such an arrangement should be noted along with costs and limitations. Having a franchise from a successful franchisor may help in securing outside financing.

The operations portion of the plan describes operating systems, such as preparation, service, inventory, purchasing, and accounting. Do they fit into a general system for the operation? Is there an appropriate information system? To what extent will the operation be computerized? The costs of the operating system will be incorporated into the amount of capital required.

If the restaurant is a start-up operation, the business plan should include a timetable for the necessary steps that must be accomplished, leading up to the opening date. If a new plan of operation is to be installed, a timetable should specify implementation of the various steps.

The Marketing Plan

Much of the information for the marketing plan can be developed in the feasibility study. Basically you want to identify potential customers or target markets and determine if there are enough of them to support the operation. What is the competition and what competitive advantages do you enjoy? Is the location good for your type of operation? This includes such factors as traffic flow, parking, foot traffic, and state of the neighborhood. Once the target markets are identified, how will you reach them? What advertising media and in what amounts will these be utilized? These can include newspapers, radio, TV, and direct mail. You also must determine what all this promotion will cost. Perhaps it will be possible to get some free publicity or promotion from various sources.

Remember that your marketing effort has the customer as its sole focus. Everything in the business, whether it is a start-up or growing concern, old or new, big or small, revolves around customers and prospective customers.

Footnotes and appendices that can support the factual data presented add to the credibility of the report. Mention any advertising agencies that you are using or plan to use.

Legal Organizational Form of the Enterprise

Every foodservice operation (or any operation) must have some legal form of organization. It might be a proprietorship (owned by one person), corporation (an artificial entity created by law), subchapter S corporation, or a partnership (two or more owners). Since forms of organization have different personal liabilities and tax considerations, the organization form should be specified in the business plan, and the proprietor, partners (limited or general), and major stockholders should be listed.

The principals in the business are those owners or others directly involved in the management. Their qualifications should be mentioned in the plan and perhaps their more complete resumes included in the appendices.

An organizational chart shows the various positions that will be required. Key personnel such as a chef or maitre'd can be described. Discuss how the various positions will be filled and review the available labor pool for these workers.

Outside consultants can include accountants, lawyers, or industry experts. If they are already involved, they and their qualifications should be mentioned.

If the organization is already in operation, permits, licenses, tax and employer I.D. numbers, or other legal requirements should be included.

Financial Data

This section is of great interest to bankers or outside investors if external funding is desired. For an operation that is developing a plan for the future without new funding, much of the financial data can be omitted.

The source and application of funds document shows where the funds will be secured and how the money will be utilized. The funds may come from owners, investors, and/or lenders, or it may be generated internally. Applications of funds can be for capital expenses or working capital purposes.

Capital expenses include major items like equipment or other big cost items. Working capital expenses include monies for payroll, inventory, marketing, and start-up costs.

Types and amounts of insurance must be determined and costed. These may require up-front payments.

Real estate may be purchased or leased. If it is owned, any mortgage requirements should be listed. A copy of a lease can be included in the appendices.

Past and present balance sheets and income statements for operations that are already functioning should be included.

Break-even analysis can show at what volumes of dollar sales, meals served, or customers served, the operation will break even financially or what losses or profits would be at the various volumes. Chapter 24 discusses break-even analysis.

Lenders may require that principals or others co-sign the loans, or pledge their assets for repayment. Therefore, they want to know the financial worth of these co-signers and will request personal financial statements. Copies of income tax forms can provide additional verification. This information can be included in the appendices.

Remember that lenders look for repayment from earnings, use of collateral, or personal guarantees.

Pro Forma Statements

Pro forma statements are prepared in advance using forecasted or anticipated data since actual data has not yet been generated. Cash flow (defined as profit minus depreciation) shows cash inflows and outflows. Expanding businesses that show good profits may have cash flow problems because they must make cash payments on new assets that will more than pay for themselves in time but may cause a current cash shortfall. Lenders want to determine if cash will be available in the future to pay off their loan and may request pro forma statements using anticipated figures for three years or some other future time period.

Pro forma statements can be prepared using percentages (say 70 percent or 80 percent) below anticipated volume or a figure over anticipated volume such as 110 percent.

Summary

This section, as its name implies, summarizes the business plan. If the business plan is for securing financing, it should help convince the lenders or investor(s) that the business plan is well thought out and that the operation is viable and can pay off the financing or provide a desired return on investment.

INDUSTRY INSIGHTS   by Walter Conti

Walter J. Conti is an International Food Manufacturers Association Gold Plate Award winner and past President of the National Restaurant Association. He is the former owner/manager of the award-winning Conti Cross Keys Inn located in Doylestown, Pennsylvania. He is a member of the Board of Trustees at the Pennsylvania State University.

YOU CAN'T ENJOY SUCCESS WITHOUT EXPERIENCING FAILURE

Question: From a personal perspective, how do you handle success and overcome disappointments?

The question is an interesting one. I don't think you can have one without the other as success and disappointment serve as measuring rods for one another. Both success and disappointment are a way of life for anyone who is involved in the day-to-day activities of the hospitality industry.

How to handle success is the more difficult part of the question. I have known people with sizable egos who seem consumed by success in that their every thought and action is geared to impress on others how successful they are. Some people talk a lot about their success rather than letting others talk about it. Some people worry that others won't think of them as successful or worry about how long their success will last.

Some successful people are not particularly successful in *managing* their own success. They want others to envy them. They make dramatic changes in their lifestyle and habits. They change the way they relate to and interact with others.

I think that truly successful people are those who possess an inner security that causes them not to think of themselves as being particularly successful. They don't think of themselves as being unsuccessful, but they retain the basic values, standards, lifestyle, and demeanor that always gave definition to their own identity. They are psychologically comfortable with themselves.

Controlling one's actions and solving day-to-day problems are all part of living successfully. I've often wondered what successful people think when their operation is running smoothly. This is the most critical time of one's professional life. It's always easier to fix or refine a wheel than to build a wheel. I suspect successful people are never satisfied. I think they keep looking to make things better and to undertake new challenges. I think they work hard to maintain the disciplines that caused them to be successful. I also think they keep abreast of what their customers want and treat their employees with the dignity they deserve.

Overcoming disappointment can be easier: you simply have to do it. There is no other acceptable alternative. You know that disappointments will occur. You may not know what specifically will be involved, but everyone experiences disappointments, so expect them. It's all part of life.

Disappointment serves a positive purpose. It brings us back to reality. It represents a challenge that we must hurdle. It enforces discipline, for it gives us a resolve that we might not otherwise exercise.

Experience can be helpful in overcoming disappointment as it gives us a confidence that we can manage whatever it is that caused the disappointment. Sometimes it's necessary to rely on outside people to assist you. They can often look at the situation more objectively and bring a different perspective to the environment. Once you realize that you can overcome disappointment, then you *must* overcome it.

Overall, you can't really understand the concept of success without understanding the concept of failure. Success gives us the confidence, strength, and ability to overcome disappointment. Disappointment is character building, which leads to resolve and confidence, which can lead in turn to success.

If the plan is to guide the operation in the future or solve some problems, it should summarize how this will be done.

Appendices

The appendices can include anything that adds to the plan but may distract or bog down the main body of the plan.

Appendices can include resumes of principals, photos of the operation, plot plans, engineering studies, floor plans, copy of the lease, equipment lists, industry studies, traffic studies, and other supporting data.

SUMMARY

A common desire is to establish a business such as a restaurant. However, the odds of failure are great: one estimate is half of all new foodservice operations fail in the first two years. A feasibility study and business plan cannot guarantee success but can greatly increase the odds of profitability. As its name implies, the feasibility study helps determine the feasibility of a project. It should include a market survey with information of the economic condition of the community, analysis of competition, a tentative description on the proposed operation, and projected volume with figures and costs.

The site analysis explores whether the site will fit the proposed operation and possible problems that could arise.

The marketing survey provides potential sales. The next step is to determine what will be required in capital and working capital investment and prepare a pro forma income statement to determine the potential and decide if this is adequate for the investment.

Once these issues are decided, a business plan can be prepared. This can utilize much information from the feasibility study after that information has been gathered. The business plan is a description of the operation and plans and policies to make it viable. It will also probably be required by lending institutions for borrowing. The business plan includes the type of financing desired. It describes the business, provides a marketing plan (based on feasibility data), describes the owners, specifies the legal form of ownership, and details financial data (again from the feasibility study).

New operations need financing, either from the owners (equity) or outside ownership (debt). Loans or credit is usually extended on the basis of the four Cs: character, capital, collateral, and capacity. Some government programs encourage new businesses or help specific groups.

For some operations, leasing may be a desirable or the only way to obtain financing.

Many new foodservice operations are franchises. A franchise may help in financing, provide tested operating procedures, and deliver an instant brand name. However, there are down sides to franchising such as costs and fees, limitations on what the franchisee can do, and potential for problems between the franchisor and franchisee.

KEY TERMS

business plan
capital costs
cash flow
current assets
current liabilities
demographics
equity financing

four Cs of credit
franchise
franchisee
franchisor
pro forma
return on investment
working capital

REVIEW QUESTIONS

5–1 How is a feasibility study for an institutional foodservice different from one for a commercial foodservice?

5–2 What does a feasibility study do?

5–3 What criteria are used to determine if an operation is financially feasible?

5–4 Discuss market aspects of a feasibility study.

5–5 List the aspects of a particular locality that should be considered.

5–6 Discuss the aspects of the competition that should be considered.

5–7 How can you determine an average check for a feasibility study?

5–8 How can you determine average sales for a feasibility study?

5–9 What is important regarding traffic patterns?

5–10 Which factors are important in determining your selling prices?

5–11 Discuss two different ways that most operating cost amounts can be determined.

5–12 Why may cash flow be more important than profit in determining an investment?

5–13 Explain the differences between debt and equity financing.

5–14 What is important in applying for a loan?

5–15 List advantages and disadvantages of leasing.

5–16 What are advantages of franchising?

5–17 What are types of debt financing?

5–18 List usual capital expenses for a new operation.

5–19 List usual working capital needs for a new operation.

PROJECTS

5–1 Prepare a business plan for a foodservice operation. It can be for an existing one possibly needing more funds or a restaurant you might like to develop. It must be in a real location.

5–2 Prepare a feasibility study for a foodservice operation. Examine the nonfinancial factors of an existing operation or develop a new operation using "best estimate" figures.

6

Management Information Systems

To best manage the efficiency of their operations, foodservice managers must have a way to track what is happening around them—from how employees are scheduled to how much food is purchased and produced.

Today, much of this information is available in manageable forms through the use of computerized management information systems.

After completing this chapter, you should be able to:

1. Define the term *management information system* and explain its importance in the foodservice industry.
2. List and discuss the five requirements of a useful management information system.
3. State four potential disadvantages in a management information system.
4. List at least six applicable functions management information systems can perform in a foodservice operation.
5. Explain what a POS terminal does.
6. Explain how access control systems operate.
7. List and describe applications available for foodservice management menu information systems.

ELEMENTS OF AN MIS

One of the most active areas in management practice recently has been management information systems. Every entrepreneur has some sort of management information system (MIS), often casual and unplanned. MIS specialists try to make communication more effective and scientific, and they also try to determine exactly what managers really need to know.

There are numerous possible definitions for MIS, but for the purposes of this book we have chosen to define it as "a system of regular or irregular data collection, selection, storage, and dissemination processes and applications." Collection and dissemination involve communication, the most important part of an MIS. The goal of an MIS is to provide accurate information to guide and produce effective management decisions. To do this, the information ideally should be precise, timely, concise, relevant, and economical. This type of information is, of course, vital to the overall control process.

The precision of the information will vary for different applications. In space flights it must be extremely accurate. In foodservice operations a manager rarely needs to go beyond a decimal point or two. Timeliness also is important. It does no good to learn that something happened long after the damage is done. Managers want to be on top of things and take appropriate action when needed. Foodservice directors can do little to recoup excessive food costs if they do not learn about those excesses until the month after they occurred.

Completeness also is crucial. Consider food preparation for an airline flight, for example. Airlines typically offer two or three menu choices for an in-flight meal. What often happens, however, is that the last people to be served are left with no choice of meal. Without knowing how many of each meal passengers would choose, it is impossible for the airline to prepare the correct number of each meal. Many foodservice managers (and other managers as well) have made less-than-ideal decisions because they could see only part of the picture.

Conciseness should be considered along with completeness, and it is an important complement on its own. Managers can be buried by too much data and can spend too much time trying to sift and analyze it rather than taking action, thus keeping them off the floor. Too much information also can confuse a situation; having the information in concise form can clarify it.

A good rule of thumb in gathering information is the 80/20 rule, which states that you can get 80 percent of the value with 20 percent of the resources. For example, if you have 100 menu items, rather than gathering and analyzing information on every item, you can look at the top 20 items to glean 80 percent of the total information impact. For most purposes, 80 percent of the total information is enough to base decisions on.

Relevancy can be associated with completeness and conciseness. What is it that a manager needs to know to make the proper decision? Some information may be nice to know but is not really relevant to the situation at hand. Many foodservice operators receive computer printouts, for example, that they do not use or do not know how to use.

Cost-effectiveness, or economy, requires that the information itself be more valuable than the cost of obtaining it. Some information might be desirable but could simply cost too much to secure.

To be a true management information system, the process or procedure must be more than just a source of information. It must be an integral unit of a larger system. A system is by definition a framework of interconnected parts through which an activity is accomplished and data travels. The MIS provides linkages for those interconnected parts. Not only is it an integral part of a larger system, but it also operates at different levels and for different purposes.

An MIS is helpful for such different management functions as planning, controlling, and resource allocation. It can be used by top management, by supervisors and other middle managers, and by regular workers, such as cooks.

Of course, the information needed by top management for strategic planning is different from that needed by the cooks in preparing a meal or supervisors controlling production. We plan to focus here more on the contributions an MIS can make to the management of control and on its use primarily by middle management.

MIS is currently an active area of management concern. Part of the reason for this is conceptual: The study of management information systems is part of the study of more effective methods of managing organizations.

We now know that an organization can be thought of as an information decision system and that every manager must have the necessary and accurate data to make decisions on a timely basis. Bad decisions are made on the basis of bad information.

Technological changes also have affected information systems. Where we once used telephones, typewriters, filing cabinets, and duplicating machines, we now use PC terminals, computer storage and retrieval devices, user-friendly computer systems that can communicate with each other, and computer graphics. Telecommunications and rapidly developing Internet technology are opening new areas of communication.

The information requirements of modern managers also have changed. In fact, change itself is more frequent, and most managers are at the mercy of the information available to them. Also, most operating units are more interdependent. In a large operation, the production manager needs information the accountant or purchaser has, and the controller needs information the food production manager has. Part of setting up an MIS is identifying the information-generating activities throughout the organization and determining who needs to receive what information. These separate activities must be recognized as parts of the whole organization, and their information must be coordinated and tied together. What do various decision makers have to know to perform their jobs? Where is this information generated and how can it be transferred? How can one establish coordination and perhaps centralization of this information gathering, information seeking, and information transfer within the organization? These questions are posed as an MIS is being designed.

FOODSERVICE MIS

A key to successful food management is control, a central concept of this textbook. Management must have the tools to control costs, and a foodservice management information system is an ideal tool for precisely this purpose. A number of software (and hardware) systems now available to foodservice managers can minimize food costs, maximize productivity, provide consistently high-quality products, and improve customer satisfaction.

An MIS is often divided into **applications**, defined as discrete and identifiable programs, for particular types of information, and the information used or developed in one application can be used in the others. For example, information developed in a forecasting application can be used in the purchasing application.

Different systems may have different applications or include different information in a particular application. Common applications in foodservice include those for sales analysis, production forecasting, purchasing, inventory, labor scheduling, back-office functions, nutritive composition, and catering.

We discuss these topics in detail throughout this book, but brief descriptions of some possible applications appear in this chapter. Remember, different systems have different applications, application titles, or information in the application.

COMPUTER APPLICATIONS IN FOODSERVICE COST CONTROL

Large-scale food production is a complex manufacturing process. Hundreds of recipes may be constructed from well over a thousand different ingredients. Vendors and their bids for raw ingredients must be evaluated, sometimes using a number of complex criteria. Demand must be forecast and adapted for recipes in the menu mix. Accurate costs should be calculated in advance of service. Menu pricing must accommodate financial goals or other constraints. Personnel must be scheduled, and cooks must be told how much to prepare and instructed in the appropriate preparation methods. Food must be ordered with optimum delivery dates and be verified on delivery. Appropriate inventories must be maintained.

Post-meal performance must be evaluated and compared to forecasts and preestablished standards. This evaluation is important not only from an accounting point of view, but also as a means of evaluating menus and production forecasts with an eye toward continually improving future performance.

Experienced foodservice managers take this process for granted, having learned from years of practice how to estimate numbers and quantities to achieve acceptable levels of performance.

The complexities and uncertainties involved in foodservice management often make gross approximations necessary. Performed manually, there may be limits on how many numbers can be crunched or how fast information can be produced. This places limitations on how tight controls can be and still assure satisfactory quality and quantity of product. It also limits how fully the foodservice operation can take advantage of opportunities for improved service and greater customer satisfaction.

Contrary to some perceptions, there is little in foodservice management that cannot be quantified, measured numerically, and directed by simple sets of decisions. The limitation is a financial one: It would cost more to manually perform the necessary calculations and apply the necessary controls than would be returned in terms of better financial performance and improved customer satisfaction. Also, it is hard to manually produce the information in time for the rapid decision making required in foodservice. Computers with appropriate software are ideal for performing these functions rapidly and accurately, freeing managers to manage with assurance of tight financial control and availability of information in time to be fully utilized.

Foodservice managers have performed surprisingly well in the past without computers. But the sheer volume of calculation, scheduling, and coordination necessary to analyze, plan, and execute a large-scale food-production process as well as it theoretically could be done is impossible using only manual methods. Various aspects of the process may be performed incompletely or skipped altogether. As a result, estimates with a degree of padding to protect against uncertainties can be facts of life in even the best-run foodservice operations.

This can result in overordering, overproduction, waste, pilferage, excess staff, and more limited menus than necessary. Using manual procedures, management often can handle only a relatively limited number of variables with accuracy and speed. This effectively limits menu variation and the ability to take advantage of opportunities.

Today, computer systems are available that can greatly extend the skills of experienced managers. Once a system is implemented successfully, the computer can make it function by ensuring that precise quantities of food are ordered and prepared. Needed for the plan are standard recipes to ensure consistent, quality products and accurate, consistent preparation and serving methods. Computer power also can handle more variables, such as patron preferences and past sales history, permitting more varied and interesting menus. The result is a more satisfied clientele at minimum cost.

Some systems can provide menu-pricing calculations, complete with profit margins, based on up-to-the-minute ingredient costs, labor costs, and the operation's own mark-up criteria. Some advantages of computer software use in foodservice production are listed in Figure 6.1.

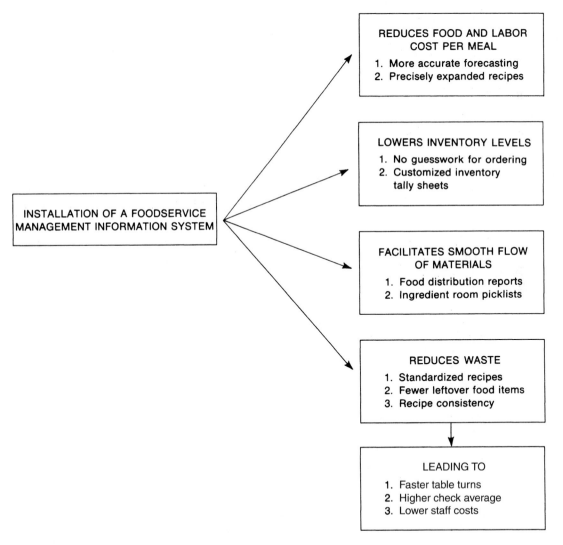

Figure 6.1
Foodservice MIS Benefits

COMPLAINTS AND MISCONCEPTIONS ABOUT AN MIS

The ability of an organization to generate information is not usually a problem. In fact, information overload may be the problem. Here are some complaints about the information an MIS provides:

- The information is not helpful or as helpful as it might be.
- It is difficult to find where the information is.
- People with other vested interests may suppress or hide information.
- The information may arrive too late for effective action.

People have certain familiar misconceptions about an MIS. One is that the communication of information comes only from the top down or is monitored and tried only by top management. In reality, the communication can be from the top down, bottom up, lateral, or in any direction at all. Who has to know what and who has what information are the important factors. An example is the type of quality circles popularized by the Japanese, where information is generated from lower levels and passed up through the hierarchy. Nevertheless, essential to MIS is a solid organization structure with positions, levels, duties, and responsibilities spelled out.

Another misconception is that all MIS information must be generated by computers. Computers have become increasingly important in MIS, but some areas remain that still cannot be computerized. Computers cannot (yet) evaluate the appearance of entrees, for example, but this is nevertheless valuable information.

Computer use has grown in restaurants in recent years, with the most striking increase occurring at smaller restaurants. By 1996, more than 8 in 10 table service restaurants reported using a computer in some fashion, whether as a stand-alone system or as part of another application in use in the operation.

The most common component is the growth in the use of **point-of-sale (POS) terminals**. The main reason for usage increase is the greatly reduced cost of the systems. Computer capabilities that cost tens of thousands of dollars a few years ago now cost only hundreds, and prices continue to drop due to the use of generic PC technology. Furthermore, in institutional foodservice operations such as those in schools and hospitals, the complexity and number of reports and information required by governmental regulatory and third-party reimbursement groups quickly made computers indispensable. The drive within all foodservice operations to control costs makes any tool that can be helpful important. Last but not least, there is growing acceptance, willingness to use, and enthusiasm for computers among foodservice managers and their line staff.

Installing a formal MIS will not automatically solve major problems and is not necessarily a quick or easy project. Employees must be taught to use the system and convinced that using technology will improve their work. However, studies have shown that restaurant employees can become proficient with most systems in one to two days. Over time, as more systems are used in primary education, this will become even less a problem.

Another misconception is that an MIS will replace the foodservice manager. A formal MIS will not replace on-the-scene management by walking around (MBWA), but it can enhance the manager's ability by giving current up-to-date information upon which to make decisions. It also can allow more unit coverage by a single manager.

For the rest of this chapter we will concentrate on MIS applications in the foodservice field. An MIS is not strictly computers, and need not even be computerized at all, but computer use has been an important development and is increasingly part of many foodservice operations. Certain recent computer developments have had an immediate effect in foodservice operations: the declining cost of hardware and software, the increase in types of software, increasing examples of successful applications, and a growing awareness and acceptance by professionals. In foodservice operations, computers can complete such general back-office functions as accounts payable (money owed to purveyors), general ledger accounts (general bookkeeping), accounts receivable (money owed to the operation), payroll (including deductions for payroll and benefits and generation of such forms as year-end W-2s), and sales and cash control (computers do this much faster than manual arrangements). Another function is business modeling, in which the system simulates different scenarios to suggest which is best for the operation. For example, the foodservice manager can readily see how a change in income or changes in costs will affect the operation. What-if games are part of business modeling, and they can be most helpful in planning and decision making. Computers also are used for word processing, which can save time producing fixed documents such as menus and manuals. Other management functions that can be handled by computers include long-term planning, budget preparation, cash flow forecasts, and variance analysis (how actual figures vary from planned or desired figures).

Computers also have many specialized uses in foodservice operations: recipe control, recipe costing, menu sales analysis, quality content, labor costing, labor analysis, inventory control, and sales analysis. In fact, many of the management processes we discuss in this book can be computerized. But this does not mean that knowing the manual systems and the theory behind them is superfluous. It does little good to press buttons and get printouts if you do not know what the information means or how to interpret it.

ELECTRONIC SPREADSHEETS

The **electronic spreadsheet**, the computerized equivalent of the accountant's worksheet, is a valuable piece of software for foodservice financial management and control. While a good deal of information will come from packaged reports as part of a foodservice computer system, the foodservice operator may need to massage this data in a way that provides the user more meaningful information.

An electronic spreadsheet consists of a grid of columns and rows that allows for the organization, standardization, and presentation of numerical information. Where a vertical column and a horizontal row intersect, a cell is created, and by using formulas, an operator can manipulate the data in these cells. For example, assume the vertical columns have information that can denote a profit. The horizontal rows can be expenses on a monthly basis with a total annual column. The formula for the vertical would be sales − total expenses = profit.

Through the spreadsheet, the computer automatically performs the calculations from inputted data. A change in a cell figure, say a new expense figure, is inserted and the new relationships (or profits) are automatically recalculated.

A foodservice operator can use spreadsheets to forecast, to compare actual results with the forecasts, to budget, and to play what-if games in which potential results are calculated on the basis of certain data.

For example, foodservice managers might want to consider what would happen if they increased the price of one of the restaurant's signature menu items. Would sales go down? Would profits decrease? What if the restaurant added a menu item that was popular but had a low return because it was costly to produce? Or if the restaurant increased the number of servers to turn tables faster? Would the increase in labor costs be offset by faster table turns (see Chapter 24, Cost-Volume-Profit Analysis)? Spreadsheets are helpful for analyzing financial statements, daily reports, productivity, food costs, inventory, and menu sales.

THE TOTAL SYSTEM

Although each of the applications described in this chapter can stand alone, their combined use, flow, and database provide a great deal of additional information for the control function. In developing the total system, one should examine and evaluate the whole operation to determine specifically why some things are done (or not done) and better ways of doing them. This examination also can lead to a consideration of what information or reports can be helpful and should therefore be generated by an MIS.

A total management information system for a foodservice operation is complex and usually expensive to develop, and not all operations need or can use some of the sophisticated systems available. Moreover, not all information systems must be computerized. However, an MIS that is supported by computerization provides information that leads to better management, monetary savings, and better overall control.

DATA INPUT AND TRANSMISSION

A major advantage of using computers is that once entered, data can be easily and quickly transferred and manipulated for analysis. For example, a waiter takes a customer's order and enters it into the system through a handheld terminal, which immediately starts the preparation cycle by sending the information to a main terminal or a printer. A guest check for the party is begun (or updated). In addition, the data is saved for analysis purposes. Sales reports, which formerly required extensive tabulations of guest checks or cash register tapes, can be prepared almost immediately. The reports can include dollar sales by period or specific personnel or counts of various items sold. The guest check, which is automatically prepared, also provides data to reconcile cash-received figures or credit card sales.

When food is received, the data is entered in the operations computer. This can lead to reports on food usage, inventory amounts, and food costs without having to maintain manual records. Paperless systems have advantages. The errors inherent in writing down information manually or having to perform manual calculations are considerably reduced, and assembling information generally can be done more quickly. At one time, foodservice operators thought they were doing well if they got out reports by the 10th of the following month. Now reports can be prepared daily per meal or for any time during the day.

GENERAL SOFTWARE APPLICATIONS

In addition to the various software packages and applications developed specifically for foodservice, literally hundreds of general-purpose software applications exist. In most foodservice operations with computer controls, the use of general-purpose software for word processing, spreadsheets, and other common purposes quickly follows. With spreadsheets particularly, managers can export data from their foodservice systems for analysis and custom presentations.

SELECTING HARDWARE AND SOFTWARE

Traditionally, when selecting new systems it made sense to choose hardware first and then choose software. However, in today's generic hardware environment, it often makes sense to choose software first and then select the hardware to support it.

When selecting either hardware or software, a good approach is to consider the functions required by the foodservice operation. To do this, it is important to break the functions into discrete major sections, such as purchasing, time and attendance, food production, dining room management, and labor scheduling.

Within each section, the specific requirements needed to perform the function must be determined. This will help in the selection of the software vendors, since vendors typically focus on specific niche areas, rather than attempting to provide all of the systems for a foodservice operation.

For each major section, a specification sheet or request for proposal (RFP) should be created. This will help in evaluating how well each vendor's system will meet the needs of the operation selecting the system. The RFP should include the top 10 or 20 features most critical to the operation, those tasks the system must accomplish. This will help weed out vendors that don't meet the foodservice operation's specific needs.

For example, if many of your employees are minors, one of your key needs might be a system that will alert a manager when a minor staff member is approaching the legal limit for the number of hours worked. This need is added to your top 20 list. Any system that does not fulfill this need is eliminated from consideration.

Be wary of promises to add functionality to a system that lacks the functions required. Betting on software that doesn't exist today often leads to trouble tomorrow. Also, avoid being the first in the industry to break in a system. Try to select a system that has been tested by another similar operation.

Selection of any system will vary depending on the foodservice operation's overall need. For example, for a single-unit operator, the best vendor might be the one that offers the best price and value. For a national chain, the decision might revolve around which vendor offers the best local customer support and service for the chain's units.

It is interesting to note that people typically buy computer systems the same way they buy food—with their eyes. However, what is behind the surface of the system is as important as what appears on the screen.

For hardware selections, it is important to keep in mind that hardware becomes obsolete fairly quickly. The most important factors to consider are processing speed, expandability, memory, the availability of peripherals such as scales or scanners, and price. When and where the hardware will be serviced is another crucial consideration.

For software, a key consideration is the ability to interface with other applications being used and the ability to generate custom reports.

LANS, WANS, AND THE INTERNET

A **local area network (LAN)** is a series of computers linked to each other either by cable or wireless communication in a closed-loop system. A closed-loop system is one in which data is only communicated internally between networked computers. Such a system does not allow input from, or output to, computers outside the loop.

Using a LAN, computers within an office can communicate with each other, or a restaurant can communicate with its central office. A **wide area network (WAN)** is a series of LANs linked to each other and communicating over a private network. A WAN might connect a very large office or several locations within a city or around the world to each other.

One of the biggest developments in communications for the foodservice industry in recent years has been the use of Internet technology as a communications vehicle. Foodservice operations are beginning to use the Internet to communicate quickly and cheaply with other affiliated locations, their central office, vendors, and the general public.

The **Internet** is a public communications system that allows computers to communicate with each other. A local user connects to the Internet via a local Internet service provider (ISP) or access company, which has a direct connection to the public Internet. Communications costs are lower than traditional means, such as satellite or phone, since data can be transmitted for the cost of a local phone call.

The difference between the Internet and a LAN or WAN is that the Internet is a public system, while LANs and WANs are private. The Internet can act as a WAN in the sense that it can connect in a closed loop many locations that are great distances apart.

In the past, computers connected via a LAN were limited to using common operating systems that were built on the same platform and could easily communicate and interface with each other. Today, many terminals or locations can be linked even though they may use different systems.

One of the newest types of Internet technology is called **point-to-point tunneling protocol**, which uses a dedicated Internet connection and allows for continual communications. In other words, the connection is dedicated to only data, rather than voice, traffic, and the switch is always left on so that communications between two specific networks are available constantly.

An intranet is a closed-loop, private network using Internet tools as the communications vehicle. It acts much like a private computer network except that it can link computers in distant locations by using the Internet to communicate between computers. Although it uses the public Internet to send data, an intranet is private because the data is protected behind firewalls, which are a combination of hardware and software that keep unauthorized people from gaining access to the network. The benefit of using the public Internet as a communication tool is that it is cheaper than using a private network. By creating an intranet, a company can send information quickly and cheaply to a select group of people without broadcasting that data to unauthorized parties. A single-location operation may choose to put its intranet on its LAN.

An extranet is a private web site using the Internet as a vehicle. An extranet uses the Internet to share part of its web site with customers, vendors, suppliers, and others. Firewalls are employed to separate internal data from information made more generally available.

All of these networks are significant for foodservice operators because they allow for cheaper, faster, and more complete communications between computer terminals within a single location and between remote locations. In addition to better internal communications, the Internet gives foodservice operators another communications avenue with their vendors and customers and can be used as a tool for competitive analysis of the marketplace.

While foodservice operations are using the Internet in limited ways now, as available bandwidth increases, the use of the Internet by the foodservice industry also will increase. Bandwidth refers to how much data can be sent through a connection simultaneously, or how "big" the data pipe is.

What's in the Future?

There are several exciting areas of technology development that are likely to see even more development in the next five years, including voice recognition technology, greater access to the Internet, and smart card technology.

Voice recognition technology enables a computer to recognize the spoken word, thereby eliminating the need to enter data via the keyboard. One application of voice recognition technology in foodservice might be in taking orders over a telephone for delivery or pickup. By completely automating the order process, an operation can reduce labor costs and improve efficiency.

The Internet, already making inroads in foodservice operations, will have an even greater impact on foodservice in the future. Eventually, the Internet may become the vehicle for all communications between a foodservice unit and its customers, a unit and its vendors, and a unit and its corporate headquarters.

Both voice recognition technology and greater access to the Internet for the general public also will help fuel a vast growth in self-service and home delivery in coming years.

Smart card technology is another area of development likely to impact foodservice. A smart card resembles a credit card but has a computer chip embedded in it. In the future smart cards may be used to replace other card technologies that have in the past depended on magnetic strips or bar codes or on information stored off site on other computers. An example of such use is in debit card systems which are frequently found in contract foodservice environments for use by students or employees. In such systems, the card contains stored value, which is deducted with use. The card can be periodically "recharged" to maintain or increase the "cash value" stored on the card. Another example of smart card use is in customer loyalty programs which can be helpful in marketing. Eventually they can house much of a customer's information thereby eliminating the need for multiple credit or identification cards.

BACK-OFFICE SYSTEMS

Accounting

Different software systems have different capabilities in this area, but generally the system is designed for the flow through of data produced from other applications. Reports generated by this application can include income and expense statements, accounts receivable,

INDUSTRY INSIGHTS   by Hughes Network Systems

Ron Magruder, FMP, is the President and COO of Cracker Barrel Restaurants, Inc. He is the former President of Olive Garden Restaurants and a Penn State Walter J. Conti Professor. In 1999 Ron will be Chairman of the National Restaurant Association.

CRACKING SATELLITE TECHNOLOGY

Cracker Barrel implements VSAT technology for improved customer service, cost-effective employee training and quality communications. When the first Cracker Barrel Old Country Store opened in 1969, it included a restaurant, a retail store and a gas station. Almost 30 years later, the restaurant chain no longer sells gas but has added satellite technology to better serve its guests, cost-effectively train its employees, and reliably facilitate quality communications between headquarters and its 365 nationwide stores.

The company previously relied on a standard dial-up network to process credit-card and personal check payments. However, as new stores opened

and the number of guests grew annually, Cracker Barrel quickly realized the need for a communications network to better address speed and bandwidth capacity. The company decided on satellite technology and implemented a very small aperture terminal (VSAT) network. During the evaluation process, Cracker Barrel discovered that VSAT networks could more quickly facilitate credit-card and personal check authorizations than other networking alternatives. At the same time, VSATs could also satisfy the company's bandwidth requirements for exchanging data between all 365 stores and corporate headquarters in Lebanon, TN.

"We kept going back to the VSAT technology during our search because we looked at it from our guests' point of view," says Mike Matheny, Cracker Barrel's CIO. "Our stores are almost exclusively located on Interstates, so the majority of guests are traveling. They don't want to stand around and wait longer than necessary at the checkout counter."

Basing its ultimate decision on cost as well as bandwidth capacity and quality of network reliability, Cracker Barrel has implemented Hughes Network Systems' (Germantown, MD) VSAT technology at its headquarters and at each of the corporate-owned

accounts payable, budgets, and property-management items. Accounting packages also can be used to make journal entries and keep ledgers.

The application may be programmed to detail sales by category or perform statistical analyses on individual profit centers. Statements can be prepared on any time basis, such as sales and expenses per meal, per day, per week, or any other period desired.

Another back-office function—cash control—can provide a reconciliation between cash register readings, cash received, and projected sales based on the sales value of consumption. Some systems include inventory control in the back-office application.

Human Resources and Labor

In the past, human resources has often been thought to be synonymous with time and attendance or payroll. In fact, a successful operation requires much more information about its employees, especially given the need to hire the right employees, retain them, and help them develop in their careers. Human resources and labor, therefore, should be broken into several distinct areas:

stores. The simple VSAT network architecture includes an HNS Personal Earth Station located at each store and a hub earth station at corporate headquarters.

Cracker Barrel's previous concerns about a reliable communications network were laid to rest with the VSAT technology. "Some of our stores are located in rural areas and we were concerned about being dependent on the local telephone company for our connections," says Matheny. "The fear of busy signals, line breaks, and natural disasters all played a part in the decision to move to a satellite-based solution. With our VSAT network, we get reliable service 24 hours a day."

In addition to faster payment authorizations, the VSAT network established a Wide Area Network (WAN) for Cracker Barrel, enabling it to develop an Intranet and provide company e-mail capabilities. In the past, stores around the country received software updates and other important information on CDs or floppy disks mailed from the Lebanon headquarters. Today, mission-critical information is exchanged electronically in real-time via the VSAT network.

Further, VSATs have the bandwidth to support interactive video broadcasting without overloading the network's capacity capabilities. By using video, Cracker Barrel brings its 40,000 employees together at the same time for meetings with key company executives, such as its president, Ron Magruder, to discuss new products, training, and other issues. Its interactive capabilities allow employees to ask questions and receive immediate responses.

The VSAT network also enables Cracker Barrel to cost effectively address its training needs. To demonstrate special preparation procedures for new menu items, the company uses the video broadcast to train the chefs, rather than send a trainer out to each store. The company plans to expand its use of video in the future to combat the high turnover in the restaurant and retail industry with an increased interactive training program.

"VSAT technology has enabled Cracker Barrel to consolidate and manage its communications network into one resource rather than a variety of vendors," says Matheny. "Cracker Barrel will continue to provide its down-home country cooked meals, but it'll also continue to expand the use of VSAT technology to better serve guests and employees."

This column is reprinted as it first appeared in the November/December issue of *Hospitality Technology*, an Edgell Communications publication.

- personnel
- labor scheduling
- time and attendance
- payroll
- training

Personnel. The personnel function consists of record keeping about the employee, including such information as hire date, birth date, education, resume, job skills, work history, professional certifications such as sanitation training, and information on warnings or performance evaluations. Ideally, all of this information is kept in one place and can tie in with other human resources and labor functions, such as training and scheduling.

One of the complexities unique to the foodservice industry is the practice of scheduling multiple jobs for individual employees. For example, a server who works in the dining room at one pay rate might also work in the kitchen at another pay rate. Therefore, a foodservice operation should track both pay rates and the employee's hours. This is especially important when dealing with minors, where the total number of hours worked is regulated by law.

Labor Scheduling.   Labor scheduling can be a simple task or very complex. In its simplest form, it can consist of merely looking at the number of customers coming in to an operation and then determining the level of staffing required to serve the expected customers. In its more complex form, the labor scheduling function factors in other types of data, such as the position for which the person is being scheduled and the training and experience the staff member has.

For example, to schedule for front-of-the-house operations, a labor schedule would have to factor in the average server's station size, the number of customers coming in, and the average table turn. Given this information, a foodservice operator can accurately plan the staffing level needed.

Labor scheduling also can factor in such considerations as skill levels. It is not accurate to assume that during slow periods you should merely schedule fewer people. The skill level of those scheduled must also be factored in. For example, in a kitchen staffed with only a few people, each person needs multiple skills. If there is just one person in the kitchen, that person must know how to perform every kitchen task required during that shift. During busier times, you might have one person who operates the grill, one who works the fryer, and one who prepares salads. Each employee would need to know only the skill he/she was required to perform that shift. A labor scheduling system can match an employee's skills with the task required for the position. Labor scheduling is covered in more detail in Chapter 12.

Labor scheduling also can be based on food production. This can be as simple as determining how much food you need to prepare to serve a specified number of customers.

For example, in a quick-service restaurant, you might assume that a hamburger can be prepared 15 minutes before it must be sold or thrown away. Given that assumption and the number of customers entering the restaurant, you can figure out how much food must be prepared in 15-minute increments and then schedule employees accordingly. Incorrectly predicting this information can result in the production of too much or too little food (Figure 6.2).

Figure 6.2
Labor Scheduling Software
Permission: Courtesy of Time
Corp. © 1998

Labor Projection for   ☒

Analysis for Workgroup [Front End Workgroup ▾]

Manager's Labor Forecast:

	Week	08/17	08/18	08/19	08/20	08/21	08/22	08/23
Sales	414702.9	95202.6	58421.1	56539.0	48570.7	44408.9	48397.6	63163.1
Hours	1289.7	249.6	184.7	179.2	165.8	159.8	160.5	190.0
Cost	12897.0	2496.4	1846.8	1792.1	1658.3	1598.3	1605.3	1899.9
Productivity	321.6	381.4	316.3	315.5	292.9	277.9	301.5	332.5
Labor %	3.1	2.6	3.2	3.2	3.4	3.6	3.3	3.0
AHR	10.0	10.0	10.0	10.0	10.0	10.0	10.0	10.0

Compared To: [System Labor Projection ▾]

	Week	08/17	08/18	08/19	08/20	08/21	08/22	08/23
Sales	416834.9	95497.9	60257.6	56539.0	48570.7	44408.9	48397.6	63163.1
Hours	1294.3	250.2	188.7	179.2	165.8	159.8	160.5	190.0
Cost	12943.2	2502.4	1886.8	1792.2	1658.3	1598.3	1605.3	1899.9
Productivity	322.0	381.6	319.4	315.5	292.9	277.9	301.5	332.5
Labor %	3.1	2.6	3.1	3.2	3.4	3.6	3.3	3.0
AHR	10.0	10.0	10.0	10.0	10.0	10.0	10.0	10.0

[Recalculate]   [Schedule]   [Close]   [Help]

Finally, labor scheduling applications also can be used to control labor costs. Such programs calculate an operation's labor costs for a defined schedule or scheduling period. By being aware of the operation's labor costs as a percentage of sales or as compared to a specified budget, the foodservice manager can make adjustments ahead of time to control costs. For example, if managers create a schedule and discover labor costs are at an unacceptable level, they can take appropriate measures, such as reducing the hours of an employee who will go into overtime during the scheduling period or scheduling lower wage employees during certain shifts. By looking at reports over a longer period of time, managers also can be alerted to labor cost problems and take appropriate action.

Labor scheduling software also can be integrated with an "intelligent" time clock, to control labor costs by only allowing employees to clock in when they are scheduled and preventing them from clocking out early without a manager's permission (see time and attendance below).

Time and Attendance.   A common assumption is that time and attendance and payroll are the same function. However, they are actually quite different, and many software applications for each function are written just for the foodservice industry. Time and attendance refers to the day-to-day transactions that occur each time an employee clocks in or out. The payroll function takes place after all of the relevant time and attendance information has been collected and the employee's paycheck is being prepared.

Since time and attendance tie in with other functions, such as labor scheduling and payroll, interfacing between these systems is very important. "Intelligent" time clocks and good time and attendance systems are critical to the efficiency of the operation. Today's time cards and clocks not only clock employees in and out, but also can be set up to only clock in employees that are scheduled to work, not allow employees to clock in early or clock out late without an override from a manager, and alert a manager when an employee is approaching overtime.

A good system also will require tipped employees to declare their tips, which are then recorded for the payroll process.

One area of technology that is seeing a great deal of development is biometrics, which uses physiological or behavioral properties to verify an individual's identity. By looking at the makeup of a person's retina, the ridges on his or her fingers, hand or face geometry, voice patterns, typing patterns or signature, biometric applications can verify a person's identity. Immediate uses are already underway in banking, welfare management, border control, and national security, but retail applications likely will follow in the near future. For example, time and attendance applications could use biometrics to clock employees in and out or to control access to limited-access areas in an operation. One foodservice time and attendance software vendor already offers a biometric application which uses a hand reader that measures more than 90 different widths, lengths, and heights of a hand. Each employee's hand is measured and the information is entered into a database. Each time the employee clocks in or out, he or she must enter a personal identification number via a keypad or optional card reader. Then, the system prompts the employee to place his or her hand on the reader. Once the hand is properly in place, the verification process takes about one second (see Figure 6.3).

Payroll.   Payroll is tightly tied to labor scheduling and time and attendance since it requires data from both to function.

Figure 6.3
Biometric Hand Reader.
Courtesy Recognition Systems, Inc.

Some payroll software comes embedded in standard industry accounting packages or payroll packages provided by companies that provide general payroll services. When using a package that is not part of an integrated foodservice system, you must be sure the data can be transferred seamlessly to the payroll system. After that, the information is sent to the paycheck processing company or agent that cuts the employee's check.

Training.   There are two distinct aspects to training systems: tracking employee training and conducting the actual training itself.

Tracking, or recording details of an employee's training history, is a back-office record-keeping function, whereas the training of employees on specific tasks goes hand-in-hand with the applications used for tasks such as food preparation, customer service, table seating, or serving. That training will be delivered via the applications that you use for those specific functions.

Tracking requires a detailed database containing the type of training employees have received and must receive to do their jobs. This ties in to the scheduling system, especially when scheduling employees based on skills. Therefore, records must be kept detailing the type of training employees have had, their scores, and their skill level. The system also should track any special certifications they have or should have.

Now, let's consider the training itself. There are different types of job training, including:

- *Administrative*—This includes training for skills such as interviewing skills, sexual harassment training, or effective management techniques. Most employees, especially those in supervisory roles, will need these general skills. This basic type of training can be available via course work, video, CD-ROM, satellite link, or the Internet.

- *General job skills*—This includes training for skills such as how to cook items, how to greet customers, or how to take orders, which can be taught by a manager or as a function of the training department.
- *Application training*—This type of training, typically computer based, teaches an employee how to operate specific systems and might be built into the specific application itself. For example, an employee might be taught how to take an order on the POS system by practicing on the real system using fabricated data.

Marketing

There are a number of ways technology can be used for marketing purposes, from creating the marketing pieces themselves to deciding who is the "ideal customer" and how to reach that customer.

Many contact databases available today help marketers track all of a business's contacts, including people you sell to and buy from or all the people you meet in the course of your business. Database programs can be general purpose or industry specific.

Industry-specific applications may be more appropriate for certain needs, such as tracking catering functions. For example, using a database application, you can track potential customers from the time they call asking for information, through the stages of the proposal process, to the actual event itself. In addition, your database might include preset templates for standard letters or event order forms so that you merely have to fill in the blanks, rather than creating a new form each time.

A database application also can be used for other types of marketing, such as frequent guest programs. These programs allow you to identify your best customers and then reward them to keep them coming back and help bring in new business. In addition to information you gather internally for frequent guest programs, data is available from credit card processing companies, which track customer purchases. Rewards for loyalty can include coupons, discounts, or birthday or anniversary cards. Databases may be kept of catering functions with such details as dates, number attending, menus, prices, contact persons, and time to contact. This data may also be kept on functions held at other foodservice operations for use in soliciting them to your operation.

In addition, frequent guests might be rewarded with special features such as newsletters or advance announcements for special events. These can often be created using a standard word processing program in the back office.

The introduction of smart cards that can store data about the frequency of guests' visits adds to the availability of information about customers and limits the amount of information that must be stored on site.

Technology also now affords more opportunities for marketing your business. The Internet can be a good marketing vehicle for foodservice operations. Restaurant guides and city and tourist bureau web sites often include lists of local restaurants.

Menu Planning

At the heart of any foodservice operation is its menu. It is the basis for other planning and for a foodservice management information system. The menu is usually not static. It must be updated periodically to keep pace with changing customer trends and preferences, changes in costs, and sometimes new products that become available. A foodservice MIS can offer a separate menu application or various menu functions included in other applications. Separate menu applications typically have four components:

- customer count forecasting
- menu preference forecasting
- past sales (history) analysis
- menu cost or margin analysis

Figure 6.4 presents an integrated model for foodservice information system modules. Remember, though, that some foodservice MISs have separate applications for these components or incorporate them with other applications.

Customer Count Forecasting.   For many types of foodservices, the computer can automatically forecast expected customer counts based on past trends and historical data. Care must be taken to be sure that managers at least review this information before the system is permitted to act on it. In some cases, human judgment can determine that a particular day is not a typical day and that the trend developed in the computer program will not hold. This interaction is discussed more fully in Chapter 8.

Menu Preference Forecasting.   Preference forecasting considers not only how much of a menu item normally will be served, but also how popular menu items sell when competing with each other. There are many ways to predict the relative preferences for various menu items. As with census forecasting, predictions reflect trends. The larger the customer base and the more fixed, or unchanging, the menu, the more accurate forecasts are likely to be. Again, manager experience should supersede the computer analysis.

Menu preference forecasting also should take into account the overall contribution to profits a menu item will have. If the profitability of each item on a menu can be determined, the profitability for the entire foodservice operation can be forecast. Therefore, it is important to look at the profit side of the equation in addition to the expense side.

Past-Sales Analysis.   The sales analysis application can differ considerably in different systems. One system determines in advance the cost of serving a combination of menu offerings and the resulting gross profit (in a profit-making operation). This analysis is a computerization of the concepts of pre-cost and pre-control, which have been in use for many years.

If the resulting figures are unsatisfactory, other combinations of menu items can be costed until one reaches the targeted costs and profits. The cost computations are generally based on the latest purchase prices using the recipes in the database. Sales analysis applications in other systems may also include such sales statistics as sales by each server, average sale per cover, and daily sales analysis.

Menu Cost or Margin Analysis.   Margin analysis software can help management determine in advance if a proposed menu is within budgetary constraints and will provide an acceptable margin of profit.

Table 6.1 shows a post-service sales and margin cost analysis. By entering information such as projected sales for the item and the selling price and unit cost, the program can analyze the profit margin for the entire menu. The program shows the selling price,

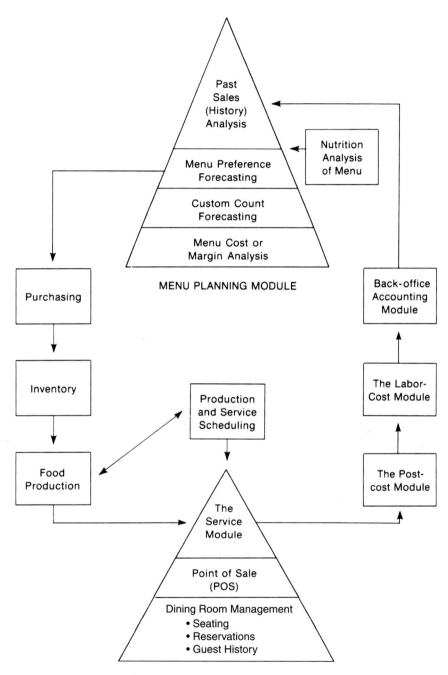

Figure 6.4
Integrated Foodservice MIS

Table 6.1
Post-Service Cost Detail

| Cafe West | | | | | | | | | | Report Period: | Post-Service Cost Detail 3/9/97–3/15/97 | |
| Date: Tuesday, January 21, 1997 | Meal: BREAKFAST | | | | | | | | | Customer Count: | 302 | |

Item Name	Per Portion			Quantity		Totals			Cost	Per Customer		
	Price	Cost	Margin	Prep	Srvd	Sales	Cost	Margin	(%)	Sales	Cost	Margin
Scrambled Eggs & Bacon	1.00	0.28	0.72	192	192	192.00	53.76	138.24	28%	0.40	0.11	0.29
Scrambled Eggs & Ham	1.00	0.37	0.63	111	111	111.00	41.07	69.93	37%	0.23	0.09	0.15
Totals For: 09 - ENTREES						303.00	94.83	208.17	31%	0.63	0.20	0.43
White Toast	0.25	0.05	0.20	58	58	14.50	2.68	11.82	18%	0.03	0.01	0.02
Wheat Toast	0.25	0.07	0.19	24	24	6.00	1.56	4.44	26%	1.01	0.00	0.01
Totals For: 12 - BREADS						20.50	4.24	16.26	21%	0.04	0.01	0.03
Orange Sections	0.50	0.35	0.15	68	68	34.00	24.12	9.88	71%	0.07	0.05	0.02
Totals For: 13 - DESSERTS						34.00	24.12	9.88	71%	0.07	0.05	0.02
Lowfat Milk (8oz Pour)(b)	0.35	0.15	0.20	72	72	25.20	10.71	14.49	42%	0.05	0.02	0.03
Lowfat Milk Crtn 8oz (b)	0.35	0.17	0.18	269	269	94.15	45.73	48.42	49%	0.20	0.10	0.10
Apple Juice (m-maid)	0.50	0.17	0.33	24	24	12.00	4.00	8.00	33%	0.03	0.01	0.02
Grapefruit Juice (m-maid)	0.50	0.11	0.39	24	24	12.00	2.74	9.26	23%	0.03	0.01	0.02
Orange Juice	0.50	0.12	0.38	216	216	108.00	25.73	82.27	24%	0.23	0.05	0.17
Tomato V-8 Juice	0.50	0.16	0.34	48	48	24.00	7.56	16.44	31%	0.05	0.02	0.03
Coffee Brewed	0.35	0.03	0.32	480	480	168.00	13.21	154.79	8%	0.35	0.03	0.32
Totals for: 15 - BEVERAGES						443.35	109.67	333.68	25%	0.92	0.23	0.70
Totals for: BREAKFAST						800.85	232.86	567.99	29%	1.67	0.49	1.1
Totals for: 3/9/97			302 Customers			800.85	232.86	567.99	29%	1.67	0.49	1.1
Totals for: Cafe West			302 Customers			800.85	232.86	567.99	29%	1.67	0.49	1.1

Courtesy of The CBORD Group, Inc. 1998

the unit price, and the profit margin for each item. It also lists the number of items prepared and served, the corresponding dollar amount in sales and the total cost for all units sold. The program then calculates the profit margin in dollars and the cost as a percentage of sales. In addition, the same information is broken down on a per customer basis.

When calculating menu cost, foodservice managers also must include all of the factors that go into producing the item, including preparation time, dishes, overhead, and any other expenses.

Food Production

At the heart of menu planning and food production are two complex databases—the food ingredient and standard recipe files.

The *food ingredient database* (inventory file) contains basic information about each ingredient used by the foodservice operation, including the name of the item, costs, purchase units, inventory units, issue units, vendors, and conversion factors. This file is the basis for successful computerized food production and will therefore require a great deal of time and care in its design. Many of today's computer software systems for foodservice management come with a universal food inventory file (containing a large and representative database assembled from the actual databases of hundreds of other food organizations), reducing much of the data entry burden of getting started. In addition, food may be already UPC coded when it is delivered by the supplier. Scanning in data via UPC codes is a quick way to update inventory database files.

The food ingredient database and ability to easily update, add, and delete items from it are crucial to food-production control and inventory management. Further information is covered in Chapters 14, 15, 16, and 17.

Standardized recipes are paramount to effective and efficient food production and cost controls. The accuracy and degree of control provided by computer systems are proportional to the accuracy of the information data entered. Recipes must be developed precisely and adhered to in the kitchen. Failure to enforce this policy in a computerized operation will result in overproduction, waste, inconsistent product, inventory shortages, and meaningless costing projections. Enforcing standard recipe use will yield the payoffs of greatly reduced food costs, minimum waste, accurate accounting, and streamlined, efficient inventory control.

Building a database of standard recipes for the initial food ingredient database is the second task in developing a computerized cost and food production control system. It can take months of laborious data entry and recipe formulation. Some software purveyors can provide precoded standard recipe files, including some of the best-known quantity cookbooks. The foodservice operation also will add its own recipes to the database and refine and reformulate recipes continually to reflect cost changes in key ingredients, cook and patron preferences, and occasionally cost-effective substitutions of key ingredients.

The food production application uses the forecasting application and menu to determine what food production orders, storeroom requisitions, and recipes will be requested for a designated period, say, for the day. After summarizing the requirements, the application can print a requisition detailing the exact amounts of raw food products to withdraw from the storeroom. It also can print recipes, extended (or "exploded") to the precise number of portions required for a particular meal, for use by kitchen personnel—even "batching" these extended recipes in amounts for the constraints of cooking equipment or recipe size limitations.

Control is imposed by having only the amounts of foods issued from the storeroom that are required by recipes (and, thereafter, having those figures stored in the database). This reduces the excess food issued or prepared and also helps ensure that the recipes will be followed. Otherwise, cooks might requisition a full unit (for example, a full bag of rice), when the exact proportion of the bag they need cannot be determined.

The system can readily compute material costs and make inventory adjustments. The application also can print production orders for the various units in the kitchen, telling what each must prepare. This can simplify scheduling and staffing.

Recipe Costing

A key ingredient to effective menu planning and food production is accurate recipe portion costs. These can be calculated relatively quickly for all of the foodservice operation's recipes. Many software packages provide a fast way of changing portion sizes and resulting costs as well. Some may also provide automatic pricing calculations, complete with profit margins, based on current ingredient costs and the price markup criteria for a cash operation.

Nutritional Analysis

Nutritional analysis traditionally has referred to the health-related function involving tracking menu items or ingredients to make sure patients get the proper nourishment and do not get foods not in their recommended diet. However, nutritional analysis increasingly refers to a broader meaning in foodservice today. People want information about the food they are eating.

This is true for quick-service and full-service operations alike. Many quick-service chains today offer breakdowns of the nutritional makeup of their key menu items. In the future, more and more information will be required. Just as grocery packages are required to contain detailed information about their contents, foodservice operations could one day be required to make available such information. Such a task is not as simple in foodservice as it is for grocery items, since consumers buying packaged items do not have a choice to combine various elements of a meal or make changes to the cooking instructions, which can often change the nutritional value of a food item.

We can assume that sometime in the future, foodservice operations will be required at least to have nutritional information available for consumers requesting it. Therefore, a foodservice operation should have the ability to break down a recipe into its nutritional components to give detailed information based on the choices a customer might make when ordering a meal.

Foodservice operations are beginning to see, in their back-office systems or their recipe planning systems, the ability to tie in nutritional analysis.

Internally, nutrition information can be stored in a database and used in a number of ways. An institution, for example, may want to compute the nutritional values of the menus and compare them with recommended dietary allowances (RDAs). Figure 6.5 shows a computer-generated nutritional analysis of a recipe for basic pasta.

Post-Cost Analysis

In **post-cost analysis**, actual customer counts and menu items prepared and used are entered into the foodservice operator's system. The computer then provides detailed consolidations and summaries of daily production results, including food usage. It also com-

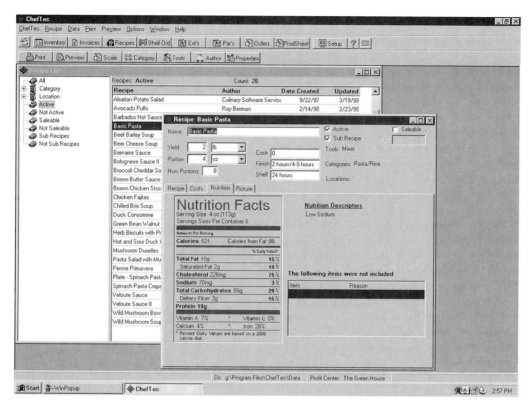

Figure 6.5
Nutritional Breakdown of a Recipe.
Courtesy of Culinary Software Services Inc. © 1998

pares forecasted to actual results as a means of making timely refinements to planned menus. This continuing feedback results in continually improving performance.

For users of customer menu item preference and customer census forecasting software packages, this postservice input also updates the database that the system uses to make future forecasts. The best of today's computer systems put control of the foodservice operation directly into the hands of management. Planned, precosted menus form the basis of a tightly controlled, efficient, and predictable foodservice operation. Post-cost applications as part of food cost accounting systems are discussed in Chapter 21.

Sales Analysis

This can be a separate application or incorporated in a menu-planning application. If separate, the application can calculate total sales, the quantity of each item, sales dollar amounts by menu item and course, sales by individual personnel, and accurate margin analysis for these and other categories.

Based on known costs, selling prices, serving trends, and other factors, these analyses can be performed with great accuracy in advance of production. This means that a financially acceptable menu plan has been constructed and approved prior to any commitments. The next step is to execute accurately the approved plan.

Sales analysis also includes reporting on the POS side of the operation. This reporting includes how cash was actually handled. Examples include accounting of cash, credit cards by type, discounts, staff meals, complimentary meals, gift certificates, and other types of payments.

Purchasing

Purchasing occurs after precosting has taken place. The system prints out the ingredients needed for a particular meal or other period to ensure that the correct amount of food is on hand at the right time to meet food production demands. The software might also offer bid analysis, which compares vendors' prices to determine which vendor offers the best price on each product.

A purchasing system calculates the amount of food to order based on exact menu needs, par stock requirements, inventory on hand, and vendor delivery schedules. The purchasing system also considers what is available from storage presently on hand. Table 6.2 shows a worksheet from the purchasing component of a foodservice management software application. The worksheet includes the number of units the operation should buy, the number actually ordered, the purchase unit, how much of the product is already on hand, and the par stock level. The data entered can then be used to order electronically from vendors.

The goals of the purchasing system include having food and other items available when needed and having an optimal amount in storage, thereby preventing tying up capital by overstocking and freeing up valuable storage space. The software can prepare purchase orders, provide data on vendors and their past prices, and indicate short or surplus conditions. The time saved by computerizing food purchasing may be used for competitive bidding, price trend analysis, or negotiation.

Purchasing is closely tied to inventory. One factor in purchasing in recent years has been the move to **electronic data interchange (EDI)**. EDI is the rapid electronic exchange of data between two parties, usually a supplier and its customer. Through EDI, many vendors today can take automated orders and have moved away from taking orders by phone, fax, or salesperson visits.

By transmitting data more quickly, accurately, and efficiently, a foodservice operation can move closer to just-in-time inventory, with the associated cost savings.

EDI allows a foodservice operation to receive a supplier's prices electronically and generate an order form that is automatically sent back to the supplier and processed. Even smaller vendors can now use EDI since the systems required to transmit and receive data are packaged with a basic PC.

Electronic purchasing can be tied to inventory and set up with par levels so that when inventory dips below a specified level, an order is automatically generated. Some suppliers have completely closed systems, but these usually apply to operations such as vending machines or mini-bars, where spoilage is not as much of an issue.

The foodservice industry is moving closer to closed-loop, totally automated purchasing, but waste, spoilage, and theft issues make it difficult to achieve a completely closed-loop system that can calculate everything solely by computer generated information.

Inventory

The inventory application is sometimes considered a separate application, but sometimes may be part of a general accounting or purchasing application. In either case it is designed

Table 6.2
Shopping List from Foodservice Purchasing Application

Corner Cafe

Item Name	Suggested	Actual Order	Purchase Unit	On Hand	On Order	Committed	Parstock	Reorder Pt	Linked
01 - Food Distributors of Central NY									
Coffee (Automatic ANF)	20	14	Gallon	10	0	4		2	Y
Virginia Baked Ham Bnless	5	7	10 Lb	0	0	2			Y
Apple Juice Conc	0	1	4/90 Oz	0	0	0	1		Y
Orange Juice Fancy Unswt	9	9	12/46 Oz	3	0	3		2	Y
Margarine Solid All-vegt	2	4	30/1 Lb	0	0	0	2		Y
Black Turtle Beans Dried	1	2	1/20 Lb	0	0	1			Y
Fordhook Lime Beans Frozen	8	8	12/2.5	2	0	2			Y
Broccoli Spears Iceless	10	12	4/3 Lb	0	0	2			Y
Carrots Fresh	1	1	50 Ct	0	0	0			Y
Celery Pascal Fresh	2	2	24 Ct	0	2	2			Y
Water Chestnuts Sliced	1	1	6/10#	1	0	1			Y
Zesta Saltine Cracker	7	7	500/2 Pk	3	0	0	3		Y
02 - Ithaca Bakery									
Wheat Club Rolls	28	28	LOAF	0	0	0			Y
Italian Bread	12	12	LOAF	0	8	8			Y
Whole Wheat Sliced	8	8	LOAF	2	0	2	2	4	Y
03 - Byme Dairy									
Lowfat Milk 2%	64	70	1/2 Gallon	4	7	7	4	4	Y
Whole Milk	6	6	1/2 Gallon	2	10	8	4	4	Y
Cheddar Cheese Mild Wht	9	6	1/10# block	3	0	0	2	3	Y

Total line items for this Requirements Worksheet: 18

Courtesy CBORD Group, Inc © 1998

to provide management with (1) a perpetual inventory of items in storage at any given time and (2) the dollar value of that inventory.

In the past, most inventories were "physical"—that is, they were taken manually. Management knew the actual quantities and values on hand only when the inventory was manually counted. A perpetual inventory keeps track of inventory additions, inventory outshipments, and the resulting current balance. Although desirable, a perpetual (constant) inventory required too much paperwork for most foodservice operations, but a computerized inventory application now makes the perpetual inventory feasible. The program records the names of items in inventory, their quantity, the unit of measurement, the cost per unit, and the total cost and their location.

The precision of today's computer systems, the degree of control they provide, and their sophisticated scheduling abilities allow inventory levels and their costs to be reduced to minimum levels. Inventory turnovers may increase by a factor of 4 or more as food is delivered on the loading dock, processed to the serving area in the least time possible, and not left in storage. An operation that turns its food inventory over twice a month may get as high as eight-times-a-month turnover with perpetual inventory.

If most food is delivered shortly before consumption and a low inventory is maintained, the costs of maintaining a total perpetual inventory may outweigh the benefits (except under special conditions, such as warehousing or large central commissaries) since so little is kept in actual inventory and such high turnover results. Applying the 80/20 rule we discussed earlier, it is safe to assume that maintaining tight inventory controls on selected high-ticket items may be a cost-effective compromise to traditional inventory management practices. With the ability to accurately pre- and post-cost the food production process and just-in-time delivery, the primary accounting justification for maintaining unwieldy perpetual management systems also may be obsolete.

For operations that maintain complex warehouse operations in which perpetual inventory management is a necessary control practice, computers can dramatically reduce the labor and clerical requirements of maintaining them. By constantly updating inventory item prices, one now can derive accurate costs of production. Some applications or software packages track purchases and can flag significant price changes for specific products or categories of products, such as meat.

It also is possible to generate item-usage reports and reorder reports. The reorder reports can be based on consumption or variances from established par stock levels. It is somewhat ironic that even though a computerized system can be helpful in inventory control, sophistication in other elements of the system, such as rapid inventory turnover, can make inventory control less important.

With better forecasting and purchasing applications and the availability of rapid data exchanges such as through electronic data interchange, operations can purchase for specific needs and only for what is needed for that night. As a result, storeroom inventories can be reduced, allowing for better management and control. Shrinkage, waste, and loss are immediately apparent in systems of this type. Consequently, shortages and overages can quickly be detected and their reasons understood. Abuses are just as quickly remedied.

Computers can simplify inventory management and reduce the time and labor cost necessary to perform and extend physical inventories. Computer systems print inventory tally sheets sorted in the order that the inventory is stored. Inventory personnel write in quantities; the computer will automatically extend them, based on a variety of cost criteria. The computer also can analyze and report the variance between actual and calculated inventories.

For organizations that require par stocking (keeping a par or predetermined amount on hand), the computer can monitor inventory levels and automatically generate purchase order indicators in specified reorder quantities, coordinating these with stocks committed to food production.

Payment Processing

Payment processing involves the processing of more than just credit cards; it includes all types of payment cards, such as debit, credit, private label, and smart cards. Regardless of the segment of foodservice, the use of some type of card, and the information that is stored on it, is an important part of any operation.

The recent worldwide move to a cashless society is making an impact on the foodservice industry. Even quick-service restaurants, which traditionally accepted cash only, are moving to accept debit and credit cards.

Institutions, especially colleges and universities, use debit cards extensively. Such payment cards not only allow students to buy food but also give them access to certain buildings or credit at the campus bookstore. This concept is discussed further in the privilege control section of this chapter.

Payment cards are particularly interesting given the amount of information that can now be stored on the card itself. As we discussed earlier, smart card technology uses computer chips to store detailed information on a card. The information is readily available and does not require foodservice operators accepting the card to store large amounts of data on their own systems since the data already is stored on the card.

Foodservice operations can use this detailed information to track preferences, which will help to improve the efficiency of their operations and provide better customer service. For example, the data can be used in determining staffing needs, menu makeup, and other decisions. Therefore, the ability to take these cards becomes more and more important.

In addition, smart card technology also will help to eliminate one of the chief complaints of consumers and retailers—the proliferation of different types of credit cards available today. Smart cards likely will lead to a move to single-source cards, which can store information relating to multiple accounts.

To accept smart cards, foodservice operations must invest in smart card readers or scanners and ensure their systems have the ability to not only read the card but also to transfer transaction data back to the card. The general move toward generic computer systems will aid in such equipment being made available to foodservice operators and in foodservice operators being able to transfer data from their other systems onto the cards. The cards may also be integrated with local banks and merchants.

Interfaces to Other Systems and Sources

It is critical that each internal system can tie into the others to make the best use of the data and applications. For example, when pricing a menu item, it is important to factor into the equation information such as labor costs or cost of supplies. Therefore, systems such as labor forecasting, payroll, and time and attendance should tie into other systems such as inventory, purchasing, and food production to pass key data between the applications. In addition to tying into other back-office systems, these applications must also tie into front-of-the-house systems, which typically are data collection devices.

Systems also should have the capability to tie into external systems, such as those used for ordering products from suppliers, paycheck processing, or credit card processing. Although these systems might be outside the foodservice operator's own closed-loop system, they hold information needed for inventory, purchasing, marketing, loyalty programs, and other functions.

Fortunately, tying systems together is made easier by the availability today of generic systems, which are being designed with "plug-and-play" capabilities. **Plug-and-play** refers to an environment in which different hardware and software elements can recognize each other and communicate with each other so that the user can simply plug in one application to another and begin using it without major modifications.

FRONT-OF-THE-HOUSE

Point-of-Sale Terminals

Point-of-sale (POS) systems are probably the single most common application of computers in foodservice. Simply put, a POS system is a network of terminals capable of capturing data at the point of sale and then processing the data.

Today's POS terminals are a far cry from the electro-mechanical cash registers (ECRs) in use during the 1980s and the traditional cash registers that preceded ECRs.

Early ECRs merely recorded every time a key was hit and then multiplied that number by the dollar amount assigned to that particular key. Early POS terminals, which took the place of cash registers, were computers that were designed to look and feel like a cash register. Today's POS terminals, on the other hand, are computers that look and feel like a PC. They may have unique features, such as a touch screen or a scanner, but they still are personal computers.

Today's POS systems typically have three primary physical components: a processor, an input device, and an output device. The processor contains the **central processing unit**, often called a CPU. The CPU contains the program operating instructions and data storage capacity. The CPU also performs the key functions of adding, subtracting, multiplying, and dividing.

The input device collects data and sends it to the processor. The most common input devices are keyboards and touch screens. The keyboard or touch screen may include specialized keys that are preset for a specific menu item or department. These are especially common in fast-food operations. Open department keys break down sales by categories such as appetizers, entrees, and desserts. **Tender keys** refer to how payment is made, and **price look-up (PLU)** keys break down sales by specific item. The input device can be used in several modes: to record sales transactions, for training purposes, or for management use to generate reports.

The output device, typically a printer, provides information to the user. One use of an output device is in the kitchen, where an order entered at a POS terminal in the dining room can be reproduced for the kitchen staff to fulfill. Other output terminals are digital displays or cathode ray tubes (CRTs), which are similar to TV screens.

In the future, we are likely to see more and more generic POS hardware in use, and increasingly we will see such hardware being bought at generic computer hardware stores rather than just through specialized POS vendors.

Software has also been geared toward the generic in recent years. Foodservice operations are using general operating systems such as Windows NT, Windows '98, Java, Oracle, and other standard databases and platforms.

Using today's generic systems means that as technology changes, POS terminals can be upgraded much more quickly and easily, either by upgrading the software and keeping the same terminals or by adding faster processing chips for additional memory. In addition, as more applications are added to a system, the system is accessible from any workstation to conduct training, run reports, or enter data. This allows the operator to get more use out of each terminal, thereby driving down the per-terminal cost.

Dining Room Management

In full-service operations, the dining room management, or table management, application is used to make the most efficient use of the dining room to increase table turns and get the highest profitability from the space available. Table management starts with taking a reservation, which can be done before a party arrives or on site in the form of a waiting list.

Each table in the dining room is assigned a number, which is recorded and charted in the computer so that the screen will show a map of the dining room with each table's location identified. Statistics are captured for each seat and each table by tying the dining room management system to the POS system. A good dining room management system should allow the operator to see the status of each table, including which course of the meal the party is in and the estimated service time for that table. To do this, the system needs to track when parties sit down at their tables, when they leave, and how long it takes to clear tables and set them up for the next party. We can use this data to determine how long the average wait will be and, by doing so, avoid turning away customers.

It is also possible to tie table status to each course being served. The system determines how much longer a table will be occupied by calculating the eating time based upon the table status and the course of the meal. This allows more accurate planning of table management.

As computers get smarter, we can tie in the actual menu items ordered with approximate eating time to better approximate how long the table will be tied up. In addition, by calculating preparation and eating times by menu item, a foodservice operator can make decisions on menu content based upon which items have the best profit margins. For example, items with longer preparation or eating times might have lower profit margins than items that are costlier to produce since they tie up a table for a longer time. In that case, it might be more profitable to change the menu makeup to decrease table turn times and improve profitability.

For quick-service operations, dining room management actually refers to queue management—producing the right amount of food at the right time to get as many people through the queue as possible (see Chapter 8 on Forecasting). In a quick-service or institutional environment, queue management is important because the food needs to be waiting for the customer. It is vital to balance between keeping the queue short and not overproducing food, which results in waste and spoilage. This ties in with production scheduling.

In quick-service, food production can be adjusted to fit demand. For example, if we know how many people are in a queue at any given time and the average amount of food they will buy, we can adjust food production so that roughly the correct amount of food is waiting for customers when they reach the counter or drive-through to order.

In the past, quick-service managers often managed the queue by counting customers as they came in the door and then adjusting the par levels in the store. However, today there are more sophisticated queuing systems, including technology known as in-store radar. In-store radar uses an infrared beam to track people as they enter an establishment. The sensors can determine, by height and weight, whether the person is a male or female adult or child.

With that data, the foodservice operator can predict more accurately exactly what items should be prepared. As these systems progress, we eventually will be able to tie a specific food item to a customer the moment that customer walks through the door.

Scheduling

Scheduling for front-of-the-house operations is closely tied to the dining room management application and consists of determining the optimal number of front-of-the-house staff to ensure smooth and efficient operations in the dining room. For full-service operations, this generally refers to servers and for quick-service or institutional operations, it refers to counter staff.

In a full-service dining room, a key factor in scheduling servers is determining how many tables each server can handle at one time. A number of factors affects this scheduling, including average table turn time, the amount of time the server can spend on the floor, and the amount of time a customer spends in the unit itself.

Table management systems can help increase the number of customers a server can handle in an evening by ensuring tables are utilized in the most effective manner. Other methods, such as having runners bring food to the server's tables and strategically placing POS terminals in the dining room, help the server spend more time on the floor. This results in higher check averages and quicker table turn times, which impact scheduling decisions.

In quick service, scheduling for counter staff focuses on attempting to get people through the line (and past the register) as quickly as possible. Just as in kitchen staffing, you will need to remember that the fewer customers coming in, the more skilled the employees have to be behind the counter. For example, an employee working the cash register at the front counter might also work the drive-through during slow periods. In this case, you will need to schedule an employee who can operate the cash register and who also has been trained to operate drive-through equipment.

Reservations

Reservation applications not only track people coming into an operation but also can help the foodservice operator determine how to best arrange available seating by putting tables together and how to even out the flow of orders to the kitchen and minimize the use of kitchen staff by decreasing the steps involved in food preparation.

In addition, reservations systems can tie into frequency or loyalty programs to give staff information such as table preferences, wine preferences, and special occasions such as birthdays.

UNIQUE SEGMENTS AND SITUATIONS

Now that we've considered the basics of traditional foodservice, let's explore some unique deviations. These include:

- institutional
- delivery
- stadiums and arenas
- multiunit operations
- salad bars and buffets
- catering
- privilege control

Many times what differentiates systems is how the information gets into the system in the first place.

Institutional

Special nutritional needs or access controls often are part of institutional foodservice operations, which include hospitals, universities, schools, and prisons. Another unique factor is bulk preparation of foods and the ability to use leftover foods in future meal periods. Institutional operations also employ unique devices such as scales or bar coding. Prison foodservice operations often offer multiple meal plans that are required by law and might not even be prepared internally.

Delivery

This unique situation requires a foodservice operation to take orders over the phone or via fax or Internet and then have the food ready when the customer arrives or in time for delivery. Delivery applications also might encompass mapping an area to find the nearest unit to the customer or plot the best delivery route for the driver.

Stadiums and Arenas

Stadium and arena foodservice is complex because it often requires different systems for different operations within a stadium. For example, the sky box area might require a catering system, while counter sales require retail POS systems and seat sales might require portable carts and handheld terminals. Tying these different systems together is difficult because the applications generally are provided by different vendors.

Multiunit Operations

Multiunit operator systems vary somewhat from those used by single unit operators. For multiunit operators, data might be stored at the unit or at a centralized location where ordering, payment processing, bank deposits, and employee information are kept.

For centralized data processing, units are polled on a daily basis and the information is stored. To be part of such a system, a multiunit operator must choose applications that have a consolidated back office but also can break out data for individual units. This is necessary whether the units are in the same city or within the same building, as in stadiums or some hotels. In hotels, for example, data must be broken out for multiple units, such as bars, room service, and restaurants, but must also be consolidated for overall evaluation.

Salad Bars and Buffets

Salad bars and buffets are hard to track and price because foodservice operators frequently are unsure of the average portion customers will take.

Typically, a foodservice operator develops averages by weighing containers or tracking the amount of food supplied to the buffet before, during, and after a meal segment. This allows for trends analysis over time. Once this type of information is gathered, pricing is more effective.

However, not all computer applications can track buffet and salad bar information. For example, POS systems can track how many times a buffet or salad bar ticket is sold but can't tell us how much food is used. Some back-office systems also have difficulty tracking this because they can't pin down the ingredients to the actual items sold.

Catering

Function room and event scheduling can be a major problem for foodservice operators. Systems are available that coordinate room and event scheduling, including generating lists of particular arrangements and reminders or checklists to perform scheduled activities.

Generally, these systems control all of the details of physical facilities used for meetings, private dining, and related activities. The system may also keep data of past catering events, including attendance, menus used, no shows, costs, and appropriate people to contact. Catering applications are available that are fully integrated with food production systems.From a food production standpoint, such catering applications should allow costing out of the production of goods for catering. This is different than costing out and scheduling food production for a restaurant, for example, which is based on just-in-time production. In catering, food is planned and ordered in advance and prepared in bulk.

For a catering operation with multiple events, the catering application can factor in specific menu items being used for other scheduled events and allow for combined purchasing and scheduling. Combining two or more catering jobs can cut costs and preparation time and increase an operation's profitability margin. In addition, a good catering system will allow an operation to schedule resources such as flowers, silverware, and china, rather than outsourcing these requirements. This provides an additional opportunity for generating revenue.

Thus, a good catering application allows the foodservice operator to plan for events, produce appropriate documents, plan the menu based on bulk purchasing and bulk preparation requirements, and track and capture incremental income from selling nonfood items for an event.

Privilege Control

Access control systems, commonly referred to as **privilege control systems**, are used not only to permit or deny access to restricted areas but also to verify dining privileges (such as in a university dining hall) and to automatically monitor, control, and provide billing for foodservice charge programs.

Operating through the use of a magnetic-strip ID card or a smart card, these systems communicate on-line with a computer that maintains a database of cardholders and their accounts.

Such systems enable managers to structure various meal programs priced for various consumer groups, often with a striking increase in cash sales. Debit cards that are encoded with various cash balances can be used to operate vending machines, copying machines, and other electronically controlled devices. In institutional environments, particularly hospitals, universities, and prisons, these cards are being used effectively to increase cash sales. Commercial operations also sometimes use meal cards to offer subsidized meals or to tie meals to an employee's paycheck.

Institutions typically use a point system, whereby a point is deducted each time a meal is purchased. For example, in a university system, a parent buys a specified number of meals per semester and each time the student uses the card to buy a meal, a point is deducted. Access also can be restricted so that a student can buy only one meal per meal period. When the points are used up, so are the meals.

SUMMARY

A foodservice MIS can be defined as a formal system for collecting, selecting, storing, and disseminating the information needed to facilitate the management of a foodservice operation. Since a manager's main responsibility is to make operating decisions, a reliable MIS is invaluable in the management process. Much of what such a system does can be computerized, and its work can be augmented by point-of-sale terminals, which are particularly useful in foodservice operations. Sophisticated management information systems include computerized applications that carry out such functions as sales analysis, production forecasting, purchasing, inventory tabulations and maintenance, labor scheduling, back-office responsibilities, nutritive analysis, and managing catering operations.

KEY TERMS

access control system
application
batching
cathode ray tube
central processing unit (CPU)
closed loop system
database
data input
debit card
80/20 rule
electronic cash register
electronic data interchange (EDI)
electronic spreadsheet
exploded recipe
extranet
fire walls

food ingredient database
Internet
local area network (LAN)
open department keys
par stock
perpetual inventory
plug-and-play capability
point-of-sale terminal (POS)
point-to-point tunneling protocol
post-cost analysis
price look-up key (PLU)
privilege control system
RFPC (request for proposal)
smart card
tender keys
wide area network (WAN)

REVIEW QUESTIONS

6–1 Define a *foodservice management information system.*

6–2 Briefly explain five things the information from an MIS should be.

6–3 Why is an MIS more important now than ever?

6–4 What are complaints about MIS information?

6–5 Why is human judgment important in customer count forecasting?

6–6 Explain LAN, WAN, and Internet.

6–7 What is new in the cost of computer technology for foodservice operations?

6–8 How can an MIS system be helpful in employee training?

6–9 Explain menu margin analysis.

6–10 Explain post-cost analysis.

6–11 What is past sales analysis?

6–12 What are the goals of a food purchasing analysis?

6–13 Why might a computerized perpetual inventory not be necessary?

6–14 Explain the use of smart cards and how they can help a foodservice operation.

6–15 How can computers help in dining room management?

6–16 How can computers be helpful in foodservice outside catering operations?

6–17 Explain how a privilege control system works.

PROJECTS

6–1 Using a local foodservice operation, determine what MISs are presently in place. Describe these systems as to what information is available, when it is available, how useful it is, who receives it, and what may be lacking in the systems.

6–2 Using this text, library research, software vendors, trade publications, or any other source, devise an MIS for one aspect of the system such as sales analysis production, forecasting purchasing, inventory tabulation, labor cost analysis, back-office responsibilities, nutrition analysis, or catering objectives.

Marketing

The best foodservice operation will flounder without customers or consumers for its products. The day has long since passed when customers might come if a restaurant was built in a particular location or because little else was available. Good food is not the only necessary ingredient to establish a clientele. Today intense competition of many different types assails any foodservice operation. Early promotion efforts usually involved simple selling. Today successful operators know they must be marketers as well as foodservice professionals. Even institutional foodservice organizations with a captive clientele must market to identify and satisfy the needs of the patrons. Marketing is not confined to restaurants. What can a hospitality dietary department do to make patients more satisfied while in the hospital? With hospitals increasingly under more stringent cost considerations and more competition, dietary departments can supply a real marketing asset by catering to the specific needs of their patrons.

After completing this chapter, you should be able to:

1. Appreciate the importance of marketing.
2. Understand the types of market segmentation and target markets.
3. Know the elements of the marketing mix that can be utilized.
4. Explain basic marketing moves.
5. Better analyze your competition.
6. Use the Importance/Performance Analysis (IPA) Technique.

Marketing can be broadly defined as those business activities involved in the flow of information to create an efficient channel of distribution of goods and services from producers to consumers. Specifically, marketing involves discovering what your customers want and need (market research and feedback), giving it to them (product and service), and telling them what is available (advertising and promotion) so they will receive value (pricing and value perception) and you will make a profit (marketability).

Marketing starts with the conception of a business, and a marketing plan should be part of any business plan. However, since change is the only constant in foodservice, the plan should be amended continually. Sometimes due to the external environment, a complete change of direction is required. Many once successful restaurants or restaurant chains, such as Howard Johnson, Childs, Stouffers, Schrafts, Longchamps, and Horn and Hardart, are no longer in business or are only minor players.

CONSUMER ORIENTATION

The most important aspect of marketing is its consumer orientation. What target market customers want, not what the management or ownership wants to provide, is all important. Ideally this orientation requires management to determine what target markets are available, which one or ones it wants to attract, and how to design a product to attract them.

CUSTOMERS

Everything involved in the business focuses on present and potential customers. The product (goods, services, and ideas), which is not just food but also such factors as decor and service, must be tailored for these people. Everything must be designed to fit their perceptions of need and value. A marketing maxim is "put the customers first and the profits will follow." Of course, there must be sufficient customers available for this maxim to hold true. Consider these questions:

a. Who are your customers?

b. What are their wants and needs?

c. What goods and services can you supply them?

d. What other markets are available to your customers?

e. Who are your competitors?

f. Are there enough customers to provide the necessary volume for profit?

g. How will customers find out about you?

If the operation is to focus on its customers, the first step is to determine who the customers or potential customers are. There may be 100,000 people in your geographic area, but how many of them will want to use your facility and how many will you separate from your competition? **Market segmentation** is the process of dividing a total market into groups of people with similar product needs or groups of customers who are homogeneous in some way. Segmentation theory assumes that segments can be determined and products can be designed for specific target segments.

MARKET SEGMENTATION

A market segment must be measurable, accessible, and substantial. Measurable means that the management can determine the approximate number of potential customers in a segment, identify their wants and needs, and identify the characteristics that determine or define the segment. Even if numerous customers exist in a segment, they are not a reasonable target if they are not accessible. Many people would probably like to eat at fine restaurants, but if they cannot afford such luxury, they are not accessible. If a segment is both accessible and measurable, it must also be substantial. It must contain sufficient numbers to warrant a marketing effort. Multimillionaires might appear to meet all the criteria for the ideal segment, but too few of them may exist to make them a practical segment for hospitality targeting. (They might, however, be a sufficiently substantial segment for fashionable jewelers or attorneys specializing in tax shelters.)

Market segments are sometimes considered according to broad geographic, demographic, or psychographic variables. Geographic variables include the region, the climate, and the population density characteristics of a market segment. A related consideration is how far patrons will travel to come to a restaurant. In the open West, people might drive 100 miles for a good meal but in a crowded city, a block may be too far for a quick lunch.

Demographic segmentation uses the study of such human population variables as age, gender, family size, income level, occupation, interests and hobbies, social class, ethnic background, religion, and family lifestyle. Through these studies, managers try to determine the size of various segments, their value, and competition for them. A particular restaurant, which has decided that upper-middle-class, professional, middle-aged couples comprise a sizable and accessible market segment, could use these demographics to decide to offer high-priced, rather exotic menus with little concern for the appetites of children. Its furnishings and service would also be designed to appeal to the tastes that demographics suggest for this market.

A third type of market segmentation is **psychographics**. This method employs such factors as lifestyles, buying motives, product knowledge, and intended product use. For the hospitality industry, lifestyle is probably the most important psychographic consideration. For example, wealthy customers were once assumed to follow conservative lifestyles. Now we realize that they may as easily be jet-setters or they may dislike the ostentation that often accompanies wealth. Segmenting by lifestyles can reveal unexpected potential markets, because customers' patronization of a particular hospitality establishment can be based on their buying motives. Are customers seeking snob appeal? Are they looking for value? Do they prefer understated luxury? Do they want fast service or pampered attention? A sports restaurant or bar is an example of using psychographic data to target sports-oriented patrons.

Once an operation researches its market segments, it must decide which target markets to broach. An operation cannot pursue all the market segments, only the most profitable ones. The ideal target market would (1) be of sufficient size to promise a profit, (2) have a potential for growth, (3) not be the target of excessive competition, and (4) exemplify some more or less unsatisfied need that can be supplied by the hospitality operation. All these criteria may not be fulfilled for any specific segment, but they may be used to measure one segment against another.

ELEMENTS OF MARKETING AND THE MARKETING MIX

Once the target markets have been determined, the marketing mix to bring them in must be established. Elements of the **marketing mix** include merchandising strategy, pricing, brand name, channels of distribution, personal selling, advertising, promotion, packaging,

INDUSTRY INSIGHTS   by Michael Berry

Michael Berry is Vice President of Food Operations and Concept Development for Disneyland Resort in Anaheim, Calif. He has been awarded the Visionary Award, the Ivy Award for Best Non-Commercial Foodservice Operation in the United States, and the IFMA Silver Plate for Foodservice Operator of the year.

DEVELOPING A CUSTOMER-FOCUSED BUSINESS

"See this?" says Michael Berry, vice president for food operations and concept development. "It's a compact bag blower." Invented for Disney, it directs a strategic puff of air into the bag, inflating it just in time to slip in a hot dog and rush it to one of six registers. The efficient process will be repeated 800 times every hour, to the tune of $6 million a year.

Few observers have ever thought of the $18.7 billion Walt Disney Co. as a restaurant operator, even though merchandise, food, and beverage accounted for $1.5 billion of last year's revenues. Even Walt himself hired outside contractors when Disneyland first opened in 1955. Five years later, Disney brought the food operation in-house, but company officials admit it's always been an afterthought, not an attraction.

It's the parks themselves that carry "eatertainment" to its ultimate conclusion. Disneyland is a hermetically sealed environment, where every detail is managed. Explains Berry, "The whole park is built inside a berm so you can't see in or out. Air traffic is not permitted to fly over. If you're in Fantasyland and a jet flies over, you have a disconnect."

Each eatery in Disneyland is assigned a story line, which dictates decor and costuming as well as food. Employees are called "cast members," with the idea that every cook and server is part of the onstage presentation for park guests.

A major challenge at Disneyland is that everything must be served at the rate of 18,000 transactions every 60 minutes. The highest-volume outlet in the park, Tomorrowland Terrace, has 18 registers serving 2,100 customers an hour.

At the center of Disneyland thematic development is the 2,200-member Walt Disney Imagineering Division, which consults on entertainment concepts for all Disney ventures. "They tell us the story of the restaurant. We give them a designed unit and the size of the box. Then they give us the creative overlay. It ping-pongs back and forth," Berry explains. The real bottom line will be whether Disney's new restaurants can add enough value to justify their prices. "There's a big opportunity to make a lot of money if we can do it right."

Berry's formula is to take McDonald's classic QSC mantra—Quality, Service, and Cleanliness—and add a fourth element: Show. "QSC plus Show equals Value," says Berry. "People will pay one or two dollars more for a unique experience."

Relative to service, Berry suggests foodservice operators need to look at business from their guests' perspective. It is an issue of quality not only service, personal contact, and display. *Merchandising* a product or service means making it as attractive as possible to potential customers. Some fast-food chains do an excellent job in merchandising, especially to children.

Pricing means the proper price in relation to the cost of providing the product or service and the appropriate profit. How should prices be fixed? A restaurant may offer a table d'hôte meal at one price that includes everything in the meal. Or it may go to the other extreme and offer an à la carte menu with everything priced separately. There are many variations. For example, the price of the entrée may include vegetables and bread but not dessert and appetizer. What is the best pricing strategy for your facility? Does the price fit in the products you provide but, equally important, in the service! Quality, like beauty, is in the eyes of the beholder, or in this case, the guest. Quality control is the measurement of goods and services against established standards of excellence.

To find out what your guests want, you must find ways to connect with them through surveys, feedback mechanisms, focus groups, anecdotes, and testing. The difference between product quality and service quality is that product quality is "what you get" and is more easily quantifiable than service quality, or "how you get it." They are two different things, and many companies have a reputation for providing one or the other. Few have a reputation for providing both.

The factors in a guest purchase in rank order are price, quality, and service. The factors in dumping a company are in rank order service, quality, and price. Consider the last time you stopped doing business with a company. Seventy percent of consumers say it was for "poor service."

The meaning of customer service is the quality of service (in terms of timeliness, dependability, communication, and convenience) provided to customers or clients. You must exceed your guests' expectations by providing high-quality products and service.

When Berry was director of dining services at Harvard University, his principles were "yes, wow, give a damn." At Disneyland his guideposts are great quality and innovative food, over-the-top guest service, exceptional cleanliness, entertainment, and show. Berry believes it is critical to saturate your company with the voice of the guests. Find as many "listening posts" as possible to stay in touch with your guests. At Disney, Berry reinforces the action

of "walk the talk." The leader must constantly reinforce the vision and the values.

Culture is defined by the organization and its leadership. If you are effective in developing a customer-focused culture, "you will be managing the culture, not the employees." Berry stresses hiring the right people: "Our people are our number one asset. At Disneyland, we consider our product to be 'happiness.' It is an intangible product, produced moment by moment through our guests' interaction with our show and our cast."

"The most integral components of our cast member training are the traditions and standards of guest service," he adds. "The first of these we call the 'personal touch.' Our cast and members are encouraged to use their own unique style and personality to provide a personal interaction with each guest. Regardless of position, all of us go by our first names. It allows us to interact on a more personal level with our guests. We know that the informality and personal work environment is ultimately reflected in a more personal style of service to our guests."

Michael Berry's steps in his leadership model include:

1. Provide clear expectations and standards.
2. Communicate those expectations through demonstration, information, and examples.
3. Hold cast members accountable for their behavior.
4. Coach through honest and direct feedback.
5. Recognize, reward, manage the culture, and celebrate success.

As Berry often says, "May you, too, find the 'happiest place on earth'!"

into your marketing scheme? Are you going to use low prices to attract a high volume or high prices to effect a high profit margin? Automobile manufacturers have become pricing experts. They offer a basic price for a car that usually seems rather reasonable. Then they persuade a buyer to order certain options that add considerably to the total price.

Pricing strategies in the foodservice industry include determining what price ranges management thinks will provide the best volume/profit mix. A break-even chart discussed in Chapter 24 can be helpful in setting prices. Value pricing is offering different items together at a lower price than they would be offered separately. However, because of the increased volume, the profit can be higher with the lower markups than less volume at higher markups. Chapter 9 discusses menu pricing in detail.

Branding involves the image you want the operation to project. A chain operation emphasizes the similarity of its units so that consumers immediately recognize the golden arches or the red tile roof even before they see the establishment. The design of the building should, in any case, portray as much as possible the type of operation it houses. Channels of distribution can include the location or site for the enterprise. Where you are geographically affects your business.

Branding has been very effective in chain operations. Instead of stopping at perfectly acceptable but unfamiliar foodservice operations, patrons may tend to visit establishments with which they are familiar as a result of a chain-fostered national reputation. The restaurant across the street may be just as good as (or better than) the chain operation but patrons prefer not to take the chance—an attitude chain operations stress in their national advertising.

For nonhospitality operations *packaging* refers to a product's wrapping, but for the foodservice industry packaging can describe the decor of the establishment. Is it strictly luxury or decidedly no frills? A steak house restaurant may have a rustic building while a convenience restaurant can have a clean, efficient, no-nonsense appearance. In the hospitality field, display is tied to packaging since the decor of the establishment is part of the product itself rather than some small, nicely wrapped gift. The physical premises, both inside and outside, should be display pieces inviting patrons to come in and enjoy the services.

Packaging can also refer to how the food or service is provided. The service of a low-cost steak house with western atmosphere, for example, is different from that of a luxurious gourmet restaurant. In the hospitality industry the service provided the customers is most important. This service must be balanced between costs and the quality of the offering. From a marketing standpoint, it is essential that the level of service desired by the target markets be determined and that this level be the goal. All the elements of the marketing mix are determined by the wants and needs of customers, and all the elements should be compatible and support each other. In foodservice, branding and packaging may overlap.

Merchandising denotes the steps taken to differentiate an establishment from the competition. In a restaurant, merchandising might include original menu items, a house salad dressing, or a specialty drink.

Channels of distribution refers to how the product gets to the consumer, such as table service, take out, buffet, or home delivery.

Personal selling can be suggestions or recommendations to the customer such as "would you like our special dessert" or "the roast beef is very good tonight." It can also be a comment by the wait person such as "an excellent choice." The great French chef, Escoffier, carried personal selling to new heights by naming dishes after good patrons, i.e. crepe suzette or peach melba.

Service of course, is how well the customer is served. Personal contact can be knowing the manager, chef, or other staff and being recognized by them.

All of these elements of the marketing mix apply to any enterprise, but their importance varies among industries and with individual situations. Marketing-oriented foodservice executives must be aware of these elements and use them constructively for their establishments. Market research should help pinpoint target markets, identify customer wants and needs, determine the proper marketing mix, and make most effective use of the advertising dollar. Because many foodservice establishments may appeal to only a small segment of the general population and thus cannot use broad outside promotion or advertising, market research is essential.

There are many ways to perform market research. Some operators may employ hospitality consulting firms, or the prospective operators might want to do it themselves. Local chambers of commerce, business groups, media, and government agencies may make demographic studies available. By spending time in an area you can do traffic counts, spot competition, and note the types of people in the neighborhood. This research also comes in handy when developing a feasibility study and business plan.

In formulating a marketing mix, you must make sure that the elements are considered as they are affected by changes in consumer attitudes and habits, competition, and government activity. For example, promotion methods that might have been acceptable, even desirable, a few years ago cannot be used now. Government controls and regulations are looming even larger for all establishments. For example, a proposed government regulation that all convenience foods be labeled as such on the menu could have implications in packaging, display, branding, and different types of promotion.

MARKETING AND THE MISSION STATEMENT

To achieve the best success in marketing, foodservice operations should have a firm idea of what they want to offer to customers. These concepts can be incorporated in the mission statement. A **mission statement** is a statement of purpose for the company. It states the business the company is in and the customers it intends to serve. It mandates how the company intends to present itself as unique in the eyes of customers and responsible in the eyes of the community and society. Goals should be specific instead of using general terms such as "quality food" or "good value." For example, the statement should specify whether the food is gourmet or low cost. It is helpful to stress whether the atmosphere is intended to be leisurely or efficient and fast.

Management should go beyond mention of these goals in the mission statement to specify how these goals will be fulfilled. The goal of friendly service, for example, might be backed up through hiring practices, training, incentives (such as recognition for friendliness), and example by management. As consumer tastes change, a mission statement may also change.

MARKET SHARE

Market share is the portion or percentage of sales that is held by a product or business in relation to its competition. It is harder for a foodservice operation to determine market share than for a more discrete product, such as a brand of cigarettes or beer. However, it is possible for a foodservice enterprise to estimate what portion of food business, such as the various meal sales, take-out business, or type of a particular foodservice business, it controls in its geographical area.

Determining market share can be helpful in measuring how an operation is doing against its competition, what a feasible goal might be to increase its market share, or how new competition has affected its share.

Setting a desired market share provides a goal. It can lead to better planning in how to achieve that specific goal and more analysis about how and what the competition is doing. If market share is slipping and no strategy seems available to reverse the trend, a change of services, products, or type of operation may be in order.

In the short run, maintaining market share may be more important than creating temporary profits, since a strong customer base is necessary for continued operation of the business. Instead of allowing competition to make inroads, an operation may accept lower profits. An operation can overcharge for a short period, perhaps increasing profits but possibly driving away opportunities for repeat business.

Some techniques used to enhance market share may be holding prices when costs are rising, lowering prices (perhaps by using coupons or other discounts), employing heavy promotion or advertising, or making menu or service changes that better correspond to the psychographic attributes of the market.

SELLING AND APPEALS

One definition of selling is the satisfaction of needs. Another is allowing someone to rationalize what he does. A person's needs may be physiological or psychological, real or imagined. (A psychologist might counter that psychological needs are real needs in the same sense that psychosomatic pain hurts.) The importance of imagined need is demonstrated by the fact that the United States could survive very well on 40 percent of what it consumes. Obviously then, much of our consumption stems from imagined, manufactured, or developed needs.

If people are hungry and have money, very little salesmanship is required to get them into the only restaurant around. A different situation arises when an area has 50 restaurants and people are not particularly hungry. To survive in this area, a restaurant must have something that appeals to customers. In part, the appeal may be food, but it can be other things as well, including decor, service, or advertising. Selling patrons may even involve providing other stimulants that make them want to eat, such as pictures of food items. If you are not particularly hungry but see a picture of a mouthwatering steak platter, your hunger threshold immediately falls. The popping of a champagne cork may stimulate others to order champagne. The mere smell of charcoal or fresh baked bread arouses the taste buds of some people.

CREATING AN IMAGE

Promotion and advertising no longer consist solely of the mention of a product's merits. Today most segments of the hospitality industry engage in brisk competition. Competitors frequently offer equal services and products. How do customers choose one (yours) over the others? Ideally, you want them to develop a strong loyalty to your operation. Thus, you must create some perception that your product is different from and better than others. This is called *creating an image*. Your image may center on luxury, fast service, economy, or some other desirable concept. The image cannot be created by advertising alone. It should involve the entire enterprise. Thus, if an operation places the picture of a colonial gentleman in its advertising, it should follow through with colonial menus, serving uniforms, and decor. Fast-food operations create an image of speed and cleanliness with their relatively small size, large windows, and strong lighting. The strong lighting and small size dramatize the fact that people go in and out quickly. Large windows allow one to observe the fast flow of traffic and much of the food preparation in a modern, clean, sanitary kitchen. Psychographic market segmentation is important in determining what image to try to create.

From a psychological standpoint, customer loyalty to various images is immensely interesting. For example, people tend to be intensely loyal to their cigarette brands. However, in blind tests, they normally cannot differentiate one brand from the others. The same is true for brands of beer. One inexpensive eastern beer—so its advertising claims—is often confused for an "aristocratic" Rocky Mountain beer when drinkers are blindfolded. Obviously, brands of cigarettes and beer have created an image. It might be the ruggedness of some cigarette brands or the boisterous good times suggested by a particular beer. A foodservice operation should consciously work at projecting and strengthening its desired image.

In determining the right image, it will be necessary again to consider potential customers and to determine what type of image they expect from the establishments they frequent. The youth-oriented image, for example, would not be wise in an area where most customers are senior citizens.

MOTIVATION AND SALES

Foodservice managers must understand two basic aspects of promotion appeals and motivation. First, people are not always logical. Second, all have certain needs. If someone can present a product that seems to fulfill our needs psychologically or physiologically, we will buy the product.

People are not logical. They buy cars they cannot afford, clothes they do not need, and equipment they may never use. Nevertheless, they can almost always rationalize their purchases. Someone purchases a new car when his old car remains in good running order. Why? He rationalizes that the new car fits needs. It gets better gas mileage. It eliminates the possibility of major repairs in the near future. The real reasons probably have more to do with status, with drawing neighborhood attention, with a desire for novelty, or with advertising that trumpets the joys of owning a new model. In promoting a service or product, remember that a logical need for something may be immaterial as long as customers can rationalize their purchase.

If a need is identified for a product or service, it can be sold. As Sigmund Freud said, "Under our simple veneer of rationality, morality, reason, and sanity is the id, which contains lust, passion, and desire." Product and service promotion focuses on the id. One definition of selling is allowing someone to rationalize what she or he does.

A number of appeals can be used in hospitality promotion. One is pride. In this case, the exclusiveness or even the expensiveness of the establishment is stressed. People to whom an appeal is addressed will consider themselves superior if they patronize an exclusive and expensive establishment, even if they feel items are overpriced. It helps even more if patrons are recognized and flattered. Rounding out the appeal is inviting patrons to call the owner, maitre'd, or chef by first name. The opposite of pride is economy, and here one stresses the value of the product or service. Patrons who could afford the best may pride themselves in using the cheapest. Thus an exclusive restaurant will not feature its prices, but a fast-food operation may stress "value pricing."

Novelty can also exert an appeal. People like to experience something new. People are curious, so an advertisement like "visit our new, unique cocktail lounge" can be very effective. In fact, the word "new" works like a magnet. A new foodservice operation can capitalize on its novelty as it opens its doors. However, if it is not prepared, suffers opening snafus, or does not provide the desired product, a new operation can turn off customers for future sales. Do not push an opening. Schedule trial runs or perhaps open on a smaller scale.

Another appeal is the recommendation of others—particularly, it seems, well-known celebrities. The testimony should come from someone whom people have confidence in. Comically absurd testimony sometimes attracts attention. A desire for "social correctness"—doing the proper thing—also sells products and services. This desire helps account for the growing habit in the United States of wine with the meal.

BASIC MARKETING MOVES

A foodservice or other operation can use four **basic marketing moves** to increase its business.

1. Sell the same products to the same customers, but maybe more often or for different uses (market penetration). If you have a loyal clientele that likes your products, this can keep you in business if there are similar potential customers willing to make up for typical customer attrition. This strategy assumes there are enough customers or potential customers who like what you are offering that the product and service mix does not have to change.

2. Sell new products to old customers (product development). What can you do to persuade your present customers to purchase more from you? Pushing more expensive appetizers or desserts is one example. Adding take-out service is another. Internal promotion can be very important with this market move.

3. Sell old products to new customers (market development). In this situation you are happy with your product service mix but want more customers. In such a situation, external promotion becomes crucial.

4. Sell new products to new customers (diversification). This is the opposite of marketing move No. 1. A long-time restaurant has had a steady customer base that is aging, causing high attrition. The restaurant has featured high priced items with elaborate service. However, there is not much of a new market for this mix in the area. Should the operation offer new products and services, probably alienating its old customers but hoping to draw in enough new patrons to compensate? A new restaurant starting out with untried product/service mix would face the same consequences.

COMPETITION

A vital factor in your marketing effort, but one over which you may have little control, is your competition. Competition may be direct (a similar restaurant down the street), indirect (people bringing brown bags to work instead of lunching with you), or in between (supermarkets offering ready-to-eat food items).

There are three times when you should be concerned with your competition.

1. When you are planning a new operation or considering purchasing an existing one. If there is little competition, it may be because the market can't support much more business. Much competition makes success harder. Bankers or financing agents are very interested in an operation's competition as they consider providing funds.

2. When a new competitor arrives on the scene. The newcomer is probably after your customers, who initially may want to try out the new enterprise. You must consider how you can cope with this new threat or perhaps how to generate new business to take care of any loss of former business to a competitor.

3. All the time. Constantly monitoring your competition is a form of preventive maintenance and a wise strategy to protect your clientele base.

Questions about your competitors include:

a. Who and what is your competition?

b. How are they doing? Is their business increasing, decreasing, or remaining steady?

c. How do their operations differ from yours? What can you learn from them?

d. How can you make your operation better than theirs?

Some foodservice operators even keep files on their competitors. Another technique is to prepare a competition comparison chart for each major competitor.

Such a chart is shown in Table 7.1. The concept of benchmarking was introduced in Chapter 3. In effect, you are rating your operation's attributes against the best of your competitors.

Table 7.1
Competition Comparison Chart

Customer Seeks	Competition Offers	You Offer	Comments
Quality food Friendly service Fast service Nice atmosphere Credit cards Low prices Name recognition Beverage service Children friendly Parking Wide name choice Specialty foods Table linens Salad bar Take-out service Smoking/nonsmoking			

New competition is not always negative. In addition to requiring established operations to react and improve, competition may draw more customers to a geographical area, creating a restaurant center and more business for all. Food courts in malls are an example of this dynamic.

ADVERTISING

Advertising involves the purchase of space, time, or printed matter to increase sales. Common types of advertising include newspapers, magazines, television, direct mail, telephone directories, and flyers. Some new types of advertising can include using fax machines and the Internet.

Advertising can be very effective, but it is not automatically so. Advertising must communicate your message. This means the message the media provides must fit your customer. John Wanamaker, the great dry goods merchant, is reported to have said that half of his advertising was wasted; the problem was he did not know which half.

Wanamaker might have benefited from understanding the general principles that can make advertising more effective. One is repetition. A single mention of a product in an advertising medium often is not enough. The customer needs to see and hear the message again and again, perhaps in several different media. Advertising should be cumulative. Past advertising should reinforce today's advertising. This investment may not appear on the balance sheet, but past advertising can be a definite asset to an organization.

Advertising cannot be indiscriminate, except for the comparatively few products used by everyone. Most of the foodservice industry has narrow target markets. Thus, advertising should be directed straight to these target markets with as little waste as possible. Advertising to people who are not potential patrons is a waste.

Unless something is drastically wrong with an establishment, it will be easier to bring back old customers than to interest new ones. Thus, its first effort should be directed to former customers. Less money need be spent educating them about what you have available. A hospitality operation which turns off regular customers must depend on new ones. If they, too, become disenchanted, the prospects for survival are bleak.

Except for large chains, most hospitality advertising is local in nature. In a large city, newspapers or television may have too much inappropriate circulation. Direct mail sent to specific addresses or flyers distributed in the neighborhood may be more effective. Classified telephone advertising has proven cost effective for many operations.

USING ELECTRONIC INFORMATION HIGHWAYS

A new marketing tool for foodservice operations is maintaining a web site. To be effective the site can offer information, entertainment, and solicitation. Try to make the web site interactive or allow customers or potential customers direct access to someone in the operation. Otherwise, the web site is just a brochure. Contents of the web site can include photos and text that allow users to visualize the dining experience, menus, daily specials, reviews of the restaurant, recipes (adjusted for smaller amounts), and related information to provoke customer interest. Some operations tie in with a weather site or other popular web destination to promote their menu items. A web site may reach audiences that were not available through other media and traditional advertising at a low cost.

INTERNAL SELLING TECHNIQUES

Many techniques or devices can be used in a foodservice operation to increase sales to customers who are already there. Foremost is the menu. It should stress what you want to sell by using artwork, photography, placement, and item description. The descriptive writing of menu items can create new desires or perceptions of value. Adjectives like "fresh" or "chef's specialty" add a certain desire for these items.

Waitpersons can employ suggestive selling: "The beef Wellington is very good tonight." "Let me run through the specials." "We're offering a special dessert this weekend." Some operations provide bonuses to employees who sell above-average numbers of desserts or high-priced entrées. Care must be taken that such selling not become too aggressive and turn off customers.

In fast-food operations large pictures of items on the walls can increase sales. Some restaurants find putting empty wine glasses with the table setting can increase wine sales. Do not launch internal selling techniques without planning. You should first decide what images you want to create for your target customers. Do the selling techniques fit in with these images?

An internal/external selling device is the sign identifying the establishment. It should be visible enough to indicate the location but also be designed to help enhance the image management is trying to create.

IMPORTANCE/PERFORMANCE ANALYSIS (IPA) TECHNIQUE

To be successful in today's rapidly changing market, it is necessary to understand and proactively address the needs of present and future customers. A traditional method for customer feedback is the use of customer surveys. **Importance/performance analysis (IPA)** provides a new dimension by plotting on a grid the importance of an attribute of the foodservice operation and the performance of the operation in satisfying this attribute. The grid displays the attributes, or what the operation is trying to provide, against how well it is succeeding in the view of customers. Since success of the analysis depends on regular feedback, the analysis may work best with a stable customer base, such as an industrial feeding facility or college foodservice operation.

Attributes considered will vary for the individual operation. Table 7.2 provides one list, but a specific operation should adapt this list by adding or deleting attributes.

Customers rate these attributes through questionnaires or other devices. A Likert scale of 1 to 3 is used to determine the importance of the attribute to the customer as "very important," "important," or "not important." The mean for the importance of each attribute forms the Y coordinate. The X coordinate is a mean of a Likert scale rating of 1 to 5 to determine how well the operation fulfills the attribute or performance. Categories in the

Table 7.2
Food Service Attributes

Menu
Choice of entrée items
Appropriateness of entrée items
Appropriateness of desserts
Choice of desserts
Menu design and appearance
Choice of beverages
Quality of coffee

Quality
Quality of entrées
Quality of desserts
Hot foods served hot
Cold foods served cold
Portion sizes—entrées
Portion sizes—desserts
Eye appeal of foods

Service
Speed of service
Courtesy of employees
Knowledge of employees
Appearance of employees

Beverages
Wine list
Wine pricing
Wine service
Choice of other drinks
Pricing of other drinks
Quality of other drinks
Bartender showmanship

Other Factors
Hours of operation
Availability of parking
Cleanliness
Ease of reservations
Dining room decor

rating are "excellent," "very good," "good," "fair," or "poor." It is then necessary to convert the 1 to 5 scales to a 1 to 3 scale. If the mean rating on a 1 to 5 scale were 2.5, it would be 1.5 on the 1 to 3 scale. This is determined by multiplying the 1 to 5 rating by .6. The Y or importance rating can be plotted directly. See Figure 7.1.

The grid has four quadrants, which are labeled on the relationship of performance and importance of each attribute. The upper left quadrant (quadrant A) is labeled "Focus Here." This indicates the operation is providing poor performance on an attribute considered important by customers. The upper right quadrant (quadrant B) is titled "Doing Great."

Figure 7.1
Importance/performance
Matrix

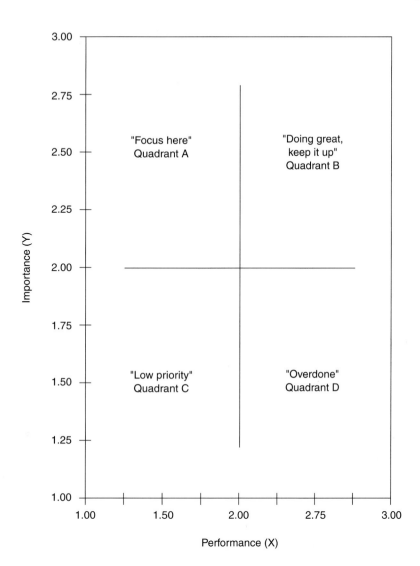

It indicates the operation is doing a good job satisfying an attribute deemed important by the customer. Quadrant C in the lower left corner is for attributes the operation is not performing too well, but they also have little importance to the customer. The lower right quadrant (quadrant D) is titled "Overdone." Although the operation is performing well on the attribute, the attribute itself is not regarded as not particularly important by the customer.

Table 7.3 provides data on 10 selected attributes for a foodservice operation. The data is plotted on Figure 7.2. Item #1, choice of entrées, has a mean rating by all customers of 3.17 on a 1 to 5 scale. The adjusting rating would be 1.86, rounded off to 1.9. The mean of customer ratings of the importance of choice of entrées is 2.59 on a 1 to 3 scale. In Figure 7.2, Item #1 is plotted at 1.9 on the performance scale and 2.59 on the importance

Table 7.3
Data on Selected Attributes for a Foodservice Operation

	A Performance Rating	B Performance Rating Adjusted	C Importance Rating
Menu			
1 Choice of entrées	3.17	1.90	2.59
2 Choice of desserts	4.05	2.43	1.51
3 Choice of beverages	3.83	2.30	2.50
Food			
4 Quality of entrées	3.05	1.83	2.76
5 Quality of desserts	3.80	2.28	1.74
6 Portion sizes—entrées	3.50	2.10	2.46
7 Portion sizes—desserts	4.17	2.50	2.08
Service			
8 Speed of service	2.65	1.59	2.95
9 Courtesy of service	2.36	1.42	1.91
10 Waiting time for table	4.20	2.52	2.80

scale. This put it in quadrant A, or "Focus Here." Its location in the quadrant indicates that this item is important to customers and the operation is close to having good performance to satisfy it.

In analyzing the data from Table 7.3 shown in Figure 7.2 we find that items that are important to our customers and that we should improve or focus on are

Choice of entrées (1)

Quality of entrées (4)

Speed of service (8)

Items that are important but where our performance is also good are

Portion sizes—entrées (6)

Waiting for tables (10)

Choice of beverages (3)

Portion sizes—desserts (7)

Items in which we do a good job but are not that important to patrons, or are overdone, are

Quality of desserts (5)

Choice of desserts (2)

An area where performance is low but customer concern is also a low priority is

Courtesy of service (9)

In general, this operation could focus on improving the quality of its entrées. The quality of desserts is good but not appreciated much by customers. Portion sizes are good.

Figure 7.2
Data Plotted on the
Importance/performance
Matrix

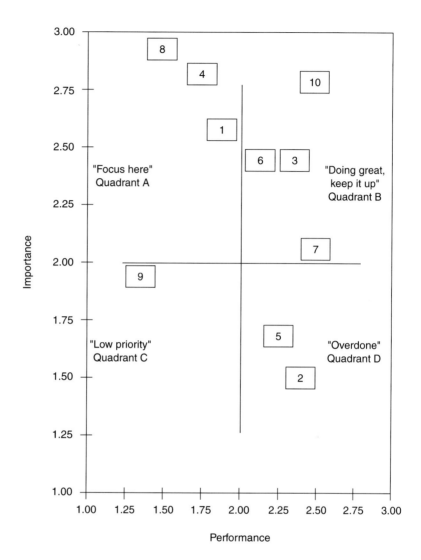

The speed of service could be increased and although courtesy of service is low, the customers do not seem to mind.

The positioning of an attribute in its quadrant is significant as it shows how much better or worse it is in its relationship to other items in the quadrant and how close it is to being in another quadrant.

An operation might also want to coordinate its importance/performance analysis with customer profiles. Information such as gender percentage of clients, income levels, frequency of patronization, age groups, types (e.g., executive, clerical, student) could lead to subanalysis. The analysis may also be performed for different meals or time periods.

SUMMARY

Marketing can be broadly defined as those business activities involved in the flow of information to create an efficient channel of distribution of goods and services from producers to customers. It is also involved in every aspect of a foodservice operation: products, pricing, employees, decor, and service. Its most important theme is consumer orientation (see Chapter 3 on Total Quality Management). To market successfully, you must know your customers and their wants and needs. Markets can be divided into segments that are measurable, accessible, and substantial. The segments can be based on geographic, demographic, and psychographic variables. Out of market segments come target markets. The marketing mix of tools such as merchandising strategy, pricing, brand name, channels of distribution, personal selling, advertising, promotion, packaging, service, personal contact, and display can be used to bring target markets to your establishment. Essential in marketing is having and believing in a mission statement that proclaims what the operation is trying to accomplish. It is also important to set a goal

of what market share in your particular market you are trying to attain and maintain.

Your food must appeal to your customers, and marketing involves creating that appeal. Part of the appeal may be the image that you reflect. Your marketing and image may create a demand that might not have been there previously.

No one markets in a vacuum. Your efforts are affected by what your competitors are doing, so it is necessary to constantly evaluate them.

Advertising is defined as the purchase of space, time, or printed matter to increase sales. Advertising can be expensive and, except for well-known chains, usually must be very selective to avoid inappropriate circulation. Although not covered by the formal definition the best advertising can be satisfied patrons who tell others about you. A new type of advertising is the electronic information highway.

The importance/performance analysis (IPA) is a relatively new tool to analyze how well you are fulfilling your customers' needs.

KEY TERMS

advertising
basic marketing moves
consumer orientation
demographic segmentation
importance/performance analysis (IPA)
marketing

marketing mix
market segmentation
market share
mission statement
psychographic segmentation

REVIEW QUESTIONS

7–1 What promotional advantages do chains have over independent foodservice operations?
7–2 How does marketing differ from promotion?
7–3 Explain the marketing mix.
7–4 "Restaurants are often more restaurant oriented than customer oriented." Discuss this statement.
7–5 How does a marketing system framework adapt to both long- and short-range planning?

7–6 What is the relationship between selling and appeals?
7–7 How is image involved in hospitality marketing and promotion?
7–8 What are the functions of a restaurant sales department?
7–9 Describe a marketing systems framework.
7–10 Discuss market segmentation.
7–11 What are the criteria for market targeting?

PROBLEMS

7–1 Collect six advertisements from foodservice operations. Analyze the advertisements in terms of appeal and effectiveness. What changes might you make?

7–2 Select a foodservice operation with which you are familiar. Describe its present marketing efforts. Your description should include present target markets and appropriate aspects of the marketing mix. Prepare a consultant's report on what changes you would recommend in the marketing approach.

7–3 Surveys taken at a restaurant indicated the following mean ratings for these attributes. The performance rating was on a 1 to 5 Likert scale and must be converted. The importance rating was on a 1 to 3 scale. Plot the data on an importance/performance matrix and comment on the results.

Attribute	Performance	Importance
Choice of Menu	3.8	2.4
Items	2.6	1.5
Quality of Food	2.5	2.7
Speed of Service	4.2	1.4
Serving Breakfast	4.5	1.2
Parking	3.0	2.8

8

Forecasting

Chapter 8 discusses **forecasting**, an establishment's process of using past data to predict future business. The chapter will explain why forecasting is vital to the foodservice industry. Additionally, you will learn what foodservice managers typically forecast for, the two types of forecasting, and several methods of calculating a forecast. Finally, this chapter will outline how to evaluate a forecast's accuracy and discuss how computers are continuing to play expanding roles in the forecasting process.

After completing this chapter, you should be able to:

1. State reasons for using forecasting in the hospitality industry.
2. Name and understand what quantities a foodservice manager may forecast.
3. Be able to calculate a popularity index and understand why it is used.
4. Understand the differences between quantitative and qualitative methods of forecasting.
5. Understand and be able to use specific forecasting methods.
6. Name and utilize two methods to measure the accuracy of a forecasting method.
7. State reasons why computers are important when forecasting.

WHY FORECAST?

Think of the town where you live. In the past couple years, how many restaurants have opened only to close their doors a short time later? If your town is like most, there have probably been several. In fact, the restaurant industry has a distinctively high failure rate; within their first five years of operation, 80 to 85 percent of new restaurants go out of business. Why? Restaurants on average have very slim profit margins (approximately 3 to 5 cents out of every revenue dollar earned go to a restaurant's bottom line). Therefore, there is little room for error: costs must be tracked and minimized for an operation to succeed. Cost overruns have resulted in failures of some promising restaurant concepts, proving that cost control in an operation is imperative. In a nonprofit foodservice operation forecasting is necessary to provide the best use of resources in service to clients.

Forecasting is an integral part of cost control in a foodservice operation and should be used for several reasons. First, forecasting helps to predict how many customers a restaurant will have and which products they will purchase on any given day. With this information, food shortages and wastage may be kept to a minimum, effectively decreasing the operation's food cost. Second, staffing problems may be avoided: the forecast's estimate of sales volume will help management to schedule employees more effectively, eliminating both the excess costs of overstaffing and employee and patron dissatisfaction from understaffing. Finally, forecasting improves an operation's efficiency. While it is impossible to predict future business with total accuracy, forecasting gives management a good idea about what to expect, so that unpleasant surprises and the difficulties that invariably arise from them may be kept to a minimum.

WHAT TO FORECAST

Foodservice managers should focus on two main forecasts. Forecasting **total covers to be sold** helps determine staffing and purchasing requirements. The forecasts for **specific menu item quantities to be sold** help with ordering and pre-preparation decisions. In all cases, **historical data** is the best place from which to start a forecast. Historical data is gathered during the same meal period last year, last month, or at some other significant time. From this figure, adjustments may be made for current trends, local events, weather, and other factors over which the restaurant's management has no control.

The most essential forecast for the property is that for total covers to be sold, or the number of guests who will visit the establishment during a given period of time. This forecast can be calculated for a meal period, a day, a week, or even a month, depending on the intended uses of the information. Calculating a useful forecast of total covers to be sold requires different information for different types of operations. An institutional foodservice operation, such as a cafeteria in an office building, will usually have a relatively constant number of guests and will not be affected by external factors such as the weather. The numbers and types of guests staying in a hotel, on the other hand, considerably affect the hotel's foodservice operation(s). Conventioneers, for example, may eat some meals in convention functions rather than in hotel dining rooms. Finally, restaurants are generally the most difficult establishments for which to forecast business. Unexpected and unpredictable factors, such as the weather, can affect even the best forecasts. Time of day, local events, and actions made by competitors are also factors that must be taken into consideration.

FORECASTING THEORY

Forecasting can be done for various periods ranging from one meal to a week or more. Forecasting is helpful in ways beyond achieving immediate control. It should be part of the initial feasibility study. It is necessary for budget preparation. And it can be used to gauge incentive payments based on how well management can meet or surpass forecasted goals. For the control process in foodservice operations, managers should be able to forecast the number of patrons being served and also the number of food items to be served from any type of selective menu. Managers must also forecast for each meal if the number of clientele varies. Thus, food operators are interested in accurately forecasting how many people will be served and how much of each food item will be served or sold.

Unfortunately, many foodservice operations consider forecasting to be more of an art than a science, and the best forecasts can indeed be altered by factors beyond the operators' control.

Some operations establish forecast committees involving different staff members. A committee could include the manager (or a representative), the dining room manager, and the accountant. An advantage in this approach is that with more people involved, more expertise is present and more accurate forecasts can result. A disadvantage is the time consumed and the coordination required. Another approach is to appoint one person to prepare the forecast and to ask others to react to it.

Forecasts may be prepared and then revised as the date or meal comes closer. Thus, an operation may forecast a month in advance but review the forecast a week before, three days before, and the day before. This approach allows managers to incorporate any new information that will affect the forecast.

Forecasting for particular meals is not an exact science, but the usual approach is to forecast the total number of customers, or covers, served and then forecast the number of each menu item that will be served. The following sections suggest how to turn this art into more of a system. Figure 8.1 shows how projected and actual figures compare. Note that comments are made about certain situations that may have affected this projection.

TOTAL COVERS TO BE SERVED

Different factors must be considered in forecasting total covers served for different types of foodservice operations. A hospital can provide an accurate count of patients. Since the number who regularly eat meals is usually a rather unchanging percentage, it is easy to multiply that percentage by the census to determine the number of meals to be served. Vagaries of the weather or events happening around the area may have little effect.

A hotel's foodservice operation is considerably affected by the number of guests staying in the hotel. The type of guests is also a factor. Conventioneers, for example, may get some meals in convention functions rather than in general dining rooms. Restaurants usually have the greatest forecasting challenge. The weather can affect the best forecasts. Days of the week, local events, and actions of competition also become factors.

The daily or meal forecast is usually based on historical data that reveals how many were served during the same meal last year, last month, or at some other significant time. Then adjustments are made for special or current circumstances. A formula that is used for this follows.

> Number served at same meal period last year
> +/− Current trends
> = Adjusted forecast
> ± Manager's adjustment
> = Final forecast

STUDENT CENTER

Date	Day	Meal	Comment		Projected Count	Actual Count	Percent of Projected
01/01/9X	WED	BREAKFAST	COUNTS ARE UP		355	365	103%
01/01/9X	WED	NOON MEAL	COUNTS ARE UP		445	451	101%
01/01/9X	WED	EVENING MEAL	COUNTS ARE UP		510	505	99%
				Meals served:	1310	1321	101%
01/02/9X	THU	BREAKFAST	EARTHQUAKE		355	365	103%
01/02/9X	THU	NOON MEAL	EARTHQUAKE		445	447	100%
01/02/9X	THU	EVENING MEAL	EARTHQUAKE		510	525	103%
				Meals served:	1310	1337	102%
01/03/9X	FRI	BREAKFAST	PAYDAY		355	375	106%
01/03/9X	FRI	NOON MEAL	PAYDAY		445	455	102%
01/03/9X	FRI	EVENING MEAL	PAYDAY		510	500	98%
				Meals served:	1310	1330	102%
				Week total:	3910	3988	101%
				Menu total:	3930	3988	101%
				GRAND TOTAL:	7860	7997	102%

END OF REPORT

CNTHSRPT PURPOSE AND DESCRIPTION:
The CNTHSRPT program will compare the projected total count for each meal with the actual total count. This report is used to review the historical count levels for any specified date range.

Figure 8.1
Projected Versus Actual Figures.
(Copyright © 1985, 1987, 1989, Computrition, Inc. Reprinted by permission.)

To know the number served in the prior period, operators must keep records of past sales. It may be helpful to break total patrons down into such specialized categories as á la carte, banquet or function, and table d'hôte customers if feasible and if these considerations will affect the forecast.

Current trends incorporate general trends that have occurred since the historical meal or meal period. If patron counts are up generally about 5 percent, for example, this increase would be a current trend.

The manager's adjustment allows for such special considerations as a shopping night (or nonshopping night), a local football game, an arts festival, or any occasion affecting patron counts more than normal.

Institutions with a stable census usually do not have trouble estimating patron counts, but weather, special events, or menu item popularity can influence the number served if there is not a captive audience.

FORECASTING MENU ITEM QUANTITIES

After the total number of patrons is forecast, the next step is to forecast the quantity of each item on the menu that will be sold. This process is more important for those items that must be prepared in advance. It is less important for food-cost consequences for those items that are prepared to order or may be constantly on hand (like ice cream). With the latter items there is little fear of overproduction.

The first step is usually to determine the number of each course that will be sold (unless a table d'hôte menu is offered with all courses included in one price). Although the percentage of customers taking each course may vary for each operation, it is usually constant for one operation. Thus, an operation may find that 50 percent of its dinner customers have an appetizer, 90 percent have an entrée, and 60 percent have a dessert. If 200 customers are forecast for the meal, this would translate into 100 appetizers, 180 entrées, and 120 desserts. The next step is to determine the number of menu items in each course and the number of each that will be sold.

Assume that you plan to feature eight entrées. How many of each should you expect to sell? Answering this question requires detailed, possibly computerized record keeping that shows how much of an item sold on previous comparable days and an estimate of how it will sell in competition with the other featured entrées. Let us assume that fried chicken, pork chops, and baked ham normally are popular and each normally constitutes 40 percent of entrée item sales. If they all appeared on the menu together, they could not each continue to constitute 40 percent of the number of entrées sold. A tool sometimes used here is the **popularity index (PI)**, or the quantity of an item sold divided by the total quantity of items sold for that menu course.

$$PI = \frac{\text{Number of an item sold}}{\text{Total number of items sold of that course}}$$

Another way to calculate a popularity index is to divide the dollar sales of that item by the total dollar sales of that type of menu item.

$$PI = \frac{\text{Sales of an item in dollars}}{\text{Total sales in dollars}}$$

As we have discussed, other items served can affect the popularity index, and individual records can be kept for the different menu items. A sample for roast beef follows:

ROAST BEEF

Date	Number sold	Popularity index	Remarks
1/8	200	40%	
1/12	210	42%	Ran out
1/16	180	36%	Steak special

The sales analysis book discussed in the precost, precontrol section of Chapter 21 also provides a system for recording sales and choosing the companion menu items. With records of how an item has been selling, it becomes relatively easy for a manager to forecast how many servings will be sold at a forthcoming meal.

We have assumed there will be 200 patrons and 90 percent of these, or 180, will have an entrée item. We can now make an educated forecast using popularity indexes and past histories about how many will choose each item.

Item	
1. Roast beef	74
2. Baked fish	26
3. Steak	20
4. Chicken	42
5. Tossed salad	12
6. Pork chops	6
Total	180

In the forecast we are concerned about those items that we must prepare in advance or purchase specially and that, if not sold, can lead to a loss. If an operation has a cyclical or rotating menu, the forecasting may be easier since the relationship between the different items probably remains fairly constant and all that must be determined is the total number of customers for that course. Figure 8.2 provides a preference percentage and extends the cost.

Forecasting Methods

There are two main categories of forecasting methods: quantitative and qualitative. **Quantitative** methods of forecasting rely on historical data alone. **Qualitative** methods are those that use historical data, but also include nonnumerical factors that are not present in that data, such as current trends and local events.

Quantitative Methods in Forecasting.   Foodservice output varies widely according to hour of the day, day of the week, week of the month, and month of the year. Random factors influencing demand for foodservices are the weather, items on sale, the economy, holidays, and days before and after holidays. Service forecasting often requires forecasts of hour-by-hour and day-to-day activities as well as longer-range forecasts. In manufacturing, weekly, monthly, and yearly forecasts are more common. In services, however, very short-range forecasts must be made frequently.

Basically, forecasting techniques can be classified under four categories: judgment, counting, time series, and association or causal.

In forecasting using judgment methods, management uses experience, mental estimates of the market, guesses, and expert opinion to arrive at a forecast for demand.

A census, or counting, is a probability sample that counts a portion of the population to estimate some characteristic of the whole population. With these surveys, forecasts may be in error because customers change their minds after the survey.

Time series are quantitative models that make predictions based on the assumption that the future of a data set is related to the past. This technique looks at what has happened over a period of time and uses past data to forecast. A limitation of this technique is that new factors in the future may alter the results.

COMPUTRITION INC.

CAFETERIA

Date	Day Meal	Category	Recipe	Recipe Description	Servings				Leftover /Short	Percent of Projected	Actual Preference	Extended Cost	Cost of Over Production
					Forecast	Prepared	Actual	Next Cycle					
03/19/9X THU NOON MEAL		FRUIT	253	APPLE	260	260	260	265	-5	100%	98%	50.50	
		SOUP	283	VEGETABLE BEEF SOUP	199	200	199	190	1	100%	75%	18.98	0.10
		CRACKERS	343	SALTINE CRACKERS PACKET	260	260	190	190	70	73%	72%	3.04	1.12
		SANDWICH	451	TUNA SALAD SANDWICH	254	250	250	260	-10	100%	94%	24.48	
		DESSERT	24	BROWNIES	176	176	176	264	-88	150%	66%	16.86	
	Meal total:				260		265			100%		113.86	
	Day total:				260		265			100%		113.86	
	Week total:				260		265			100%		113.86	
	Menu total:				260		265			100%		113.86	
	GRAND TOTAL:				260		265			100%		113.86	

***** END OF REPORT *****

PREFRPT PURPOSE AND DESCRIPTION:

The PREFRPT program will compare the projected meal preferences with the actual meal preferences for a specified menu(s), date range or meal. The following information will be provided on the PREFRPT report for individual menu item, menu total, daily total, weekly total and grand total:

The date, day, & meal specified by the user.
The beginning and ending time of the specified meal.
The category, recipe description of each menu item.
The percent of projected servings.
The actual number of servings.
The time-ran-out of served Recipes.
The cost-per-serving and extended costs.

Figure 8.2
Preference Listing.
(Copyright © 1985, Computrition, Inc. Reprinted by permission.)

Association or causal methods, such as linear regression, also are mathematical models. They incorporate the variables that may influence demand. Many mathematical forecasts involve subjective input. However, many believe that forecasters should rely more on quantitative forecasts than on their own qualitative judgment.

The following are explanations of some quantitative methods of forecasting. Formulae for calculating the forecasts, as well as advantages and disadvantages of each method, will be discussed. Some statistical background is required and not all will want to employ the formulae.

Random Walk.   Random walk is the simplest method of forecasting. The idea behind random walk is essentially that what happened yesterday will happen again today. A formula for this method is

Today's Forecasted Sales = Yesterday's Actual Sales

Simplicity is random walk's greatest advantage. However, look at the Actual and Forecast columns in Table 8.1. As these calculations clearly illustrate, the numbers that the random walk method generates are far from accurate. Therefore, the only circumstance where random walk could be a useful forecasting tool would be in an establishment, such as an office building's cafeteria, where the number of customers varies little from day to day. However, it would be more beneficial in that case to use the data from the same day of the week prior as the basis of the forecast, rather than the data from the previous day. In other words, if you want to forecast for Tuesday, use the data from the previous Tuesday rather than the data from Monday.

Moving Average.   How can we improve on the random walk forecasting method? One way to make the forecast more accurate is to incorporate more data. This is the purpose of the **moving average** form of forecasting. In a two-period moving average forecast, the average of the previous two periods' business volume becomes the current period's fore-

Table 8.1
Forecast Using Random Walk

Date	Actual	Forecast	Difference	|Difference|	Difference Squared
13	156				
14	221	156	65	65	4225
15	286	221	65	65	4225
16	156	286	−130	130	16900
17	244	156	88	88	7744
18	429	244	185	185	34225
19	268	429	−161	161	25921
			SUM =	694	93240
			MABE =	115.67	
			MSE =		15540

casted volume. In a three-period moving average, the average of the previous three periods becomes the current period's forecast. The formula looks like this:

$$\text{Today's Forecast} = \frac{\text{The sum of the previous } n \text{ periods' actual sales}}{n}$$

$$n = \# \text{ of previous periods}$$

Notice that in Table 8.2 and Table 8.3 the moving average methods of forecasting indeed result in better forecasts for the same data than the forecast calculated by the random walk method. In this example, the three-period moving average resulted in a more accurate forecast; however, that finding is not absolute and results will differ for each establishment and each individual forecast. Note also that the term *period*, rather than *day*, is used; with the moving average forecast, managers have the option of using a greater range of data. For example, if a restaurant typically has an extremely busy lunch period

Table 8.2
Forecast Using Two-Period Moving Average

Date	Actual	Forecast	Difference	|Difference|	Diff^2
13	156				
14	221				
15	286	188.5	97.5	97.5	9506.25
16	156	253.5	−97.5	97.5	9506.25
17	244	221	23	23	529
18	429	200	229	229	52441
19	268	336.5	−68.5	68.5	4692.25
			SUM =	515.5	76674.75
			MABE =	103.10	
			MSE =		15334.95

Table 8.3
Forecast Using Three-Period Moving Average

Date	Actual	Forecast	Difference	Abs Diff	Diff^2
13	156				
14	221				
15	286				
16	156	221	−65	65	4225
17	244	221	23	23	529
18	429	229	200	200	40133
19	268	276	−8	8	69
			SUM =	296	44956
			MABE =	74.17	
			MSE =		11239.22

on Wednesdays, the dining room manager may opt to forecast for next Wednesday by using data from the past two Wednesdays, rather than data from the previous Monday and Tuesday. However, even in that instance, this method of forecasting does not account for unusually low or high periods of business. If used in a forecast, unusual data will skew the prediction, resulting in a grossly inaccurate, and therefore useless, prediction.

Exponential Smoothing.   A third quantitative method of forecasting is **exponential smoothing**. Exponential smoothing is the most complicated and, in some cases, the most accurate time series method of forecasting we will discuss in this chapter. To use exponential smoothing, you must first forecast using one of the methods previously explained. The reason for this is that to exponentially smooth data you must already have calculated forecasts for two preceding time periods. The first step when using exponential smoothing is to find α (alpha), the **smoothing constant**, by using the following formula:

$$\alpha_t = \frac{F_{t-1} - F_{t-2}}{A_{t-2} - F_{t-2}}$$

A = Actual Results
F = Forecasted Results
t = Present Time Period

The smoothing constant is a value, between zero and one, which will help to minimize the effects of unusually high or low values in the forecast calculation. This value may also be modified: when α has a higher value, recent data carries more weight, and less recent data has more influence when α is lower. For example, when $\alpha=0.5$, the new forecast is largely determined by data from the last three periods. When $\alpha=0.1$, the forecast places little weight on recent figures and takes many periods of historic values into account. Once the smoothing constant has been found, you can use the following formula to calculate the forecast:

$$F_t = F_{t-1} + \alpha_t (A_{t-1} - F_{t-1})$$

A = Actual Results
F = Forecasted Results
t = Present Time Period

What can you tell from the example in Table 8.4? For one thing, it is easily seen that, in this case, exponential smoothing is not the best forecasting method to use. The deviation from actual results is larger with this method than with the moving average method, proving that, while exponential smoothing uses a larger amount of data in its calculation, it is not necessarily the most exact method to use. This formula, like all others, is subject to uncertainty. Two-period, three-period, and seasonal forms of exponential smoothing also exist. However, these calculations are complicated and time-consuming and are best done using advanced statistical software on a computer. In many cases, the results of these forecasts are more accurate and, since the computer is completing the calculations, simple to determine. As the accuracy of the forecasting method increases, though, the costs associated with the process will also increase due to the length of time, amount of effort, and tools needed to complete the forecast.

Table 8.4
Forecast Using Exponential Smoothing

Date	Actual	Forecast	Difference	Abs Diff	Diff²	
13	156					SC = Smoothing Constant
14	221					
15	286	189	98	98	9506	SC = Forecast 2−Forecast 1
16	156	254	−98	98	9506	Actual 1−Forecast 1
17	244	189	56	56	3080	
18	429	226	204	204	41412	SC = 0.666667
19	268	361	−93	93	8680	
			SUM =	549	72184	
			MABE =	109.43		
			MSE =		14437.01	

Qualitative Forecasting

Regression. Regression is a form of qualitative forecasting. We mention it here but for specific calculation and application the reader is referred to a statistical text. Strangely enough, it is debatable whether it is a qualitative method at all. Regression can be used by simply employing historical values, or forecasts may be calculated by taking into account nonhistorical data as well. Earlier in the chapter, we defined qualitative forecasting as a type of forecasting that takes into account nonhistorical data such as current events and industry trends.

Why then do managers use regression analysis for forecasting purposes, if the process is so time-consuming and expensive? The main argument for regression is that this process is far more sophisticated, takes more data into consideration, and minimizes the discrepancy (or error, which will be discussed in the next section) between forecasted and actual figures.

Two advantages of regression analysis are that predictions can be made with the utmost accuracy and managers can discover whether or not a set of data is helpful in calculating the forecast. With this information, managers may eliminate tracking information that is not helpful. The greatest disadvantage to the regression model of forecasting, on the other hand, is that it is tedious and time-consuming. To get the most accurate predictions, it is often necessary to track many different pieces of information. Another drawback to regression is that it must be done using a computer, especially when using multiple factors.

Evaluating the Accuracy of Forecasting Methods

To find out which form of forecasting is best for a given situation, it is necessary to have a means by which to measure the forecast's accuracy. The two most recognized ways of evaluating a forecast are **MABE (mean absolute error)** and **MSE (mean squared error)**. To find MABE, also known as *MAD (mean absolute deviation)*, first find the differences between the forecasted values and the actual quantities, otherwise known as the **absolute**

error. Next, sum the absolute values of these differences. Finally, divide the sum by the number of periods that were added together. This number reflects the average number of covers or sales dollars the forecast was off by; therefore, the lower the MABE, the more accurate the forecasting method. Symbolically expressed, the equation for MABE looks like this:

$$MABE = \frac{\Sigma \ |e|}{n}$$

For example, refer to Table 8.1. Notice the column labeled |Difference|. The numbers in this column are the absolute values of the differences between the actual and forecasted amounts for each day. These differences are then added together and divided by 7, or the number of values added. This result, 115.67, is the MABE.

The other form of evaluating a forecasting method, MSE, is found in a slightly different manner. Like MABE, the first step is to find the absolute error. Next, you sum the squares of these differences, rather than their absolute values. Finally, divide the sum by the number of periods that were added together. If you have taken an introductory statistics class, you can think of MSE as the average variance of a forecasting method. The equation for MSE looks like this:

$$MSE = \frac{\Sigma \ e^2}{n}$$

The calculations for MSE in Table 8.1 may be found in the column labeled Difference Squared. As you can clearly see, the MSE was 15540 in this case—undeniably a substantially high number.

Why do we use two different methods of determining error? These methods are both useful but are appropriate to use in different situations. MABE is most frequently used when an increase in error results in a proportional increase in costs. For instance, if a forecast is inaccurate by 10 covers, resulting in a cost of $10.00 to the establishment, and a 20-cover error results in a $20.00 cost, then MABE is the best calculation to use. However, if a 10-cover error results in a $10.00 cost, but a 20-cover error costs the restaurant $45.00, then MSE would probably be better to use since the error is magnified and the forecasting method may be scrutinized based upon those considerations.

COMPUTERIZED FORECASTING

As discussed, many methods of forecasting for the hospitality industry are becoming more complex and computers have become helpful, and even necessary, tools for restaurants. Different types of forecasts have many dimensions which must, because of the time and labor involved, be calculated by computer. For this reason, many programs and software packages have been created to aid foodservice managers. For the less complicated time-series forecasts such as random walk and moving average, a program as user-friendly as Microsoft Excel can be a sufficient forecasting aid. While these forecasts may easily be done by hand, with the help of a computer they can be performed more quickly and with smaller margins of error. For the more complicated forecasts, such as exponential smoothing and regression, many versions of statistical software have been developed that can compute instantly and precisely what would take a person days to calculate. Many hospitality establishments have even implemented computer systems that integrate all aspects of their businesses. For example, in a restaurant, the servers' terminals are connected with the manager's office, which is in turn connected with the corporate office. Every level of management knows the current situation at any given time. This way, nothing can be hidden or missed, and when a problem arises everyone can work together to fix it. Increasingly, computers are becoming vital to the hospitality industry.

CAPACITY MANAGEMENT OF THE FOODSERVICE DELIVERY SYSTEM

Tied in with forecasting is **capacity management**, or making full use of the capacity of the operation. This goes beyond forecasting by determining during which periods more patrons can be handled or how to accommodate occasional periods when the facilities are overtaxed and more customers could be available if they could be served.

The **foodservice delivery system** is a comparatively new term and considers factors such as the following:

- types and sophistication of the menu and table service
- reservation capabilities
- parking availability and ease of use
- patron arrival tracking to serve patrons
- available production facilities
- dining space capabilities
- queuing capability
- availability and effectiveness of employees

Each can affect the number of patrons that can be handled at a specific time. Most of the factors, such as labor scheduling or production management, will be discussed in detail elsewhere in this book. Dealing with these factors may allow you to serve more patrons when desired. With a capacity management strategy, operators try to control either demand or delivery to allow a maximum use of services and facilities. Two types of general strategies can be employed for this: flexible capacity strategy and smoothing demand strategy.

Flexible Capacity Strategy

Flexible capacity strategy is designed to handle customer demands of varying volumes without increasing overhead expense to handle high volumes all the time. Tools that can be used include increased patron participation or requiring patrons to do some of the serving work. Buffets or self-service stations such as salad or dessert bars or customers dealing directly with a cashier are examples. At some fast-food operations patrons do almost all of the table serving.

Another strategy is faster patron turnover. The more rapidly you can get your patrons in and out of an operation in a given time, the more patrons you can handle. Bright lighting and hard seats are designed to increase turnover. Handheld terminals for ordering can decrease time necessary to order and dine. Eliminating entrée items with longer preparation time can help. Giving fewer tables to servers or having more busing support can be effective.

Another option is to optimize kitchen capacity, which means that the faster food is delivered from a kitchen, the more patrons can be served. A menu may be simplified for peak periods. Again, consider eliminating long preparation time or labor-intensive items. A fine-dining operation in a college town scraps its regular menu during football weekends and serves only four entrées, each prepared in advance. Be sure the menu will not overload particular kitchen stations such as broiling or deep frying, which can cause bottlenecks. Pre-preparation can be performed in slower times, or perhaps the kitchen staff can use cook-and-chill techniques to allow food items to be prepared ahead of time. It may be possible to use items prepared commercially outside of your kitchen at peak times. Management must be careful that using these techniques does not undermine the factors that attract the patrons to the operation.

Optimize employee capacity by adjusting employees to varying needs. Variable rather than standard or flat staffing (a standard staff at all times) may help. Cross-training employees to fill different jobs can be effective. Dishwashers may be trained as bus persons; after the rush they can go back to the dishwasher, though perhaps at the cost of incurring overtime, a short dish supply, or a dirty dish storing problem. Some operations increase an employee's base payroll rate if that person can supply multiple capabilities. Can automation or efficient equipment be substituted for manual labor? One operation found that more tray racks in the dining area and using movable racks to bring dirty dishes to the dish room reduced labor requirements and speeded up service. Any personnel policy that helps efficiency, such as reducing turnover or having better trained or motivated workers, is helpful.

Smoothing Demand Strategy

The second general strategy is **smoothing demand**, or encouraging patrons to come at slower periods rather than at peak times. Tools include price incentives. Offer a price break for off-peak times. Florida restaurants that cater to senior citizens do this (but they have a major traffic problem when many patrons try to arrive just before the cut-off time). Another approach is to offer a free food item such as a beverage or dessert, or have free or reduced valet parking if patrons come at slower periods.

Stress the use of reservations. If patrons call for reservations, they can be better scheduled to the facility's availability. There is, of course, danger that a patron who cannot get a desired time will not come at all, or there may be excessive no-shows. On the other hand, telling patrons they could avoid a long wait by reserving earlier or later might make a happier patron. There are also techniques such as calling to confirm reservations or educated overbooking that can compensate for no-shows.

Customer queuing involves feeding customers into an operation at a rate management desires. Few patrons like to wait in a queue, so the trick is to make the waiting as pleasant as possible by diversions or other means. Inviting patrons to wait in a lounge may placate some. Providing complimentary hors d'oeuvres or beverages may help. Some operations charge for this. Taking the patrons' orders while they are waiting provides a diversion and can speed later service. Some operations have customers fax their orders in advance so that they can be immediately available upon arrival.

Amusement parks have made a science of disguising queue lines. A restaurant does not want long lines or waiting masses of patrons in evidence. Try to disguise queues so that the problem does not appear as bad to newcomers. This can be accomplished by locating different waiting areas away from the main entrance or using lounges and other facilities. Providing diversion to queues by music, video screens, or circulating entertainers can make the queuing more enjoyable or palatable.

Running Out of an Item

Involved in forecasting quantities is the management decision of whether or not to run out of a menu item. Some operators believe that patrons should have the same menu choice a minute before closing that would have been available a minute after opening. They think it reflects poorly on the operation if menu items are crossed off or become unavailable, and they know that it causes patron dissatisfaction.

Other operators feel that maintaining a complete menu choice throughout the service period causes overproduction and subsequent waste, particularly for items prepared in advance. Planning to run out assures patrons that each day's offerings will be freshly prepared. It is also possible to incorporate prepared-to-order substitutions or to use other leftovers at the end of the service period.

Successful operators can use either approach, and the choice they make will be a factor in production forecasts.

SUMMARY

With increasing competition in the hospitality industry, it is necessary for managers to keep costs as low as possible, while still producing a quality product. By using forecasting, both food and labor costs may be controlled, enabling managers to produce a greater profit margin and ensure the success of the business.

There are two categories of forecasting: quantitative and qualitative. Quantitative methods of forecasting use only historical data. These methods cover a wide range of difficulty and effectiveness levels; overall, however, they are less effective than qualitative forms of forecasting, which take into account events that occur in the world outside the office.

KEY TERMS

capacity management
exponential smoothing
flexible capacity strategy
foodservice delivery system
historical data
MABE
moving average
MSE
popularity index

qualitative forecasting
quantitative forecasting
random walk
regression
smoothing constant
smoothing demand strategy
specific menu item quantities to be sold
switches

REVIEW QUESTIONS

8–1 Provide a format or formula to determine the total number of covers that will be served at a particular meal.

8–2 Show two ways of expressing a popularity index.

8–3 What are advantages of planning to run out of an item even though it may not be available for late customers?

8–4 Explain capacity management.

8–5 List the elements of a foodservice delivery system as applied to forecasting.

8–6 How do flexible capacity strategies and smoothing demand strategies differ?

8–7 List ways to improve customer queuing in a restaurant.

8–8 Explain four categories of forecasting techniques.

8–9 What are advantages and disadvantages of regression analysis in forecasting.

PROBLEMS

8–1 A sales history analysis for a restaurant provides the following average Saturday night sales of various menu items and selling prices:

Menu item	Amount Sold	Price
Appetizers		
Shrimp cocktail	45	$5.25
Smoked trout	25	$6.25
Salads		
Greek salad	55	$4.25
Caesar salad	65	$5.50
Entrées		
Swordfish steak	80	$11.50
Veal and shrimp	50	$14.00
Prime rib	110	$16.50
Filet mignon	70	$17.50
Lobster tail	90	$22.00

Because of a holiday, management predicts the average number of covers will be down 25 percent for the following Saturday night.

Calculate:

a. the number of Caesar salads that will be sold

b. the number of total appetizers that will be sold

c. the total sales revenue for entrée items

d. referring to c, the percentage of entrées sold and entrée dollar sales that lobster tail sales represent.

e. the gross profit if food cost is expected to be 35 percent.

8–2 Prime rib has a popularity index of 15 percent of entrée items. In terms of dollars it has a popularity index of 20. The selling price is $15.

a. If 300 entrées are expected to be sold, what would be the dollar value of prime rib sales?

b. If entrée sales are $600, how many prime rib dinners could be expected to be sold?

8–3 A restaurant forecasts 200 covers for a Friday. Two hundred twenty covers are actually served. An alpha of 0.5 is midway between recent trends and trends of a few months ago. Using exponential smoothing, make a forecast for the next Friday.

Menu Pricing and Control

Effective menu pricing strategies are extremely important to commercial foodservice operations. Too-high prices can deter customers, and too-low prices will limit the operation's profit potential. If prices are too high, the operation may lose customers to its competition. Moreover, any food-cost percentage or labor percentage will be distorted if menu pricing is inappropriate.

The overall goal of menu pricing is to maximize profits while encouraging the steady continuation of the business. Menu pricing is not a science, but the strategies and principles discussed in this chapter can help make the procedure more reliable and predictable.

After completing this chapter, you should be able to:

1. Briefly explain what a menu should accomplish for a foodservice operation.
2. List ways to reduce leftover food.
3. Briefly explain how a contribution margin influences menu pricing.
4. Explain the nine factors involved in menu pricing.
5. Name and describe the five traditional methods of listing prices on a menu.
6. Briefly discuss at least three nonquantitative approaches to menu pricing, including "perceived value to customers."
7. Describe seven quantitative menu pricing methods.
8. Explain how one might incorporate labor and energy costs in a menu pricing scheme.
9. Name and thoroughly describe two methods of measuring menu effectiveness.
10. List advantages in using cyclical menus.

In the past, many operations designed and built their facilities and then wrote a menu. Today the menu determines the type of facilities used, the number and type of personnel required, and the merchandise ordered. In short, the menu should be one of the first decisions made in a proposed food operation. It is a prime sales tool, and it is essential to sales promotion, production planning, and labor requirements.

A menu can affect an operator's cost in many ways. Purchasing, storage, preparation, payroll, food cost, service, and scheduling are all heavily dependent on it. The trend toward short-order specialty operations with standard menus is in part attributable to the desire to simplify problems caused by elaborate menus and the high costs associated with them.

THE MENU

The menu is the heart of any foodservice operation. It determines (if planning an operation) or controls (for an existing operation) such factors as layout, equipment, number of personnel, skill level of personnel, pricing, and scheduling. It is most important in marketing as it can be a sales tool to allow for market segmentation or market differentiation.

Not too long ago, menus were based on "three squares," or three regular meals a day. With today's hectic lifestyle, some individuals depend on only coffee and a bagel for breakfast. Others grab a hurried take-out lunch at work or graze by eating food throughout the day rather than at specific meals.

Methods of serving, such as salad or dessert bars or other self-service, affect a menu. The rapid pace of life, or "poverty of time," causes many to limit the time they want to spend eating or dining. The result is that the menu must offer items that can be prepared and served fast or be of a grab-and-go nature.

Another trend is more emphasis on specialty foods, especially of an ethnic nature, which also affects what a foodservice operation puts on its menu.

MENU PLANNING

Menu selection has a very definite effect on sales, ease of production, and costs. It is easy to draw up an attractive list of foods without considering the physical and personnel resources in the kitchen or the cost of the food compared to what patrons are willing to pay, but it is both foolish and costly to do so. A menu must be planned.

A menu should:

1. Depict an appetizing and appealing array of foods that diners will want to buy and consume.

2. Achieve the best use of personnel and equipment. Too often, a menu may overburden one section of the kitchen while another area remains relatively idle.

3. Incorporate the best seasonal buys. Generally when foods are at their peak of quality, they are also cheapest.

4. Offer foods that will either keep the operation within cost limits or produce the desired profit. In planning a menu, operators must take care to see that food items do not go over the budget or are not too expensive in relation to what customers are willing to pay.

MENU ROTATION

Fast-food operations usually have a standard or **static menu**, which does not change from day to day. Operations that have very transient or temporary patronage may also employ a static menu. A static menu may be changed seasonally. A static menu may be necessary when expensive menu cards with picture are employed.

Many operations use a **cyclical menu**, which rotates daily menus on a cycle such as 8 or 15 days. Some operations that use a cyclical menu prefer to have the daily menus appear on different days of the week so that Tuesday, for example, is not known as "liver and onions night." Other operations like their patrons to be accustomed to certain foods being offered on the same day of the week. This would indicate a cycle divisible by seven. Cyclical menus may also be changed seasonally.

Cyclical menus have many advantages:

1. They eliminate much of the time necessary to prepare several menus, so more time is available to analyze and plan better menus to be used in the cycle.

2. They simplify purchasing, since the menu pattern is definite for the cycle period. There is more lead time for purchasing than when the menu is made up a day or so before the food is prepared. Quantity purchasing is also facilitated.

3. They ease employee scheduling problems. Menus and workloads are known in advance and employees needed for the production of certain items can be scheduled.

4. They improve forecasting, since continuous experience over an extended period gains knowledge of the amounts of the various choices consumed.

5. They allow training or instructional periods to be arranged in advance.

6. They provide for the systematic use of leftovers.

7. They improve labor efficiency since workers become more familiar with the menu items.

Single use menus, as the name implies, are changed every day. Operations that have banquet or other catering business may try to have menus that can tie in with this business.

WRITING THE MENU

The primary goal of any food operation is to plan, prepare, and serve attractive, appropriate meals at a reasonable cost for the type of operation. In many institutional operations, the manager must also consider the nutritional needs of the patrons. Menu writing is related to cost control, consumer preference, market availability, sales promotion, kitchen layout, personnel capabilities, and food budgets or food selling prices. Although menu preparation often is done hurriedly in the midst of the kitchen activity, it is much better to prepare a menu in a quiet place with files of past records, ideas from trade publications, item sales history cards, and sales forecasts all readily accessible. Many operations that offer a new menu daily maintain standard items and à la carte selections; they actually change only a portion of their menu each day. Other operations feature specific items on different days of the week as a merchandising plan. Thus, Tuesday may be steak day and Wednesday fish day, with different customers attracted to these specific items on the designated day.

Two main pitfalls in menu writing are the temptation to include items on the basis of their appeal to the writer and the habit of listing the same selections over and over. Meatball stew may be your favorite food, but your patrons probably do not share the preference and should not be subjected to it too often. With attractive new menu items appearing constantly in publications and being advertised by food distributors, there is no reason not to try some of them on your menu. These can be a rewarding adventure in eating for your patrons and a lively challenge for your personnel. Some operators offer the same food favorites for years, feeling that they must be satisfactory if no complaints arise. Perhaps there would be more patrons—and happier ones—if the menu changed occasionally. The menu should also be modified seasonally; seasonal food should be included when it is best, cheapest, and customary.

NUMBER OF ITEMS

In the past, fine restaurant menus offered an elaborate number of courses and several choices for each course. This was possible when food and labor costs were lower. Today there is a definite trend toward limiting the number of prepared items on the menu, for both cost savings and quality control. If a large selection of items must be kept and prepared for a relatively small turnover, the quality and freshness of many of these items frequently suffer. The larger the selection, the more labor required, since more items will need separate, time-consuming preparation. Some operations are using convenience foods and pre-prepared items to expand their menu selection, and these operations can sometimes offer a greater variety with limited personnel and facilities. In planning the menu, a manager should take into careful account the time needed to prepare the items and the difficulty of this preparation.

LEFTOVER FOOD CONTROL

Overproduction always affects the profit of an operation adversely. Good managers know in advance how they can use their overproduction, but in almost every case, the reuse leaves much to be desired. Using the food in other dishes—leftover roast beef in beef pot pie, for example—takes care of the leftover roast beef but makes for expensive pot pie because of the lower selling price and the double labor involved in preparation. Serving leftovers to the staff can also be expensive. Often, leftover food is placed in containers under refrigeration, which at least removes it from sight. If it is not used promptly, however, it must be dispensed with, resulting in a complete loss and a high food cost. Overproduced items may also be run as specials at a later period. Not only does this practice often result in substandard food, it also increases the possibility of other first-run leftovers on the day the leftovers are added to the menu.

The ideal in terms of overproduction is not to have any. Some operations achieve this ideal by planning to run out of their prepared items toward the end of the meal. Other items, usually of a short-order nature that can be kept on hand, are then substituted easily. Advocates of this system feel that it serves the needs of both their operation and their customers. Without the cost of leftovers, more food and fresher food can be provided to customers. Other operators believe, however, that as part of their total service to their customers they should be able to serve substantially the same menu items just before closing that they offered at opening. To these operators, a menu with a number of items not available, even near closing time, is bad public relations. They believe leftovers are part of the cost of doing business, and they include this cost in their menu prices.

Much can be done to reduce overproduction. Accurate forecasting can help. In addition, continuous small-batch cookery not only gives better quality but allows production to match demand. Freezing prepared items provides more flexibility and greater production control. Some operations prepare many food items in advance, freeze them, and then reconstitute them according to demand. Newer techniques are better in retaining quality.

The more prepared-in-advance items on a menu, the greater the potential leftover food problem. Thus, limited menu selections help control leftovers. Limiting the amount of advance preparation and stocking more short-order or prepared-to-order items reduces overproduction. Management should have an inventory of leftovers each day to decide on their use. Some operations have a specific area in the refrigeration unit for leftovers so that the manager can readily see them. In these operations, dates are placed on the trays so the ages of the items are apparent.

CONTRIBUTION TO OVERHEAD AND PROFIT

Chapters 1 and 24 discuss the contribution margin, which affects menu pricing. Every menu price must make a contribution to profit and help meet the overhead. In fact, appropriate menu prices or combination of prices are those that maximize the menu's contribution to profit and overhead. The *contribution margin (Cm)* can be defined as the difference between the revenue a product generates and the variable costs of producing it.

$$Cm = Sp - Vc/\text{unit}$$

where Sp = selling price and Vc = variable costs (such as food and direct labor).

Contribution to profit and overhead is not simply raising the selling price in relation to variable costs. If the resulting price is too high and people do not buy it, there is little gross contribution to overhead. Even if lower prices stimulate overall sales, the lower contribution per item can cause financial difficulty. It is important to remember in menu pricing that the pricing mix must cover overhead costs and a provision for profit.

MENU PRICING FACTORS

Although menu pricing is not yet a science, some important factors must be considered when menu prices are set. There are also quantifiable and nonquantifiable approaches to accomplish menu pricing decisions. However, no single method exists to set menu prices. Thus, a foodservice operator may want to consider different approaches in deciding menu prices or different approaches for pricing different items.

Some factors involved in menu pricing include:

- elasticity of demand
- perception of value

- a consideration of competition
- relationship between menu, sales prices, and volume
- profit in dollars, not percentages
- inclusion of all costs involved
- a consideration of contribution to profit and overhead
- difficulty of uniform pricing margins
- the long-term implications of menu pricing

Elasticity of demand means that demand can fluctuate in response to such other factors as changes in pricing, food quality, or the environment. With respect to menu pricing, when managers consider elasticity of demand, they must gauge whether changes in selling prices will have a major effect on customer demand. With a captive, affluent clientele, an increase in prices might not affect consumption. But with patrons who balk at new prices, who can go elsewhere or find dining alternatives, higher prices could cause a significant decrease in sales. This can occur in restaurants with many competitors.

On the other hand, could significant new volumes of sales and a larger contribution amount be obtained if a restaurant lowered its prices, increased its portion sizes, or made other moves to increase sales? If there is no additional demand to be influenced by these moves, they would be useless.

Perception of value is what a consumer feels the meal is worth. You may offer items with low cost to you but with a relatively high selling price. Nevertheless, if customers think they are receiving a good value, there is little problem. On the other hand, if customers think menu prices are too high—even if viewed objectively, they are fair or even low—the operation has a problem. Different geographical areas or classes of society can have different perceptions of value. Sometimes it is possible to impose higher prices for prestige and price-sales appeal (just because something is expensive it appeals to some customers, regardless of its real value or quality). People may pay more simply because others know that the operation's prices are high. In this case, psychological factors become more important than objective value considerations. Adding a pickle slice and potato chips to a hamburger may enhance its value in the purchaser's eyes far more than the additional cost. Menu terminology may help. Beef barbecue can sound more impressive than "sloppy joe." A cheap extra course such as a small amount of sherbet to cleanse the palate may be seen as value enhancement. Try to be sure the value is enhanced more than the cost, and the contribution to profit and overhead are increased.

Unless you have a captive clientele or a monopoly, you must be aware of what your competition is doing. The competition does not have to be nearby or direct. Bringing a lunch from home is a type of indirect competition. In some cases, it may be necessary to drop or substitute menu items if the competition's prices are too low. Just because your competition is headed for financial trouble does not mean you must follow.

The relationship between menu prices and volume has several aspects. One is whether you are trying to make a small profit per item but selling many items or a high profit per item selling fewer items. The cost-volume-profit analysis presented in Chapter 24 explores this area more thoroughly. Elasticity of demand is also involved in how many customers you can serve. If you cannot handle more business, you have little incentive to lower menu prices.

Many operations stress percentages in their menu pricing. But as the old saying goes, "You bank dollars, not percentages." A menu item may be very profitable on a percentage basis, but because of a lower selling price, it may bring in little profit. You would rather sell a steak at $20 with a 50 percent food cost, which provides a $10 gross profit, than a chicken dinner at $12 with a 40 percent food cost, which provides only a $7.20 gross profit.

In setting their menu prices, many operations concentrate primarily on the raw food prices involved. This approach may have had more validity when raw food prices were more of a factor in total costs, but other costs are now more significant and should be considered. A focus on the contribution to profit and overhead recognizes that the selling price must provide for the item's adequate share of overhead and for a profit.

It might be nice to have a uniform pricing policy for all menu items, but this idea has never proven feasible for a number of reasons, including elasticity of demand, perception of value, competition, and relationship between menu prices and volume. Occasionally you might be able to offer an item at four times your purchase price; other times you might not be able to double your food costs in the selling price.

Finally, the long-term implications of menu pricing are important. If an operation has a reputation for high or low menu prices, it can be difficult to change that reputation in the short run. Some commercial operations create financial difficulty for themselves when they try to raise their prices. Conversely, other operations try unsuccessfully to increase volume by lowering menu prices. They have difficulty gaining acceptance because of their previous reputations.

Listing Prices on the Menu

Closely related to menu pricing is how the prices appear to customers on the menu. This presentation can affect total sales. The problem is not unique to foodservice. Automobile manufacturers often vary what they offer as standard equipment and what must be purchased as an additional extra. They concern themselves, in short, with which arrangement provides greatest sales appeal and brings in the most dollars.

Some common ways of listing prices on a menu include:

- Charge one price for all entrées.
- Offer a completely à la carte menu.
- Set prices based on the entrée.
- Price appetizers, entrées, and desserts à la carte.
- Offer the choice of a platter or a complete dinner.
- Include children's or smaller portion prices.
- Set one price for all menu items.

With the final pricing option, all dinners, including all courses, are one price. The method may be used in expensive establishments where it is sometimes listed as "prix fixe." This arrangement simplifies menu pricing, but it raises the concern that the established price will not provide an adequate gross profit for items offered that have different costs. A one-price arrangement may also be established in low-price establishments that offer few choices or for banquet or function meals.

INDUSTRY INSIGHTS   by Stephen Michaelides

Stephen Michaelides is President of Words, Ink. He is recipient of several awards for editorial excellence from the American Society of Business Press Editors. Michaelides also received the Diplomatic Award from the Educational Foundation of the National Restaurant Association. Courtesy of Restaurant Hospitality Magazine.

YIELD MANAGEMENT

How many pounds of ground meat can you squeeze into a 10-pound sack? OK. Next: how many hamburgers will a 10-pound sack of ground meat yield? Depends on how big you make the burger.

You knew that.

What you charge for the burger depends on lots of variables: the cost of the meat, the cost to produce the burger, its size, your level of service and decor, your menu mix, and the demand for burgers in your market.

You weigh all the variables, decide on a size and price for your burger, and order enough ground meat to satisfy the demand for your burger. If it's important to sell burgers, you'll do whatever it takes to sell them. If nobody buys them, you delete them. If you insist on putting them on the menu when nobody is buying them, you end up throwing away lots of meat.

Yield management. It works for food and for labor. Anything else? How about seats? Seats? Absolutely. They're as perishable as ground meat: lost forever if you can't sell them.

Airlines have practiced yield management for years. So what if they're not too successful at it? Airlines aren't successful at doing much of anything.

Airlines sell seats. Correction: they try to sell seats. Airlines prefer to fly full, so they offer all kinds of deals to do just that: weekend deals, red-eye deals, supersavers, maxisavers, enough to drive you nuts. "I have seats to sell," says the airline CEO. "The more I sell, the better off I am."

Who subsidizes the deals? Who pays a fortune to sit next to daddy with diapered kids from coast to coast? Businesspeople, that's who. They fly when they have to, not when they want to, paying through the nose to keep airlines flying.

What do airlines do to keep them happy? Frequent flyer programs. For forking over $20,000 for trips that everyone else pays $5,000 for, you get a

---

An à la Carte Menu.   Technically this means every item on the menu is prepared to order and is individually priced. Although à la carte may give the illusion of low prices for individual items, the total dinner price may be quite high when all prices are added together. This type of pricing may appeal to those who like to "pick and choose" what they want. It does, however, cause more work in pricing and totaling checks.

Entrée Prices Determine the Price of the Meal.   This method assumes that the major difference in the cost of a meal is in the choice of the entrée. All makeup items or other courses are assumed to cost about the same, so the price is determined by the choice of entree or main course.

A **table d'hôte** (literally "table of the host") meal is defined as a complete meal consisting of specific courses at a set price. This method is sometimes modified by charging more for a special appetizer, such as shrimp cocktail, or for an especially expensive dessert.

Appetizers, Entrées, and Desserts à la Carte.   This is a modification of an à la carte menu. It does not base everything completely on à la carte but gives the à la carte choice for free coach round-trip ticket to use any day of the week, except Monday through Sunday, in months without Rs, provided you don't order oysters.

Airlines love businesspeople. They give them prizes in exchange for fares that border on extortion.

Likewise, you love businesspeople. Hang the cost: they order everything from appetizers to desserts and wash down everything with pricey beverages. So passionate is your love affair with businesspeople, some of you jilt everyone else in your market.

Result? In times of economic firestorms, you get burned more than others. To wit: When the recession forced many companies to rethink their business entertaining, those of you who in happier times had banked on expense account dining to fill your coffers suffered the most. Maybe yield management techniques could have prevented the suffering.

You are a restaurateur. You don't fill your seats Monday through Thursday. You're lucky if you do half a turn those days. You'd like to do more. Remember, your seats are as perishable as your food. If you don't sell them, they're lost forever.

You know that. You've known that for years, so you've come up with ways to sell seats. Here's what you've come up with: early bird specials. That's it. OK: happy hours. Neat, eh?

Did you know you can fiddle with prices whenever you want to? For crying out loud, airlines have done it for years. Why not you? You don't do it because you think your menu prices are inviolate—etched in stone like the Ten Commandments. Thou shalt not charge less than $25 for prime rib. Thou shalt not charge less than $6 for a bloody Mary.

Every one of your menu prices is based on costs and margins. "Let's see, if I run a 28-percent food cost, I can laugh all the way to the bank." Not if you don't fill seats with customers, you can't. You tell me: is it better to sell nothing at a 28-percent food cost, or a lot of something, every once in a while—say, for the sake of argument, Monday through Thursday—at a 50-percent food cost?

Michael Hurst, this year's NRA president, owner of The 15th Street Fisheries in Ft. Lauderdale, Fla., and one of the best speakers ever, insists restaurateurs overrate the impact of costs on their sales and profits. "Want to know how to cut your labor costs to zero?" he asks. "Fire all of your employees."

Why not offer bonuses to regulars—even businesspeople, for Pete's sake—who spend fortunes on prime rib and bloody Marys, who are the backbone of your business? Why not offer frequent dining deals? Why not manipulate your menu prices according to the laws of supply and demand: high prices on weekends, discounted prices weekdays?

Why not yield management? Why not, indeed.

main items. All other makeup items such as breads and vegetables are included. There can be other modifications to the à la carte menu.

A Choice of Platter or Complete Dinner.   This method allows the patron who does not want a complete meal to order only a platter while other patrons can have the complete meal if they desire. The recent emphasis on calorie counting has made this method more popular. A variation is offering smaller entrée portion sizes at a lower price. However, since the entrée cost is only a fraction of the meal cost, this does not reduce the selling price significantly.

MENU PRICING METHODS

Setting menu prices is, as you can see, a constant problem for foodservice operators. A commercial operation wants to make the highest possible profit but still attract returning patrons. Nonprofit operations want to serve the best food that their resources permit. Unless they find subsidies, this may require a pricing strategy that covers all costs.

Two broad approaches to menu pricing are used. These are sometimes called either quantitative and nonquantitative, or rational and nonrational. Combination approaches are also possible.

Some nonquantitative approaches include intuition (what the operator "feels" is the right price) and follow-the-leader (what the leading competitor in the area charges). McDonald's, for example, often sets the local standard for hamburger prices. Competition, or what other operations are charging, is taken into consideration even though competitors themselves may not know that their prices are off. Trial-and-error is another approach: If there is money left over, it can be assumed prices are correct. This reasoning has obvious faults.

Nonquantitative approaches usually have some quantitative basis. Marketing, or psychological concepts, is involved in the nonquantitative field. Here, a primary concern is the perceived value to customers. This concept assumes that customers do not care what the cost of the product is to the operation, but only how much it appears to be worth to them. If you know the value of your product to the customer, you know how much you can charge. Fast-food operations serving deep-fried items such as French-fried potatoes often employ this idea. These items can be difficult to prepare at home and can have a higher perception of value than their actual costs. This idea can also lead to creative merchandising where such inexpensive frills as garnishes or potato chips may be thrown in to enhance perceived value. Another psychological or marketing approach is to advertise specials or loss leaders to attract customers or to develop a new market or market share.

It is obvious that some aspects involved in pricing must be nonquantitative, such as location, hours, or friendliness of the staff. These are very difficult to quantify or assign a dollar value.

QUANTITATIVE OR RATIONAL APPROACHES TO MENU PRICING

A number of quantitative, rational, or "figure" approaches to menu pricing exist as well. No one method predominates. Different operations can use different methods for different items or different methods to provide a price for the same item. The level of management sophistication can also determine the methods used. It is important to note that quantified data input—such as item sales records, standardized recipes, standardized portions, and cost history—is most important. But in the end, menu pricing is not a science, and factors other than those that can be measured come into play.

The quantitative methods we consider here include:

- the factor system
- the prime-cost system
- the actual-pricing method
- the overhead-contribution method
- the gross-profit method
- the base-price method
- the Texas Restaurant Association method (modified)

The Factor System

Also known as the multiplier, or mark-up, system, the **factor system** has been very popular, probably because it is simple to use even though it is difficult to apply uniformly to all items. The raw food cost (*Rfc*) is multiplied by a pricing factor (*Pf*) to provide a menu selling price (*Msp*), or $Rfc \times Pf = Msp$. This method considers a food-cost percentage. Multiplying raw food cost by 2 gives a 50 percent food cost, by 2.5 gives a 40 percent food cost, and by 3 gives a 33.3 percent food cost. With an *Rfc* of $4.00 and a factor of 3, a $12.00 *Msp* is determined.

The factor is determined by dividing the desired food-cost percentage into 100. If a 40 percent food cost is desired, dividing 0.40 into 100 produces a factor of 2.5.

Although simple to use, the factor system has disadvantages. It does not consider any other costs besides *Rfc,* and it disregards perception of value and the fact that customers will not pay a uniform markup on all items.

The Prime-Cost System

The prime-cost system considers not only raw food cost but also direct labor cost (*Dlc*). Direct labor cost includes only those costs that are involved in preparation; it does not include service, sanitation, or administrative labor costs. Because another cost is included, the pricing factor can be less.

This algebraic equation would be

$$\text{Prime cost } (Pc) = \text{Raw food cost } (Rfc) + \text{Direct labor cost } (Dlc)$$
$$\text{Prime cost } (Pc) \times \text{Price factor } (Pf) = \text{Menu selling price } (Msp)$$

If the *Rfc* is $4.00, the *Dlc* for the item is $1.00, and a factor of 2 is used, the *Msp* calculation would be

$$(Rfc + Dlc) \times Pf = Msp = (\$4.00 + \$1.00) \times 2 = \$10.00$$

Although the prime-cost method includes direct labor costs in its pricing, it does not consider other costs, profits, or any perception of value.

The factor is determined by dividing the total of the desired food-cost percentage and the percentage of direct labor cost. If the desired food-cost percentage is 40 percent and direct labor costs are 10 percent of sales, the factor would be 50 percent divided into 100, or 2. Direct labor costs per item are estimated.

The Actual-Pricing Method

This method includes all costs plus a desired profit to determine the menu selling price (*Msp*). Its components are

Rfc = Raw food cost in dollars

Lc = Labor cost in dollars per meal

Vc = Variable costs (other costs that vary with production), expressed as a percentage of sales

Fc = Fixed costs, such as overhead, that remain constant regardless of volume, expressed as a percentage of sales

P = Profit, expressed as a percentage of sales

Msp = Menu selling price

Vc, Fc, and P are obtained from the income statement, where the various dollar amounts are divided by the sales figure to provide the percentage. The fixed-cost percentage, for example, is found by

$$\text{Fixed cost/sales} = Fc\%$$

The formula would be

$$Rfc + Lc + [(Vc\% + Fc\% + P\%)]\, Msp = 100\%\, Msp$$

or

$$100\%\, Msp - (Vc\% + Fc\% + P\%) = X\%$$

or the total percentage for the food and labor cost portion of Msp.

$$X \text{ divided into the total of } Rfc + Lc = Msp, \text{ or}$$
$$(Rfc + Lc)/X = Msp$$

Expressed in words, this means the percentages for variable costs, fixed costs, and profit are added, and this total percentage is subtracted from 100 percent, which represents the total Msp. The resulting percentage figure (X) would give the percentage available for food and labor. Dividing the dollar food and labor cost by this percentage (or X) would give the Msp. Let us assume the following data for a meal:

$$
\begin{aligned}
Rfc &= \$4.00 \\
Lc &= \$1.75 \\
Vc &= 10\% \\
Fc &= 15\% \\
P &= 15\% \\
Rfc + Lc &+ (Vc + Fc + P)\, Msp = 100\%\, Msp \\
\$4.00 + \$1.75 &+ (10\% + 15\% + 15\%)\, Msp = 100\%\, Msp \\
\$5.75 + 0.4\, Msp &= Msp \\
\$5.75 &= 0.6\, Msp \\
\$9.58 &= Msp \text{ (rounded to } \$9.60)
\end{aligned}
$$

The actual-cost method has the advantages of including all costs and the desired profit in the menu selling price. Like other methods so far explored, it does not consider any nonquantitative factors, nor can it be used on all items.

The Overhead-Contribution Method

This is a modification of the actual-pricing method. Percentages for profit and all nonfood costs including labor are subtracted from 100 percent. Let us assume that these costs total 70 percent, leaving 30 percent for raw food cost (Rfc). The desired 30 percent food cost is divided into 100 to give a factor of 3.3. The raw food cost of a menu item or meal is multiplied by this factor to provide a menu selling price. If Rfc is $4.00 and the factor is 3.3, the selling price would be $13.20, or $4.00 × 3.3.

The Gross-Profit Method

This method assumes that it costs a certain amount to serve any meal exclusive of the food cost and that every customer would contribute a uniform amount to cover nonfood costs and profit. Assume, for example

Item	Entrée Cost (Erfc)	+	Makeup Items Cost (Muc)	+	Average gross Profit/customer (Agp/C)		Menu Selling Price (Msp)
A	$1.50	+	$1.00	+	$6.00	=	$8.50
B	$2.00	+	$1.00	+	$6.00	=	$9.00
C	$2.50	+	$1.00	+	$6.00	=	$9.50

Operations using the gross-profit method sometimes find it desirable to lower the price of more expensive items and raise the price of less expensive items since the nonfood costs of providing more or less expensive items is the same.

The system can also be used for different types of foods, such as desserts. An *Agp/C* for desserts is found by subtracting dessert food costs from dessert sales and dividing this by the number of dessert customers. To this *Acp/C* figure is added the individual dessert food cost to determine the selling price. Unfortunately, this formula does not recognize that some desserts have high labor-production costs and others do not. It would work better if all desserts were pies, ice cream, and other items that could be purchased in prepared form. The gross-profit method has the virtue of including all costs and profit (even though they are considered the same for all items) and food costs in the *Msp*.

The Base-Price Method

This method varies considerably from those already discussed in that it is primarily concerned with desired selling prices rather than with costs or profits. It takes perception of value into consideration rather than basing selling prices strictly on costs. Guest checks or some other data are used to identify the most popular menu prices or desired menu price ranges. Managers then decide what to offer for these base prices. Thus, the desired selling price determines the choice of items. Of course, items must be selected that have appropriate costs and can be sold at the desired prices. It is necessary to have percentages of sales for profit (*P*), labor cost (*Lc*), and fixed costs (*Fc*). Let us assume that $10.00 seems to be the *Msp*, or the price that many patrons are willing to pay. The desired profit is 15 percent, labor cost is 30 percent, and fixed costs are 15 percent.

$$100\% \ Msp = [(P + Lc + Fc)Msp] + Rfc$$
$$100\% \ Msp = 60\% \ Msp + Rfc$$
$$40\% \ Msp = Rfc$$
$$\$4.00 = Rfc$$

The *Rfc* ($4.00) is the amount that can be spent on raw food because $4.00 is 40 percent of the *Msp* ($10.00).

A simplified approach to the base-price method is multiplying a desired menu selling price (*Msp*) by the desired food-cost percentage. This shows the dollar amount that can be spent for raw food (*Rfc*). If a menu item selling for $10.00 is desired and a 40 percent food cost is desired, $4.00 can be spent for food. The operation must find some items for which it can purchase the food for $4.00.

The base-price method has the advantages of considering what people will pay and including all costs and profit in the *Msp*. There can be a number of different menu selling prices, but each would have to have the amount available for Rfc calculated separately. The determination of the most profitable and popular price ranges can be difficult, but most operators develop a feeling for what their customers want and what they will pay. In using the base-price method, management must be careful to include foods that have appeal to customers and not consider only the costs of the food.

The Texas Restaurant Association Method (Modified)

This method is considered by some to be the best quantitative method of menu pricing. It uses a factor, but the factor is modified for competitive pricing, low- or high-volume items, and the amount that an operation must charge to stay in business. The data necessary to use the system includes:

Oc = Percentage of sales allocated to other costs (identified as nonfood and labor costs)
Lc = Percentage of sales allocated to total labor costs
Pm = Percentage of Msp desired for profit markup (which varies for different items)
Rfc = Raw food cost in dollars

$Oc + Lc + Pm$ = the total percentage of Msp allocated to nonfood costs and profit. By subtracting the total of these percentages from 100 percent Msp, the percentage of the Msp available for Rfc is provided. The Msp selling price is calculated by dividing this percentage into the Rfc, or

$$\frac{Rfc}{100\% \ Msp \ - \ (\text{Total of nonfood cost percentages} \ + \ \text{profit percentage})} = Msp$$

In this method the percentage allocated for profit markup is important, since this will vary according to the volume of the item sold, competitive prices, or other factors the food operator believes important.

The following ranges are sometimes used:

Menu category	Profit markup range
Appetizers	20–50%
Salads	10–40%
Entrées	10–25%
Vegetables	25–50%
Beverages	10–20%
Breads	10–20%
Desserts	15–35%

Managers can change these ranges if they think the particular circumstances warrant it. They must also determine where each particular item is in the general range.

For example, let us assume that an operation serves a hamburger platter. It is fast moving, has little risk of being left over, and must be priced competitively. Therefore, a profit markup of 10 percent (the minimum entrée markup) is selected. Labor costs (Lc) for the operation are calculated to be 25 percent of sales. Other costs (Oc) are 25 percent of sales. Total costs and profit percentages are

$$Lc + Oc + Pm = 25\% + 25\% + 10\% = 60\% \ Msp$$

allowing 40 percent of the *Msp* to be available for raw food cost (*Rfc*). The raw food cost (in dollars) is divided by this percentage to provide a menu selling price (*Msp*). For example, if the *Rfc* is $4.00, the *Msp* is $10.00.

$$\frac{Rfc}{\%\ Msp\ \text{available for food}} = Msp$$

or

$$\frac{\$4.00}{40\%} = \$10.00$$
$$0.4\ Msp = \$\ 4.00$$
$$Msp = \$10.00$$

COMPUTERIZED MENU PRICING

Tables 9.1 and 9.2 are part of a computerized food management system used in menu planning. The menu writer enters the various menu items with anticipated portion counts. The system then provides portion sizes, selling prices, item costs, and resulting cost percentages and total-cost percentage. The menu writer can change figures and the system automatically recalculates the other figures. The sales figures can be by meal, day, or any other period. Total costs and profit margins are provided along with cost per customer and margin per customer.

LABOR-COST CALCULATIONS

Labor costs are as important as food costs, and managers should strive to have prices directly reflect the cost of the labor involved in producing a menu item. In general manufacturing, it is usually practical to calculate the labor necessary to produce a product, especially when employees work at a steady rate. If one worker's part of the production sequence takes 15 minutes, he or she should complete the work on four objects every hour. The kitchen, however, produces uneven periods of activity; a cook may produce many objects during meal-preparation periods but do relatively little in between. Moreover, the variety of items produced makes it difficult to allocate production time to each.

Table 9.1
Calculation of Production Labor Cost per Serving of Pot Roast with 30 Servings per Roast

Time Required[1]	Labor Classification	Cost per Hour	Cost per Roast	Cost per Portion
20 minutes	Skilled	$12.00	$ 4.00	13.3¢
40 minutes	Semiskilled	$ 9.00	$ 6.00	20.0¢
20 minutes	Unskilled	$ 6.00	$ 2.00	6.7¢
Total			$12.00	40.0¢

[1]The time required includes preparation, cooking, and slicing the roast.

Table 9.2
Preservice Cost Detail

Cafe East									Preservice Cost Detail	

| Date: Saturday, May 02, 1998 | | | Meal: Breakfast | | | | | Report Period: 5/2/98 - 5/2/98 | | |
| | | | | | | | | Customer Count: | | 225 |

Item Name	Per Portion			Qty Fcst	Totals			Cost (%)	Per Customer		
	Price	Cost	Margin		Sales	Cost	Margin		Sales	Cost	Margin
Lowfat milk (8oz pour)(b)	0.35	0.15	0.20	33	11.55	4.91	6.64	42%	0.05	0.02	0.03
Lowfat milk crtn 8oz (b)	0.35	0.17	0.18	126	44.10	21.42	22.68	49%	0.20	0.10	0.10
Apple juice (m-maid)	0.50	0.17	0.33	11	5.50	1.83	3.67	33%	0.02	0.01	0.01
Grapefruit juice (m-maid)	0.50	0.11	0.39	11	5.50	1.26	4.24	23%	0.02	0.01	0.01
Orange juice	0.50	0.12	0.38	101	50.50	12.03	38.47	24%	0.22	0.05	0.17
Tomato V-8 juice	0.50	0.16	0.34	22	11.00	3.46	7.54	31%	0.05	0.02	0.03
Coffee brewed	0.35	0.03	0.32	225	78.75	6.19	72.56	8%	0.35	0.03	0.32
Totals for: beverages					206.90	51.10	155.80	25%	0.91	0.24	0.67
White toast	0.25	0.05	0.20	27	6.75	1.25	5.50	19%	0.03	0.01	0.02
Wheat toast	0.25	0.07	0.19	11	2.75	0.72	2.03	26%	0.01	0.00	0.01
Totals for: breads					9.50	1.97	7.53	21%	0.04	0.01	0.03
Orange sections	0.50	0.35	0.15	31	15.50	11.00	4.50	71%	0.07	0.05	0.02
Totals for: desserts					15.50	11.00	4.50	71%	0.07	0.05	0.02
Scrambled eggs & bacon	1.00	0.28	0.72	90	90.00	25.20	64.80	28%	0.40	0.11	0.29
Scrambled eggs & ham	1.00	0.37	0.63	51	51.00	18.87	32.13	37%	0.23	0.08	0.15
Totals for: entrees					141.00	44.07	96.93	31%	0.63	0.19	0.44
Totals for: breakfast		225 customers			372.90	108.14	264.76	29%	1.65	0.49	1.16
Totals for: 5/2/98		225 customers			372.90	108.14	264.76	29%	1.66	0.48	1.18
Totals for: Cafe East		225 customers			372.90	108.14	264.76	29%	1.66	0.48	1.18

204

At present, the cost of raw food is probably the main determinant in setting menu prices, but a high or low labor cost for a particular item should cause some adjustment in its pricing, especially if the item requires considerable skilled labor. It would be helpful if direct labor costs could be unerringly included, but, as we have seen, they cannot be calculated reliably.

Nevertheless, some operations consider the relative labor time necessary to produce the different menu items and may use this time as a factor in pricing (and also in production scheduling). To calculate accurately, a manager should break the time required to produce a menu item into skilled, semiskilled, and unskilled labor. By multiplying the average wage of each class by the amount of time required, the manager can arrive at an approximate labor cost. Table 9.1 shows the calculation for a pot roast. Notice, however, that this cost assumes that workers will work at a steady rate all day, usually a faulty assumption since food preparation has peaks and valleys of activity. This type of calculation would give the unit labor cost used in the prime-cost method of menu pricing.

Another approach involves the number of meals served and hours required to produce them. The following format could be used: the number of labor-hours multiplied by the average hourly wage divided by the number of meals will give the average labor cost for each class of meal.

Meal	Number of labor-hours	Average hourly wage	Total labor cost	Number of meals	Labor cost per meal
Breakfast	40	$6.00	$240	480	50¢
Lunch	80	$6.00	$480	640	75¢
Dinner	60	$6.25	$376	396	95¢

This type of analysis can also be broken down into the various labor segments of food operation, such as production, service, sanitation, and administration.

Another type of labor-cost-per-meal calculation places all items into production time classifications. Let us assume that the items in one operation can be divided into those requiring 5, 10, and 15 minutes of production time. During the period, 6,000 items were served and production labor costs were $2,000. Using a base unit measurement of labor of one item produced per 5 minutes, the following analysis could be utilized:

Category	Production labor time required	Number of items served	Labor units	Production labor cost	Production labor cost per category
A	5 mins.	1,000	1,000		15.5¢
B	10 mins.	3,000	6,000		31.0¢
C	15 mins.	2,000	6,000		46.5¢
Totals		6,000	13,000	$2,000	

Producing 6,000 items with a labor cost of $2,000 required 13,000 labor units. The unit labor cost of 5 minutes was $2,000/13,000, or 15.5 cents. A 10-minute unit cost would be twice this, or 31.0 cents; a 15-minute cost would be 3 × 15.5 cents, or 46.5 cents. Categories B and C are based on the time required compared to category A. In the example, category B is 10 minutes or 2 times category A. If category B were 7.5 minutes, it would be 1.5 times category A.

All labor costs shown are approximate, but even an approximation is helpful in menu control and pricing.

ENERGY COST CALCULATIONS

With energy becoming a more significant foodservice cost, it may be desirable to consider it when pricing an individual menu item. Let us assume that a recipe for 16 portions requires 2 hours of baking in an electric oven with the energy rating of consumption 10 kilowatts (kW) per hour. The electric rate is $0.08 per kilowatt-hour (kWh).

- Energy consumption is 2 hours $\times$ 10kW, or 20kWh.
- Energy cost is 20 $\times$ 0.08, or $1.60.
- Energy cost per recipe is $1.60 for 16 portions, or 10 cents per portion.

The figure admittedly is only a guide since preheating time or the time the equipment is turned on but not actually cooking food is not included. However, it may be desirable to consider high or low energy costs for particular menu items in the menu selling price.

MEASURING MENU EFFECTIVENESS

It is difficult to measure the effectiveness of one particular menu against another of the operation's own menus. One might be more popular, whereas the other is more profitable.

Some operators find it helpful to analyze their guest checks for price ranges for main dishes this way:

$ 9–$11 range

$11–$13 range

$13–$20 range

Once managers have identified the ranges of what people are buying, they can compare those numbers with the price ranges on the menu. This can reveal if the general pricing agrees with the pattern of purchases. A similar approach is to determine what the average check should be from items on the menu and then compare this with the average check based on total guest checks divided by the number of customers.

MENU PROFITABILITY AND POPULARITY COMPARISONS

A foodservice manager always is concerned with which of the menus or potential menus, or which of the menu items, is best for the operation. A menu may be profitable but not popular, or vice versa. How does one compare one menu with another? Two tools that can be used to accomplish this comparison are menu scoring and menu engineering, which analyze the profitability and popularity of individual menu items.

Menu Scoring

Menu scoring can be used to analyze one menu of one operation against other menus of the same operation. It determines the profitability of the menu and then combines it with the popularity to provide the menu score. The higher the score, the better the menu should be for the operation. An operation can use scoring to analyze its current menus. It can be used to analyze possible menu changes by estimating sales of the new items and projecting what the new menu score will be. One can also change menu prices and forecast how menu popularity and profitability and the resulting menu score are affected. Menu scoring considers food costs only. Labor and other costs require other methods of evaluation.

After the menu score is calculated, management can determine why one score differs from another. Does one menu have too high or too low check averages? Does a menu have too high a food cost percentage? Is the popularity of a menu too low?

The popularity of a menu is measured by the proportion of customers who eat the featured items compared to the total number of customers. Scoring assumes that management would like customers to eat its featured items. If customers choose à la carte items or otherwise skip the featured items, the indications are that the featured items are not as popular as they should be. However, sometimes à la carte items are more profitable than regular menu items but may be more time-consuming to produce.

The six steps in menu scoring are:

1. Decide which menu entrées or major items are to be counted, making sure that this represents the major portion of your sales; enter in column 1.
2. Obtain the number of orders for each item being counted; enter in column 2.
3. Enter the item sales prices in the space provided in column 3.
4. Calculate the food-cost percentage (to selling price) of each item selected.
5. Find out the *total* number of meals served (entrées being scored and all other entrées) for the menu scoring period; enter this figure in the space provided in column 11.
6. Begin calculations for the menu score following instructions given at the top of each block, beginning with column 5.

The scoring of two sample menus, A and B, is shown in Figures 9.1 and 9.2.

Comparing menus A and B, we note that menu B has the higher score of 5.51 compared to menu A's score of 4.81. Analyzing further, we see that their popularity is different. Menu A is 80 percent and menu B is 84 percent. The meal check average for menu A is $10.21 and the gross profit average is $6.01. Menu B's meal check average is $10.40 and gross profit average is $6.56. The items that are different on the menus are rainbow trout and filet mignon on menu A and baked ham and lobster tail on menu B. The baked ham and trout affect the profitability and popularity in the menus about the same. The filet, although a little more popular as a high-profit item than lobster tail, was not as profitable and gave Menu B the higher score along with its higher popularity.

Menu A

1 Menu item	2 Number sold	3 Item sales price	4 Food-cost percentages	5 Total sales (2 × 3)	6 Total food cost (4 × 5)
Roast beef	85	$11.00	38.2	$ 935.00	$ 357.17
Rainbow trout	58	8.50	42.1	493.00	207.55
Filet mignon	85	12.00	50.0	1,020.00	510.00
Roast turkey	100	9.00	33.3	900.00	300.00
Totals	328			$3,348.00	$1,374.72

7	8	9
Meal check average (Total 5 ÷ Total 2) $10.21	Gross profit (Total 5 − Total 6) $1,973	Gross profit percentage (Block 8 ÷ Total 5) 58.9%

10	11	12
Gross profit average per meal (Block 7 × Block 9) $6.01	Total meals served 410	Percentage of customers eating meals counted (Total 2 ÷ Block 11) 80%

13	
Menu score (Block 10 × Block 12) <u>4.81</u>	Remarks:

Figure 9.1
Scoring of Sample Menu A

Menu Engineering

A tool used to analyze individual menu items on a menu is **menu engineering**. It assumes that two factors, the popularity of an item and its profitability, determine its desirability as a menu item. Menu engineering defines these factors as

1. **menu mix** (MM), which is concerned with consumer demand or popularity, and
2. contribution margin (CM), which is concerned with the gross profit of menu items.

Menu B

1 Menu item	2 Number sold	3 Item sales price	4 Food-cost percentages (%)	5 Total sales (2 × 3)	6 Total food cost (4 × 5)
Roast beef	120	$11.00	38.2	$1320.00	$ 504.24
Baked ham	65	8.50	36.5	552.50	201.66
Roast turkey	110	9.00	33.3	990.00	330.00
Lobster tail	45	15.00	40.0	675.00	270.00
Totals	340			$3,537.50	$1,305.90

7 Meal check average (Total 5 ÷ Total 2) $10.40	8 Gross profit (Total 5 − Total 6) $2,231.60	9 Gross profit percentage (Block 8 ÷ Total 5) 63.1%
10 Gross profit average per meal (Total 7 × Total 9) $6.56	11 Total meals served 405	12 Percentage of customers eating meals counted (Total 2 ÷ Block 11) 84%
13 Menu score (Block 10 × Block 12) 5.51	Remarks:	

Figure 9.2
Scoring of Sample Menu B

Based on these factors, menu items are divided into four classifications (Figure 9.3):

Stars—menu items that are both popular and profitable. This is the classification you like menu items to be in.

Puzzles—menu items that are profitable but not popular.

Plow horses—menu items that are popular but not overly profitable. They can generate a lot of business.

Figure 9.3
Menu Engineering Matrix

Plow Horses
  High Popularity
  Low Contribution
	Stars
	  High Popularity
	  High Contribution

Dogs
  Low Popularity
  Low Contribution
	Puzzles
	  Low Popularity
	  High Contribution

Dogs—menu items that are neither profitable nor popular. Managers should consider taking dogs off the menu.

Another system describes menu items as primes, sleepers, standards, and problems.

The menu mix assumes that an item is acceptable if it brings in 70 percent of the average sales per item. If 10 items are on the menu, the average menu sales would be 10 percent (100%/10). Seventy percent of this (or 7 percent of sales) is minimum acceptable popularity for many operations. An individual operation might want to change this figure. This 70 rate factor is also known as the **hurdle rate**.

The contribution margin for an item would be raw food cost subtracted from the unit selling price. This can be compared with the average contribution figure, which is found by dividing the total contribution figure by the total number of items sold.

In Figure 9.4, we analyze a six-entrée menu that sells 500 entrees for total sales of $6,710 and a food cost of $2,322. Subtracting the food cost from sales provides a total contribution (K) of $4,388. Dividing this by the 500 entrées sold provides an average contribution (L) of $8.78. If six entrées are sold, the average percentage of sales per entrée (M) is 16.7 percent. Multiplying this by 0.70 provides an MM category standard of 11.7 percent.

The chicken item has a CM of 8.25, which is lower than the average of 8.78. Its 130 sales (or 26 percent) are above the MM category standard of 11.7, so this entrée is rated high. A high popularity and low CM puts it in the plow horse classification. The sole has a CM of 8.10 and a percentage of sales of 10, which are both lower than standard, putting it in the dog classification. The prime rib has a higher MM and a higher CM, making it a star. Lasagna, with a $5.80 CM, is low, but 16 percent of sales is acceptable to make it a plow horse. Petit steak generates a high CM of $12 but has a low percentage of sales to become a puzzle. Veal parmesan's CM of $8.75 is just under the standard of $8.78. At 20 percent of sales, it becomes a plow horse.

Day 11/16/9X Meal *Dinner*

Menu Item	A Number Sold	B % of Sales	C Item Selling Price $	D Food Amt $	E Item CM (C − D)	F Sales (A × C)	G Total Food Cost (A × D)	H MM Category	I CM Category	J Menu Item Class
Chicken	130	26	12.50	4.25	8.25	1,625	553	High	Low	Plow Horse
Sole	50	10	14.50	6.40	8.10	725	320	Low	Low	Dog
Prime Rib	90	18	18.00	7.20	10.80	1,620	648	High	High	Star
Lasagna	80	16	8.00	2.20	5.80	640	176	High	Low	Plow Horse
Petit Steak	50	10	16.00	4.00	12.00	800	200	Low	High	Puzzle
Veal Parmesan	100	20	13.00	4.25	8.75	1,300	425	High	Low	Plow Horse
Totals	500	100%				$6,710	$2,322			

K

Total sales (F)	$6,710
− Total food cost (G)	2,322
Total contribution	$4,388

L

Total contribution	$4,388
÷ Number of covers (A)	500
Average contribution/meal	$ 8.78

M

Total percentage	100%
÷ Number of entrees	6
Average % for entree	16.7%

N

Average % for entree	16.7%
× MM Popularity standard	0.7
MM Category standard	11.7%

Figure 9.4
Menu Engineering Worksheet

In Figure 9.5, the data is graphed to better show the relative positions of the items in their categories and how close they are to being in a different category. Here, the horizontal axis is 59, which is our MM of 11.7 percent times 500 customers, and the vertical axis is at $8.78, our average CM for entrée items. We see that chicken and veal parmesan, with a little more profitability, could become stars. Could the CM be increased with a higher price (perhaps more garnish) or a lower cost (perhaps with smaller portions)? The problem here is not with popularity. Prime rib is a star, and we want to push stars in every way, including menu placement and suggestion. Perhaps it could be made a signature item. The fresh sole is a dog but close to being either a puzzle, a star, or a plow horse. Often the dog category means the item should be dropped, but this appears to be so close that management may want to include a fish entrée in every menu. The petit steak is a puzzle. It has a high CM but lacks popularity. Could it be better marketed? For this item, with its high CM, would reducing the selling price create enough additional sales to make it a star?

Figure 9.6 shows a computerized menu engineering analysis for the beef and veal items of an operation. Figure 9.7 is a graph of Figure 9.6.

Figure 9.5
Menu Engineering Graph

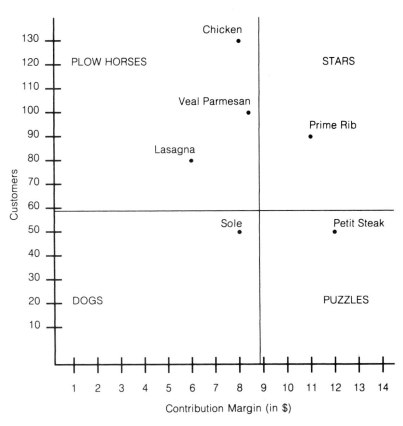

Figure 9.6
Computerized Menu Engineering Analysis. Courtesy of The CBORD Group, Inc.

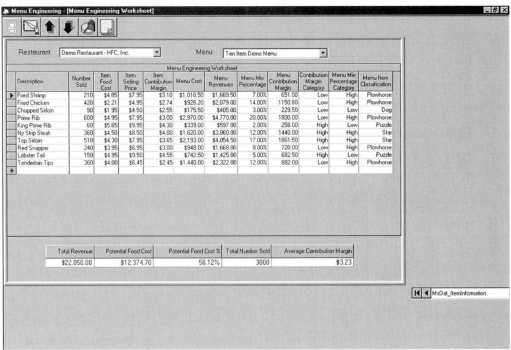

Menu Engineering - [Menu Engineering Worksheet]

Restaurant: Demo Restaurant - HFC, Inc.   Menu: Ten Item Demo Menu

Menu Engineering Worksheet

Description	Number Sold	Item Food Cost	Item Selling Price	Item Contribution Margin	Menu Cost	Menu Revenues	Menu Mix Percentage	Menu Contribution Margin	Contribution Margin Category	Menu Mix Percentage Category	Menu Item Classification
Fried Shrimp	210	$4.85	$7.95	$3.10	$1,018.50	$1,669.50	7.00%	651.00	Low	High	Plowhorse
Fried Chicken	420	$2.21	$4.95	$2.74	$928.20	$2,079.00	14.00%	1150.80	Low	High	Plowhorse
Chopped Sirloin	90	$1.95	$4.50	$2.55	$175.50	$405.00	3.00%	229.50	Low	Low	Dog
Prime Rib	600	$4.95	$7.95	$3.00	$2,970.00	$4,770.00	20.00%	1800.00	Low	High	Plowhorse
King Prime Rib	60	$5.65	$9.95	$4.30	$339.00	$597.00	2.00%	258.00	High	Low	Puzzle
Ny Strip Steak	360	$4.50	$8.50	$4.00	$1,620.00	$3,060.00	12.00%	1440.00	High	High	Star
Top Sirloin	510	$4.30	$7.95	$3.65	$2,193.00	$4,054.50	17.00%	1861.50	High	High	Star
Red Snapper	240	$3.95	$6.95	$3.00	$948.00	$1,668.00	8.00%	720.00	Low	High	Plowhorse
Lobster Tail	150	$4.95	$9.50	$4.55	$742.50	$1,425.00	5.00%	682.50	High	Low	Puzzle
Tenderloin Tips	360	$4.00	$6.45	$2.45	$1,440.00	$2,322.00	12.00%	882.00	Low	High	Plowhorse

Total Revenue	Potential Food Cost	Potential Food Cost %	Total Number Sold	Average Contribution Margin
$22,050.00	$12,374.70	56.12%	3000	$3.23

MsDat_ItemInformation

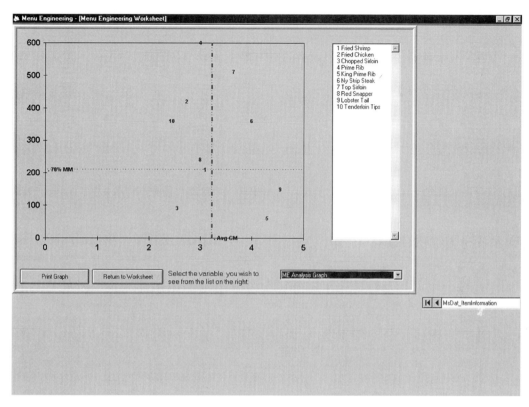

Figure 9.7
Graph of the Computerized Menu Engineering Analysis Shown in Figure 9.6. Courtesy of The CBORD Group, Inc.

SUMMARY

The menu affects almost every aspect of any food-service operation; thus, a restaurateur must decide how to list prices on the menu and, more importantly, what those prices should be. Menu pricing can involve both quantitative and nonquantitative approaches. Chief among the nonquantitative approaches are considerations of the prices charged by the competition and of customers' perceptions of food value. The quantitative (or the more "scientific") approaches include the factor system, prime-cost analysis, the actual-pricing method, the gross-profit method, the base-price method, and the Texas Restaurant Association method.

With the ever-increasing cost of labor, it becomes desirable for the menu price to incorporate food production and other labor expenses. The chapter discussed several ways to do this, in spite of the inherent difficulty for foodservice organizations to determine labor costs per menu item precisely. The chapter also discussed ways to make some allowances in the menu for energy costs.

In evaluating menus, managers should consider the relative popularity and profitability of the products the operation serves. A high-priced menu can appear to be very profitable, even as the high prices gradually work against the restaurant's long-term popularity and reputation. Menu scoring and menu engineering are two techniques restaurateurs use to determine menu item popularity and to measure the overall success of a menu.

KEY TERMS

actual-pricing method	menu scoring
à la carte	overhead-contribution method
base-price method	perception of value
cyclical menu	plow horses
dogs	prime-cost system
elasticity of demand	puzzles
factor system	stars
gross-profit method	static menu
hurdle rate	table d'hôte
menu engineering	Texas Restaurant Association method
menu mix	

REVIEW QUESTIONS

9–1 What should you try to accomplish with your menu?

9–2 Why is it important to consider contribution to overhead and profit in menu pricing?

9–3 Discuss perception of value in menu pricing.

9–4 Differentiate between à la carte and table d'hôte with advantages and disadvantages of each.

9–5 Explain the concept of the gross-profit method of menu pricing.

9–6 Explain the concept of the prime-cost system of menu pricing.

9–7 You would like to determine the direct labor and production cost of a serving of pot roast. Various employees of different skill (and salary) levels are involved. Provide a format to do this.

9–8 You would like to find your labor cost for each type of meal served. Provide a format to do this.

9–9 What is menu scoring?

9–10 Menu engineering divides menu items into plow horses, stars, dogs, and puzzles. Explain each of these categories.

PROBLEMS

9–1 *Menu Scoring Problem*

The following information was taken from three menus of the Nittany Restaurant.

a. Determine how these menus compare by means of menu scoring.

b. Analyze the reasons for the differences in scores.

Items	Number sold	Selling price	Food-cost percentages
MENU A			
Steak	90	$15.00	50%
Fried chicken	120	$ 9.50	30%
Broiled flounder	80	$12.00	33.3%
Roast beef	120	$14.00	40%
Totals	500		Total served 700

MENU B			
Pork chops	130	$10.00	40%
Broiled trout	90	$11.00	33.3%
Roast turkey	150	$11.00	30%
Roast beef	200	$14.00	40%
Totals	570		Total served 680
MENU C			
Steak	120	$15.00	50%
Roast turkey	100	$11.00	30%
Seafood Newburg	130	$14.00	40%
Roast beef	150	$14.00	40%
Totals	500		Total served 550

9–2 *Menu Engineering Worksheet*

a. Using the partial menu engineering worksheet, determine the menu engineering category for each of the menu items.

b. Show the results on a menu engineering graph.

	A	B	C	D	E	F	G	H	I	J
Menu Item	Number sold	% of sales	Item selling price $	Food cost	Item CM (C-D)	Sales (AXC)	Total food cost (AXD)	MM Category	CM Category	Menu Item Class
Liver and onions	40	8.7	9.95	2.20	7.75	398	88.00			
Mixed grill	74	16.1	14.00	5.10	8.90	1,036	377.40			
Chef's salad	35	7.6	10.00	2.00	8.00	350	70.00			
Sirloin steak	80	17.4	15.00	7.00	8.00	1,200	560.00			
Seafood platter	69	15.0	14.00	7.00	7.00	966	483.00			
Pot roast	88	19.1	12.00	3.30	8.70	1,056	290.40			
Chicken divan	74	16.1	11.00	3.00	8.00	814	222.00			
	460	100.0								

K

	Total Sales (F)	$
−	Total Food Cost (G)	
=	Total Contribution	$

L

	Total Contribution	$
÷	Number of Covers	
=	Average Contribution/Cover	$

M

	Total Percentage	
÷	Number of Entrées	
=	Average % for Entrée	

N

	Average % for Entrée	
×	MM Popularity Standard	
=	MM Category Standard	

9–3 *Menu Pricing Exercise*

The following data are presented. Calculate the menu selling price of a small steak by using:

Factor method

Prime-cost method

Actual-pricing method

Gross-profit method

Base-price method (Calculate the dollar food cost.)

Texas Restaurant Association method

Entrée cost	$2.00	Income statement	
Makeup item cost	1.00	Sales	$100,000
Direct-labor cost	0.50	Cost of goods sold	40,000
Number of patrons	15,000	Gross profit	$ 60,000
Desired food cost %	40%	Other expenses	
Prime-cost factor	2	Labor	30,000
Markup percentage	20%	Other	10,000
(Texas Restaurant only)		Fixed	10,000
Selling price	$8.00	Total other	$ 50,000
(Base-price method only)		Profit	$ 10,000

The Problem of Labor Costs

This chapter explores the familiar and general labor problems along with those that uniquely affect the foodservice industry. The chapter focuses on ways to control and reduce labor costs and to increase productivity. Some of these approaches include (1) convenience foods; (2) limited menus and efficient layout, design, and equipment in the workplace; (3) improved employee benefits; and (4) the following seven-step system for streamlining a labor force:

1. personnel policies
2. job analysis
3. work simplification
4. work production standards
5. forecasting work load
6. scheduling
7. control reports

These steps will receive even closer attention in the four chapters that follow this one.

After completing this chapter, you should be able to:

1. Explain why labor costs have become so crucial in the foodservice industry.
2. Discuss at least four labor problems characteristic of the foodservice industry.
3. List the elements typically included in a calculation of total labor cost.
4. Explain the relationship between worker productivity and labor cost.
5. Compare and contrast the typical labor costs in a kitchen and in a factory.
6. Name and discuss at least four approaches to labor-cost savings.
7. Discuss the connection between employee morale and labor productivity.
8. Outline and briefly explain the seven-step system for enhancing employee productivity as described in this chapter.

Labor cost is the most important cost in hospitality operations. At one time, food cost was generally thought to be more important, but that was back in the era of cheap and abundant labor and relaxed governmental regulation. At that time, foodservice operators could afford surplus labor if it was not very expensive. But that period has passed, and if management is to generate a profit for commercial operations or provide the best services its resources permit for institutions, it must now work hard to control labor costs.

Perhaps ironically, controlling labor costs can be good for the employees. If the main control is to pay as little as possible (often the minimum wage in foodservice operations), employees receive compensation that may be difficult to exist on. But if management can make employees more productive and lower labor costs as a percentage of sales, more money becomes available to employees. The foodservice industry is labor intensive and has some peculiar labor problems. Not the least of these is the fact that other industries usually compensate their employees more generously, leaving the less competent workers for foodservice. Also, foodservice work often is only temporary or part-time work that employees hold while seeking better opportunities in other fields.

For a long time, many foodservice operators and managers believed that little could be done about high labor costs other than to raise menu prices to compensate for them. Food operations needed a certain number of people to staff the different positions, and the fluctuations from high peaks to low valleys of activity resulted in inefficient use of labor. However, the cost-price squeeze and the difficulty in passing high labor costs on to consumers forced the industry to search for ways to lower labor costs, increase employee productivity, and provide a satisfactory wage that attracts and retains competent employees.

The public often fails to appreciate the cost of the labor in the foodservice industry and compares it to the household, where the homemaker receives no wages. With the public associating a restaurant with the home dining room and the family food budget, it becomes difficult to convey the fact that the cost of wages must be included in the menu price. Still, with the current low percentage of profit in foodservice operations, there is little room for abnormal labor costs.

UNIQUE FOODSERVICE LABOR-COST PROBLEMS

The foodservice industry presents a number of unique labor-cost problems. As previously mentioned, the low compensation typical of the industry does not tend to attract the most competent workers. The lower wages also attract many teenagers, who tend to be less reliable than older workers. Fast-food operations, in particular, employ many teenagers; one survey found that fully a quarter of all foodservice employees are teenagers. But current demographics suggest that this age group will become less of the population. It has even been predicted that partly because of our dwindling teenage population, the foodservice industry will experience a serious shortfall of up to 1 million workers in the near future. The number of entry-level teenage employees shrank by 11 percent between 1986 and 1990. Some economic forecasters suggest that the elderly and the handicapped may help take up this employment slack. In addition, foodservice employee-hours may be long and odd, and the peaks of activity complicate scheduling and productivity. The hours of operation do not lend themselves to all having a 9 to 5 job or a Monday through Friday work week.

Finally, foodservice is unique in that some employees are partially paid by customers in the form of tips rather than by management.

Although foodservice operations are labor intensive, the relatively small size of most, the limited profit of many, and the other demands on management can limit what many operations can do to use their personnel more effectively, even though this is vital to their success.

PAYROLL DETERMINANTS

Payroll is the result of two factors: the time required, both indirectly and directly, for performing the job and the rate of pay for doing the job. If either factor is too high, the payroll cost will be excessive. If someone takes four hours to do a job that can be done in two, or if he or she is paid $14.00 an hour instead of $7.00 (the amount that should be paid for that type of work), the labor cost in each case will be twice what it should be. In the foodservice industry, the problem is usually one of either decreasing the time requirement or raising productivity, rather than paying excessive wages. An unduly high wage cost results, however, when highly skilled people consistently do the work that lower-paid workers could perform. A chef should not spend time pre-preparing vegetables unless no other gainful work is available. A highly trained waiter or waitress should not normally have to bus dishes, a job that a bus person with little training can do, probably with less effort.

ACTUAL LABOR COSTS

Many foodservice operations are not aware of their true hourly wage costs. Fringe benefits and other indirect costs can easily be 50 percent and often more of the base hourly wage. (One school district that provided full benefits to foodservice employees who worked about five hours a day during the school year actually paid out considerably more in benefits than in base wages.) Table 10.1 shows a worker at the $5.15 minimum wage had benefits of $2.27, not including overtime, local taxes, uniforms, and other frequently incurred costs. If employee is only actually doing productive work 50 percent of the time he or she is working, which is not unusual for foodservice workers, the actual hourly cost for productive time is $14.74, or nearly three times the base wage.

PRODUCTIVITY

Probably the most important element in labor-cost control is employee productivity. High productivity can provide both a high wage rate and higher profits. The foodservice industry has generally lagged behind other industries when it comes to improving productivity. In many instances, workers use the same methods and the same type of equipment to produce the same amounts as they did years ago. Traditionally, productivity increases have been less in foodservice than in manufacturing or many other industries. If the foodservice industry is to prosper, offer its patrons better service, and provide adequately for its employees, it must increase its productivity with the application of new and creative methods, and this increased productivity must be reflected in fewer work hours or increased production. The study of productivity is complicated. For our purposes, the basics of productivity are the people doing the work, the equipment they use, and their work methods. If the workers are enthusiastic

Table 10.1
Actual Costs of Employees to Employers

	Base Pay Rate	$5.15/hr	$7.50/hr	$10.00/hr
Other Employer Costs				
Vacation (two weeks paid)		.20	.30	.40
Social security		.37	.56	.74
Workers compensation		.10	.15	.20
Unemployment compensation		.08	.12	.14
Sick pay (three days paid)		.06	.09	.12
Holiday pay (seven days)		.10	.15	.20
Medical/other insurance (average $20/week)		.50	.50	.50
Breaks (1/2 hour)		.36	.54	.72
Meals (two at $4.00 each)		.50	.50	.50
Other (employer paid)		—	—	—
Other (employer paid)		—	—	—
Other (employer paid)		—	—	—
Subtotal (other costs per hour)		2.27	2.91	3.52
Total hourly cost		7.42	10.41	13.52
If 100% productive		7.42	10.41	13.52
If 50% productive		14.84	20.82	27.04

and devoted, if mechanization has relieved as much hand labor as possible, and if the most efficient work methods are used, productivity should be high. Total Quality Management, discussed in Chapter 3, has also led to high productivity increases.

Many factors affect productivity, and some are inherent in foodservice. We have mentioned the peaks and valleys of production, the many small enterprises, the many items to be produced, the daily menu changes, and the typically inexperienced workforce. A foodservice operation sells more than just food; it also sells service, decor, and ambience. There are some inherent conflicts in providing the best service and obtaining the highest productivity, and the best decor or ambience may not be conducive to productivity. Still, the industry can do much to increase its productivity. A major influence regarding productivity has been fast-food operations, some of which can serve 100 patrons with 10.5 hours of labor input compared to 72.3 hours of labor input for full-service establishments. Fast food has achieved this productivity with specialized and simplified menus, specialized and automated equipment, dependence on more self-service, use of pre-prepared food (often distributed by central commissaries), and simplified work processes. Not all foodservice operations can use all these approaches, but some of them can be effective for some operations, and all operations can consider ways to make their labor more productive.

KITCHEN VERSUS FACTORY

A commercial kitchen has been compared to a factory, since it produces goods for quantity consumption. If industrial factories have been able to increase their production efficiency, should not those kitchens that use the same methods and theories show the same gains?

Figure 10.1
Typical Factory Production
Compared to a Foodservice
Operation

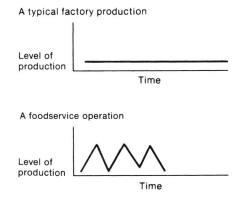

A typical factory production

Level of
production

Time

A foodservice operation

Level of
production

Time

Unfortunately, kitchens and factories have several inherent differences. A factory usually has long production runs of uniform items. A kitchen prepares many different items, often in small amounts and with frequent variations. If it cannot sell its goods immediately, a factory can produce for inventory. Food generally must be sold when produced and, unless it is frozen, cannot be held for long periods. Nor is it in the nature of the foodservice business to sell its excess production by offering lower prices or running sales to move unsold items. With food, there is an almost immediate obsolescence. Instead of producing at a constant steady rate, the kitchen must be ready to serve peak loads at meal times. At certain times of the day there is relatively little activity in the kitchen, and its personnel and facilities are not fully used, as Figure 10.1 illustrates.

The foodservice operation experiences production peaks and valleys, but the typical factory can have long production runs of few items. The kitchen, of course, has short runs of many different items.

Approximately 500,000 operations provide food in the United States. The variety and differences in these many operations preclude standardization of output or quality. In such a situation, a major problem in combating low productivity is trying to determine what a fair output would be per worker. By its nature, a service industry requires a great deal of personnel time and effort. Obviously, it is also much easier to regulate a machine that will control production volume—a common practice in general industry—than it is to deal with individual employee speeds and temperaments. Employees too often set the standards, and **Parkinson's law**, which states that workers adjust their pace to the work available, may apply. If there is less work, they work at a slower pace.

COST-SOLVING APPROACHES

The fast-food business has provided a new way of looking at the food business and new labor-cost-saving and productivity approaches that may be adopted by others. One is a food system using pre-prepared convenience foods produced under factory conditions for inventory, regardless of the immediate consumption requirements. A normal restaurant operation that offers a wide choice of items produces comparatively few foods in quantity, which discourages this specialization. But the food could come from an operation's own commissaries or from outside vendors that employ longer production runs of individual items. Cook/chill systems (or sous vide), where foods are prepared in advance to a just-done state and stored up to 45 days, are becoming more popular. This is sometimes referred to as cooking to inventory. Another approach is to serve a limited menu. Specialty (limited-menu) operations have become popular; they appeal to customers who prefer the specialty foods and help an operator reduce labor requirements and costs. Even those operators who pride themselves on preparing their own foods and who like to serve a variety increasingly are turning to convenience foods and gradually are beginning to limit their menu offerings. Menus containing an excessive number of items create higher food and labor costs and also make it difficult to maintain the quality of each of the many items.

Providing less service can also reduce labor usage. Self-service salad bars and buffets and self-busing are examples of this option.

The labor already present can be used more efficiently. For example, using bus persons to carry trays can make servers both more efficient and more attentive since they need not leave the serving area.

Physical factors involved in productivity include layout, equipment, and working conditions. Too often, production-facility planning takes second place to merchandising considerations in the planning of commercial operations. Too often, especially in institutional foodservice operations, supply companies install superfluous equipment that actually impedes efficiency. Layouts are often unnecessarily large, requiring miles of extra walking and extra employees as well. Or they may be too small, crowded, confused, or downright tense with employees bumping into each other. Frequently, operators plan their kitchens without first considering the expected menu, types of service, periods of service, and most efficient labor use. The menu is most important—the pivotal point of the whole operation. From it the type of service, period of service, and quality of labor are determined, along with the equipment and other facilities.

New, more efficient equipment is now available. Point-of-sale registers and terminals can move orders directly into the kitchen, and handheld computers can do this in the dining area. Microwave ranges can be helpful where only a few items are required. Computer-controlled or automatic equipment also can reduce manual effort.

Developments in food processing and preservation will almost certainly be helpful. By reducing spoilage, handling, and refrigeration concerns, production facilities can be smaller and more efficient.

Employees may be cross-trained to do several jobs. A dish worker could, when necessary, act as a bus person or a wait person or do some kitchen work. This can keep employees busy in one section when another section where they work has slow activity. Cross-trained employees may receive a somewhat higher wage. Cross-training can make scheduling and substitution easier.

EMPLOYEE MORALE

The most vital asset of any foodservice organization is its employees, and their psychological needs can be vital to productivity. Unfortunately, employees too often are treated as commodities, like the food they prepare and serve. Too little thought is given to incentives that encourage workers to produce more and feel good about their work. Attendance is often taken for granted. Employees are criticized if attendance is poor, but go unrewarded for faithfulness. To increase morale and cut absenteeism, some hospitality employers now give bonuses for good attendance. These bonuses may come in the form of additional money or extra wages paid out for unused sick time. Since employees often feel that sick time is something they have coming to them, they tend to take advantage of it whether or not they are actually ill. If they are not really sick, most workers prefer the extra money. Moreover, their continued presence on the job causes less confusion, and production remains at a higher level.

The foodservice industry is notorious for its lack of incentive or profit-sharing plans, which are readily adaptable even in nonprofit organizations. Certainly, there should be some reward for exemplary service, and people tend to exert themselves more when they share directly in the endeavor. Motivation can take psychological, rather than purely financial, forms. Many operations develop a feeling of cooperation and esprit de corps while actually paying employees less than competing organizations. They create this feeling by making sure that employees realize someone is interested in them and they are vital to the operation. Fairness is all-important: Employees regard inequality and partiality within the organization as more demoralizing than differences in material benefits among organizations.

Some external factors may help productivity. As more people eat out more often, some operations can achieve larger volumes, which are inherently more productive. The tendency to eat three meals a day has, in part, given way to a tendency to eating more snacks, also called **grazing**. Spreading consumption more evenly through a day theoretically could help productivity, even if longer hours are required.

MANAGEMENT AND PRODUCTIVITY

The quality of management has an important influence on employee productivity. Management functions of screening, hiring, orienting, training, and supervising all affect productivity. Too often, management hires the first person available and immediately throws him or her at the job. This practice usually results in poor productivity and high turnover rates. Management often fails to plan the production activities of its employees in advance and merely instructs someone to do something as the need arises. With the constantly changing variety of items produced, foodservice operations require a high degree of supervision. Industry finds that one supervisor for 10 employees is often a desirable ratio, but in foodservice, the ratio often is one to 30. Another problem is that foodservice operations may employ many part-time employees. More people may be required than their full-time equivalents (FTEs), which adds to the complexity.

Often, managers find themselves overwhelmed. They must spend long hours at the job and do not have the time to analyze its labor costs adequately to identify areas for improvements. The concentrating of food operations into chains has led to increased competency in management.

A SYSTEM FOR EMPLOYEE CONTROL AND PRODUCTIVITY

Unfortunately, in foodservice and hospitality, the most efficient use of employees often proves to be a matter of pure chance. Most employees are hired and assigned to jobs where management hopes they will produce. Operators give little thought to the broader

INDUSTRY INSIGHTS   by Don Smith

Don Smith is one of the hospitality industry's most desired speakers; he captivates audiences all over the world. He has consulted for many of America's most successful hospitality chains. He is a professor for the University of Houston.

LEADERSHIP

What is this quality called *leadership?* I would have liked to address the subject within the realm of the business of hospitality although I use athletics as a metaphor. It is the capacity to get ordinary people to work together to accomplish extraordinary results.

What are the components of leadership? I suggest four:

1. The number of championship seasons produced, wins vs. losses. Professionals are paid to get results. However, results in themselves do not a leader make.
2. The number of disciples that follow in the wake of their coach to become leaders themselves.
3. The tendency to show up in difficult times. As Bear Bryant said, "I never inherited a warm bed."
4. A legacy. Leaders leave their worlds (whatever the size) changed because they were there. They made a difference. This is often both technical and systemic. They have the drive to achieve mastery of their fields.

How do you know leadership when you see it? Results! Not by appearance, sound, or sight because the research shows that leaders take on many styles.

Examples are Kroc, Harman (KFC), Schuler, and Brinker, to mention only a few.

How much of leadership is genetic and how much environmental? Genetics does play a small part, I am sure, in one's energy and raw intelligence, for example. However, these birth-given gifts will not hold leaders back. Their lack of drive will. Most of leadership, like one's constant need to create an altered and improved state, self-awareness (read *emotional intelligence*), and empathy, optimism (a positive expectation of outcomes), persistence, and mastery are all learned. Most of the character traits, values, and beliefs are learned very early in life (before eight years).

Can leadership be taught? No, but it can be learned. Learning begins in the home in most cases. Certainly, some mentor shows up to shape the individual's self-esteem. Learners trust, respect, and ultimately love this mentor so much that their core values and beliefs are reinforced, changed, and acted upon for the rest of their life. I call these mentors "coaches." I think lucky people will have met three of them in their lives.

How is it learned? First, leadership is a state of continuing development. It is not a place or a course to conquer. Thus, leadership is a journey, not a destination. (Thank you, Herman.) In other words, most people begin their journey in leadership as followers, move into small positions of responsibility of achieving outcomes through others, and develop from there. Perhaps, one day, they become super leaders. In any case leadership learning begins like that old game, Follow the Leader.

What skills should be included in leadership development? This is a subject for great discussion, but I would list communication skills first.

overall picture of productivity and efficiency. This lack of concern has caused two of the major problems facing the industry today: low productivity and comparatively low wages. In an attempt to relieve these interrelated problems and offset increasing labor costs, managers and experts have been trying to devise systems that will help motivate employees and increase their productivity. A number of these systems, called *personnel staff control, staff planning, manpower scheduling and development,* or *professional staff planning,* have come into being, each with the same goal: getting the greatest production from employees, not by imposing undue demands on them (the work itself may even become easier) but by better work organization, better planning of jobs, tighter scheduling of employees, and more thorough reviews of employee productivity.

These systems could create short-term labor-cost reductions that might then be sustained. They should also maintain or improve the quality of service or product within the operation. The latter is crucial. Anyone can cut costs by reducing the number of employees; the trick is to not reduce the quality of service. Some chains have rigid quality standards and inspections with ratings given in areas such as cleanliness and sanitation, length of time food is held, and length of time until the patron is served. Management bonuses or incentive pay may be based on these criteria.

A system or method for employee control and productivity might employ the following seven steps:

1. personnel policies
2. job analysis
3. work simplification
4. work production standards
5. forecasting work load
6. scheduling
7. control reports

To be most effective, the system must be reinforced by strong supervision with good personnel administrative policies, up-to-date management policies, and modern techniques. The productivity of employees depends partly on such personnel practices as recruiting, hiring, orienting, training, supervising, and evaluating, together with the operation's compensation and termination policies. Management affects productivity with its kitchen layout, the equipment it provides, the type of foodservice it runs, the standards it expects, its scheduling, and its interest in and concern for its employees.

A job analysis usually contributes to the development of a job description and a job specification. The **job specification** lists the qualifications necessary to hold the job, such as the educational, physical, mental, and age requirements. The **job description** lists the tasks and duties that are performed in the job. It is extremely helpful in training and orienting new employees. The **job analysis** is very important for the control system. Management must take the entire work load, determine which divisions should do which jobs and how much each position should be expected to accomplish. A job analysis eliminates questions of who does what and permits less chance of someone being overworked or underworked in relation to others. Job descriptions are discussed further in Chapter 13.

Work simplification involves studying and analyzing a job to find the easiest and most productive way to perform it. It might involve changes in the layout, introduction of labor-saving equipment, introduction of preprocessed food, or changes in other methods currently being followed. Determining whether the employees are producing a maximum output commensurate with their labor input and whether an easier way of performing the work may be available is part of work simplification.

Work production standards provide a gauge that measures what to expect from an employee or position. These standards can be measured either in dollars of sales per day per employee or position or in units or covers produced or served each day (or hour) per employee. The workload forecast is based on an estimate of the sales expected each day. Management calculates the number and the kinds of meals that it expects to sell. Dividing the forecasted volume of sales by work production standards (or the normal workload per each type of employee) should provide a basis for determining the number of each type of employee the operation requires.

In institutional foodservice operations that have a definite census, the forecasting of volume is easy. In commercial operations where volume may fluctuate considerably, the problem is much more difficult. For commercial operations, an individual or a committee may be assigned the task of forecasting sales for subsequent days or meals. In addition to its importance for determining personnel requirements, the forecasting of activity is necessary for food purchasing and production planning.

Too often, scheduling is done routinely and without change. The same number of employees report in and leave at the same time every day. Some food service authorities suggest that up to one-third of all labor time may be either wasted or severely limited by poor scheduling alone. Foodservice scheduling is complicated by the fact that meals are usually served during three peak periods during the day, and that production and service must be geared for these three periods rather than for steady production throughout the day. In our model control system, the volume in covers was forecast, and the number of employees required was determined by work production standards. Scheduling ensures that the proper number of employees will actually be on hand for the volume of work required at the times needed.

Control reports are definitely the responsibility of management. The system will not succeed unless management checks its results carefully. The control reports indicate how accurate the forecasting has been and whether the operation had been over- or understaffed for the level of activity. These reports must be current, and management must take action on them immediately for optimum effectiveness.

SUMMARY

An efficient system provides for the proper use of employees, for analyzing jobs to determine who should do what, for eliminating overlapping responsibilities, and for covering all necessary tasks. The jobs are then analyzed to find the easiest and most efficient ways of performing them. There is no one best way to perform any job, but there is always a better way, and management must always be looking for that better way. Production standards or goals must be established to provide a basis for determining a fair day's work. The volume of activity and consequent workloads are then forecast. By knowing the production expected from each job position and the total amount of work expected, the number of people necessary for each job can be determined. Knowing whether a position is fixed (with some employee time required regardless of volume) or variable (where employee times vary with volume) is critical. Once the number of employees required for the different times is determined, it becomes necessary to schedule them for those times. This may involve changing regular hours. By means of control reports, management can constantly review the system and the results reported. It must make sure there is no excess labor to increase labor costs or, conversely, too little labor, which would result in poor service and perhaps increases in other costs.

The system is simple and logical. When operating properly, it can provide an alternative to random and potentially wasteful personnel practices. The system can definitely increase productivity, lower labor costs, and help boost employee satisfaction and morale.

KEY TERMS

grazing   Parkinson's law
job analysis   work production standards
job description   work simplification
job specification

REVIEW QUESTIONS

10–1 How can labor-cost control benefit   10–6 Explain Parkinson's law.
       foodservice workers?   10–7 Explain four approaches suggested to reduce
10–2 List four unique labor-cost problems for the   or help control labor cost.
       foodservice industry.   10–8 List the seven steps suggested for employee
10–3 What determines payroll cost?   control and productivity.
10–4 List the three basics of productivity as   10–9 Explain the two parts of job analysis.
       presented in the text.
10–5 What are five factors that cause lower labor
       productivity in foodservice?

PROJECT

10–1 Contact a local foodservice organization.   categories shown in Table 10.1 and any other
       Determine the actual hourly labor cost for a   direct or indirect labor cost.
       specific employee using local figures for the

11

Analyzing Labor Costs

The cost of labor is a major consideration in foodservice operations, and progressive operators must know how to analyze and control this cost if they expect to maintain the profit margins they desire. Nonprofit operations such as hospitals and schools must also analyze their labor costs so that they can convert any savings into the best possible foodservice for their patrons.

After completing this chapter, you should be able to:

1. Explain the two major functions of labor-cost analysis, and explain why labor costs can be particularly difficult to determine in a foodservice operation.
2. List the three classes of foodservice employees.
3. Calculate labor cost as a percentage of sales.
4. Arrange a foodservice's labor costs into appropriate categories.
5. Explain the expression *work production standards* and discuss how you might determine these standards for a foodservice worker.
6. Perform a typical payroll analysis.
7. Demonstrate how to apply bar charts in labor analysis.
8. Explain how computer technology can be used.

Labor-cost analysis has two major functions: (1) to determine whether labor costs are excessive or insufficient and (2) to identify where these inadequacies occur. A number of tools can help managers analyze labor costs, including ratios such as labor-cost percentages and work production standards such as dollar sales per labor input, covers served per labor input, or meals per labor-hour. Bar charts are helpful in analyzing personnel scheduling.

Once managers determine that labor costs are excessive, the problem is to find out why. High labor costs can be caused by factors such as poor scheduling and resulting idle time, inefficient employees, excessive overtime, high turnover, and high absenteeism.

A difficulty in analyzing labor costs is that discrepancies in different parts of the operation can balance each other out. Labor costs may be too high in preparation and too low in the service area, so that the overall figures look good. Thus, it is necessary to examine the various labor components of a foodservice operation separately. Discrepancies over time can also balance each other out. An operation can be in trouble if ratios or percentages are "too good" since that may indicate that the level of service is too casual, which may cause a long-term loss of patronage.

Another problem can arise in the difficulty of measuring service quality. Industries can establish exact, measurable quality standards and reject those products that are not up to the standards. In foodservice, one server may not be able to serve as many patrons as another, but might radiate more pleasantness and be much more appreciated by patrons. Thus, an optimum level of service quality can resist productivity measurements.

In analyzing employee labor costs, an operator should keep in mind that different classes of employees are affected differently by changes in sales volume. These classes are sometimes labeled *fixed, semivariable,* and *variable.* A **fixed employee** is someone necessary to the operation regardless of the volume of business. Whether business is heavy or light, the operation will still need a manager's secretary, a cashier, or a porter, for example. The only way to produce a lower unit-labor cost on these fixed positions is to increase the sales volume or add tasks to the employees' usual work. Dishwashers might be considered **semivariable employees**, since there is usually a significant change in volume before fewer or additional dishwashers are required.

Servers and preparation personnel are **variable employees** in most operations. Their numbers fluctuate according to changes in sales volume. Some operators have chosen to turn these variable employees into fixed employees by keeping a constant number of servers on duty regardless of the forecasted volume. This practice may help explain why up to a third of all labor time in the foodservice industry is wasted.

LABOR COST AS A PERCENTAGE OF SALES

The first labor-cost analysis simply compared the amount paid for labor with sales dollar volume. This approach led to the calculation of labor cost as a percentage of sales, a simple and frequently used approach. The statement that labor costs are 30 percent of sales refers to the total cost of labor as 30 percent of the sales dollar volume. If sales were $100,000, labor costs would then be $30,000, or 30 percent.

$$\frac{\text{Cost of Labor (\$30,000)} \times 100}{\text{Sales (\$100,000)}} = \text{Labor-cost percentage (30\%)}$$

Calculating labor cost simply as a percentage of sales may be common and helpful, but it is limited in scope. If the percentage is calculated over a particular period, such as a week or a month, daily discrepancies often balance. During this period the labor cost might have been too high at certain times and too low at other times, but the overall percentage for the period might be acceptable. A single overall percentage, without a careful breakdown, makes it difficult to pinpoint profit drains.

A change in menu pricing will also change the labor-cost percentage. If menu prices increased 10 percent on the $100,000 volume, and if the number of covers served remained the same, a new volume of $110,000 would result. If the labor cost remained at $30,000, the new labor percentage would be 27.3 percent instead of 30 percent. This new figure would seem to indicate an improvement in labor productivity, when productivity and efficiency actually remained the same. Conversely, when employees receive wage increases and dollar volume is constant, the labor-cost percentage rises even though the efficiency and productivity may remain the same. Operations such as hospitals, institutions, and American-plan hotels, which serve food without receiving payment for it directly, often assign an arbitrary dollar value for food sales. The resulting percentage is only as accurate as the arbitrary value.

A labor-cost percentage may also be distorted by sick or vacation relief. When extra help is needed, the labor-cost percentage goes up. This does not necessarily indicate a labor-cost problem, only that previous labor costs had been understated.

It is difficult to compare the labor percentages of apparently similar operations accurately. The labor cost of an operation depends on such factors as the menu (that is, choice of food and its selling price), amount of convenience food used, layout, equipment, labor market in the area, and services provided. Seemingly similar operations may produce different labor-cost percentages.

To refine and increase the usefulness of a labor-cost percentage, many operations calculate percentages for different labor categories. These categories usually include administration and general labor costs, preparation labor costs, dining room service labor costs, and sanitation (including dishwashing) labor costs. The labor cost for each of these groupings may be calculated as a percentage of sales or as a percentage of the total labor cost. If total sales were $100,000, total labor costs $30,000, and preparation labor costs $12,000, then preparation costs would be 12 percent of total sales and 40 percent of total labor costs.

$$12,000/100,000 = 12\% \text{ of sales}$$
$$12,000/30,000 = 40\% \text{ of total labor costs}$$

With sanitation labor costs at $3,000, service labor costs at $9,000, and supervision at $6,000, percentages of category labor cost to total labor cost are

Preparation	$12,000	40%
Sanitation	3,000	10%
Service	9,000	30%
Supervision	6,000	20%
Total labor cost	$30,000	100%

It is possible to break the groupings down even more. If desired, one could obtain the labor-cost percentage for customer service separately for servers, bus persons, and captains. The preparation personnel could be divided into the various cooks, bakers, salad makers, and pantry workers. (The breakdown conceivably could proceed until each employee was considered separately.)

The value of calculating labor costs as a percentage of sales is enhanced when percentage figures are available for past weeks and months. These can be correlated with future sales forecasts to be used in employee scheduling and as a guide to control future labor costs. It must not be assumed, however, that since labor costs have always been a certain percentage of sales, this percentage is the best one for the operation.

Despite their limitations, labor-cost percentages are helpful in determining whether labor costs are within desired limits, and they can help to pinpoint where labor costs may be excessive. At best, however, the percentage figure shows the relationship between costs and sales; it is not, itself, a positive control. Although it is commonly used as a labor cost control, it might better be used as a menu-pricing tool by considering a labor-cost percentage in setting menu prices. When relying on a labor-cost percentage, the operator must remember to maintain standards for customer service. It is possible to reduce a labor-percentage figure by providing unsatisfactory service to customers. But this practice creates a long-range business survival problem. An unduly low percentage thus is not necessarily desirable since it can indicate that not enough employees are on hand to render the appropriate service. The percentage may also vary for different levels of sales volume. For low volumes, the necessary number of fixed employees may cause a higher percentage than that calculated during a higher volume of business. For an operation with few employees, the addition or elimination of one employee may have a marked effect on the percentage figure and may make a standard percentage difficult to maintain.

WORK PRODUCTION STANDARDS

The establishment of work production standards and detailed job analyses constitutes the next logical development in the attempt to analyze labor costs in foodservice operations. Work production standards are simply the amount of work that a worker with a certain type of job is expected to accomplish in a specified time. These standards can then be compared with the average amount of work that a person on that job actually performs. Work production standards can be used to pinpoint the area in which labor costs are abnormal; in some cases they will indicate the individuals or the particular jobs causing the discrepancies. Work production standards are goals established for each type of job. They often provide an upper limit which, if surpassed, may mean that the employee is being overworked and that the quality of service is therefore compromised. They may also establish a lower limit suggesting the minimal fair day's output.

Work production standards are most useful with variable employees, or when the number of employees varies with the sales volume. They are less helpful in analyzing the contributions of the semivariable or fixed employees, since it may not be feasible to increase or decrease their numbers even though the sales volume may change. However, if fixed employees do not meet work production standards, this can indicate that job duties should be reevaluated.

Generally, production standards are based either on dollar sales generated during an employee's time period or on units served or produced during the period. A server may be rated on the dollar volume of business handled, or might be rated in the number of covers handled. A coffee shop server might be expected to handle from 45 to 60 covers in a two-meal period, whereas a server in a more formal dining room could be expected to handle only from 25 to 30 covers. The coffee shop server might be expected, for example, to produce sales of from $200 to $400, while the dining room server might reasonably produce sales of from $240 to much more, depending upon the menu prices and meal period. Unit production standards can be expressed in covers served by server, dishes washed per dishwasher, covers prepared per cook, and patrons served by a cashier. The production standards may be measured on an hourly, daily, or weekly basis. An hourly analysis pinpoints hourly output per work unit. Activity usually fluctuates, however, between the peak meal periods during the day. An hourly analysis thus becomes less meaningful in the foodservice industry than in general industry. Foodservice often uses the workday as the production standard. A **workday** is determined by dividing the total number of hours spent in each job category by eight. If 100 hours of the wait staff time is used during a day, the number of workdays would be 12.5.

Some managers use the work production standard of profit per labor hours or profit for a period divided by the number of labor hours worked in the period. If the profit for a period is $10,000 and 4,000 hours are worked, the profit per labor hour is $2.50. The use of the standard suffers from the fact that labor cost is only one of the variables in producing a profit. Also, the type of profit—operating, net, etc.—must be determined and the types of employees whose hours will be counted specified.

The productivity index is calculated by dividing sales per employee by the payroll per employee. If an employee produces $10,000 in sales for a period and her payroll cost is $2,500, the productivity index is 4.0. The index indicates how efficiently labor is used. Gross payroll and gross sales can also be used. The index can be compared to other operations or the index for the same operations over different periods.

Analysis on a daily basis is most appropriate to the foodservice field. It provides production standards (daily covers or dollar sales) for each day's activities and permits fast corrective action. Weekly analysis is not as helpful as daily analysis, but it can be a guide and certainly takes less effort to compute. The analysis can be computed on a monthly basis, but by the end of the month it is too late to correct the month's discrepancies. Also, there is more chance of high and low cost days canceling each other and giving a satisfactory figure, even though individual days were unsatisfactory.

Obviously, to employ work production standards effectively and to secure all of their benefits, one must forecast the volume accurately and schedule personnel accordingly. It is useless to determine how much a worker should produce if this standard is not then divided into the total production expectation to determine how many workers of each type should be on hand. If 600 covers are forecast for a period and a server is expected to handle between 45 and 60 covers, then 10 or 11 servers should be scheduled. As employees are scheduled on a daily basis, it is obvious that labor costs will not be controlled effectively unless daily production standards are established. A regrettable tendency is to schedule the same numbers of employees every day regardless of daily volume.

DETERMINING WORK PRODUCTION STANDARDS

The first problem, and one of the greatest difficulties in using work production standards, is establishing those standards. Because of the diversity and individuality of foodservice operations, it is usually impractical to use standards developed by other food operations. The menu, production methods, layout, equipment, service, pricing, and type of patrons will contribute to differences in work production standards among various operations. In setting standards, the past productivity records of the better employees should be used. If a satisfactory dishwasher averages a production range of from 135 to 270 covers per day over a specified period (say, a month), one can assume that the proper production standards are somewhere within this range. The low of 135 may have been too low and the high of 270 might have required undue effort and thus be unreasonably high. If a number of observations show the dishwasher to be consistently busy handling between 190 and 220 covers, this may be considered a fair workload. There may be times when circumstances (special events or poor weather, for example) cause these standards to fall or to be exceeded, but at least management has a fairly sound basis for determining the amount of dishwashing help it needs after forecasting its volume.

Larger operations, such as chain restaurants in which the units are similar, may employ more sophisticated techniques such as time studies to set their standards. However, despite the many similarities in operations, differences in the local workforce and in the character of the customers can affect work production standards differently in different units.

Operations that have used work production standards over long periods have found that their standards can often be revised upward. When managers and supervisors begin to look at jobs more critically when setting and maintaining the standards, they tend to discover new ways of doing the work better, faster, and more easily. Sometimes labor-saving equipment must be developed and installed. Some operators have been able to introduce a competitive spirit, pitting their employees against the standards. Some chain restaurants have recognized the value of this approach and pay special monthly bonuses to workers in the units or publicly compare statistics between units. However, care must be taken to see that quality standards have been maintained in the wake of these lower costs. An unduly low cost may be cause for investigation. A change in standards may also involve union negotiations.

USING WORK PRODUCTION STANDARDS IN SCHEDULING

Work production standards and labor-cost percentages are often involved in advance scheduling. One method of scheduling in advance requires an operator to forecast the volume of anticipated business in dollar sales for the following week (or for any other convenient period). This figure is then multiplied by the desired labor-cost percentage to provide a budgeted labor cost. The payroll for the period should not exceed that dollar amount.

Here's an example: 1,000 covers are forecast for a certain period at a check average of $20.00, or $20,000 in sales. If a 35 percent payroll figure is desired, the dollar cost of labor scheduled should not exceed $7,000, or $20,000 multiplied by 35 percent. (There can be variations, usually centering on whether to use the total labor-cost percentage or a figure that excludes some fixed employees and better reflects the volume for variable employees.) Another system for scheduling in advance requires an operator to set an expected dollar return per hour of labor expended. If, for example, $60.00 in sales is desired for every labor-hour and forecast sales are $6,000, the number of hours scheduled should not exceed 100, or $6,000 divided by $60.00.

Labor-cost percentages and work production standards both help in analyzing and controlling costs, but each shows different measurements, so one may supplement the other. One advantage of work production standards over labor-cost percentages is that the labor-cost percentage shows only the relationship between labor costs and sales, and it

INDUSTRY INSIGHTS   by Norman Brinker

Norman Brinker is Chairman of the Board of Brinker International and CEO of Chili's Inc. He is the founder of Steak & Ale. In 1982, Brinker was named President of Pillsbury Restaurant Group, which includes Burger King, Steak & Ale, Bennigan's, and Poppin Fresh Restaurants.

LABOR COST CONTROL

One of the most critical components of any service-oriented business is labor. In the restaurant business, 9 out of 10 new concepts don't survive more than five years. While labor costs are the second-highest expense component behind food costs, they are the single highest factor in determining our success.

Brinker International has a 21-year history in the restaurant industry, and labor has always been an essential component in everything from the way food is prepared to the cleanliness of the restaurant. Scheduling can be a time-consuming part of a manager's job, and adequately forecasting labor needs is a delicate and essential task when turnover and dependability are issues. The challenge is how we manage and control labor costs in an ever-changing, competitive environment.

We face two key labor issues in the restaurant industry: finding the right people and keeping them. Turnover in this business is high, and the jobs that are required for our kitchen staff, servers, and managers to run a restaurant efficiently are not always the easiest or most glamorous. Compare jobs in the restaurant industry to those in retail, and it's easy to see why it's tough to keep good employees.

Shortage of available labor is another consideration. The labor pool has always been consistently low in the restaurant industry, due in large part to the minimum wage standard and the difficulty of retaining high levels of staff motivation and morale. Our main source of restaurant employees comes from the 18- to 24-year-old range. Many of these people see their work in our restaurants as a temporary stop on the road to another career. They may be working their way through college or in need of a second job. Initially, they're not considering a position in the restaurant industry as a potential career, so their motivation to stay is minimal. Higher labor costs are usually the result because employee retention becomes an issue.

To help combat this problem, we make sure our restaurants offer many opportunities for development. Often, our employees become developers who train new employees to the restaurant. Or, they become in-store trainers who travel to other restaurants to help open new stores, getting a first-hand glimpse of what it takes to run a restaurant. We also have a management training program that actively recruits from within our restaurants.

Of course, compensation is always a great motivator. Considering the incredible amount of competition in the restaurant industry for quality people, it becomes apparent that keeping current with industry compensation standards is *de riguer*. A necessary component of managing labor costs is rewarding employees, and this element must be factored into the equation.

As a restaurateur and businessman, I have always believed that people are our most important assets. It is essential to create and maintain a culture that is "can-do" in every respect. It is our responsibility to make the workplace a fun and enjoyable place to be. At that point, the enthusiasm of our employees will become second nature, and we will be rewarded with employees who have a real interest in the business and in watching it grow.

varies with changes in either. The standards provide a definite standard or goal to achieve, and it is easy to determine how close each job comes to the predetermined standard. With the standards, it is a simple matter for management to determine if there is an excess or deficiency of workers in the variable job categories. The work production standard can also relate to the overall quality of service, since it can establish whether personnel have adequate time for their work. Whether to use a work standard based on covers served or on dollar sales per job (or both) is up to the individual operator. Some believe that the number of covers served is a more objective standard, while others contend that dollar sales per workday is a criterion more related to profit, the main goal of the business. Adjustments in menu selling prices will require changes in a standard based on dollar sales.

EXAMPLES OF TYPICAL ANALYSES OF PAYROLL

To illustrate the preceding discussion, a number of examples are presented that show some typical methods and standards used to analyze payroll costs.

Table 11.1 presents a simple format to prepare on a weekly basis. It requires a minimum of information: the number of full-time employees, the number of covers served, the total sales, and the weekly payroll by classification. It divides employees into the four major classes and computes, weekly for each class, the number of covers served, the sales for each employee of a certain class, and the ratio of payroll costs to food sales. These three indexes can indicate whether payroll costs are excessive and where discrepancies occur. They may also be expanded to show details for different groupings of employees within the respective major classes.

Used on a weekly basis, the form cannot reveal daily discrepancies. However, the form does reveal unfavorable trends, and even a weekly analysis is better than no analysis.

Table 11.2 was designed for a different type of operation and is somewhat more detailed than Table 11.1. The example is prepared on a weekly basis, but the format could also be used on a daily or monthly basis. Unlike Table 11.1, which indicates covers per employee classification per week, Table 11.2 indicates the covers per workday of time per job type during the week—a more specific approach. It also provides a total labor-cost percentage, percentages for each of the four major employee classifications, and percentages for each job. These percentage calculations can be eliminated, if desired.

In using this control, managers would first consider the total labor-cost percentage (33.3 percent) and total covers per workday (17.8). These figures provide an indication of overall productivity and a comparison of labor costs to sales. Managers would then look at the figures for the various classifications, concentrating on the preparation and service categories, since they have both the largest number of employees and the most variable employees.

Table 11.3 can be used both as a forecast for scheduling personnel and as a report of labor costs during the period. First, an average hourly wage is calculated (the total wages for the last payroll period divided by the number of hours worked in the period). Multiplying the average hourly rate ($5.00) by the number of hours (B) will give labor costs (C). Dividing sales (A) into the labor cost (C) will give the labor-cost percentage (D). Dividing the number of hours (B) into sales (A) provides the sales per work-hour (E). If this form is prepared before the actual period begins, management can see subsequently

Table 11.1
Analysis of Weekly Payroll

	Number of Employees	Weekly Payroll Cost	Number of Covers per Employee	Sales per Employee	Ratio of Payroll to Food Sales
			Week Ending _____		
Administrative					
Manager	1	$ 800.00			
Bookkeeper	1	200.00			
Cashier	2	360.00			
Total	4	$1,360.00	760	$6,400	5.3%
Preparation					
Cooks-cook's helper	4	$2,000.00			
Baker	1	500.00			
Pantry	2	640.00			
Total	7	$3,140.00	434	$3,656	12.3%
Service					
Host/hostess	1	$ 320.00			
Servers	10	1,780.00			
Buspersons	2	500.00			
Total	13	$2,600.00	234	$1,968	10.2%
Cleaning					
Dishwashers	2	$ 680.00			
Porter	1	340.00			
Total	3	$1,020.00	1,013	$8,534	4.0%
Grand Total	27	$8,120.00	113	$946	31.8%
Statistics					
Food sales	$25,600				
Covers served	3,040				
Average check	$ 8.42				

if labor costs are in line with the projected volume. After the period, actual figures rather than projected ones are used, and management can see how labor costs compared with sales and productivity as shown by sales per work-hour.

Some modifications in the form include figures by work shifts rather than total daily, and breakdown by various classes of employees. Management's compensation may or may not be included in the average hourly wage, but it is important that a consistent policy be followed regarding its inclusion.

In Table 11.3 the format is used as a forecast report. Management wants the scheduled labor percentage to be not higher than 33 percent. To maintain this percentage with anticipated sales, no more than the number of hours indicated on the Hours Today line can be scheduled. The average hourly rate of $5.00 was determined by dividing the payroll for the previous period by the number of hours worked. If this is thought to be too high, a

Table 11.2
Labor-Cost Percentage Analysis by Workday

Number of Employees	Position	Salary (S) or Hourly Wages (H)	Total Amount	Work-Hours	Work-Days	Covers Workday	Ratio of Payroll to Sales (%)
	Administrative and General						
1	Manager (S)	$ 800.00	$ 800.00	40	5	1417	1.9
1	Office (S)	500.00	500.00	40	5	1417	1.2
2	Cashier (H)	10.00	720.00	72	9	747	1.7
1.5	Storeroom (H)	8.00	512.00	64	8	884	1.2
4	Total		$ 2,532.00	216	27	263	6.0
	Preparation						
1	Head cook (S)	$ 700.00	$ 700.00	40	5	1417	1.6
4	Cooks (H)	12.00	1,720.00	160	20	254	4.5
4	Pantry (H)	10.00	1,600.00	160	20	254	3.8
1	Utility (H)	8.00	320.00	40	5	1417	.1
10	Total		$ 4,540.00	400	50	142	10.1
	Service						
1.5	Host/hostess (H)	$ 10.00	$ 640.00	64	8	884	1.5
14	Servers (H)	5.00	2,800.00	560	70	101	6.6
4	Bus persons (H)	4.00	640.00	160	20	354	1.5
19.5	Total		$ 4,080.00	784	98	72	9.6
	Sanitation						
6	Dishwashers (H)	$ 8.00	$ 1,932.00	240	30	236	4.6
1	Porter (H)	7.00	280.00	40	5	1417	.6
7	Total		$2,212.00	270	35	202	5.2
30	Totals		$13,364.00	1,672	209	34	30.9
	Statistics						
	Food sales	$42,500.00					
	Food covers	7,083.00					
	Average check	$ 6.00					

goal figure for the hourly rate could be used instead. Since this is the first week of the month, the week-to-date figures and month-to-date figures are identical.

Table 11.4 shows sales per work-hour and compares them with a sales goal per work-hour and the sales per work-hour during the previous week. The sales/hour figure is calculated by dividing the number of hours worked into the dollar sales for the period. The sales goal per hour figure represents the amount of sales desired for each hour worked in the various categories. The sales/hour last week figure represents the sales/hour of the previous week and permits a comparison of the two weeks.

Table 11.3
Sales and Labor Forecast and Report

Week Ending	June 1			Average Hourly Rate		$5.00	
Date	6/1	6/2	6/3	6/4	6/5	6/6	6/7
Day of Week	Mon	Tues	Wed	Thurs	Fri	Sat	Sun
(A)Sales							
Today	$1,000	$1,050	$1,000	$1,030	$1,100	$1,200	$1,175
Week-to-date	—	2,050	3,050	4,080	5,180	6,380	7,555
Month-to-date	—	2,050	3,050	4,080	5,180	6,380	7,555
(B)Hours							
Today	60	63	65	63	70	80	75
Week-to-date	60	123	188	251	321	401	476
Month-to-date	60	123	188	251	321	401	476
(C)Labor cost ($)							
Today	300	315	325	315	350	400	375
Week-to-date	—	615	940	1,255	1,605	2,005	2,380
Month-to-date	—	615	940	1,255	1,605	2,005	2,380
(D)Labor-cost percentage							
Today	30	30	32.5	30.6	31.8	30	32
Week-to-date	30	30	30.8	30.78	30.98	30.8	30.9
Month-to-date	30	30	30.8	30.78	30.98	30.8	30.9
(E)Sales/work-hour							
Today	16.7	16.7	15.4	16.3	15.7	15	15.7
Week-to-date	16.7	16.7	16.3	16.3	16.2	16	16.0
Month-to-date	16.7	16.7	16.3	16.3	16.2	16	16.0

Table 11.5 is a simple form that can be of assistance to a hospital dietary department by relating the number of covers served per eight-hour workday. The hospital food administrator can readily see how the dietary department is staffed for the current patient load. In the example, a monthly evaluation is made, but the analysis could be made on a daily basis. A daily analysis is desirable, but because of the amount of paperwork involved and because hospital dietary workers usually work the same number of hours regardless of changes in the patient census, a monthly analysis may be acceptable.

Tables 11.6, 11.7, and 11.8 are examples of computer-generated reports that can be used in labor-cost analysis.

BAR CHARTS

Bar charts are a great help in analyzing the use of labor in foodservice establishments. Not only do they present the information in a form that may readily be analyzed, they also provide a unique visual presentation that makes the information easier to absorb. Bar

Table 11.4
Weekly Analysis of Employee Productivity

Positions	Payroll	Hours	Week Ending June 6 Sales/hour	Sales Goal per Hour	Sales/hour Last Week
Administrative and General					
Manager	$ 600	44	589	600	551
Office	375	40	648	650	662
Cashier	390	52	499	500	502
Storeroom	304	45	576	575	564
Total	$1,669	181	143	150	138
Preparation					
Chef	$ 525	48	540	550	522
Cooks	1,170	130	199	200	196
Pantry	807	99	262	265	261
Pastry	280	40	648	650	635
Utility	264	51	508	510	500
Total	$3,046	368	70	75	68
Service					
Host/Hostess	$ 390	60	432	435	427
Servers	887	400	65	65	63
Bus persons	568	105	247	250	252
Total	$1,845	565	46	50	45
Sanitation					
Dishwashers	$1,200	200	130	140	129
Porters	245	40	648	650	642
Total	$1,445	240	108	110	105
Grand Total	$8,005	1,345	19	20	18

charts can help determine how busy employees are, how well they are scheduled in relation to workloads, and whether or not too many employees have been hired.

Through the use of bar charts, management quite often discovers, for example, that employees are arriving for work before they are actually needed (as when dishwashers come on duty at 7 a.m. but the dishes do not arrive at the dishroom in any quantity until 9 a.m.).

Management may find too many employees are on hand for the volume of activity at one time during the day and too few at another time. Employees may have been properly scheduled originally, but conditions or workloads may have changed although the working hours remained the same. Under changing conditions, alert managers will reschedule their employees.

How well employees are scheduled (as demonstrated by bar charts) can also be used as a criterion to help evaluate supervisory personnel, sometimes for possible merit salary increases.

Table 11.5
Dietary Department Monthly Performance Standard

Positions	Work-Hours	Workdays	Number of Covers Served per Workday
Administration and general			
Administrator	184	23	977
Dietitian (diet aide)	192	24	937
Receiving and storeroom	184	23	977
Total administration	560	70	321
Preparation			
Cooks	704	88	255
Potwashers	356	44½	505
Vegetable cleaners	188	23½	957
Pantry	344	43	523
Pastry	176	22	1,022
Total preparation	1,768	221	102
Service			
Tray persons	2,776	347	65
Servers	584	73	308
Total service	3,360	420	54
General			
Warewashing	1,856	232	97
Porter	208	26	865
Total general	2,064	258	87
Grand total	7,752	969	23
		Month	Week
Total meals served		22,480	5,190

PREPARING BAR CHARTS

Bar charts are easy to prepare. Charts appear as graphs with the working hours of the operation plotted along the top. Names of employees or the various jobs are listed along the side of the form. The hours that each employee or job classification is on duty are then drawn across the appropriate time intervals. These lines need not necessarily be solid; different shadings can be used to indicate the nature of the work and the nature of the time off: serving, production, or sanitation on the one hand; lunch break or rest period on the other. Different shadings might also be used to indicate how busy the employee actually is. The chart can also show information about the volume of activity by superimposing a graph on the chart or by listing the appropriate figures.

Figure 11.1 shows the activity in one hotel kitchen. The manager who prepared it observed kitchen activity, evaluated it on a scale ranging from 0 to 100 percent, and plotted this graph. Plotting points using such specific measurements as covers served per hour

Table 11.6
CBORD Dining Hall Labor Analysis By Day

June 09, 1998 PROD COOK1 Cook Lead							Week Beg	1 April 30, 1998
	Thu	**Fri**	**Sat**	**Sun**	**Mon**	**Tue**	**Wed**	**Totals**
CUST								
Forecast	$1,104.00	$1,208.00	$1,181.00	$1,072.00	$1,229.00	$1,104.00	$1,188.00	$8,090.00
Actual	$1,226.00	$1,219.00	$1,172.00	$1,180.00	$1,261.00	$1,220.00	$1,206.00	$8,486.00
Difference	$ 122.00	$ 11.00	−$ 9.00	$ 108.00	$ 32.00	$ 116.00	$ 18.00	$ 396.00
Actual/forecast %	111.05	100.91	99.24	110.07	102.60	110.51	101.52	104.89
Hours								
Required	16.50	16.50	16.50	16.50	16.50	16.50	16.50	115.50
Scheduled	16.00	16.00	27.00	24.00	25.00	42.00	35.00	185.00
Worked	16.00	16.00	27.00	24.00	25.00	42.00	35.00	185.00
Difference								0.00
Overtime						1.50	6.50	8.00
Dollars								
Required	$165.00	$165.00	$165.00	$165.00	$165.00	$165.00	$165.00	$1,155.00
Scheduled	$164.00	$164.00	$275.88	$244.00	$256.13	$437.19	$396.00	$1,937.19
Worked	$164.00	$164.00	$275.88	$244.00	$256.13	$435.69	$389.50	$1,929.19
Difference						−$ 1.50	−$ 6.50	−$ 8.00
Overtime						$ 69.19	$295.88	$ 365.06
Actual+salaried	$164.00	$164.00	$275.88	$244.00	$256.13	$435.69	$389.50	$1,929.19
Actual+sal+tax	$164.00	$164.00	$275.88	$244.00	$256.13	$435.69	$389.50	$1,929.19
Performance								
Absolute variance	1.50	1.50	10.50	8.50	9.50	25.50	18.50	75.50
Labor/CUST								
Required	14.93	13.65	13.97	15.39	13.41	14.94	13.88	14.28
Scheduled	14.84	13.57	23.36	22.76	20.82	39.59	33.31	23.95
Actual	13.38	13.44	23.54	20.68	20.30	35.71	32.27	22.73
Actual+salaried	13.38	13.45	23.54	20.68	20.31	35.71	32.30	22.73
Actual+sal+tax	13.38	13.45	23.54	20.68	20.31	35.71	32.30	22.73
CUST/hours ($)								
Required	$66.96	73.26	71.58	64.98	74.54	66.92	72.06	70.04
Scheduled	$69.06	75.55	43.74	44.67	49.20	26.29	33.97	43.73
Actual	$76.63	76.25	43.41	49.17	50.48	29.05	34.48	45.87

Source: Courtesy of The CBORD Group, Inc.

is not practical in this preparation department. To measure preparation activity in this operation, it is necessary to actually observe the activity and subjectively estimate the various levels of activity. In this operation, pre-preparation and preparation activities reach a peak just before noon and hold rather steady until about 6 p.m.

Eight people were scheduled for the production unit, four on a 7-to-3 shift and four on a 3-to-11 shift, as shown in Figure 11.2. This scheduling did not coincide with the activity. By rescheduling according to the bar chart shown in Figure 11.3, it was possible to eliminate the need for two workers and yet have the same number of employees on hand for the key periods necessary to complete the work adequately. In addition, the person preparing the graphs could see ways in which the work peaks could be leveled somewhat and some work eliminated. There were also benefits in not having a complete change in

Table 11.7
Schedule Violation Report

Doug's Diner #1
Report Dates: Sunday, September 13, 1998 through Sunday, September 20, 1998

Employee Number - Employee Name

Date	Job Name	Punch Type	Scheduled Time	Actual Time	Violation	Severity Level	Manager Name
225 - Alcot, Andrew							
09/13/1998	Servers	In		07:52	Early	0	
09/13/1998	Servers	Out		15:52	Early	0	
09/14/1998	Servers	In		09:06	Early	0	
09/14/1998	Servers	Out		17:07	Early	0	
09/15/1998	Servers	In		08:00	Early	0	
09/15/1998	Servers	Out		16:00	Early	0	
09/16/1998	Servers	In		08:00	Early	0	
09/16/1998	Servers	Out		16:00	Early	0	
09/17/1998	Servers	In		11:02	Early	0	
09/17/1998	Servers	Out		19:00	Early	0	
325 - Andreta, Mario							
09/13/1998	Dishwashers	In		12:59	Early	0	
09/13/1998	Dishwashers	Out		19:00	Early	0	
09/16/1998	Dishwashers	In		12:02	Early	0	
09/16/1998	Dishwashers	Out		19:00	Early	0	
09/18/1998	Dishwashers	In		11:02	Early	0	
09/18/1998	Dishwashers	Out		18:00	Early	0	
09/19/1998	Dishwashers	In		14:00	Early	0	
09/19/1998	Dishwashers	Out		19:00	Early	0	
523 - Hawkes, Kitty							
09/13/1998	Cashiers	In		14:58	Early	0	
09/13/1998	Cashiers	Out		19:00	Early	0	
09/14/1998	Cashiers	In		08:01	Early	0	
09/14/1998	Cashiers	Out		16:00	Early	0	
688 - Hernandez, Wendy							
09/14/1998	Hostesses	In		09:00	Early	0	
09/14/1998	Hostesses	Out		16:00	Early	0	
09/15/1998	Hostesses	In		09:00	Early	0	
09/15/1998	Hostesses	Out		16:00	Early	0	
09/16/1998	Hostesses	In		09:00	Early	0	
09/16/1998	Hostesses	Out		16:00	Early	0	
09/17/1998	Hostesses	In		09:00	Early	0	
09/17/1998	Hostesses	Out		16:00	Early	0	
09/18/1998	Hostesses	In		09:00	Early	0	
09/18/1998	Hostesses	Out		16:00	Early	0	
753 - Jackson, Jackie							
09/13/1998	Cashiers	In		09:00	Early	0	
09/13/1998	Cashiers	Out		15:00	Early	0	
995 - Kosta, Bob							
09/13/1998	Bussers	In		07:53	Early	0	
09/13/1998	Bussers	Out		15:00	Early	0	
09/15/1998	Bussers	In		10:00	Early	0	
09/15/1998	Bussers	Out		15:00	Early	0	
09/16/1998	Bussers	In		11:00	Early	0	
09/16/1998	Bussers	Out		17:00	Early	0	
09/18/1998	Bussers	In		10:30	Early	0	
09/18/1998	Bussers	Out		16:00	Early	0	
886 - Valdez, Juan							
09/13/1998	Cooks	In		10:57	Early	0	
09/13/1998	Cooks	Out		19:00	Early	0	
09/16/1998	Cooks	In		08:57	Early	0	

Table 11.8
CBORD Dining Hall Projected Labor Cost Summary

		Thu	Fri	Sat	Sun	Mon	Tue	Wed
Page 1								
Date December 04, 1997								
Position		**Thu**	**Fri**	**Sat**	**Sun**	**Mon**	**Tue**	**Wed**
PROD	**Production - BOH**							
COOK 1	Daily totals	$ 64	$ 80	$ 116	$ 90	$ 115	$ 90	$ 90
	Week to date	$ 64	$ 144	$ 260	$ 350	$ 465	$ 555	$ 645
COOK 2	Daily totals	$ 85	$ 76	$ 179	$ 179	$ 76	$ 153	$ 150
	Week to date	$ 85	$ 161	$ 341	$ 520	$ 597	$ 751	$ 902
Department Total								
	Daily	**$149**	**$ 156**	**$ 296**	**$ 269**	**$ 191**	**$ 243**	**$ 240**
	Week to date	**$149**	**$ 305**	**$ 602**	**$ 871**	**$1,063**	**$1,307**	**$1,548**
SERV	**Service - FOH**							
CASHR	Daily totals	$130	$ 135	$ 135	$ 128	$ 152	$ 178	$ 135
	Week to date	$130	$ 265	$ 400	$ 529	$ 681	$ 860	$ 995
DELI	Daily totals	$ 55	$ 55	$ 55	$ 49	$ 49	$ 47	$ 48
	Week to date	$ 55	$ 110	$ 166	$ 215	$ 264	$ 312	$ 361
LINE	Daily totals	$198	$ 174	$ 172	$ 140	$ 203	$ 201	$ 210
	Week to date	$198	$ 372	$ 544	$ 685	$ 889	$1,091	$1,301
RUNNER	Daily totals	$ 97	$ 115	$ 103	$ 105	$ 133	$ 112	$ 110
	Week to date	$ 97	$ 212	$ 315	$ 420	$ 553	$ 666	$ 777
Department Total								
	Daily	**$482**	**$ 479**	**$ 466**	**$ 423**	**$ 538**	**$ 541**	**$ 504**
	Week to date	**$482**	**$ 961**	**$1,427**	**$1,851**	**$2,390**	**$2,931**	**$3,436**
Grand Total								
	Daily	**$631**	**$ 636**	**$ 762**	**$ 693**	**$ 730**	**$ 784**	**$ 745**
	Week to date	**$631**	**$1,267**	**$2,030**	**$2,723**	**$3,454**	**$4,238**	**$4,984**

Source: Courtesy of The CBORD Group, Inc.

shifts at one time. Because people tend to slow down as they approach the end of their workday, and since it usually takes a little time to get started, there was less work being performed at change-over time. With personnel starting and stopping at different times, this problem was largely eliminated.

Another method, using bar charts to determine how hard employees are working and whether the number of scheduled hours is reasonable, was developed by a hospital food supervisor. The various positions and the on-duty hours are shown by the charts. The supervisor made ratings of the level of activity in each position over a specified period of time using a scale of 1 to 6. A 1 on the scale indicated that the employee was working much too slowly or was underutilized; a 6 indicated that the employee was overworked. A rating of 4 was considered the proper level of activity for the job. The ratings for all positions were totaled for each hourly period and divided by four (as shown in Figure 11.4).

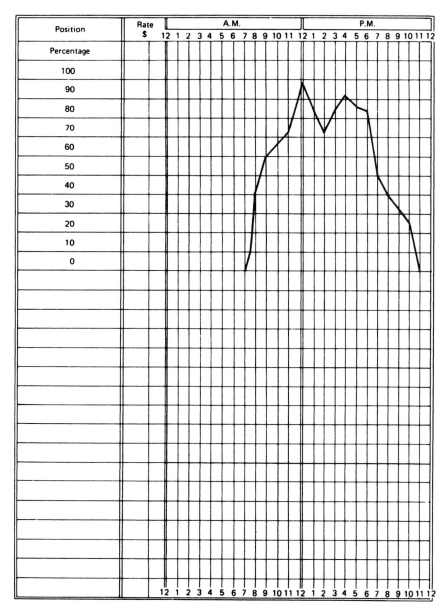

Figure 11.1
Kitchen Production—Level of Activity

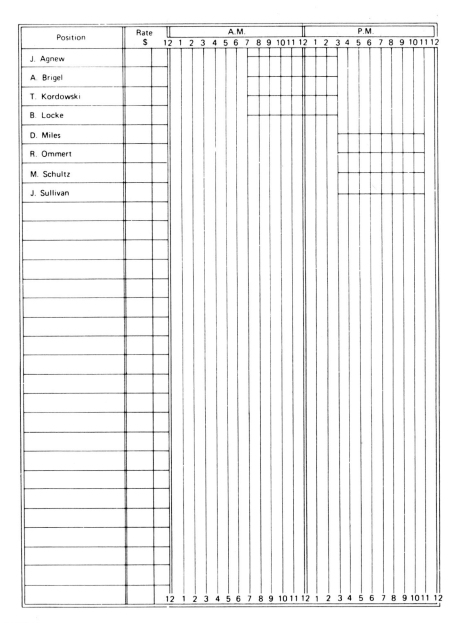

Figure 11.2
Kitchen Production—Original Scheduling

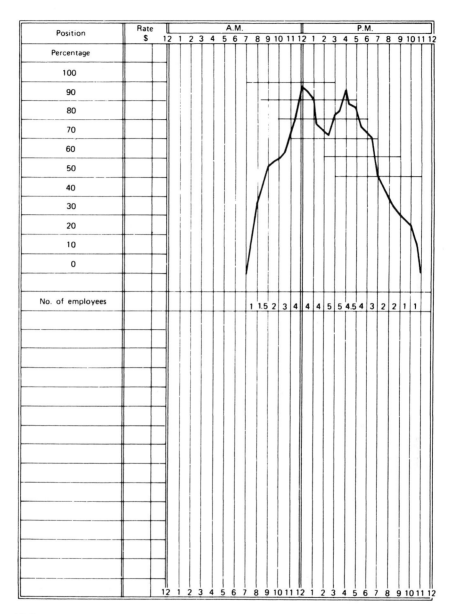

Figure 11.3
Kitchen Production—Rescheduling to Production

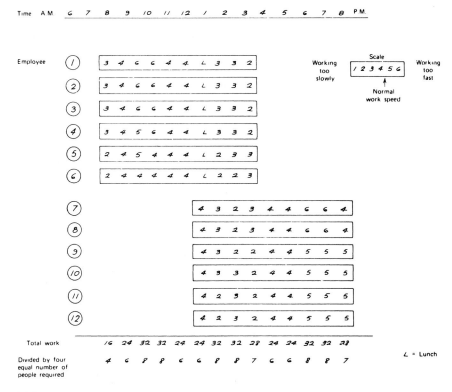

Figure 11.4
Evaluation of Tray Room Workload

The resulting figure suggested the optimum number of people who should be on duty during any specific hour. By indicating times of surplus labor, the supervisor was better able to coordinate labor hours with production needs and to make a sizable reduction in the labor required.

Figure 11.5 shows the bar chart scheduling of a small hospital. Table 11.9 provides a format for comparing regular time and overtime with scheduled hours and the resulting variation and dollar difference on a weekly basis.

Figure 11.6 demonstrates another application of bar charts. In this figure, the work-hours of four dishwashers are shown on bar charts. The level of activity of each is determined visually and is indicated by a different shading. This helps indicate where there may be excess labor. Different scheduling allowed the workload to be handled by three people instead of four and one of the three was available for other work between 3 p.m. and 5:30 p.m. Not only were savings in payroll achieved, but the morale of the dishwashers increased with more consistent work levels replacing alternating periods of activity and idleness.

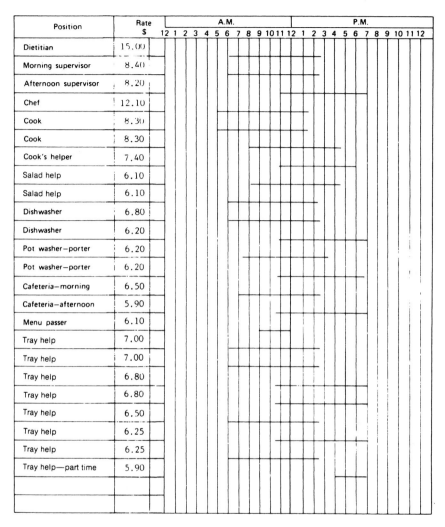

Figure 11.5
Typical Daily Staffing Schedule

COMPUTERIZED TECHNOLOGY FOR LABOR RECORDS

The computer, in the form of computerized time clocks and some POS register functions, is being used more and more by foodservice operations to keep track of employees' workhours. A problem for some operations is employees who punch in before they are supposed to start working. Many states require that employees be paid for the actual time recorded on their time cards, which means that an employee can be paid for time not worked. This can be a financial drain, especially if that time becomes overtime paid at a premium rate.

Table 11.9
CBORD Dining Hall Daily and Week-to-Date Labor Summary

		Page 1									
		Date	May 06, 1998								

		Regular Time		Overtime		Total		Scheduled		Variance	
Position		Hours	Dollars	Hours	Dollars	Hours	Dollars	Hours	Dollars	Hours	Dollars
PROD	**Production - BOH**										
COOK 1	Daily totals	28.50	$ 290	6.50	$ 98	35.00	$ 389	35.00	$ 396	0.00	($ 7)
	Week to date	177.00	$1,807	8.00	$121	185.00	$1,929	185.00	$1,937	0.00	($ 8)
COOK 2	Daily totals	6.00	$ 48	0.00	$ 0	6.00	$ 48	6.00	$ 48	0.00	$ 0
	Week to date	94.50	$ 798	1.50	$ 18	96.00	$ 817	96.00	$ 818	0.00	($ 1)
Department Total											
	Daily	34.50	$ 339	6.50	$ 98	41.00	$ 438	41.00	$ 444	0.00	($ 6)
	Week to date	271.50	$2,606	9.50	$140	281.00	$2,746	281.00	$2,756	0.00	($ 9)
SERV	**Service - FOH**										
CASHR	Daily totals	15.75	$ 93	0.00	$ 0	15.75	$ 93	15.75	$ 93	0.00	$ 0
	Week to date	127.50	$ 749	1.00	$ 9	128.50	$ 758	128.50	$ 759	0.00	($ 1)
DELI	Daily totals	9.00	$ 53	0.00	$ 0	9.00	$ 53	9.00	$ 53	0.00	$ 0
	Week to date	63.00	$ 384	0.00	$ 0	63.00	$ 384	63.00	$ 384	0.00	$ 0
LINE	Daily totals	25.25	$ 154	0.00	$ 0	25.25	$ 154	25.25	$ 154	0.00	$ 0
	Week to date	176.25	$1,095	0.00	$ 0	176.25	$1,095	176.25	$1,095	0.00	$ 0
RUNNER	Daily totals	11.00	$ 66	0.00	$ 0	11.00	$ 66	11.00	$ 66	0.00	$ 0
	Week to date	76.75	$ 483	1.50	$ 14	78.25	$ 497	78.25	$ 499	0.00	($ 1)
Department Total											
	Daily	61.00	$ 367	0.00	$ 0	61.00	$ 367	61.00	$ 367	0.00	$ 0
	Week to date	443.50	$2,711	2.50	$ 24	446.00	$2,736	446.00	$2,738	0.00	($ 2)
Total for All Departments											
	Daily	95.50	$ 707	6.50	$ 98	102.00	$ 805	102.00	$ 812	0.00	($ 6)
	Week to date	715.00	$5,318	12.00	$164	727.00	$5,482	727.00	$5,494	0.00	($12)

Summary Statistics

Sales	Projected	Actual	Variance
Sales daily	$1,188.00	$1,206.00	$ 18
Sales week to date	$8,090.00	$8,486.00	$396

Scheduled labor	Projected Hours	Projected $$
Labor daily	102.00	$812.15
Labor week to date	727.00	$5,494.55

Scheduled labor vs. forecast	Productivity ($$/Hours)	Labor $$/ Sales %
Daily	$11.65	68.36
Week to date	$11.13	67.92
Actual labor vs. sales		
Daily	$11.82	66.80

Source: Courtesy of The CBORD Group, Inc.

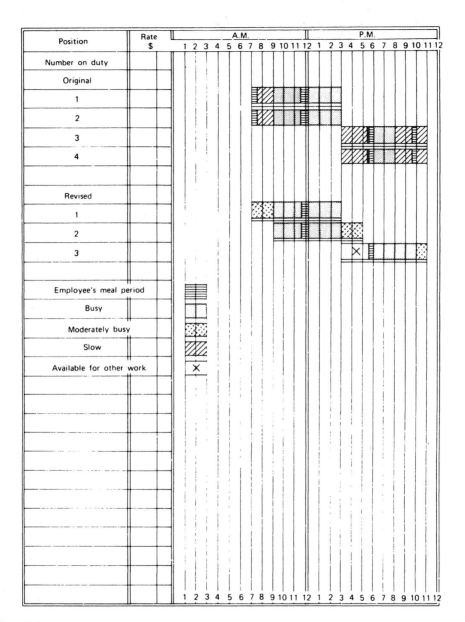

Figure 11.6
Dishwashers' Work Schedule

A computerized time clock with an employee's work schedule in its memory can refuse early or late time punches. The computerized time clock can also total the daily hours on cards, which can save the manpower required to do this manually. The time clock can be connected to a personal computer or a central computer to compute payroll data, including payroll checks and required reports.

Some other features of computerized time systems include an ability to allow employees to punch in their tips, to produce reports indicating approaching overtime, to produce reports on absences and tardiness, to show who is working at any given time, to print new cards at the end of a period, and to track overtime automatically. The clock can more easily allow managers to daily monitor labor costs and track their labor budget. Some of the calculations include revenue per labor-hour on the clock both for individuals and for totals, labor dollar cost, labor-cost percentage, and summary information. Daily and period labor-hours and dollars can be calculated by various cost or profit centers.

There is no best way to do anything but always a better way. Job analysis and consideration of new developments in technology, equipment, and products may provide for more efficient use of labor. Once managers are satisfied they are providing goods and services, they can establish labor needs and set goals. This can involve bar charting and may result in work production standards to better schedule personnel. However, scheduling also involves forecasting of business, which may be difficult (Chapter 8 may be helpful). The results of scheduling should be calculated. With POS or other technology this can be done very easily. The final step is the comparison of actual and desired results. If this is not satisfactory, then corrective action is indicated.

SUMMARY

Foodservice operators must know whether their labor costs are excessive, insufficient, or appropriate and—if either of the first two—where and why these costs are out of line. This chapter discussed a number of approaches to bring labor costs into balance with an operation's goals. The most familiar, even though it has some conceptual disadvantages, is the labor-cost percentage. An overall labor-cost percentage can be broken down into different labor divisions. Preparation, service, sanitation, and administration are the four typical divisions within a foodservice enterprise.

Another approach is to determine and then establish work production standards, the amount of labor a worker can be expected to complete in a specified time. This work can be expressed in dollar sales or in units produced, such as covers served or plates washed.

Both labor-cost percentages and work production standards mean little by themselves, but they become helpful when they are compared with a standard such as budgeted or historical figures. Labor-cost percentages and work production standards can be presented in a number of formats described in this chapter.

A third approach is the use of bar charts that show the number of employees on hand compared to the volume of business. Bar charts can also be used to show graphically how busy (or idle) employees are during their work periods.

Computer technology can add new dimensions to analyzing labor costs.

KEY TERMS

bar charts
fixed employees
semivariable employees

variable employees
workday

REVIEW QUESTIONS

11–1 What are the two functions of labor-cost analysis?

11–2 Briefly describe three difficulties in analyzing labor costs in foodservice operations.

11–3 Differentiate between fixed, semivariable, and variable employees.

11–4 List four disadvantages in using a labor-cost percentage in foodservice labor-cost analysis.

11–5 Show the four categories that a foodservice labor cost may be divided into.

11–6 On what are work production standards usually based?

11–7 Describe how you might determine the work production standard for a waiter or waitress.

11–8 What is a major advantage of using work production standards rather than labor-cost percentages for labor-cost analysis?

11–9 How are bar charts helpful in labor-cost analysis?

11–10 Show how the number of employees necessary in a tray room can be determined.

PROBLEMS

11–1 Prepare bar charts with the following data, using Figure 11.6 as an example. Revise the scheduling so workers can be working more efficiently. For example, from 8:00 to 8:30 both Mr. White and Mr. Green are working at a slow rate, but Mr. White on duty by himself would be working at a moderately busy rate. Indicate the number of labor-hours eliminated or saved with the new scheduling.

The following assumptions can be made:

a. Workers can be rescheduled or laid off.

b. Part-time workers can be used after 4:00 p.m. (when school is over), but they must be used or paid for at least four hours.

c. Times may be indicated when workers can be used elsewhere and not charged to this cost center. Such breaks in the schedule must be in half-hour increments and be for at least two hours.

11–2 Figures 11.7 and 11.8 show the level of activity and present block scheduling for a unit of a foodservice operation. Revise the schedule to better conform to the levels of activity. Use Figure 11.6 as a reference. Assume that if four personnel are necessary at the peak of activity, only two will be necessary at 50 percent of peak activity. Use assumptions from problem 11.1 and also assume at least one employee must always be on duty.

Labor Control Problem

Dishwashers Schedules:
Number Employed: (4)

Mr. White	Mr. Green	Mr. Brown	Mr. Gray
7:30 a.m. On duty	7:30 a.m. On duty	3:00– On duty	3:00– On duty
7:30–8:00 Meal	7:30–8:00 Meal	3:00–3:30 Meal	3:00–3:30 Meal
8:00–8:30 Slow	8:00–8:30 Slow	3:30–4:00 Slow	3:30–4:00 Slow
8:30–9:00 Mod. busy	8:30–9:00 Mod. busy	4:00–4:30 Slow	4:00–4:30 Slow
9:00–9:30 Very busy	9:00–9:30 Very busy	4:30–5:00 Mod. busy	4:30–5:00 Mod. busy
9:30–10:00 Very busy	9:30–10:00 Very busy	5:00–5:30 Mod. busy	5:00–5:30 Mod. busy
10:00–10:30 Mod. busy	10:00–10:30 Mod. busy	5:30–6:00 Very busy	5:30–6:00 Very busy
10:30–11:30 Slow	10:30–11:30 Slow	6:00–6:30 Very busy	6:00–6:30 Very busy
11:30–12:00 Lunch	11:30–12:00 Meal	6:30–7:00 Very busy	6:30–7:00 Very busy
12:00–12:30 Mod. busy	12:00–12:30 Mod. busy	7:00–7:30 Mod. busy	7:00–7:30 Mod. busy
12:30–1:00 Very busy	12:30–1:00 Very busy	7:30–8:00 Mod. busy	7:30–8:00 Mod. busy
1:00–1:30 Very busy	1:00–1:30 Very busy	8:00–8:30 Slow	8:00–8:30 Meal
1:30–2:00 Very busy	1:30–2:00 Very busy	8:30–9:00 Meal	8:30–9:00 Slow
2:00–2:30 Mod. busy	2:00–2:30 Mod. busy	9:00–9:30 Mod. busy	9:00–9:30 Mod. busy
2:30–3:00 Slow	2:30–3:00 Slow	10:00–10:30 Slow	10:00–10:30 Slow
3:00–3:30 Slow	3:00–3:30 Slow	10:30–11:00 Slow	10:30–11:00 Slow
3:30– Off duty	3:30– Off duty	11:00– Off duty	11:00– Off duty

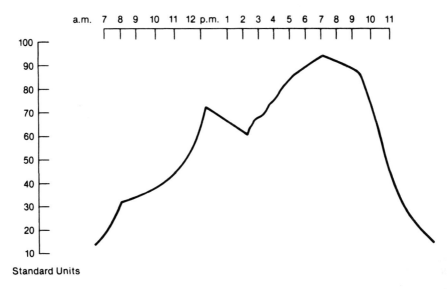

Figure 11.7
Level of Activity in Kitchen Production Unit

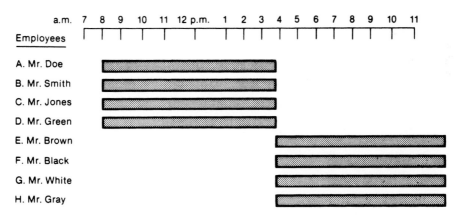

Figure 11.8
Original Scheduling of Production Unit

12

Staffing and Scheduling

This chapter discusses staffing and scheduling as they affect labor-cost control. The importance of scheduling is emphasized by the fact that in some food operations it is estimated that one-third of the hours paid are wasted because people are not scheduled according to the time their work is required.

After completing this chapter, you should be able to:

1. Distinguish between staffing and scheduling.
2. Use a job number control list.
3. Explain staff equivalents.
4. Consider the use of part-time workers.
5. Appreciate difficulties in scheduling in foodservice operations.
6. Explain nine steps involved in the scheduling process.
7. Know the relationship between production schedules for products, for work stations, and for individual hours.
8. Differentiate between block and staggered scheduling.
9. Incorporate scheduling guides.
10. Appreciate the advantages of computerized scheduling.

DEFINING STAFFING AND SCHEDULING

The terms *staffing* and *scheduling* are sometimes used interchangeably, but they refer to separate functions. **Staffing** entails the determination of the appropriate number of workers needed for the operation for the work that must be accomplished. This determination can be worked out objectively in advance by using work production standards and job analyses. **Scheduling** entails having the proper number of workers on duty, as determined by the staffing needs. Scheduling presents special problems since the volume of activity, and consequently the labor need, varies during the working day. Bar chart techniques, discussed in Chapter 11, can be helpful in scheduling.

Of help in staffing is the use of a **job number control list**. This list requires that each job be analyzed, described, formalized, and numbered with the payroll or time card number. New employees must be hired for a specifically numbered and classified job with a job description and job specification, and not just to work where needed. Those who use a job number control list system must plan the duties and responsibilities of each job in advance. Overlapping jobs is decreased; control is increased because no one is added to the payroll on a permanent basis unless to a definite numbered position and need. (Too often, employees are hired for a temporary requirement and remain when they are no longer needed.) Listing jobs on the job control form does not mean that every number must be filled. Ten cook positions may be listed, but if business warrants only eight, only eight are employed.

Work production standards are very helpful in determining the number required in each position. Table 12.1 shows a sample job control form for the dining room department of a table service restaurant. Not all the positions would be filled unless business had reached its maximum. The dining room service positions are numbered in the 100s. Positions in preparation could be numbered in the 200s, sanitation in the 300s, and administration in the 400s. Positions are further classified with hosts or hostesses and cashiers being listed from 100 to 109, servers 110 to 149, and bus persons 150 to 170. This system allows for easy identification. The use of a job control list also helps to eliminate dissatisfaction about scheduled hours. Workers are hired for a definite job with specified hours. They may eventually move into another job number with more desirable hours.

Scheduling is the assigning of employees to specific working hours and workdays. One goal in scheduling is having enough staff to handle busy meal periods without having excess help in the slower periods between meals. Advance preparation can help achieve this goal. Employees should do as much advance work as possible during the slow periods so that they will not have to perform it during the peak meal periods. The menu can be changed for large-volume days to eliminate time-consuming food items. For example, a fine restaurant in a university town finds itself swamped after football games. It discards its regular diversified menu and serves only roast beef, which requires little effort in the kitchen during the serving period. Some operations use convenience foods to reduce the labor demand during their busiest periods. This practice may provide a more expensive food cost, but it does not require expensive and inefficient temporary help; thus, the payroll and overall costs may be kept low. In some locations it is possible to find part-time help to supplement peak periods. A hospital may hire full-time tray persons to cover two meals and part-timers for the third meal. Split shifts can be very useful if employees can be found who will work the staggered hours. However, many employees do not like the off time in between, and double transportation costs can be a problem.

Managers should be careful not to schedule employees before they are needed. It is a rare foodservice operation where all employees are needed at the same time; staggered times of starting and stopping may do much to increase productivity. Some operations with a five-day work week schedule a six-day work week during busy periods and pay overtime. During slow periods, some employees welcome voluntary time off, which helps lower labor costs. The adoption of the 10-hour day, 4-day week may help some operations cover three meals with some of their employees.

Table 12.1
Job Number Control List

Predetermined Job Numbers	Classification	Hours
Dining Room Service		
101	Host/hostess	8:00 A.M.–5:00 P.M.
102	Evening host/hostess	4:30 P.M.–11:00 P.M.
103	Assistant host/hostess	Variable
104	Relief host/hostess and relief cashiers	Variable
105	Cashier	8:00 A.M.–5:00 P.M.
106	Evening cashier	4:00 P.M.–12:00 A.M.
110	Server	7:30 A.M.–4:30 P.M.
111	Server	7:30 A.M.–4:30 P.M.
112	Server	7:30 A.M.–4:30 P.M.
113	Server	11:00 A.M.–7:30 P.M.
114	Server	11:00 A.M.–7:30 P.M.
115	Server	11:00 A.M.–7:30 P.M.
116	Server	11:00 A.M.–7:30 P.M.
117	Evening server	4:30 P.M.–12:00 A.M.
118	Evening server	4:30 P.M.–12:00 A.M.
119	Evening server	4:30 P.M.–12:00 A.M.
120	Evening server	4:30 P.M.–12:00 A.M.
121	Evening server	4:30 P.M.–12:00 A.M.
122	Relief server	Variable
123	Relief server	Variable
124	Relief server	Variable
125	Relief server	Variable
126	Relief server	Variable
150	Bus person	8:00 A.M.–5:00 P.M.
151	Bus person	8:00 A.M.–5:00 P.M.
152	Bus person	8:00 A.M.–5:00 P.M.
153	Bus person	5:00 P.M.–12:00 A.M.
154	Bus person	5:00 P.M.–12:00 A.M.
155	Bus person, P.T.	5:00 P.M.–9:00 P.M.
156	Relief bus person	
157	Relief bus person	

Scheduling and staffing are so important that large organizations have staff planners or operation analysts who devote much of their time to it. By using job control lists and ensuring that the work schedules conform to the times when help is most needed, the small operator can go far in equalizing the advantages of those specialists.

STAFF COVERAGE

For everyday coverage, it is usually necessary to have about 1.55 personnel for every full-time everyday position. The mathematics for this are

Days in a year to be covered	365
Subtract	
Days off (52 × 2)	104
Sick days	7
Holidays	8
Vacation	10
Total days not worked	129
Total days worked	236
Ratio of days not worked to days worked	0.55
Requirement for full-time coverage	1.55

Employing a full staff capable of filling all schedule needs may not be feasible. It may be better for an operation to have a smaller permanent staff supplemented by relief employees such as part-time employees, temporary employees from an agency, or, if unionized, from a union hiring hall. In some locales, better restaurants, private clubs, and hotel foodservices lend each other employees when business is slow at one enterprise but help is needed at another.

PART-TIME WORKERS

A common problem in the foodservice industry is the need to serve three meal periods a day, which do not fit into the normal eight-hour shift. Some operators use part-time workers to provide workers throughout the day. This is especially feasible when high school workers can be scheduled after school hours or on weekends.

Besides providing for employee coverage, part-time workers can provide some other benefits. They usually do not receive all the benefits full-time workers do, especially expensive medical and pension coverage. On weekends they can be scheduled to provide more weekend time off for regular full-time workers.

Problems with using part-time workers include:

1. transportation costs, which are the same for a four- or eight-hour shift
2. more people on the payroll
3. additional accounting
4. the problems involved in scheduling more people.

FULL-TIME EQUIVALENTS (FTEs)

In analyzing labor costs, **full-time equivalents,** or the number of hours worked by part-time workers which translates into having equivalent full-time employees, can be more important than the number of employees on the payroll. If full-time employees work 40 hours per week for 52 weeks, they would work 2,080 hours without consideration for vacation, holidays, or sick leave. Dividing total part-time employees' hours by 2,080 provides the FTE. For example, four part-time employees' time totals 4160 hours, or two FTEs.

If the standard work week is not 40 hours but some other figure, that figure should be multiplied by 52. For example, if a 37.5-hour work week is standard, multiply 37.5 by 52. The FTE is 1,950 hours.

Holidays, sick leave, vacations, and other paid time off are not considered in FTE since that is time paid for but not worked. If part-time employees receive similar time benefits, they would be added to the hours worked.

THE IMPORTANCE OF SCHEDULING

Probably the most important factor in controlling labor costs in most foodservice operations is the scheduling of workers. In addition to excessive labor costs, poor scheduling has other implications. Besides possibly affecting quality, scheduling too few workers can make workers resentful about being overworked or can be the cause for excessive overtime. Scheduling too many workers can leave workers dissatisfied because they are not kept busy (even though they may adapt to the work available), or they may enjoy the low level of work needed from them and resent it when work returns to a normal level. Workers who earn tips suffer when there are too many to share the available tipping opportunities. Overscheduling may cause some employees not to be concerned if they do not show up for scheduled work.

DIFFICULTIES IN FOODSERVICE SCHEDULING

The foodservice industry presents some unusual problems in scheduling. If an operation serves three meals, it is usually impossible to include them all in one shift, yet the hours between breakfast and supper do not lend themselves to two full shifts. In addition, typical shifts have peaks and valleys of activity, not the steady production of an industrial line.

The level of expected activity may not be certain. It is difficult to forecast, in some operations, how much or how little business may appear on a future day. Changes in the weather or other factors beyond the operator's control may change the best forecasts.

A foodservice cannot generally produce for inventory and release from inventory when needed. If personnel are on hand but there is not enough business to keep them busy, their efforts cannot be stored for another time. It may also be difficult to determine what scheduling is necessary for the optimum level of service or quality. In other words, determining how many should be on hand at one time can be a problem since the levels of good and poor service have qualitative aspects that are not well defined.

Despite these difficulties, operations have found that they can greatly improve their scheduling with no loss and perhaps an increase in quality.

THE SCHEDULING PROCESS

The scheduling process includes these steps:

1. development of work production standards
2. plotting patterns of activity of various units of the operation

3. forecasting levels of activity

4. determining the number of personnel or hours needed according to forecast and work production standards

5. consideration of employee time requests and factors that management considers important, such as the number of experienced workers, rotation, wage rates, or legal considerations such as hours for minors

6. development of a schedule

7. approval by management after evaluation by criteria such as sales per hour, labor-cost percentage, customers served per labor-hour, labor costs per hour, or any other criteria appropriate for the operation

8. distribution to affected employees

9. review of scheduled and actual performance after the time periods

The scheduling process fits into the framework of the system for employee control and productivity discussed in Chapter 10, and some of the steps are similar.

Work production standards, or the amount of work expected for labor input, are discussed in Chapter 11. The various units of a foodservice facility usually have different patterns of activity during the day or shift that require different levels of scheduling. Even though the patterns of activity may be the same regardless of the amount of business, it is necessary to forecast anticipated business since busier days will require more people on duty and slower days will require fewer. If the work production standards are divided into the anticipated number of customers (or dollar sales), the number of personnel required can be determined. For various reasons management may want different or specific personnel on duty at one time, and employees will have their own requests for time off. These must be incorporated into the schedule.

A tentative schedule may now be drawn up. Management will want to check that it meets any criteria it has established. However, if work production standards were used in developing it, the criteria have already been built into the schedule. After approval, the schedule can be posted or otherwise delivered to employees.

As part of the control process, management should review scheduled hours with actual hours worked and compare forecast projections to actual business. If hours paid for during the period are different from what was scheduled, management should know why. There can be very legitimate reasons, such as unexpected business, that can cause this.

TYPES OF SCHEDULES

Different types of scheduling can be used in a foodservice production operation, and the different schedules are related to each other. Common schedules include:

1. production schedules for individual items

2. station production

3. staff coverage

The **production schedule** specifies what must be produced for the day, meal, or period. It may include items that will be produced ahead for future meals. A format for such a schedule could be

DAILY PRODUCTION SCHEDULE

Date_____   Day of week_____

Items	Quantity	Recipe number	Meal or time needed	Assigned
Apple pie	12	B-605	5 p.m.	Bake shop
—	—	—	—	—

The items from the daily production schedule are assigned to a work station such as the bake shop, which may have its own schedule. Smaller operations may combine a production schedule and a station work guide.

STATION: BAKE SHOP

Items	Quantity	Recipe number	Time required	Start	Ready	Assigned
Apple pie	12	B-605	2 hours	2:30	4:30	Robert
—	—	—	—	—	—	—

The staff coverage schedule provides coverage for the various units in the operation. A problem can arise when individual work schedules are prepared in advance of production schedules and station work guides and the individual times scheduled do not conform to them. If the operation is sophisticated enough to prepare these at the same time as individual time schedules, the production labor requirements can be coordinated with individual scheduling. Dining room scheduling is based primarily on the forecast number of patrons divided by work production standards of dining room personnel. The peaks of activity during the regular meal periods rather than steady volume through a shift complicate this scheduling.

SCHEDULING PATTERNS

There are two basic scheduling patterns. One is to use **block scheduling**, or stacked scheduling, in which everyone on a shift starts and stops at the same time. A block schedule could look like this:

7 a.m.   3 p.m.   11 p.m.

_____

_____

_____

                                        _____

                                        _____

                                        _____

The other method is **staggered scheduling**, in which employee schedules correspond to the work pattern.

7 a.m.	10 a.m.	3 p.m.	6 p.m.	11 p.m.

In this example it is possible to cover the work station with five employees rather than six by using staggered scheduling. Staggered scheduling makes it possible to save considerable labor time and cost since most units of a foodservice operation do not have uniform volumes of activity throughout the day.

Although more inefficient, block scheduling has some advantages. It is easier to check that everyone is present and on time. It is also easier to give common information to everyone at once. Employees may also prefer to start and stop together.

ACTIVITY PATTERNS

In scheduling it is important to realize that the different units of a foodservice have different patterns of activity throughout the day. Activity is typically highest in a pre-preparation unit before it peaks in a preparation unit.

Normally, activity is highest in the kitchen before it is in the serving areas, and the dishwashing units' activity peak may be 15 to 45 minutes after that of the serving area. When individual time schedules are designed, managers must consider what unit the individual is working in and the activity pattern for that unit.

SCHEDULING GUIDES

Some multiunit chains with many similar operations have provided scheduling guides for the operations that not only show how many personnel are required and when, but also provide the times that employees should perform their various activities.

The first step is for the manager to forecast the dollar volume for a particular shift. The chart in Table 12.2 shows the scheduling required for various volumes, and the closest one to forecast sales is chosen. Employees are then scheduled for the various jobs and times. Depending on which schedule is chosen, the duties of each job will change. Table 12.3 shows the daily duties of the roaster-slicer working 8 A.M. to 5 P.M. on schedule #5, or a daily volume of $2,250. (Instead of dollar sales, the number of customers could also be used.)

The schedules for various volumes are also divided into day and night shifts. It is very easy to use one schedule for the day shift and another for the night shift.

Advantages in using such a system include help in scheduling for the unit manager and a well-thought-out scheduling plan adapted for various volumes. Each employee receives a chronological list of duties, which can also make supervision easier. The fact that all the necessary work and who should do it must be decided before making up the schedules can often allow for improvements in the work division.

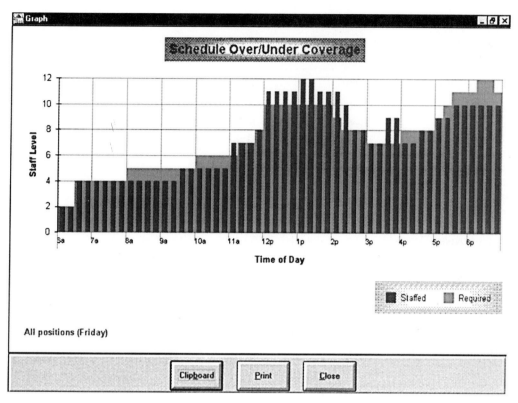

Figure 12.1
Scheduled Coverage Graph Comparing Actual Staffing to Level of Staffing Desired

COMPUTERIZED SCHEDULING

Scheduling personnel can consume a lot of management time. Managers of medium-size operations, with 50 to 70 employees, may spend 5 to 10 hours a week preparing schedules, so it is natural that some have turned to computer software for help. It is possible to enter specific information such as staffing requirements, employee availability, hourly sales projections, and available shifts. A computer can then be programmed to select the optimum weekly labor schedule; schedules for each employee can be set up considering time preferences, available job classifications, and performance ratings. The result can be a printout with individual schedules for the week, stations to be worked each day, and total number of hours. If a required position is not filled, the computer will call attention to the need. Management can then determine if it needs more of a specific type of worker. Tables 12.4 and 12.5 show examples of computer-generated daily and weekly schedules.

One food chain has a program designed to consider nine items when composing a schedule.

Table 12.2
Work Schedule

Schedule	1	2	3	4	5	6	7	8
Sales per Day	1,050	1,350	1,650	1,950	2,250	2,550	2,850	3,150
A.M.								
Roaster–slicer	8–4	8–4	8–4	8–5	8–5	8–5	8–5	8–5
Grill and french fry			11–2	11–3	11–5	11–5	10–5	10–5
Register 1	10–5	10–5	10–5	10–5	10–5	9–5	9–5	9–5
Counter 1	12–3	12–3	12–3	12–3	12–3	12–3	12–5	12–5
Beverage 1	12–2	12–2						12–3
Register 2			11–2	11–2	11–2	11–2	11–2	11–2
Counter 2				11–2	11–2	11–2	11–2	11–2
Beverage 2						11–2	11–2	11–2
No. employees—lunch	3+1	4+1	5+1	6+1	6+1	7+1	7+1	8+1
No. employee hours	19.0	19.0	23.0	28.0	29.5	33.5	36.0	39.0
P.M.								
Roaster-slicer	5–12:30	5–12:30	5–12:30	5–12:30	5–12:30	5–12:30	5–12:30	5–12:30
Grill and french fry			5–8	5–9	5–10	5–10	5–11	5–11
Register 1	5–12:30	5–12:30	5–12:30	5–12:30	5–12:30	5–12:30	5–12:30	5–12:30
Counter 1	5–8	5–8	5–8	5–8	5–9	5–9	5–10	5–10
Beverage 1	5–7	5–7						5–7
Register 2			5–7	5–7	5–7	5–8	5–8	5–8
Counter 2				5–7	5–7	5–7	5–8	5–8
Beverage 2						5–7	5–8	5–7
No. employees—dinner	3+1	4+1	5+1	6+1	6+1	7+1	7+1	8+1
No. employee hours	19.0	19.0	22.0	26.0	26.5	29.5	32.0	34.0

1. Performance ratings or evaluation of the capabilities and competencies of the work force: This allows for a mix of experienced and nonexperienced workers, helps the training of new workers, and avoids a disproportionate ratio of the better or poorer workers on duty at the same time.

2. Restrictions: Some employees may have restrictions on their work, such as not being bonded to handle cash or perhaps having physical limitations; they are not scheduled for jobs they cannot handle.

3. Wage rates: Lower paid workers of equal performance levels are scheduled first. (This could present problems with higher seniority and higher paid workers losing out.)

4. Individual time requests: An individual's requests for time off are honored.

5. Minimum and maximum hours: An employee's desire to work a minimum or a maximum number of hours during a period is considered.

6. Minors: The program includes constraints regarding hours that minors can work.

7. Rotation: It can be desirable to schedule workers to different work areas to reduce boredom, provide more training, and avert favoritism for preferred stations.

8. Qualifications: Workers are not scheduled for stations or jobs for which they are not qualified.

Table 12.3
Daily Duties of Roaster-Slicer

SCHEDULE #5	
Roaster-slicer, 8–5	
8:00–8:30	Weigh, season, pin roasts for lunch service Return to walk-in box.
8:30–9:40	Clean lot. Scrub spills from sidewalks and patio. Empty and wipe trash cans. Wipe tables and benches.
9:40–9:55	Put deliveries away.
9:55–10:00	Put seasoned pinned roasts in oven.
10:00–10:30	Warm chicken, make egg batter, set up chicken station. Flour chicken, drop first run of chicken at 10:30.
10:30–10:40	Continue chicken preparation if needed.
10:40–11:00	Remove roasts when ready from oven and make au jus. Store cooked roasts in thermocontainer. Remove chicken from fryer and store.
11:00–11:30	Clean kitchen area: pots, pans, and sink area.
11:30–12:00	Lunch.
12:00–1:30	Customer service. Slice and make roast beef sandwiches as needed. If needed, additional roasting and chicken preparation. Back up grill and french fry employee.
1:30–2:00	Weigh, season, pin, and put in oven roasts for afternoon business; return to walk-in.
2:00–2:45	Clean and boil out chicken fryer. Watch roasts that are cooking; when ready, remove from oven and make au jus.
2:45–3:15	Scoop, weigh, mold hamburgers for evening preparation.
3:15–3:55	Mix and cup coleslaw for evening preparation.
3:55–4:00	Put roasts in oven for evening business.
4:00–5:00	Clean kitchen: pots, pans, sink, storeroom floor. During this time watch roasts in oven; when ready, remove from oven and make au jus.

Table 12.4
Daily Employee Schedule

ReMACS Grill
Monday, December 01, 1997

Employee Name	Job	Begin	End
Andreta, Mario	Cash	09:30	14:00
Vettner, Rebecca	Cash	11:30	14:00
Zappa, William	Cash	11:30	14:30
Perkins, Julee	Cash	16:00	22:00
Hernandez, Wendy	Cash	17:30	22:00
Sacks, Jonathan	Cook	09:00	16:00
Ozmond, Donald	Cook	16:00	22:00
Hanson, Jacob	Cook	17:30	22:00
Benson, Theresa	Mgr	08:00	14:00
Williams, Mary Joe	Mgr	08:00	17:00
Williams, Laura	Mgr	15:00	22:00
Valdez, Juan	Pack	17:30	22:00

Table 12.5
Weekly Employee Work Schedule

ReMACS Grill
For Monday, December 01, 1997 through Sunday, December 07, 1997

Name	Monday 12/1/1997	Tuesday 12/2/1997	Wednesday 12/3/1997	Thursday 12/4/1997	Friday 12/5/1997	Saturday 12/6/1997	Sunday 12/7/1997	Total Hours
Alcott, Andrew	-Off-	Cook 1600–2200	-Off-	Cook 1600–2200	-Off-	Cook 0900–1600	-Off-	17.50
Andreta, Mario	Cash 0930–1400	Cash 0930–1400	Cash 0930–1400	Cash 0930–1400	Cash 0930–1400	-Off-	-Off-	22.50
Benson, Theresa	Mgr 0800–1400	Mgr 1500–2200	Mgr 0800–1600	-Off-	-Off-	Mgr 0800–1500	Mgr 1600–2200	31.50
Hanson, Jacob	Cook 1730–2200	Dish 1730–2200	-Off-	Dish 1730–2200	Dish 1730–2200	Dish 1730–2200	Dish 1730–2200	27.00
Hawkes, Kitty	-Off-	-Off-	Cook 1730–2200	-Off-	-Off-	-Off-	Cook 1600–2200	10.00
Hernandez, Wendy	Cash 1730–2200	Cash 1600–2200	Cash 1600–2200	Cash 1600–2200	Cash 1600–2200	-Off-	Cash 1600–2200	32.00
Jackson, Jackie	-Off-	-Off-	-Off-	-Off-	Cash 1700–2200	Cash 1600–2200	-Off-	10.50
Lakeson, Julie	-Off-	Cash 1700–2200	-Off-	-Off-	Cash 1730–2200	Pack 1700–2200	-Off-	14.50
Ozmond, Donald	Cook 1600–2200	-Off-	Cook 1600–2200	-Off-	Cook 1600–2200	Cook 1600–2200	Cook 0900–1600	28.50
Perkins, Julee	Cash 1600–2200	-Off-	Cash 1600–2200	Cash 1600–2200	-Off-	-Off-	-Off-	16.50
Perkins, Kathy	-Off-	Cash 1730–2200	-Off-	-Off-	Cash 1730–2200	Cash 1600–2200	Cash 0930–1600	20.50
Sacks, Jonathan	Cook 0900–1600	Cook 0900–1600	Cook 0900–1600	Cook 0900–1600	Cook 0900–1600	-Off-	-Off-	32.50
Siefert, David	-Off-	-Off-	-Off-	-Off-	Cook 1700–2200	-Off-	-Off-	5.00
Valdez, Juan	Pack 1730–2200	-Off-	-Off-	Pack 1730–2200	-Off-	Pack 1730–2200	Cash 1600–2200	19.00
Vettner, Rebecca	Cash 1130–1400	Cash 1130–1400	Cash 1130–1400	Cash 1130–1400	Cash 1130–1400	-Off-	-Off-	12.50
Washburn, Rachelle	-Off-	-Off-	Cash 1730–2200	Cash 1730–2200	-Off-	Cash 1130–1400	Cash 1730–2200	16.00
Wilkins, Jennifer	-Off-	Cash 0930–1400	Pack 0930–1500	Cash 0930–1500	Pack 0930–1400	Cash 0930–1600	Pack 1200–1500	29.00
Williams, Laura	Mgr 1500–2200	-Off-	-Off-	Mgr 1 500–2200	Mgr 0800–1700	Mgr 1500–2200	Mgr 0800–1600	35.50
Williams, Mary Joe	Mgr 0800–1700	Mgr 0800–1700	Mgr 1400–2200	Mgr 0800–1700	Mgr 1500–2200	-Off-	-Off-	39.50
Zappa, William	Cash 1130–1430	-Off-	Cash 1130–1400	Cash 1130–1430	Cash 1130–1430	-Off-	-Off-	11.50

9. Tax credits: The program can consider which employees may qualify for federal job tax credits or any other tax benefits.

Tables 12.6 through 12.8 illustrate various work plans and reports detailing essential information to guide scheduling decisions.

Table 12.6
Detailed Hours Staffing Guide

	Unit Number 3202											For Bus. Date THU–8/15/9X Prepared Date 8/11/9X	
TIME	EI/CO FCST	DEL FCST	C&M	PREP	PROD	DISP	SERV	TELE	DRIV	ADMN	TOTAL	DAY PART	PLAN DIR HRS
08:00				2.0							2.0		
08:30				2.0							2.0		
09:00			1.0	3.0							4.0		
09:30			1.0	3.0							4.0		
10:00	0		3.0	2.0							5.0		
10:30			4.0							1.0	5.0	OPEN–11	11:00
11:00	3		3.0		1.0		1.0				5.0	OPEN–11	11:00
11:30	12		1.5		1.5		2.5	0.5			6.0		
12:00	20				2.0		5.5	0.5			8.0		
12:30	16		1.5		2.0		4.0	0.5			8.0		
01:00	12		3.0		1.5		2.5	0.5		0.5	8.0		
01:30	7		0.5	0.5	3.0		1.5	0.5		1.5	7.5	11–2	12.25
02:00	6			0.5	1.0		1.5				3.0	OPEN–2	32.25
02:30	6		1.0		1.0		1.0				3.0		
03:00	5		1.5		0.5		1.0				3.0		
03.30	5		2.5		1.0		1.0				4.5		
04:00	4		1.5	1.0	2.5		1.0	1.0			7.0		
04:30	4		3.0		2.0		1.0	1.0			7.0	2–5	13.75
05:00	6		2.5		2.0		1.5	1.0			7.0	OPEN–5	46.00
05:30	10				2.0		2.0				4.0		
06:00	8				2.0		2.0				4.0		
06:30	9				2.0		2.0				4.0		
07:00	8		1.0		1.0		2.0				4.0		
07:30	7		0.5	0.5	1.0		1.5	0.5			4.0	5–8	13.50
08:00	4		1.5		1.0		1.0				3.5	OPEN–8	59.50
08:30	3		1.0		1.0		1.0				3.0		
09:00	4				2.0		1.0				3.0		
09:30	4		2.0				1.0				3.0		
10:00	3		2.0				1.0				3.0		
10:30	2		2.0					0.5		0.5	3.0		
11:00	1		2.0								2.0		
11:30	0		1.5		0.5						2.0	8–CLOSE	11.75
12:15					1.0					1.0	2.0	OPN–CLS	71.25

Table 12.7
Employee Availability List

Employee Information		Day of Week	Can Work?	Prefer to Work	Unavailable Time Frame 1	Unavailable Time Frame 2	Preferred Shift
Joe's Diner For All Active Employees							
Name:	Rivera, Norma	Monday	Yes	Yes			
Number:	1479	Tuesday	Yes	Yes			
Phone 1:	914-682-2246	Wednesday	Yes	Yes			
Phone 2:		Thursday	Yes	Yes			
Emergency:		Friday	Yes	Yes			
		Saturday	Yes	Yes			
		Sunday	Yes	Yes			
Salaried/Management Active Employees							
Name:	Gonzalez, Genaro	Monday	Yes	Yes			
Number:	4637	Tuesday	Yes	Yes			
Phone 1:	914-934-2046	Wednesday	Yes	Yes			
Phone 2:		Thursday	Yes	Yes			
Emergency:		Friday	Yes	Yes			
		Saturday	Yes	Yes			
		Sunday	Yes	Yes			
Name:	King, Michael	Monday	Yes	Yes			
Number:	2957	Tuesday	Yes	Yes			
Phone 1:	203-438-9893	Wednesday	Yes	Yes			
Phone 2:		Thursday	Yes	Yes			
Emergency:		Friday	Yes	Yes			
		Saturday	Yes	Yes			
		Sunday	Yes	Yes			

Table 12.8
Schedule Violation Report

<table>
<tr><td colspan="9" align="center">ReMACS Grill
Reports Dates: Monday, December 01, 1997 through Sunday, December 07, 1997</td></tr>
<tr><td colspan="9" align="center">Employee Number–Employee Name</td></tr>
<tr>
<th>Date</th>
<th>Job Name</th>
<th>Punch Type</th>
<th>Scheduled Time</th>
<th>Actual Time</th>
<th>Violation</th>
<th>Severity Level</th>
<th>Manager Name</th>
</tr>
<tr><td colspan="8">7610–Alcott, Andrew</td></tr>
<tr><td>12/6/1997</td><td>Cook</td><td>In</td><td>09:00</td><td>08:41</td><td>Early</td><td>2</td><td></td></tr>
<tr><td colspan="8">2087–Andreta, Mario</td></tr>
<tr><td>12/3/1997</td><td>Cashier</td><td>In</td><td>09:30</td><td>08:58</td><td>Early</td><td>2</td><td></td></tr>
<tr><td>12/5/1997</td><td>Cashier</td><td>In</td><td>09:30</td><td>09:10</td><td>Early</td><td>2</td><td></td></tr>
<tr><td colspan="8">8068–Benson, Theresa</td></tr>
<tr><td>12/7/1997</td><td>Manager</td><td>In</td><td>16:00</td><td>15:05</td><td>Early</td><td>2</td><td></td></tr>
<tr><td colspan="8">1210–Hanson, Jacob</td></tr>
<tr><td>12/1/1997</td><td>Cook</td><td>In</td><td>17:30</td><td>16:25</td><td>Early</td><td>2</td><td></td></tr>
<tr><td>12/2/1997</td><td>Dishwasher</td><td>In</td><td>17:30</td><td>16:26</td><td>Early</td><td>2</td><td></td></tr>
<tr><td>12/4/1997</td><td>Dishwasher</td><td>In</td><td>17:30</td><td>15:52</td><td>Early</td><td>2</td><td></td></tr>
<tr><td>12/5/1997</td><td>Dishwasher</td><td>In</td><td>17:30</td><td>15:52</td><td>Early</td><td>2</td><td></td></tr>
<tr><td>12/6/1997</td><td>Dishwasher</td><td>In</td><td>17:30</td><td>15:33</td><td>Early</td><td>2</td><td></td></tr>
<tr><td>12/7/1997</td><td>Dishwasher</td><td>In</td><td>17:30</td><td>15:25</td><td>Early</td><td>2</td><td></td></tr>
<tr><td colspan="8">4764–Hawkes, Kitty</td></tr>
<tr><td>12/3/1997</td><td>Cook</td><td>In</td><td>17:30</td><td>16:53</td><td>Early</td><td>2</td><td></td></tr>
<tr><td>12/7/1997</td><td>Cook</td><td>In</td><td>16:00</td><td>08:48</td><td>Early</td><td>2</td><td></td></tr>
<tr><td colspan="8">5201–Jackson, Jackie</td></tr>
<tr><td>12/5/1997</td><td>Cashier</td><td>In</td><td>17:00</td><td>17:34</td><td>Late</td><td>2</td><td></td></tr>
<tr><td>12/6/1997</td><td>Cashier</td><td>In</td><td>16:00</td><td>16:51</td><td>Late</td><td>2</td><td></td></tr>
<tr><td>12/7/1997</td><td>Cashier</td><td>In</td><td></td><td>16:23</td><td>Unscheduled</td><td>5</td><td></td></tr>
<tr><td colspan="8">7359–Lakeson, Julie</td></tr>
<tr><td>12/6/1997</td><td>Packer</td><td>In</td><td>17:00</td><td>17:24</td><td>Late</td><td>2</td><td></td></tr>
<tr><td colspan="8">9054–Perkins, Julee</td></tr>
<tr><td>12/1/1997</td><td>Cashier</td><td>In</td><td>16:00</td><td>16:20</td><td>Late</td><td>2</td><td></td></tr>
<tr><td colspan="8">9986–Valdez, Juan</td></tr>
<tr><td>12/7/1997</td><td>Cashier</td><td>In</td><td>16:00</td><td>16:24</td><td>Late</td><td>2</td><td></td></tr>
<tr><td colspan="8">9571–Vettner, Rebecca</td></tr>
<tr><td>12/1/1997</td><td>Cashier</td><td>In</td><td>11:30</td><td>10:54</td><td>Early</td><td>2</td><td></td></tr>
<tr><td colspan="8">0835–Washburn, Rachelle</td></tr>
<tr><td>12/3/1997</td><td>Cashier</td><td>In</td><td>17:30</td><td>17:04</td><td>Early</td><td>2</td><td></td></tr>
<tr><td>12/4/1997</td><td>Cashier</td><td>In</td><td>17:30</td><td>17:09</td><td>Early</td><td>2</td><td></td></tr>
<tr><td colspan="8">4350–Wilkins, Jennifer</td></tr>
<tr><td>12/2/1997</td><td>Cashier</td><td>In</td><td>09:30</td><td>09:58</td><td>Late</td><td>2</td><td></td></tr>
</table>

SUMMARY

Staffing is critical to a foodservice operation. Staffing is defined as having an appropriate number of workers available for the work to be done; scheduling is having them actually on duty at the necessary times. Toward this end a job number control list can be helpful. Part-time workers may be invaluable in foodservice staffing and scheduling. Foodservice presents unusual problems in scheduling. There often are three peaks of activity rather than a steady volume.

The scheduling process can involve nine steps. In scheduling for production, schedules may be prepared for individual items and for work stations. Personnel hours must be adapted to these production schedules. An operation must decide if it wants block or staggered scheduling patterns. The latter is often more efficient. Computerized scheduling is becoming commonplace.

KEY TERMS

block scheduling
full-time equivalents (FTEs)
job number control list

production schedule
staffing
staggered scheduling

REVIEW QUESTIONS

12–1 Why use a job number control list?
12–2 Differentiate between staffing and scheduling.
12–3 All your workers are full-time, and you normally require 40 each day. Approximately how many should be on your staff?
12–4 Discuss advantages and disadvantages of using part-time workers.
12–5 What are particular difficulties in foodservice labor scheduling?

12–6 List nine steps involved in foodservice labor scheduling.
12–7 Explain three types of schedules used in foodservice operations.
12–8 Differentiate between block and staggered scheduling patterns.
12–9 List nine items that can be included in a computerized labor scheduling program.

PROBLEM

12–1 *Weekly Time Schedule Problem*

Purpose: To prepare a weekly time schedule for variable employees based on forecast sales. The operation is a fast-food restaurant in a college town, with the variable employees able to interchange in the various positions.

Guide Hours: The operation's policy is that for each variable employee-hour worked, $48.00 in sales be produced.

Sales Forecast: The sales forecast for the following week is

	Hours: 11 A.M.–3 P.M.	Hours: 3 P.M.–7 P.M.	Hours 7 P.M.–11 P.M.
Mon.	$450	$750	$600
Tues.	$600	$750	$600
Wed.	$600	$900	$450
Thurs.	$600	$750	$450
Fri.	$750	$900	$750
Sat.	$450	$600	$900
Sun.	$900	$750	$450

Problem: Prepare a time sheet for incorporating the sales forecast and guide hours. The following personnel are available:

Mary and Barb can't work after 4 P.M. or on weekends.

Allen and Carl are students and have classes on Tuesday and Thursday.

Jean can work only Monday, Wednesday, and Friday.

Mike can work only Friday, Saturday, and Sunday.

Bob, Tom, and Dave are all full-time employees. It is management policy that at least one of them be working the night shift each evening.

Ken has classes all day Monday, Wednesday, and Friday.

Jim can't work any weekdays before 2 P.M.

Pete can't work on Wednesday or Friday.

Stan has all his classes before 11 A.M. and can work any hours.

Management policy establishes a 40-hour work week for full-time employees and a maximum of 30 hours per week for part-time help. All employees must be off two days each week. Full-time help are not given split shifts or schedules of more than eight hours per day. Part-time help must be scheduled for not less than three-hour periods. Overtime is discouraged.

13

Other Factors That Influence Labor Costs

L abor-cost control is the logical projection of labor-cost analysis, and many of the techniques and formats of analysis discussed in Chapter 11 are also applicable to controlling costs. In this chapter we are especially concerned with correcting some of the causes of high labor costs in foodservice.

Labor-cost control does not end with a one-time correction of problems. A labor-cost management system should establish an immediate or short-term reduction of labor costs, provide sustainable results, and maintain or improve the quality of service and product for your operation. It is a continuous process. The better the routine cost-control procedures, the less chance corrective action will be necessary. As with so many aspects of cost control, a management information system can be very helpful.

The labor costs of an operation result from many factors. Some labor costs arising from layout design, equipment, and union restrictions, for example, are built into the operation from its beginning. Others result from management decisions involving other aspects of the operation, such as menu selection, use of convenience foods, prices to be charged, and amount of employee training required. Still others frequently are caused by lack of direct control over the workers and poor labor practices generally. All factors are important, and the neglect of any one can cause costs to rise.

In this chapter we will discuss some specific causes of high labor cost apart from scheduling and staffing.

After completing this chapter, you should be able to:

1. Explain how factors such as layout and design, union agreements, the menu and its prices, and employee selection and training can influence labor costs.

2. Briefly explain how a sound personnel program, including careful orientation and training, generally reduces labor costs.

3. Define *job evaluation* and explain its role in controlling labor costs.

4. List at least four advantages of a job analysis.

5. Prepare an organizational chart for a hospitality workplace and explain its importance.

6. Explain the importance of a fair wage and salary structure and define the following terms: *simple ranking system, classification system, point system,* and *factor-comparison system.*

7. List at least 10 typical reasons for employee turnover.

8. Discuss the value of the termination interview.

9. Name six common causes of absenteeism and six ways a manager can combat this problem.

10. Calculate a monthly turnover rate and absentee rate.

11. State two ways to control overtime.

12. Outline a formal safety program for a hospitality operation.

13. List and discuss at least five elements of an alcoholic employee's assistance program.

14. Explain the purpose and value of a *daily payroll report,* a *staffing table,* a *daily payroll summary,* a *daily cost report,* and a *staffing guide.*

15. Discuss *fringe benefits* and list at least five fringe benefits commonly offered in the hospitality industry.

16. Name the two categories of employment benefit plans and briefly describe the concept known as *profit sharing.*

17. Discuss wellness programs.

18. Discuss employee assistance programs.

19. Know signs of substance abuse.

20. Discuss workers' compensation insurance.

JOB EVALUATION

The increasing cost of employees and the ever-growing scarcity of skilled and competent workers has brought labor to the forefront of the hospitality industry's problems. Job evaluations, which have long been used by industrial firms, have been adopted by many hospitality operations with considerable success. A **job evaluation** has been defined as a broad analysis of the operating goals affected by the employees. A typical job evaluation has three parts:

1. the job analysis, which consists of preparing job descriptions and job specifications for every job in the organization,

2. the organizational structure, and

3. wage and salary administration, or the determination of a proper wage for a job or employee in comparison with other jobs and employees.

JOB ANALYSIS

Job analysis is a description of the work the employee does, including a complete summary, or job description (Figure 13.1), of the work to be performed. It should indicate what tools, equipment, and materials are involved with the job and the supervision given and received. The second part of job analysis is the job specification, which lists the human or physical requirements needed to do the job successfully. These requirements can include education, experience, physical capabilities, and mental attitudes. The job analysis can also list specific employment factors required by the job, which may not be covered under the broader requirements. Hours worked, days off, and vacation are usually spelled out along with the salary range. In some cases, avenues of possible job promotions or advancements are also noted.

Why use job analysis? It takes a fair amount of work to compile the descriptions and specifications in a job analysis, and many operations have successfully operated without them. However, today's high wage costs make job analyses practically mandatory for control purposes. Before preparing the forms, one must study and evaluate the actual

---

Code No.   22-252A-01-10

Dept.:   Housing and Food Services

Grade: 10

Job Title: Food Production Worker B

The following description covers the typical duties to be performed and/or assigned:

Under normal supervision, performs the following duties:

1. PREPARE salads, salad dressings, appetizers, fruit, jello, and sandwich spreads; FOLLOW simple recipes in cooking fruits, vegetables, and other ingredients.
2. CHECK menus to determine salads required and PREPARE such salads.
3. CHECK products to ensure that they meet desired standards of appearance and portion size.
4. DISASSEMBLE and STORE salad ingredients in proper manner.
5. WORK on serving counter and other areas of food production as required.
6. MOVE foods to and from serving counter as required.
7. Under the direction of the first or second cook, PREPARE vegetables and other food items following methods of food preparation, menus, and recipes.
8. OPERATE and CLEAN equipment such as mixers, choppers, cutters, and slicers; CLEAN refrigerator, tables, sink, and pans.
9. Occasionally INSTRUCT one other person in the preparation of salads, etc.
10. PERFORM periodic and special cleaning duties as required.

Date: 8/24/9X

Figure 13.1
Job Description

jobs. This frequently brings to light cases where employees do not have a full day's work allotted although they may be giving the impression of always being busy. Conversely, it can help identify employees who might be overloaded. Responsibility for work to be accomplished is specified. The forms are a great help to both interviewers and applicants in hiring, orienting, and training new personnel. Interviewers know for which job they are hiring and the qualifications necessary for the job, which have been determined in advance. Applicants can see exactly what the duties are and should not be dissatisfied should the job be different from what was expected. Overlapping of jobs and the resultant bickering are reduced, and a great deal of time is saved on explanation when everything is written down.

Job analysis may be accomplished with outside professional help, but many organizations prefer to do their own, both to save money and because they are already familiar with the jobs. One procedure is to decide first on the content of the evaluation forms. The employees are then asked to write down on a questionnaire what they do on their jobs and what they think the job's qualifications are. The employees' supervisors are also asked to submit the same material. Managers or their representatives then observe the employees on the job. They combine these observations with the other material and write the job analysis in a standard format. This is then reviewed by a committee. The makeup of the committee can be critical. It should include informed members who are willing and capable of asking pertinent and probing questions. Employees and supervisors may be asked to comment before the form becomes official. In securing employees' help, one should assure them that the job analysis will in no way jeopardize the job and that the improved work situation will probably be beneficial. It may also provide employees job satisfaction in the feeling that they are participating with management.

ORGANIZATIONAL STRUCTURE

Any operation with two or more people is an organization and to be efficient must have specified lines of authority, accountability, and lines of responsibility. If not, an informal organization, which always exists in larger operations, will prevail, and much of the power and control will be in the hands of those not designated by management. Although an informal organization with a positive view toward the operation can be very helpful, a situation may occur where the employees are actually running the business. The organizational structure should provide that every employee knows how he or she is involved in the total operation in terms of authority, responsibility, and communication. Each employee should know his or her position, the person(s) to whom he or she is responsible, and the employee(s) who report to him or her. If this is not clear, employees may have several conflicting supervisors telling them what to do, work may be left undone with different employees blaming each other for the deficiencies, and management may face an inefficient or even chaotic situation. Managers cannot do everything themselves and must delegate work to other employees. In doing so, they must specify exactly what employees are to do and must provide the necessary authority for them to do it. A common fault of management is holding an employee responsible for something the employee did not realize was his or her responsibility or did not enjoy the necessary authority to take responsibility.

A job analysis spells out the details of authority and responsibility for an individual job. An **organizational chart** shows in graphic form the relationships of jobs to each other and lines of authority, responsibility, and communication. Chapter 1 discusses organization more fully.

WAGE AND SALARY ADMINISTRATION

One of the greatest causes of employee dissatisfaction, low morale, and turnover occurs when employees believe they are paid an inadequate salary or unfair wages compared to other employees. Inequalities within an operation can be more critical than inequalities between different organizations. In general, three factors determine how much an employee should be paid (apart from funds available and union or other external pressures):

1. what other workers are being paid in the area for the same kind of work
2. the difficulty and demands of the job compared to jobs of others in the operation
3. recognition of the standard of work performed by the individual in his or her job

Managers employing **wage and salary administration** consider these factors and try to provide a salary schedule that can be explained and accepted as fair by employees.

This type of administration is a specialized area, and we suggest that an individual operator either call in outside help or secure more detailed literature dealing with the subject. There are four basic systems, and the operation should adopt the one that best meets its needs.

1. **Simple ranking system**. All jobs are ranked in order of difficulty or importance. Grade levels are determined for appropriate portions of the list, and the compensation for a job depends on its grade level, which in turn depends on its position in the list. This system is usually found in smaller foodservice organizations.

2. **Classification system**. Grades and categories are established, and the various jobs are inserted into the most appropriate grade or category. This system is considered more refined than the ranking system. Salaries vary in more detail according to the grade. This system is used by the federal government.

3. **Point ranking system**. Significant factors common to all jobs under evaluation are specified. Typical factors include mental and physical effort, required type of working conditions, amount of responsibility, education, knowledge required, and need for accuracy. A maximum number of points to be given to any one factor is determined. Each job then receives points in relation to the importance of each factor. The points for each factor are then added and converted into money units. A job that totals 200 points might be paid $8.00 per hour, or a point might be worth 5 cents for a $10.00 hourly wage.

4. **Factor-comparison system**. Significant factors that pertain to all jobs are determined. Key jobs thought to have an appropriate wage schedule are selected as models or measuring standards. The key jobs are ranked factor by factor, and a portion of the wage is allocated to each factor. Other jobs are compared to the models on a factor basis, and an appropriate amount for each factor is awarded, depending on the worth of the factor

INDUSTRY INSIGHTS   by Michael Hurst

Michael Hurst is owner of the renowned 15th Street Fisheries Restaurant. He also teaches at Florida International University.

~

FIVE MYTHS THAT COST BIG BUCKS

Management myths of yesterday are creating turbulence in today's marketplace. Let's look at five of those myths that could lead to the death of your business. They are:

- The budget is your bible.
- Training is a variable cost.
- People are different today.
- The economies of scale mean huge savings.
- Standardization must be 100 percent.

The budget is your bible. The very nature of a competitive marketplace cries out for a guest-focused reward system. Ultimately, a restaurant concept will have longer life if it keeps its eye first on the guest and then on the bottom line. Both are important. The chef who won't allow his service staff

to taste test the food because his bonus is based on food cost has his eye on the bottom line and not the guest. Your servers are salespeople who must know the product to increase profits.

In a perfect world food costs are zero. The only way to accomplish that is to leave the doors locked all day. Or you can forbid your staff to taste the food, cut portions and quality, and avoid offering higher costing items. All that, of course, will gradually erode your customer base.

Keep in mind that a happy guest who spends $50 a year will likely recommend your restaurant to two friends, and those two guests, if they're happy with the dining experience, will each bring two more guests to your place. At the end of 10 years, the original guest has a value to your business of $1,476,200. That price tag alone should tell you that it's foolish to keep your eye on the budget at the expense of your customers.

Training is a variable cost. When guests really are at the top of a modern organizational chart, employee training is a fixed cost. Teaching new employees the basics, while teaching existing employees new skills and reminding them of old lessons, puts an organization in the position of hiring superstars at every level. Employees who are con-

---

in the key job. The total amount of all factors is the wage rate for the job. Since it is assumed that the key jobs were in line with the wages paid in the area, the jobs based on the key jobs will also be in line. This system is more difficult to explain to employees.

The systems are very helpful in comparing the value of one job to another within the organization. Except for the factor-comparison system, the established rates for practical purposes must conform with the wages of the local labor market and wage policies of the operation.

Wage and salary administrations rank the various jobs. Consideration must also be given to how well the individual performs in a particular job. Merit raises may be given, or there could be a range of rates in the job for levels of performance. Seniority or length of service may also be considered. Often, long-term employees are the most efficient. However, some operations that consider seniority have found their labor costs to be higher if they have many long-term employees, especially if they do not care to work as hard as they once did. Other compensation can involve bonuses, tips, and profit sharing.

tinually trained may very well grow beyond you. That growth affords an opportunity to secure the services of someone with even more potential. Thus, turnover is not a cost but an investment in enhanced guest experience.

Training, retraining, and coaching are a continuing and fixed responsibility of management. Raising the bar in terms of higher expectations stimulates the staff and enhances the guest experience. Leadership is about bringing out the best in people, not abusing them.

People (employees) are different today. The theory that there is something uniquely different about people today doesn't hold water. It's been the crying towel of control-focused management for generations. People aren't different. As always, they need training, coaching, understanding, and flexibility. You must understand that the work we provide our employees is secondary to the rest of their life. Their outside responsibilities, particularly their families, take precedence.

Management focused on control doesn't work, certainly not with positive, long-term results. Management that serves the interests of employees leads to secure, happy workers who pay you back with enhanced performance results. The world may be changing, but human needs do not.

Economies of scale mean huge savings. People building—staff and customers—ensures a long and healthy business life. Centralization creates short-term savings at the expense of a long business life in a rapidly changing marketplace. Leaner, flatter organizations are in a position to react faster to change. In terms of restaurant expansion, a simple structure is more efficient than the centralized administrative behemoth of yesterday. Marketing, accounting, human resource management, purchasing, recipe development—handled with limitations on a local basis—offer quicker, more precise solutions. Point-of-sales polls at each unit and high-speed data transmission will keep headquarters advised of pertinent data.

Standardization must be 100 percent. A need to change quickly is mandated by intense competition, populations shifts, new food trends, and an evolving foodservice market. Standardization at 100 percent in multiunit operations may be appropriate for trademarks, signature dishes, layout, design, color, theme, and service items, but menu flexibility may be necessary to adapt to the local community. Promotions geared to the locality are also more effective at times. An organization cannot afford to standardize all functions of its operation because what works in one unit may not in another unit.

ABSENTEEISM

Absenteeism is a major problem for American industry as a whole, and the hospitality industry is no exception. National figures show that the average worker takes off six days for sickness or injury and three days for personal reasons per year. Absenteeism can, of course, lead to reduced output (which is especially troublesome in foodservice, where meals are prepared on demand rather than from inventory), increased record keeping, a need to substitute untrained workers, poorer service and products, increased overtime, and understaffing. All of these increase costs.

Absenteeism, sickness, and leaves without permission cause many problems in the hospitality industry. Since most operations are relatively small, the absence of even a few employees has a serious effect on work schedules, duties of the other employees, and sales volume. Generally, operations that have the most casual attitude toward absenteeism have the highest rates of absenteeism, whereas those that make an effort to curb it usually meet with some success. Some estimate absenteeism unrelated to a legitimate illness may account for 50 to 70 percent of total absenteeism.

Causes of absenteeism vary considerably from place to place. Some authorities have tried to classify the many reasons under three broad categories: on-the-job causes, community causes, and personal causes. On-the-job causes might include poor supervision, kitchen heat, fatigue, dirty working conditions, or poor morale. Community causes could include poor public transportation, inadequate police protection, or lack of child-care facilities. Personal causes can include illness, alcoholism, family responsibilities, or psychological problems. The employer can do much about on-the-job causes and can sometimes help in personal causes. A common problem is when both spouses work and one must take off to care for children who are sick; single parents do not have the luxury to trade off that responsibility.

Some techniques that have been found helpful in combating absenteeism follow.

1. *Checking on the absentee.* A quick telephone call or a short visit to the absentee's home may reveal that the employee is not really sick but has gone fishing. It also indicates management's concern for the employee and his or her absence. A negative factor is that the employee may think, "What's the big deal? Don't you trust me?" Checking should be done as a matter of policy and not sporadically.

2. *Bonuses for attendance.* These can be given to employees for a period of perfect attendance. Unused sick time may be given as a Christmas or year-end bonus. Supervisors may also be rewarded for high attendance in their departments.

3. *Preventive medicine.* Employees might be required to have regular physical examinations. These may expose some physical conditions before they become severe and cause absenteeism. The exams should be given at the time of hiring and periodically during employment, and the employer might pay for them.

4. *Use of social agencies.* Many communities have agencies to which hospitality managers might refer employees who have problems. Alcoholics Anonymous, for example, has rehabilitated many people with alcoholic problems. Instead of summarily discharging alcoholic employees, management could require them to use the services of such an agency as a condition of continuing employment. Other groups have been organized that use the collective self-help techniques of Alcoholics Anonymous for those having difficulty with drugs or gambling urges. Large industrial concerns are beginning to employ the industrial chaplain or psychologist more and more to assist their employees and reduce turnover and absenteeism.

5. *Use of child-care centers.* Finding someone to take care of young children while the parent (or parents) is working can be a real problem for otherwise productive employees. The increasing number of single-parent families or families where both spouses work magnifies the problem. By providing or arranging for regular child care, the employer can go far toward eliminating this cause of absenteeism. However, the costs to the employer can be high.

6. *Flex time.* Making an employee's working hours as flexible as possible can eliminate many reasons of absenteeism. Some smaller foodservice operations have gone so far as to let the employees schedule themselves as long as the normal shifts are covered. This requires a very cooperative group of workers.

7. *Four-day weeks.* Four 10-hour days equals 40 hours. Three free days a week allow more time for personal matters. One problem with the four-day work week, however,

is that some employees might try to get another part-time job during the extra period and perhaps overwork themselves.

8. *Paid leave banks.* Pooling all time-off benefits, such as vacation, sick leave, and bereavement leave, together tends to reduce unexcused absences and thus makes scheduling easier. Unused time is not carried over into the next year, but employees may cash out, or be paid for, any leave not used.

9. *Monitoring reasons for absenteeism.* Tracking may help managers determine if something can be done to alleviate underlying causes.

To control absenteeism or to determine if it is a real problem, one must analyze how much absenteeism there is. A standard formula for determining absenteeism (the **absenteeism ratio**) is

$$A \text{ (Rate of absenteeism)} = \frac{(\text{Number of daily absentees during period}) \times 100}{(\text{Average number of employees}) \times (\text{Number of working days})}$$

Let us assume

Number of absences during period	6
Average number of employees	22
Number of working days in period	30

The calculations would then be

$$A = \frac{6 \times 100}{11 \times 30} = 0.9\%$$

Once the general rate of absenteeism is determined, it may be desirable to use other ratios to pinpoint specific problems. There are at least 41 ratios that can be used for this purpose, but common ones are the incidence ratio, inactivity ratio, and severity ratio. These ratios are used to further indicate the specific absenteeism problem.

The **incidence ratio (Icr)** helps show how widespread absenteeism is. It can be helpful to know if it is spread over a large number of workers or is confined to a smaller number:

$$Icr = \frac{\text{Number of employees absent}}{\text{Total number of employees}} \times 100$$

If there were seven employee absences during a month (an absence is defined as 1 hour or longer) and there are 100 workers, the calculations are

$$Icr = \frac{7}{100} \times 100 = 7\%$$

The **inactivity ratio (Iar)** shows what percentage absenteeism is to total hours worked.

$$Iar = \frac{\text{Number of hours of absenteeism}}{\text{Number of hours worked in a period (often, 1 week)}}$$

If there were 40 hours of absenteeism in a week where 1,000 hours were worked, the calculations are

$$Iar = \frac{40}{1,000} \times 100 = 4\%$$

A **severity ratio (Sr)**, or average length of absence, is found by dividing the number of hours of absences by the number of absences, which indicates how severe or time-consuming the average absence is. An operation might have a high absenteeism ratio for a period, but this ratio could show that it was caused by relatively few absentees with long-term absences. If there were six absences amounting to 90 hours, the average absence would be 15 hours.

TURNOVER

A major problem in the food industry—one that has a direct effect on costs and productivity—is turnover of employees. Turnover occurs when employees leave the operation and are replaced by new ones. In the foodservice industry, turnover is far above that of general industry. One figure sometimes quoted is 10.4 percent per month, or about 125 percent per year. Despite these high percentages, many individual operations have low turnover rates, proving that high turnover is not necessarily inherent in the food industry and that it can be alleviated. Estimates of the cost of replacing a rank-and-file employee range from $1000 to $2000 or more. The problem of employee turnover is exacerbated in foodservices by the low income generated by each employee—$45,000 is a figure sometimes used. (In the automobile industry, each employee contributes $250,000 or more in income.) The cost of employee turnover in foodservice is a much higher percentage of revenue than in most other industries.

One fast-food company determined that 20 percent of its units with the lowest turnover had double the sales and 55 percent higher profits than the 20 percent of units with the highest turnover.

It may take $8,000 to $25,000 in sales to make up for the turnover of one employee. Filling vacated positions can involve time expended for exit interviews, administrative functions, separation pay, and unemployment taxes. Prior to leaving the organization, an employee can have behavioral and attitude problems that are manifested in tardiness, poor performance, low morale, and absenteeism. These problems can also affect other employees adversely. Turnover abrades managerial effectiveness, stifles competitiveness, and is disruptive to the operation's sanguine atmosphere.

Filling vacated positions can involve entrance interviews, testing, training, preemployment physical, advertising, employment agency fees, and preemployment administrative functions.

Turnover also results in the intangible nonmonetary cost of poorer service to patrons, risking dissatisfaction and loss of patronage. The greatest turnover usually occurs within the first two weeks of employment, and any long-term benefit of training and supervision is wasted. The following list discusses some of the major causes of turnover among foodservice employees:

1. *Poor selection, hiring, and orientation.* Management hires the first "body" to apply without adequately checking qualifications or references.

2. *New employees placed in jobs that are not compatible with their capabilities.* Employees will become bored if the work is not challenging or interesting, or they will be frustrated if the job is too difficult.

3. *Inadequate information about the job or its requirements.* New employees may find the job vastly different from what they had imagined. The use of job descriptions and job specifications can be very helpful in preventing this problem. New employees should be fully informed about their job.

4. *Inadequate or poor supervision, causing a potentially good worker to give up early on.* New workers need help, guidance, and assurance.

5. *Lack of a proper wage rate structure.* New employees should not be hired at a higher rate than that being paid to current workers in similar positions. Violating this rule leads to resentment and employee turnover. A definite wage rate policy is necessary.

6. *Lack of a training program.* The more highly trained employees are, the more likely they are to stay on the job. An operation with a continuous training program will retain employees for a longer period of time. Training instills a feeling of status and professionalism and increases efficiency, productivity, and loyalty.

7. *Lack of a grievance outlet.* If an employee has a grievance, there should be a procedure whereby it can be expressed without future prejudice. A grievance may be real or imagined and can smolder and then flare beyond rational importance. Misunderstandings should be cleared up before they become major problems.

8. *Poor working conditions.* Substandard working conditions and inadequate facilities can contribute to a high turnover rate. Proper restrooms and washroom facilities are most important to the food industry and help to increase morale and sanitation standards.

9. *Lack of advancement.* Ambitious new employees like to see a path by which they can advance. The bus person who can reasonably expect to become a server and then the head server, or the scullery person who can conceivably become a chef, will be less likely to leave the place of employment.

10. *Lack of financial incentive.* A worker likes to earn as much as possible and will gravitate toward the highest wage. Higher wages alone may not retain employees. If an adequate wage is already being earned, then other considerations, both psychological and material, become more important when considering a change of jobs.

11. *Apparent lack of supervisory interest.* Sensitive, good supervisors and department heads and good employee relations will lower employee turnover. Incentive plans of recognition, awards, sports teams, picnics, company activities, comfortable working conditions, and pleasant surroundings all contribute to employee satisfaction. In fact, all of the 10 previously mentioned causes of high turnover rates are closely tied to the lack of the human factor.

Measuring Turnover

Turnover may be lowered by good personnel administration and by reducing the causes of high turnover where possible. To combat turnover, it is very important to know what is causing it. Termination interviews often are used for this purpose. Departing employees are interviewed by management to determine their reasons for leaving (even if they are being fired). Quite often the reason for leaving may not be the one first mentioned; unfavorable situations such as poor working conditions or an unfair or incompetent supervisor may be brought to light only reticently. Larger organizations have regular report

Name:	Date:	Dept.	Shift	Date hired
Address:	Sex	Marital Status	Age	Dependents

Present job	Previous training and experience

Supervisor's name	Type of separation Quit ☐ Discharge ☐ Lay-off ☐ Mil. ☐ Misc. ☐ sep. sep.

Reason for separation—employee's statement:

Reason for separation—supervisor's statement:

Indirect causes or conditions contributing to this separation—foreman's statement and his suggestions for correcting these conditions:

Reason for separation—interviewer's statement:

Final action taken:

Would you rehire?

    Yes ☐   No ☐

                                            Signature of Interviewer

Figure 13.2
Termination Interview Report

forms for the termination interview and summarize the prevalent reasons for turnover regularly. Since employees may have strong feelings about leaving, some managers prefer to send a letter the following week containing a form to be filled in with the reasons for the departure and a stamped, self-addressed return envelope. The theory behind this practice is that employees may be more objective about their departure at a later time.

Figure 13.2 shows a termination interview report. These should be summarized periodically to determine whether trends or curable situations are behind terminations. To control turnover, it is necessary to establish the current **turnover rate** for comparison purposes. There are a number of different formulas that may be used to compute the turnover rate, but whichever one is chosen, it is important that the same formula be used each time. One formula for determining a monthly turnover rate divides the number of separations during the month by the total number of workers on the payroll in the pay period ending nearest the 15th of the same month:

$$T\,(\text{Turnover rate}) = \frac{S\,(\text{Number of separations})}{M\,(\text{Midmonth work force})} \times 100$$

If 50 employees were on the payroll at midmonth and six were terminated during the month, the turnover rate would be 12 percent.

$$T = \frac{6}{50} = 12$$

The formula can also be done on an annual basis or by using the average workforce for the period.

To best evaluate turnover, more specific data may be desired, such as rate of those employees who quit, were fired, or laid off. It may be desirable to analyze the rate for different types of employees such as production, service, or sanitation.

It may be helpful to calculate how long the average new hire stays on the job. Often operations have steady corps of employees with little turnover and if the turnover is with new hires, management should try to determine why.

Reducing Turnover

Reducing turnover involves tackling the problems that cause people to leave. Increasingly turnover is being linked to social reasons as well as economic ones such as wage levels. Some recommendations for reducing turnover include:

1. Know your turnover rate and cost of turnover.

2. Institute a quality program of recruitment and retention. A direct, cost-effective way to reduce turnover is to use valid, reliable employment selection tests that determine which applicants fit the model of the long-term, effective employee.

3. Implement a socialization process that involves management to ease employees into the organization and making their transition comfortable. This can be accomplished by orientation programs for new hires that help them understand the organization. An orientation follow-up can also be of significant help. Supervisors of new employees can serve as role models and set expectations. The positive influence created by this is known as the *Pygmalion effect.* Supervisors who believe new employees can do well will convey this to the employees who will be prone to live up to expectations.

4. Offer profit sharing and share ownership. As the organization grows because of the efforts of its employees, the employees are also rewarded.

5. Provide a realistic job preview. Such previews can give applicants a realistic view of the job prior to entry so they are less likely to have unrealistic expectations once hired. It can show them company policies and organizational behavior. It should explicitly show tasks that applicants will be expected to perform.

6. Help employees achieve job satisfaction. Job satisfaction as it relates to turnover has been mentioned repeatedly and has been found to have a consistent negative relationship to turnover. Those who are dissatisfied on the job have been found to be more likely to leave than are their satisfied counterparts.

7. Offer cross-training programs to help reduce boredom and absenteeism.

8. Implement a job enrichment program to give workers more pride in their jobs and a broader appreciation of their importance to the company. This program can combine subparts of a job so that the resulting job offers more skill variety.

INDUSTRY INSIGHTS   by The Coach, Don Smith, Washington State University

Don Smith is a well known hospitality educator who appears frequently before industry groups.

HIRE FRIENDLIES

We work in a caring business where hiring "friendlies" is essential. Some people are as warm as sunshine and as welcome as a sunrise. You see it in their smile, hear it in their voice, and feel it in their walk. You can tell they enjoy life and find their work rewarding. Friendlies are gifted in the art of relating. They have mastered the skill of communicating, most often without words. Most of all they have mastered the art of listening and observing.

Let me share an example of a dinner my wife and I enjoyed on her birthday. We had been seated for only a couple of minutes when our server glided up, made a soft landing on one knee, put his elbows on the table, and with an impish smile said, "My name is Harold. My job is to make you happy tonight and whatever you do, don't lose me. For if you lose me, you lose a really good thing." What an entrance!

I have spoken out against rote "Steak and Ale" introductions by service people for over 25 years. They are tiring and insincere. Frankly, I do not go to restaurants to be on first name basis with a waiter. But this was not an ordinary waiter. Harold was truly an artist of influence. As the laughter subsided and a little repartee exchanged, he continued: "Listen! Before I take your drink order, I want you to think about three 'not on the menu' items tonight." He described them with the enthusiasm of their inventor and went on. "But whatever you do, don't eat too much. You must save room for our famous Black Raspberry Cheesecake. It's to die for." Harold's magic had begun. Of course, we were in the mood for cocktails and calamari and onion loaf and a good time.

As a guy who makes his daily bread in this business, I was fascinated by Harold and observed him

carefully as he interacted with his three other tables that evening. What was most interesting was that his approach was a little different at each table, always cheerful, but different. At one table Harold's enthusiasm was more subdued, even a bit formal. At another he supplied a quick little joke, and at the third all I could hear was their laughter. Ours was the only table where he came down to one knee to greet us or made the "don't lose me" statement. He either had many dramas from which to draw or made them up as he went along. This was a true artist at work and a joy to watch and learn from.

Somehow Harold picked up on our reason for celebrating and surprised us with a complimentary dessert, candle and all, after which we had a special coffee. As the evening fun and celebration ended and the credit card with a 25 percent gratuity was signed, I had to stop Harold for a moment to thank him. My true agenda was to ask how he knew to use the different approaches for each of his tables. His answer was honest, even if a bit disappointing from a scientific perspective. He said, "I don't know. I just feel it."

This story is almost true. It really was my wife's birthday, but I don't remember what we ate. I still remember the restaurant, though. It was one of the first Victoria Stations in Atlanta. More importantly, the waiter's name really was Harold and "If you lose me, you lose a very good thing" were his opening words. It happened 30 years ago. How's that for making a lasting impression?

How did Harold manage to create such happiness for others while at the same time making a buck for himself and his employer? If we can identify the characteristics, perhaps we can teach it. Certainly in this business of hospitality where the quality of service and relationship building is key to repeat business, we should give this subject much thought.

What Harold Had

We could discuss many characteristics, such as Harold's energy, communication skills, training, appearance, and motivation. The two traits I believe are most important are empathy and optimism.

The first time I ever heard the word *empathy* was in 1957. It was a concept put forth in the book,

New Ways in Discipline by Dorothy Baruch. She likened empathy to one's ability to sense another person's feelings and mirror them back to that individual. Generally, the degree we are sensitive to what another person is experiencing emotionally determines our interpersonal effectiveness. Empathy is at the heart of understanding, caring, relating, bonding, and influencing others. Harold was on track when he said, "I just feel it." Empathy is experiencing another person's feelings.

Empathy differs from *sympathy* in that sympathetic words are empty of feelings. How many times has someone failed in an attempt to ease some distress or problem by saying the words, "Believe me, I know how you feel." When the words are empty of true feeling, they are meaningless and can even exacerbate the problem. Recently, for example, a pilot with a low level of empathy for passengers announced, "We appreciate your patience for putting up with the delay." The jetliner had been sitting on the tarmac at Houston International Airport for over an hour. The disgruntled passengers had been sitting in the overheated 727 cabin with no information about the problem, no progress report, and no apology. How insincere and ridiculous he sounded. We had no choice but to sit there. Patience had nothing to do with it.

This brings us to the concept of *readers*. I have employed many excellent service people over the years and the level of their effectiveness related to their ability to read the nonverbal behavior of others. Some people can read others so well they seem to have ESP. They can pick up on problems and opportunities by the intonation in guests' voices, eye movements, facial expressions, and body language. Thus, at the root of empathy is one's ability to read the nonverbal cues of others and not just their words. If service people or anyone responsible for influencing others (salespeople, teachers, parents, etc.) are not good readers, they will be order takers and deliverers at best and creators of misunderstanding and customer problems at worst.

Once I likened readers to chameleons, but now I realize they do much more. The chameleon is a slow-moving lizard that can quickly change colors to match its surroundings, thus making itself virtually invisible. Figuratively speaking, exceptional readers

begin by changing their style to match patrons' moods; however, they eventually change the color of their patrons' mood. When Harold said his job was to make us happy that evening, it was clearly his reason for being there, no matter what our mood.

Friendlies are optimistic people. Optimism can be a powerful asset. I encourage anyone who is responsible for hiring, training, and developing people, particularly in the hospitality business, to read Martin E. P. Seligman's *Learned Optimism.*

Dr. Seligman makes a serious distinction between people who tend to be successful and those who tend to be unsuccessful. He persuasively argues that optimistic people have distinctly different ways of viewing the world. When viewing the possibilities of outcomes of events, optimists tend to see results in positive ways. When optimists are confronted with a bad situation, they tend to see it as a temporary setback. They don't see it as their fault and will most often see hard knocks as a challenge they can correct. Pessimists see bad events as lasting a long time, and they tend to blame themselves for negative situations. The two habits of thinking become self-fulfilling prophecies. Seligman's research indicates that "optimists tend to do much better in school and college, at work and on the playing field." His research indicates that they are healthier and live longer than pessimists. The good news is that even deeply rooted pessimism can be changed. It will suffice for our purposes to say that we need optimistic people in our business.

Can You Train Friendlies?

For years I have argued that small business operators, even if they could, don't have the time to train for the job. Empathy and optimism are hired, not trained. We must have friendlies to build a loyal family of customers. In addition, we must keep them once we hire them. I am not suggesting it is easy in today's labor market but nothing worth having comes easy. If you think it can't be done, you might rush out to purchase *Learned Optimism.* We are not looking for rocket scientists. We need nice people, and there are lots of nice people.

In his book *Emotional Intelligence,* Daniel Goleman stresses the importance and power of one's emotional IQ, or EQ. He suggests we have two minds, two different ways of knowing. One is the rational mind, the mode of conscious comprehension with which we are most familiar. With this mind we think, question, and evaluate. The emotional mind, on the other hand, is impulsive, powerful, and sometimes illogical. Dr. Goleman explains, "The emotional/rational dichotomy approximates the folk distinction between 'heart' and 'head'; knowing something is 'right in your heart' is a different order of conviction—somehow a deeper kind of certainty—than thinking so much with your rational mind." While the two minds operate in *harmony,* the emotional mind becomes more dominant the more intense the feelings. Harold's rational mind might have put aside the words, "Don't lose me. For if you lose me, you lose a good thing." However his emotional mind, sizing up the situation, felt it was the right thing to say and dominated the moment.

Where does empathy development begin? What is being learned today is that the power of the emotional mind begins developing at birth, and perhaps even before. Empathy develops in early childhood. Most people have empathy or at least the brain circuitry for it. The earliest experiences we have as babies and children make us more or less adept at reading the feelings of others. Dr. Goleman's research suggests that the nature of an adult is cast at a very young age. Some people are wonderfully tuned in to reading others' emotions, and other people are emotionally tone deaf. Emotional IQ has nothing to do with innate intelligence.

Dr. Goleman explains that "evidence suggests that the higher one's empathetic acuity the better adjusted, more popular, more outgoing and sensitive." What can you do to improve your EQ? Dr. Goleman offers these suggestions:

1. Work to be in touch with your feelings. Emotional intelligence begins with a high level of self-awareness. Be aware of feelings such as anger, joy, jealousy, and fear. Think about your feelings and tendencies to react to each of these conditions.
2. Attempt to understand how people you interact with feel. What signals their feelings? The more

you understand your feelings, the more skilled you become at reading the feelings of others.
3. Control your feelings. Empathy is of little value unless it is expressed effectively. Reading another person's feelings is only effective if you can control your feelings to bring about the desired interpersonal response. This does not mean you should withhold feelings, but you must be in control to express them.

In closing, employers should recruit service personnel with signs of high EQ. If in interviews prospects have difficulty in making eye contact, don't smile easily, or are unable to read your nonverbal cues, you should not consider them for positions of guest services. Even if we could change habits developed in early childhood, businesses that depend upon people for service and goodwill do not have the time to do so.

Empathy can be nurtured. Most people are not emotionally tone deaf. Their level of empathy and optimism can be enhanced. Managers can enhance empathy at every opportunity through positive reinforcement and reward.

Where Do You Find Friendlies?

Begin inside your place of business. Go to those people who you know come to work and make it a better place to work. Watch customers or workers at the local laundry. Always carry a business card like the one I include here that reads, "I Like Your Style." It can be your best recruiting tool. I met one of the best managers I have ever known while picking up laundry. I was waiting in a line of four people on a hot summer afternoon at a cleaners in Elgin, Illinois. I watched as this dynamo of positive energy raised the spirit of each customer as they interacted. Her eyes, smile, and initial greeting would pierce customers' attitudes as they approached the counter. Her enthusiastic "Good afternoon!" seemed to be at a different level for each of us. Without lost motion in doing her job, she found time to kid one customer, notice some point of dress for another, and call them by name as if they were old friends. By the time it was my turn I had my "I Like Your Style" business card in hand. I introduced myself as the owner of the Chateau Louise up the road and asked her name. Giving her the card, I remarked that we were looking for someone with her gift of people and, if she had a friend that might fit that description, asked her to refer them to me. One day a few weeks later, Mara came in to talk to me about a part-time job. Within three years, Mara Palmer, an immigrant from Rome with no education beyond high school, was managing the most successful restaurant at the Chateau Louise.

Develop Your Own Screening Device

In addition, listening and observation are most often key indicators. For example, how well does an individual understand and express their own feelings? How effective are their nonverbal cues? What do they find funny and do they have the capacity to laugh at themselves (a sign of confidence)? How easily do they give up on a goal and how persistent are they?

Here is one system to develop a benchmark for screening job candidates.

1. Identify your most effective service personnel. Who would you choose to serve your best friends if they were coming to the restaurant for the first time? Then identify your least effective service personnel.
2. Observe a variety of guests in service situations. The pictures should provide insights into guest feelings. They may be pleased or angry, thrilled or unhappy with the product or service.
3. As a basis for a benchmark, show your most effective service personnel the pictures of facial expressions, eye movements, and expression and body language without audio. Use the audio without pictures and finally the combined audio and pictures. Then do the same for the low performers.
4. Evaluate the responses of each. This evaluation becomes the benchmark for candidates.

It takes more than empathy to become a leader. When I first met Mara, I was impressed with her high level of empathy and customer service. I had no plans to place her in a position of authority. Leadership requires additional talents. In addition to vision, courage, and persistence, one must have a strong sense of ego and clarity of purpose. Leaders must balance empathy with ego. While it takes empathy and caring to relate to people, a will to survive economically and a burning desire to compete and win are needed to survive in today's brutal business environment. Too much empathy creates pushovers. Too much ego creates tiresome bores. Leadership requires a balance.

This is a copy of a folding business card developed by Dirk Smith, a marketing manager for Taco Bell. It is given to people who exhibit a highly positive customer-making talent.

(Business Card Cover)

I LIKE YOUR STYLE

(Inside)

HELLO OPPORTUNITY!

I am impressed by your service style. You are the type of individual that will be successful in the hospitality industry and the kind of person we want on our Taco Bell team!

Taco Bell is one of the fastest growing and successful food companies in the world with nearly 3,000 restaurants and building 250 to 300 a year. The career opportunities are exceptional!

Obviously, you are happy with your present job, but perhaps you know someone like yourself who is not so content and would be interested in discussing career opportunities with Taco Bell. If so, please pass along this card and suggest a quick phone call to myself.

We know what it takes to be #1.

(Back)

List the manager's name, business address, phone and fax number.

9. Train continuously. Quality training within the operation can significantly cut down on turnover.

10. Develop a program of continuous quality improvement (CQI). This program seeks quality through the efforts of everyone in the organization and is a never-ending process which seeks to improve operational standards. It provides a systematic approach that uses methods and tools to enhance the practice of quality within the organization and empowers at all levels to construct the framework for success (see Chapter 3).

An extremely low turnover rate is not necessarily good. Management may be tolerating employees who, although very satisfied, should be contributing more. Low turnover may also signal that managers are intimidated by employees. While a good function of management is to encourage cooperation and cordiality among all employees, this can be carried to an extreme. Employees who do not contribute their fair share to the organization or receive favoritism can cause resentment in others.

Date _8/2_   Section _Sanitation_   Supervisor _Green_

Name	Position	Time	Elapsed time	Reason
John Jones	Dishwasher	8-9-45 p.m.	1¾ hours	Dishwasher breackdown caused delay

Figure 13.3
Overtime Report

OVERTIME CONTROL

One of the best ways to encourage high labor costs is to allow uncontrolled overtime work. It may be necessary occasionally for employees to work beyond their normal hours, but if uncontrolled, overtime becomes a substitute for proper scheduling or planning. Employees may try to create overtime conditions to earn extra money. To avoid overtime, management must forecast workloads and schedule the staff for the workload within the normal period. It is almost axiomatic that if management accepts overtime claims without question, the privilege will be abused.

Two practices can be very helpful in controlling overtime. One is to require a requisition in advance for overtime personnel. This requisition should include the name and job of the employee involved, the amount of overtime the job requires, and the reason for the overtime. Management approves the requisition by signing it. In addition to its function as a control device, the form requires supervisors to correlate accurately personnel with the workload since they must determine in advance whether overtime assistance will be needed.

There are, of course, reasons for overtime, such as breakdowns or unexpected business, that cannot be predicted in advance. In such cases, management should insist that an overtime report be prepared within 24 hours showing the amount of overtime worked and giving the reason for it. It is much easier to evaluate the need for overtime when the facts are current than at the end of the month when reasons may have been forgotten by management or invented by employees. Figures 13.3 and 13.4 illustrate typical forms used to control overtime.

AUTHORIZATION FOR OVERTIME OR EXTRA WAGES

Number

Function __________ Date Scheduled __________

Number of Persons or Overtime Hours Required	Job Classification	Rate	Per
Remarks			

Date filed __________ Department head __________

Date approved __________ Manager __________

Figure 13.4
Authorization Form for Overtime or Extra Wages

SAFETY AND ACCIDENT PREVENTION

Besides humane considerations, safety and accident prevention can provide economic benefits and help eliminate possible legal problems. It is perfectly possible for a $100 accident to wipe out the profit from $5,000 in sales. Moreover, the Occupational Safety and Health Act (OSHA) requires compliance with safety standards. A kitchen can be a dangerous place in which to work. It has hot surfaces, possibly an open fire, sharp knives and cans, slippery floors, constant movement, and machinery such as mixers, choppers, and slicers.

The most common kitchen injuries include slips and falls, lifting strains, burns, cuts, and food machinery injuries. Some sensible ways to reduce these causes include:
(for slips and falls)

- nonslip floors
- wide aisles
- no blind corners
- immediate mopping of spills
- a no-running policy
- repairing cracks and holes
- proper ladders for reaching shelves
- tight carpets that do not bunch up
- general and constant housekeeping and cleanliness

(for lifting strains)

- showing employees how to lift properly
- limiting weights that can be lifted (often to 25 pounds)
- using carts or other mobile equipment instead of carrying

(for burns)

- supplying uniforms with sleeves
- requiring use of hot pads
- providing a cooling area at pot sink
- using handles on pots
- insulating pipes on hot surfaces
- supplying instructions on filtering cooking oil

(for cuts)

- keeping knives sharp (a dull knife is more likely to slip)
- never throwing knives to be washed into a sink with soapy water
- storing knives with handles up in racks
- never keeping food in open cans with jagged edges

(for food machinery injuries)

- training employees in use of equipment
- using the machinery guards

- grounding all appliances
- unplugging machines when cleaning them
- insisting that employees not wear loose clothing or dangling jewelry around equipment
- keeping fingers from guiding the food into slicers, grinders, or choppers
- posting instructions near the equipment
- keeping blades sharp

A FORMAL SAFETY PROGRAM

Some operations have a formal safety program. Common elements of such programs include a management policy statement specifying management's concern for and commitment to safety and a safety committee whose members can include management, union representatives, a personnel representative, employee representative, and the chief engineer or maintenance person. The committee's responsibilities might include:

1. *Preparing for emergencies.* Employees should be instructed what to do when an emergency or accident occurs, such as summoning an ambulance, calling the fire department, evacuating the premises if necessary, giving cardiopulmonary resuscitation, and applying the appropriate procedures when someone is choking.

2. *Establishing safety inspection procedures.* The premises and equipment should be regularly monitored for unsafe conditions. Many checklists are available for these inspections. The inspections may be conducted by staff or by professionals from the outside.

3. *Developing safe work procedures.* Every job or work station should be analyzed and safety procedures developed for it. In some cases these procedures should be posted in the area or by the equipment. All employees should be instructed how to use these procedures.

4. *Providing safety education instruction.* This instruction could include preventing accidents from slips, falls, burns, and machinery. The instruction should be continuous so new employees receive it and longer-term employees receive reviews. Many training aids are available from insurance companies, OSHA, and local agencies.

5. *Investigating accidents and completing reports.* Every accident should be investigated and usually a report prepared, including pictures if appropriate. This is necessary to prevent additional accidents and to discourage unwarranted legal action. Questions that should be covered in the report include:

- What happened?
- Why did it happen?
- Who was injured?
- When did it occur?
- What was the employee doing immediately before the accident and at the time of the accident?
- What materials, machines, equipment, or conditions were involved?
- What can be done to prevent a recurrence?

Witnesses should be identified and asked to provide a description of the accident.

6. *Complying with governmental safety codes.* Federal, state, and local jurisdictions are enacting more laws to improve safety in the workplace. A manager on the committee should have the responsibility for remaining constantly aware of these laws and seeing to it that the operation is in compliance.

7. *Auditing the safety program.* This task again is a responsibility of management. Appointing a safety committee does not by itself ensure an effective safety program. Management should periodically check to see if the committee is performing its function. If the safety record is lower than similar establishments, there should be concern.

The government has provided a measurement known as the **accident incidence rate (AIR)**, to analyze the number of accidents. The formula is

$$AIR = \frac{(\text{Number of accidents in period}) \times 200,000}{(\text{Number of employee-hours worked in period})}$$

Assume 10 accidents and 800,000 hours worked.

$$AIR = \frac{10 \times 200,000}{800,000} = 2.5$$

Because the ratio considers only hours worked, different time periods such as months or years can be compared. (The 200,000 figure represents 100 workers working a normal 2,000 hours a year.)

WELLNESS PROGRAMS

Wellness programs were almost unknown a few years ago. Today they are being considered and used more and more. A wellness program is concerned with the various combinations of specific activities or interventions initiated by an organization with the intent of enhancing the overall physical or psychological health of its people. Wellness programs emphasize preventive medicine rather than a focus on detecting and correcting health problems. This includes creative awareness and providing health-promotion opportunities to employees. Activities are designed to alter employees' lifestyles in the direction of positive health practices and to head off preventable illnesses and injuries. Impetus for such programs has increased with the awareness that the more sedimentary American lifestyle has been identified as a major contributor to the 10 leading causes of death. One large nonhospitality company stated that nearly half of its annual $40 million health-care budget resulted from ailments related to lifestyle.

Labor is a very expensive cost to an operation, so it pays to make labor as productive as possible; a healthy worker should generally be more productive than an ailing one. One would also hope that an employer, out of concern for employees, would like to see them as healthy as possible. Employees who are in poor physical condition are more prone to accidents, and in some situations, employees who are infected with a disease can transmit it to other employees or patrons.

Probably the biggest impetus to wellness programs is the rising cost of health care and health-care insurance and the indirect costs of wages paid to substitute employees.

This is not just a business problem, but a national social problem. Furthermore, the cost is likely to balloon in the future. Yet, 42 million Americans (up from 37 million in 1992) lack access to health-care insurance. Surely there can be improvements in the health-care delivery system and its funding.

EVALUATING CORPORATE WELLNESS INVESTMENT

Cost-Effectiveness Analysis

Cost-effectiveness (C/E) analysis identifies the cost of producing a unit of effect within a given program. To illustrate, look at an example. Suppose a workplace weight-control program has an annual cost of $20,000 for a 100-employee population. The average reduction in weight per individual is 10 pounds. The C/E ratio is

$20,000/100 divided by 10 lbs. = $20.00 for each pound reduced

or

Cost-effectiveness = $20,000/10 lbs. × 100 employees or again $20 per pound lost

C/E analysis permits comparisons of alternative intervention programs designed to achieve the same goal. For example, the $20.00 cost per pound achieved by this program could be compared to alternative programs not offered, such as at a weight loss clinic. Unfortunately, C/E analysis fails to offer a financial perspective—whether the program is financially beneficial. The benefits of the program are not expressed in monetary terms. Cost-benefit analysis can be used instead.

Cost-Benefit Analysis

Cost-benefit (C/B) analysis is similar to C/E analysis in that both focus on goals, costs, and benefits. The difference is that C/B analysis expresses benefits in monetary terms. One of the most popular forms of C/B analysis is return-on-investment (ROI) analysis. Although traditionally associated with investments in hard assets, ROI analysis also can be used to evaluate returns on investments in wellness activities by relating program profits to invested capital. It does so in terms of a ratio in which the numerator expresses some measure of profit related to the project, and the denominator represents the firm's investment in the program.

Suppose a wellness program costs a firm $75,000 during its first year of operation. The measured saving from reduced absenteeism is $5,000, from reduced employer health-care payments (assuming a self-funded plan) is $7,000, and from reduced employee turnover is $3,000. The ROI before interest and taxes would be calculated as follows:

Benefit type	Benefit amount
Reduced absenteeism	$ 5,000
Reduced health-care payments	$ 7,000
Reduced employee turnover	$ 3,000
Total expected benefits	$15,000

ROI = Total expected benefits/program investment

ROI = $15,000/75,000 = 20%

As a measure of return, the ROI statistic can be compared with other investment opportunities inside or outside a company. If an expected return of 15 percent on invested capital is desired, the 20 percent return from the wellness program would be very favorable.

More sophisticated techniques emphasizing the time value of money such as net present value (NPV) or internal rate of return (IRR) can also be used.

LEVELS OF WELLNESS PROGRAMS

The scope of wellness and fitness programs offered by businesses can vary tremendously. One classification of these programs has three levels.

The first level consists of awareness programs that include newsletters, health fairs, screening sessions, posters, flyers, and educational programs. Although these programs may or may not directly improve someone's health, they are helpful in making individuals aware of the consequences of unhealthful habits and in motivating them for positive behavior possibly in the next level.

The next level involves lifestyle modification with specific programs. The programs may last 8 to 12 weeks and are available on an ongoing basis. They are intended to provide long-term health benefits through formation of new health habits. Examples of programs at this level include self-administration fitness programs, access to local health facilities, and classes teaching the proper performance of physically demanding work tasks. Management can also review design of the workplace to provide the safest and most healthy arrangement. For example, are heights and distances in the work area optimum for the worker?

The third level has as its goal the creation of an environment that assists individuals in sustaining their healthy lifestyles and behaviors. Physical workout facilities may be provided. Healthy food is made available at the workplace. Smoking is not permitted, and perhaps a bonus is paid to nonsmokers.

It may be harder to create a wellness and fitness program in the foodservice industry than in some other industries. Many of the operations are small, making it difficult to finance programs with few participants. The high turnover can limit the payoff from such programs. Some workers may be hard to motivate. The industry has its share of workers with health problems, such as alcoholism, chronic smoking, and drug use.

However, even the smallest operation can do something. It can arrange physical exams that can reveal health problems before they become worse. Ideally, it would provide real health insurance coverage. It can encourage employees with problems to go to self-help organizations such as Alcoholics Anonymous. It can discourage smoking on the job. It can send employees to health-screening clinics. Some operations have found it worthwhile to help employees who might not or cannot take care of some of their health problems. One small operation, for example, helps employees who need dental work by initially financing it and then letting the employees pay it back in small amounts. (One must be selective, however, when offering this arrangement.)

THE COST OF SMOKING

Discouraging employee smoking is one of the keystones of a wellness program. The surgeon general has called it the chief preventable cause of death in our society and the most important public health issue of our time. Tobacco is responsible for one of every six deaths, killing about 390,000 Americans annually. This is the equivalent of two or three jumbo jets crashing every day with no survivors. Smoking has an economic cost to employers. One study shows the additional cost of employing smokers and allowing smoking at the workplace to be $2,853 per smoker in 1990 dollars. These costs include increased absenteeism, costs of medical care, costs due to premature death, insurance, time lost while on the job, property damage, and increased ventilation.

EMPLOYEE ASSISTANCE PROGRAM (EAP)

An **employee assistance program (EAP)** is defined as a human resource program based on the concept that employers can help their employees by enabling them to cope with their personal problems, including substance abuse, and thereby improve their on-the-job performance. The fundamental objective is to help restore impaired employees to full productivity in the workplace and to allow them to regain a satisfactory level of emotional and physical well-being.

When successful (some plans report up to an 80 percent success rate, although others are not nearly as optimistic), employees may be salvaged. The employer and employee are working together, which helps limit adversary factors. Benefits claimed for EAP include:

- less absenteeism
- reduced turnover
- improvement in work quality and productivity
- lower medical costs
- fewer workers' compensation claims
- fewer patron complaints
- an example of employer commitment to employee welfare
- improved morale

The program may be performed for an employer by outside agencies. Each organization must consider its needs for such a program and obtain management commitment if it is to be implemented. A policy statement should be formulated and disseminated through the organization. Although the cost may be high, the salvaging of good employees, less absenteeism, and alleviation of other problems may go far to offset this cost.

A typical EAP focused on alcohol and other drug abuse might employ the following steps:

1. *Train supervisors to recognize problems.* Other people may be aware of the problem before the employee with a problem with alcohol or other drugs. Symptoms can include lateness, excessive arguments, and feelings of depression or rejection.

2. *Implement a monitoring procedure.* Supervisors should watch for instances of nonconforming behavior that could be due to alcohol or other drug problems.

3. *Appoint a nondisciplining coordinator.* Someone not in a direct supervisory capacity talks with employees. This individual should have some counseling skills and be comfortable talking with all employees. Someone effective with a white-collar worker might not be effective with a blue-collar worker.

4. *Present employees with an option.* The counselor tells employees they have been referred because of their performance. Employees can either correct the deficiencies or enroll in the EAP program supported by the employer. Some employees may view this as a veiled threat, whereas others may view it as an opportunity to face the facts.

5. *Provide an opportunity for treatment.* A specific course of medical treatment often lasting a month is recommended. (Costs vary considerably, and sometimes health insurance will pay part of it.) Before reentry into the job, employees should be interviewed by the counselor or other employer representative to discuss their return. If possible, an in-house support group is arranged. If not, membership in Alcoholics Anonymous or a similar group may be required.

6. *Continue monitoring.* The coordinator monitors employees to try to prevent a relapse.

SUBSTANCE ABUSE

Abuse of alcohol and other drugs is a national problem, but the foodservice industry has more than its share. It is estimated that at least 10 percent of the nation's workforce is afflicted with alcoholism or drug addiction. Among 18- to 25-year-olds, where the hospitality industry draws many entry-level workers, 65 percent have used illegal drugs.

Substance abusers have three to four times as many accidents on the job, four to six times more accidents off the job, are absent from work two to two and a half times more often than nonabusers, and have three times the medical costs. Forty percent of all hospital admissions are due to health problems that result from chemical dependency.

To deal with employees who have substance abuse problems, it is necessary first to recognize these employees. Some symptoms of drug or alcohol abuse are

- slurred speech or unsteady gait
- bloodshot or watery eyes
- dilated or constricted pupils
- noticeable sudden weight loss or gain
- tremors and excessive perspiration
- frequent trips to a restroom or water fountain
- drug paraphernalia nearby
- erratic mood swings
- lack of concentration
- arguments and fights with others
- attendance and tardiness problems
- poor-quality work and more accidents or near accidents
- evidence of theft

None of these symptoms are, by themselves, proof that a problem exists, but they can indicate that further investigation is appropriate.

At one time, most foodservice operators thought they had two options in dealing with employees with a substance abuse problem. One way was to tell employees to "shape up or ship out." In other words, the behavior would not be tolerated. The other way was to simply tolerate the situation. Many organizations are now using a third option, which involves trying to help employees overcome the addiction. Tools for this option can include drug testing, supervisory training programs, drug education programs, and employee assistance programs.

The costs of these programs can range considerably, especially in considering how extensively they are used. In 1989, the cost of an alcohol education program could be as little as $150, and a medically intensive intermediate rehabilitation as high as $50,000.

Drug testing can be a controversial issue. Historically, job performance has been the only legitimate issue on which to base disciplinary action, and there are problems in administrating and evaluating the tests. Some labor organizations have fought against requiring their members to submit to the tests, claiming they are an invasion of one's privacy. However, tests that may confirm that someone is abusing alcohol or other drugs can be helpful in assisting the individual. Where legally feasible, some employers are using drug tests as part of the employment process.

Supervisory training programs can include recognizing the symptoms of alcohol or other drug abuse, dealing with those employees, and knowing how to refer them for therapeutic help.

Drug education programs cover a wide range of options that can be developed in-house or supplied by outside vendors. Using strong disciplinary action against substance abusers in the hope that the action will be a deterrent to other employees can have some negative consequences. Supervisors may be averse to reporting their employees, peers may remain silent about coworkers, and substance abusers may not admit (perhaps even to themselves) to a problem. This can lead to less chance to decrease substance abuse in the organization. It also can create an adversary relationship between management and employees.

WORKERS' COMPENSATION INSURANCE

One of most rapidly rising health benefit costs to an employer is workers' compensation insurance. This insurance program is designed to provide a safety net for employees who suffer job-related absences, injuries, and illnesses. Whereas health costs are rising about 12 percent a year, workers' compensation is increasing about 20 percent a year. Reasons for the increase include allowing more intangible stress-related claims and abuse by some insurance companies, doctors, and lawyers. Workers' compensation programs are administered by the individual states, and there are great differences between states.

Costs can be reduced through safety and safety-conscious programs including incentive-based risk-reduction programs and political action to reform the state systems and eliminate fraud. Rates generally are based on accident experience, so the fewer the accidents, the fewer the claims and therefore the lower the rates. Employers should also challenge employee claims they believe to be unrealistic. The insurance can be provided by a state agency or private companies, or large organizations may self-insure.

ELDER CARE PROGRAMS

As the country's population ages, the need for workers to care for older relatives increases. One study shows that 20 percent of today's workforce has elder care responsibilities. These responsibilities can cause absenteeism, lower productivity, or absence from the workforce altogether. Employers are beginning to offer elder care programs to help with these problems and their related costs.

Various elements of such programs include part-time work options, extended leave, contributions to community agencies, work-at-home arrangements, and counseling services. It has been estimated that companies without elder care programs spend $2,500 a year for each caregiver, in the form of absenteeism, missed overtime, and lost productivity.

CONTROL REPORTS

One of the responsibilities of management is constant awareness of its labor costs. For this feedback, control reports are indispensable. Many of the formats in Chapter 11, Analyzing Labor Costs, and Chapter 12, Staffing and Scheduling, can also be used for control purposes. Different operations have different central control information needs but common information desired can include:

- labor-cost percentages (both total and departmental)
- work production standards (both total and departmental)
- differences between forecasted, or desired, and actual figures
- overtime (both dollar amount and percentage of payroll)
- turnover ratios
- accident incidents (brief details and costs)
- workers' compensation claims
- unemployment compensation claims

A report can be prepared on a daily, weekly, or monthly basis. At least weekly reports are the most effective approach.

FLEX (OR CAFETERIA) BENEFIT PLANS

It has been estimated that only about 20 percent of today's workers follow the traditional pattern of a working husband with a wife at home "keeping house." Now both spouses often work, and there are more single-parent families and more women in the workforce. This trend has led to **flex (or cafeteria) plans.** If an employee is covered by a spouse's medical plan, for example, there is little need for duplicate coverage. Some workers might like to trade some other benefits for more vacation time. Some employees need more medical coverage; others would like more pension contributions; some would like more life insurance coverage. Generally employees in a flex plan receive certain core benefits along with a "budget" of a certain dollar amount to buy more benefits they desire.

Items for which more or less coverage may be negotiated generally include medical coverage (a certain amount is required), life insurance (including dependents), disability insurance, vacation days, larger pensions, and child care.

MEDICAL BENEFITS

One of the fastest rising and most expensive benefits for employers is medical benefits. One approach in trying to curb medical costs is the use of managed care programs. In 1987 slightly more than 25 percent of employees received care through such plans. Ten years later the figure was more than 67 percent.

Managed care is based on a contract between an insuring organization and groups of doctors and other health service providers. The fees are predetermined and usually discounted. This allows the providers to be assured of a predictable pool of clients and income while employers pay lower premiums.

Service is most usually provided by either health maintenance organizations (HMOs) or preferred provider organizations (PPOs). Employees served by HMOs select a primary care physician in the HMO who becomes the "gatekeeper" for patient services such as specialists, hospitalization, and surgery. An HMO may provide preventive medicine services in its fee. The PPO does not appoint a gatekeeper but employees must use health providers in the system who charge a discounted fee for their services. PPOs provide more flexibility in choice of physician.

The managed care plans may also offer an out-of-network or point-of-service (POS) option. This provides for use of health service providers who are not in the network. However, deductibles are usually higher and the amount covered is less, usually 10 to 20 percent, than the amount provided using in-network providers.

Although managed care organizations have proven they can help control costs, there have been many complaints, even horror stories, about pressure on doctors to see a great volume of patients with less quality care, too short hospitalization stays, or nonreferrals not paying for some treatments (perhaps because they are considered experimental). Since the managed care organizations are usually profit driven, some wonder if medical care might be sacrificed for profit.

Although many employees may not particularly like managed health care plans, resistance may drop when a POS option is available.

Strategies for reducing health care costs include: implementing managed health care plans, raising employee service co-pays (or costs the employee pays), increasing deductibles, and encouraging preventive measurement actions. Preventive measurement can include wellness campaigns and required physicals to reveal health problems before they become critical.

Increasing employee co-pays and higher deductibles may reduce unnecessary requests for service. They may also cause resentment and force some employees to postpone medical care.

DEFERRED COMPENSATION AND RETIREMENT PLANS (PENSIONS)

Payments into qualified pension plans provide tax deductions for the employer but are not treated as taxable income by employees until the funds are distributed. At that time the employee is usually in a lower tax bracket so taxes paid are lower. Also, the income generated by these funds is not taxable until distributed.

Pension plan difficulties often arise in today's highly mobile labor market where workers frequently change jobs over the course of a career and do not build up large pension benefits. One study indicated that the average male worker works for his current employer for only seven years and females work only an average of five years in one place. With workers nearing retirement, more than half have been working for their current employers less than one-third of their adult lives.

Almost half of all employees would lose benefits if they shifted jobs tomorrow, so it would be better for employees to have a plan that can be moved from employer to employer. Generally speaking, employment benefit plans fall into two categories.

1. **Defined-benefit plans**. Benefit amounts are predetermined and contribution amounts are based on actuarial methods; employees know what their retirement income will be.

2. **Defined-contribution plan**. The contribution by the employer is defined as a percentage of payroll, profit sharing, or a stock bonus. In such plans the employer specifies what will be contributed, but there is no definite benefit amount guaranteed to employees upon retirement.

From a cash flow standpoint, the defined-contribution plan is better for an employer. Contributions may be related to the ability to contribute, and there is not an obligation to contribute to retired employees beyond payments already made.

Some retired workers in defined-benefit plans now face problems. If their former employer goes out of business, the benefits may be curtailed. Federal insurance for private pension plans is provided through the Employment Retirement Income Security Act of 1974 (ERISA) operated by the Pension Benefit Guarantee Corporation. However, there are problems regarding the resources available for this insurance and its coverage.

PROFIT SHARING

A hospitality establishment's employees are vital to its success, but these employees can present problems such as high turnover, low productivity, a lack of interest, inadequate skills, poor quality work, and a lack of responsibility. Every hospitality manager wants to improve the quality and performance of workers. This improvement often requires increased motivation among the workers and possibly higher benefits in return for higher productivity.

At the very least, employees desire from an employer a living wage, recognition, job security, and a challenge. To reach both the employer's and employees' goals, one must have employee job motivation and employees who believe they are part of the business. This may be accomplished through profit sharing, savings sharing, or productivity motivation. The goals of these types of plans include:

1. increased remuneration over and above regular wages and basic fringe benefits but within the capacity of the firm to pay
2. the establishment of an essential link between workers' self-interest and the employer's objectives
3. motivation to cut costs and increase productivity
4. the possibility that employees can become part owner of or participate in the earnings of a productive facility
5. an expression of management's concerns for employees
6. the establishment of a retirement nest egg
7. a way to reduce turnover

Profit-sharing plans usually earmark a certain percentage of earnings for employees. The amount to each employee can be based on salary and perhaps length of service. The profits can be distributed immediately in a cash or immediate payout plan. They can also be deferred by depositing them into employees' accounts. With compound interest earned on the savings, these accounts can grow and be used instead of a pension for retirement income through a defined-contribution plan. There may also be a combination where some money is dispensed immediately and the rest is placed in a deferred account. Additional contributions by an employee to a defined plan may be required, optional, or not possible. Generally, the money contributed to a deferred plan and the income earned by it are not taxable until distributions are made.

Labor Management Audit

Table 13.1 is a labor audit that allows grading of an operation's labor policies.

Table 13.1
Labor Management Audit

Date:	Account/Unit:	Weight Total 100	Actual Score
	Name		
A	**Review of Planning Data**		
	1. Has supervisor thought through the job positions in an orderly fashion?	6	
	2. Do the budgeted labor positions match established guidelines?	6	
	3. Are schedules updated and modified to meet business changes?	6	
	4. Is projected sales (or transaction) information available on an as-needed basis?	6	
	5. Are projected labor hours and labor expenses available on an as-needed basis?	6	
	Total Points Possible:	**30**	
B	**Review of Actual Labor Productivity Activities**		
	1. Are positions staffed with favoritism and according to customer needs and guidelines?	6	
	2. Is continually planned overtime not scheduled?	6	
	3. Are appropriate resources scheduled when needed?	6	
	4. Is actual sales (or transaction) information available?	6	
	5. Are actual labor-hours and labor expenses available?	6	
	Total Points Possible:	**30**	
C	**Statistical Review**		
	1. Is statistical analysis completed?	15	
	2. Are correction action plan(s) in place?	15	
	Total Points Possible:	**30**	
D	**Review of Compliance**		
	1. Are all client contract guidelines followed?	3	
	2. Are all company guidelines followed?	3	
	3. Are all federal, state, and local guidelines followed?	4	
	Total Points Possible:	**10**	
	Total Score:	**100**	
	If your score is less than 80 points, you should review your labor management programs.		

SUMMARY

This chapter has introduced the various costs associated with hiring and maintaining a workforce, along with practices to limit these costs while encouraging employee productivity. Hospitality managers can, as we have seen, control labor costs by analyzing and specifying the procedures associated with the jobs in the workplace, by establishing and enforcing a reliable hierarchy on the job, and by distributing compensation fairly. Managers should also attempt to reduce employee turnover, absenteeism, overtime, on-the-job accidents, and stress-related illnesses such as alcoholism. A modern manager also provides not only a traditional selection of fringe benefits but also some sort of incentive for maintaining productivity and an allegiance to the operation, possibly in the form of deferred payments or profit sharing.

Having current information on labor costs is essential. With medical costs skyrocketing, many operators are considering wellness programs to help employees remain healthy. Tied in with this are employee assistance programs and substance abuse programs.

KEY TERMS

absenteeism ratio (formula)
accident incidence rate (formula)
classification system
cost-benefit analysis
cost-effectiveness analysis
defined-benefit plan
defined-contribution plan
employee assistance program (EAP)
factor-comparison system
flex plan
health maintenance organizations (HMOs)

inactivity ratio (formula)
incidence ratio (formula)
job evaluation
organizational chart
point ranking system
preferred provider organizations (PPOs)
severity ratio
simple ranking system
turnover rate (formula)
wage and salary administration

REVIEW QUESTIONS

13–1   Explain the elements of a job evaluation.
13–2   How may turnover be lowered?
13–3   How many days are employees absent, on average?
13–4   List six techniques to combat absenteeism.
13–5   Differentiate between the purposes of the general formula for absenteeism
           incidence ratio
           inactivity ratio
           severity ratio
13–6   What practices are helpful in controlling overtime?
13–7   What may be done to prevent burns in a kitchen?

13–8   List the steps of a formal safety program.
13–9   List steps of an employee assistance program (EAP).
13–10 Differentiate between defined-benefit and defined-contribution pension plans.
13–11 Why are foodservice operations considering wellness programs?
13–12 What are three levels of a wellness program?
13–13 Who can provide workers' compensation insurance?
13–14 List tools for combating substance abuse.

PROBLEMS

13–1 The Nittany Restaurant has 50 employees. During one week there were five absences amounting to 60 hours. Total hours worked were 1,800. Calculate: the incidence ratio (Icr), the inactivity ratio (Iar), and the severity ratio (Sr).

13–2 During a month six employees were terminated. What is the monthly separation rate?

13–3 *Assumption:* You are the president of a restaurant corporation that has developed a very successful concept involving full meals and full service at low selling prices. The concept is especially popular with the elderly. In two years the organization has grown from three operations geographically close together to an expected 12 in three states with some over 200 miles from headquarters. Your organization is not large enough to have extensive regional or area management or management hierarchy. The local managers have a great deal of autonomy as long as they operate under company policies. They report directly to you. With the expansion, the time you can spend discovering labor cost problems and helping individual managers is becoming more and more limited. This weakening of supervision and remoteness of operations has caused labor costs to increase significantly where you are not on top of things. Because of low selling prices, strong control of costs is most important. It is vital that you develop a better management informant system regarding labor costs, labor productivity, and labor-cost problems at the individual operations.

Assignment: Devise a format for a labor analysis and control form that would be prepared by each operation on a weekly basis. This form should help reveal what operations may have labor-cost and productivity problems (and which have no problems) and is in part a substitute for personal visits. It is necessary to consider what information is really necessary and not to include all possible information. What do you as CEO really need to know? The format should include blanks for the appropriate data and you may simulate numbers and data for the blanks if you like. Areas covered can include labor costs and comparison standards, labor productivity indices and standards if appropriate, and other information that would help in interpreting the figures. Other information such as turnover, absenteeism, accidents, and overtime can be included, if appropriate. The format should be more of "fill in the blanks" rather than a largely written report. It would be helpful to explain on a separate sheet the logic of including or omitting certain information. The heading for the format could be:

Labor Cost and Productivity Report
_____Restaurant   For Week Ending_____

PROJECT

13–1 Tour a foodservice operation and list all potential safety problems or unsafe practices. Make recommendations to correct these problems.

Food Purchasing

ood purchasers in foodservice operations aim to

1. have an appropriate amount of various food items on hand when needed,
2. ensure the food is of appropriate quality for the operation,
3. buy the food at the lowest cost to the operation, and
4. keep the quantities in inventory or storage as low as possible so the dollar investment in merchandise and storage-facility upkeep will remain low.

Some of these goals raise certain difficulties. It may not be clear-cut what the lowest cost is. Some food items that require advance preparation, such as frozen vegetables, may actually cost less once the additional labor necessary to handle fresh vegetables is figured in. Keeping low quantities in inventory may preclude savings on bulk purchases or produce vulnerability during a sudden shortage of an item. Some larger operations that cut their inventory levels back stop before reaching the minimum level because they want a safety margin on hand, typically a one-week supply.

After completing this chapter, you should be able to:

1. State the four main goals of food purchasing.
2. List at least 10 recent trends causing changes in traditional purchasing procedures.
3. List at least six advantages of one-stop purchasing.
4. Explain different types of distribution systems.
5. Briefly discuss the ideal qualifications for an efficient food purchaser.
6. List seven factors that affect the quality of food to be purchased.
7. Briefly explain how to calculate an EOQ.
8. Briefly explain open market, sealed bid, cost-plus, co-op, and warehouse club buying.

9. Explain the advantages of purchasing specifications.
10. Discuss the potential advantages and disadvantages of purchasing food bargains in large quantities.
11. Describe the advantages of forecasting food needs, maintaining standing orders, scheduling hours for visiting salespeople, using written purchase orders, and conducting can-cutting sessions.
12. Use yield conversion factors.
13. Explain how the cost of deliveries can be reduced.
14. Discuss ethics in food purchasing.
15. List elements of procurement planning.

CHANGES IN FOOD PURCHASING

Food purchasing procedures have changed dramatically in recent years, and more changes are imminent. Formerly, the buyer would contact the purveyors who handle different food items, discover the best deal, and make the purchase. The typical purveyor specialized in one type of product, and one foodservice operation would deal separately with purveyors that specialized in fresh produce, meats, frozen foods, poultry, eggs, groceries, and baked goods. But marketing innovations and high delivery costs are forcing the one-line purveyor to change. The evolving nature of the foodservice industry and the many new products available are also changing purchasing procedures. Here are some factors causing changes in the traditional buying procedures:

1. Food distributors are expanding their lines. The purveyor who formerly handled only fresh produce can now stock frozen foods. In fact, some food distributors are developing a **total shopping capability**; that is, they are trying to supply a complete range of food items, nonfood supplies, and kitchen and dining equipment.

2. Purveyors are providing more nonmerchandise services, such as menu planning, marketing advice, computer time sharing, and data processing.

3. The small, local distributor is either growing or merging into a distribution chain that can serve much larger geographical areas.

4. New products change purchasing procedures. It is easier to purchase and store a package of frozen peas than a bushel of fresh peas. It is more convenient to buy preportioned meat items than primal cuts. Moreover, purchasing preprepared convenience items does not present the problems found in purchasing a variety of individual components.

5. Multiunit operations have begun central preparation facilities or commissaries. Thus, a unit's purchasing becomes centralized. It orders prepared food from its commissary.

6. Many operations, especially the fast-food variety, are built around comparatively few menu items that are not routinely changed. Even when it does not actually supply much of the food (and it often does), a central organization may establish standards, make specifications, and choose the purveyors. This centralized authority leads to simplified food purchasing.

7. Similar kinds of foodservice operations—hospital and school cafeterias, for example—band together in buying combines. Their volume purchases can bring economic benefits and eliminate much purchasing at the operational level.

8. Food marketing is changing. Some companies have started selling directly to the operation rather than to the distribution systems, the traditional middlemen.

9. The structure of the foodservice industry has changed with many more multiunit chains as opposed to single independent operators. This has led to different methods of distribution and purchasing of foods.

10. Rising delivery costs limit the amount of service a purveyor can provide. Food industry distribution costs are thought to be higher than in almost any other industry, and fewer and larger deliveries are becoming more desirable. Accordingly, more product lines are now being handled by fewer suppliers.

11. Supermarkets, which once were concerned almost exclusively with home business, are becoming more active in the institutional supply field.

12. Food shortages due to weather or other conditions can make purchasing more of a scramble than an organized process. In times like these, the assurance of a food supply may well outweigh cost considerations. Moreover, those operators who have established sound, reliable, businesslike dealings with purveyors tend to get taken care of first when normal competitive buying procedures must be suspended.

13. Recent developments have improved the shelf life or storage capabilities of some products.

14. Faxes and e-mail have provided new and different methods of communication, and suppliers can display their wares on the Internet.

The computer has, of course, changed food purchasing. The better forecasting that one can achieve with a computer can lead to more exact purchase quantities. A menu planning module can use recipes stored in the computer to determine the quantities necessary for forecasts and the amounts to order by vendor. The computer can provide vendor bid lists and vendor price-quote comparisons. It can keep track of the number of items in inventory and provide a low-inventory warning report. Chapter 6, Management Information Systems, discusses computerization of purchasing.

FOOD DISTRIBUTION SYSTEMS

Food is purchased through a food distributor. A distributor may be defined as a merchant wholesaler who secures products from various sources for resale and delivery to retail or individual or chain operations. Because of economies of size, distributing companies have been forced to become larger. In 1992 the top five companies accounted for about 20 percent of food distribution sales, although there were a great number of competitors in smaller companies. There are four typical distribution types used by larger organizations in food service: broad line distributor, primary vendor, systems distributor, and self distributor.

The broad line distributor sells many different types of products and can be described as a supermarket for foodservice operators to individual or street accounts.

There may be a primary vendor relationship in which an account or food operation agrees to purchase most of its products from the vendor in exchange for specified savings in prices and delivery costs. This is called a program account and the foodservice operation typically agrees to buy 70 to 80 percent of its food items and supplies from the vendor over a specified period, often one year. Under this arrangement, the operator could also buy lesser amounts from other vendors.

The systems distributor does not handle individual accounts but is a delivery specialist for large chains. The chains negotiate price agreements with suppliers, and the systems distributor keeps an inventory of the items and delivers them for a per-case fee to units of the chain.

The self distributor, as the name implies, has food delivered to its own warehouses and/or picks up the food from vendors. It is a method that a franchiser might use to provide items to franchisees.

A food distributor may provide service under the different types of distribution systems to different types of foodservice organizations.

The purpose of a food distributor is to have available and deliver items needed by foodservice operations. Profit margins are low with fixed costs rather stable, and delivery costs are relatively high so vendors want the highest volume and largest delivery amounts possible. Profit margins vary for different items so the low and high profit mix of items handled is important.

Foodservice distributors are also classified as broadline, full-line, and specialty. As discussed, the broad line distributor, in addition to food items, also handles supplies and equipment. It tries to function as a one-stop service. The full-line distributor handles food items and supplies for foodservice operations. The specialty distributor, as the name implies, specializes in one type of food item. A meat provider would be of the specialty type. Large foodservice operations may be involved with food brokers who are independent sales representatives that offer suppliers sales representation. They receive a commission on the sales they make for the suppliers and may handle products from different suppliers. They normally do not maintain inventory or provide delivery service.

Somewhat similar to brokers are manufacturers' agents for a specific geographical area. A manufacturers' agent may be one producer who agrees to handle products of another producer that cannot provide its own distribution and marketing arrangements. A manufacturers' representative may act as a broker but carry inventory and make deliveries. Manufacturers' agents, representatives, and brokers may sell to distributors.

ONE-STOP PURCHASING

The need for greater volume from accounts and larger delivery quantities has led to one-stop purchasing. **One-stop purchasing** requires that one purveyor be available to handle a wide enough variety of products to cover a large portion of the operation's needs. The salespeople for such a purveyor may not even take orders; instead, they introduce a client to new products and show how the operation can use the products in their menus. They also may spend time trying to solve problems for the clients. The client phones an order in to a specific order taker at the purveyor's office, and three or four sales representatives often work as a team with one order taker. The order taker uses a computer to show what the purveyor has available and to process orders. Computer-generated pricing sheets may be sent to the client to help in the ordering (see Table 14.1). One-stop purchasing provides a number of advantages to a foodservice operation. First, there is ease in ordering. Salespeople do not have to be seen or interviewed. At their convenience, buyers call a familiar person who is equipped for the most efficient order taking.

Second, dealing with only one purveyor or with fewer purveyors lessens the accounts payable, accounting work, and accompanying costs.

Table 14.1

Supplier Price Report Generated by the Purchasing Module of a Foodservice Management System

Supplier Price List
For Diamond Dairy, Inc. (117)
For June 29, 1998
For All Diamond Dairy, Inc. (117) items

Item Description	Current Purchase Description	Price Date	Price	Item Yield	Supplier Item Number
Bev juice V8 10 oz bottle	case	03/05/1998	15.750 per case	100.00%	843982
Cheese blu crumble	5 lb box	04/28/1998	13.700 per 5 lb box	100.00%	0552
Cheese cottage	lb	10/22/1997	1.290 per lb	100.00%	0093
Cheese cottage low fat	5 lb tub	10/22/1997	6.350 per 5 lb tub	100.00%	96
Cheese cream blk 3 lb	3 lb blk	10/22/1997	4.000 per 3 lb blk	100.00%	565
Cheese feta	1 lb	03/30/1998	2.280 per 1 lb	100.00%	0570
Cheese neufchatel	box	02/25/1998	2.990 per box	100.00%	98888
Cheese parm grtd	5 lb bag	04/02/1998	17.000 per 5 lb bag	100.00%	0556
Dairy chocolate Quik	case	02/25/1998	0.620 per bottle	100.00%	0045
Dairy chocolate Quik	case	02/24/1998	12.000 per case	100.00%	0114
Dairy lite cream cheese	each	02/24/1998	1.350 per 1 lb	100.00%	333
Dairy yogurt plain bulk	tub	02/27/1998	4.550 per tub	100.00%	55555
Egg med wht gd A	15 dozen	03/26/1998	0.710 per 15 dozen	100.00%	124578
Eggs broken ready	12 Ct	03/02/1998	1.380 per 12 ct	100.00%	55555
Milk 1% 1/2 pt	carton	10/21/1997	0.160 per carton	100.00%	0031
Milk 2% 1/2 pt	carton	10/21/1997	0.160 per carton	100.00%	0025
Milk 2% gal	gallon	10/21/1997	2.440 per gallon	100.00%	0028
Milk 2% qt	quart	10/21/1997	0.660 per quart	100.00%	0026
Milk bulk (poly)	bag	10/21/1997	16.390 per bag	100.00%	0019
Milk bulk (poly) 2%	box	10/21/1997	16.150 per box	100.00%	0029
Milk bulk (poly) skim	box	10/21/1997	16.150 per box	100.00%	0038
Milk buttermilk qt	quart	10/21/1997	0.690 per quart	100.00%	0049
Milk choc 1/2 pt low fat	carton	10/21/1997	0.170 per carton	100.00%	0041
Milk half/half qt	quart	10/21/1997	1.200 per quart	100.00%	0065
Milk heavy cream	quart	10/22/1997	2.830 per quart	100.00%	0062
Milk heavy ultra cream	quart	10/22/1997	2.830 per quart	100.00%	0063
Milk homo 1/2 gal	1/2 gallon	10/21/1997	1.290 per 1/2 gallon	100.00%	0015
Milk homo 1/2 pt	carton	10/21/1997	0.170 per carton	100.00%	0011
Milk homo gal	gallon	10/21/1997	2.440 per gallon	100.00%	0016
Milk homo pint	carton	10/22/1997	0.420 per carton	100.00%	0013
Milk homo qt	quart	10/22/1997	0.670 per quart	100.00%	0014
Milk skim 1/2 pt	carton	10/22/1997	0.160 per carton	100.00%	0035
Milk skim 1/2 pt	1/2 pint	02/24/1998	0.170 per 1/2 pint	100.00%	035
Milk skim 1/2 pt	carton	02/25/1998	0.170 per carton	100.00%	0035
Milk skim gal	gallon	10/22/1997	2.440 per gallon	100.00%	0039
Milk skim qt	quart	10/22/1997	0.680 per quart	100.00%	0036
PC cheese cream cup 100 ct	box	10/22/1997	15.500 per box	100.00%	562
PC creamer H&H	box	10/22/1997	8.500 per box	100.00%	0066
PC creamer milk	box	10/22/1997	7.980 per box	100.00%	00

Third, foodservice operators can get more service from sales representatives, who can spend more time on a client's problems, including determining what products may be best for that client.

Fourth, in some cases the purveyor's computer can keep track of consumption by the foodservice operation, which can help determine purchase quantities. It is possible for a purveyor's computer system to keep track of the foodservice operation's inventory and related functions.

Fifth, by receiving larger orders, the purveyor (theoretically at least) should be able to provide more frequent delivery service.

Sixth, an operation that gives all of its business to one purveyor should expect savings from that purveyor. This may or may not be true, but purchase costs should certainly not be higher. A purveyor with a standard price list may not be able to offer discounts on specific items, but the foodservice operation may be able to negotiate a later rebate based on large volumes of purchasing.

Seventh, the large, one-stop purveyor is often in a stronger financial position to help a foodservice operation work itself out of financial difficulty. For example, instead of suing and perhaps forcing the operation out of business, the purveyor could arrange a repayment plan with current deliveries strictly cash on delivery. In those cases, the purveyor might require the client to sign a judgment note, which makes it easier to sue later if necessary and perhaps collect on the owner's other assets. The purveyor might also require that the operation buy all of its items through the purveyor.

The purveyor also gains advantages by offering one-stop purchasing. The larger volume of business leads to a larger profit potential. It also allows a purveyor to buy larger quantities and follow more efficient warehousing procedures. Larger deliveries to an operation permit lower unit delivery costs. Selling costs can come down because the order taking is automated and the salespeople do not spend all of their time selling. With a steady one-stop customer, the purveyor can better forecast business and purchases since it knows that the customer will not be dealing with other purveyors.

In short, with one-stop shopping the foodservice operator can obtain lower purchase costs and offer better all-around service. If not, an operator is always free to try other purchasing methods or go with another one-stop operator.

A disadvantage to one-stop shopping is that the operator does not have contact with different vendors' sales personnel who may have different information or new products or ideas. It is harder to take advantage when a different vendor has an unusually good deal. It is also imperative that this operator confirm that the best prices and service are being given by the selected vendor. If the one-stop vendor is located some distance away, it may be difficult to get emergency deliveries or to fill in when there is a discrepancy in the delivery.

WHO SHOULD PURCHASE?

The job of food purchaser has been simplified in some ways in recent years. It requires less expertise to purchase frozen or other prepared foods than foods in the raw. One-stop shopping or other contract purchasing can remove much of the daily negotiation once common.

The size of the operation, the variety of its purchases, the training and interest among the staff members, and company policy will determine who does the purchasing. Larger operations may have purchasing specialists. Regardless of who assumes the job, some general considerations are involved. Purchasers must understand food grades and prices, quantity specifications, and market fluctuations. They must have the time to perform the duties properly. To determine purchase quantities, buyers must have access to records of past purchases, yield computations, formulas to determine portion breakdown, and sales forecasts. Food purchases can be divided into categories such as:

- meat
- poultry
- fish
- fruit
- vegetables
- dairy products
- bakery items
- coffee
- ice cream
- desserts
- groceries (condiments and packaged foods)

Some smaller operations find it desirable to divide the purchasing duties. The manager, for example, might purchase meats and leave the vegetable, produce, and grocery purchasing to the steward. (Since meat usually represents by far the greater part of food cost, it deserves the most consideration and care.)

Most operations relieve the chef of purchasing and give this responsibility to an administrative person. A chef often is too busy to do an adequate job of checking prices and quality and may be tempted merely to call in the orders. An administrative assistant to the chef, sometimes called a purchasing steward, is not directly involved in preparation and service deadlines and thus has the time to do the job efficiently and economically.

For control purposes, the purchaser should not also be responsible for receiving and preparing food. Employees who seek to defraud the operation could do so quite readily if they both purchase and receive food. Deficits in quality or in quantity would be less easily detected. Also, when the preparation function is separate from purchasing, the preparation personnel are likely to call attention to instances where the food quality does not meet specifications.

Although it may not be feasible for management to do the purchasing directly, it should specify—or at least approve—the purveyors from whom food is secured. This practice provides an element of control and limits the possibility of undesirable purchases. Many managers periodically check their merchandise costs against those of similar operations to see that the prices they pay do not exceed those paid by others for comparable quality and service.

PURCHASE QUANTITIES

A major problem that arises when management orders standard nonperishable food items is determining the quantity to order. No operation wants to run short, but too much on hand increases the amount of money needed to finance it, the space required to store it, and the chances of spoilage.

```
REPORT#: 3      * * * CBORD FOODSERVICE MANAGEMENT SYSTEMS * * *      PAGE:    1
OPTION : 2.5.3.            MENU MANAGEMENT SYSTEM - 4.1.36              Nov 08 9X
USER#  : 1                          HENDERSON HALL                    1327 HOURS
                                 PURVEYOR QUOTE FORM
```

Vendor   : _____

Purchase Group: 01 MEAT REQUIREMENTS

Item Name	Purchase Spec Ref	Purchase Unit	Purchase Unit Wgt	Order Quantity	Item Nmbr	User Item Nmbr	Bid Price (per PU)	Brand Name	Vendor Order #
BEANS & PORK IN TOM SAUCE	_____	6/#10 CN	39.750	0.000	68	_____	< _____ ><	_____ ><	_____ >
BEEF BASE	_____	12/1# CS	12.000	50	30	_____	< _____ ><	_____ ><	_____ >
BEEF BONES CRACKED	_____	LBS	1.000	7	36	_____	< _____ ><	_____ ><	_____ >
BEEF BULK GROUND	_____	LBS	1.000	11	155	_____	< _____ ><	_____ ><	_____ >
BEEF CHUCK	_____	LBS	1.000	0.000	234	_____	< _____ ><	_____ ><	_____ >
BEEF CORNED	_____	4/6# CN	24.000	0.000	61	_____	< _____ ><	_____ ><	_____ >
BEEF CORNED ROUND	_____	LBS	1.000	0.000	163	_____	< _____ ><	_____ ><	_____ >
BEEF DICED STEW FRZN	_____	LBS	1.000	0.000	152	_____	< _____ ><	_____ ><	_____ >
BEEF HAMBURGERS CAN	_____	6/12 OZ	4.500	0.000	158	_____	< _____ ><	_____ ><	_____ >
BEEF LIVER WHOLE FRZN	_____	LBS	1.000	0.000	153	_____	< _____ ><	_____ ><	_____ >
BEEF RD CKD	_____	LBS	0.980	0.000	260	_____	< _____ ><	_____ ><	_____ >
BEEF RIBS SHORT	_____	LBS	1.000	0.000	314	_____	< _____ ><	_____ ><	_____ >
BEEF RIBS SHORT - COOKED	_____	LBS	1.000	0.000	316	_____	< _____ ><	_____ ><	_____ >
BEEF ROLL BNLS	_____	LBS	1.000	0.000	156	_____	< _____ ><	_____ ><	_____ >
BEEF ROUND	_____	LBS	1.000	113	157	_____	< _____ ><	_____ ><	_____ >
BEEF ROUND FRZN	_____	LBS	1.000	0.000	154	_____	< _____ ><	_____ ><	_____ >
BEEF STOCK	_____	GALLONS	10.480	2	254	_____	< _____ ><	_____ ><	_____ >
BEEF TRIMMINGS	_____	LBS	1.000	3	70	_____	< _____ ><	_____ ><	_____ >
CHILI CONCARNE COOKED	_____	6/#10 CN	39.750	4	58	_____	< _____ ><	_____ ><	_____ >
FRANKFURTERS FRZN	_____	LBS	1.000	0.000	171	_____	< _____ ><	_____ ><	_____ >
HAM BUFFET FLAT	_____	LBS	1.000	33	170	_____	< _____ ><	_____ ><	_____ >
HAM SLICED CAN	_____	LBS	1.000	0.000	161	_____	< _____ ><	_____ ><	_____ >
HAM WHOLE CAN	_____	LBS	1.000	0.000	160	_____	< _____ ><	_____ ><	_____ >
LAMB RIBLETS	_____	LBS	1.000	0.000	159	_____	< _____ ><	_____ ><	_____ >

Figure 14.1

Example of a Purchase Order Created in the Purchasing Module of a Foodservice Management Application. (Reprinted courtesy of The CBORD Group, Inc.© 1992.)

For items kept regularly on hand, these factors should be considered when the purchase quantity is determined:

1. the usage rate for a certain time period
2. the lead time or number of days from placing the order to receipt
3. the safety level, or the minimum amount that you would like always to have on hand
4. the order point, or inventory when a new order should be placed
5. the maximum stock level, or the maximum amount you would want on hand at any time
6. the space available for storing inventory
7. the money available for inventory

These factors have led to the **usage method** of ordering. Let us assume that applesauce is a standard item. When should it be ordered and in what quantity? Examine this chart:

Item	Unit	Purchase unit	Serving per unit	Usage rate	Lead time	Safety level	Max, stock	Order point	Order amount
Applesauce	#10 can	Case (6 #10)	25	2 #10/day	8 days	6 cans	36 cans	22 cans	3-4 cases

An operation may purchase its applesauce by the case, which is six No. 10 cans, and the usage rate averages two cans a day. This does not mean that two cans are used every day, but that two cans are used per day on average over an eight-day period. Management has decided that it never wants fewer than six cans in inventory for unexpected use or in the event of delayed deliveries. But to control inventory, management does not want more than 36 cans (six cases) on hand at any one time. The logical time to order is when the inventory reaches 22 cans. A logical order amount would be 18 to 24 cans, or three or four cases. A computer can be used to calculate usage and also keep track of inventory and indicate when the order point is reached.

Another approach to ordering, called the **forecast method,** is to forecast usage and then order that quantity. If the item is used more than once during the delivery period, the different serving times can be batched together.

Item	Forecasted servings	Unit	Serving per unit	Units needed	Size of order list	Order amount
Applesauce	150	#10 can	25	6 cans	1 case (6 cans)	1 case

A computer can go over the menus and recipes in its memory and determine how much of an item will be needed. An arbitrary safety factor can also be built into the computer program to ensure that a supply is always on hand.

The following table lists the capacities of various-sized cans used in restaurants.

Some Common Can Sizes

Can Name	Diameter (Inches)	Height (Inches)	Volume (Ounces)	Approximate Cups	Number per Case
No. 211 cylinder	$2\text{-}\frac{11}{16}$	4	10.5	1.25	14, 48
No. 300	3	$4\text{-}\frac{7}{16}$	13.5	1.75	24, 36, 48
No. 2 cylinder	$3\text{-}\frac{7}{16}$	$5\text{-}\frac{3}{4}$	23	3	24
No. 2-$\frac{1}{2}$	$4\text{-}\frac{1}{16}$	$4\text{-}\frac{11}{16}$	28.5	3.50	12, 24
No. 3	$4\text{-}\frac{1}{4}$	$4\text{-}\frac{7}{8}$	33.6	4	12, 24
No. 5	$5\text{-}\frac{1}{8}$	$5\text{-}\frac{5}{8}$	56	7	12
No. 10	$6\text{-}\frac{3}{16}$	7	103.7	12.75	6
Gallon	$6\text{-}\frac{3}{16}$	$8\text{-}\frac{1}{4}$	130	16	4, 6

THE BEST COST

In purchasing, the cheapest price does not necessarily mean the best buy. A case of eggs can weigh from 34 to 60 pounds. In this case, the price per pound can be more useful than the cost per dozen (grade and quality aside). The amount of bone and fat in a piece of meat may make the lower price for a bone-in, poorly trimmed piece of meat actually higher than that for a similar, higher priced piece that is trimmed and boneless. The optimum cost is partially determined by the yield of the product, not just by the price per pound.

PURCHASING METHODS

There are many methods by which food can be purchased. In addition to one-stop purchasing, here are the five main traditional or conventional methods:

1. open market buying
2. sealed bid buying
3. cost-plus buying
4. co-op buying
5. warehouse club buying

Open Market Buying

This type of purchasing was the traditional method for foodservice operations to secure their food. After determining needs, purchasers obtain prices from purveyors. Then they give the order to the purveyor, who quotes the lowest price commensurate with the quality specified. This ordering is usually done by telephone, but orders may be given to a purveyor's sales representative. It is a good control procedure to obtain price quotations from more than one purveyor for each food item, although a shortage of local purveyors might make this impossible. If the order is large and contains a number of items, it may be split among several different purveyors, with each supplying the items that are offered at the most advantageous price. This is also sometimes referred to as line-item purchasing.

Open market buying has disadvantages. It is labor intensive in securing and requesting quotes. Delivery costs are high for small deliveries and many suppliers are not set up for daily price negotiation, although this practice can be computerized.

In open market buying a **steward's market order sheet** may be used. This printed form has various food items listed, with the quantity desired and spaces to list prices from purveyors.

Sealed Bid Buying

This purchasing method is used mainly by large organizations and governmental institutions. This method requires purchasers to (1) determine how much of an item will be needed for an extended period of time, (2) prepare detailed specifications for the item, and (3) ask purveyors to submit sealed bids. It eliminates the problems of frequent pricing and buying and permits large quantity discounts. The sealed bid method tries to eliminate partiality or favoritism and, therefore, conforms with published institutional policies. But the system is cumbersome and does not let a manager take advantage of price fluctuations as they occur in the market.

Cost-Plus Buying

This purchasing method is not used frequently, but it does offer certain advantages. The operator agrees to buy all of a certain kind of food from a purveyor at a selling price that is fixed at a specific percentage over the dealer's cost. Usually, the operator agrees to phone in all orders at a definite time, and a definite delivery schedule may be agreed upon as well. The advantage to the food operator is that the dealer's markup is usually only a fraction of the normal markup. Moreover, the operator need not go to all the bother of getting competitive bids and keeping records on different purveyors. The advantage to the purveyor is getting all of a customer's business. The purveyor knows in advance what the customer wants and so does not have to risk stocking food that customers may not need or want. Moreover, time spent soliciting business is kept at a minimum. But a problem may arise when it comes time to verify the purveyor's costs, and a manager may have to supply more motivation for the purveyor to seek the best prices because the purveyor knows the percentage has been guaranteed no matter what price is charged. Reports issued by the U.S. Department of Agriculture are helpful in determining current prices, and a subsidiary agreement may be made whereby the purveyor provides the customer with a copy of its invoices. If given access to the distributors' records, some organizations will for a fee provide audit reports. Normally, cost-plus buying is used by large organizations or chains.

A problem in cost-plus buying is that the distributor may receive rebates and incentive programs for attaining certain volumes of sales that do not show up on regular invoices. Distributors may also sponsor trade shows and rent booths to suppliers and generate a profit to them but not reflect this in their individual billings.

Co-op Buying

This purchasing method involves a group of similar operations (such as schools, hospitals, or fraternities) that band together to secure, through mass purchasing, quantity discount prices. The group may employ a manager who investigates prices and quality on behalf of all the members of the group. The members indicate to the co-op the quantities and qualities desired, and the co-op combines the orders to get the lowest prices it can.

Theoretically at least, purveyors can offer lower prices because they do not have to send sales representatives to call regularly on the various members. Many co-ops purchase other items in addition to food for their members, and many offer other services as well.

Warehouse Club Buying

This purchasing method is helpful to smaller foodservice operators. The first ones were originally founded primarily for retail consumers, but they are now being used more and more by foodservice operators.

Restaurant owners purchase a membership that allows them to make purchases. Other employees can purchase associate memberships that allow them to make purchases. The club is actually a large warehouse that sells in high volume and provides no extras. There is no credit, sales personnel, or fancy displays, and the merchandise is stacked on pallets. Advantages to foodservice operators include prices that run even lower than wholesale, an ability to buy in cans rather than cases, and the fact that traditional wholesalers may not want to serve the small operator.

The clubs carry many nonfood items, but they cannot be used as a total source of supply. However, they may be helpful to the small operation where they are available.

CONTRACT PURCHASING

Contract purchasing can loosely be defined as a process whereby a buyer signs an agreement with a supplier to provide certain food or other supplies for a set period of time, often one year. It is most feasible for large operations or those with multiple outlets. It can incorporate elements of purchasing that have already been discussed, such as cost-plus or co-op buying or sealed bids.

Advantages of contract purchasing include bidding the contract infrequently, such as once a year. Often only one truck delivery is made a week, saving considerably on delivery costs. If used effectively, there is a potential to reduce costs with the larger definite orders and the fewer deliveries. Both the purveyor and the purchaser may have considerably less paperwork.

In contract purchasing, purveyors usually are compensated in one of three ways: reimbursable cost plus a fixed fee or percentage for service, formula pricing, and fee for service.

The reimbursable cost is a form of cost-plus. Purveyors are reimbursed for their costs plus a fixed or percentage amount over this.

Formula pricing is best for bread and dairy products. The price paid is governed by a third-party pricing structure. For milk, this could be the USDA Milk Marketing Board or a state milk board. Bread prices are keyed to the price of the flour. Manufacturing and delivery costs remain constant through the life of the contract, and the milk and flour prices can change as determined by the third party.

In the fee-for-service method, the user buys the product and has it shifted to the purveyor's or distributor's warehouse sites. The user pays the packer directly for the product, and a fixed fee per unit to the purveyor who is now primarily a distributor or contractor for delivery or distribution services. This method is used primarily by large, multiunit chains that can negotiate national purchase contracts and separate local delivery ones. This could be a systems distributor.

PURCHASE SIZE DETERMINATION

To purchase properly, a manager must know both what and how much to purchase. Normally, the menu offering and sales forecast determine the types and amounts of food to be purchased. A number of food operations work from an inventory exclusively, and the kitchen merely requisitions food from the storeroom. Purchasing groceries, bread, dairy products, ice cream, and certain vegetables can become routine and even scheduled. If a par stock of each item is maintained, an order of a predetermined size is placed when the inventory declines to a predetermined point. Foods that are not regularly and routinely needed require special purchasing care, and the maintenance of par stocks here may not be feasible.

The determination of quantities in purchasing is a difficult task. After managers establish a menu, they must calculate the expected sales of each entrée on the basis of past experience and future expectations. A record of entrees sold is a valuable help when the time comes to determine quantities to be purchased and to schedule production. In too many cases there are no records, and the quantity to be served becomes guesswork. Prepared-to-order items can be held in storage in raw form and used as needed, but this is not feasible with items normally prepared in advance, such as roasts, fowl, and fish. A miscalculation could mean overproduction, underproduction, waste, a higher food cost, and dissatisfied guests.

ECONOMIC ORDER QUANTITIES

A quantitative approach to the ordering of staple or regularly stocked items is the **economic order quantity (EOQ)**. The EOQ attempts to find the quantity that minimizes purchase costs and also minimizes inventory costs. It is just as easy to order a large quantity as a small quantity, so economics would suggest buying in large quantities to reduce the costs of making purchases. However, buying in large quantities requires a large investment in inventory. So, what is the best mix of reducing both purchasing and inventory costs? The EOQ can tell you. The formula for EOQ is

$$\text{EOQ} = \sqrt{\frac{2FS}{CP}}$$

where

$F =$ the fixed cost of making an order (let us assume $10.00; this includes the time of ordering, receiving, and the resulting paperwork);

$S =$ sales or usage in number of units over a year (let us assume 100 cases of napkins);

$C =$ carrying cost, which represents the money involved in carrying the inventory (let us assume 20 percent); and

$P =$ purchase price per unit (let us assume $10.00 a case).

Using the formula, we find

$$EOQ = \sqrt{\frac{2 \times \$10 \times 100}{0.20 \times \$10}}$$

$$= \sqrt{1,000}$$

$$= 31.62$$

Because the square root of 1,000 is 31.62, the economic order quantity to buy at one time is 31 or 32 cases.

STANDARD SPECIFICATIONS

A necessity in food purchasing is the use of standard specifications. With standard specifications, purveyors can bid knowledgeably according to quality or size. Specifications provide a basis for all purveyors to bid equally on the same item. Specifications also provide a basis for standard yields and production. A seven-rib roast of beef, for example, can weigh anywhere from 7 to 34 pounds. The number of servings from each of these seven-rib roasts could, therefore, vary tremendously. Specifications should be used by receiving clerks as a basis for accepting or rejecting items. Without them, clerks are forced to use their own judgment, which might or might not coincide with management policy. With specifications, it is much easier for a new employee to take over the ordering. To be most effective, specifications must be available to the buyer, to the purveyor, and to the receiver. Many sets of specifications are available; what is important is that purchasers develop or adopt the best ones for the particular operation and intended use. They may want to accept standard published specifications but should be sure to experiment first to see that they are the most suitable for the operation. A 20-pound roast may give the highest yield, but there is no sense in buying this roast if the operation can sell only two-thirds of it at a time.

Items included in specifications often include:

1. The name or nomenclature of the item. When possible, use a name or standard of identity formulated by the government or a trade association.
2. Standard of quality, which ideally is an official classification. In using a company's own brand name, the term *same as sample* may be appropriate.
3. The size of the product in weight, number of containers, can size, or count (usually the number per pound).
4. Any special instructions, such as current pack.
5. Origin of the product, such as Washington State apples.
6. Class, style, kind, or variety, if appropriate.

BARGAINS AND OVERBUYING

There is a strong temptation to overbuy when a good deal appears, but the temptation tends to cloud some of the hidden costs involved in a bargain. Money, both interest and principal, that could be invested or put to other profitable use is tied up in the large pur-

INDUSTRY INSIGHTS   by Neil S. Reyer

Neil Reyer is the Vice President of Corporate Dining Services, Chase Manhattan Bank and a Penn State Conti Professor

SPEC IT RIGHT

In foodservice there is a plenitude of costs that provide for easy and obvious targets of opportunity for management control. Remember that on any profit and loss statement there are more cost components that can be quickly reduced than revenue line items that can be readily increased. The problem, however, is that after management goes after the low hanging fruit—the *easy* targets, if you will—the tendency is to consider the task complete. But wait, cost control is not some kind of chore that one does just to make someone else at the next level of the organization happy. It is an ongoing process that ensures that we are operating efficiently, that our business is operating in an optimum fashion. That makes sense! After all, it doesn't take a rocket scientist to tell us not to waste money.

Conventional wisdom would have us believe that first and foremost we must strive to lower food and labor cost. That has always amazed me since *food* and *service* are our products. They are our raison d'etre and therefore should not be haphazardly singled out in some capricious cost-cutting scheme. Take food cost as an example. An egregious mistake is the belief that paying the lowest price and minimizing all waste is the panacea to reducing this expense.

It is my contention that the single most important focal point for the proper exercise of food cost control is an effective understanding, use, and management of the specification process. All too often the specification process is taken to mean the establishment of food product purchase standards that ensure the continued acquisition of the lowest priced commodities. However, I suggest it is almost axiomatic that buying right is more important than buying low. Hypothetically, if you could get a product for free it is of no use if it isn't the right product. When my wife claims that she saved me a bundle on a new recliner that was on sale, that may sound fine. However, since I didn't need a recliner, she didn't save me a dime—on sale or not. Suffice it to say that my wife's notion of saving money could put me in the poor house.

Let's say your purchaser buys an engineered, round turkey product that will significantly lower the food cost on your hot turkey sandwich entrée. You've priced it to sell even though you wouldn't eat that stuff yourself. You produce 100 portions. At the end of the day only 25 portions are sold and three-fourths of the batch are tossed to the local feed the hungry program. That same rocket scientist who we didn't need to tell us not to waste money also doesn't have to tell us that we just did. Your purchaser will continue to cut costs looking to save you money and, like my wife, will save you into the poor house!

An effective specification must hit the target dead center. As we can see, shooting too low can cost money just as shooting too high or overspecifying can have the same effect. Let's say, for example, that you need canned peaches for a fruit salad. You're going to slice, dice, cut, or otherwise mutilate the little fellows, so why specify AA fancy, whole, unblemished, peaches in a heavy syrup, when a grade or two lower would serve as a perfect complement to the dish at a much lower cost? At one time or another all of us in this business have been guilty of overshooting the target and establishing a standard that was overkill and just didn't make sense for the final use of the product.

Expense management is a process that demands an in-depth understanding and analysis of the relationship between what an expense is supposed to produce and what it actually produces. It is not some mindless task of random cutting, controlling, reducing, or avoiding costs. It is a process that begins and ends with an effective product specification.

chase. It costs money to maintain and to refrigerate or heat storage space. The greater the supply of food on hand, the easier it is to pilfer. Costs may also go up because employees exercise less care when apparently unlimited amounts are available. Outright spoilage or deterioration in quality may occur. Finally, there is always the chance that the price of your "good deal" will drop even further.

Sometimes, of course, it is necessary to buy more than the normal amounts. Climatic conditions may be such that a shortage can be definitely assured, and it may be necessary to buy to protect prices or even to ensure a supply. Temporary food shortages may, therefore, justify some overbuying that in usual times would be ill advised. Unfortunately, it is often difficult to beat the wholesalers who raise prices in anticipation of food shortages.

YIELD FACTORS (AP AND EP COSTS)

For some purchases, including prime cuts of meat, it is necessary to consider the yield that will be available from the gross amount purchased. The letters **AP** (or **as purchased** weight) and **EP** (or **edible portions** weight after preparation) are used in this context. A rib of beef may weigh 20 pounds when purchased, but after trimming and cooking loss there may only be 12 pounds of available EP meat. Some fresh vegetables, such as peas, carrots, lettuce, or potatoes, if not baked in their skins, have a much lower yield after peeling, shelling, trimming, or discarding outer leaves.

In determining purchase quantities, the buyer must be aware of these losses and purchase accordingly. For many operations the problem is not as acute as it once was since preportioned meats are more common and frozen vegetables have no trimming loss.

To convert AP to EP, a yield percentage, yield factor, or **yield conversion factor** figure is used. For the beef rib, it would be 12/20 pounds, or 0.60.

A rib banquet for 100 people is scheduled. The EP serving is 9 ounces. How many pounds of beef ribs should be purchased and prepared? First, it is desirable to convert the portion size to a decimal by dividing the portion size by 16 (the number of ounces in a pound), or $9/16 = 0.562$. The formula is

$$\text{Quantity} = \text{Number of portions} \times \text{Portion size (decimal)}/\text{Yield factor}$$

or

$$\text{Quantity} = 100 \times 0.562/0.6 = 93.7 \text{ pounds}$$

In this situation, 93.7 pounds should be purchased and prepared.

The yield factor can be used in costing menu items. The reciprocal of 0.6 is 1.67 (1.00/0.6). If the AP is $3.00, the EP cost is $5.01 ($3.00 × 1.67). A 9-ounce portion, or 0.562 of a pound, would cost $2.82 (0.562 × $5.01).

This can also be figured as

$$\text{Reciprocal yield factor} \times \text{Portion size (decimal)} \times \text{AP cost (lb)} = \text{Cost per portion}$$

or

$$1.67 \times 0.562 \times \$3.00 = \$2.82$$

If the AP price per pound changed to $3.25, the new cost per portion would be

$$1.67 \times 0.562 \times 3.25 = \$3.05$$

If the portion size was cut to 7 ounces EP and the price remains at $3.25 per pound, the cost per portion would be

$$1.67 \times 0.437 \text{ (or 7/16)} \times \$3.25 = \$2.37$$

In using yield factors there must be strict purchase specifications so the products are always the same. A 12-pound rib may have a different factor than a 20-pound one. Products from different purveyors can have different factors. In this case, the factors can be used in determining the best buy. One purveyor's product has a yield factor of 0.60 and the other 0.57. Their prices are $3.00 and $2.95 a pound, respectively. Which is the better buy?

	Factor	Reciprocal	Price/lb AP	Price/lb EP
Purveyor A	0.60	1.67	$3.00	$5.01
Purveyor B	0.57	1.75	$2.95	$5.16

The EP price per pound for Purveyor A is $1.67 \times \$3.00 = \$5.01$. The EP price per pound for Purveyor B is $1.75 \times \$2.95 = \$5.16$. Purveyor A offers the better buy using this analysis.

In performing a yield test, cost consideration must be given to any by-products that may be produced. Scraps of trimmed meat can be used for other purposes or trimmed fat may be sold. The yield factor for meats requires two types of tests. The first is the batches test results, which show the net weight after trimming, cutting, and giving credit for any part of the purchase used in other ways. The second test involves losses or shrinkages in cooking. For yield factors to be accurate, cooking procedures and temperatures must always be the same.

FORECASTING FOOD NEEDS

Knowing the number of patrons to be served is essential to wise purchasing. Purchasing too much food often results in waste or spoilage; purchasing too little food leads to dissatisfied customers. Thus, many operations prepare a business forecast to help alleviate both problems. The forecast may be prepared by an individual or by a committee. One effective system starts with an estimate of the total number of covers to be served during a meal, day, week, or other period. Factors involved in this forecast include records of, for example, the number of people served on the same day of the week during the previous year, the weather conditions, and other miscellaneous factors that affect local business and general business trends. Percentages of total customers ordering the various courses—appetizers, salads, á la carte items, and desserts, or the sales mix discussed in Chapter 8—are usually rather constant for a specific operation, and it is easy to obtain the number of servings for each course by multiplying total covers by the percentage for each course. It is somewhat more difficult to determine the sales of individual items in each course, particularly if the menu constantly varies. Fried chicken might be very popular with one set of companion items but not nearly as popular with another set. A cycle menu can be very helpful in this regard, and it simplifies forecasting sales if records are kept of the relative popularity of items. Chapter 8 discusses forecasting in more detail.

STANDING ORDERS

Standing orders can help organizations with a steady volume. These orders are prepared in advance, often on a monthly or weekly basis, and they eliminate the need to call in frequent orders on regularly used foods such as bakery and dairy products.

Standing orders may also be used with par stocks. The delivery would correspond to the amount needed to raise the stock to a predetermined level. The standing orders specify how much of each item automatically should be delivered each day of the week or month, or the amount to maintain a predetermined par stock. It is usually convenient to have the standing-order items supplied by only one vendor. Where volume fluctuates, standing orders should not be used; moreover, consideration must always be given to holidays or special occasions when fluctuations can be expected in even the most steady operations. Frequent checks of supplies on hand and tabulations of current needs must also be made to prevent spoilage.

SALESPEOPLE'S VISITS

Calls by salespeople can be of considerable help to the food purchaser. Sales representatives can provide market trend information, introduce new products, and provide information about unusually good buys. Many purchasers find it expedient to specify the times when salespeople should make their visits or telephone calls. This practice is helpful to both parties; purchasers can organize their day without being interrupted by unplanned visits, and sales representatives can expect purchasers to be prepared to discuss an order when they call.

PLACING ORDERS

In the past, most purchasing was done through phone contact, written purchase orders, or salespeople taking orders. Now it is possible to use computers for purchasing. In the future, an operation's computers will interact with the suppliers' computers in order making and taking. POS registers that analyze consumption and computerized forecasting techniques will be very helpful in determining order quantities.

WRITTEN PURCHASE ORDERS

Some larger organizations employ written purchase orders for food items. These purchase orders are sent to the vendor and usually specify quantity, price, and delivery time. They may also include quality specifications and payment information. The purchase order helps eliminate errors in pricing and quantities and may be useful in the receiving process. The frequency of ordering, the short time between ordering and delivery, and the clerical work involved do not make purchase orders feasible for the typical operation, except possibly in the special case of large orders of canned goods or nonperishable items where a great deal of money is involved and complete agreement on quality and purchasing details is important.

CAN-CUTTING TESTS

When purchasers buy large quantities of canned goods, they may want to have an occasional can-cutting session. Purchasers ask different purveyors to send samples of their products that meet the operation's specifications. The containers are emptied and the label net weight, the actual weight, and the drained weight are noted, along with a count of the items in the can or the yield by portions. Unlabeled samples are inspected by a panel of at least three people who rate the items according to quality, color, yield, syrup, absence of defects, and taste. Price may or may not be considered at this time, depending upon whether the operation's emphasis is on cost or quality. Many operations conduct can cuttings for each new pack or new crop of food items.

TRADE CREDIT AND PAYMENT POLICIES

Having money available to buy and pay for food purchases affects the amount of money an operation needs for working capital (current assets minus current liabilities). When a seller extends credit to a buyer, a loan is made. Normally, purveyors would like to be paid as soon as possible and may offer a discount to encourage quick payment or a penalty for longer-term payments. The buyer, on the other hand, would like to make use of the purveyor's credit or loan as long as possible.

Common payment terms are

1. **Cash on delivery. (COD)** The merchandise is paid for when delivered or before delivery.

2. No cash discount and limited time for payment. An example would be N-30, or a net (or total) of 30 days to pay the bill.

3. Penalty for late payment. This term has no cash discount and a limited payment period. A penalty such as 1.5 percent per month, or 18 percent annually, may be added to the unpaid balance each month that the account is not paid after the stated payment period.

4. Cash discount. This could be expressed as 2/10, N-30, which means a 2 percent discount if paid within 10 days and a maximum of 30 days to pay. The percentages for early payment and time periods can vary tremendously with different purveyors.

It may be helpful to consider the actual interest percentage involved with discount percentages. A formula for calculating this percentage is

$$\text{Discount (\%)} = \frac{\text{Savings (\$)}}{\text{Net cost (\$)}} \times \frac{365}{\text{Time (in days) allowed beyond discount period}}$$

Assume a $500 purchase with terms of 2/10, N-30; savings equal 2 percent of $500, or $10; net cost is $500 − $10 = $490; and time beyond discount is 30 − 10, or 20 days:

$$\text{Discount (\%)} = \frac{\$10}{\$490} \times \frac{365}{20} = 37.2\%$$

This means that, on an annual basis with a discount of 2 percent for paying within 10 days, the interest rate is 37.2 percent; phrased another way, it would be advantageous to borrow money at a rate up to 37.2 percent to take advantage of the discount if the money was not otherwise available.

The credit standing of an operation can affect the amount of credit and terms a purveyor might offer. Therefore, it benefits an operation to maintain as good a credit standing as possible. Purveyors can subscribe to credit rating services such as Dun and Bradstreet, which prepare credit reports on individual operations. The reports may also be available through a bank. The reports can include data on credit experiences other companies have had, an indication of bank balances and loan balances, the principals involved in the business, bankruptcies, fire losses, and other financial data.

Purveyors often analyze their accounts receivable as current, 30 to 60 days past due, or 60 to 90 days past due. It is not unusual for a food operation to experience difficulty paying its bills. This may be due to poor business, nonprofitable business, seasonal fluctuations, delay in third-party payments (for institutions), or slow payments by their own customers. It is usually best to discuss the situation with the purveyors and try to work out a repayment schedule. Purveyors who expect slow payment may raise their prices to cover the cost of money that they are, in effect, lending to customers. Although purveyors want to be paid, they do not want to put a customer out of business, which could happen in a lawsuit for repayment. Thus, purveyors often are amenable to some sort of settlement.

COST OF DELIVERIES

Usually, after the cost of the food itself, the largest single cost in food marketing is the cost of delivering the orders to the buyer. Adding to the expense is ensuring that the order has the right products, comes at the right time, and is in the right condition. Delivery costs vary considerably. The variance can be because of distance, traffic congestion, cost calculations, size of the order, types of foods being delivered, and other factors.

A rule of thumb is that a delivery drop cost should not be more than 10 percent of the value of the drop order. In other words, if the cost of a delivery drop is $75, the order should be at least $750.

For the benefit of purveyors and eventual benefit of purchasers, everything should be done to make delivery costs as low as possible. If purveyors can make cheaper deliveries, they can, at least in theory, offer cheaper prices, which can be a factor in negotiating prices. Some ways to reduce delivery costs include:

- Delivering larger orders, which can include consolidation of orders or fewer deliveries if the operation can function without more frequent service.
- Planning the delivery time to fit in with a route schedule and having the operation ready to receive it to reduce waiting time for delivery personnel.
- Using a 24-hour inspection limit that gives the operation a full day to inspect and notify the purveyor of irregularities. This limit allows the delivery personnel to be immediately on their way without having to wait for someone to check on the merchandise. Larger operations may want to have the capability of accepting orders packed on pallets that can speedily be removed from the delivery vehicle. This involves having a forklift available and a pallet-exchange system.

Simplifying deliveries has some trade-offs. Having the order just dropped off and the delivery people immediately on their way can create security problems and difficulties in resolving disagreements.

ETHICS IN PURCHASING

A food purchaser can have considerable discretion in placing orders. A purveyor may seek to influence purchases from the buyer apart from price, service, and quality. This leads to the possibility of collusion between them to the detriment of the operation. Although a friendly relationship is desirable between a purveyor (or the salespeople) and the buyer, how much should one give the other? Certainly the buyer should be cordial and exercise proper courtesy.

Gifts from purveyors pose potential problems. The operator should establish a policy or guideline on limiting gifts buyers can accept. One commonly used rule is that a gift should not exceed a stated dollar value. Another is to accept no more than one bottle of an alcoholic beverage.

Another problem arises when purveyors want to give buyers hard-to-get tickets to sporting events. Should there be limits on after-hours fraternizing? Some definite taboos are under-the-table deliveries to the buyer's home or under-the-table payments. Each operation should decide its own policies and notify both its purveyors and its buyers.

Another ethical aspect can involve the sale of items from the operation, such as rendered fats, waste grease, recycled cans or bottles, or old rags. Tradition may be that the chef or some other person other than the operation is the recipient of any gain. The operator should be aware of the amount involved and may decide to change the tradition.

PROCUREMENT PLANNING

In the past, purchasing or procurement was reactive. The operation realized it needed certain items in certain quantities by a certain time and then went out to secure the items. Now, more operations are considering purchasing as part of the overall operating system and are doing some long-range purchasing planning. Some elements of longer-range **procurement planning** include:

- Long-range menu planning that allows for determination of how much of an item will be needed over an extended period. This does not necessarily mean larger deliveries, but it does allow for price negotiations on larger amounts, perhaps with a planned delivery schedule. This can also help purveyors, since by knowing in advance what an operation's needs will be, they can negotiate earlier with suppliers.

- The seasonality of food. When foods are at their peak is generally the best time to use and purchase them. At other times you may want to use frozen or other preserved items.

- Current interest rates. Normally, you want to have as little working capital as possible tied up in inventory. However, when interest rates are low, it often is a recessionary time when bargains can be picked up, and the lower interest rates contribute to lower carrying costs. Six percent or lower generally is considered a low interest rate.

- The best grade or quality of a food item to use with different products. Lower-priced grades may be perfectly acceptable, or even better, for some products.
- Purveyor options. You may be tied in now with one or more purveyor, but there may come a time for change. What are their product lines, delivery arrangements and schedules, payment policies, reliability, and physical facilities? Visit their premises and talk with some of their customers and sales personnel. This is not to imply that you constantly should change purveyors, but it is only prudent to know what is available if you should consider a change.
- Services of commodity associations such as the Produce Marketing Association, American Meat Institute, American Dairy Association, National Processors Association, and National Fisheries Institute. These groups can be very helpful regarding specifications, recipes, new uses, availability of products, and even merchandising tips.
- Trends of availability and possible shortages of food items. Trade publications will help an operation keep on top of these. Some national distributors have newsletters that they send to noncustomers. Weather or other disruption of supply can cause shortages and higher prices. Perhaps because of this, some items should be temporarily removed or not pushed on the menu.

VALUE ANALYSIS

Value analysis can be defined as determining the best value in services and features for the price obtained. Is it better to buy fresh or frozen foods? Are trimmed meats at a higher price than a primal cut a better value? Will paying higher wages procure a better workforce that could be more economical?

A formula for value analysis is

$$V = Q/P$$

where

V = value,

Q = quality, and

P = price

If the quality (Q) increases and price (P) remains constant, the value (V) increases. On the other hand, if P increases and Q decreases or does not increase as much as P, V goes down.

Although the formula can express the concept of value analysis, it may be hard to use quantitatively. Managers may not be able to quantify the many variables in V. How much value can be placed on superior delivery service, for example?

However, food purchasers (and others) should be aware of the concept and consider:

1. Price is only one factor, and not necessarily the most important one.

2. Many factors, including some that may not be immediately obvious, affect value.

3. Product and service improvements must be cost-effective and responsive to customer demand.

4. Standards of quality and their importance vary from operation to operation. Fresh fruit may be considered of a higher quality than canned fruit, but does it matter in some prepared foods such as fruit gelatin?

In summary, value analysis may be thought of as considering other factors besides prices in determining the best value regarding a purchase.

SUMMARY

This chapter explored the many considerations involved in the foodservice purchasing function and the responsibilities a purchaser assumes. The chapter included a discussion of trends that currently are changing the traditional purchasing procedures, including the capabilities of computerization. It discussed methods of distribution, purchasing arrangements, and one-stop purchasing at some length. Both forms and formulas were offered for determining purchase quantities and evaluating food "bargains." Forecasting food needs was explained. Also discussed were payment and credit policies, yield conversion factors, ethical considerations, cost of deliveries, and procurement planning.

KEY TERMS

as purchased (AP)
cash on delivery (COD)
contract purchasing
co-op buying
cost-plus buying
economic order quantity (EOQ)
edible portions (EP)
forecast method (of food purchasing)
one-stop purchasing

open market buying
procurement planning
sealed bid buying
standing order
total shopping capability
usage method (of food purchasing)
value analysis
warehouse club buying
yield conversion factors

REVIEW QUESTIONS

14–1 Describe the total shopping capability concept.

14–2 How can a computer help in food purchasing?

14–3 List advantages of the one-stop shopping concept to a purveyor.

14–4 Provide the captions for a form that uses the usage method of ordering.

14–5 Differentiate between the usage and forecasting methods of food purchasing.

14–6 What information must you have to use an EOQ?

14–7 Explain open market buying.

14–8 What are the advantages of sealed bid buying?

14–9 What are advantages of cost-plus buying to the purveyor?

14–10 Why use specifications in food purchasing?

14–11 Briefly discuss four common payment terms.

14–12 Food merchandise worth $1,000 is purchased at 2/10, N-30. Utilizing the discount equates to what interest rate?

14–13 What is the purpose of using yield factors?

14–14 Explain two tests that may be required in determining yield factors.

14–15 What can be done to help a purveyor reduce the cost of a food delivery?

14–16 Prepare an ethical policy for your operation regarding food purchasers.

14–17 List factors involved in procurement planning.

14–18 Explain the formula for value analysis.

14–19 Differentiate between the main types of food distribution methods.

14–20 What is a broad line food distributor?

PROBLEMS

A prime rib banquet for 200 people is scheduled. The EP is 10 ounces. The yield factor is 55.

14–1 How many pounds of roast beef should be purchased for the banquet?

14–2 The cost per pound of the beef from one purveyor is $2.80. What is the cost per portion?

14–3 Another purveyor's price is $2.90 per pound. You have found from experience that the yield conversion factor for this purveyor is 58. Determine the total cost of the meat for each purveyor.

Receiving

The receiving function is as vital in food-cost control as purchasing. If an item is ordered and paid for but never arrives, the situation is the same as someone's stealing money from the cash register.

After completing this chapter, you should be able to:

1. List in order the six traditional functions of the receiving role.
2. Discuss the six essentials for effective receiving.
3. Explain the uses and advantages of the receiving clerk's daily report and the daily list of deliveries.
4. List six advantages in meat tagging.
5. Explain the advantages in marking cans and cartons with their original prices, using invoice stamps, placing standing orders, blind receiving, and using credit memorandums.
6. Define the expression *short delivery*.
7. List 10 ways an unscrupulous purveyor or receiver can defraud a foodservice operation.
8. Repeat a 10-point procedure for effective receiving.

FUNCTIONS OF RECEIVING

The traditional receiving functions include:

1. verifying that the quantities actually delivered are the same as those specified on the invoice and ordered
2. verifying that qualities and sizes meet specifications
3. verifying that the price is the same as the price quoted

4. processing the invoice initially

5. informing the kitchen of nondeliveries and possible shortages

6. delivering the food to the kitchen or into storage

In some ways, receiving is one area of food-cost control that has become easier in recent years. It is easier, for example, to check in packages of frozen vegetables and fruits than cases or baskets of the raw items. Preportioned meat servings are easier to receive and control than primal or large cuts. One-stop purchasing and the expansion of purveyor lines have led to fewer (if larger) deliveries. Refrigerated transportation has eliminated much of the need to pack food in ice, which once caused many receiving problems.

Nevertheless, a foodservice operation must ensure that the quantities ordered and paid for actually arrive and that the quality of those goods meets specifications. Receiving is an area where alert management, or management by walking around (MBWA), can prevent a great deal of grief. The more consistent and more routine the receiving function, the less chance that attempts will be made to defraud the operation during the delivery of merchandise.

ESSENTIALS FOR EFFECTIVE RECEIVING

Competent Personnel

Receiving personnel must have the four I's: intelligence, integrity, interest, and information about food. A conscientious employee who takes enough interest and time to detect old merchandise, excess shrinkage, short weights, and foods that fall short of specifications is an essential member of the management team. Such a person is valuable and should be paid accordingly. Accepting poor quality and paying for short measure costs money any way you look at it. If the operation is too small to afford a regular receiver, deliveries should be arranged for definite times so that a competent person can be assigned to receive them. Many operations require that all meats, poultry, and seafood (the costly items that amount to about half of all food expenditures) be delivered at a specific time and received by the manager or a responsible employee.

Facilities and Equipment

The first requirement for good receiving is a proper receiving area. In some food operations, the receiving area may also serve as an employees' entrance, a trash deposit area, the salespeople's entrance, or a place for general storage. Coping with this inherent clutter and confusion requires good backdoor management. Ideally, the receiving area should be uncluttered and located near the storeroom and refrigerators so that the movement of food takes a minimum of time and effort and remains in plain sight.

The receiving department requires certain equipment. Accurate scales in good working order are a must. One survey discovered that 30 percent of the scales used in receiving departments could not give correct weights, yet management thought shipments were being properly weighed. Why not test your scale periodically with a known weight to check its accuracy? Both platform and counter scales should be available, but a platform scale is more important. Large operations have begun to use scales that print the weight on the reverse side of the invoice or packing slip; other scales print a tape that is then attached to the merchandise. This system removes any doubt in the weighing-in process. New electronic scales are close to 100 percent accurate, but a problem can arise when they show fractions as a decimal rather than in ounces.

There should be a loading dock of a convenient height for unloading trucks and a ramp to facilitate the unloading of other vehicles. The receiver should have a desk to keep invoices, forms, and other paperwork in order. Some receiving areas have photocopy machines that can be used to make copies of invoices that have been marked "received" and stamped numerically. Copies can then be sent to the bookkeeping department for payment, to the cost department, and to the storeroom, and the originals can be retained in the receiving department as a permanent receiving record. Proper dollies and hand trucks are important to a receiving department; they help to expedite the movement of merchandise with the least amount of effort. If frozen foods are held for any length of time in the receiving area, enough freezer capacity should be provided to prevent food deterioration.

Specifications

The person who receives orders should know the standards that the purveyor must meet and be instructed to accept nothing below this standard. The purchaser's written specifications should also be in the hands of the purveyor. The specifications are usually given to the receiving clerk in one of two ways. Either a memorandum or purchase order of the food ordered showing the quantity, price, and quality or grade is handed to the clerk, or specifications for main food items may be posted on the wall near the scale so that weights, sizes, and qualities can be checked.

Sanitation

The facilities should be arranged so that they can be cleaned easily. A faucet that permits a hosing down of the area is almost a necessity. If insects congregate, there should be adequate screening and fly protection.

Supervision

Receiving should be checked by management at irregular intervals. It is just as important to recheck weights, quantities, and qualities occasionally as it is to audit the cash, and receivers should be aware of management's concern for their work and the importance attached to it.

Scheduled Hours

If possible, purveyors should make deliveries at specified times. This practice makes it easier to have a qualified receiver available and helps avoid the confusion when too many deliveries come in at the same time. With the drivers all eager to be off for the next delivery, the receiving clerk may be pressured, and the goods may not be properly checked. Some operations require that perishable foods be delivered in the morning and other groceries in the afternoon. Most purveyors, however, route their trucks for the most efficient use of time and fuel, which can limit individual time preferences. Even if the purveyor cannot adjust the delivery schedule, agreeing on an appropriate time for the delivery can allow the operation to have a capable person available.

INDUSTRY INSIGHTS   by Joseph Fassler

Joseph Fassler has been a Chairman of the Board of the National Restaurant Association. He is President and Chief Operation Officer of Restaura, Inc., one of the nation's leading dining service companies and a subsidiary of the Dial Corporation.

EIGHT STEPS TO CONTROL
Ordering

Use cycle menu and production records as a guide for completing order/receiving log.

- Order only what you need from authorized vendors.

- Adhere to specifications.

Receiving

Compare your order/receiving log with vendor's invoice.

- Are prices the same as quoted?

Check, weigh or count items received:

- for quality
- pounds ordered—pounds received
- number ordered—number received

Get what you pay for. Do not accept substitutions unless they meet or exceed specifications. Lock back door and all storage areas after each use! Make one person responsible for keys on each shift.

Storage

Date, price, rotate—first-in, first-out. Store all perishables immediately upon delivery. Store all other items as soon as possible after delivery. They may grow legs and walk away if you don't!

Be sure to check temperature of coolers and freezers: coolers must be 34°F–38°F, freezers must be 0°F or below.

Issuing

One person responsible for issuing all food products on each shift. Set up usage box or boxes for each day's or shift's productions.

Production

- Adhere to cycle menu.
- Use approved recipes.
- Use food production/order records.
- Use leftovers as soon as possible.

Portioning

- Adhere to Price and Portion Book and use portion scale.
- Hold Line School daily to assure proper selling price and portion size.
- Use correct size of dishes and glassware.
- Use correct serving utensils, scoops, and ladles.

Pricing

- Adhere to Price and Portion Book.
- Check raw food costs monthly
- Update recipe cost analysis form to be sure selling price is within food cost percentage limitations.
- Request price change if necessary.
- Price menu boards correctly.

Cash Collection

- Train cashiers.
- Take periodic cash register audits.
- Have Price and Portion Book available for cashier's reference.
- Check cash register sales and production record:

FOOD SOLD = FOOD PRODUCED − LEFTOVERS

THE RECEIVING CLERK'S DAILY REPORT

A main receiving record is the **receiving clerk's daily report** (Figure 15.1). This form has a number of uses. It provides an accurate record of all food received, the date of delivery, the vendor's name, and the food's quantity, weight, and price. This data can be helpful in checking and paying bills. For controlling costs, one should know the unit prices of all food delivered to the kitchen and storeroom. In the purchase journal distribution section of the receiving report, there are three columns: Food Direct, Food Stores, and Sundries. These columns are required in some food-cost control systems. Items in the Food Direct column indicate that the food has been delivered to the kitchen to be used that day (**direct purchases**) and should be included in that day's food cost. Items in the Food Stores column indicate that the food went to the storeroom rather than to the kitchen (**storeroom purchases**). (Food sent from the storeroom is charged by requisition.) The **Sundries** column includes nonfood items such as cleaning and paper supplies.

Checking the receiving report is an easy way to determine how much food went directly to the kitchen on any one day from sources outside the storeroom. The receiver who signs the report is responsible for seeing that the food has all been received by the operation and measures up to the specified quality. This record usually is prepared in duplicate. One goes with the invoices to the food-cost accounting department, and one remains in the receiving department for reference. Invoices or shipping orders of goods listed on the report may be turned in with the report.

DAILY LIST OF DELIVERIES

It can also be helpful for the receiver to have a pre-prepared list of expected deliveries. Prepared by the purchaser at the end of the previous day, these often are put together on a clipboard that can be hung in the receiving area.

On the clipboard are a list of deliveries expected and a copy of any orders or memos to the supplier. Included in the list of deliveries should be quantities, brands, sizes, weights, and prices. The receiver marks off the items on the list as they are delivered and received. This makes it easy to notice if any ordered items are absent and to warn management in time to prevent a crisis when an expected food item is not on hand.

A pre-prepared daily list of deliveries can be used in conjunction with a receiving report, or it can be used instead of a receiving report. If a receiving report is not used, at the end of the day the prepared list of deliveries with items checked should be sent to the food-cost accounting office with invoices and any credit memorandums attached.

Table 15.1 is a computer generated receiving report.

DATING PERISHABLES AND GROCERIES

In many well-run operations, food items are dated with a marker or crayon or by a tag. The dating can be put on the case or crate or on the individual container. Such a system permits the use of the older merchandise first and helps to ensure quality.

WILLIAM ALLEN & CO., N.Y. STOCK FORM 9184

RECEIVING CLERK'S DAILY REPORT

DATE_____   NO._____

QUAN.	UNIT	DESCRIPTION	✓	UNIT PRICE	AMOUNT	TOTAL AMOUNT	PURCHASE JOURNAL DISTRIBUTION		
							FOOD DIRECT	FOOD STORES	SUNDRIES

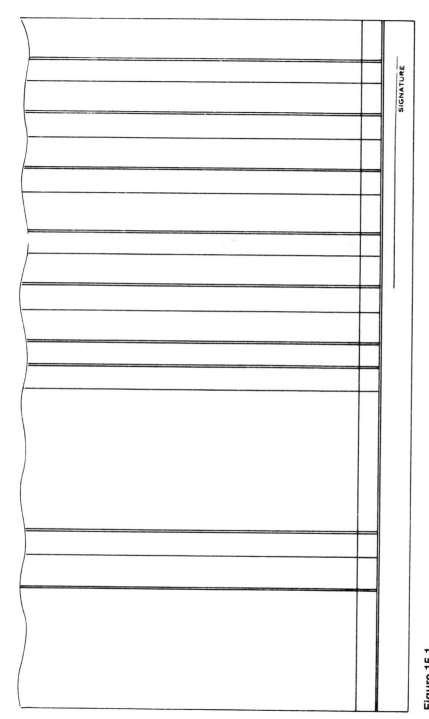

Figure 15.1
Receiving Clerk's Daily Report

339

Table 15–1

Example of Receiving Report by Inventory Item from a Foodservice Management Software Application

Receiving by Inventory Item—Detail
Joe's Diner
Thursday, April 23, 1998 thru Thursday, April 30, 1998
Mandatory Products/All Receipts

Supplier	Supplier Item	Yield	Receipt Date	Priced In Unit	Units Received	Unit Cost	Discount	Extended Cost
Inventory Item								
Food - Meat/Poultry - Beef								
Beef grnd bulk 80/20								
Long Island Beef Co. (50)	Beef grnd bulk 80/20 cryo	100	4/24/98	Lb	40	$1.390	$0.00	$ 55.60
Rykoff Sexton (390)	Beef ground bulk 80/20	100	4/27/98	Lb	40	1.130	0.00	45.20
							$0.00	$100.80
				Meat/Poultry Totals			0.00	$100.80
Food - Dairy - Cheese								
Cheese american 120 sliced								
Walker Butter & Egg Co.	(4 Cheese american 120 sliced	100	4/23/98	Lb	15	$1.820	$0.00	$ 27.30
Cheese blu crumble								
Diamond Dairy, Inc.(117)	Cheese blu crumble	100	4/27/98	5 Lb Box	1	$13.700	$0.00	$ 13.70
				Cheese Totals			$0.00	$ 41.00
				Dairy Totals			$0.00	$ 41.00
Food - Produce - Fresh Fruit								
Fru banana								
Baldor Enterprises (238)	Fru banana	100	4/24/98	Lb	10	$0.500	$0.00	$ 5.00
Baldor Enterprises (238)	Fru banana	100	4/28/98	Lb	20	0.500	0.00	10.00
							$0.00	$ 15.00
Fru kiwi								
Baldor Enterprises (238)	Fru kiwi	100	4/28/98	Case	1	$9.900	$0.00	$ 9.90
				Fresh Fruit Totals			$0.00	$ 24.90
Food - Produce - Fresh Vegetables/Salads								
Veg broccoli whl								
Baldor Enterprises (238)	Veg broccoli whl	100	4/4/98	Case	2	$11.900	$0.00	$ 23.80
Baldor Enterprises (238)	Veg Broccoli whl	100	4/28/98	Case	1	11.900	0.00	11.90
							$0.00	$ 35.70
Veg onion spanish								
Baldor Enterprises (238)	Veg onion spanish	100	4/28/98	Bag	1	$15.290	$0.00	$ 15.29
Veg pepper green whl								
Baldor Enterprises (238)	Veg pepper green whl	100	4/28/98	Case	1	$25.900	$0.00	$ 25.90
Veg spinach cello								
Baldor Enterprises (238)	Veg spinach cello	100	4/24/98	Case	3	$12.000	$0.00	$ 36.00
Baldor Enterprises (238)	Veg spinach cello	100	4/28/98	Case	1	12.000	0.00	12.00
							$0.00	$ 48.00
				Fresh Vegetables/Salads Totals			$0.00	$124.89
				Produce Totals			$0.00	$149.79

MEAT TAGGING

In food cost, meat is the largest expense in food purchasing, and many operations use a meat tag system to control this cost better. The **meat tag** is a card that can be attached to the individual meat item or to poultry or seafood shipments (Figure 15.2). The standard card consists of two duplicate parts. Each half has a printed number and spaces for the date received, the dealer's name, the item, the weight, the price per pound, and the total price. A procedure for using meat tags follows:

1. Both parts of the tag are filled out for each piece, box, or package of meat, fish, or fowl.
2. The left half of the tag is fastened to the merchandise.
3. The right half is sent to the person responsible for food-cost accounting.
4. The tag is removed and usually is placed in a locked box when the items are used in the kitchen; tags are then sent to the food-cost controller, who totals the used tags to determine the meat cost for the day.
5. The food-cost controller matches his or her copy of the tag with the tag that has come from the kitchen. There should be merchandise in storage for every unused tag; if not, the merchandise has "walked away" or has not been properly charged.

Using a meat tag system offers several advantages:

1. The receiver has to fill in a tag for each individual piece of meat, which requires the receiver to weigh the meat.
2. With the item already having the weight marked on the tag, a second weighing when issued is eliminated.
3. It is very easy to determine the meat cost for a day or for any other period.

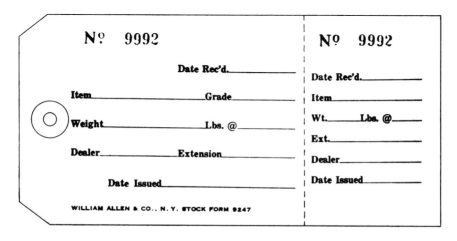

Figure 15.2
Standard Meat Tag

4. Shortages and disappearances of meat are brought to light when there are more duplicate tags than items in storage.

5. The tagged items make inventory very easy, and, if desired, an inventory or dollar value of the items on hand can be determined just by totaling the duplicate tags.

6. The name of the dealer on the tag makes it easy to trace the item back to where it was purchased.

7. The date on the tag makes it easier to use the older items first, or to age meats.

Instead of using a manual method such as meat tags, an operation can enter all receipts and disbursements of an item in a computer. The computer can then tell what should be in storage and can provide the other functions of meat tags.

PRICING MERCHANDISE

Some operations follow the practice of marking every can or carton with the price of the item, just the way prices are stamped on supermarket items. Proponents of the practice claim it makes pricing inventories much easier and also makes employees more cost conscious. With the price stamped on it, the item is no longer just a piece of merchandise to the employees; it becomes an article of value. Bar coding may substitute for putting prices on or make pricing easier.

INVOICE STAMPS

To facilitate the process of handling and checking invoices, some operations stamp the delivery slip or invoice with a rubber stamp, and the person performing each function indicates it by initialing the appropriate line. This practice ensures that all the steps have been performed, and it fixes the responsibility for any errors.

```
Date Received  _____
Quantity       _____
Price OK       _____
Extension OK   _____
Entered        _____
Paid           _____
```

BLIND RECEIVING

To force receiving personnel to weigh or count incoming merchandise, a number of operations employ the **blind receiving** system. The purveyor is instructed to list only the items on the shipping invoice and to omit quantities or weights. The receiver must then count or weigh the items to fill in the invoice or the receiving report. The receiver's figures are then checked with the invoice containing counts or quantities that is mailed to the accounting office by the purveyor. An operation may supply the blind invoice forms to the purveyor.

```
┌──────────────────────────────────────────────────────────────────────┐
│                           Credit Memorandum                            │
│                           Nittany Restaurant                           │
│                       Request for Credit or Adjustment                 │
│     No. 404                                      Date: August 24, XXXX │
│                                                                        │
│          To:              ABC Meats                                    │
│                           123 Main Street                              │
│                           Anytown, PA                                  │
│          Re:              Your Invoice Number _____                   │
│          Date 8/24                                                     │
│                            X  Your Shipping Voucher Number 762         │
│          Reason:          25 lbs hamburger not in shipment             │
│          Amount of Credit: 25 lbs @ $1.00 = $25.00                     │
│                                                                        │
└──────────────────────────────────────────────────────────────────────┘
```

Figure 15.3
Credit Memorandum

CREDIT MEMORANDUMS

Occasionally, merchandise not ordered may be included in the delivery. Delivered goods may be short of weight or unsatisfactory in quality, or invoices may have arithmetic errors. In all these cases, credit should be received. A printed form may be used that should be prepared in triplicate (Figure 15.3). One copy should be attached to the invoice, initialed by the deliverer, and sent to the bookkeeping department. Another copy should be given to the delivery person to take to the purveyor. The third copy should be kept by the receiving department. In addition, the invoice should be properly marked, as should the driver's receipted copy showing the discrepancies. A phone call to the vendor may also be in order.

The credit memorandum should contain the name of the purveyor, the date, the number of the invoice, the discrepancy, and the amount of credit if determined. Formal credit memorandums are used more generally where times for deliveries have been scheduled and the receiver has an opportunity to fill them out properly. Regardless of whether a printed form is used, it is important that application for credit be made as soon as possible while the facts are clear. Regardless of the form used, each operation should establish a definite procedure to be followed.

COLLUSION

Unfortunately, collusion between receiving people and purveyors or their delivery personnel occurs now and then in the foodservice industry. Also, management personnel occasionally defraud their operation by allowing short deliveries, having goods delivered elsewhere for their personal use, or receiving a personal commission or rebate for sales to their operation.

Auguste Escoffier was one of the most influential chefs of all times, the "king of chefs and the chef of kings." However, an article in *The Wall Street Journal* revealed that he was not immune to this kind of greed. Testimony from the year 1900, when Escoffier was chef at the Savoy in London and Cesar Ritz was the manager, quotes a food purveyor this way:

> During the whole of the time I was at the Strand branch the eggs supplied to the Savoy were always delivered short. For instance if 700 eggs were ordered, about 450 to 500 would be delivered. I know from talk I heard in the shop that everything was delivered short to the Savoy Hotel. For instance, until Mr. Escoffier left the hotel the hams were delivered under weight. I weighed them sometimes and they weighed short. Mr. Escoffier always had a regular five percent commission. Besides the five percent commission paid Mr. Escoffier, which was common knowledge in the shop, large presents consisting of packages of goods were sent out every week addressed to Mr. Boots, Southsea.

Short deliveries may be discovered when consumption does not match purchases. New computer systems that determine how much should be purchased according to the computer's own forecasts make short deliveries more apparent.

Sending rebates or gifts to purchasers may be harder to control. At the very least, management should have a policy against it. The difference between a kickback and a token gift of appreciation may be hard to determine, but some operations place limits on the value of gifts their purchasing people can receive from those with whom they do business.

RECEIVING PITFALLS

There are many ways in which an unscrupulous person can successfully defraud an operation. Here are some of the tricks:

1. packing merchandise in excessive moisture, wrappings, or ice to make weighing more difficult and to add more weight.
2. repacking produce and putting a lighter weight in the new crates while keeping the price the same as for the heavier, original crates. (It is wise to spot check the weights of crates and cartons.)
3. placing satisfactory merchandise on the top level that is visible, but inserting merchandise of poorer quality underneath.
4. not sending the grade specified in the hope that it will not be noticed.
5. sending incomplete shipments with the full bill and neglecting to send the remainder.
6. supplying short weights. (Insisting that merchandise be weighed is one of the most important parts of receiving.)
7. charging for boneless meats but leaving the bone in, substituting larger-boned cuts than specified, or leaving excessive fat on the meat. (Specifications and the insistence on their use can help eliminate this practice.)
8. using excessive packaging to increase weights, a practice somewhat akin to the old-time butcher leaving his thumb on the scale.

9. trying to get the receiver to make a bulk weight for all items under the pretense of saving time so that, for example, the amount of hamburger can be increased and the amount of sirloin decreased by a similar amount, with the total weight remaining the same as the total weights indicated on the invoices.

10. delivering merchandise directly to the kitchen without passing it through the receiving department.

11. allowing deliverers to place merchandise directly from the truck into the storeroom or refrigerators without checking quantity and quality in the receiving area.

12. providing delivery personnel the opportunity to "lift" other items when they are on your premises.

RECEIVING PROCEDURES

It is management's responsibility to see that proper receiving procedures are established and adhered to. It is easy to establish procedures but may be difficult to adhere to them. A good set of procedures includes the following steps:

1. A daily list of anticipated deliveries is prepared for the receiving department.

2. All items are counted, weighed, and marked.

3. All pieces of meats, fish, and poultry are weighed and inspected individually, and their tags are prepared.

4. Cartons of fruits and vegetables are opened at random and inspected for quantity and quality.

5. All items are checked against purchase specifications.

6. Invoice prices are checked against the purchase order or the buyer's quotation sheet.

7. After verification, all receiving invoices are stamped and signed by the receiving clerk.

8. All merchandise, food, and supplies are indicated on the receiving report.

9. The unit price is put on each item and then the items are placed in storerooms or refrigerators.

10. Management periodically checks its receiving procedures.

COMPUTERIZATION

Although there will always have to be some sort of human visual verification, some areas of receiving will undoubtedly be computerized. A daily list of deliveries can be prepared at the same time a computer is used to order the merchandise and the receiver only has to check off items on the list. Bar codes on merchandise can be automatically scanned on incoming goods. These components can form a complete integrated computerized system of determining needs, ordering and purchasing, receiving, paying vendors, and providing cost reports.

SUMMARY

This chapter stressed the importance of systematic receiving in the cost-control program of a foodservice operation. The chapter focused heavily on the need for a receiver to verify that the operation receives exactly what it has purchased, which requires close checks on quality, sizes, weights, and prices. The more consistent and routine the receiving function becomes, the less chance that someone will try to defraud the operation.

The chapter outlined the essentials for effective receiving and analyzed two documents—the receiving clerk's daily report and the daily list of deliveries—that promote effective receiving. Also discussed were additional methods, including meat tagging, merchandise pricing, invoice stamps, blind receiving, and credit memorandums, that increase receiving efficiency. The chapter also discussed the problem of collusion and provided typical examples with a view toward reducing the opportunities and temptation to defraud a foodservice operation.

KEY TERMS

blind receiving
direct purchases
meat tag

receiving clerk's daily report
storeroom purchases
sundries

REVIEW QUESTIONS

15–1 List the six functions of the receiving role.
15–2 What are the six essentials of effective receiving?
15–3 What are the uses of the receiving clerk's daily report?

15–4 Differentiate between food direct, food stores, and sundries on the receiving clerk's daily report.
15–5 How does a daily list of deliveries work?
15–6 Why use meat tagging?

PROBLEM

15–1 You are having difficulties regarding the receiving function of your foodservice operation. The quality of goods is not always what you pay for or desire. Deliveries for specified standard recipes do not provide the standard yield. You are receiving bills for items you do not think you have received. Items seem to disappear before being placed in storage. How would you go about investigating the receiving function?

Food Storage Management, Issuing, and Inventory Control

After food items have been purchased and received, they must be stored (if they are not used immediately) and issued to production units when necessary. In addition to the physical security of the food items, there must be inventory control. Management wants to keep the lowest feasible quantities of food items on hand to reduce its investment in inventory and handling costs. It also needs to know what is on hand and what is needed.

After completing this chapter, you should be able to:

1. Discuss the importance of effective food storage, issuing, and inventory procedures in controlling food costs.
2. Describe the requirements for an adequate dry storage area.
3. Define *FIFO*.
4. Describe the requirements for adequate refrigerated storage.
5. Describe the requirements for frozen food storage.
6. Define *freezer burn*.
7. Define the terms *direct purchase or issue, storeroom purchase, storeroom issue,* and *daily food cost*.
8. Name seven typical inventory control functions.
9. Define the expressions *shrinkage, opening and closing inventory,* and *physical inventory*.
10. Show the formula for determining a food cost.
11. Calculate an *inventory turnover rate*.
12. State five advantages in using a perpetual inventory.
13. Discuss how food storage management and issuing can be computerized.

FOOD STORAGE MANAGEMENT

Vital to any foodservice establishment is the operation of its food storage facilities, and in any evaluation of such an establishment, the adequacy of its storage area should be one of the prime considerations. Here, the food items that represent money must be kept until needed. They must be protected from theft and kept in prime physical condition. Contents should be placed in an organized manner, and the premises should be clean. Too often, food storage is synonymous with disorder. Food is piled helter-skelter, and sanitation may be largely overlooked. Management cannot tell what is on hand, and chances of both wastage and spoilage are greatly increased.

The food storage area is usually divided into two sections: a place for the dry-food items, those in cans, bags, and cartons that do not require refrigeration, and a refrigerated section where frozen foods and foods susceptible to spoiling are kept. A large foodservice operation might have the following types of storage areas:

- frozen foods
- canned, dry, and boxed goods
- wet produce
- dry produce
- dairy products
- meat and poultry
- seafood
- pathway area for frozen food
- paper supplies

THE STOREROOM (DRY STORAGE)

Too often, when planning a food facility, the architect relegates any leftover space in the floor plans to storage without any real thought to precise storage needs. Considerations in planning for dry stores should include:

- adequate space
- proximity to receiving and preparation areas
- security of contents
- temperature, humidity, and lighting
- types of shelving (for arrangement of contents in the storage area)
- protection from vermin and insect infestation

Adequate Space

The space required for dry stores depends on many factors: type of operation, menu, volume of business, purchasing policies, and frequency of deliveries. An operation that serves a varied and changing menu will have different storage requirements than one that serves a fixed, limited menu. Operations that can have food delivered daily and readily do not have the problems of an operation that is isolated and may receive only weekly, or even more infrequent, deliveries of certain items. Other operators like to purchase large quantities of foods at one time, and they must make extra provision for food storage.

Although each type of operation is different, several general rules may be used as guidelines. One approach is to specify necessary floor space in terms of square footage per meal served. Proponents of this method often recommend one-half to one square foot of floor space per meal served. Another method is to determine storage needs in terms of the supply on hand. A two-week supply is generally suggested; after calculating the amount of dry stores that will be used in a two-week period, the manager calculates the amount of space it will occupy.

Although many food operators believe they can use as much dry food storage space as they can get, too great a storage area presents problems. Every square foot of storage area costs money to heat and maintain, so too great an area will require a larger capital expenditure. There is a tendency to want to fill up a storeroom, so an overly large area may promote an overly large inventory. If the area is not filled with foodstuffs, other supplies may be stored there. This habit complicates security, because it encourages more goings and comings, perhaps by people not controlled by the food department. Obviously, too small a storage area also presents problems by retarding ready access to items. Some items may be hidden, while others must be stored in open areas. It is more difficult to keep crowded, disorganized premises clean.

A trend that has affected many foodservice operations, especially larger ones, is the effort to cut down on inventories. This not only reduces costs of maintaining larger inventories, it also frees up space formerly used in storage for other purposes. A downtown hospital with no space to expand, for example, can find this approach very useful and can free up valuable working capital. Some factors that make lower inventories possible are better forecasting, faster ordering (perhaps by fax or e-mail), more limited menus, use of convenience foods, and one-stop shopping, which may allow for more frequent deliveries by one purveyor. A foodservice operating plan should incorporate factors that allow less storage area.

Location

Theoretically, the storage area should be located between, and adjacent to, the receiving area and the preparation area. Sometimes this is impossible. Many storerooms are located below the kitchen, with an elevator or a dumbwaiter providing access. Unfortunately, in some large institutions, the dry stores area may be located blocks away from preparation, necessitating much hauling. If space is severely limited, it may be desirable both to have limited storage facilities close at hand and to utilize bulk storage elsewhere.

Security

A prime purpose of the storage area is to protect the contents, which, after all, represent money in the form of merchandise. For tightest security, access to the storeroom should be strictly limited. Ideally, only the storeroom personnel and management are permitted in the room. Merchandise should be delivered by delivery persons to porters at the storeroom entrance or to storeroom personnel who are solely responsible for deliveries. A Dutch door that has a top half and a bottom half with a counter or ledge over the bottom half may be very helpful. This adjustment permits merchandise to be handed out and also keeps people from entering. Operations that allow personnel to enter the storeroom indiscriminately invite trouble. Not only are they apt to experience more pilferage, but they will find it practically impossible to pinpoint the guilty individuals. The open storeroom may also be used as a lounging place, away from the eyes of supervision.

Security is also promoted by installing only a limited number of entrances. Having only one is desirable. Some operations with doors opening to the outside have found pilferage greatly reduced by locking the outside door and throwing away the keys.

Temperature, Humidity, and Lighting

Some operators feel that although care must be given to raw or perishable items, there is little need to worry over canned or boxed items. This is not true. With few exceptions, almost every food begins chemical deterioration immediately after processing. Infestation by roaches, flies, weevils, and rodents is also possible, and there is a definite natural deterioration in the quality of canned foods stored over long periods. This deterioration is accelerated by high temperatures or sudden fluctuations in temperatures, which can cause condensation in the products. The dry-food storeroom should be kept relatively cool; a 60° to 70° F temperature is satisfactory, but a 50° F temperature will help to maintain better quality in most foods. One study showed that foods in general keep three times as long at 70° F as they do at 100° F. Other studies have revealed that nutritional losses in foods increase as storage temperatures rise. Unfortunately, many storerooms have heating and water pipes running through them. The heating pipes may cause excessive heat, especially if there is little ventilation. The water pipes may cause condensation in the summer. This condensation creates dripping and humidity problems. It is desirable that relative humidity be around 50 to 60 percent, and lower for cereals. Operations with excessive humidity may want to install a mechanical or chemical dehumidifier. On the other hand, if the relative humidity is too low and the air is too dry, a humidifier or basins of water distributed around the storage area may be helpful.

The storeroom should be ventilated, and four air changes per hour are desirable. Ventilation haphazardly installed may cause security, insect, and dust problems.

A problem in many dry-food storerooms occurs when refrigeration compressors and condensers for refrigeration units are installed in the dry storeroom. These not only give off heat but also require periodic servicing, which creates still another security problem. Moreover, in some closed storerooms the compressors raise the temperature high enough in the closed area to cause mechanical problems.

Some products, such as beer and beets, are affected adversely by direct sunlight, so storeroom windows should be frosted. Clear glass can also transmit radiant heat to sealed containers and raise the temperature inside them higher than the surrounding room temperatures. Of course, the storeroom should have adequate illumination. One good rule of thumb dictates two or three watts of light for every square foot of floor area. Low ceilings and high shelves can hinder proper light distribution.

Shelving and Arrangement of Contents

Shelving is required whenever less-than-case lots must be stored or where management does not want to leave canned goods in full cases. Shelving should be adjustable and can be either metal or wood. Metal shelving takes up less space than wood, is easier to clean, can be adjusted more easily, and eliminates danger of splinters. Wood shelving, on the other hand, is somewhat softer than metal and better suited to storing glass jars, but it requires more care. Shelving space usually depends on the size of a No. 10 can, which is 7 inches high and $6\frac{1}{4}$ inches in diameter. Shelves 19 inches wide and 16 inches high will permit three rows of No. 10 cans to be stacked two tiers high, or four rows of No. $2\frac{1}{2}$ cans stacked three tiers high. Unless special equipment (a rolling ladder, for example) is available, items should not be stored above $7\frac{1}{2}$ feet or, in any case, beyond normal reach. Bulk supplies, such as cartons of breakfast food, case lots of canned goods, and bags of flour, may be stored on pallets that are raised 6 to 7 inches above the floor. Any merchandise stored directly on the floor or against outside walls may absorb moisture, create cleaning problems, and cut down ventilation. For this reason, merchandise on shelves should be kept 2 inches away from outside walls. If bags or crates of goods are kept on pallets on the floor, those bags and crates should be piled in a crisscross arrangement. This allows for better ventilation and, in some cases, easier stacking. Bags and crates should not be stacked more than six tiers high.

Arranging foods in the storeroom involves several considerations. First, each item should be assigned a definite place. Second, the fast-moving items should be stored close to the entrance. One effective system breaks the foods down into groups and then arranges them in that group alphabetically on the shelves. If fruit juice is one of the groups, the cans would be placed on the shelves, apple juice first, then cranberry, grape, and grapefruit, for example. The various groups do not necessarily need to be placed alphabetically; for example, frequently used items should be stored so that they may be easily reached.

One classification of groups is:

1. beverages, milk products, and mineral waters
2. candies
3. cereals (prepared)
4. cereals and flour
5. chocolate and cocoa
6. cookies, cakes, and crackers
7. colorings
8. condiments and spices
9. extracts
10. fats and oils
11. fish, shellfish, and seafoods
12. fountain and ice cream supplies
13. fruits (canned)
14. fruits (dried and glazed)
15. fruit juices and cocktails
16. fruit preserves and jellies
17. fruits (spiced and pickled)
18. gelatin and gelatin desserts

19. leavening agents

20. nut meats and nut products

21. pickles and olives

22. sauces and relishes

23. sugar and related substances

24. vegetables (canned)

25. vegetables (dried)

26. specialties

Assigning a definite space for each type of food item requires somewhat more space than if foods were placed haphazardly in an empty area, since foods may not require all the space allotted to them at one time. However, a great deal of time is saved by not having to hunt for items, which most likely would be necessary if they were stored randomly. In addition, if the foods are stored systematically, the operator can readily determine exactly what is on hand. If inventory sheets are made up to correspond with the allotted spaces on the shelves, a great deal of time can be saved in taking inventory.

Too often, new merchandise gets used while the old merchandise gets older and staler. **FIFO (first in, first out)** is the process of rearranging the merchandise so that the older containers are in front and issued first. It takes extra work to implement FIFO, but it pays off by eliminating the problem of stale merchandise. Some operations use a dating stamp on containers or cases to help show which merchandise is the oldest.

Protection from Vermin and Insect Infestation

Food must be protected from infestation by flies, roaches, weevils, and rodents. Grains and cereals are especially vulnerable to such vermin. Protection from pests requires the elimination of all holes or openings in the walls, ceilings, and floors of the storeroom. Some mice can enter a half-inch hole. Windows should be tightly screened. Provision should be made for regular cleaning and spraying so that insects can be controlled. Trash—especially garbage—should never be placed in the storeroom. If pipes must penetrate the walls of the storeroom, the walls should be tightly sealed around the pipes.

Bulk supplies of cereals, dried fruits, and vegetables should be kept in metal or heavy plastic containers with tight fitting lids. The cans should be labeled and perhaps mounted on rollers.

Dry Storage Essentials

Following are some basic guidelines for dry storage.

1. A thermometer to indicate excessively high temperatures should be kept in the storeroom.

2. People allowed in the storeroom should be strictly limited and controlled.

3. Goods should be marked with the date of delivery, and the FIFO system should be employed.

4. Merchandise should be stored 6 to 10 inches above the floor and 2 inches from walls.

5. Each food classification should be assigned a definite space.

6. Employees' personal belongings should not be kept in the storeroom.

7. The storeroom should be locked when authorized personnel are not manning it. An emergency key in a sealed envelope may be kept in the manager's office.

8. The storeroom should be cleaned and sprayed regularly, with particular attention given to dark corners and to the areas under the shelves.

9. Foods packed in glass should not be exposed to direct sunlight or to any strong light.

10. "G.I." cans or large plastic containers that are used for bulk storage should have tight lids, and it may be desirable to mount them on rollers for easy maneuverability.

REFRIGERATED STORAGE

Refrigeration is absolutely necessary for perishable items and extends the quality and life of some semiperishable foods. In addition to maintaining quality, refrigeration is necessary to curtail the growth of bacteria and control the food poisoning that results. Storage is generally classified as *refrigerated* when temperatures above freezing are maintained; frozen food storage exists when a temperature of 32° F or lower is maintained. Equipment is usually classified as *reach-in* when food is removed from outside and *walk-in* when it is necessary actually to enter the unit. Specialty refrigeration units, such as beer coolers, salad refrigerators, and milk dispensers, are also in common use.

Amount of Refrigeration

No established rules dictate how much refrigeration is required in an operation. The number of entrées, the amount of convenience food in use, the frequency of deliveries, the policy on leftovers, and fluctuations in business will all affect the amount of refrigeration required. To determine the size of the unit, one must determine the quantity of food that will be stored and its volume. Refrigeration space is sometimes divided (somewhat arbitrarily) into a third for meats, a third for fresh produce and vegetables, a sixth for dairy products, and a sixth for frozen foods, but again this allocation depends on menu deliveries, the amount of frozen convenience food used, and other factors.

It is difficult to be exact in these calculations unless one expects to serve a very standard menu to a constant number of customers. Refrigeration storage space is rated in cubic feet, and some designers recommend 1 to 2 cubic feet per each meal served or 3 to 5 cubic feet per seating capacity. Obviously, an excessive amount of refrigeration increases capital costs and operating expenses, but an equally important result is that it encourages a tendency to allow leftovers to accumulate and spoil. Some operations have found that by strictly limiting the amount of refrigeration, they curtail overproduction and overordering.

Reach-in refrigeration is very efficient because no space is needed for personnel to maneuver; however, walk-in units are necessary for storing large quantities of food. Many operations provide relatively small reach-in refrigeration handy for cooks in the preparation area while maintaining larger, walk-in refrigeration some distance away. Issues for the day, or for the meal, can be delivered at one time to the smaller units, and subsequent trips are largely eliminated. Efficiency in storage can be increased by installing adjustable shelves and racks that can be arranged according to the size of the articles stored. These adjustable shelves also help to eliminate unused storage space.

Physical Construction

It is poor economy to try to save money on cheaply constructed refrigeration units. Proper insulation is vital since outside heat can enter the unit by direct transmission. Vapor barriers are necessary to prevent water vapor from condensing in the insulation and making it less effective. All openings should be tightly fitted with some sort of stripping or gasket. Doors on walk-in units should be able to be opened from the inside, and a light or some other signal should be provided so that people trapped in the unit can indicate their presence there. Glass and plastic refrigerator doors are becoming more popular. The inside construction of walk-ins should include walls that allow easy cleaning. Durable floors are especially important. The floor of the unit should be flush with the outside hall so that carts can readily be wheeled in. Portable shelving is very desirable. Stainless steel casing outside is very attractive and very durable, but it is also very expensive; cheaper finishes can be just as efficient, though possibly less attractive. Vinyl finishes provide a great flexibility in aesthetic design. The handles, latches, releases, and other hardware used in the units should be the best available, and spare parts should be readily accessible.

Temperatures and Humidities

Some large operations maintain over a dozen different temperatures in at least as many units. Optimum temperatures have been established for different foods, but most operations with a limited number of units must compromise. A prime function of refrigeration is to prevent the growth of bacteria, which usually multiply most readily in the 50° to 120° F temperature range; therefore, all refrigerated foods should be kept colder than 45° F. Humidity also affects refrigerated foods. An excessively high relative humidity allows food to become slimy, encourages bacteria growth, and enhances spoilage. Too low a relative humidity causes food to dry out. Too low a relative humidity can often be overcome by covering items with a wet cloth or dampening them directly. However, open containers of water should not be kept in the units to increase humidity because of the sanitation problems they create. Separate refrigeration is often provided for three types of products: meats, fruits and produce, and dairy products.

Other Refrigerated Storage Considerations

Cleanliness of the refrigeration unit is vital for good management, housekeeping, and sanitation. The contents of the unit should be put in order daily, and any spilled foods should be wiped up immediately. Warm, soapy water can be used to wash inside walls, but they should be rinsed quickly. Walk-in floors should be mopped daily.

If food items become "slimy," the temperature may be too hot or air movement may be inadequate. These problems may be caused by a blocked evaporator or frosted coils. Normally, a unit should be defrosted when a quarter-inch of ice accumulates. In addition to maintaining efficiency, defrosting reduces electrical power costs. Self-defrosting units further reduce labor cost.

If the food appears to be dried out, the temperature may be too low or there may be too much air movement. If there is no fan control, blocking part of the evaporator (the coils inside the unit) may help.

A germicidal or ultraviolet ray lamp can help. Some operations recommend them because they reduce the mold that accumulates on aging meat. However, others feel this advantage is outweighed by their tendency to speed fat breakdown.

Some operations have an alarm light or a buzzer that is activated when temperatures rise above a certain level. This system helps prevent food loss by alerting personnel. If the trouble takes time to repair, temperatures may be kept down by placing ice or dry ice in the highest part of the unit. One common refrigeration trouble is the loss of refrigerant. Since replacing the refrigerant is relatively expensive, it is wise to locate and correct leaks as soon as any difficulty is detected. Every unit should have a thermometer installed, and it should be checked regularly. Sometimes the thermometer gauge is installed outside the unit for easier visibility.

Frozen Food Storage

The most important factor in frozen food storage is, of course, the temperature, which normally should be from $0°$ to $-10°$ F. Even though foods stored at $32°$ F may technically be frozen, chemical changes and microorganism growth can occur in this temperature range. It is sometimes said that every temperature rise of $10°$ F in frozen food storage cuts the storage life in half. Vegetables such as peas and lima beans will become discolored and lose flavor in two months at $10°$ F, but they can be held up to a year at $0°$ F. Frozen peas deteriorate 60 times faster at $30°$ than at $0°$ F.

Frozen food should be wrapped in moisture- or vapor-proof material; this will prevent the food from losing moisture and suffering freezer burn. **Freezer burn** occurs when fat under the surface becomes rancid, causing a brown discoloration. A high humidity should be maintained in the freezer area because the cold dry air will seek moisture from the foods stored in it.

Foods that have been allowed to thaw should not be refrozen. Rejuvenated microorganisms can cause spoilage, and changes in the food cell structure can cause a loss of quality. Most frozen foods can be cooked or reconstituted directly from the frozen state. Large pieces of meat, however, must be thawed, or partially thawed, before further processing. To prevent rapid growth of bacteria, these items should be thawed under normal refrigeration temperatures, rather than at room temperature. There may be less shrinkage when unthawed meats are cooked, but cooking times may be longer and fuel costs higher.

As in the regular refrigeration process, a thermometer gauge to check the temperature of the freezer units should be visible, and it is very desirable to have an alarm system that activates if the freezer temperature rises above a certain safety level. Air circulation should be provided inside the units. Circulation is facilitated when items are not placed directly against the walls and ceiling or on the floor. To ensure FIFO, it is helpful to have items stamped with the date of storage.

ISSUING

Issuing, or requisitioning, is the process used to supply food to the preparation units after it has been received by the operation. It also entails controlling food sent to preparation, providing information for food-cost accounting, and, in some cases, providing information for a perpetual inventory system. In a **perpetual inventory** quantities of an item coming in and going out and the amount on hand are kept constant. This is opposed to a **physical**

INDUSTRY INSIGHTS   by Dick Cattani

Dick Cattani is President of Development and Management Services for Restaurant Associates. He has served as the Chairman of the Board of Paul Smith's College in upstate New York.

Dairy products	38° F
Fish and seafood	38° F
Meat	35° F
Preparation/sauce box	38° F
Pastry box	38° F
Garbage refrigerator	40° F

Storage areas should be maintained at the following temperatures:

Freezer	−10° F

FOOD STORAGE MANAGEMENT

The primary purpose of food storage management is to receive, store, issue, and control product and prevent its loss through theft and/or spoilage.

To prevent theft, there should be an adequate lock and key control. Strong locks are to be used and keys to the storeroom should be issued only to individuals designated by the unit's director. Only authorized persons should be permitted in the food storage area at any time. Someone should always be on duty during the hours the storeroom is scheduled to be open.

Exposure to vermin and bacteria causes rapid deterioration of food and possible disease. Therefore, a fixed schedule of cleaning and extermination of the food storage areas must be developed and followed.

The most important control in preventing food spoilage is low temperature. Perishables are stored in a refrigerator with temperature above the freezing point of food. Refrigerator storage is intended to prolong the life of the product for a comparatively limited period. Freezers with temperature below freezing point are used for longer storage.

Food should be stored at the following temperatures:

All fresh fruit and vegetables with the exception of unripe fruit, bananas, potatoes, yellow onions, and garlic	38° F

It is recommended that the kinds of foodstuffs stored and the proper temperatures to be maintained be painted on refrigerator doors, such as: Diary 38° F.

A designated person should read the temperature of the refrigerators and freezers daily, and record the readings in the refrigerator temperature book. An erratic thermostat can endanger large quantities of food stored in a refrigerator or freezer, particularly when meat becomes unfit for use because of alternate freezing and thawing. This condition may not be observed until after the damage has been caused by faulty thermostats. Problems with refrigeration units must be reported to the Maintenance Department immediately.

All received food items must be dated at the receiving location. Date all cartons, bags, crates, etc., upright on the labeled side to insure proper rotation. The dating should be done with wax crayon, indelible marker, or tags.

Excessive delays between time of receipt and proper storage must be avoided. Any item requiring refrigeration must be placed under proper refrigeration as soon as possible. Any deterioration of quality should be noticed while taking the daily inventory and during cleaning periods or special inspection trips. The unit's chef should be notified, in writing, of all slow moving items. There is a danger of spoilage when no action is taken on slow moving stock.

Fresh fish should be kept constantly at 38° F to ensure maximum storage life. Proper icing has most to do with retaining fish quality. Refrigeration on its own is not sufficient. The cooler is not cool enough and not damp enough. After accepting delivery, the fish should be washed and re-iced. The old ice will be building up bacteria from the fluids dripped from the fish and the bacteria will speed decomposition. Fish needs the wet coldness of ice if it is to be kept in peak condition.

All fresh fruit must be thoroughly checked for ripeness prior to storage. If this inspection must be delayed, store merchandise in the refrigerator until such inspection can be made on the same day. With the exception of bananas and pears, fruits do not ripen fully after they have been harvested. Never store ripe fruit in close proximity to other fruit. Separate by use of egg type dividers. Do not put anything on top of ripe fruit. On a daily basis, carefully check for spoiled fruit.

For best protection, vegetables and greens should be covered with wet towels or clean cloths and/or placed into a plastic bag or tightly closed container. Vegetables and greens in the field or in storage are continually going through processes of growing. Frozen vegetables must be handled in the same way as other frozen food; that is, they should be dated and sorted in the freezer as soon as received.

Egg shells are highly porous and absorb odors readily. They must be separated from foods with strong odors. Keep them in their individual cartons in the shipping case, closed, in the coldest part of the walk-in refrigerator. Keep them dry. Wet eggs develop mold and spoil. To allow for air circulation, stack with strips of wood between cases. Store away from refrigerator pipes, as freezing spoils eggs. Eggs freeze at 32° F. Store eggs right side up, never on their sides or tops, since turning the eggs may break the air sack in the egg which will cause spoilage. Store away from direct air flow from fan or blower; this would dry out the eggs and cause them to deteriorate. Eggs begin to deteriorate as soon as they are laid. If they are properly processed and stored, egg components may be held for many months retaining the same quality of fresh eggs. An egg component stored at 29° F to 31° F for six months will have the same quality of a fresh egg held at room temperature for one week.

Cheese should be stored at 38° F. Cheese must be stored away from eggs, especially the strong, highly flavored cheeses such as Parmesan, Roquefort, blue, Liederkranz and Gorgonzola. Soft unripened cheese, such as cottage, cream, or Neuchatel, is perishable and should be used within a few days. Other cheeses keep well in the refrigerator for several weeks if protected from mold contamination and drying out. When possible, the original wrapper or covering should be left on.

Storeroom space permitting, it is advisable to repack grocery items, bought in bulk form, into smaller units. This procedure will make it easier to correctly weigh and cost items as requisitioned. These items include flour, sugar, salt, spices, coffee, rice, and nuts, which are weighed exactly and put into paper or plastic bags in quantities generally requisitioned.

Canned foods generally known to contain acid (vinegar, olives, some specially prepared vegetables) must not be stocked in close proximity to steam or hot water radiators or directly under an exterior metal roof. While putting cans on shelves, watch for swells or leaks. Do not take chances with cans that are not sound. Promptly discard them.

A special cabinet under lock and key should be used for high-priced items such as truffles, saffron, caviar, and goose liver. The last two items should be kept in a locked cabinet in the refrigerator.

inventory, where the items are manually counted. Issuing can be done directly from the receiving dock or from the storerooms. If the issues are sent from the receiving area to the kitchen without going through a storeroom, they are called *direct purchases,* or *direct issues*. Direct purchases are presumably used on the day they are purchased, since the kitchen is not a storeroom. The dollar value of direct purchases is found in the Food Direct column of the receiving clerk's daily report, as shown in Chapter 15 (15-1) and from this report management can also determine the various items that are sent directly into the preparation unit.

All food items that are received but are not used the day they are purchased are considered *storeroom purchases*. They are storeroom issues when delivered from the storeroom. Thus, if a food item is received, sent to the storeroom, issued from the storeroom, and used the same day, it would be considered a storeroom issue. The control for storeroom issues is the requisition, and no food should be issued from the storeroom unless it has been recorded and ordered on a requisition form. By adding the total direct purchases and the total value of the requisitions, it is relatively easy to determine the food cost for the day or for the period under examination. Direct purchases plus storeroom issues for the day equal daily food cost.

Direct Purchases

To maintain accurate food-cost information and better control, it is necessary that direct purchases (or issues) be limited to food that will be used on the day of delivery. If the food is not used the same day, the recorded food cost for the day of delivery would be unrealistically high, and the recorded food cost on the day it is used would be unrealistically low. Some incoming purchases may have a portion of their value charged as direct purchases sent directly to the preparation units and a portion charged to the storeroom and sent there.

Storeroom Issues

All food provided by the storeroom should be recorded on a requisition. Figure 16.1 provides a computerized requisition. If the requisitions are prenumbered, duplicates and missing requisitions can be more easily traced. Although most operations do not need numbered requisitions, the numbering may have some psychological value in that workers tend to be more careful with them. The name of the ordering department—the kitchen, pantry, or bake shop, for instance—should be filled in along with the date. The requisition should provide columns for the quantity of each item, the size of the unit desired, and the name of the item. There should also be spaces for the unit price and the total cost, or *extension,* which is determined by multiplying the number of units and the cost of each unit. A line should be included for the person authorized to request the articles to sign or initial. The storeroom should not give out any merchandise without this authorizing signature. There should also be space for the person issuing the food or filling the requisition to sign. In addition, it may be desirable to provide a space for the person entering the requisition on the bookkeeping records, or extending the costs, to sign or initial. If there is trouble regarding deliveries, the person delivering the food from the storeroom may also have to sign.

Some operations use only one original requisition, whereas others feel that control is facilitated by the use of duplicate copies. Duplicate copies may be used to provide a copy of the requisition for the ordering department, to supply a duplicate to the food-cost controller, to provide a copy for perpetual inventory, and to allow a copy to be returned

Cafe East				*Issue Requisition*

Date: 4/1/98   **Reason:** Production Request   **Meal:** Dinner
Unit: Cafe East   **Prep Area:** Hot Food Prep
Reference: Meal cycle 3, day 5   **Approval:** rrg

                                                    Attention: Jim

               Type: Issue   **Status:** Issued   **Number:** 2

Item	Quantity	Unit	Cost	Extended Cost
Bean Green Fr Cut Fz Grb	3.88	20 LB	12.82	49.74
Bread Baguette Mini	228.0	6 OZ	0.38	86.69
Coffee (automatic Anf)	9.38	Gallon		
Coffee Decaf Inst Indiv	113.31	Each	0.07	8.33
Milk Lowfat 1/2 Pint	185.00	1/2 PINT	0.17	31.45
Water	7.04	Gallon	0.01	0.07

Number of Items: 6   **Total Cost:** 176.28

Issued by _____ Date _____ Time _____ Initials _____
Received by _____ Date _____ Time _____ Initials _____

Figure 16.1
Issue Requisition

with the order. The duplicates may be made out with the original requisition, or they may be made out by the issuing storeroom. Since the duplicates are largely informational, they would not need to be signed by the person making out the original.

Difficulties sometimes arise when food is requisitioned for preparation prior to the actual serving day. These difficulties are best handled by making two requisitions: one with the date that the food is issued, and the other with the date that the items will be used. The food is released on the basis of the first requisition, but only the second requisition is recorded on the date of use for cost-control purposes. Care must be taken at the end of an inventory period that items issued but not charged be given credit on the inventory.

If the storeroom cannot supply an item on the requisition, it should be marked "out." In some cases, it is desirable to call the person requesting the item immediately so substitutions or purchase arrangements can be made. The storeroom should not make changes on requisitions or accept requisitions over the telephone.

Pricing the requisitions and calculating extensions may be done in the storeroom or elsewhere. With constantly changing prices, finding the exact cost of the item may be a problem. An effective and easy way to determine this cost is to stamp or mark the containers with the unit cost when they are received. When filling out a requisition, it is simple to record the cost. This also simplifies pricing inventories. It eliminates the necessity of checking back through the receiving report, the invoices, or the perpetual inventory cards to find the purchase cost. Some operations cost out the requisition at the last purchase cost, but this practice can lead to some difficulties in resolving inventory valuations.

Table 16.1
Correlation of Requisition with Standard Recipe Card

		Requisition		
Date _____			Item _____	
Ingredients	Quantity	50 Servings	100 Servings	150 Servings
Eggs	_____	9 eggs	1½ dozen	2¼ dozen
Shortening	_____	¾ pound	1 ½ pounds	2¼ pounds
Vanilla	_____	⅛ cup	¼ cup	⅜ cup
Salt	_____	¾ teaspoon	1½ teaspoons	2¼ teaspoons
Sugar	_____	2 pounds	4 pounds	6 pounds
Flour	_____	2 pounds	4 pounds	6 pounds
Baking powder	_____	1¾ ounces	3½ ounces	5¼ ounces
Dry milk	_____	3 ounces	6 ounces	9 ounces

If a meat tag system is employed, the meat tag can be used for costing purposes. It saves reweighing the item and also eliminates inventory shrinkage calculation, since the item is issued at the weight on the tag, which is the weight received.

Table 16.1 correlates the requisition with the standard recipe card. The items required are already listed, and only the quantities need be entered for the number of servings desired. This system, of course, requires that a standard recipe sheet be used every time the item is prepared.

COMPUTERIZED ISSUING

Much of the issuing process can be computerized. Once the menu and number to be served have been entered, the computer can determine from the standard recipes in its memory the amount of food that will be required or must be requisitioned. It can combine the amounts in recipes when the same ingredient is used in several items. The computer can print the requisitions, cost them, and at the same time remove the value and number or quantity of the items from inventory counts. The requisitions can also be used to determine food costs for the meal or period.

The computerization of requisitioning provides some additional control elements. For example, bogus requisitions become harder to prepare. The computer may also render the necessary quantities more precisely than manually prepared requisitions do. It may be able to keep track of requisitions and provide an audit trail if necessary. A computer program can also expand or condense quantities in a recipe to meet production needs.

INVENTORY CONTROL

Inventory control has become an increasingly important food-cost control element. Its functions can include:

1. having the smallest dollar investment possible in inventory
2. providing quality and security protection for the goods
3. providing variances between actual quantities and calculated quantities on hand
4. providing the dollar value of inventories necessary for financial reports
5. providing the usage figures of various food items or tracking their consumption
6. alerting management to slow-moving items
7. alerting management when replacements to inventory are needed
8. providing a safety factor for unexpected problems in deliveries

With increasing cost pressures, a sound strategy is to keep inventories as low as possible to reduce both the amount of money invested in inventory and the storage and handling costs. With efficient forecasting of consumption and purchasing geared to the forecast, one can dramatically reduce inventory quantities by purchasing specifically for a meal or period. This is somewhat akin to the practice among Japanese automobile manufacturers of making frequent deliveries instead of keeping large inventories. How successful this is in foodservice can depend on the frequency and reliability of the purveyors' deliveries. Also, some inventory may be kept in reserve for unexpected circumstances.

Management should know the quantities (and value) of inventory items on hand, but they can do this with a perpetual inventory system, which may be computerized. Otherwise, someone has to go to the storeroom and physically count the items. A knowledge of quantities on hand is necessary to determine purchase quantities or to tell if there is enough on hand so purchasing is not required.

It is desirable to know the **shrinkage**, or the difference between what should be on hand based on purchases and issues and what is on hand by actual count. Shrinkage may occur because of theft, because of poor posting, or because of items "walking out." It is also desirable to know the shrinkage on individual items. On an overall basis, too-high figures may balance out too-low figures on different items. Some operations calculate shrinkage only on high-cost items such as steaks or high-volume items such as coffee.

To prepare an income or profit-and-loss statement, one must know the value of the opening and closing inventories to determine the cost of sales. The opening inventory value is the closing inventory value of the previous period.

Operations with varied and frequently changing menus may have many slow-moving items in inventory that are served only infrequently. Or, some items may no longer be served but are still in inventory. Management should be aware of these items and try to use them. A problem arises when the items cannot be used but are taken off inventory. This reduces the value of the closing inventory for the period, which increases the cost of goods sold and shows a lower profit, even though management is simply taking care of prior purchasing mistakes.

PHYSICAL INVENTORY

Without proper physical inventory, it is possible for one to maintain a misleadingly low food cost by not recording requisitions and not replacing food taken from storage. This practice will eventually come to light when the storeroom grows bare and requires extensive restocking. The restocking will return inventory to normal levels, requiring more expenditures, and the understating of prior costs will be revealed. In calculating food cost, one needs an opening inventory value figure (the closing inventory of the previous financial period) and a closing inventory value figure. These figures can be accurately determined only by counting the merchandise in storage and determining its value. The formula for determining food cost is:

> the value of the opening inventory
> + food purchases
> = total inventory available
> − closing inventory
> = cost of the food consumed during the period

The cost of food consumed is known as the *gross cost*. If employees' meals are deducted from this amount, the resulting figure is referred to as cost of goods sold. Although food cost can be ascertained on a daily basis by adding direct purchases and storeroom requisitions, inventory fluctuations must be taken into account for a truly accurate figure.

Normally, inventories are taken once a month, usually at the end of the month or whenever the financial period ends. An inventory at the end of December would be the closing figure for the year (and the opening inventory for the next year) if the financial year runs from January 1 to December 31. However, physical inventories are taken whenever management needs an accurate food-cost figure. This can be for an accounting period, ordering time, end of a 13-week cycle, or any other time period.

Two people can take inventory more easily if one counts while the other records the figures. To ensure control, at least one inventory taker should be free of connections with the storeroom or the kitchen and should not be influenced by their personnel. Someone from the manager or food controller's office usually does the work. The inventory is sometimes taken on looseleaf inventory sheets, which list the items in the same order as they are placed on the shelves. Space should be left on the inventory sheets for new items that might be added during the period. To facilitate pricing, unit prices, if marked on the merchandise, should be noted when the merchandise is counted. No more than one food group should be listed on each inventory page, and each page should be subtotaled. These subtotals are combined for a grand total on a recap sheet, and the personnel taking the inventory should sign it to fix responsibility.

Storeroom inventories should be taken after the close of business on the last day of the financial period, but this is not always possible. In any case, they should not be taken until the day's purchases are in the storeroom and issues have been made.

Some operations with a very stable inventory have found that their count of items in the storeroom varies little from month to month. In some cases, it has proven economical not to count most items but to assume that they remain constant. Only expensive and fast-moving items are counted. This method sacrifices some accuracy and control but does eliminate much of the tedious job of inventory taking. It should be employed only where experience has shown little variance from month to month, and, of course, a full inventory should be taken periodically.

Kitchen or production inventories represent goods that have been charged to preparation departments but have not yet been consumed. These inventories usually are taken by the person in charge of the unit or department, but spot checks should be made by personnel responsible for food-cost control. Meat is usually the item of largest cost in production inventories, so food-cost control personnel may want to take part in this inventory, which in some operations is done daily. Kitchen inventories are added to storeroom inventories for a total inventory value figure. Instead of physically counting kitchen inventory, it may be calculated as a percentage of other inventory.

Figure 16.2 shows a computer-generated physical inventory form. The Units on Hand blank would be filled in by those taking the inventory. Table 16.2 shows a computerized extension of inventory value by different storage locations. Figure 16.3 shows computer calculations of the entire inventory value.

Following are some tips for taking inventory:

1. Count inventory only after the operation is shut down.
2. Be sure that no food is being prepared while inventory is in progress.
3. Organize storage areas, labeling shelves whenever possible.
4. Use two-person teams: One counts and one records and double checks.
5. Count items in their appropriate units.

```
REPORT#: 271   * * * CBORD FOODSERVICE MANAGEMENT SYSTEMS * * *        PAGE:   1
OPTION : 7.5.1.6.1.  MENU MANAGEMENT SYSTEM - 4.1.36                    FEB 01  9X
USER#  : 1                        HENDERSON HALL                        1035 HOURS
                               INVENTORY TALLY SHEET


Unit Name: _____                          Taken By: _____
Code: ____                                           Date: ___/___/___ Time: _____
.
Storage Location: 01 MEAT COOLER  1
.
--------------------------------------------------------------------------------
Bin              Item                  Item   Units      Stock             Price per
Nmbr             Name                  Nmbr   on Hand    Unit              Stk Unit
--------------------------------------------------------------------------------
A05    CHILI CON CARNE               350 <_____.__>  BAG 2 GL              14.04

A15    BEEF BASE                      30 <_____.__>  12/1# CS              14.40

A15    HAM WHOLE CAN                 160 <_____.__>  LBS                    1.90

A15    SAUSAGE PASTRAMI              168 <_____.__>  LBS                    1.51

B15    SAUSAGE SALAMI                173 <_____.__>  LBS                    1.01

B35    HAM SLICED CAN                161 <_____.__>  LBS                    1.73

C15    BEEF HAMBURGERS               158 <_____.__>  2 LBS                  2.36

D10    BEEF CORNED                    61 <_____.__>  4/6# CN               16.32

D10    HAM BUFFET FLAT               170 <_____.__>  LBS                    1.45

SUBTOTAL NUMBER OF RECORDS PRINTED  9
--------------------------------------------------------------------------------
```

Figure 16.2
Physical Inventory Form
(Reprinted courtesy of The CBORD Group, Inc. © 1992.)

Table 16.2
Extension of Inventory Value

<table>
<tr><td colspan="5" align="center">Extension Report—Detail
Joe's Diner
By Inventory Department/For Inventory Group Mandatory Products
Costing Method: Default
As of Thursday, April 30, 1998 End of Week Inventory</td></tr>
<tr><td colspan="5" align="center">Reported in Unit</td></tr>
<tr><td>Inventory Item</td><td>Count</td><td>Name</td><td>Cost</td><td>Extension</td></tr>
<tr><td colspan="5">Food—Meat/Poultry—Beef</td></tr>
<tr><td>Beef corned brskt raw</td><td>20.00 lb</td><td></td><td>$ 1.590</td><td>$ 31.80</td></tr>
<tr><td>Beef eye round</td><td>6.00 lb</td><td></td><td>2.190</td><td>13.14</td></tr>
<tr><td>Beef frank footlong</td><td>10.00 lb</td><td></td><td>2.620</td><td>26.20</td></tr>
<tr><td>Beef grnd bulk 80/20</td><td>80.00 lb</td><td></td><td>1.130</td><td>90.40</td></tr>
<tr><td></td><td></td><td></td><td>Beef Total</td><td>$161.54</td></tr>
<tr><td colspan="5">Food—Storeroom—Bulk Condiment, Dressing, Oil</td></tr>
<tr><td>Dressing italian</td><td>1.50 1 gallon</td><td></td><td>$ 8.050</td><td>$ 12.07</td></tr>
<tr><td>Dressing ranch</td><td>4.00 1 gallon</td><td></td><td>10.850</td><td>43.40</td></tr>
<tr><td>Dressing thousand island</td><td>2.00 1 gallon</td><td></td><td>10.850</td><td>21.70</td></tr>
<tr><td>Oil coating pan spray</td><td>7.00 can</td><td></td><td>2.000</td><td>14.00</td></tr>
<tr><td>Oil olive</td><td>4.50 1 gallon</td><td></td><td>14.000</td><td>63.00</td></tr>
<tr><td></td><td></td><td colspan="2">Bulk Condiment, Dressing, Oil Total</td><td>$154.18</td></tr>
<tr><td colspan="5">Food—Storeroom—Pasta, Cereals & Flours</td></tr>
<tr><td>Rice arborio</td><td>14.00 lb</td><td></td><td>$ 1.450</td><td>$ 20.30</td></tr>
<tr><td>Rice jasmine</td><td>10.00 1 lb</td><td></td><td>0.000</td><td>0.00</td></tr>
<tr><td>Rice wild</td><td>5.00 1 lb</td><td></td><td>6.000</td><td>30.00</td></tr>
<tr><td></td><td></td><td colspan="2">Pasta, Cereals & Flours Total</td><td>$ 50.30</td></tr>
<tr><td colspan="5">Food—Storeroom—Spices & Special Blends</td></tr>
<tr><td>Base soup chicken no msg</td><td>11.00 1 lb</td><td></td><td>$ 2.483</td><td>$ 27.32</td></tr>
<tr><td>Base soup clam no msg</td><td>14.00 1 lb</td><td></td><td>4.583</td><td>64.17</td></tr>
<tr><td></td><td></td><td colspan="2">Spices & Special Blends Total</td><td>$ 91.48</td></tr>
<tr><td colspan="5">Food—Storeroom—Bakery & Dessert Supplies</td></tr>
<tr><td>Bake cake mix devil's food</td><td>5.00 box</td><td></td><td>$ 7.892</td><td>$ 39.46</td></tr>
<tr><td>Bake mousse chocolate</td><td>0.50 1 ct</td><td></td><td>2.862</td><td>1.43</td></tr>
<tr><td>Bake pancake & wfl mix</td><td>5.00 box</td><td></td><td>3.813</td><td>19.07</td></tr>
<tr><td>Bake pudding inst chocolate</td><td>0.50 1 ct</td><td></td><td>2.756</td><td>1.38</td></tr>
<tr><td>Bake pudding inst vanilla</td><td>0.50 1 ct</td><td></td><td>2.582</td><td>1.29</td></tr>
<tr><td>Bake sugar confectioners</td><td>18.00 box</td><td></td><td>0.659</td><td>11.86</td></tr>
<tr><td></td><td></td><td colspan="2">Bakery & Dessert Supplies Total</td><td>$ 74.48</td></tr>
<tr><td colspan="5">Food—Storeroom—PCs (Portion Control Packets)</td></tr>
<tr><td>PC coffee inst indv sanka</td><td>1.00 box</td><td></td><td>$18.000</td><td>$ 18.00</td></tr>
<tr><td>PC honey</td><td>0.60 case</td><td></td><td>17.650</td><td>10.59</td></tr>
<tr><td>PC salt pkt</td><td>0.50 case</td><td></td><td>4.350</td><td>2.17</td></tr>
<tr><td>PC sugar in the raw</td><td>0.30 case</td><td></td><td>17.050</td><td>5.12</td></tr>
<tr><td>PC sugar pkt</td><td>7.00 case</td><td></td><td>7.950</td><td>55.65</td></tr>
<tr><td></td><td></td><td colspan="2">PCs (Portion Control Packets) Total</td><td>$ 91.53</td></tr>
<tr><td></td><td></td><td></td><td>Storeroom Total</td><td>$461.97</td></tr>
</table>

```
REPORT#: 295   * * * CBORD FOODSERVICE MANAGEMENT SYSTEMS * * *        PAGE:   1
OPTION : 7.5.1.9.2.        MENU MANAGEMENT SYSTEM - 4.1.36             FEB 01 9X
USER#  : 1                        HENDERSON HALL                      1248 HOURS
                              INVENTORY EXTENSION SUMMARY

Inventory Date : 02/01/9X
------------------------------------------------------------------------------
Product Group         Inventory  Value        Storage Location    Inventory  Value
------------------------------------------------------------------------------

 4 DAIRY FOODS AND EGGS    581.86    9.22%
 5 FRUITS, FRESH           892.84   14.15%     1 MEAT COOLER  1      640.85   10.16%
11 BAKERY & CEREAL PRODUCTS 404.49   6.41%     2 MEAT COOLER  2       72.57    1.15%
23 SUBASSEMBLIES            43.02    0.68%     4 DAIRY COOLER        937.65   14.86%
27 SPICES                  165.00    2.61%                         ----------------
35 BREADS AND BREAD PRODUCTS 75.82   1.20%     COOLER TOTALS       1651.07   26.16%
52 MISCELLANEOUS            36.00    0.57%                         ----------------
                        ----------------       8 FREEZER, VEGETABLES  80.72    1.28%
UNSPECIFIED ROLLUP GROUP  2199.03   34.85%     9 FREEZER, JUICES     277.27    4.39%
                        ----------------      10 FREEZER             448.30    7.10%
 1 MEAT & MEAT PRODUCTS    699.89   11.09%                         ----------------
 2 POULTRY                 353.26    5.60%     FROZEN TOTALS        806.29   12.78%
 3 FISH                    329.04    5.21%                         ----------------
                        ----------------       5 STOREROOM         2870.65   45.49%
MEAT ROLL UP             1382.19   21.90%       7 BREAD RACK         131.77    2.09%
                        ----------------      11 DRY STORES         850.82   13.48%
 9 JUICES, FROZEN, FRESH   277.27    4.39%                         ----------------
10 NONPER. FRUIT, VEG, JUICE 133.42  2.11%     DRY TOTALS          3853.24   61.06%
12 GROCERIES, DRY GOODS   1920.88   30.44%                         ----------------
14 SOUP AND BOUILLON       167.67    2.66%
17 FOOD OILS & FATS        140.03    2.22%
18 CONDIMENT & RELATED PROD  90.11   1.43%
                        ----------------
STAPLES ROLL UP          2729.38   43.25%
                        ----------------
                        ----------------                          ----------------
    TOTALS               6310.60  100.00%                         6310.60  100.00%
```

Figure 16.3
Computer Calculations of Inventory Value
(Reprinted courtesy of The CBORD Group, Inc.© 1992.

6. If the inventory unit is "lb," weigh it unless it is in sealed packages.

7. Be sure scales are properly calibrated, and the right scale is used for the item to be weighed.

8. Set up the inventory book to follow the shelf order to maximize efficiency.

9. Write legibly.

10. Don't rush. Accuracy, not speed, is the main objective.

11. Use a tape recorder if that would improve accuracy and efficiency.

When the inventory has been completed by the counter and recorder, each item must be reviewed by the food-production manager (or a person knowledgeable in purchasing, receiving, and production) prior to the count being given to the input clerk.

1. Review the current inventory count. Is the ending count appropriate for the inventory unit?

2. Review the new inventory prices.

3. Review the deliveries for frequency and amounts.

Table 16.3
Storeroom Reconciliation

Beginning inventory value	$ 2,000.00
Food stores purchased	8,000.00
Total	$10,000.00
Issues per requisition	8,050.00
Balance	$ 1,950.00
Ending inventory value	1,925.00
Over or (short)	$ (25.00)

4. Request verification of all items that do not look proper.
5. Review the unreceived orders.

STOREROOM RECONCILIATION

Table 16.3 shows a format for storeroom reconciliation. In addition to opening inventory, purchases, issues, and closing inventory, other credits are subtracted and debit transfers are added. It may be desirable to reconcile commodity groups, especially if there is a large discrepancy. It is important to discover where this discrepancy occurred.

There will usually be some difference between the value of the physical inventory and the figure that could be calculated if purchases were added and issues subtracted from an original figure. Normally, an overage or shortage of one-fourth of 1 percent of the cost of goods sold is considered acceptable.

Computerized systems not only can give gross over and short figures but also can indicate over and short figures on individual items.

INVENTORY TURNOVER

Slow inventory turnover may indicate an excessive amount of goods on hand, often stale or unusable goods still carried as assets. Many operations figure that their inventory should turn over three to five times a month. Thus, an inventory value of $5,000 should be reflected in a monthly cost-of-food-consumed figure of $15,000 to $25,000. Inventory turnover is calculated by dividing the value of the inventory into the cost of food consumed during the period. If the cost of food consumed is $25,000 and the value of inventory is $5,000, the inventory turnover is five times. This figure will vary according to the operation; a limited-menu fast-service operation, for example, will have a considerably higher turnover.

$$\text{Inventory turnover} = \frac{\text{Cost of food consumed}}{\text{Inventory value}} = \frac{\$25,000}{\$5,000} = 5\times$$

Almost every food service organization should try to increase its inventory turnover. Some operations using the latest technology have increased the turnover from two to eight times a month.

A factor that can negatively affect inventory turnover is having items that have been in storage for a long time, such as items used for discontinued menu items, and may never be used. Managers hate to write these off since that would increase food cost for the period and reflect badly on them, or they may not even know those items are still around.

There are situations where high inventory turnover is not always desirable. For example, an operation that has insufficient working capital and must operate hand to mouth probably pays more for buying the smallest amounts and may pay for poor credit.

PERPETUAL INVENTORY

A perpetual inventory keeps purchases and issues constantly recorded for each item in storage so that the balance on hand is always available. Perpetual inventories require considerable labor to maintain and typically were used only by very large operations that make purchases for several months' consumption. With the use of computers increasing, perpetual inventories for purchase determinations and cost analysis are more routine. In a noncomputerized operation, advantages that may accrue from the use of a perpetual inventory include the following:

1. It guides buying. The perpetual inventory indicates when it is necessary to reorder.

2. It controls overbuying and underbuying. It is easier to see how much food has been used and how much will be needed.

3. It provides a constant inventory figure. Although the perpetual inventory should be checked periodically against a physical inventory, it is possible to take a quick inventory from the cards or printouts at any time.

RECEIVED						ISSUED						BALANCE	
DATE	RECEIVED FROM	QTY.	UNIT	PRICE	AMOUNT	DATE	ISSUED TO	REQ NO.	QTY.	AMOUNT		QTY.	AMOUNT

WHITNEY DUPLICATING CHECK CO., NEW YORK, N. Y. FORM 760

Figure 16.4
Perpetual Inventory Card

Table 16.4

Example of an Inventory Usage Report Detail from a Foodservice Management Application

Inventory Usage Report—Detail

Joe's Diner

By Inventory Department/By Unit/For Inventory Group Mandatory Products
Costing Method: Default
4/23/1998 End of Period Inventory thru 4/30/1998 End of Week Inventory

Inventory Item	Reported in Unit	Ending Cost	Begin Count	+ Received Count	+ Transfer Count	+ Production Count	− End Count	Usage Count	= Usage Value
Beverage—Beverages—Bottled & Canned Beverages									
Bev Arizona 16oz	case	$14.500	13.00	0.00	0.00	0.00	10.60	2.40	$ 43.50
Bev crystal ice	case	14.500	2.90	0.00	0.00	0.00	2.00	0.90	0.00
Bev Perrier 6.5oz	1/24 ct	12.850	4.00	0.00	0.00	0.00	4.00	0.00	0.00
Bev San Pellegrino Spark 8.5oz	case	13.050	2.00	0.00	0.00	0.00	2.00	0.00	0.00
Bev soda bottle Coke 7oz	case	9.400	7.00	0.00	0.00	0.00	5.00	2.00	18.80
						Bottled & Canned Beverages Total			$ 62.30
Beverages—Beverages—Juices									
Bev juice orange 10oz	case	$13.200	7.30	6.00	0.00	0.00	10.30	3.00	$ 39.60
						Beverages Total			$101.90
Beverage—Liquor—Wine									
Wine burgundy cooking	1 gallon	$ 5.250	3.50	0.00	0.00	0.00	3.50	0.00	$ 0.00
Wine sherry	1 gallon	3.338	2.00	0.00	0.00	0.00	1.50	0.50	3.34
						Wine Total			$ 3.34
Beverage—Dairy—Cheese									
Cheese american 120 sliced	lb	$ 1.820	5.00	15.00	0.00	0.00	20.00	0.00	$ 0.00
Cheese blu crumble	lb	2.740	1.00	5.00	0.00	0.00	5.00	1.00	2.54
Cheese cream cheese bulk 3lb	1 lb	1.360	8.00	0.00	0.00	0.00	12.00	−4.00	−5.44
Cheese feta	1 lb	1.690	5.00	0.00	0.00	0.00	2.00	3.00	5.07
Cheese mont jack	lb	1.990	12.00	0.00	0.00	0.00	10.50	1.50	2.98
Cheese swiss alpine lace	lb	3.500	1.00	0.00	0.00	0.00	1.00	0.00	0.00
						Cheese Total			$ 5.15
Beverage—Dairy—Eggs, Butter, Yogurt, etc.									
Dairy margarine solid	lb	$ 0.420	27.00	0.00	0.00	0.00	26.00	1.00	$ 0.42
Dairy sour cream tub	tub	0.740	0.80	0.00	0.00	0.00	8.00	−7.20	−5.92
						Eggs, Butter, Yogurt, etc. Total			$ −5.50
						Dairy Total			$ −0.35
Beverage—Meat/Poultry—Beef									
Beef corned brskt raw	lb	$ 1.590	20.00	0.00	0.00	0.00	20.00	0.00	$ 0.00
Beef eye round	lb	2.190	6.00	0.00	0.00	0.00	6.00	0.00	0.00
Beef frank footlong	lb	2.620	10.00	0.00	0.00	0.00	10.00	0.00	0.00
Beef grnd bulk 80/20	lb	1.130	10.00	80.00	0.00	0.00	80.00	10.00	24.80
						Beef Total			$ 24.80
Beverage—Produce—Fresh Fruit									
Fru banana	lb	$−0.500	5.00	30.00	0.00	0.00	2.00	33.00	$ 16.50
Fru grapes green seedless	case	16.890	0.50	0.00	0.00	0.00	0.10	0.40	0.00
Fru grages red seedless	case	19.290	0.50	0.00	0.00	0.00	0.10	0.40	0.00
Fru kiwi	case	9.900	0.50	1.00	0.00	0.00	1.00	0.50	0.00

Courtesy of Radiant Corporation

4. It shows item variations. The perpetual inventory indicates how much of each item should be on the shelves, and it helps to pinpoint items that show unusual variances.

5. It helps move old items. By glancing at the cards, one can see which items are not being used so that they can be incorporated into menus.

To be effective, a perpetual inventory must be constantly kept up to date. Some operations keep a perpetual inventory on fast-moving items like butter or coffee. Such ratios as pounds used per $100 of sales, or pounds used per 100 customers, will indicate whether food usage is within bounds.

The perpetual inventory can be kept on cards (Figure 16.4), or it can be easily computerized (Table 16.4).

UNIFORM PRODUCT CODE (UPC)

A procedure that has been adopted by some larger foodservice operations is the **universal product code (UPC)** or bar codes, which have been used in supermarkets for some time. UPCs are expected to become increasingly common in foodservice operations. These codes can be scanned by a hand scanner that counts the items and with data stored in a computer quickly determines the value of the goods. This eliminates the need for labor intensive and slow visual counting inventory sheets, human mistakes, and laborious calculations to determine the value of the item. If exact quantities are desired, the scanner and a programmable scale can provide exact amounts.

The bar codes provide information about the various items, such as size, packaging, producer, and date of production. This can be tied into cost information to give inventory valuations. Some operations have developed their own bar codes and different organizations are trying to develop codes for the industry that could greatly simplify purchasing, ordering, storing, and payment. Using bar codes, scanning, and computers that provide printouts is much easier than actual counting and manual cost calculations.

SUMMARY

This chapter addressed food storage, issuing, and inventory control, respectively, and it discussed the elements of each. Effective food storage requires adequate dry storage, refrigeration, and frozen food storage areas and facilities, all of which have definite requirements. Issuing, also called requisitioning, is the process used to supply food from storage (or, occasionally, receiving) to the preparation areas. Control here is essential because of the need for accurate records of food used and food available for use.

The chapter also included several procedures for ensuring this accuracy. It listed eight functions of inventory control, defined and discussed physical inventory and perpetual inventory, provided a formula for determining an operation's food cost, and discussed inventory turnover. Finally, the chapter discussed the specific advantages of both a perpetual inventory system and computerization in the inventory control process.

KEY TERMS

FIFO (first in, first out)
freezer burn
inventory turnover
perpetual inventory

physical inventory
shrinkage (inventory)
uniform product code (UPC)

REVIEW QUESTIONS

16–1 List six considerations for dry-food storage.
16–2 How much light (in watts) is suggested for every square foot of dry-storage area?
16–3 At what refrigerated temperature should meats, fruits and vegetables, dairy products, and general-purpose refrigerated areas be kept?
16–4 Provide a formula to determine the cost of food for a period.

16–5 Provide a formula to determine the amount an inventory is over or short.
16–6 How is inventory turnover calculated?
16–7 List five advantages of using a perpetual inventory.
16–8 How can bar coding help a foodservice organization?

PROBLEMS

16–1 Using the following figures, determine how much the food inventory was over or short for the month of March:

Physical inventory, March 1	$ 2,900
Physical inventory, March 31	$ 3,000
Food purchased for storeroom	$12,000
Food issues	$11,800
Direct purchases	$ 4,000

16–2 Using the figures in problem 16–1, determine the monthly food cost or cost of goods sold for March.
16–3 Using the previous figures, determine the inventory turnover for March.

Preparation and Portion Control

Preparation and kitchen control implies both the most efficient use and scheduling of personnel and equipment and the production of a predetermined amount of food ready at a designated time. Overproduction and waste should be kept to a minimum, and the food should be the highest quality suitable for the operation.

Control is a basic function of management, and kitchen control is most particularly a management and supervisory concern. For control to be effective, management must constantly inspect, check, instruct, and evaluate. No operation that "runs by itself" has effective control. Production is a major subsystem of the general operation system, and the production unit or kitchen should be considered as such. Food, equipment, labor, recipes, and other inputs should be considered with the desired outputs, the processes to obtain these outputs, and necessary feedbacks (see Chapter 4).

After completing this chapter, you should be able to:

1. Design a food production sheet.
2. Appreciate the importance of quality control.
3. Provide five advantages of standard recipes.
4. Know five areas to help control loss in meat cooking.
5. Compare a kitchen with a factory.
6. Provide six advantages to using an ingredient room.
7. Implement portion control.

FORECASTING

Estimating how much to produce is vital to kitchen control. In institutions with a definite patron census, these estimations are relatively easy to make; however, in operations that serve varying volumes of different items, it becomes a problem to forecast total sales volume and the volume of individual selections. As noted in Chapter 8, forecasting is usually

Table 17.1
Sales History Card

			Fried Chicken				
Date	Day	Price	Lunch (number sold)	Percent	Dinner (number sold)	Percent	Comments
6/1	Monday	$8.00			40	20	5 over
6/3	Wednesday	$8.00			40	18	Ham out 7:15
6/5	Friday	$7.50	25	12	15	5	Special for dinner—out 6:30
6/18	Thursday	$8.00			50	22	6 over
6/22	Monday	$8.00			45	20	15 over—heavy rain—150 entrees

of three types: (1) dollar-sales forecasts, (2) forecasts of number of patrons to be served, and (3) number of the various items to be served. In this chapter we are concerned with the number of various menu items to be prepared. Production estimates must be performed in advance so that scheduling of personnel and, possibly, equipment and purchasing can be more exact. Forecasting the number of each item that will be sold requires past performance records. Forecasting is tied in with labor scheduling, which is covered in Chapter 12.

A sales history card or record, such as that shown in Table 17.1, can be used to track past consumption or sales and any factors that might have influenced consumption or sales.

FOOD PRODUCTION SHEET

The food production sheet is prepared after quantities to be used are forecast. Table 17.2 illustrates one type of food production sheet, although there are many variations of this performance record. The food production sheet shows forecasted orders, the quantity actually prepared, the number of orders sold, the number of leftovers, the discrepancy (the difference between the number sold plus leftovers compared to the number prepared), and space for comments. The information may be used in future forecasts.

WORK ASSIGNMENT SHEET

After total food production is determined, station or individual work assignment sheets (Table 17.3) can be prepared for those individuals (or stations) in the kitchen who are responsible for advance food preparation. (If designed for a station, the work assignment sheet should indicate the personnel assigned to the station.) With a work assignment sheet, a supervisor does not need to instruct employees personally what to produce. Since

Table 17.2
Food Production Sheet

Date and Day: Monday, June 1
Weather: Fair
Total Meals Served: 200
Meal: Supper

Item	Forecasted	Prepared	Number sold	Percent	Leftover	Discrepancy	Comments
Fried Chicken	45	45	40	20	5		Employee meals
Filet of sole	30	25	22	11	3		
Baked ham	70	70	61	31	2	7	Poor portioning
Pot roast	80	75	67	33	8		
Lamb chop	5	10	10	5			Employee meals
	230	225	200	100	18	7	

Table 17.3
Work Assignment Sheet

Work Assignment Sheet

Station: _____
Employee(s): _____
_____
_____
_____

Date: _____

Item	Recipe No.	Quantity	Preparation Time	Needed	Comments

the orders are written, there is less chance of error and confusion regarding quantities. In making out a work assignment sheet, the supervisor must give thought to the equalization of workloads. In the example shown, there is a column for listing items that the individual or sections must prepare, the recipe number (if a numbering system is used), and the quantity desired. Listing the preparation time helps the supervisor determine workloads and also gives employees an indication of the time required to produce the item. The Needed column shows when the product should be ready. When small-batch cooking is desired, a time schedule is shown for the required amounts needed. The Comments column provides space for special instructions, other jobs to be performed, equipment to be used, or any additional information the supervisor might want to transmit.

QUALITY CONTROL

Not only is **quality control** difficult to achieve, it is also elusive to define. One definition is getting it right the first time, every time.

In some operations, there is a feeling that quality costs; in reality, what costs is a lack of quality, which may result in rejects or dissatisfied customers. One of the reasons for the success of the fast-food industry is the standard quality of goods and service that customers expect and generally receive.

A shortsighted concentration on the bottom line distracts attention from a company's long-term constancy of purpose and leads to neglect of the process of continued improvement, which results in lasting profitability. Quality is an investment. One may make more profit by cutting quality in the short run, but the operation also may not be in business for the long run. What counts is how customers, not producers, perceive quality. Producers may know that a quality product is produced, but if buyers do not perceive this, there is no recognition of quality.

Quality is achieved with cooperation between employees and management. Adversarial relationships affect general quality. Decisions should be made as low as possible in the organization. Define responsibility for quality inspection. Total quality management techniques as discussed in Chapter 3 are being adopted by the foodservice industry. At one time, quality control was informally thought to be descriptive of only highly skilled personnel using the finest ingredients to produce a consistently superior product. Now it is recognized that the ingredients do not have to be the finest available, but that they should be the best for the level of quality desired. Skilled help is not always readily available, so other ways must be found to substitute for the missing skills and artistry. Moreover, consistency has become as important as quality. Now quality control implies that every product measures up to a predetermined standard and sells at an appropriate price, rather than necessarily being outstanding. Quality control today is just as important for a hot dog stand as it is for a gourmet restaurant. At one time, the industry stressed periodic and final inspections to discover defects and maintain quality; today it recognizes that quality control comes, in large measure, with the proper planning of facilities and production processes, the motivation of employees, and the careful instruction of these employees who carry out these processes.

Quality control requires the proper equipment and its correct use. Some tools of quality control in foodservice include measuring scales, written specifications, standard recipes, accurate thermostats, and modern, light, cool, spacious working conditions.

In addition to planning and providing the physical equipment, it is the job of management to motivate employees to be conscious of product standards. Concern for and insistence upon quality is mandatory. With the relative abundance of good jobs in other industries and the low esteem in which many foodservice jobs are held, it is difficult to create in an employee a sense of pride in his or her work. Therefore, some operators try to motivate their employees by exposing them to other operations. They encourage cooks to visit, at company expense, other restaurants with their spouses to get ideas and to evaluate the quality of the competition. Hostesses and other key employees should also be sent to view competitive operations.

Quality control may be somewhat easier in the future, with the increase of mechanization and convenience foods. The more automatic the equipment, the easier it is to maintain quality. Convenience foods that are produced in large production runs in a central plant can develop a high level of quality control and product standardization.

INDUSTRY INSIGHTS   by John Farquharson

John Farquharson is the President of the Industry Council on Food Safety. He is Executive Emeritus of ARAMARK and past President of the National Restaurant Association.

FOOD SAFETY

The time in which we now live may well be the critical time we have experienced when it comes to the crucial issue of food safety. The manner in which we approached food safety in the past is just not good enough today.

My father ate soft boiled eggs every morning for breakfast and to my knowledge *never* had a problem with the food-borne illness salmonella enteritidis. Today, he well might.

As a family, we ate very rare hamburgers at picnics and cookouts and never had a problem with the food-borne illness *E. coli*. Today, we might. Why might we have a problem with food-borne illness today involving these aforementioned pathogens but not in the past?

Because they're new!

These pathogens are mutations of ones that were apparently controlled in the past by nature, sanitary practices, or antibiotics given to the source at feeding time. But, these practices don't seem to work anymore.

Faced with these new threats, it becomes vitally important that the people preparing food in kitchens are properly educated in the area of food safety.

We must know how and why to wash our hands properly with an antibacterial soap to prevent cross-contamination. We must be educated to know what cross-contamination is and how to prevent it. We must be educated to know what temperature to cook foods to, for how long a period of time, and why.

Education and training are the only answer to the issue of food safety today. The way it was done in the past is just not good enough today. We all must be made aware how critical proper food safety practices are.

We need to know where education and training are available and be motivated to become educated. We must be motivated and disciplined to practice these learned standards.

Remember: just one incident of food-borne illness can be the most devastating thing that can happen in a foodservice operation. It can put you out of business.

STANDARD RECIPES

At one time, standardized recipes were the anathema of chefs and fine cooks. Their reputation, after all, rested on their ability to prepare a wide variety of food products relying solely on their own ability and experience. Because they were proud of their training, it would have been an insult to place a recipe in front of them. At one time, cooks had to be able to make allowances for variations in raw food quality, and these allowances could not be incorporated into a recipe. However, the quality of today's processed raw food products is very uniform and rarely presents problems in recipes. The master cooks who could work strictly from their own knowledge are vanishing; where they remain, they must often admit that they can produce even better dishes with the help of standard recipes.

Standard recipes are useful to a foodservice operation for these reasons:

1. They facilitate uniform quality and taste. Patrons who order a product and smack their lips in fond remembrance of past enjoyment will again enjoy the same taste, not another cook's different interpretation. Your patrons have a right to expect the same item each time they order it.

2. They give predictable yields. The recipe specifies how much it will produce. That information affects portion control, since the number of servings from a particular recipe can be determined in advance. Portion control, in turn, is necessary for accurate costing.

3. They require less supervision. The standard recipe gives instructions that supervisors might otherwise have to give orally and oversee in person.

4. They require less trained help. Not only do standard recipes substitute, in part, for the lack of staff expertise, but they also serve as a medium of staff instruction. Employees can learn from clear-cut instructions as they do the work.

5. They establish food-cost control. With standard recipes it is possible to secure accurate food costs, since qualities and kinds of ingredients are established in advance. Standard recipes make possible the calculation of labor and time costs when they specify the preparation procedure.

6. They create independence. With standard recipes, other people can produce items that may be the speciality of one employee, and the operation is not dependent solely on that one employee. To be candid, though, one must admit that even with standard recipes, some employees do a better job than others on particular items.

At one time standardized recipes were on cards. Now they can be listed in a computer as part of the management information system. As such, purchasers have ready access to recipes, and managers can adjust them automatically for varying production amounts. With a printer, a copy can be produced to give to the individual producing it. Some operations have provisions for displaying the copies in work areas.

There are many sources of standard recipes, most of which are very good, but each recipe should be tested and then adapted to your particular operation. In testing, it is necessary to judge the quality of the product according to the standards of your operation. Decide on seasoning or flavoring changes that would make it more appealing to your patrons. Convert the amount of ingredients used to produce your desired yields (the conversion process may also cause some changes in the ingredient proportions). Cost out the recipe, and determine the necessary selling price appropriate for you.

Figure 17.1 illustrates a standard recipe taken from a computerized food management system. Quantities of ingredients are given. Columns are provided for ounces or other measurements. The preparation procedure is listed in sequence with appropriate temperatures and times included. The total yield in weight or portions, the yield per pan, the type of pan, and the size of the portions should be included. Cooking temperatures and times should be specified, and so should special equipment, such as a particular kind of oven, that might be required. Preparation times are very helpful for planning workloads. It may be desirable to have a numbering system of recipes for easier reference, and many standard recipes include the ingredient and portion costs to facilitate pricing and cost control. Finally, it is important that the date of the last testing or revision be shown to indicate if the version is the most current.

```
REPORT#: 30    * * * CBORD FOODSERVICE MANAGEMENT SYSTEMS * * *        PAGE:   1
OPTION : 7.1.7.3.    MENU MANAGEMENT SYSTEM - 4.1.36                    FEB 01 9X
USER#  : 1                    HENDERSON HALL                           1223 HOURS
                         KITCHEN PRODUCTION RECIPE

Production Unit : 1  MAIN KITCHEN              Prod Date : THURSDAY  02/18/9X
Preparation Area:10  CENTRAL PRODUCTION        Cust Count:   410

==================================================================================
0012  LASAGNA SICILIAN                     Yield   :  16   2" FULL PANS
----------------------------------------------------------------------------------
Prepare Main Batch  1 TIME(S)          Cooking Time : 1 Hour
Ptn Desc :3"x4" CUT                    Cooking Temp   350F
Prep Time:1 Hour                       Cooking Equip: CONVECTION OVEN
Portions :384        10.00 OZ
----------------------------------------------------------------------------------
      Ingredient          |------ Main Batch -------||----- Partial Batch -----|
                                  Quantity                      Quantity
----------------------------------------------------------------------------------


_____  MEAT SAUCE  _____


<GROUND BEEF             28 LBS   13      OZS
 GROUND PORK SAUSAGE     12 LBS   13      OZS

    1. Cook meat in its own fat, stirring to break apart.  Drain off
       excess fat.

HOT WATER                 4 GAL

       Add hot water to cooked meat then bring to a boil.

 OLIVE OIL                          1 2/3 CUP
<CHOPPED ONIONS           9 LBS    10     OZS
<MINCED FRESH GARLIC                6 1/2 OZS
 TOMATO SAUCE                       6 1/2 #10 CANS
 GROUND OREGANO                     1 3/4 TSP
 WHOLE LEAF THYME                   1 3/4 TSP
 SWEET GROUND BASIL                 1 3/4 TSP
 COLD WATER               3 QT        3/4 CUP

    3. Mix the above ingredients into the meat mixture.  Cook over
       medium heat until the sauce comes to a boil, then remove from
       heat.  KEEP MIXTURE IN BAIN MARIE OR 170 DEGREE OVEN.

    _____  FILLING: REMOVE INGREDIENTS FROM COOLER JUST PRIOR TO MIXING ___

EGGS, SLIGHTLY BEATEN     9 DOZEN   8      COUNT
COTTAGE CHEESE           35 LBS     4      OZS
ITALIAN CHEESE GRATED     4 LBS
<CHOPPED PARSLEY                    1 2/3 CUP

    4. Combine eggs, cheeses, and parsley.  Mix well, then cover and
       return to the cooler.

LASAGNA NOODLES          19 LBS     4      OZS

    5. Cook noodles until al dente.  Drain and rinse in cold water.

<SLICED MOZZARELLA CHEESE 12 LBS

 ITALIAN CHEESE, GRATED   1 LBS     4      OZS
```

Figure 17.1
Standard Recipe

```
                    KITCHEN PRODUCTION RECIPE               PAGE:   2
                           CONTINUED
Production Unit : 1  MAIN KITCHEN           Prod Date : THURSDAY   02/18/9X
Preparation Area:10 CENTRAL KITCHEN        Cust Count:    410
```

```
================================================================================
0012  LASAGNA SICILIAN                   Yield    :    16.00 2" FULL PANS
--------------------------------------------------------------------------------
```

```
         6. LAYER:   1. 1/2 Qt meat sauce
                     2. Noodles, flat and in rows
                     3. 3 Cups filling (cheese/egg)
                     4. 6 Ozs mozzarella cheese
                     5. 1 Qt meat sauce
                     6. Noodles, flat and in rows
                     7. 3 Cups filling
                     8. 6 Ozs mozzarella cheese
                     9. Noodles, flat and in rows
                    10. 1 1/2 Qt meat sauce
                    11. Sprinkle with parmesan cheese.
                    12. Cover and return to cooler or oven.

         7. Bake until internal temp of 150 degrees and top is bubbling,
            about one hour.
```

```
   -----------------------------------------------------------------------------
                          RECIPE DISTRIBUTION
   =============================================================================
          Unit            Date         Meal      Yield       Portions    Service Pan/Utensil/or Main Recipe
   -----------------------------------------------------------------------------
CAFETERIA CENTER        FRIDAY   02/19/9X  DINNER   15.83 2" F PAN  380  10  OZ   2" FULL PAN
                        Actual Distribution          <_____><_____>        6" TONGS
   -----------------------------------------------------------------------------
ROUNDING OVER-PRODUCTION THURSDAY 02/18/9X ALL MEALS  0.17 2" F PAN  4  10  OZ *
                        Actual Distribution          <_____><_____>
   -----------------------------------------------------------------------------
NOTES:  1.   '*' FOLLOWING PORTION INFORMATION INDICATES ROUNDED QUANTITY
   -----------------------------------------------------------------------------
```

Figure 17.1
Standard Recipe (Continued)
(Reprinted courtesy of The CBORD Group, Inc.© 1992.)

FACTORY PRODUCTION TECHNIQUES

A kitchen is a type of factory, but where the usual factory has long production runs of generally few items, a kitchen has short production runs of many items that may change with each meal. Also, some items must be individually prepared, making for craft rather than mass production.

Foodservice operators have tried a number of strategies to make their kitchen factories more like industrial factories. One approach is to limit the number of menu items. Another is not to change the items so frequently or not to change the items much throughout the day. Fast-food chains used these strategies in the beginning of the fast-food revolution.

Another is to make large quantities and then put them into inventory rather than primarily prepare them for immediate use. The inventory concept can be used by buying items from producers that can have long production runs or by making long production runs in the operation's own kitchen or commissary and then putting items into storage. Thus, one day all the beef stew needed for, say, three months can be prepared; the next day a different item would be prepared. Improved refrigeration or freezing equipment and better reconstitution equipment may be helpful, but some foodservice professionals believe the quality does not equal freshly prepared items.

In addition to evening out production through a day, the longer production runs usually have less waste. Leftovers are less of a problem, because it is easier to pull from inventory more exact consumption quantities. With the longer production runs, start-up and cleanup efforts must only be done for the run rather than each time the item is prepared.

Purchasing outside convenience foods can provide other advantages. Food items that a kitchen does not have the capacity to prepare may be purchased and served to customers. Kitchens can handle an increase in business that might otherwise tax their limits by using outside convenience foods.

Cook/Chill Systems

An application of factory production techniques is a **cook/chill system**. With this method, a food item is cooked to a just-done state, packaged in casing (often Cryovac) at or above pasteurization temperature, then chilled rapidly in 33° F ice water. Most food items can be stored from 21 to 42 days at 28° F to 32° F and can be reheated or rethermalized in the same package.

Two production techniques are used in cook/chill: tumble chill and blast chill.

Tumble Chill. Tumble chill systems have been designed to cook and store foods 30 to 45 days in advance of serving. Foods that are "pumpable" (e.g., chili, spaghetti sauces, and soups) can be prepared with the tumble chill food production system that utilizes larger steam kettles (Figure 17.2).

Another cooking component of this system is a cook tank, which is a large stainless steel tank designed to cook large quantities of roasts at low temperatures (200° F), usually overnight. Shrinkage is reduced by 50 percent, and the product is juicier and more tender due to the retention of natural juices.

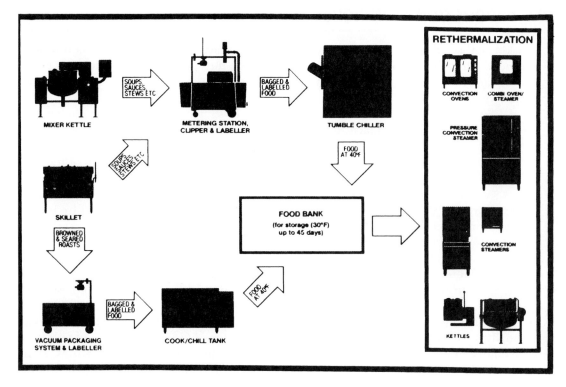

Figure 17.2
Tumble Chill Food Production System

Blast Chill.   A blast chill system is used for foods that are not pumpable (e.g., pork chops, Salisbury steak, and stuffed peppers). Food can be prepared conventionally, placed on individual trays or in bulk pans, and chilled to −10° F to −15° F in a blast chiller that quickly pulls the temperature of the food down within approximately 60 minutes. Food is then rolled directly into a walk-in cooler and stored for three to five days prior to serving (Figure 17.3).

Rethermalization can be accomplished in a convection oven, pressure convection steamer, combination oven/steamer, convection steamer, or kettle.

Some specialized equipment used are cook/chill mixed kettles, metering filling stations, tumbler chillers, cook/chill tanks, and ice builders. The Cleveland Cook/Chill System claims the following advantages:

- high quality
- production labor costs reduced up to 50 percent
- food costs reduced 8 to 15 percent
- eight-hour shifts, four or five days a week, rather than 12-hour shifts, seven days a week
- improved quality and consistency

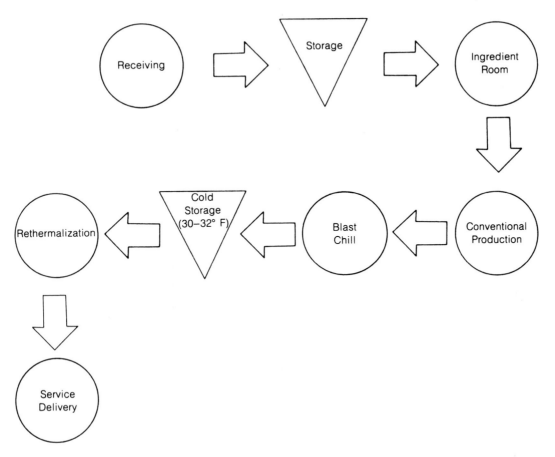

Figure 17.3
Food Production System: Cook-to-Inventory (Blast Chill)

- centralized production for satellite operations
- reduced kitchen space requirements
- excellent sanitation/food safety information

One study claims that a full-service dining room or cafeteria can reduce its back-of-the-house space by 50 percent, equipment cost by 75 percent, and kitchen staff by 50 percent by using meal components produced in central production facilities.

A variety of food operations can use cook/chill systems. Private-sector restaurants of all types are potential customers. Hotels with convention facilities can use the systems for banquets or other functions. Operations with wide swings of activity, such as country clubs, may find cook/chill systems helpful. Any mass-feeding institution, such as a school, university, prison, or hospital, would be an ideal user of such systems. Chains would find that the cook/chill systems provide consistency, and retail food chains could also use them.

High-volume production generates economies of scale, and it is suggested that production facilities produce upwards of 200,000 to 300,000 meal components per day. This could lead private-sector operators not only to produce for themselves but also to contract with other organizations to help use the large capacity. Cook/chill can also be used by facilities that do take-out business. The food items can be rethermalized before being sold or by the customer off the premises.

COMPUTERIZED APPLIANCE CONTROLS

In 1970 the first solid-state cooking computer was introduced to standardize and enhance the cooking of French fries and to improve product quality. Since then, controls have been developed for many other types of cooking and baking equipment.

Cost savings claimed for these devices include:

- *Food quality/waste reduction.* The key benefit of precise control of times and temperatures, aside from food safety, is enhancement of food quality and consistency. When food quality is sustained, waste is virtually eliminated through automation of recipe consistency.

- *Labor savings.* Touch-and-go operation offers simplified crew training and operations along with reduced need for manager oversight of cooking and other procedures.

- *Shortening/oil life extension.* When frying, precise temperature control greatly reduces overheating and overshoot to extend overall shortening life. There is a direct connection between shortening life and total exposure time to extremely high temperatures. This is a significant factor for quick-serve restaurants where shortening is a major food cost.

- *Appliance life extension.* Precise temperature control enhances appliance performance and extends its useful life.

- *Energy savings.* In appliances which idle at a set temperature (fryers, holding cabinets, etc.), maintaining a precise idle temperature and, more importantly, reducing overheating lowers the ambient temperature of the kitchen and reduces HVAC consumption. In ovens, controllers eliminate the need to constantly open the door to check product status or remove product in various stages. The controller prompts the operature precisely when the product is done. Therefore, less heat is released into the kitchen.

KITCHENLESS KITCHENS

In 1991, Cedars-Sinai Medical Center in Los Angeles closed its very efficient central production kitchen and switched to a novel **kitchenless** approach. Reasons for closing the facility included difficulty in finding skilled staff, difficulties in finding suppliers who would adhere to their stock specifications, cost of replacing some equipment, and the nearly 5,700 square feet of space used by the production facility that could be converted to revenue-producing space by the hospital.

The switchover plan involved closing the central production facility. Instead of cooking and freezing their own entrées as previously, the hospital foodservice operation now orders appropriate frozen retail products on a just-in-time basis to match orders placed the previous day by patient units or galleys. The frozen retail items are stored in the walk-in cold storage units adjacent to the former production area; each evening, the galleys are restocked with food necessary for patient trays and nourishments.

During the switchover, the hospital discovered that manufacturers of food products prefer to sell a limited number of items suitable for bulk plan service. However, suitable non-bulk items were available in supermarkets. After some persuasion, a local distributor agreed to sell the hospital the large amounts of these products that are needed. Some single-stage (heat-and-serve) items are prepared in the cafeteria and coffee shop during down times. These are preconditioned through searing, packaged frozen, and distributed with the commercially prepared items to the patient floors.

As a result of the switchover,

- 15 FTEs were cut,
- nonwage expenses were cut 5 percent (probably in part because of less waste and spoilage),
- about $1.5 million worth of real estate space was released for revenue-producing activities, and
- high foodservice standards were maintained.

MCDONALD'S

After suffering from lackluster sales and plunging stock prices, McDonald's in 1998 introduced a new production system called "Made for You." Previously an order would have to be rung up, a receipt produced, and then someone would have to get the food.

Now, the customer's order is sent electronically from the cash register to a monitor near the sandwich maker, telling him or her what item to begin assembling. New buns that can tolerate more BTUs of heat and a new high tech, three second toaster start the process. A special order, such as a Big Mac without pickles, gets its own slip of paper from the computer. The slip rides along as the sandwich goes from one work station to another. After the bun is toasted, the condiments are ordered. The meat, the only element stored in a heated holding cabinet, goes on the sandwich last, just before it is wrapped and served.

Between orders, workers replenish supplies of buns, meat patties, sliced tomatoes, etc.

Only a small percentage of the company's 12,400 U.S. stores are currently using the system. McDonalds believes its new system generates a hotter, fresher product delivered "just in time" for the customer.

INGREDIENT ROOMS

Some operations, especially large hospitals, have found that ingredient rooms, or food production control centers, as they are sometimes called, increase efficiency and effectively implement a food delivery system. The **ingredient room** is an area where pre-preparation is performed on food items before they are issued to cooking personnel. Pre-preparation can include weighing, measuring, cleaning, chopping, slicing, and peeling. After pre-preparation, the items are delivered in the quantities needed for the recipes at the time preparation begins.

Conventional handling of materials differs from an ingredient room. Under the former, food is requisitioned according to the various recipes. The food is then issued in standard amounts, rather than the exact amounts listed in the recipes. After issuance, food must be stored in the preparation unit until it is needed. Exact weighing to conform to recipes must be done in the kitchen. Excess amounts from issues must be returned or be kept in the kitchen until they are used in other items. This complicates requisitioning for new items because consideration must be given to the goods already in the kitchen. Because pre-preparation and preparation are mixed, cooks must often perform the work that less skilled workers could perform. With conventional materials handling, there is also considerably more handling and moving of items, which can result in higher costs and a need for more labor.

The first step in the operation of the ingredient room involves food quantity planning. The operator determines the production quantities from patron forecasts. Then, determining the quantities of specific items needed from the standard recipes for the various menu entries, the operator requisitions the ingredients from the storeroom, making sure to consolidate the ingredients that are duplicated in different recipes on one requisition.

In the ingredient room, the amounts of the various ingredients for each recipe are exactly weighed or measured, and pre-preparation such as cleaning or trimming is performed. Both the ingredients and a copy of the recipe are then delivered to the proper work center or area in the kitchen at the time preparation is scheduled to begin. All pre-preparation has been finished, and final preparation can start immediately.

A daily production schedule is prepared that conforms to both the ingredient room and kitchen operations. Consideration is given in the production schedule to meal times, personnel use and availability, equipment use and availability, and advance preparation necessary.

The advantages in using an ingredient room are:

1. *Better use of personnel.* In many operations, skilled cooks spend less than half their time actually cooking. They often spend valuable hours weighing, cleaning, trimming, and performing other pre-preparation work. With an ingredient room, unskilled personnel do more of the less skilled work, so fewer skilled personnel may be required.

2. *Less handling of materials.* Exact quantities are sent from the ingredient room to the proper kitchen area. Differences between recipe amounts and issue quantities do not often occur; therefore, the need for storage space in the preparation unit is also reduced.

3. *Better quality.* With more exact weighing and ingredients control, the quality of the meal can be enhanced. Cooks are no longer liable to misjudge amounts, and they becomes less liable to proceed carelessly. Because the cooks primarily are cooking and do not have to bother with pre-preparation duties, they can concentrate on the preparation. Food items are delivered only when preparation is to start, and cooks cannot prepare the food ahead of time, which might cause deterioration in quality while waiting to be used.

4. *Lower food costs.* Food issues in excess of the required quantity are eliminated. Sending exact amounts to the kitchen reduces opportunities for pilferage. The ingredient room often can be located closer to storage areas than the kitchen, which can significantly reduce transporting distances.

5. *Better control.* By separating weighing, counting, and other pre-preparation steps from final preparation, an operator can achieve better control in both phases and can give more attention to the weighing of ingredients.

6. *Easier costing.* With exact amounts rather than approximate requisitions determined in the ingredient room, it is much easier to cost production. Instead of many requisitions (and trips) between the kitchen and the storeroom, relatively few consolidated requisitions from the ingredient room are necessary.

An ingredient room may require extra clerical help to combine quantities needed for the same items used in different recipes. However, this requirement is more than offset by the handling and processing of fewer requisitions. Moreover, an ingredient room lends itself to automatic data processing. Computers may be efficiently used to determine item and total food costs, provide nutritional analyses, keep inventory counts, and determine purchasing needs when the operation uses exact quantities of ingredients. Finally, since the delivery time from the ingredient room to the kitchen must be specified, supervisors can give more thought to the most efficient scheduling of personnel and tasks both in the ingredient room and in the kitchen.

PORTION CONTROL

Portion control is vital in the operation of a foodservice facility. It requires two definite steps: determining a specific size to be served and making certain that this designated portion is always served.

A facility may have excellent control in all other phases of its operation, but if it serves a 5-ounce portion of an entrée instead of the planned 4 ounces, its profit has been considerably reduced. Serving meager portions or uneven portions will cause customer resentment and dissatisfaction. The serving personnel in cafeterias may occasionally show partiality for favorite patrons to the dismay of others. Unfortunately, portion sizes are too often left to the discretion of the serving or preparing personnel, with little thought given to what might be the ideal portion size.

Determining the Proper Portion Size

The proper portion is one that has been determined by a consideration of the type of operation, customer satisfaction, cost of food and service, and merchandising issues. Published standard-portion charts can be used as a guide, but specific standard-portion charts should be developed for the individual operation.

The cost approach involves determining what your clientele will pay for an item and determining how much of the item you can provide for that price. If roast beef will sell for $12.00 á la carte and a 40 percent food cost is your goal, the portion of roast beef should cost around $4.80.

The quantity approach requires a determination of the amount of food your average patron prefers to consume. Unfortunately, average portions may be too much for some and not enough for others. Cost, quantity, quality, and sales prices all affect the determination of portion sizes. Unusually large portions, such as a 9-inch-high piece of cake, may be served for merchandising purposes—that is, to attract attention. Some operators serve large portions to secure more sales, which they hope will compensate for their higher costs. With rising costs, some operators cut their portions until they encounter visible or audible customer resentment. This is a dangerous practice as one can never tell how much resentment and lost patronage have occurred before they become evident.

One of the least effective ways to set portion size is to blindly copy those of the competition. Your competitors may be in error, and there is no reason for you to suffer for their mistakes. In any case, portion sizes must satisfy customers. Since sales volume will signal this approval, it is important to analyze the sales and the cost of the best-sellers. If the profit is acceptable and if the item is selling briskly, portion sizes are probably correct. Also, it is good to observe the food that is returned to the dishwashers. Such informal observations sometimes give clues as to whether or not the quality of the food is acceptable and the portion sizes are too small or not enough for typical customers, too large or more than typical customers desire, or just right for most customers.

Some foodservice operators use techniques to make portion sizes look larger. Slicing a 4 oz. portion of meat into two slices spread side by side may appear to offer more meat. Using a smaller plate may make the contents appear larger. Fast-food operators put French fries into small packages that appear overflowing.

Serving the Proper Portion Size

After the proper portion size is determined, it must be served as specified. Personnel must be made aware of this proper size, and written instructions containing the information should be readily available to all personnel who portion food. Large institutional operations serving a single menu may ask a supervisor to demonstrate the proper portions before the serving period and to make up sample platters for the benefit of serving personnel.

Portion control scales are invaluable. They can be used to measure portions of such meat items as steaks, chops, and patties when they are cut or formed and before they are cooked. Often, preparation personnel feel that they can judge sizes and weights without the aid of a scale, but even the most experienced cook will do a better job if what is being cut or formed is weighed. It may not be necessary to weigh every steak or patty, but it would be wise to weigh every third or fourth. Scales can also be used to weigh prepared entrées. Some scales on the market can be adjusted to account for the weight of the platter, thus showing the weight of the portion directly on the dial.

The dish or glass size often controls portions. A 4-ounce glass will serve about $3\frac{1}{2}$ ounces of liquid. Vegetable dishes can determine the amount of vegetables served. Desserts may be controlled by the size of their containers. The serving plate is most important. A smaller serving plate should be used for small portions that would look incongruous on a large plate.

Paper service is popular for portion control. Paper souffle cups are very handy for side garnishes such as applesauce and mint jelly. Paper creamers and condiment and jelly containers are also useful in controlling portions, figuring costs, and reducing labor. Not only do they help determine portion size, but they also prevent garnishes from mixing into the other foods.

Specific-sized ladles, scoops, or serving spoons can standardize the portion. For instance, a No. 8 scoop will serve a half-cup, or 4 ounces. (Scoop size is determined by the number of scoops per quart.)

Cooking utensils can be used in portion control. An 8-inch pie tin yields six slices. Uniform sizes can be obtained by using a marker or scoring the pie tin. If a standard recipe is used for hard puddings, gelatin, or sheet cakes, a marked pan can delineate standard quantities and sizes. Portion sizes are often determined by cut lines along each side of the pan. Casserole dishes automatically control portion sizes.

Portion control is closely tied to purchase specifications. A half-crate of fresh grapefruit weighing 36 pounds can contain from 18 to 48 grapefruits, depending upon their size. Therefore, it is necessary to determine what size of grapefruit is desired and to specify this size in purchasing. A half grapefruit from the 48 count is far smaller than one from the 18 count, and, presumably, it would command a lower menu price. Frankfurters and bacon strips come in various sizes, so the number per pound should be specified. Baked potatoes and many other vegetables depend on precise specifications for portion control.

Effective portion control requires five steps:

1. determining the desired size per portion
2. making sure these portion sizes are known and used by all personnel
3. requiring the use of specifications in all purchases for properly sized food items
4. providing the means for measuring portions
5. checking and constantly rechecking to see that your personnel are serving the specified portions, which can be the hardest part of the whole process

SUMMARY

A foodservice operation must have control over the preparation and portioning process. Included in production control can be production sheets, standard recipes, proper meat cookery, and an ingredient room. More efficiency in production is gained by using factory production techniques such as cook/chill or even kitchenless operations. Portion control is a five-step process that involves determining the proper size of a portion, ensuring that portion sizes are known to personnel, using specifications in food purchasing, providing a means for measuring portions, and checking to see that personnel are serving proper portions.

KEY TERMS

blast chill system
cook/chill system
ingredient room
kitchenless kitchens

quality control
standard recipe
tumble chill system

REVIEW QUESTIONS

17–1 What are advantages in using a work assignment sheet?
17–2 List tools that can help in quality control.
17–3 Briefly explain four reasons to use standard recipes.

17–4 What information should a standard recipe contain?
17–5 Describe the ingredient room concept.
17–6 List advantages of using an ingredient room.
17–7 List five devices that can help in portion control.

17–8   List the steps in portion control.
17–9   What is a cook/chill system?
17–10 Explain the difference between a blast chill and a tumble chill system.

17–11 Why would a large hospital consider using a kitchenless kitchen approach in its dietary department?

PROBLEM

17–1 Using a multiunit foodservice operation (perhaps a college foodservice), devise a plan that would centralize production. Recommend procedures to be used, such as cook/chill, and facilities that could be eliminated. Explain the advantages and disadvantages of such a system to the operation, and discuss whether the plan would be feasible.

Beverage Control

In many foodservice operations, sale of alcoholic beverages can represent a significant portion of sales and can be more profitable than food sales since the costs of beverages as a percentage of sales is usually much lower than the food-cost percentage and requires proportionately less labor and equipment. However, the sale of alcoholic beverages also requires cost-control procedures to ensure their full contribution to the bottom line. In theory, beverage control is easier than food-cost control. Production is to order—eliminating waste. Liquor does not spoil. One person usually does all production at one time, not a battery of cooks perhaps with production in different areas. Once received, the liquor is usually only in the storeroom and then at the bar.

Beverage control does present some special problems. The beverages are valuable and desirable, leading to theft temptations. One individual may take the order, prepare it, serve it, and receive payment with no control from division of duties. The same beverage may have different sales values in different drinks or at different times of service, such as happy hours and regular bar service. Because of the value of the beverage, consistent over- or underpouring can amount to sizable differences of money.

After completing this chapter, you should be able to:

1. Briefly describe at least five ways a beverage service operation might be defrauded.
2. Discuss nine general beverage control practices.
3. Discuss cash register control.
4. Discuss three differences between beverage purchasing and food purchasing.
5. Calculate beverage inventory turnover.
6. Name four considerations when selecting a liquor purveyor.
7. Briefly describe a sensible and practical beverage receiving procedure.
8. Describe a sensible and practical beverage storage procedure.

9. Explain the difference between a physical inventory and a perpetual inventory, and explain how to apply both in controlling beverages.

10. Briefly explain the importance of careful beverage pricing and how to incorporate service and ambience expenses in beverage pricing.

11. Explain five approaches to establishing a beverage cost-control system.

12. Describe four components in an integrated beverage control system.

13. Discuss dram shop liability.

DEFRAUDING AN OPERATION

There are many ways a bartender or serving person, perhaps in collusion, can defraud an operation. In fact, a bartender can, in a way, go into partnership with the operation, but with the operation paying all expenses. One defrauding approach can involve not ringing up sales and then pocketing the money. One can accomplish this in a number of ways and still maintain an appropriate bar cost (or percentage). Drinks may be underpoured and the difference used for drinks that go unrecorded. Someone may bring in his or her own bottle and not record sales for it. One can dilute liquor in opened bottles, permitting proper pouring amounts but not recording the excess sales.

Nonrecording of sales can also take place in various ways. The bartender may not ring up each order as prepared, but ring up several orders together, conveniently missing some. It is not unknown for a bartender to pocket guest checks (if they are not accounted for) and also pocket the money from them. Perhaps a bartender might reuse a check and collect payment more than once, but record payment only once. A hint of possible fraud is the surreptitious use of counting devices such as matches (watch for a bartender who constantly relights cigarettes), which allow one to keep track of manipulations. Tipsy patrons also make check manipulation or overcharging easier, or extra, uncharged drinks may be served to knowing customers who reward the "service" with more generous tips.

A perhaps apocryphal story tells of the bar owner who, believing he was being defrauded, employed a specialized service to investigate. The service reported that all sales were being rung up on one of the two registers and there should be no loss of revenue. The confused owner replied that he knew of only one register in his bar!

A particularly dangerous situation can arise when servers "buy" the beverages from the bartender by paying for them when they are delivered at the bar and then use their own bank when they collect from the customer. There is no oversight of what they may try to collect from the customer. There are, in short, no perfect systems for preventing fraud, and determined personnel can always devise ways to counter the controls. But control can indeed greatly reduce and discourage fraud.

GENERAL BEVERAGE CONTROL PRACTICES

Regardless of an overall bar control system, some general practices are helpful in any system. They include the following measures.

Par Stock Control

Each bar has a certain **par stock**, or level of inventory, for each beverage item. Requisitions, which amount to the empty bottles returned, must be made to bring each item back to its par amount. The use of this par stock method has certain advantages. It makes possible a simple and accurate percentage system since there are no inventory fluctuations. The quantity at the bar remains constant, and since the purpose of the requisitions is to maintain par, the value of the requisitions equals the beverage cost for the period, which helps prevent an excessive amount being on hand.

Par stock can also help eliminate some physical inventory since the par that is maintained is the quantity that should be on hand. However, occasionally the specified par quantities should be checked with a physical inventory to discourage outright theft.

The par stock of each item on hand should be enough to handle normal sales. Managers sometimes use a figure of 1.5 times the quantity usually served. Excessive par amounts mean excess money tied up in inventory and a greater possibility of loss. Sometimes unusually heavy business will render the par for particular items inadequate, and special requisitions must be used. They should be added to the regular requisitions in calculating the amount of the par replenishment used.

All Bottles Identified

Every bottle sent from the storeroom to a bar should have some distinct identification for the operation, a stamp or seal that cannot be peeled off. This helps prevent someone from bringing his or her own bottles to the bar and making unrecorded sales while keeping a desirable cost percentage. An operation with different bars should have a different seal or stamp for each operation.

Return of Empty Bottles

To get a full bottle, a bartender should return an empty one (with the appropriate identification). This practice facilitates par stock inventory, makes it harder for someone to bring in his or her own bottle, and can help prevent someone from trying to defraud by constant underpouring. Care must be taken so that, in the disposal or breaking of bottles, none is allowed to get out, be refilled, and be used again. Occasionally printing the requisition number on the bottle can show up reused bottles since old requisition numbers should not be on bottles currently in use.

Use of Guest Checks

In some bar operations, guest checks may not be feasible. But guest checks add an element of control as opposed to just ringing up sales on the register with no "paper trail" to audit. If guest checks are not used, a tape receipt can be given to the customer.

Red-Lining Guest Checks

After the orders on a check are filled, the bartender can make a red mark on the check so that it cannot be presented again.

All Drinks Rung Up When Served

Busy bartenders who are pushed to get drinks out may claim it is better to get the drinks out and ring them up later. But this batch processing invites a bartender to conveniently forget some. Each order should be rung up when it is served.

Use of Code Numbers

It may be easier to refer to beverage items by code numbers rather than by name and size. One size bottle or one brand will have a different code number than a different size. The code number may be the storage or bin number of the beverage, and different numbers or symbols in the code can indicate the type of beverage, storage location, size, and brand.

Signed Requisitions

To replenish the bar stock, one should use a formal requisition (when returning the empty bottles) signed both by the person who requisitions the beverages and by the person who receives them. The person who fills the order may also sign. The requisition can be used for inventory purposes, to calculate beverage cost, and to assign responsibility.

Standard Drink Recipes

Standard drink recipes or formulas are even more important than they are in food-cost control. A variance of a quarter-ounce of liquor in a recipe can greatly affect its cost and its quality. Standard recipes also help one present uniform drinks and allow the employment of less experienced mixers. This is especially important if one experiences high personnel turnover or uses many part-timers. However, operations offering a wide and changing variety of drinks—or where one of the amusements is "stumping the bartender"—cannot standardize recipes for every possible drink.

Standard Glassware

Standard glassware includes the use of both standard measuring devices, such as shot glasses, and standard serving glassware. A drink that has normal strength (with mix) in a 6-ounce glass would taste weak with the same amount of alcohol in an 8-ounce glass. Management should specify shot sizes, drink recipes, and glassware sizes if special glasses are not used.

Cash Register Control

A cash register or POS register can be an essential part of beverage control and newer systems can provide a great number of control and analysis features. Although it can slow production, each sale should be run up individually and not batched. The cash drawer should be closed after each transaction to record that transaction and record when the drawer is opened. Bartenders should not be allowed to clear the register (money could be collected after clearing and not recorded). Some operations do not allow bartenders to take readings even at the end of the shift. Their cash return is compared to readings taken by management. Bartenders should have their own bank to make change, which can be issued at the beginning of the shift. If more than one bartender is using a register, try to have a separate cash drawer for each. All employees using a register should have a key to indicate the transactions they have recorded. If possible, all voids should be accomplished by management. If this is not feasible, have a record of voids or mistakes in ringing items up. Have a control over free drinks or drinks on the house.

Full Bottle Sales

Selling a full bottle of liquor can present problems since the sales price of the full bottle is usually less than the sales value of individual drinks from the same bottle. Also no bottle can be returned for replacement. An unscrupulous bartender trick is not to record individual sales that would come from a bottle but ring up a full bottle sale and pocket the difference. Sales of full bottles should be recorded separately, and they should not be included in the general liquor cost percentage.

BEVERAGE PURCHASING

In a number of ways, beverage purchasing (except for fine wines) is easier than food purchasing. There are no seasonal vagaries in prices and quality, and the merchandise arrives in sealed bottles, eliminating any concern about spoilage. Prices may be more uniform, and though deals may be negotiated in systems not controlled by states, they usually operate on a quantity or long-term basis rather than using daily competitive price comparisons.

A major aspect of beverage purchasing is the selection of **house** or **well brands**. Unless a customer specifies another brand, often called a **call brand**, these are the brands normally served. The selection of the house brand can involve factors such as cost and customer acceptance. Some operations serve high-quality house brands as a marketing tool; others prefer the lower selling prices and profit afforded by an inexpensive brand. Beers are sometimes classified as premium or regular.

The quantities to purchase is another purchasing decision. A good business practice is to have as small an amount as possible invested in inventory, but enough so as never to run out of an item. Many operations use a par system for their liquor storerooms, wine cellars, and/or bars. This makes purchasing easier since the quantity purchased is the amount required to bring inventory up to par. But quantity or case lot discounts may require a manager to purchase more than the par amounts.

One measure of purchasing efficiency can be inventory turnover. Normally, the faster the inventory turnover, the more efficient the operation.

$$\text{Inventory turnover} = \frac{\text{Cost of beverages used (beverage cost of sales)}}{\text{Average beverage inventory (\$)}}$$

The figure can vary tremendously among different operations. Sales of beer and a fine-wine inventory can affect the turnover. For example, an operation that has cash flow problems has to buy in lower quantities, missing opportunities for discounted prices and unable to afford to have all desired beverages on hand. Such an operation would have a high beverage inventory turnover, but for the wrong reasons.

Table 18.1 provides a format for par stock ordering out of the storeroom. The sheets may be printed with much of the information already included, such as the code number, item name, pack and size, and par. The items are listed on the sheet as they are stored in the storeroom. Once a week (or some other specific period) the amounts on hand are noted, and the difference from par becomes the normal order. As the items are ordered, the person in charge fills in the date, purveyor, quantity, and cost. A perpetual inventory can be used to determine the quantity on hand, and the entire procedure can of course be computerized.

Some operations like to use written purchase orders for their beverage purchasing. These purchase orders can be used to help control the receiving process. Other operations simply transmit orders to salespeople in person or by telephone.

Table 18.1
Beverage Purchase Sheet

Code Number	Item	Pack & Size	On Hand	Par	Needed	Date	Purveyor	Ordered Quantity	Cost

Date	_____
Received by	_____
Prices checked	_____
Entered	_____

Purveyor selection (where the law allows) can involve the lines of liquor carried, credit available, discounts available, quality of the delivery service, and the provision of dispensing equipment (such as beer taps and automatic pourers).

RECEIVING

The receiving function in beverage control is similar in many ways to food receiving, but it is even more important that the delivered beverages be secure. It would be bad enough to leave a case of lettuce in the receiving dock, but leaving a case of fine scotch would offer a substantially greater temptation. When received, the beverages should be counted and checked against the invoice. The invoice may be stamped to provide spaces to show who completed the various processing steps.

If one buys established brands, there should be no need to check quality or specifications. A receiver should examine cases for broken or missing bottles. (Some operations actually weigh incoming cases to spot this.) If purchase orders or purchase lists are used, incoming goods should be checked against them. Credit memorandums, if necessary, should be prepared at receiving and signed by the purveyor's delivery person.

Most purveyors deliver on a routine weekly basis, so there are usually fewer beverage deliveries than food, but there should be a receiving form indicating which and how much of the beverages were received. The receiving report is necessary to help determine what should be on hand, to help with bill paying, and to help guarantee that the goods were actually received. Many different beverage receiving report formats exist, ranging from

Table 18.2
Receiving Report

| | Purveyor and Invoice | | | | Unit | | Invoice | Checked | Breakdown | | | | |
Date	Number	Item	Size	Quantity	Cost	Extension	Total	by	Spirits	Wine	Beer	Mixes	Supplies

Period Ending _____

a simple list of invoices received and their amounts with the invoices stapled to it to sophisticated forms with an abundance of information. Table 18.2 shows the format for one form. The Period Ending can be a day, week, or month; the length of the period would depend on the frequency of deliveries. The Date column is used if the receiving period is more than just one day. The purveyor's name is listed with the number of the invoice. This information is helpful if more than one delivery comes in from a purveyor during the period.

The item, size, and quantity are indicated, with the unit cost for that size. The extension is the quantity multiplied by the unit cost. The invoice total is the total of all items on the invoice and what will normally be paid. The Checked By column is helpful if more than one person receives the beverages.

The Breakdown columns provide a handy way to separate beverage costs into spirits, wines, and beer. It may be desirable to compare the sales of these items to their costs. Mixes would include nonalcoholic beverages, and supplies include stirrers and napkins that are received but are not included in beverage costs. Fruits and garnishes may be separate or may be included under mixes.

If the operation picks up the beverages from the purveyor in its own vehicle, the goods are entered on the report when delivered at the operation.

BEVERAGE STORAGE

Security for the beverage storeroom or wine cellar is especially important for alcoholic beverages. The contents must be protected from theft and, in some cases, adverse temperatures. Security is maintained by limiting access to the liquor. Only those authorized to issue the liquor should be allowed in the storage area. Some operations use a Dutch door; the top opens to distribute liquor, but the bottom half remains closed to prevent the people who pick up the merchandise from coming farther into the storage area. Ideally there should be only one entrance, but in any case the entrance should be locked when the area is not manned. At least one operation uses a former bank vault door for this purpose. There are also devices that record the time when a door is opened, which may be helpful.

Each beverage should have its own space in the storeroom, and beverages should be stored with like beverages: bourbons with the bourbon, scotches with the scotch, gins with the gin, and so forth. Exceptions can be made for fast-moving items, which should be moved close to the serving door. Unless beverages are issued in case lots, they are usually stored uncased on storage shelves. The items are kept on bin shelves with a separate number for each item or bin.

An operation with a sizable wine inventory may have the problem of necessarily frequent visits to the wine cellar and perhaps frequent changes on its wine list. Temperature considerations are also associated with wine storage. Sparkling and white wines should be stored in cool areas. If no special areas are available, store these wines below red wines since the temperature may be lower close to the ground. For short periods, one may use chill facilities at 40° F for sparkling wines and other wines served chilled. Corked wines with an alcoholic content of less than 14 percent should be stored on their sides to keep the cork moist. Special racks may be used for this. Fine wines should be handled as little as possible before serving to keep the sediment settled. In suspension, sediment can affect the clarity of wine.

Beer kegs should be handled as little as possible and kept between 40° F and 50° F. Higher temperatures cause "wild" beer and lower temperatures reduce effervescence and cause flat beer. Beer stored in bottles should not be exposed to direct sunlight, which can cause the temperature in the bottle to rise and produce "skunky" beer.

INVENTORYING

As with food, there are two types of beverage inventories. One is the physical inventory, where an actual count is made; the other is a perpetual inventory, where a continuing count is maintained. It is easy to computerize a perpetual inventory, but periodically it is desirable to check it with a physical inventory. The inventory can be in terms of both dollar value and quantities on hand. The dollar value is necessary to determine the cost of goods sold, and the quantity inventory is helpful in ordering and replenishment.

If the perpetual inventory is not computerized, a perpetual inventory form can be kept in the cost controller's office. The form can be simple (Table 18.3) or more complete (Table 18.4).

Beverage purchase prices do not change as frequently as food prices, so requisition costing is not such a problem. An operation can use the last purchase cost price for requisition costing or may keep track of amounts purchased at different prices and use the actual cost.

The formula for beverage inventory reconciliation is

Opening inventory value	$ 3,000
+ Purchases	10,000
+ Returns from special functions	200
= Total	$13,200

Table 18.3
Simple Perpetual Inventory Form

Item _____	Size _____	Bin number _____
Min. _____	Max. _____	Order point _____

Suppliers _____		Telephone _____
_____		_____
_____		_____

Date	In	Out	Balance
6/1	12		12
6/2		2	10

Table 18.4
More Complete Perpetual Inventory Form

Date	In	Unit Cost	Extension	Out	Cost	Balance	Value
6/1	12	$8.00	$96	___		12	$96
6/2				2	$16	10	$80
6/3				2	$16	8	$64

− Requisitions sent to bars		9,500
− Kitchen requisitions		100
= Closing inventory value		$ 3,600
+/− Physical inventory value		3,100
= Difference		500

This formula can be broken down by spirits, wines, and beers to find their separate values, and it can also be applied to quantities of individual beverages:

Grand Dad (750 ml bottle)

Opening Inventory	18
+ Purchases	96
= Total	114
− Requisitions	80
= Calculated closing inventory	34
+/− Physical inventory	32
= Difference	2

Normally, two people should take a physical inventory, and one of them should not be regularly involved with the beverage storeroom. The inventory book or inventory sheets generally have items listed the same way they appear on the storage shelves. Beverages in the storeroom will usually be in filled bottles, with the exception of beverages that have been returned from function bars. There will, of course, be open bottles when the beverages at the bar are inventoried, and these open bottles can be measured in various ways. One way is to determine the fraction of the amount in the bottle—one-half or three-fourths, for example. Another way is to divide the bottle by tenths. Special rulers can be made for different type bottles, and by holding the ruler against the bottle, one can read off the quantity. Another practice is to count open bottles that are half filled or more as a full bottle and not count bottles less than half filled.

ISSUING

Unless the operation is very simple, beverages must be issued from the storeroom to the bar. This issuing usually involves a requisition. If one uses a par stock, the requisition will be the same as the empty bottles returned.

Following is a standard requisition form.

REQUISITION					
Bar _____			Date _____		
Item	*Brand*	*Quantity*	*Size*	*Cost*	*Extension*
Bourbon	J.W. Dant	4	750	8.40	32.60
Blend	Seagram 7	10	L	12.00	120.00
		48			502.00
Authorized _____		Filled _____		Received _____	

There may also be a column for the bin number, since it can be used instead of the item description. Some operations may not require three signatures. Separate or different requisitions can be used for spirits, wines, and beer so that the total cost of each of these categories can be ascertained.

PRICING

As with food, pricing alcoholic beverages presents some problems. If the price is too high, sales may be lost; if it is too low, potential profits are lost. Entertainment, decor, service, and competition are all involved in the pricing decision. In some bars, perception of value is all-important. In bars that stress snob appeal, overpricing may actually turn into a marketing tool.

Beverage pricing may be accomplished in many ways. Since the beverage ingredients are standard, community pricing or what the competition is doing can be important. If patrons think prices are too high, they can try to get the same drink elsewhere. Some operations try to sense what their patrons will pay and charge accordingly. Trial and error may be used. What is the effect on sales when prices are changed? Various beverage promotions such as happy hours, two-fors, or a free glass with an exotic drink may be used and affect pricing.

Whatever the method of determining prices, the operation should know its costs. It is easy to find the cost of the goods sold or cost of beverage and mix (if used), but this is only one of the costs. What is the cost of labor involved? How much should be appropriated to general overhead or marketing? Following are some other costs that may vary with different types of drinks or beverages sold. Management can calculate these costs as a percentage of the cost of the beverage and add it to the beverage cost or as a money amount. The goal is to have a clearer idea of the actual cost to the operation when setting a selling price. Some of the principles discussed in Chapter 9 on menu pricing can be helpful. Total sales consist of two factors, the item selling price and the quantity of each item sold. More than with food, beverage prices can affect consumption. Bar operators face the challenge of knowing when or if pricing will affect consumption of patrons who may go to the competition or switch to less profitable drinks.

Interest cost on inventory	1%	$0.02
Cost of space	5%	0.15
Cooling or ice	3%	0.06
Bartender cost	10%	0.20
Service labor cost	10%	0.20
Glassware	5%	0.10
Breakage	2%	0.04
	36%	$0.77

This is an illustration only; costs would vary with the type of operation and type of beverage. Interest costs for fast-moving beverages would be far less than for expensive wines kept in an extensive inventory.

One system of beverage pricing, called the bottom-up approach, considers profit as a type of cost, either as a percentage or dollar amount, and includes it in the beverage price. A top-down approach is to forecast sales and expenses and determine if the resulting profit is adequate. Some rules of thumb exist regarding wine pricing. One suggests that operators double the cost of cheaper wines and charge one and one-half times the cost of expensive wines. Other operators claim that the cost of serving all but special wines is about the same, and they add a flat amount to the purchase cost.

BEVERAGE COST-CONTROL SYSTEMS

Different approaches also exist to establish a beverage cost-control system, and one can find some overlapping among them. These approaches include:

- percentage systems
- inventory or quantity control
- standard cost systems
- standard sales
- integrated or automatic dispensing systems

More and more beverage control systems are yielding to computerization, often through a point-of-sale (POS) register or a backroom computer. However, even if much of the detail is computerized and the reports are printouts, it is helpful to know the concept being used.

Percentage System

The **percentage control system** is similar to the food-cost percentage system discussed in Chapter 21. The concept is that beverage cost should be a certain percentage of beverage sales:

$$\text{Beverage cost percentage} = \frac{\text{Beverage cost}}{\text{Beverage sales}}$$

A beverage-cost percentage differs from a food-cost percentage system in that bar requisitions rather than beverage purchases are used. (The purchases go to the beverage storeroom.) If a par stock control is used, the system can be accurate on a daily basis since there is no fluctuation of inventory with the par amounts maintained. Table 18.5 provides a format for a daily beverage-cost percentage.

An operation that has the capability and desire for more specific cost percentages can break its beverage costs and sales into type of beverage with a percentage for each—spirits, wines, and beers—or into types of one beverage and find the percentage for each brand, such as Ancient Age, Banker's Club, Beam's Choice, Bellows, and J. W. Dant (bourbons). As with a food-cost percentage, the beverage-cost percentage might better be used as a pricing device than as a control device. Factors affecting the percentage include bottle sales (which may be handled separately), price promotions, types of business, and ratio of mixed drinks to straight drinks or highballs.

Table 18.5
Daily Beverage-Cost Percentage

		Liquor Cost Month of June 1989					
		Sales ($)		Cost ($)		Bar Percentage	
Date	Day	Today	To-date	Today	To-date	Today	To-date
6/1	Mon.	1000	1000	250	250	25.0	25.0
6/2	Tues.	1200	2200	330	580	27.5	26.4

Inventory or Quantity Control

The **inventory control method** depends on bar checks, a register, or a system that can keep count of all the different drinks served. Knowing the amount of beverage in the drink recipe and the number of drinks served, one can easily determine the amount of beverage that should have been consumed. This figure can then be compared to the amount of replacement requisitions, and any differences can be noted. Normally, the requisitions will be more than the amount indicated by checks because of spillage, returned drinks, complimentary drinks, and so forth. A percentage may be included to cover these.

This concept originally was used only as a special control because of the detail involved, but POS registers and other electronic systems have greatly reduced much of the work, making the system more feasible. The system can be used for all beverages served, for only the fast-moving beverages, or for specific types of beverages. The following format illustrates its use for the house whiskey (Schenley Reserve).

Drink	Quantity	Number Sold	Total Ounces
Manhattan	2 oz	80	160
Old Fashioned	2 oz	40	80
Highball	1.5 oz	60	90
.	.	.	.
.	.	.	.
.	.	.	.
Total			618

Assume that the bar uses the 750 milliliter bottle, which contains 25.4 ounces. Checking inventories and requisitions (in bottles) for Schenley's Reserve, we find

Opening inventory	6.5
+ Requisitions	24.0
= Total	30.5
− Closing inventory	4.5
= Consumed	26.0
Ounces used	$(26 \times 25.4) = 660.4$
Ounces used per guest checks	618.0
Difference	42.4

In this situation we find a difference of 42.4 ounces out of 618 used, which is significant. Management would then be warned of a potential problem.

Standard Cost Systems

This approach determines what the cost of the beverages for the period should have been (the **standard cost**) and compares it with the cost of the beverages actually requisitioned or used. These amounts can also be shown as actual and standard cost percentages. To use a standard cost approach, one must calculate the cost for each drink.

Following is a format for calculating a standard cost system.

| Sales $1,000 | | Period Ending June 1 | | |
Drinks	Cost ($)	Selling Price ($)	Number Sold	Standard Cost ($)
Manhattan	0.40	1.50	60	24.00
Old Fashioned	0.50	2.00	20	10.00
Martini	0.35	1.50	30	10.50
.	.	.	.	.
.	.	.	.	.
.	.	.	.	.
Total				240.00

This table shows that for all the beverages, ingredient costs should be $240. If replacements or requisitions come to $250, the difference is $10. If sales are $1,000, the actual cost percentage is 25 and the standard cost percentage is 24. The closer the standard and actual percentages are to each other, the better.

Standard Sales

The **standard sales method** is used to calculate the potential sales values of the beverages used and then to compare these standard sales with actual sales. This can be accomplished by assigning a dollar sales value to each bottle, an easy process for operations that sell only one type of drink from that bottle. For example, if 1-ounce shots are served from a quart (32-ounce) bottle at a $1.00 (1 ounce) selling price, the sales value of the bottle would be $32.00, without consideration for spillage. Problems occur, however, when the bottle is used for different drinks, such as a highball or a cocktail, which can have different sales values per unit of the beverage. Also, differences in sales values occur when a complete bottle is sold or when an operation offers a special price promotion, such as a happy hour.

One way to handle this problem is to determine the number of drinks and sales revenue for a particular beverage during a test period. Knowing the amount of the beverage used in the various drinks, one can determine the amount in ounces of the beverage used (the sum of the number of each drink times the beverage content). Dividing this figure by the size of the bottle (in ounces) will provide the number of bottles required. Dividing the number of bottles into the revenue from that drink will provide a sales value per bottle.

Assume that during the test period 1,000 ounces of the house whiskey were sold. The whiskey came in 750 milliliter (25.4-ounce) bottles. It can be determined by dividing 25.4 ounces into 1,000 ounces that 39.4 bottles were used, with no consideration for spillage. This can be compared with requisitions during the period.

With consideration for spillage, assume we get 25 ounces from a bottle. Dividing this into the 1,000 ounces sold shows that 40 bottles were used. If sales involving the house whiskey were $2,400, the sales value per bottle would be $60.00. If one does these calculations over a test period, one can generally assume that the sales mix (the relationships of beverages sold) will remain about the same for all other periods. Calculations such as these once required a great deal of work, but POS registers and integrated or computerized systems can readily provide most of the data.

Another method of handling differences in varying sales value is the **differential method**. A standard sales value per ounce is determined, say $1.00. If, in a particular drink, the sales value is $1.50, a 50-cent positive differential is established. If the drink is sold for less than the standard sales value, a negative differential is calculated. Multiply the number of each drink that has a differential by the differential, then add or subtract this figure from the standard sales value, and you have a net sales value.

Following is a standard sales format.

Bar Requisition and Worksheet

Date _____

Bottle Code	Item	Bottle Size	Number Required	Unit Values Cost ($)	Unit Values Sales ($)	Extensions Cost ($)	Extensions Sales ($)
4-023	Canadian Club	750	3	9.00	36.00	27.00	108.00
	Total extended costs and sales value			$450.00	$1,800.00		
	+ Other requisitions			15.00	75.00		
	+ Bottle sales			18.00	68.00		
	= Total sales			$483.00	$1,943.00		

This format can include preprinted information on the commonly used items so that only the number required and the extensions must be filled in. This format results in a summary like that in Table 18.6.

Integrated Beverage Control Systems

An **integrated beverage control system** can combine an automatic dispensing system with a computer or POS register. Although these systems are relatively new, they already enjoy widespread popularity. Not long ago, operators wondered whether customers would accept drinks they could not see being mixed or would miss the bartender's showmanship. Bartenders, too, resisted the systems, perhaps from a natural fear of change or perhaps from a fear that more control would discourage finagling for personal gain.

Manufacturers of the system, meanwhile, claim the dispensers lower labor costs since a bartender can produce more drinks; reduce spillage, waste, and overpouring; and, since the dispensers use larger bottles, produce drinks of more uniform quality. There is indeed more control since everything poured through the system is recorded. Pricing errors are also eliminated for drinks that are handled through the system. Because so much is done automatically, the bartender does not have to be as skilled or as quick. In fact, the systems

Table 18.6
Summary of Actual and Standard Results

Date	Day	Beverage Cost Today	Beverage Cost To-date	Standard Sales Today	Standard Sales To-date	Percentage Cost Today	Percentage Cost To-date
6/1	Mon.	483	—	1943	—	24.8	—
6/2	Tues.	500	943	2000	3943	25.0	23.9

generally justify themselves financially in about 24 months. Many different integrated systems are available, but most have certain common components.

The Entry Unit.   The entry unit is where drink orders are entered into an electronic cash register, a POS register, a keyboard, or any other POS device. An entry unit can also include conventional controls such as cash drawers, operating keys, tender keys, and amount-of-sale displays. The unit can total bills, calculate taxes, and add tips. Some systems will not operate unless a guest check is registered.

The keys on its keyboard may be automatic drink keys for specific drinks such as a bourbon Manhattan. When its key is pressed, the following can happen:

- The drink and correct price are recorded.
- A journal record (audit tape) is printed for audit purposes.
- A guest check is printed.
- The liquor inventory is updated.
- A drink is dispensed in accordance with exact portions and recipes.
- The appropriate accounting information is accumulated.

If there is no automatic drink key, there may be preset price keys for hand-poured drinks. These, again, can automatically print the correct price and reduce inventory quantities. Some usual preset price keys designate standard liquor, premium liquor, special liquor, a standard cocktail, and a premium cocktail.

The Logic or Control Unit.   This unit contains the electronics to time and control the system. To produce information from the system, it must have tracking and reporting features to keep track of the data and to produce the desired information and reports. This unit can computerize many of the beverage controls already discussed in this chapter. Tracking and reporting, moreover, can be done through a POS register.

The Storage and Delivery Unit.   This unit stores the beverages and transmits them to the dispensing units. Storage is usually accomplished by placing the bottles in racks, often located a considerable distance from the dispensing unit. Larger bottles can be used, which may be cheaper and may reduce handling costs. Each liquor must have a separate line to the dispensing head.

Wines can be stored in multigallon containers, if necessary in a cooled location. Beverages are forced through the system under pressure supplied by compressed air, nitrogen, nitrous oxide, or carbon dioxide. Beer presents some special problems, and it usually requires a separate dispensing system.

The Dispensing Unit.   Another component of the system is the dispensing unit. Common dispensing units for integrated or automated systems include the bundled tower unit, which can cover 100 delivery lines and dispense simultaneously, and the hose and gun, which can deliver both the beverage and the mix. Hose and gun units may be used separately by serving personnel to add mixes.

The automated systems can save labor, reduce beverage costs, speed service, provide a drink of uniform quality and quantity, and allow one to employ less skilled personnel. The computer or POS register also provides considerable data on various drinks sold, total sales, sales by period, server productivity, reordering needs, and inventories. Different systems make different claims, such as:

- controlling up to 72 different brands
- dispensing 1,200 different drinks
- pouring all programmed cocktails
- pouring a drink in less than three seconds
- printing the guest and journal tape
- providing complete inventory control
- allowing substitution of brands in cocktails
- including modifier buttons for drinks (for example, a very dry martini)
- allowing price changes through the day
- providing interim and final totals ($X + Z$ reports)
- varying quantities from one drop to 64 ounces

DISPENSING DRINKS

A major area of beverage control is control over dispensing drinks, or getting the beverage from the bottle to the patron's glass. There are a number of ways to accomplish this. The old-fashioned way is simply to pour it from the bottle, perhaps getting more control by using jiggers or shot glasses, but bottle pourers are probably the most prevalent and popular form of dispensing alcohol in bars today. Bottle pourers, made of metal or plastic, fit in the neck of the bottle and have a stopper. Two types, regular pourers and speed pourers, can regulate the flow of liquid out of the bottle.

Measured pourers are a variation on the bottle pourer. They utilize a system of ball bearings inside the plastic housing of the pourer to shut off the flow of spirits after a certain amount has been poured. They are preset and are available in shot sizes from 5/8 ounce to 2 ounces. Some of the measured pourers, in addition to dispensing a measured shot, can count shots dispensed and may come with special attachment systems that cannot be removed by the bartender.

Optics are common in Europe and Great Britain. **Optics** are inverted bottle dispensers that release measured shots. The dispensers are preset and are sealed at the factory. Operators simply invert the spirits bottle into the device and dispense by pushing a glass up against the three-pronged release lever.

Electronic dispensers can be part of an integrated system. The liquor can be stored up to 500 feet away from the bar. Spirits are dispensed as measured shots from a gun. Some systems can be programmed to pour different-size shots at different times of the day, pour doubles, or even prevent anyone from pouring (after the last call, for example).

There is some debate over which pouring system to use. From a marketing standpoint, spirits companies and customers will tell you they would rather see spirits poured from a bottle. Bartenders like the showmanship of free pouring and believe they can make more tips. Electronic dispensing systems can cost a great deal of money, but they offer control features and can speed up production.

DRAM SHOP LIABILITY

A major cost and major problem for operations serving alcoholic beverages has been dram shop liability and the greatly increased liability insurance costs associated with it. **Dram shop liability** is the responsibility of an establishment that serves alcoholic beverages to patrons for damages caused by patrons after they leave the premises. The concept was started in New Jersey in 1979 but has spread rapidly. Under common law, the voluntary consumption of alcohol held only the consumer, not the seller, responsible for subsequent behavior. The concept is tied in with **joint and several liability** and the **deep-pockets theory**. In these, not only may the intoxicated person be sued but also the establishment that served the person; the establishment may have "deeper pockets" in the form of financial resources or insurance coverage. With both actual damages and punitive damages included, multimillion-dollar awards are not uncommon. Not surprisingly, liability insurance rates have soared, and in some cases the insurance has become difficult to obtain.

It behooves the bar operator to eliminate, as much as possible, the potential for claims. This includes training personnel to recognize signs of intoxication and cut off affected drinkers, monitor consumption, provide foods high in protein, serve nonalcoholic drinks, and arrange transportation for drivers who appear incapable of driving themselves. Various organizations have programs to train and educate bar personnel. The two most common infractions are serving underaged patrons and already-intoxicated patrons.

SUMMARY

Beverage control is a specialized, potentially profitable, and highly sensitive area of foodservice control. There are many ways to defraud a beverage service operation, but fortunately practices can be used to reduce or discourage this potential loss. Alcoholic beverages are expensive, highly desirable, and easily transportable; thus, liquor is a prime target for thieves. Special purchasing, receiving, storage, issuing, and inventory controls can protect the valuable liquor stock.

The various beverage accounting systems include percentage, quantity, standard-cost, and standard-sales approaches. Some of these systems overlap.

Beverage control may also utilize computerized and automatic dispensing systems. These systems may lower costs because they (1) reduce spillage and virtually eliminate overpouring, (2) can speed service, and (3) provide records of sales and amounts of beverages served. Dram shop liability and the associated increase in insurance costs have become a major problem for many operators.

KEY TERMS

call brand
deep-pockets theory
differential (beverage)
dram shop liability
house brand
integrated beverage control system
inventory control method (beverage)
joint and several liability

optics
par stock
percentage control system
red lining
standard cost method (beverage)
standard sales method (beverage)
well brand

REVIEW QUESTIONS

18–1 Explain four ways in which an operation serving alcoholic beverages can be defrauded.

18–2 Explain how a par stock control system works.

18–3 Why is beverage purchasing easier than food purchasing?

18–4 What is the formula for beverage inventory turnover?

18–5 Explain red lining guest checks.

18–6 Provide a formula for reconciling the quantity of one beverage item.

18–7 What is a rule of thumb for pricing a better wine?

18–8 Provide the format for a percentage beverage control system.

18–9 Explain how a beverage inventory or quantity control method works.

18–10 Explain how a standard-cost method works in beverage control.

18–11 Explain how a standard-sales method works in beverage control.

18–12 Explain the components of an integrated beverage control system.

18–13 Why would a bar want to install an integrated beverage control system?

18–14 Explain dram shop liability.

PROBLEMS

18–1 The following data is given:

Beginning beverage inventory	$1,000
Beverage sales	$8,000
Ending beverage inventory	$ 900
Cost of goods sold	25% of sales

a. Calculate the beverage purchases.
b. Calculate the beverage inventory turnover.

18–2 A sales analysis of your beverage operation shows the following:

Liquor	Drink	Number sold	Portion size (oz)	Selling Price ($)
Scotch	A	30	1.25	2.25
	B	75	2.00	3.50
Vodka	A	25	1.00	1.50
	B	70	2.00	2.75
	C	35	1.50	2.00

a. What is the sales price per ounce for scotch?
b. What is the sales price per ounce for vodka?
c. What is the weighted-average sales price per ounce for both liquors together?
d. The total ounces used from a physical inventory is 500 ounces. What is the variance in ounces?

e. What is the variance in dollars (referring to the previous question)?

18–3 Calculate beverage purchases for a period using the following data:

Beginning beverage inventory	$ 2,000
Beverage sales	10,000
Ending beverage inventory	2,200
Beverage cost percentage	25%

18–4 Using the data from problem 14–3, calculate the beverage inventory turnover.

18–5 Using the following data, calculate the closing beverage inventory value:

Beverage sales	$20,000
Beverage purchases	6,000
Beginning inventory	1,000
Beverage cost percentage	20%

18–6 Using data from problem 14–5, calculate the beverage inventory turnover.

18–7 A 15.5-gallon keg of draft beer costs $40.00. Pouring and spillage losses are 2 gallons, a 12-ounce glass is used, and selling price is 75 cents. Calculate:
a. the number of glasses expected from the keg
b. the operations cost per glass
c. the sales-dollar potential of the keg

19

Some Aspects of Property Management

Property management covers many different areas. In this chapter we are concerned with five of these as areas of controlling costs: energy management, water management, preventive maintenance, risk management, and waste management. The discussion of risk management considers some aspects of insurance protection that go beyond strictly property management.

After completing this chapter, you should be able to:

1. Define *Btu.*
2. Explain the two basic factors of electric rates.
3. Compare gas and electric rates.
4. Define sensible and latent heat.
5. Discuss seven areas in foodservice operations from which energy savings can be accomplished.
6. Compare fuel costs for HVAC.
7. Find causes of excess water usage.
8. Appreciate treating water for "hardness."
9. Explain the importance of preventive maintenance.
10. Explain the four general types of preventive maintenance contracts.
11. Identify the areas of risk management.
12. Understand the role and securing of insurance.
13. Explain a standard fire policy, extended coverage, and coinsurance.
14. Appreciate business interruption insurance.
15. Discuss methods of controlling waste.

ENERGY MANAGEMENT

At one time, energy costs were considered a minor factor in foodservice operations, and many operated as if little could be done to control them. However, a number of factors have driven these costs up considerably. One is the control other nations have over our oil supply. Another is the substitution of machines for human labor, causing lower labor but higher energy costs. The increased use of air conditioning and brighter lighting has also contributed to higher energy use.

With the higher energy costs came the recognition that much could be done to reduce the use of energy. Some organizations have been very successful at this. Some esoteric ideas (such as using outside cold air in colder climates for cooling in refrigeration) and some high-tech ideas (such as using the heat in wastewater from dishwashing for heating purposes or sophisticated computer energy control systems) have been successful. Some operations are even factoring in energy costs in the selling prices of items.

Measurements of Heating Energy

To understand energy costs, it is necessary to understand how the energy is measured. The unit of measurement for heat is the **British thermal unit (Btu)**. A Btu is the amount of heat required to raise 1 pound of water 1° F, or roughly the heat given off by a wooden match. Natural gas is usually sold in units of 1,000 cubic feet (mcf) or by 100,000 Btu, or a **therm**. The heat value of natural gas is approximately 1,000 Btu per cubic foot, or 1 million Btu per mcf, or 100,000 Btu per therm. Electricity is usually sold by the kilowatt-hour (kWh), and each kWh provides 3,412 Btu of heat. Oil is sold by the gallon, with about 142,000 Btu per gallon. On the basis of cost per input Btu, natural gas is usually cheaper than electricity. However, gas cooking equipment requires more Btu to produce the same amount of heat as the comparable electric cooking equipment. The gas industry can produce figures showing that it takes 1.6 Btu of gas in gas equipment to equal 1 Btu of heat from electricity in electrical equipment. The electrical industry can produce figures showing that it takes closer to 3 Btu of gas in gas equipment to equal 1 Btu of electricity in electrical equipment. The industries would agree that different equipment has different ratios. The smaller the energy ratio—the number of Btu of gas to match equivalent results in electricity, which requires fewer Btu—the more attractive gas looks.

In summary, gas fuel for the kitchen is cheaper in terms of input Btu per dollar, but gas equipment requires more input Btu than comparable electric equipment. Gas and electricity costs can be compared by determining the number of Btu required by gas equipment and dividing this by the cost per 1,000 cubic feet to derive cost per therm. This would give the cost for gas. The total number of Btu required by electricity, once determined, could be multiplied by the rate per kWh (including demand charges). The result would be the cost of electricity as fuel. The rate per kWh is sometimes hard to determine, since the increased use of electricity could affect the rate. It could also change the maximum demand, which could affect the rate as well.

Electrical Rates

Electrical rates are usually based on two factors: (1) the amount of electricity actually used and (2) the **demand charge**, which is the price the utility charges for being able to supply the maximum amount of electricity an operation might require during its peak demand periods. Although the peak demand periods may occur infrequently, the electric utility nevertheless must have the capacity available to meet them whenever they occur. Since large quantities of electricity cannot be stored, the demand charge helps defray the expense of maintaining a generating capacity that, much of the time, is not needed. Therefore, it may help a foodservice operation to plan its use of electricity so as to avoid peak loads. For example, it could use electric water heaters only during off-peak periods and store the hot water, or it could arrange to operate large electric appliances only during off-peak periods.

Sensible and Latent Heat

In considering the energy in heat, it is necessary to recognize there are two types. It takes energy to produce the heat, and sometimes more energy to remove it or cool the premises.

Sensible heat is measured by a thermometer, and latent heat is water vapor in the air. A boiling pot gives off heat, which raises the temperature (sensible heat), but it also adds hot vapor to the air (latent heat), causing an increase in humidity. Since temperature and humidity are definitely related, both types of heat can be uncomfortable. In kitchens, the open bain-marie is a prime offender. Cooking pots, steam tables, and steam kettles should be kept covered. Only a small portion of the fuel needed to boil the contents of an uncovered pot is required to boil the contents of a covered pot, and the kitchen will be considerably more comfortable.

Controlling Kitchen Fuel Costs

Let us examine areas of possible energy savings in the typical food production facility. Some will cost little to implement; others will require only comparatively modest expenditures. We will divide dietary department energy usage somewhat arbitrarily into

- cooking equipment,
- refrigeration equipment,
- hoods and ventilation,
- dishwashers,
- lighting,
- climate control, and
- recipe and preparation modification.

A survey of different types of foodservice operations showed the following average percentage consumption of energy:

Heating, ventilation, air conditioning (HVAC)	25%
Lighting	11%
Refrigeration	7%
Sanitation	24%
Food preparation	33%
	100%

Cooking Equipment

This is probably the most productive area to find energy savings. Some foodservice professionals suggest that up to 50 percent of the energy used to heat foods is wasted.

Scheduling Equipment

This probably causes the most flagrant waste of energy. Cooking apparatus are turned on in the morning and left on all day. Many operations have developed time schedules as to when to turn on and off equipment. For example, not all ovens need to be turned on at once. Determining preheat times is necessary in scheduling when equipment should be on or off. Sometimes the scheduling or cycling of equipment is performed by computers or automatic timers. Equipment now in development will automatically determine how long a piece of equipment should be on for the load it has and make adjustments if the load is changed. Operators should schedule food production for the most efficient use of equipment. Cooking equipment is generally more efficient when used to capacity: Using a full oven is more efficient than using an oven twice for half loads. Generally, there is also considerably less shrinkage when an oven is filled to capacity. Determine if preheat times are really necessary, or necessary for all items. Can the preheat energy be used to cook the food? You may find it desirable to attach timers to equipment if they are not installed. (Preheating may be necessary for baked goods to activate yeasts.)

Maintenance and Cleaning of Equipment

Some energy audits have shown that thermostats may be inaccurate by 30 degrees or more. This can waste energy. Check thermostats by using a separate oven thermometer and, if necessary, have them recalibrated or replaced. In some operations this is part of a general maintenance program. If gas equipment is used, be sure the burners are properly adjusted. A yellow flame is often a sign of poor adjustment. Cleanliness and housekeeping are also important for energy savings. Grease or encrusted material inhibits heat transfer and thus requires more heat. A grill should be cleaned at the end of every shift. Clogged burners cannot operate efficiently.

Choice of Equipment Usage

The most energy-efficient methods of cooking are steaming, microwaving, baking, and stir-frying. Ranges are relatively inefficient. Open-burner ranges are more efficient than hot tops since the whole surface has to be heated for the latter. One test between the two showed a 59 percent savings of energy on bringing a pan of water to boil. If hot tops are used, practice cluster cooking and keep all the pots and pans in one area. For single portions or small amounts, use a microwave oven or a high-speed hot plate.

Cooking at lower temperatures over longer periods saves energy and also reduces shrinkage. Some ovens are now available that are designed to cook roast beef overnight at 225°F. If feasible, cook in large volumes; this is more efficient.

Try not to open ovens or other equipment to check foods. For every second an oven door is open, an estimated 1 percent of heat is lost. When purchasing new equipment, you might want to specify windows to observe the cooking. In older equipment, try to depend on cooking times.

Use lids on open pots and pans to save energy. This will also keep the kitchen more comfortable by eliminating extra latent and sensible heat. Pans should be somewhat larger than the burners on which they are being heated. This will use the heat more effectively.

Some new designs of hot tops will heat the area only where the receptacle is. Sometimes kitchens have equipment that is too large for current needs. Often a smaller mixer can do all the work a larger mixer is doing. A food processor may be able to take over from a large Buffalo chopper. Putting the smaller equipment on carts may also make workers more productive by bringing the equipment to where it is needed rather than having to bring everything to the equipment.

Try to cook in the largest volume possible for your operation. Steaming several pans of different vegetables in a steamer or heating them in an oven that is timed to finish them together uses space efficiently and saves energy.

Refrigeration

Maintenance is especially important in keeping refrigeration equipment efficient. Keep the coils defrosted and compressors and condensers clean. See that gaskets around openings are in good shape and clean. Compressor and condenser units should have proper air circulation. Use refrigeration units to defrost food. Not only is it better from a sanitation standpoint, but it effectively adds cooling power. Your purchasing and delivery procedures can affect cooling. If you keep large quantities of food for longer periods than necessary in refrigeration or freezing areas, you will use energy unnecessarily. Frequent purchases and deliveries, if possible, can lessen this. But be careful not to have deliveries come all through the day, thereby necessitating frequent trips to refrigeration units; this will only waste the energy you are trying to save.

Walk-in units are generally more efficient than reach-in units. Hopes of better labor usage with reach-ins have not been realized. Walk-in units can be even more efficient with the use of plastic strips to help keep the units cool when doors are open. Although it is generally better to have the refrigerated space filled, the contents should be arranged to permit proper air circulation around perishable items. Stacking the contents in even columns increases efficiency. Goods should not be placed too close to the evaporator units in the cooled areas. Lights should be turned off when not needed. A 100-watt light bulb generates 341 Btu of heat per hour. A light outside indicating that the light is on may be desirable. Temperatures in the cooled and frozen areas should be monitored to see that they are not too low. It takes 15 percent more energy to maintain a temperature of $-20°$ F than $0°$ F. Too-low temperatures can increase the chances of perishables drying out or freezer burn.

Although this must be determined when planning the facilities, entering the freeze-temperature storage areas through the refrigerated boxes can save energy. Also, specifying walk-ins rather than reach-ins can be helpful.

Hoods and Ventilation

Ventilation hoods are another area where maintenance and cleaning are especially important for energy savings and fire prevention. Hoods that have filters clogged with grease are both energy users and fire risks. It is not necessary to have ventilation hoods over ovens because there are no grease-laden vapors to remove and the hoods only take heat from the ovens. Ventilation fans are sometimes left on when not needed. For example, a fan might be left on in an empty restroom; sometimes it might be left on all night.

When hoods are being planned, it is desirable to specify double- rather than single-walled hoods. In the single-walled hoods, 100 percent of the air that has been conditioned in the kitchen is exhausted. A **double-walled hood** uses a separate supply of untempered makeup air (which takes no energy to treat) and introduces this air at the perimeter of the exhaust hood. Thus, most of the air drawn out by the exhaust fans has not been conditioned. The auxiliary makeup air (which requires a makeup air fan) can save approximately 70 percent of the conditioned air normally lost through the hoods. This arrangement also allows the hoods to be more effective in collecting cooking grease and oil.

When deciding what hoods to use, one must evaluate what equipment really requires ventilation. It might be more cost-efficient to have several smaller hoods, only some of which are ventilated, rather than one large ventilated hood over all the equipment.

Lighting

One of the first steps in reducing energy used in lighting is to check the wattage of the bulbs. Many fixtures produce more light than necessary. A 25 percent wattage reduction can approximate a 12.5 percent reduction in energy consumption.

Are lights on when they are not needed? Can timers, automatic or otherwise, be used to turn off lights when not needed? Assuming a lighting period of 12 hours, if lights are off for three of these hours a 25 percent reduction in energy is required. Some operations have found savings by simply posting "Please turn off the light" notices.

Lamps that are not clean can cut emitted light. Incandescent bulbs decrease in efficiency over time. Replacing them before they burn out can provide a savings. One study showed a 50 percent decrease in two years. One technique is to replace all bulbs when the first one in an area burns out.

The color of walls and ceilings also affects the amount of light required. Light surfaces are more reflective and need less energy.

Fluorescent lighting is more efficient than incandescent lighting, especially when lights are not turned on or off frequently. On a subjective note, many people believe that incandescent light gives a "warmer" light and a better appearance to the food.

Recipe and Preparation Modification

There is more and more interest in saving energy by recipe planning and preparation techniques. Results appear promising and, although initial modification requires much work, the savings go on as long as the recipes are used.

Five energy modification principles are used in modifying recipes:

- ingredient temperature
- flavor development
- preheating time
- efficient heat transfer
- time-temperature relationship

Ingredient temperature involves making the ingredients as warm as possible before heating. An example would be thawing frozen goods before processing. Even better is thawing them in ordinary refrigeration to reduce the cooling required by other items.

Preheating time can be eliminated for many items. Baked products may require heat immediately for leavening and rising actions.

Efficient heat transfer considers the most efficient way of transmitting heat to the product. One study showed that browning beef cubes in a trunion kettle required almost 80 percent less energy than browning them in a convection oven.

Time-temperature relationships specify that the precise time and temperature relationship be considered. Can the heat be turned off for a product in the oven, completing the baking with the heat already in the oven? Common practice is to take the product from the oven when finished. The heat in the oven then dissipates into the surrounding area.

Climate Control (HVAC)

Heating, ventilation, and air conditioning are sometimes referred to as **HVAC**. For space and climate control, heating and cooling degree-days are used. A heating **degree-day** is the difference between the mean daily temperature and 65° F. If the daily mean temperature is 45° F, there would be 20 degree-days that day. The total of the degree-days gives the total heating load for that heating season. Energy use can be compared to this standard in various ways. If one heating season is 2,000 degree-days and another 2,400 degree-days, the second energy or fuel expenditure should be around 20 percent more than the first. It is possible to calculate fuel or energy consumption per degree-day and, by multiplying by the number of degree-days, have an approximation of fuel or energy consumption. The number of degree-days that have occurred is often published in local newspapers. A cooling degree-day is a measure of the need for air cooling. It is calculated by subtracting 65° F from the mean daily temperature. If the outdoor temperature is 80° F, 15 cooling degree-days are recorded.

A first step is to check the thermostats (assuming that the area has separate ones). Are they accurate? People sometimes put more faith in a thermostat reading than in their own feelings; if the thermostat shows a reasonable temperature, they are comfortable even if it might objectively be too hot or too cold. Often 68° F provides comfort. Each degree reduction in the temperature called for will reduce energy consumption by about 1.5 percent. Timed thermostats, which can cut down heat when the area is not occupied, usually have a very fast payback of costs. If the premises are air-conditioned, each degree increase in temperature setting saves about 3 percent in cooling costs.

Ventilation can also affect climate control. Unnecessarily venting treated air means energy required to treat the replacing air. Are ventilation fans operating when not needed? As in other areas, housekeeping and maintenance can have an effect. Are heating units blocked, thereby preventing air circulation? It is estimated that a cooling system that is not properly maintained and adjusted can require 10 percent more energy to operate. Faulty control valves and traps or loose windows that are letting heat escape need to be repaired.

Savings in fuel consumption may be obtained by proper insulation, which often pays for itself. Another source of loss is incomplete combustion. Besides wasting fuel, incomplete combustion will build up soot on the heating surfaces of the furnace, which sharply reduces its efficiency. A layer of soot $\frac{1}{32}$ of an inch can cause a 2.5 percent increase in fuel consumption; a $\frac{1}{8}$-inch layer can cause an increase of 8.5 percent. A three-step preventive maintenance program to achieve proper combustion includes:

1. maintaining the proper fuel-air ratio as specified by the burner manufacturer,

2. keeping the burners and orifices clean, properly aligned, and in good mechanical condition, and

3. maintaining the fuel oil temperature and pressure at recommended levels.

The furnace and burner should be periodically checked, adjusted, and cleaned for efficient trouble-free operation. In addition to promoting economy, efficient combustion will help minimize air pollution.

Cost Comparison

It is easy to determine the approximate relative costs of various fuels by determining the number of Btu received for each cent expended. Other considerations include energy conversion efficiency, availability and continuity of energy supply, space for fuel storage, operating expenses, labor, comfort standards, and physical plant investment. These factors cannot be so readily compared.

Water

Water, an essential commodity for life, is indispensable in foodservice operations, which have traditionally been careless with water. Half of the water used in connection with foodservice is probably wasted. With water shortages occurring, it may become necessary to eliminate this wastage not only to control costs but also merely to maintain the supply. Adding to the cost of the water can be the cost of dispensing it as sewerage. In some localities sewerage rates are higher than the water rates.

Common causes of wasted water are leaky faucets and running toilets. Both problems can lead to costly damage beyond the cost of the wasted water, but fortunately both problems are easy to remedy. Usually, all that is needed for a leaky faucet is a new rubber washer. For the running toilet, it is usually necessary to replace only the flush tank ball. Parts are available at any hardware store, and the work does not require a plumber. Table 19.1 outlines the cost of various sized leaky faucets—and at a very low water rate. A toilet may be silently leaking water. A simple test is putting a few drops of food coloring in the tank. If, without flushing, it appears in the bowl, there is a leak.

Cleaning with **hard water**, which contains excessive calcium and magnesium salts, also increases the use of water. Hardness of water is measured by the number of grains of these mineral salts in a gallon. "Three grains hardness" means that there are three grains of mineral salt per gallon, or fifty parts per million. Water-softening systems usually pay for themselves with soap or detergent savings, longer wear for fabrics, and easier cleaning. Softening also prevents the buildup of hard water scale in pipes, which both curtails the flow of water and decreases the efficiency of heating systems. In many areas about the country it is not necessary to purchase a water-softening system, since the water-softening

Table 19.1
Amount of Water Lost and Cost per Month through Various Size Openings

Opening	Gallons Lost	Cost
$\frac{1}{2}$ in	1,230,800	$430.85
$\frac{3}{8}$ in	692,400	242.20
$\frac{1}{4}$ in	307,700	107.80
$\frac{1}{8}$ in	76,900	26.93
$\frac{1}{16}$ in	19,200	6.65
$\frac{1}{32}$ in	4,800	1.80

Figures assume 40 pounds pressure and a rate of 35 cents per 1,000 gallons.

ion-exchange tanks and their necessary replacements can be secured on a service basis. If it is not feasible to supply conditioned water to the whole operation, it may be desirable to supply softened water at least to the dishwasher and laundry. Not only will there be water savings, but cleaner dishes, brighter linens, and a smaller detergent expense should also result. (Most detergents contain a large amount of water-softening compound, so pre-softened water requires less of it.)

Some operations waste a great deal of water in their air conditioning systems. By using cooling towers, an operator can cycle cooled water over and over again.

Energy Committees

Many large facilities with foodservice and other operations have energy committees. These committees often arrange for an energy audit to determine where energy may be saved and costs reduced. The energy audit is a detailed analysis of energy use, consumption, and consumption patterns. In hospitality operations the audits often result in savings of 8 to 30 percent. (One survey resulted in a 70 percent savings.) Usually the surveys do not lower the operation's energy bills, but they do allow the operation to better absorb the increasing costs of energy.

PREVENTIVE MAINTENANCE

A sound preventive maintenance program is essential to avoid expensive failure of equipment or facilities. Some of the maintenance is low-tech, such as cleaning activities. Other maintenance can require some degree of sophistication, such as pest and rodent control or maintenance on refrigeration, air conditioning, kitchen equipment, fire alarms and fire suppression systems.

Although larger operations may have maintenance managers and maintenance departments, most foodservice operations are too small for this even though the maintenance activity is equally important. Some foodservice chains have more complete maintenance activities. Provision must be made for preventive maintenance whether it is done in-house or contracted out.

Preventive maintenance can be defined as any work performed to an operational device or facility to continue operating at its proper efficiency without interruption. With the increasing sophistication of the physical systems and facilities in foodservice operations, it is becoming more and more important.

There are a number of reasons for implementing a preventive maintenance program. One is simply to maintain operations. A restaurant that uses china plate service may have difficulty continuing if the dishwashing system breaks down because of lack of preventive maintenance. Service life can be extended. Equipment is expensive, so it is prudent to keep it operating as long as it is efficient. There is a definite financial advantage in not having to replace the dishwasher prematurely.

Identifying degradation through preventive maintenance should alert the operation that repairs, replacement of parts, or other procedures should be performed before a serious situation arises. Sometimes the degradation appears in a minor form, such as leaks, before becoming a more serious problem.

Elements of a Preventive-Maintenance System

Preventive maintenance systems have many facets. Operations should maintain histories for equipment and facilities. The history for a dishwasher could include the following data: equipment designation, type of equipment, manufacturer, model number, location, date purchased or installed, preventive maintenance history and schedule, history of repairs, and source of parts.

Foodservice facilities should be inspected regularly to note safety hazards, needed repairs, or attention to upkeep requirements. The scheduling for inspections could be on a computer or on a tickler file.

Another aspect of preventive maintenance is loss prevention. This can also be protection to personnel or the facility itself. A nonworking fire alarm system could lead to injuries and damage to property.

A foodservice facility must comply with various local, state, and federal standards. The operation's insurance company may also impose some standards. Working conditions can depend heavily on systems such as heating, ventilating, and lighting. The Occupational Safety and Health Act (OSHA) provides for fines for failures to meet OSHA standards. Preventive maintenance may be necessary to maintain those standards.

Preventive maintenance order (PMO) forms can be used. These can include information such as description of the equipment, model number, priority, frequency, location, tools required, material required, safety procedures, maintenance procedures, completion date, name of the person who performed the work, time required, comments, and a blank for the manager or supervisor to initial.

Maintenance Contracts

Instead of the operation performing the work itself, it may want to contract maintenance work. This is especially helpful with specialized equipment that requires specific expertise. However, some operators find that even routine functions such as cleaning or grounds care can best be contracted out. This can allow the operation to maintain a small regular staff. In negotiating the contract, management should be sure emergency service is available if it is for vital equipment.

Maintenance contracts usually fall into one of four general classes:

- long-term fixed-price contract
- one-time fixed-price contract
- cost-reimbursement contract
- fixed-cost and retainer

A long-term fixed-price contract establishes the responsibility for each party at a firm price, which helps budgeting. It lends itself to competitive bidding, and the single contractor can gain familiarity with the specified equipment. However, it is difficult to charge or terminate early, and changes can be costly. It may also be difficult to express fully the problems that may occur. This contract is used primarily for maintenance needs that can be predicted well in advance. A one-time fixed-price contract rigidly establishes the scope of the work with very specific responsibilities. As its name implies, it is for one use.

Cost-reimbursement contracts are unpriced, with actual labor and material costs reimbursed plus an additional percentage or amount provided for the contractor's overhead and profit. These contracts are particularly useful in breakdowns of unknown cause or scope. A disadvantage is that the contractor has no incentive to provide a quick low-cost project, and there must be some oversight to ensure that all costs are fair.

A fixed cost and retainer are helpful when there is predictable routine preventive maintenance and a possibility for major repairs, which are inevitable even if unpredictable. This contract has routine service requirements paid for at a fixed price with repairs performed at labor rates established in advance. A retainer may be provided to compensate the repair contractor to be ready for emergency repairs. The retainer can be a dollar amount or an agreement that the contractor will get all the business involving that type of repairs.

The Preventive Maintenance Cycle

Preventive maintenance operates in a continuous cycle. Steps in this cycle include the following:

1. After initial installation, the preventive maintenance requirements are determined and written down. These may come from the manufacturer.

2. A system of showing the dates the activities are to be performed is implemented. One simple system is marking on a calendar; a tickler file or computer may also be employed.

3. When the due date for performance arrives, a designated person takes responsibility to assign the work or see that it has been performed.

4. Information that the work has been completed and any comments by the person doing it, such as signs that would affect future performance of the equipment, are noted.

5. If appropriate, action is taken in response to the comments. This could include further inspection, calling in an outside expert, or scheduling nonroutine maintenance.

The cycle resumes at step 2.

RISK MANAGEMENT

Insurance, which is included under the topic of **risk management,** is another cost that has gone from being rather insignificant to being one of concern. Foodservice has more than a normal need for insurance protection. It has the problems of a retail business that deals primarily with customers and the problems of a manufacturing concern that has production risks from the kitchen.

Insurance is only one of the methods to handle risk management. Four others are:

- *Risk avoidance.* Can a risk be eliminated? One restaurant abandoned its flambé cooking in the dining room because of the fire hazard.

- *Risk retention.* This is somewhat analogous to a speeder on the highway who continues to speed even though there is a chance of being caught and fined. In risk retention, management must decide that the chances of loss do not merit the cost of insurance protection. It may also give increased attention to preventing a potential accident or loss. Although not always used this way, risk retention is best suited to smaller losses, not catastrophic ones. Risk retention sometimes is unfortunately used when an operation does not have funds to purchase insurance.

- *Risk transfer.* Risk transfer involves transferring the cost of loss to another party, often an outside contractor that should have the necessary insurance coverage for the risk involved. An example is an operation that believes it could remove some trees from its property with its own personnel but hires a contractor (who assumes any risk) to do it. A type of risk transfer is changing the legal form of operation from a proprietorship or partnership to a corporation so that the proprietor or partners would not risk losing their personal assets.
- *Loss control.* As its name implies, **loss control** is an attempt at preventing losses. Safety programs and safety training for workers are examples of loss control.

Reasons for Insurance

Insurance trades the possibility of a loss for the certainty of reimbursement for that loss for a certain but small cost called a premium. Nothing may ever happen, but if it does, you pay a premium to recover the amount of the loss.

Insurance is used to:

- Replace asset losses through such causes as fire, theft, or flood. When the asset is damaged or destroyed, insurance can help replace it.
- Cover liability claims. A foodservice operation can be sued for various reasons, and insurance can be used to fight or reimburse these claims.
- Cover such costs as unemployment compensation or workers' compensation, which are mandated by law. This coverage, called social insurance, can also be used for voluntary causes such as health insurance or retirement annuities.

Other insurance includes types of coverage not cited in the preceding categories. An example would be business interruption insurance, which provides funds when a business cannot operate because of a fire or other cause.

Purchasing Insurance

There can be differences in the costs and quality of insurance secured. An operation wants to secure insurance at a low premium cost, but low cost is not the only consideration. It is important to choose a stable insurance company that will not go out of business or have financial difficulties. *Best's Insurance Reports* publishes the financial rating and an analysis of major insurance companies and information about their financial stability. Different insurance companies can specialize in different types of insurance, serving specific industries or types of organizations. Insurance agencies also may specialize. Areas of specialty can give insurers experience that can be helpful in tailoring insurance to an operation's particular needs. Other factors include availability of agents and ease in settling claims.

Insurance is distributed in one of two principal ways: through an independent agent or through the direct routing system. The independent agent has the right to represent the insurer in a particular territory and usually represents a number of companies. Theoretically at least, the independent agent can look for the best deal for its client from the various companies it represents. The independent agent is compensated with a commission arrangement. Insurance agents are not all equal. Some will go further than others in trying to help their clients. In **direct routing**, the insurance is sold through employees of the insurance company who do not handle other companies. Proponents of direct routing cite the fact that theoretically it can be cheaper because of lack of commissions; in addition, employees can be more familiar with their company and its procedures than agents and therefore would offer better service. Both systems have worked satisfactorily.

Other insurance personnel include the **insurance broker**, who represents the insured rather than the company and is the legal representative of the insured. Since they are not beholden to a company, insurance brokers theoretically can work in their clients' interests. An independent agent can be a broker. The broker may also represent the insured regarding claims or disputes.

An organization may want to use an insurance consultant to analyze and make recommendations on its insurance needs, coverages, and costs. The consultant is paid by the organization and can provide an independent viewpoint apart from those who have an interest in selling the insurance.

An **insurance adjuster** is an employee or agent of the insurance company who works on determining the amount of the loss from the insurance company's side. Insurance companies may use appraisers to determine the value of an asset for insurance purposes.

Insurance companies may provide other services such as inspecting boilers, elevators, or other equipment they insure. They may also provide some safety or fire prevention recommendations.

Types of Insurance

Many different types of insurance can be secured; we will consider here some of the most important ones to a foodservice organization.

The owner of a building needs fire insurance to compensate for a loss due to fire. A **standard fire policy** is used throughout the country to insure against loss from fire, lightning, and losses to goods that were temporarily removed from the premises because of the fire. A standard policy does not cover theft, actions resulting from war or civil disorders, or losses due to failure by the insured to use all reasonable means to save the property after a fire loss. It is often desirable to supplement the basic fire policy with an **extended coverage** endorsement for such perils as windstorms, hail, explosions, riots, vehicle damage, and smoke damage.

The standard policy is usually written with a **coinsurance clause**. Using the idea of risk retention, an operator may figure that most fires are not total, so the property needs to be insured for only a portion of its insurable value (let us say $500,000). An insurance policy of $250,000 with an 80 percent coinsurance clause is purchased. The coinsurance clause states the minimum percentage of the value of the premises that the insurance company wants to be insured before it pays the full amount of any loss up to the limits of the policy. For an 80 percent coinsurance clause on a $500,000 property, the insurance carried should be at least $400,000. A $50,000 loss occurs. Even though this is less than the value of the policy, the company pays only half the loss, or $25,000.

It is important that if the insurable value of a property increases, the fire insurance should also increase to at least the coinsurance amount. Insurance companies and agents can be helpful in periodic reappraisal of insurable amounts needed. Operators should take care not to purchase too much insurance. They should consider reducing premiums through better fire protection, such as a sprinkler system or an automatic fire suppression system in the kitchen.

If a fire occurs, indirect costs arise when the business cannot operate and generate income. Financing costs or real estate taxes must be paid, and it may be desirable to continue paying the manager or key employees so that they do not look for other jobs.

Business interruption insurance is designed for these circumstances. It can cover the profit the operation could have been expected to earn or the fixed expenses it may incur. This coverage can also be secured on a coinsurance basis.

Four conditions must be satisfied to collect business interruption insurance:

1. A property loss from the insured peril must occur.
2. The business must be partially or totally shut down because of the loss.
3. The loss must be the cause of the shutdown. The insurance would not cover a shutdown caused by lack of business, for example.
4. It must be shown that if the business had not been damaged, it would have been able to pay expenses and generate a profit (if covered).

With the increase in crime, it may be desirable to have crime insurance to cover losses from robbery or burglary. Comprehensive crime policies can cover other crime losses as well. Inside crime may be covered by fidelity bonds. These are designed to reimburse an operation for embezzlement or misappropriation of funds by an employee.

A foodservice organization is subject to both common law and statutory law covering injury to customers and employees arising out of the organization's negligence. Examples are foreign articles in food served, food poisoning, and certain injuries on the job. A fertile area for litigation is operations that serve alcoholic beverages being sued for injuries or damages perpetrated by intoxicated customers after they leave the premises. The operation may secure insurance to protect itself against these liability and negligence situations.

There are many types of social insurance, including workers' compensation, social security, unemployment compensation, and employee group life and health policies. These are beyond the scope of this book except to note that by contesting unemployment claims by former employees, employers can often show that they are not entitled to benefits and can lower their premium rate. There are consultants who specialize in these cases.

WASTE MANAGEMENT

A relatively new area of concern for foodservice operators is waste management for products such as food waste, paper, plastics, metals, glass, and landscape waste. Sometimes this waste matter is referred to as **municipal solid waste (MSW)**. Several factors are behind this increased concern. One is cost. During the '90s the cost of placing waste material in a local landfill, called a **tipping fee**, more than tripled in some localities in a few years. There is increasing difficulty in some areas in finding suitable landfills. Another is concern for the local environment. Methane gases from landfills can pollute the area. Toxic leachates can contaminate water supplies. Approximately 80 percent of MSW is landfilled, 10 percent incinerated, and 10 percent recycled. Not only is there concern for the local environment but also about polluting the land, oceans, flora, and fauna of the whole planet. There is a finite limit of resources to produce many products and wasting those resources may harm future generations.

The three methods that are considered effective in waste management (WM) are the three Rs: reduce, reuse, and recycle. Reduce is involved in purchase considerations.

Is there packaging that produces less waste? Must products be in aerosol cans or can they be bought in concentrate (often cheaper) with less disposal problems? Reuse refers to reusing the product. Can old linens be cut up for cleaning rags? Can polyethylene pails that some products arrive in be used elsewhere? Recycling is another component of good WM. Experts estimate that about 60 percent of waste is recyclable but present programs handle a much smaller percentage. Some recyclable materials have value and can produce limited income. Recycling may be primary, secondary, or tertiary. Primary is actual reuse, with glass bottles probably being the best example. Secondary recycling includes processes such as reforming aluminum cans. Tertiary recycling involves breaking down the products and producing something else, such as plastics being made into road materials.

Probably the first step in effective waste management is taking a good look at your trash, garbage, and other wastes. Once you have an idea of its composition, you can think about what can be done to reduce, reuse, or recycle it.

Management may want to do a cost analysis between reusables and disposables. Although disposables often cost more, there are substantial costs in using reusables, such as china and silverware inventories, dishwashing labor, equipment, supplies, dishwashing space required, and water and electric costs.

Fast-Food Operations

Fast-food operations have been targeted as prime offenders in producing MSW. However, an analysis of U.S. landfills shows only about 0.3 percent per volume can be attributed to fast-food operations. Proponents of using disposables claim they are more sanitary than reusables and do not require the water and energy of reusables, which helps balance the environmental equation.

Waste Removal

No foodservice operation wants to have food and garbage standing around. In some areas waste removal may be handled by local government and in others by private contractors that may be small local independents or affiliates of national chains. Where there is a choice, some factors to consider are:

1. Cost of service.
2. Frequency of service.
3. Suitable equipment, including pickup and storage equipment, such as dumpsters.
4. Quality of service. Do the contractors leave a mess when picking up?
5. Security. Could the waste pickup be a conduit to take stolen food or other items out of the operation?
6. Possibility of retrieval. Can the contractor salvage and return silverware inadvertently mixed with waste? (This may not be feasible.)
7. Other options. Could there be value in the waste, such as pig farmers paying for garbage or cash for recycling cans?

SUMMARY

The basic unit of measurement for heat is the British thermal unit, or Btu. It is possible to use Btu to compare gas and electric fuel costs for a kitchen. Electricity charges are based on two factors: the amount of electricity used and the electric demand charge. In comparing space heat amount, it is necessary to realize that it can be measured by temperature (or sensible heat) or by latent heat (or the amount of water vapor in the air). Either can cause discomfort.

Kitchens present many areas to control fuel costs. Included are cooking equipment, refrigeration, hoods and ventilation, dishwasher, lighting, climate control, and recipes and preparation modification.

Foodservice operations use a great deal of water, and much can be wasted. Water can also be treated to remove hardness. Hard water uses more soap or detergent, is harder on fabrics, clogs pipes, and makes cleaning more difficult.

Another aspect of property management is preventive maintenance or work performed to an operational device or facility to keep it operating at its proper efficiency. This includes maintaining operations, extending service life, and identifying degradation. Preventive maintenance can be contracted out. Contracts are usually one of four different classes: long-term fixed-price contract, one-time fixed-price contract, cost-reimbursement contract, or fixed cost and retainer.

Risk management is also part of property management. Included in risk management are risk avoidance, risk retention, risk transfer, loss control, and insurance. Insurance trades the possibility of a loss for the certainty of reimbursement for that loss in exchange for a premium cost. A foodservice operation needs different kinds of insurance, including fire insurance, if property is owned. When fire insurance is purchased, it is important to be aware of any coinsurance clause.

KEY TERMS

British thermal unit (Btu)
business interruption insurance
coinsurance clause
degree-day
demand charge
direct routing (insurance)
double-walled hood
extended coverage
hard water
HVAC
insurance
insurance adjuster

insurance broker
latent heat
loss control
municipal solid waste (MSW)
preventive maintenance
risk avoidance
risk management
risk retention
sensible heat
standard fire policy
therm
tipping fee

REVIEW QUESTIONS

19–1 Define *Btu*.
19–2 What are generalities in comparing gas and electrical rates for kitchen equipment?
19–3 What are the two components of an electric rate?
19–4 Differentiate between sensible and latent heat.

19–5 How can energy be saved in refrigeration units?
19–6 How can energy be saved regarding lighting fixtures?
19–7 Define a heating degree-day.
19–8 What are two easy ways to conserve water?

19–9   What are advantages of using water-softening systems?

19–10 Define a preventive maintenance program.

19–11 List reasons for having a preventive maintenance program.

19–12 What should be included in the preventive maintenance history of a dishwasher?

19–13 What is the difference between a long-term fixed-price contract in preventive maintenance and a fixed cost and retainer contract?

19–14 List the steps in the preventive maintenance cycle.

19–15 What are the elements of risk management?

19–16 What are elements to consider when you are purchasing an insurance policy?

19–17 Explain a fire insurance policy coinsurance clause.

19–18 What conditions must be satisfied to collect business interruption insurance?

19–19 Explain the three techniques of waste management.

PROBLEMS

19–1 A restaurant has an insurable value of $1 million and maintains an $800,000 fire policy with an 80 percent coinsurance clause. A fire causes complete destruction. How much can be collected from the insurance policy?

19–2 A restaurant has an insurable value of $600,000 covered by a $500,000 fire insurance policy with an 80 percent coinsurance clause. There is a $200,000 fire loss. How much will be recovered from the policy?

19–3 A restaurant is insured for $600,000 with an 80 percent coinsurance clause. Over the years the insurable value has increased to $900,000 with no change in the policy. A $300,000 loss occurs. How much will be recovered from the policy?

19–4 *Energy Problem* A walk-in refrigerator operates for 18 hours per day. The wattage consumption per hour is 250. The kilowatt-hour cost is 5 cents. The restaurant is considering the purchase of a new, energy-efficient refrigerator that will consume 275 watts per hour but operates only 16 hours per day. What is the operating cost per year for each unit, and which has the lowest electrical consumption? Calculate the percentage difference between the two.

19–5 *Energy Problem* A restaurant is considering changing from incandescent lamps to fluorescent lamps. There are presently 200 incandescent lamps. Each lamp is 75 watts and is in operation eight hours per day seven days per week. If the restaurant changes to fluorescent it would need 60 lamps. Each is

100 watts. The cost of electricity is 5 cents per kWh. What is the annual cost of each type of lamp, and what is the percentage difference?

19–6 *Case Problem* I am a hotel chief engineer and I thought my boss, the manager, didn't look very happy when he walked into my office yesterday. I was right! It seems that he'd had lunch with one of his cronies, that chap who manages the old fire trap they call the Eastbourne Hotel over on the East Side.

Anyway, the old man sits down beside my desk, see . . . and without a word, he hands me this list. It's written on a scrap of hotel stationery—the Eastbourne's—and it's got a whole bunch of figures on it.

"What's up?" I asked, glancing at the sheet.

"Read it and weep, Denney!" The old man was in a foul mood. "I had lunch today with Sol Litenboyer. Seems he's hired a new chief engineer for that dilapidated dive of his." (It isn't that bad, really; the Boss was just jealous.) "Look at those figures! In every category we're spending more than he is!"

"Look, Boss!" I tried to reason with him. "You can't compare properties like that."

He came right back at me. "Why not! They were both built about the same time—early 1950s. They both have about 200 rooms, have about the same occupancy and food business, are heated electrically with individual room temperature controls, have room air conditioning units, have the same kind of construction [brick outside], and the climate is the same over on the East Side. For crying out loud, take a look!!!" He points to the list.

Then he went on. "I want a 10 percent cut in the cost of running this place, Denney boy!! Otherwise. . . ." I was sort of glad he didn't finish that last sentence. Well, that was yesterday. Problems like this I don't need. Here, let me show you the list. See if you can make anything out of it. It shows how much higher our costs are on a percentage basis than at the Eastbourne.

1. Heating +7%
2. Air conditioning +4%
3. Hot water +6%
4. Other electricity +2%
5. Equipment repair +10%
6. Lost time due to accidents +3%
7. Average time per work order +7%
8. Refrigeration +6%

OK! You've seen enough! Get the point? Maybe I've been a little lax, but suppose you HR&IM hotshots in the university show me how to do it right. Obviously you don't know my building. I can't even show you a picture, but what I really need is a checklist. What should I be looking for in each of the listed categories? What are the likely reasons for my higher costs? Do a good job for me, will you? My neck is on the line!!

By the way, what do you think of the old man's management style? Isn't he a peach of a human being? How would you have approached me?

19–7 Examine as much as possible the waste products of a foodservice operation. What can you suggest be done to reduce, reuse, and recycle this waste?

Financial Statements and Their Analysis

To evaluate the financial status and progress of its operation and to control costs, management must understand and use its financial statements. Financial statements are also necessary for preparing tax forms, arranging loans or credit, and determining how much can be withdrawn from the business. Anyone thinking of buying an operation would certainly want to examine its financial records.

After completing this chapter, you should be able to:

1. Describe the two basic accounting statements.
2. Explain the value of *The Uniform System of Accounts for Restaurants* and the *Restaurant Industry Operations Report*.
3. Define the following terms having to do with a restaurant's income and expenses:
   - gross profit
   - other income
   - operating expenses
   - administrative and general expenses
   - marketing, energy, and utility service
   - repairs and maintenance
   - rent and occupation costs
   - depreciation
   - interest
   - general taxes paid
4. State and explain the fundamental balance sheet equation, and briefly explain the expression *net worth* (or equity).

5. State the three broad financial categories displayed on a balance sheet.

6. Define the following terms associated with a restaurant's balance sheet:
   - current assets
   - inventory
   - prepaid expenses
   - long-term debt
   - shareholders' equity
   - retained earnings

7. List the three basic components of a statement of income.

8. Prepare a cash flow analysis via the direct and indirect methods.

9. Explain comparative, common size, and ratio analyses.

10. List and briefly describe at least three sales analysis ratios.

11. Name the three general classifications of expenses.

12. Explain how to calculate these three ratios:
    - earnings ratio (or net profit to net sales ratio)
    - net profit to net equity ratio
    - net profit to total assets ratio

13. Name the two typical "cash accounts" and briefly explain their importance.

14. Define *accounts receivable,* and briefly explain its importance.

15. Calculate an accounts receivable turnover and an average collection period.

16. Define the terms *current ratio, fixed assets,* and *current liabilities.* Briefly explain their importance.

17. List types of records necessary in a foodservice operation.

FINANCIAL STATEMENTS

There are three basic accounting statements. One, the **statement of income** (formerly called the profit-and-loss statement, or the income statement), shows whether the operation has made or lost money over a specific period. From sales or revenues are subtracted the costs of food and every other expense item. The difference between the total sales or income and the total costs is the profit or loss.

The second major statement is the **balance sheet**, which portrays the financial condition of an enterprise at a particular time. One discovers how much money an operation is making or losing during a period by examining the income statement. The financial condition or value of an operation on one particular day (December 31 is often used) is found on the balance sheet.

A third helpful statement is the statement of **cash flows** which shows how cash was generated and dispensed during a period to provide the cash position as of a certain date. Cash (or cash equivalents) is generated or dispensed in three categories. Cash inflows and outflows come from:

- operating activities
- investing activities
- financing activities

Although accounting should be numerically correct, the statements are rarely 100 percent accurate in all respects. It is impossible, for example, to say at what precise rate a piece of equipment will depreciate or what its exact salvage value will be. Inventories may have values considerably different from original costs. A value given to such an intangible asset as goodwill, for example, is strictly an estimate. Financial statements cannot show assets such as managerial competence, employee morale, and patron satisfaction, which are no less important to success for their imprecise value. There is truth in the saying that "the devil can quote figures in his own behalf." Although figures are vital for information, one should not rely entirely upon financial statements for information.

Moreover, since there is considerable leeway in the preparation of statements, it is often important to know who prepares them. A good accountant does not have to be a certified public accountant, but the letters **CPA** after the accountant's name indicate that he or she has fulfilled certain requirements to gain this status and must adhere to the rules and regulations prescribed by the American Institute of Certified Public Accountants.

The usual analysis procedure is using comparisons. These comparisons may be with past figures of the operation, with general industry figures, with budgeted figures, or with goals. The dollar figures may be converted into percentages or ratios to help the comparison process.

The foodservice industry is fortunate to have an important resource regarding its financial statements. *The Uniform System of Accounts for Restaurants* has been adopted and recommended by the National Restaurant Association and prepared by the accounting firm of Deloitte and Touche LLB. The system provides a carefully thought-out accounting system so a foodservice operator does not have to hire an accountant to devise an individual system. Because the accounting system is used by many operations, it is possible to compile figures for the industry knowing that each individual operation calculated its figures the same way. If an individual operation prepares its statements in compliance with the *Uniform System,* meaningful comparisons can then be made.

A source of comparison for figures and ratios is presented in the yearly *Restaurant Industry Operations Survey* prepared and issued by the National Restaurant Association among others. The industry reports provide detailed information, which is broken down by type of operation, geographical location, age of operation, volume, menu theme, and affiliation. Similar accounting systems are available for other types of foodservice operations.

Statement of Income and Retained Earnings

An example of a statement of income and retained earnings appears in Table 20.1. This statement lists revenue and other income. It then deducts all expenses to find the profit before taxes. For better interpretation, each item is also calculated as a percentage of sales. The operation has earned a profit of $74,000 (or 7.4 percent of its sales) before provision for taxes. The *cost of sales* (food) is calculated in the following manner:

Inventory of food on hand at beginning of period	$ 30,000
+ Purchases of food during period	330,000

= Total value of available food	$360,000
− Inventory of food on hand at end of period	40,000
= Value of food used during period	$320,000

To find out how much food has been used, one must conduct an opening and closing inventory. The closing inventory for one period is the opening for another. Where possible, inventories should be taken on the same day of the week since they can vary through a week or period. Otherwise, an operation could show an unrealistically low food cost by using inventory on hand; if the operation accumulated a higher inventory during the period, it would show an inaccurately high food cost and lower profit. Some operations use 13 four-week periods for interim statements. This procedure includes the same number of busy or slow days, such as weekends, with each period having the same number of days.

Let us discuss the items on the statement of income in Table 20.1. The dollar figures for each category are shown along with the percentage of these figures to total revenue (except for cost of sales). More detailed schedules are often prepared showing the individual items under each classification.

The statement shows revenue for the one-year period ending December 31. Sales (formerly called revenue) are largely the revenue from food and beverage sales. Since beverage revenue is generally more profitable than food revenue, a high percentage of beverage revenue to food is usually good for the bottom line. In any case, it is helpful to know the division if both are served.

Cost of sales is the cost of the raw food and beverage sold. Since food and beverage will have different percentages, it is desirable to compare the cost of food to food income, and cost of beverages to beverage income. The total cost of food and beverage sales of $370,000 (compared to $1 million) gives a total cost-of-sales percentage of 37 percent.

Gross profit is the profit shown after a deduction of the cost of raw food and beverages from sales and before any consideration of other expenses. *Operating expenses* (formerly called ***controllable expenses***) were those expenses that are the direct responsibility of management and can be influenced and controlled by competent management and efficiency. The new format now includes depreciation. Salaries and wages paid to service, preparation, and administrative personnel might also be called *payroll*.

Employee benefits include items such as employee meals, social security taxes, workers' compensation insurance, medical insurance programs, and any expenses furthering employee goodwill. It should be noted that although employee benefits are only 4 percent of sales in the example, they are 15.4 percent of total payroll ($40,000 of $260,000). Many hospitality operations have a much higher percentage, sometimes going up to 40 percent. **Direct operating expenses** are items directly involved in service to customers. Included would be costs such as uniforms, laundry, china, glassware, silver, flowers, licenses, decorations, and parking fees.

Music and entertainment expenses are self-explanatory and vary considerably in different types of operations. Comparing with standard figures has limited utility because of these variances.

Marketing was once listed as advertising and promotion. It can include expenses for selling and promotion, advertising, publicity, public relations, fees and donations, and commissions (including franchise fees).

Table 20.1

Sample Statement of Income and Retained Earnings

Nittany Restaurant Statement of Income and Retained Earnings Year Ended December 31, XXX2		
	Amounts	**Percentages**
Sales		
Food	$ 800,000	80.0
Beverage	200,000	20.0
Total sales	$1,000,000	100.0
Cost of sales		
Food	$ 320,000	40.0
Beverage	50,000	25.0
Total cost of sales	$ 370,000	37.0
Gross profit		
Food	$ 480,000	60.0
Beverage	150,000	75.0
Total gross profit	$ 630,000	63.0
Operating expenses		
Salaries and wages	$ 260,000	26.0
Employee benefits	40,000	4.0
Occupancy costs	57,000	5.7
Direct operating expense	50,000	5.0
Music and entertainment	2,000	0.2
Marketing	20,000	2.0
Utility services	40,000	4.0
Depreciation	20,000	2.0
General and administrative	35,000	3.8
Repairs and maintenance	20,000	2.0
Other income	(1,000)	(.10)
Total operating expenses	$ 546,000	54.6
Operating income	$ 84,000	8.4
Interest	$ 10,000	1.0
Income before income taxes	$ 74,000	7.4
Income taxes	$ 11,000	1.2
Net income	$ 63,000	6.3
Retained earnings, beginning of this period	$ 101,600	
Less dividends	($ 20,100)	
Retained earnings, end of period	$ 144,500	

Utility services include fuel costs, light bulbs, water, removal of waste, engineer supplies, and ice and refrigeration supplies. Comparable figures can be very helpful in analyzing an operation.

General and administrative expenses are overhead expenses not directly connected with the service and comfort of customers. Included in this category are telephone, postage, office supplies, data-processing costs, outside accounting and legal assistance, liability and other general insurance, credit card commissions, cash shortages, and provisions for accounts receivable that may not be able to be collected.

Repairs and maintenance are self-explanatory (except that repairs and maintenance expenses paid by a landlord would be classified under "rent and other occupation costs"). Total operating expenses together with raw food and beverage costs are those costs over which a manager has some control, excluding depreciation. Expenses such as occupancy, depreciation, and taxes are usually of a fixed-type nature, and a unit operation manager has little control over them even though they are now listed as operating costs.

Occupancy costs are expenses necessary to present the premises to the management ready to operate. Included in this category are rent, real estate taxes, and property insurance. These costs are usually beyond the control of unit management. The dollar cost of the physical assets, financing arrangements, interest rates, and rent all result from the type of structure built or acquired. These costs are considered fixed overhead and cannot readily be changed. A major problem for many foodservice operators is excessive rent. Rent figures may or may not be expressed as net of insurance, net of property taxes, and net of maintenance costs. (These are referred to as "net net net leases.") Rent costs may also include a percentage of sales. Before signing a lease, the operator should check that cash flow or profit will be adequate for the rent required and what renewal terms will be.

Every physical object incurs wear and tear and may become obsolete. If one does not consider this expense, profits are overstated since they are an actual cost even if not paid out every month. An operator without funds set aside for depreciation expenses can be in difficulty to supply replacements. **Depreciation** (or *capital cost recovery*) is defined as the systematic and rational means by which the costs associated with the acquisition and installation of an asset are allocated over the estimated useful life of an asset. Different assets will have different estimated lives. The Tax Reform Act of 1986 lists eight classes of depreciable property based on anticipated life under the accelerated cost recovery system (ACRS). These are based on the type of asset and its anticipated life. A foodservice operator might use a required depreciation method for tax calculation but choose another for other types of statement preparation, such as a regular income statement. Besides the ACRS, other methods of depreciation include straight-line depreciation, with or without a consideration of salvage; declining-balance depreciation; sum-of-the-digits depreciation; and units-of-production depreciation. For more specific information on these methods, refer to an accounting text. Since depreciation is a noncash but tax-deductible expense, depreciation moneys are available to the operation in its cash flow even though they are shown as an expense and are tax deductible.

Interest is the cost of using borrowed capital, and interest costs can vary tremendously. An operation with a mortgage on its property will have interest costs that an operation that rents its property or has no mortgage does not have. Whether or not the operating equipment is leased can affect interest costs.

Although not shown in Table 20.1, other additions or deductions from net income may occur. Included in this category could be

- income or losses on sale of equipment,
- income from outside investments,
- judgments or settlements of claims, and
- tax refunds or assessments.

These are shown in the Statement of Cash Flows and since these are atypical and often one-time occurrences, it is not feasible to convert the amount to a percentage of sales.

Taxes.   Taxes are a cost of doing business every profit-making operation must pay. If the operation is a proprietorship or partnership, the taxable income would be included with the owner's other taxable income (or losses) and the taxes paid by the owners personally. If the operation is a corporation, it must pay state corporation taxes and federal income taxes. Taxes must be paid and records kept for those taxes. Types of taxes include:

- *Income taxes.* These can be federal, state, or local.
- *Sales taxes.* Most states have some sort of sales and use tax. Although the sales tax is paid by customers, it is collected by sellers.
- *Property taxes.* Real property taxes can be a major expense and may be imposed by state or local jurisdictions. They are based on assessed value of the property. If an owner believes the assessments are too high, an appeal can be made.
- *Personal property taxes.* This could include such categories as kitchen equipment and improvements, small wares such as china, glassware, and dining room equipment, and construction in progress. The tax is often based on an assessment of a certain date. It might be profitable to acquire property after that date and delete obsolete equipment from the list. Record keeping of the covered items is important.
- *Payroll taxes.* Payroll taxes can be considered in two categories. One is tax money that is withheld from employees' paychecks and then paid by the employer. These are taxes paid by the employee (the employee must match the FICA taxes). The other payroll taxes are such as federal unemployment insurance, workers' compensation, and unemployment compensation. Since workers' compensation is usually based on accident expense, the employer should for tax (and other) reasons have as safe a premises as possible. Federal unemployment insurance (FUTA) is also based on claims experience. It behooves an employer to contest what it believes to be groundless unemployment claims from employees who voluntarily leave.

Balance Sheet

An example of a balance sheet appears in Table 20.2. The balance sheet portrays the financial condition of the business at a particular day or time. A balance sheet is based on the **fundamental equation:**

$$\text{Assets} = \text{Liabilities} + \text{Equity}$$

One part of the balance sheet shows the assets—things of value—owned by the operation. The other half lists all the liabilities—the debts—of the operation. The difference between the assets and liabilities is the operation's net worth, or equity.

Foodservice operations should differentiate among the values of its food, beverage, and supplies inventories. The value of food on hand depends on the type of operation. A fast-service, limited-menu operation may turn over its inventory every few days, whereas

Table 20.2
Sample Balance Sheet

Nittany Restaurant
Balance Sheet as of December 31, XXXX
(in Dollars)

Current Assets

Cash			
House banks	$ 8,500		
Cash in bank	30,000	$ 38,500	
Accounts receivable			
Customers		$ 10,000	
Inventories			
Food	$ 40,000		
Beverage	25,000		
Other	10,000	$ 75,000	
Prepaid expenses		$ 9,000	
Total current assets			$ 132,500
Fixed assets			
Land-parking lot		$120,000	
Building improvements	$700,000		
Less accumulated depreciation	$105,000	$595,000	
Furniture and fixtures	$400,000		
Less accumulated depreciation	200,000	$200,000	
Operating equipment and uniforms		$ 95,000	
Total fixed assets			$1,010,000
Other assets			45,000
Total assets			$1,187,500

Liabilities and Shareholders' Equity

Current liabilities			
Accounts payable	$145,000		
Current portion of long-term debt	50,000		
Accrued expenses	65,000		
Other current liabilities	44,000		
Total current liabilities			$ 304,000
Long-term debt (less current portion)			$ 450,000
Other noncurrent liabilities			89,000
Total liabilities			$ 843,000
Shareholders' equity			
Capital stock	$200,000		
Retained earnings end of year	144,500		
Total shareholders' equity			$ 344,500
Total liabilities and shareholders' equity			$1,187,500

an operation that serves a varied menu and has widely spaced deliveries may have an extremely slow inventory turnover. Food inventory turnover is determined by dividing the value of the food inventory into the cost of the goods sold. If the food inventory figure is $40,000 and the cost of goods sold is $320,000 per year, the inventory turnover is eight times per year. A turnover of three, four, or five times a month is usual for many operations. But too high a turnover may mean that the operation is living from hand to mouth, which may be expensive. If cash is short, for example, too high a turnover may indicate that the operation cannot afford to buy in sufficient quantities. It may also signify that the operation cannot secure credit from purveyors, which limits its competitive buying power.

On the other hand, too slow an inventory turnover can indicate that management is not turning over this asset fast enough to attain its highest profitability potential but is instead incurring the extra costs involved in protracted storage. It may also indicate that the inventory is loaded with old merchandise that cannot be moved. It is helpful to examine the storeroom shelves to see if there is a large quantity of old, unusable merchandise still carried at purchase value.

Alcoholic beverage inventory turnover must also be evaluated. The rate of turnover here will be affected by the overall volume of business, the amount of slow-moving "show" merchandise, and the volume of beer sold.

Fixed Assets. The major fixed assets usually include land and buildings, if the operation owns its premises. If an operation does not own its premises but has made improvements to them, the improvements are shown as leasehold improvements. Land is not considered to be depreciable, although it can change in value.

Liabilities and Shareholders' Equity. *Current liabilities* are obligations that will become due within one year. Accounts payable usually make up the bulk of this item. Accrued payroll is a current liability.

Long-term debt, once called fixed liabilities, is those obligations or parts of obligations that will not be paid during the current year. It can include mortgages payable, bonds payable, long-term notes payable, and equipment contracts payable. The portion of these debts payable in one year appears under current liabilities.

The shareholders' equity nomenclature in the table indicates that the operation is owned by a corporation that has issued shares of stock. An operation owned by one proprietor or by two or more partners could have its equity expressed by the term *capital account.*

Retained earnings represent profits kept in the business rather than distributed to the owners as dividends or withdrawals. The format for retained earnings that may be part of the statement of income is

> Retained earnings at the beginning of period

+ Net earnings

= Total

− Dividends or profits dispersed during period

= Retained earnings at end of period

Table 20.3
Statement of Cash Flows (Direct Method)

Nittany Restaurant Statement of Cash Flows (Direct Method) For Year Ending December 31, XXXX	
CASH FLOWS FROM OPERATING ACTIVITIES:	
Cash received from customers	$996,000
Cash paid to suppliers and employees	(906,400)
Interest costs	(10,000)
Income taxes paid	(11,100)
Net cash provided by operating activities	$ 68,500
CASH FLOWS FROM INVESTING ACTIVITIES:	
From sale of equipment	$1,000
Payment for new equipment	(15,000)
Net cash used in investing activities	($ 14,000)
CASH FLOWS FROM FINANCING ACTIVITIES:	
Payment on long-term debt	($ 18,000)
Dividends paid	(20,000)
Net cash provided by financing activities	($ 38,000)
Net increase (decrease) in cash	$ 16,500
Cash, beginning of period	$ 22,500
Cash, end of period	$ 38,500

Statement of Cash Flows

The statement of income and retained earnings shows the profit or loss over a specified period and the balance sheet shows the financial position of the operation on a specific date, but neither shows the inflow and outflow of funds, which is very important information to the management and ownership. There are many differences between an income statement and a cash flow statement. For example, depreciation is shown as an expense on the income statement but since no payment is regularly made, it does not affect the cash position. A major expense may be incurred and paid at one time but charged off over a period of years on the income statement. Additional capital may be secured, which is not reflected on the income statement. Although cash is shown as a current asset on the balance sheet, there is no indication how the cash position was calculated.

The statement of cash flows shows cash receipts and cash payments in three categories although some listings in the category may not be appropriate for individual operations.

The cash flows in the operating category come from the sale of goods and services of the operation that produce net income but not from transactions that are defined as investing or financing. Cash flows in the investing category come from making and collecting loans and acquiring and dispensing of fixed assets. Cash flows from financing activities come from resources from owners such as issuing more stock, loans or repayment of loans by owners, and payment of profits or dividends to owners.

The statement of cash flows can be prepared in two ways, which differ in how the cash flows from operating activities are treated. The **direct method** shows operating cash

Table 20.4
Statement of Cash Flows (Indirect Method)

Nittany Restaurant
Statement of Cash Flows (Indirect Method)
For Year Ending December 31, XXXX

CASH FLOWS FROM OPERATING ACTIVITIES:	
Net income	$62,900
Adjustments to reconcile net income to net cash provided by operating activities:	
Depreciation and amortization	$11,000
Provision for doubtful accounts	200
Loss on sale of equipment	500
Change in assets and liabilities:	
Decrease in accounts receivable	1,000
Increase in inventory	(1,200)
Increase in prepaid expenses	(400)
Increase in accounts payable and accrued expenses	2,200
Increase in interest and income taxes payable	300
Decrease in other liabilities	(8,000)
Total adjustments	$ 5,600
Net cash provided by operating activities	$68,500
CASH FLOWS FROM INVESTING ACTIVITIES:	
From sale of equipment	$ 1,000
Payment for new equipment	(15,000)
Net cash used in investing activities	($14,000)
CASH FLOWS FROM FINANCING ACTIVITIES:	
Payment on long-term debt	($18,000)
Dividends paid	(20,000)
Net cash provided by financing activities	($38,000)
Net increase (decrease) in cash	$16,500
CASH, BEGINNING OF PERIOD	$22,000
CASH, END OF PERIOD	$38,500
Supplemental disclosures of cash flow information	
Cash paid during the year for:	
Interest (net of amount capitalized)	$10,000
Income taxes	11,100

receipts and payments, the sum of which is the cash flow from operating activities. The **indirect method** adjusts the net income for revenue and expense items that were not the result of operating costs. Either method is acceptable from an accounting standpoint. The indirect method, while simpler to prepare, requires more explanatory information. Probably more foodservice firms use the direct method. The investing and financial sections are the same in either method. Table 20.3 shows a format for a cash flow statement using the direct method. Table 20.4 shows a cash flow statement using the indirect method.

INDUSTRY INSIGHTS   by Jim Sullivan

Jim Sullivan is an award-winning trainer and restaurateur.

THE BIGGER TRUTHS OF THIS BUSINESS

I've been in the business 28 years, a relatively ancient amount of time in this turbo-changing industry. Along the way, I've helped open and operate 184 restaurants for someone else, owned six of my own, supervised hundreds of hourlies, and trained thousands of operators. I can honestly say that after all this experience, I've only learned one thing for sure: Any dope with a checkbook can buy a restaurant. It's what you do afterwards that matters.

On the seminar circuit I meet and literally talk to tens of thousands of owners, operators, and managers every year. Many of them try to get my advice on how to solve their most pressing challenges on topics ranging from turnover to marketing to cash flow to site selection. And while I sincerely empathize with each and every one of their concerns, the sad truth is that there are no quick solutions. Still, while there are no quick fixes, there are bigger truths in this business that, when properly applied, can produce better results for every restaurant operator, big or small.

I've spent months articulating these thoughts and humbly offer them up to my fellow servants of the industry. Read 'em and reap.

- There is no "labor crisis." It's a turnover crisis. Focus your energies on keeping your people and you won't have to worry about finding new ones.
- Keep it fresh, keep it focused, remember to say thank you. These 11 key words keep your good people with you and keep your customers coming back.
- The difference between restaurant reality and fiction is simple. Fiction has to make sense.
- Next time you hear that everyone's buying a certain restaurant stock, ask who's selling.
- Don't spend too much time beating up your vendors on price when you could be training your staff to sell more and serve better. I've never met a restaurateur who "saved himself" to profitability.

The factors that change the cash position of a restaurant are profit (or loss, depreciation), investing activities including purchasing or selling long-term physical assets, and short-term financing, which includes long-term borrowing and funds to and from owners. Factors that can affect the operating income besides depreciation include changes in:

- accounts receivable
- inventory
- prepaid expenses
- accounts payable
- accrued expenses
- interest
- income taxes payable

Cash flow analysis is important. A foodservice operation can have plenty of cash from investments by owners, sale of assets, or loans, etc. but be losing money and headed for disaster. Another operation may be very successful but short of funds, especially if

- Make it idiot proof and somebody will make a better idiot. The difference between genius and stupidity is that genius has its limits.
- We don't own our restaurants. The customer does. We work for our customers because if we don't satisfy them, somebody else will. And when we're done working for them, we work for our employees.
- How do you make a small fortune in the restaurant business? Start with a large one.
- Torture the hell out of numbers and they'll confess to anything.
- People want economy and they will pay any price to get it.—*Lee Iacocca*
- When someone gets something for nothing, someone else gets nothing for something.
- Don't ever practice on the guest.
- Our real bottom line is not how much we get from our customers, but rather how much they get from us.
- The customer is not always right, because that would mean the employee is always wrong. Keep in mind, though, it's all right for the customer to be wrong.
- The two words *information* and *communication* are often used interchangeably, but they signify quite different things. Information is giving out;

communication is getting through. Make training fun, experiential, and interactive. What we learn with pleasure we never forget.
- Different is not always better, but better is always different. I don't know the key to success, but the key to failure is trying to please everybody.
- Last but not least, you want the best piece of advice I could give for running a successful operation? Here it is: the most powerful weapon on earth is the human soul on fire. If you're no longer driven, find a new way to steer your business. If you're no longer passionate, rediscover the romance of hospitality. If you've lost the spark, let the sheer *joie de vivre* of this business relight your fire. You're never a loser until you quit trying.

If your employees and customers are anything like ours, they smell complacency and inertia. Then they go somewhere else. They'd rather work for or patronize the inspired leader, the single person carrying a blowtorch, than a half a dozen uninspired people holding candles.

This column is reprinted with permission from *Restaurant Hospitality,* December 1998.

there is rapid growth. The cash funds analysis can show when more funds will be needed, allowing different alternatives to be investigated or if and when funds can be taken out of the business by owners. It shows where the funds have been derived and indicates whether they will be forthcoming from these sources in the future. The statement of cash flows ties in with cash budgeting described in Chapter 23.

ANALYZING FINANCIAL STATEMENTS

Different analysts may examine financial statements for different purposes. A banker may analyze a statement to see if enough potential earnings exist to repay a loan or if sufficient assets exist to provide security for a loan. An investor may analyze the statement to estimate the rate of return on the investment, the chances for the investment to appreciate, and the projected earnings. A purveyor may check a statement before extending credit. Management looks at financial statements to determine the profitability of its operation. Management may also use a financial statement to judge the efficiency of its operation, to determine where its costs have gotten out of line, and to make basic management decisions.

The analysis of a financial statement is basically a comparison process. The amounts, for example, may be expressed as a percentage of sales. These percentages may then be compared with prior percentages, projected percentages, general industry percentages, percentages released by trade associations or specialized accounting firms, or budgeted percentages.

TYPES OF FINANCIAL ANALYSIS

There are three general types of financial analysis:

- comparative analysis, sometimes called horizontal analysis,
- common size analysis, sometimes called vertical analysis, and
- ratio analysis, which separates ratios into different classifications or formulas such as liquidity, solvency, activity or operating, and profitability.

Comparative Analysis

Comparative analysis shows the dollar difference in line items on statements for two or more financial periods (income statement) or for two or more financial dates (balance sheet) and the percentage changes. Table 20.5 illustrates this by using the income statements of the Nittany Restaurant for the current year XXX2 and the preceding year XXX1.

In analyzing the XXX1 and XXX2 comparative income statement, we note that total revenue increased an anemic $40,000, or 4.2 percent ($40,000 ÷ 960,000). The food revenue increase of $50,000 was adversely affected by a $10,000 (4.8 percent) decrease in beverage revenue. Management would surely investigate to determine the reason for this drop. In the cost of sales for food, there was an increase of $35,000 (12.3 percent). This indicates that food cost increases were greater than the increase in dollar food sales. Beverage costs increased $4,000 or (8.7 percent). How this could happen with a 4.8 percent decrease in beverage sales is a critical question. The small increase in sales and the higher food and beverage costs lead to an almost identical gross profit.

Under operating expenses, salaries and wages increased $10,000 (4.0 percent), which is close to the increase in revenues. Employee benefits, as expected, were higher but appropriate for the salaries-and-wages figure. The direct operating expenses increase of 4.1 percent is in line with revenue increases and less than the increase in food revenue, which is positive. Direct operating expenses are usually higher for food revenue than beverage revenue. Music and entertainment remained the same. Energy, administrative and general, and repairs and maintenance all increased by a higher percentage than did revenue. Total operating expenses were $40,000 (7.9 percent) higher. This is higher than the 4.8 percent increase in revenues and led to a $39,000 or (31.7 percent) decrease in income before operating income. Provision for income tax was lower by 60.7 percent, but unfortunately this was due to lower taxable income. Net income was lower by $24,000 despite the 4.8 percent increase in total revenue.

Often, a comparative income statement analysis shows where costs are out of line and what corrective action should be taken. However, there may be reasons that are beyond the control of management. The above bad situation could have been caused by a recession that limited management's ability to raise selling prices even though its own

Table 20.5
Sample Comparative Income Statement

	Nittany Restaurant **Comparative Income Statement** **December 31, XXX1 and XXX2**			
	XXX1	**XXX2**	**Difference ($)**	**Difference (%)**
Sales				
Food	$750,000	$ 800,000	$50,000	6.7
Beverage	210,00	200,00	(10,000)	(4.8)
Total sales	$960,000	$1,000,000	$40,000	4.2
Cost of sales				
Food	$285,000	$ 320,000	$35,000	12.3
Beverage	46,000	50,000	4,000	8.7
Total cost of sales	$331,000	$ 370,000	$39,000	14.8
Gross profits	$629,000	$ 630,000	$ 1,000	0.02
Total income	$629,000	$ 630,000	$ 1,000	0.02
Operating expenses				
Salaries and wages	$250,000	260,000	10,000	4.0
Employee benefits	37,000	40,000	3,000	8.1
Occupancy costs	60,000	57,000	(3,000)	(5.0)
Direct operating expenses	48,000	50,000	2,000	4.1
Music and entertainment	2,000	2,000	0	0
Marketing	20,000	20,000	0	0
Utility services	36,000	40,000	4,000	11.8
Depreciation	20,000	20,000	0	0
General and administrative	34,000	38,000	4,000	11.8
Repairs and maintenance	18,000	20,000	2,000	11.1
Other income	(1,000)	(1,000)	0	0
Total operating expenses	$506,000	$ 546,000	$40,000	7.9
Operating income	$123,000	$ 84,000	($39,000)	(31.7)
Interest	10,000	10,000	0	0
Income b/income taxes	$113,000	$ 74,000	($39,000)	(34.5)
Income taxes	28,000	11,000	(17,000)	(60.7)
Net income	$ 87,000	$ 63,000	($24,000)	(17.5)

operating costs increased. An alcohol awareness program and a switch to less profitable drinks could be largely responsible for the decrease in beverage sales and increase in beverage costs.

Common Size Analysis

Common size analysis of statements is performed by dividing each item on two or more statements by the total revenue for the respective year. Table 20.6 illustrates this for the Nittany Restaurant. Analyzing the table reinforces the findings from the comparative statements.

Table 20.6
Sample Common Size Income Statement

			Common Size ($)	Common Size (%)
	XXX1	**XXX2**		
Sales				
Food	$750,000	$ 800,000	78.1	80.0
Beverage	210,000	200,000	21.9	20.0
Total sales	$960,000	$1,000,000	100.0	100.0
Cost of sales				
Food	$285,000	$ 320,000	38.0	40.0
Beverage	46,000	50,000	21.9	25.0
Total cost of sales	$331,000	$ 370,000	34.5	37.0
Gross profits	$629,000	$ 630,000	65.5	63.0
Operating expenses				
Salaries and wages	$250,000	260,000	26.0	26.0
Employee benefits	37,000	40,000	3.9	4.0
Occupancy costs	60,000	57,000	6.8	5.7
Direct operating expenses	48,000	50,000	5.0	5.0
Music and entertainment	2,000	2,000	0.2	0.2
Marketing	20,000	20,000	2.0	2.0
Utility services	36,000	40,000	3.6	4.0
Depreciation	20,000	20,000	2.0	2.0
General and administrative	34,000	38,000	3.4	3.5
Repairs and maintenance	18,000	20,000	2.0	2.0
Other income	(1,000)	(1,000)	(1.0)	(1.0)
Total operating expenses	$506,000	$ 546,000	52.7	54.6
Operating income	$123,000	$ 84,000	12.8	8.4
Interest	10,000	10,000	1.0	1.0
Income b/income taxes	$113,000	$ 74,000	11.8	7.4
Income taxes	28,000	11,000	29.2	1.1
Net income	$ 85,000	$ 63,000	9.1	6.3

Nittany Restaurant
Sample Common Size Income Statement
December 31, XXX1 and XXX2

The more profitable beverage sales percentages are lower in comparison to food sales. The cost-of-sales percentage is higher. (In common statement analysis, comparing the cost of food and beverage to total sales rather than to food and beverage sales can be distorting since the relationship is with either the food or the beverage sales and not total sales.) The gross profit percentage is accordingly lower. The controllable expenses have inched up by 2 percentage points. The net result has a net income percentage of 6.3 percent compared to the previous year's 9.1 percent.

Ratio Analysis

Ratios can be separated into different classifications or formulas such as liquidity, solvency, activity or operating, and profitability.

Liquidity Ratios.   **Liquidity ratios** show the organization's ability to meet its short-term obligations. Banks and creditors can be very interested in this data for determining whether an operation's short-term debt can be repaid. Managers should be concerned about liquidity. If it is a problem, they may seek more capital long-term debt or take less out of the business.

Common liquidity ratios include the **current ratio** (current assets/current liabilities). This shows how **current assets**, defined as cash or assets that are readily turned into cash, can be used to cover **current liabilities**, which are defined as debts that must be paid within the next 12 months. From Table 20.2, the current ratio for the Nittany Restaurant as of December XXXX is $132,500/$304,000 = 0.44 to 1.

The current ratio indicates how well an operation can pay off its short-term creditors and is therefore an indication of financial strength. In many businesses a ratio of 2 to 1 is considered desirable. However, in foodservice operations it is often closer to 1 to 1. Factors that cause this lower ratio are lack of accounts receivable, relatively small inventories, and a fast inventory turnover. By living on the credit of their purveyors, some operations exist on less than a 1 to 1 ratio, but this practice can hardly be recommended. The 0.44 to 1 ratio is too low.

The current ratio can be misleading. By incurring long-term debt, an operation may receive more cash and improve its current ratio, but its overall financial position remains unchanged. Too high a current ratio may indicate that management is not turning over its current assets or not using them in other ways to the best advantage.

The dollar difference between current assets and current liabilities is the working capital. If this amount is limited, there will be a high turnover. (Turnover is determined by dividing the amount of working capital into sales.) Excessive turnover indicates a shortage of working capital, which could cause severe problems in a financial emergency and which limits purchasing and bill-paying capability. A slow turnover indicates that working capital may be excessive and is therefore not being used to its best advantage.

The **acid test ratio**, also called the **quick ratio**, is cash, accounts receivable, and marketable securities divided by current liabilities. This ratio gives an even better indication of how readily current debts can be paid off, since inventory and prepaid expenses (which can be harder to convert to cash) are removed from current assets. Calculations for the Nittany Restaurant would be 48,500/304,000 = 0.16. This again is very low and indicates the operation may have a cash flow or liquidity problem.

The accounts receivable ratios tell how well accounts receivable are being managed. Accounts receivable represent the amounts customers owe the operation. Operations with sales strictly on a cash basis will have no regular accounts receivable. Others may allow their customers to charge meals. This is, of course, an added expense to the operation because it does not have immediate use of the money owed to it, and it incurs extra bookkeeping costs, interest expenses, and possibility of bad debts. An operation needs to determine if these costs outweigh the increased sales to be gained by providing this service. The increased use of credit cards has greatly affected the accounts receivable in many operations. For a commission, the credit card company assumes these costs and risks. A large banquet or business function, for example, can vastly increase accounts receivable. One can evaluate accounts receivable in terms of their turnover, average collection period, percentage to sales, and the number of sales days tied up in accounts receivable. The following formula shows **accounts receivable turnover**. The faster the turnover, the better.

$$\text{Accounts receivable turnover} = \frac{\text{Total sales}}{\text{Average accounts receivable}}$$

If total sales are $1 million for the period and accounts receivable are $10,000, the calculations would be $1 million divided by $10,000, or 100. The period can be for a week, a month or a year.

The average collection period formula is

$$\text{Average collection period} = \frac{365 \text{ days}}{\text{Accounts receivable turnover}}$$

If the turnover is 100, the average collection period would be 365 divided by 100, or 3.65. The shorter the collection period, the better the operation is controlling its accounts receivable. Sometimes an analysis is made of the number of days of sales tied up in accounts receivable. For example, an operation that averages $500 in daily sales and has $2,000 in accounts receivable would have 4 days of sales tied up in its accounts receivable. Sudden and marked changes in the character of the accounts receivable are as important as the total amount of money in the accounts receivable. If the percentage of accounts receivable to sales, or the number of days of sales represented by accounts receivable, should increase suddenly or considerably, there is cause for immediate investigation. The "quality" of the receivables is defined by the willingness of customers owing to pay promptly, and this quality may be determined by aging the receivables. Assume total accounts receivable are $2,000; the following chart helps establish the quality of these accounts receivable.

Aging Accounts Receivable
Balance in Each
Classification
Summarized from
Individual Accounts

Classification by Due Date	Dollars	Percentage	Expected Percentage Uncollectible	Estimated Uncollectible Amount
Not yet due	$1,200	60.0%	1%	$12.00
Less than 30 days past due	350	17.5%	5%	17.50
31–60 days past due	300	15.0%	10%	30.00
61–120 days past due	150	7.5%	10%	15.00
Over 120 days past due	—	—	—	—
Total	$2,000	100.0%	—	$74.50

Normally, the longer the accounts are past due, the less the chance of eventual collection. It may be desirable, then, to create a reserve for doubtful accounts so that the net accounts receivable figure will be more accurate.

Accounts receivable from established credit card operations normally do not present a problem except for commissions paid to the credit card companies. Accounts receivable from employees usually are individual situations and are therefore analyzed differently.

Solvency Ratios. Whereas liquidity ratios are used to evaluate how well a company can meet its short-term obligations, **solvency ratios** indicate how well the company can meet its long-term debt requirements. They also can be used to indicate the amount of leverage. **Leveraging** is the use of borrowed money to make more money for the operation. Leveraging is a way to make a lot of money in good times. In bad times, an operation can be overleveraged and cannot meet debt requirements on the borrowed money; in this situation, very serious problems can result. One solvency ratio is comparing total assets to total liabilities.

Using Table 20.2, total assets to total liabilities = $1,187,500/ $843,000 = 1.41. This indicates that total assets are 1.41 times total liabilities for the Nittany Restaurant. The difference between total assets and total liabilities is shareholders' (or owners') equity. A highly leveraged operation will have a lower ratio. Normal ratios are usually between 1.5 and 2.0.

A second solvency ratio is total liabilities to total assets, which expresses in reverse the previous ratio. For the Nittany Restaurant on December 31, XXXX, this figure is $843,000/$1,187,500 = 0.71.

Another ratio, total liabilities to total equity, compares the amount of liabilities to the financial investment of ownership. The higher the ratio, the more leveraged the operation. For the Nittany Restaurant, it would be $843,000/$344,500 = 2.45. For every dollar the owners have in the operation, others have lent it $2.45, which is high.

A fourth solvency ratio compares long-term debt to total capitalization. Capitalization is long-term debt plus the ownership equity. How much of this capitalization is in long-term debt would be leverage. For the Nittany Restaurant, long-term debt/(long-term debt + owners' equity) = $450,000/$794,500 = 0.57. This is on the high side; a normal figure is 40 to 50 percent. A final solvency ratio is times interest earned, or the earnings before income taxes (EBIT)/divided by interest expense. From Table 20.1, we get $74,000/$10,000 = 7.4. This indicates that the operation can meet its interest payments with EBIT by a factor of 7.4, which gives creditors fair protection.

Operating Ratios. Operating ratios use data from the income statement and are important in cost control. For analysis purposes, one can divide a profit-and-loss statement into three parts. The first part shows sales, or the amount of business. The second shows expenses, which are subtracted from sales to provide the third category, profit. Although the three parts are related, each can be analyzed separately.

Analyzing Sales

In analyzing sales, operators want to determine several things. Are sales increasing or decreasing? If so, why? They may also want to know if the sales are appropriate to the value of the physical facilities, the number of seats for the operation, or the size of the investment in it.

A yearly sales increase or decrease is shown by comparative figures, and it is important to know the makeup of sales. The number of customers served in each period can be significant. If alcoholic beverages are sold, total sales should be broken down to show their contribution. If other merchandise is handled, it should be separated. Sales may be broken down into the different meal periods so that each meal can be examined separately. Total sales for the current year and for past years can be shown in this way.

Although dollar sales have shown an increase each year in the following example (Table 20.7), the amount is small and probably reflects higher selling prices attributable to higher costs. There may in fact have been a decrease in real volume.

Sales may also be compared on a monthly basis. The current month could be compared with the past four months, or with any other appropriate period. Such a sales comparison appears in Table 20.8.

Table 20.9 shows a format using a comparative income approach to compare sales for different periods. The current period could be this month compared with the same month last year, or this week compared with the same week last month, or any period that seems appropriate. Often year-to-date (YTD) figures for the current year are compared with these from the previous year. The format shows not only dollar changes but also percentage increases or decreases.

Table 20.7
Yearly Sales Analysis

	Year X		Year X + 1		Year X + 2	
	Amount	Ratio to Sales	Amount	Ratio to Sales	Amount	Ratio to Sales
Net food sales	$ 800,000	80%	$ 820,000	77.4%	$ 840,000	76.4%
Net beverage sales	$ 200,000	20%	$ 240,000	22.6%	$ 260,000	23.6%
Net sales	$1,000,000	100%	$1,060,000	100.0%	$1,100,000	100.0%

Table 20.8
Monthly Sales Comparison

	Current month			Last month		
	Food Sales	Covers	Average Check	Food Sales	Covers	Average Check
Breakfast	$ 5,600	1,068	$ 5.24	$ 5,300	1,108	$ 4.78
Lunch	$26,000	2,210	$11.76	$24,500	2,194	$11.67
Dinner	$35,400	2,020	$17.50	$36,900	2,045	$18.04
Total	$67,000	5,298	$12.65	$66,700	5,347	$12.47

Table 20.9
Sales Comparison for Different Periods

	Current Period	Previous Period	Amount of Increase or Decrease	Percentage of Increase or Decrease
Net food sales	$800,000	$750,000	$50,000	6.67%
Net beverage sales	$200,000	$210,000	($10,000)	(4.76%)

If food sales are increasing, it is desirable to know why they are on the rise. Increases can reflect one or both of two factors: more menu items served or higher prices received per cover. An operation may be showing an increase in sales while serving fewer customers. Dollar volume may rise while customer volume declines. This information is determined from recording the number of covers served. Dividing this number into sales provides the amount of the average check, a very significant figure because it indicates whether prices have increased enough to absorb costs. If sales are decreasing, it is most important to discover why. It is usually desirable to analyze each meal, or even each menu item, separately. Perhaps one segment of the business, such as breakfast, is unprofitable. Discontinuing it may lower sales, but the profit may nevertheless rise. The question is whether the contribution to overhead and profit is increased. Generally, decreasing sales are serious in a period when all costs are rising.

SALES ANALYSIS RATIOS

One can use a number of ratios to analyze the sales of a foodservice operation. It is usually best to calculate the following ratios separately for each meal period.

Average Check

This is perhaps the most basic ratio and is found by dividing sales by the number of customers.

$$\text{Average check} = \frac{\text{Sales}}{\text{Number of customers}}$$

This ratio is especially helpful in revealing trends in a particular operation. If the average check is lower than the presumed normal, perhaps different menu items or more dessert and appetizer promotion could cause an increase. There is, after all, a danger in driving customers away if prices are too high for the market.

Seat Turnover

This ratio indicates how well an operation is filling its dining facilities. A low turnover means that more customers are needed or can be accommodated. A high turnover can indicate need for expansion. The ratio is found by dividing the number of customers per meal by the number of seats available.

$$\text{Seat turnover} = \frac{\text{Number of customers}}{\text{Number of seats}}$$

Sales per Square Foot

Retail sales establishments use this ratio to determine the amount of revenue from every square foot of sales space. It is especially helpful when alternative uses for the footage—such as serving space, take-out order space, or perhaps outside sales of food items such as bakery items prepared by the operation—present themselves.

$$\text{Sales per square foot} = \frac{\text{Sales}}{\text{Number of square feet}}$$

ANALYZING EXPENSES

Since controllable expenses are related to sales, the normal procedure in analyzing an expense is to calculate the expense item as a ratio to sales. The sales figure is considered 100 percent, and the amount of the expense divided by the sales figure will give the expense percentage. So, if salaries and wages are $270,000, and food sales are $1 million, the labor-cost percentage is 27 percent.

$$\frac{\text{Salaries and wages}}{\text{Food sales}} = \frac{\$270,000}{\$1,000,000} = 27.0$$

The amounts of various expense items are difficult to analyze by themselves, but as a percentage of sales they become more meaningful. A considerable increase in one particular expense over a previous period could be cause for concern. However, a proportionate increase in sales would alleviate any cause for alarm.

Analyzing Cost Percentages

The cost percentages of the various expense categories can be compared with percentages for similar periods in the history of the same operation, with budgeted percentages, with goals set by management, or with industry averages. Table 20.10 supplies the industry data from the 1997 *Restaurant Advisory Services Pennsylvania Report* that one might use for these comparisons. The full study provides very detailed figures for types, sizes, geographical locations, ages, and types of ownership. Table 20.11 suggests a format managers can use to analyze foodservice operations. For the meal period, it might be better for some operations to divide the day into time periods rather than by specific meal—breakfast, lunch, or dinner. Sales, number of customers, and employee-hours can readily be determined from point-of-sales registers or other means. From this information the average check, dollar sales per seat, turnover per seat, customers served per employee-hour and dollar sales per employee-hour can readily be determined. Many POS registers can provide these calculations. Figure 20.12 analyzes sales and amount per seat if beverages are served.

In comparing the cost category percentage figure of the present period with past periods, an operator should notice all trends, especially upward ones. These might indicate some lack of control in the area under analysis. Sharp variations both upward and downward should be resolved. If utility costs have remained a constant percentage for a period of time, for example, a sudden increase or decrease calls for an immediate explanation.

Table 20.10
Ratio to Total Sales and Amount Per Seat by Sales Volume**

	Ratio to Total Sales**				Amount Per Seat***			
	Under $500	$500–$999	$1,000–$1,999	$2000 & Over	Under $500	$500–$999	$1,000–$1,999	$2,000 & Over
Sales								
Food	75.8%	87.7%	79.5%	83.0%	$2,495	$5,553	$5,199	$9,429
Beverage	24.2	12.3	19.4	16.5	179	500	1,005	1,187
Total	100.0	100.0	100.0	100.0	3,668	6,453	6,588	10,091
Cost of sales								
Food	41.3	33.6	36.0	33.6	815	1,570	1,733	2,837
Beverage(1)	38.4	35.9	31.0	30.6	453	334	369	518
Total	39.8	34.5	34.2	33.3	1,396	1,865	2,109	3,059
Total gross profit	60.2	65.5	65.8	66.7	2,058	4,498	4,484	7,320
Other income	0.1	0.5	0.5	0.0	3	31	30	0
Total income	60.2	66.2	69.2	67.0	2,109	4,541	4,545	7,320
Controllable expenses								
Payroll	24.5	30.9	31.3	31.7	751	1,841	1,785	2,832
Employee benefits	3.7	7.0	6.4	6.7	120	366	339	617
Direct operating expenses	4.0	5.3	4.9	5.3	121	347	263	593
Music and entertainment	0.0	0.1	0.0	0.0	0	3	0	0
Advertising and promotion	1.1	1.4	2.9	1.7	33	65	143	136
Utilities	4.7	4.0	4.2	2.3	165	272	179	270
Administrative and general	4.7	3.2	3.4	1.7	157	202	175	147
Repairs and maintenance	1.5	1.7	1.6	1.1	65	72	80	168
Total controllable expenses	47.2	53.2	54.7	53.2	1,626	3,328	3,445	5,240
Income before occupation costs	14.8	13.1	12.3	13.8	440	632	622	1,419
Occupation costs								
Rent(2)	4.1	5.9	6.7	6.1	98	375	337	789
Mortgage interest(2)	0.7	7.1	0.6	0.5	30	362	20	116
Property taxes	1.8	0.9	0.7	0.6	80	60	26	50
Other taxes	0.8	0.4	0.1	0.3	24	13	8	31
Property insurance	1.6	0.8	1.2	1.0	10	40	62	140
Total occupation costs	3.9	7.0	6.5	8.2	110	468	332	807
Income before interest & depreciation	8.3	4.6	6.9	9.0	244	281	305	1,353
Interest	0.4	0.9	0.6	0.2	13	102	27	200
Depreciation	1.5	3.6	1.5	1.9	52	204	98	193
Restaurant profit	2.7%	1.3%	4.5%	9.0%	$67	$107	$218	$1,353
Other deductions	1.5	3.9	2.1	1.9	48	242	99	279
Income before income taxes	5.0%	1.3%	2.6%	6.4%	$70	$107	$97	$944

**All amounts are medians
***Sales volumes expressed in (000's)
(1)Beverage cost calculated only for those respondents who declared beverage revenue.
(2)Survey respondents who leased their space declared rent; building owners declared mortgage interest.
Source: Restaurant Advisory Services Pennsylvania Report

Table 20.11
Restaurant Analysis Format

Meal Period	Sales ($)	Number of Customers	Number of Seats	Employee Hours	Average Check ($)	Sales per Seat ($)	Turnover per Seat	Customers Served per Employee-Hour	Sales per Employee-Hour ($)
8–11	600	150	100	20	4.00	6.00	1.5	7.5	30
11–3	1,200	200	100	30	6.00	12.00	2.0	6.7	40
3–8	800	150	100	25	5.33	8.00	1.5	6.0	32
8–11	250	100	100	10	2.50	2.50	1.0	10.0	25
Total	2,850	600	100	85	4.75	28.50	6.0	7.1	33.53

Expense categories may be classified as variable, semivariable, and fixed. Variable dollar expenses should change more or less directly with volume. Food cost is an excellent example. Semivariable expenses, such as some types of labor costs, change with sales volume, but not as directly as the variable food cost. Fixed expenses, such as administrative and general, remain relatively constant despite changes in volume. The more variable the expense, the more significant its percentage figure as related to sales.

The two largest expense categories are salary and wages and cost of food sold. These two are sometimes referred to as *prime costs*. Management should have a definite idea of what percentage of labor expense to sales it considers comfortable for its operation. If the percentage should rise above the desired ratio and selling prices are adequate, the rise could indicate the need for better labor-cost analysis and control. (Chapters 11 to 13 provide a good deal of guidance here.) The use of work production standards such as meals served per labor-hour or dollar sales per labor-hour can show where the increase is occurring. If, on the other hand, the labor-cost percentage is significantly lower than planned, the operation may be understaffed, and as a result, it may be providing substandard food and service to its patrons. Quality control is just as important as labor and food-cost control.

Food cost, as already mentioned, is one of the most variable expenses. As the number of meals changes, the total cost of food used should also change. Chapters 14 to 17 on the various aspects of food-cost control should help you learn how to combat an excessive food cost. Although the prime costs, food and labor, account for the major portion of total costs, the other categories deserve serious study. One way to keep from spending money in the short run is to defer needed repairs and upkeep and maintenance, but these savings must be made up later, perhaps at considerably higher cost. Thus, an unusual decline in expenses in this category may be suspicious.

In analyzing the cost percentages, care must be taken not to compare the percentage in question with only one standard. An operation that uses a great many convenience and prepared foods may have a high food cost, which may, however, be more than offset by lower labor costs. An operation may be willing to bear a higher than normal food cost if it believes that its low menu prices can bring in more than enough additional business to provide a higher profit despite a higher food-cost ratio. The same may hold true of relatively high entertainment and advertising costs.

In comparing the cost percentages of two operations, it is important to notice whether they are of similar types. The percentages for a fast-food hamburger stand and a

Table 20.12
Ratio to Total Sales and Amount Per Seat by Beverages Served*

	Ratio to Total Sales		Amount Per Seat	
	Food Only	Food & Beverage	Food Only	Food & Beverage
Sales				
Food	100.0%	77.0%	$6,122	$4,181
Beverage	0.0	21.9	0	1,054
Total	100.0	100.0	6,507	5,938
Cost of sales				
Food	33.8	36.0	2,082	1,291
Beverage[1]	25.5	34.5	0	365
Total	33.8	35.2	2,303	1,766
Total gross profit	66.2	64.8	4,264	3,816
Other income	0.1	0.4	2	29
Total income	66.2	66.2	4,266	3,816
Controllable expenses				
Payroll	24.6	31.3	1,608	1,703
Employee benefits	4.2	6.9	245	314
Direct operating expenses	4.1	5.3	201	283
Music and entertainment	0.0	0.1	0	1
Advertising and promotion	0.6	2.0	35	101
Utilities	4.3	4.1	259	202
Administrative and general	3.3	3.6	173	175
Repairs and maintenance	1.0	1.7	59	84
Total controllable expenses	45.0	53.4	2,822	3,280
Income before occupation costs	22.0	11.3	1,104	574
Occupation costs				
Rent[2]	6.0	5.0	305	320
Mortgage interest[2]	*	0.6	*	30
Property taxes	0.4	0.9	31	57
Other taxes	0.7	0.3	27	14
Property insurance	1.8	0.9	73	45
Total occupation costs	6.7	6.5	305	321
Income before interest & depreciation	12.3	4.7	625	198
Interest	0.5	0.6	30	24
Depreciation	1.6	2.3	79	128
Restaurant profit	10.2%	2.1%	$ 500	$ 94
Other deductions	1.6	2.6	108	114
Income before income taxes	8.0%	2.3%	$ 351	$ 91

* Insufficient response

**All amounts are medians

[1]Beverage cost calculated only for those respondents who declared beverage revenue.

[2] Survey respondents who leased their space declared rent; building owners declared mortgage interest.

Source: Restaurant Advisory Services Pennsylvania Report

luxury restaurant will vary considerably. It is also very important that each operation use the same accounting classifications. (Once again, *The Uniform System of Accounts for Restaurants* permits excellent comparisons.) The volume of sales will also affect the cost percentages, especially those in a fixed category. The administrative or general expenses may make up a certain percentage of sales. If sales double and no new expenses are incurred, that percentage figure should be cut in half. It is also important to know if menu prices are appropriate. Too-low menu prices affect sales, which affect percentages.

The controllable expenses are the most important indication of a manager's proficiency. There may be little the manager can do about occupation or depreciation expenses, but there is always a great deal that can be done about controllable expenses, such as reducing food or labor costs.

Instead of just using percentages for analyzing costs, some operations determine the cost per seat for a particular cost category. Thus, for example, energy, marketing, or occupancy costs can be divided by the number of seats to provide a cost per seat instead of the amount of the costs as a percentage of sales. This may provide a better measure for some costs than percentages. There may also be specific calculations for specific costs, such as energy cost (Btu used per meal, for example) or pieces of linen (or pounds of linen per meal).

Profitability Ratios

The third area of the statement of revenue is profit, what is left when expenses are deducted from sales. What is an appropriate profit? Apart from any ratio analysis, profit must be adequate for the business to continue and to satisfy its operators. Ratios might indicate a favorable profit, but if the operator is not satisfied with the profit and could do better in another endeavor, the profit is simply insufficient. Three ratios are often used to analyze profit: net profit to net sales, net profit to total net equity, and net profit to total assets.

Net Profit to Net Sales.   The net profit to net sales is often called the **earnings ratio**, **operating ratio**, **operating margin**, or **profit ratio**. It is found by dividing the net profit before taxes by the net sales.

$$\frac{\text{Net profit}}{\text{Net sales}} = \text{Operating ratio} = \frac{\$74,000}{\$1,000,000} = 7.4\%$$

Adaptations of this ratio include the substitution of gross profit, operating profit, or net profit after taxes for net profit before taxes. Generally, though, this ratio is the most important one used by foodservice operators, since it shows the profitability of the operation compared to the amount of sales. The higher the ratio, the more effective management has been in controlling costs. Like other ratios, the operating ratio may be used to compare different financial periods and to compare the operation's performance to that of other operations.

Net Profit to Net Equity.   Net profit (usually after taxes) to net equity represents the owner's return on the investment. Equity investment is the difference between assets and liabilities, or theoretically, the equity amount that is invested in the business. A return is expected from any investment, and the higher the investment risk, the higher the expected return. If the operator could take the money invested in the business and invest it in another business or in securities that offer a higher return at the same risk or at a smaller risk, the inclination would be to do so, assuming the first investment could be readily liquidated. In some fast-food operations with high-volume sales compared with a relatively small percentage of investments to sales, it is possible to have a low operating ratio but a high net-profit-to-equity investment percentage. The calculation of the ratio of net profit to net equity is

$$\text{Net profit to net equity} = \frac{\text{Net profit (after taxes)}}{\text{Net equity}} = \frac{\$62,900}{\$344,500} = 18.3\%$$

Net Profit to Total Assets.   The ratio of net profit to total assets is sometimes called the **management proficiency ratio.** It shows how much profit management can make with the total assets (not just the investment of net worth) at its disposal. The greater the percentage, the more proficient the management. At least this is the assumption. Following are the calculations for this ratio:

$$\text{Management proficiency ratio} = \frac{\text{Net profit (after taxes)}}{\text{Total assets}} = \frac{\$62,900}{\$1,187,500} = 5.3\%$$

Earnings per Share.   If the operation is a corporation and has issued capital stock, it can be helpful to determine the earnings for each share. If the Nittany Restaurant had 1,000 shares stock outstanding, the calculation would be $74,000/1,000 = $74.00. It is helpful to compare **earnings per share** from one year (or other financial period) to another as it shows how much is made on each share of stock. Ideally, the earnings per share increase.

RECORDS AND FORMS

In addition to the general journal and ledger systems and appropriate financial statements, a foodservice operator will probably want to keep subsidiary records (which may supply the information to the accounting system) to help in operations. Although these may vary depending on the type of operation, common ones include:

- *Daily sales and cash receipts*—This could include monies collected, type of collection (i.e., cash, credit cards, or charges), sales taxes, and adjustments. This can be reconciled with bank deposits.
- *Daily report*—This indicates total sales and type of sales such as food, bar, or gift shop. It can be further broken down such as type of beverages, regular menu or á la carte sales, sales by meal or other period. It can be prepared daily or other period.
- *Tip records*—Underreporting of tips by employees in foodservice operations has received considerable attention from the IRS, which employs different approaches to this problem. An employer with tipped employees should be aware of their liability and ways to comply with tax laws.

- *Employee payroll records*—It is very important that employee work-hours be recorded, including overtime and rate of pay. An employer must withhold federal and state income taxes paid by each employee and these must be deposited on a regular basis. It is also considered good practice to keep a file for each employee with appropriate personal information, employment information, warnings of poor performance, absences, etc. In today's environment where employees commonly sue their employers, the documented information in the file may help in a legal defense if a lawsuit develops.

- *Budgeting*—As discussed in Chapter 23, budgeting is part of good management to help determine what you anticipate to do in the future and to compare how well you have succeeded. There may be subsidiary budgets such as for food (in an institution), labor, repairs, or new equipment.

- *Control reports*—These may be specialized control reports regarding food or labor costs or other cost centers. In addition to providing dollar figure comparisons, percentages, work production standards, and other comparisons can be helpful.

- Information and formats for these reports are discussed throughout the book. Many of them can be part of a management information system and may be part of a computerized system.

SUMMARY

This chapter explains three basic accounting statements: the statement of income, which shows whether an operation has made or lost money over a specific period; the balance sheet, which portrays the financial condition of an operation at a particular time; and statement of cash flows, which shows how funds were received and dispersed. The foodservice industry is fortunate to be able to consult *The Uniform System of Accounts for Restaurants,* which provides an excellent accounting system for restaurants and also allows an operator to compare the financial performances of different types of restaurants. In addition, various restaurant industry operations reports provide figures and statistics from across the industry.

Finally, one can use a number of specific analyses, including comparative analysis, common size analysis, and ratio analysis, to evaluate one's position and the financial health of the enterprise.

KEY TERMS

accounts receivable turnover
acid test ratio
balance sheet
cash flows
common size analysis
comparative analysis
controllable expenses
cost of sales
CPA

current asset
current liability
current ratio
depreciation
direct method (cash flow)
direct operating expenses
earnings per share
earnings ratio
fundamental equation

gross profit
indirect method (cash flow)
leveraging
liquidity ratios
long-term debt
management proficiency ratio
operating margin
operating ratio

profit ratio
quick ratio
ratio analysis
solvency ratios
statement of income
Uniform System of Accounts for Restaurants
working capital

REVIEW QUESTIONS

20–1 Define *income statement* and *balance sheet*.

20–2 What are advantages of using *The Uniform System of Accounts for Restaurants?*

20–3 How does depreciation affect profit and cash flow?

20–4 Explain the fundamental accounting equation.

20–5 Provide the formula for retained earnings.

20–6 Explain what the following would look for in financial statements: a banker, an investor, a purveyor, a manager.

20–7 Explain two ratios used in analyzing sales.

20–8 How are expenses usually analyzed?

20–9 Provide three ratios used to analyze profit.

20–10 What does a slow food inventory turnover indicate?

20–11 Why is a cash flow analysis important?

PROBLEMS

20–1 Using the following information taken from the books of the Happy Valley Restaurant, prepare a statement of income for the year ending December 31, 20XX, using the approved format.

Food sales	$80,000
Food inventory, January 1, 20XX	2,500
Food purchases	31,000
Current assets	
Cash	6,000
Inventory food	1,500
Inventory supplies	500
Prepaid insurance	600
Deposit with electric company	200
Fixed assets	
Building less accumulated depreciation	22,500
Equipment less accumulated depreciation	10,500
Fixtures less accumulated depreciation	8,200
Land less accumulated depreciation	6,000
Current liabilities	
Trade accounts payable	2,200

Accrued wages payable	3,000
Accrued employee benefits payable	1,200
Mortgage payable—20XX	800
Long-term liabilities	
Notes payable to bank	14,800
Mortgage payable	8,000
Owners' capital account	
Owners' capital account, January 1, 20XX	25,000
Net profits, 20XX	10,000
Owners' withdrawals	9,000
Owners' capital account	26,000
Depreciation expense	4,000
Occupation expense	2,200
Salaries and wages	18,000
Employee benefits	1,800
Repairs and maintenance	1,200
Direct operating expense	4,800
Administrative and general	2,000
Marketing	1,600
Energy and utility service	2,400

All account balances are as of December 31, 20XX unless otherwise stated. Cost of goods sold must be calculated.

20–2 Using the preceding information, prepare a
balance sheet for the Happy Valley
Restaurant.

20–3 Using the information from the preceding
problems for the Happy Valley Restaurant,
calculate:
  a. Current ratio
  b. Operating ratio
  c. Return on investment
  d. Inventory turnover using the amount
     calculated for Problem 20-1. If this is not
     calculated, use $25,000.
  e. Management proficiency ratio

20–4 Using the following data, calculate the
monthly profit for April 20XX for the FSHA
337 Restaurant. Assume all costs are paid the
month incurred except for food and direct
expenses, which are paid the following
month. Use a proper format.

April 1 cash balance	$ 5,000
April food sales	30,000
March closing food inventory	2,000
April closing food inventory	3,000
Accounts receivable	4,000
Depreciation expense	3,000
Withdrawals by owners	2,000
Occupation expense	2,000
Direct expense—March	900
Direct expense—April	800
Other controllable—March	3,100
Other controllable—April	2,900
Loan repayment—Interest Loan	200
Repayment—Amortization	1,900
Food purchases—April	10,000
Food purchases—March	11,000

20–5 From the following data of a foodservice
operation,

Profit	$ 10,000
Opening food inventory	5,000
Sales	100,000
Labor cost	25,000
Fixed liabilities	20,000
Equity	30,000
Closing inventory	$ 4,000
Food purchases	35,000
Occupancy costs	6,000
Depreciation	10,000
Fixed assets	50,000
Total assets	80,000

calculate and show all calculations for the
following:
  a. Operating ratio
  b. Return on investment
  c. Current ratio
  d. Working capital

20–6 Using the following data, prepare common
size and comparative monthly income
statements in the proper format for The Lions
Restaurant.

	XXX1	XXX2
Food sales	$80,000	$90,000
Beverage sales	40,000	44,000
Food cost	26,000	27,000
Beverage cost	15,000	16,000
Salaries and wages	30,000	32,000
Employee benefits	6,000	7,000
Direct operating expenses	5,000	6,000
Music and entertainment	1,000	1,000
Marketing	3,000	2,000
Energy and utilities	5,000	6,000
Administration and general	5,000	5,000
Repairs and maintenance	2,000	1,000
Rent and occupation	8,000	9,000

20–7 Describe an actual foodservice operation in a
short paragraph (type, size, customers, etc.).
Prepare a list of subsidiary records that would
be appropriate for this operation with a brief
reason for each (management does not want
information overload).

Food-Cost Accounting Systems

Food-cost accounting is a specialized type of management cost accounting designed to give timely data about whether food costs are in line. If the data indicates food costs are too high, management can then check other areas of food management such as purchasing, receiving, storing, issuing, pre-preparation, preparation, and serving. If an operation pays too much for food or purchases quantities that cannot be used, food costs will, of course, rise. Employee waste or theft may also be the cause of excessive food costs.

After completing this chapter, you should be able to:

1. List the functions of food-cost accounting.
2. Explain the differences between food-cost accounting and industrial-cost accounting.
3. Describe the development of food-cost accounting.
4. Calculate the cost of food used.
5. Calculate cost of food for employee meals.
6. Calculate a food-cost percentage.
7. Explain the importance of inventory fluctuations in food-cost accounting.
8. Use food-cost accounting percentage systems.
9. Appreciate the importance of sales mix.
10. Perform sales analysis.
11. Explain and use standard-cost systems.
12. Identify the steps in a manual precost-precontrol food-cost accounting system.
13. Identify the steps in a computerized precost-precontrol food-cost accounting system.
14. Calculate a market price index.

FOOD-COST ACCOUNTING FUNCTIONS

The functions of food-cost accounting include:

1. determining whether food costs are in line with predetermined goals
2. determining if food costs are excessive
3. determining if costs of different food groups are appropriate
4. helping in menu costing and pricing
5. providing individual costs of menu items
6. providing information to help in forecasting

Food-cost accounting, once merely an analysis of past data on cost and sales, can now be also concerned with potential profits involving both sales and costs. It can provide data for managers to price a menu for the greatest sales and profit. Food-cost accounting can determine whether it is better to sell lower-cost food items or items with a high cost that may produce a higher gross profit and total gross contribution. Using these methods, managers can keep track of customer preferences and the relative popularity of menu items. This type of analysis can help determine how much cost should be added for special touches and specialty items such as chafing dish service, exotic foods, and off-season foods. In sales analysis, the food-cost accountant must forecast sales volumes, demands, and menu selections.

A kitchen is a type of factory, but there are significant differences between food-cost accounting and general factory-cost accounting. In factory-cost accounting, the finished product may be broken down into its various cost components and appropriate allocations made for different materials, labor, overhead, and factory burden.

A factory usually has long production runs of comparatively few items and produces for inventory instead of for immediate sales. A kitchen, on the other hand, cooks many items to order or has only short production runs for limited periods. Food is perishable and normally must be disposed of rapidly, rather than put into stock or inventory. An excess amount of production and inventory cannot be moved readily by clearance sales or price reductions. Some foods must be purchased, prepared, and consumed within a period of a few hours, which does not allow time for elaborate cost records.

Pricing of menu food items is usually chaotic compared to most other products. A dessert costing 25 cents may be sold for $1.50, but milk costing 35 cents may be sold for only 65 cents. Food operations find it impossible to perform cost analyses on the finished product and instead have developed methods of cost accounting based on the total cost of the raw food.

FOOD-COST ACCOUNTING HISTORY

Prior to Prohibition, many food operations were often subsidiaries of a beverage operation; food was actually given away in the "free-lunch" bars. Food was an attraction to draw people then, just as underpriced food and entertainment are used today to draw people to casinos, where more profit lies in gambling. With beverages outlawed, some operations by necessity had to survive on their food business, and every assistance was needed. Food-cost accounting provided such assistance, and its importance has grown steadily through the years.

Until the beginning of the twentieth century, many food operations had one price for as much as could be eaten. Many food operations were located in commercial hotels operated on the American plan, which included the cost of meals in the room rate. The dining room was a merchandising tool to attract people to the hotel. Many hotel owners were far more concerned about their reputations for fine table fare than about the cost of their food. Food and labor were cheap; profit was in the sale of guest rooms, so why bother with food costs as long as restaurant operations broke even? Other operations had a "meal ticket" system, permitting bearers to eat as much as they wanted in a sitting.

The chef could be a despot in the kitchen, often more concerned with the creations than with their cost. Perhaps by using sauces to cover up cheaper foods and by astute buying, the chef might be able to show, if so inclined, a profit—or at least minimize the loss. The total amount available for food expenditures was the only control. Menu pricing was often erratic and was based on what the customer would pay or what competition might be charging rather than on any relation to the cost of the food.

The one-price meal plan gave way to selective prices, á la carte items, and different prices for different meal course arrangements, such as a lower price for just a platter and dessert than for a full-course meal. The American plan in commercial hotels was replaced by the European plan, in which meals were not included in the room rate. This required more cost accounting, control, and information. The chef's intuition was no longer sufficient to control pricing. Management found it necessary to send food-cost accountants, or "bean counters," into the domain of the autocrat of the kitchen to learn where costs were excessive, perhaps to learn where better purchasing techniques could be employed or to learn how waste, overproduction, and overly generous portioning could be controlled. Also, menu selection and pricing policies often needed changing.

Not surprisingly, there is no one universal system of food-cost accounting; different operations have different requirements and have reached different levels of sophistication in their systems. The first food-cost accounting system simply considered the gross amount of food purchases. A manager might decide that $10,000 in food purchases should provide $30,000 in sales, or for every $100 of beef sales, beef purchases should be $35. Then it became logical to relate food cost to food sales as a percentage:

$$\text{Food-cost percentage} = \frac{\text{Raw food cost}}{\text{Food sales}}$$

As long as the food-cost percentage was satisfactory, the food cost was considered under control. Many commercial food operators are still at this stage of food-cost accounting.

The overall percentage could be refined, however, by breaking down the total cost into various food groups. This level of food-cost accounting is very helpful, but it does not include sales analysis and relates only what has happened instead of what should have happened.

The next logical step was to analyze food sales according to the dollars received in the different food categories and producing departments. These sales analyses were then compared to the costs. This was still mere historic information, but with the trends in mind, the chef could make adjustments in future food preparation.

As these techniques developed, some operations began to forecast future sales and their costs. The costs of different food items, called **standard costs**, were determined in advance from standard recipes. Actual costs were compared with the forecast costs and sales. Analysis could then be made to determine whether any difference resulted from overproduction, poor preparation methods, or other factors.

Computerization becomes more useful in food-cost accounting as new systems are designed. With their vast memories and rapid calculation abilities, computers can correlate purchasing inventory, issuing, standard recipes, sales, forecasting, and food-cost accounting. Their speed permits almost instantaneous reports. Not only can food costs be considered, but labor and other costs can also be analyzed. Point of sale registers can also gather and calculate data.

In this chapter we are especially concerned with the principles of food-cost accounting that can be used by computers and management information systems.

THE COST OF FOOD

Normally a food operation will not use all the food delivered on a specific day; nor will it use only the food delivered on a specific day. Some food will probably be used that day, some will be put in storage for future use, and some food used will be taken from storage. To determine the food cost accurately on a particular day, it is necessary to know the value of the food that was delivered and consumed on that day and the value of the food that was taken from storage. The foods that were delivered and sent directly to the kitchen for use the same day are called *direct purchases*. The value of these foods is usually obtained from the receiving report, which breaks down all food received into direct purchases or stores. **Stores** refers to food items that are received but are put into storage rather than sent directly to the kitchen. The value of food that is obtained from storage, or *stores food cost,* is usually obtained by costing requisition slips. Total food cost for a day (or for any other period) is the sum of direct purchases and storeroom issues, or

> Direct purchases
> + Storeroom requisition
> = Food cost
> +/− Adjustments
> = Net food cost

The adjustments can be anything that affects food cost. For some operations it could include the cost of the raw food consumed by employees. Other adjustments could include food items sent to an operation's bar, beverages sent from the bar to the kitchen to be used in food preparation, or stewards' sales (where food is sold to nondiners through the kitchen).

In some operations with a fast turnover and little inventory, all food received may be considered direct purchase.

Cost of Food for Employee Meals

One line of reasoning is that the income from restaurant patrons should be compared only to the raw food consumed by the patrons. In other words, compare apples with apples. Cost of food consumed by employees is a personnel benefit expense and should be charged as such; including it in the food cost distorts the food cost. This line of reasoning is valid only if the value of food consumed by employees can be determined accurately. If the value given to employee meals is unrealistic, there may be little rationale for segregating it.

Most operators prefer to deduct the value of employees' meals from the total cost of food consumed and to use only the value of food sold to patrons for a food-cost percentage. Determining the value of the food consumed by employees can be accomplished in several ways. Some operators try to calculate the value of the food consumed per average employee meal. Multiplying this figure by the number of employee meals should give at least an approximate value of food consumed by employees. Different average values can be used for breakfast, lunch, or supper. Very large operations may have separate kitchens and facilities for employees, which makes determining the cost much easier, but these operations are the exception.

If guest checks for employees are used, several other methods may be employed. One is to determine the sales value of food consumed by employees. Multiplying the sales value by the normal food-cost percentage will give a value for employees' food consumption. However, if employees are restricted from consuming the more expensive items, employees' meals would have a different cost percentage than customers' meals. An accurate method is to tally the number of each item served to employees. By multiplying the number of each item by the food cost of the item and adding the total of all items, an operator can obtain the employees' food cost accurately.

THE FOOD-COST PERCENTAGE

One very important part of most food-cost accounting systems—perhaps even the goal of the system—is the determination of the **food-cost percentage**, the ratio of the cost of food sold over the dollars received from selling the food. Dividing the cost of food sold by sales provides the food-cost ratio, which is expressed as a percentage. If food costs are $1,000 and sales are $3,000, the percentage would be $1,000 over $3,000, or 33.3 percent.

It is also possible to calculate the markup figure by dividing food cost into sales. Many food operators use a markup method that increases or multiplies the cost of the food item by two and a half or three times as a guide in determining the selling price of some items. This technique will automatically yield a food cost of 40 percent or 33.3 percent, respectively, for the item.

For an accurate food cost, it is necessary to consider the fluctuations in food inventory. Without an inventory, it is possible to show (for a limited period) a lower food-cost percentage by using more food from inventory than is replaced. Conversely, if the food inventory value is increased, the food-cost percentage will increase unless the increase in inventory is considered. Following is the usual formula for calculating food cost and for incorporating inventory into food cost:

> Value of opening inventory
>
> + Food purchases
>
> = Total available
>
> − Closing inventory
>
> = Value of food consumed during period
>
> − Value of employees' meals
>
> = Cost of food sold during period

If a requisition system that prices food items from storage is used, it is not necessary to know the opening and closing inventories because the value of the food from storage can be determined from the requisitions. However, the food cost must be determined periodically with the inventory values in order to adjust for requisition errors and to reveal any inventory losses.

TYPES OF FOOD-COST ACCOUNTING SYSTEMS

The objective of a food-cost accounting system is to show whether or not the cost of food used is within predetermined or desired limits. There is no one universal system, but several general systems each have appropriate applications for different types of foodservice operations. A small owner-manager operation may want to know only if the food cost is reasonable for the amount of sales; a larger operation needs a system that reveals the specific items on which the food cost is excessive and that provides production and forecasting controls. Although a food-cost accounting system may indicate that the food cost is excessive and may even identify what food category is responsible, it generally will not tell why it is excessive. Management then tries to find out if the fault is in purchasing, receiving, pricing, portion sizes, waste in preparation, pilfering, forecasting, or any of the many other facets of the foodservice operation.

Percentage systems are based on the premise that food cost should be within a definite percentage range of food sales. If food costs exceed desired percentage limits, corrective action should be taken. The percentage by itself means little until compared with some goal. As mentioned, standard cost systems, also referred to as *precost systems,* are based on the industrial technique of determining in advance what the cost of materials (food items) should be and comparing this precalculated cost with the actual cost as shown by food purchase costs, with changes in inventory values taken into account. If the actual cost is significantly higher than the predetermined calculated cost, the difference (or variance) is an unanticipated loss. If the actual cost is lower than the predetermined cost, there is an indication that standard recipes or portions are not being followed or that the cost data used is erroneous.

In the past, a standard cost was difficult to implement because of the difficulty in updating food costs. Computerized systems can show this with ease in a timely (often daily or by meal) and cost-efficient manner.

Sales analysis is a major factor in containing food cost, and it can be used in standard cost and cost-analysis systems. Records are kept of past sales for specific items and then used for more accurate forecasting of future sales and production. The estimated sales of an item are then compared with actual sales to gauge the accuracy of the forecast and to provide a basis for future forecasting. (Forecasting is discussed in Chapter 8.)

A low food-cost percentage does not necessarily mean a high contribution to profit and overhead. A $20.00 steak dinner with a 50 percent food cost generates $10.00 toward profit and overhead, whereas a $12.00 chicken dinner with a 40 percent food cost generates only $7.20. Higher unit volume at a high food-cost percentage can sometimes generate more contribution to profit and overhead than lower unit volume with a higher unit profit. Lower cost of sales does not necessarily generate a higher contribution.

In any food-cost accounting system, it is necessary for management to keep track of the **sales mix**, or how the different items on the menu sell in relation to each other. If a number of high-profit items are on the menu but they are not a high percentage of sales, the operation may have profitability problems. Menu engineering, discussed in Chapter 9, may be helpful in analyzing these problems.

Percentage Control Systems

Table 21.1 illustrates a format for a simple food-cost percentage control system. It has columns to record food sales and food cost on a daily and to-date basis. This particular example uses the cost of the food delivered for a day as that day's food cost. Not considered is the fact that some of the food may be taken from storage or that food delivered on one day may not be used on that day. If an operation receives the bulk of its food on certain days, the food cost would be overstated for those days and understated on days when there are fewer deliveries and food that has been delivered previously is used. An accurate food cost for the month or period is found when inventory is taken. Whether or not more food has been taken from the inventory than added to it can be determined by comparing opening and closing inventory figures. The inventory change can then be incorporated into the food cost for the period. Because there is no consideration of daily inventory fluctuations, the today cost percentage is only a guide, and the to-date figure, especially after the 10th day, more accurately reflects the true cost. During the latter part of the period, the days with more deliveries are balanced against days with fewer deliveries.

Table 21.1
Simple Food-Cost Control (Whole-Dollar Calculations)

A A		B	C D	E	F G H		I
				Simple Food-Cost Control			
1				**Month of** _____			
2							
3			**Sales**		**Food Purchases**		**Food–Cost Ratio**
4							
5	**Date**	**Today**	**To-date**	**Today**	**To-date**	**Today**	**To-date**
6							
7	1	683		365		53.4%	
8	2	969	1,652	275	640	28.4%	38.7%
9	3	1,112	2,764	446	1,086	40.1%	39.3%
10	4	480	3,244	165	1,251	34.4%	38.6%
11	5	557	3,801	120	1,371	21.5%	36.1%
12	6	633	4,434	164	1,535	25.9%	34.6%
13	29	702	19,413	362	6,833	51.6%	35.2%
14	30	954	20,367	255	7,088	26.7%	34.8%
15	31	1,318	21,685	507	7,595	38.5%	35.0%
16	Total purchases			7,595 @SUM(E6..E15)			
17	Add beginning inventory			2,563			
18	Total			10,158 +E16+E17			
19	Less ending inventory			2,752			
20	Net cost of food for the month			7,406			
21	Food–cost ratio for the month			34.2% +E20/C15			

The system in Table 21.1 would be suitable for a small operation closely supervised by an owner or manager who does not purchase large quantities for long-term future operations. It gives a helpful, if not entirely accurate, approximation of the food-cost percentage. The system is simple, requiring only the value of daily deliveries, the daily sales, the to-date additions, and two simple ratio calculations.

In the table, the daily food cost varies between 21.5 percent and 53.4 percent in the first six days. The reason for the wide fluctuation is that food is charged as cost on the day it is delivered. If not all the food delivered is used that day, a high food cost results. If the food used comes partially from previous deliveries, there is a lower food cost. The To-date column is considerably more accurate, and the last to-date figure of 35 percent is very close to the actual food-cost ratio of 34.2 percent for the month, which considers inventory fluctuations. In this example, the value of the inventory increased from $2,563 to $2,752.

Institutions such as hospitals, which do not have direct food sales (except for pay cafeterias), cannot calculate percentages. Management must establish what it considers proper food costs before these operations can determine if their costs are in line. In other hospitality food operations, this may be the ratio of food cost to sales (or food-cost percentage). In institutional operations, the proper food cost is the amount that management has budgeted for dietary department operations. The budgeting can be done on a flat amount, such as $200,000 for food for a specified period or a certain amount for every patient-day. The latter method is more realistic. If the daily amount is $6.00 and the average census is 200, an operation would have a food budget of $36,000 for a 30-day month ($6.00 × 200 × 30). After the food budget is established, management then must have accounting to show if it stays within its budget.

Table 21.2, which is a modification of Table 21.1, illustrates this on a monthly basis. Column 1 gives a line for each day of the month. Column 2 provides the daily food budget. This could be a figure for each patient (or guest) or a flat amount. Column 3 gives the cumulative food budget, and column 4 lists the food purchases for the day. These can depend on daily deliveries and may not relate directly to food revenue for that day. For example, there may be no food delivery on a Sunday but meals could be served from prior deliveries. Column 5 gives the cumulative food purchases. Column 6 shows the difference on a daily basis, and column 7 is the difference on a cumulative basis. Column 7 becomes more accurate as the month or period goes along.

Table 21.2
Simple Food-Cost Control System

(Col. 1) Date	Budgeted Food Cost		Food Purchases		Differences	
	(Col. 2) Today	(Col. 3) To-date	(Col. 4) Today	(Col. 5) To-date	(Col. 6) Today	(Col. 7) To-date
1	$800	—	$850	—	($50)	—
2	$760	$ 1,560	$700	$ 1,550	$60	$ 10
3	$812	$ 2,372	$830	$ 2,380	$18	($ 8)
30	804	$24,000	820	$23,600	(16)	$400

This type of format can give the institutional food manager a basis to compare budgeted food revenue and actual food purchases. However, since it assumes that food is used on the day it is purchased and does not take into account requisitions from already purchased food in storage, the method has a serious conceptual fault.

Summary of Food Cost and Sales

Figure 21.1 gives an accurate daily food-cost percentage; it takes into account daily inventory fluctuations. To use the format of Figure 21.1, it is necessary to have some record, usually the receiving clerk's daily report, which shows which food items received during the day are sent directly to the kitchen and should be included in the day's food cost. It is also necessary to have a costed requisition system for foods sent from the storeroom so that a daily value can be determined. The daily food cost would be the value of the food sent from receiving directly to the kitchen for use that day and the value of food used from the storeroom. Column 1 shows the dollar value of the goods in storage at the beginning of the day. Column 2 indicates purchases, which are placed in storage rather than used immediately in the kitchen. This total can be obtained from the food stores column of the daily receiving report. Column 3 shows the total of the opening inventory plus stores purchases or additions to the inventory. Column 4 shows the value of the issues taken from the storeroom. This value is obtained by pricing and totaling the storeroom requisitions. Adding purchases to the beginning inventory and then subtracting requisitions will give a new storeroom inventory value that should be shown as the beginning storeroom figure for the second or subsequent day. Column 5 shows the value of foods that are purchased and sent directly to the kitchen to be used the same day. The amount can be obtained from the food direct column of the receiving report. Column 6 shows the value of the food consumed, both the food from the storeroom and the food sent directly to the kitchen. Such an item should be included in the food cost. Column 7 refers to beverage transfers. Column 8 shows the net food cost today after considering transfers. Column 9 shows the total food cost for the period to date. The figures in column 10, which shows the day's food sales, are obtained from a source such as the sales record, the cash register reading, or the total of the guest checks. Column 11 refers to the cumulative food sales in the period. Column 12 shows the ratio of the day's food cost to the sales for the day. Column 13 indicates the ratio of the cumulative food cost to the cumulative food sales.

Figure 21.1 has definite advantages over Table 21.1. It provides a more accurate daily food cost and an inventory valuation figure that is helpful in controlling the inventory. It is possible to judge whether the inventory is higher or lower than the desired inventory, and this information can influence the volume of purchasing. It also brings an excessive inventory to the attention of management on a daily basis.

Sales Mix

Important in food-cost accounting and analysis is consideration of the sales mix. The **sales mix** is the number or quantity of the various menu items that are sold during the time period being analyzed. If relative quantities of these items change, there can also be a change in the dollar amount of food sales and the food-cost percentage. In the interest of simplicity, let us assume that we have only two items on our menu. One hundred portions are sold: 40 steak and 60 chicken.

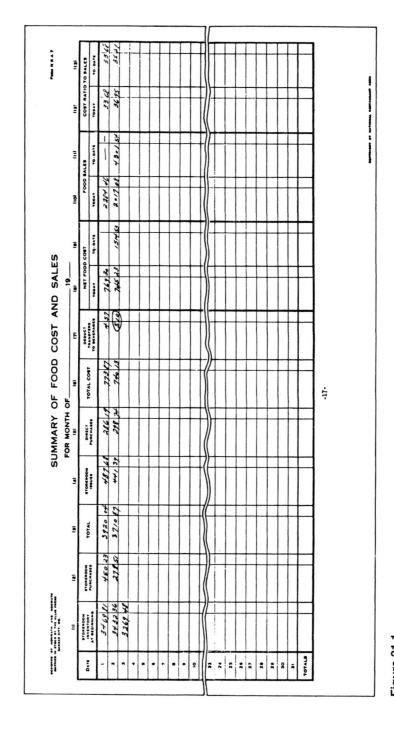

Figure 21.1
Daily Food-Cost Percentages

466

	Selling price	Item cost	Number sold	Total sales	Total cost	Gross profit	Food-cost percentage
Steak	$20.00	$10.00	40	$ 800	$400	$400	50.0%
Chicken	12.00	4.80	60	720	288	432	40.0%
Total				1,520	688	832	45.2%

Now let us assume that the quantities sold of each item are reversed, and 60 steak orders and 40 chicken orders are sold.

	Selling price	Item cost	Number sold	Total sales	Total cost	Gross profit	Food-cost percentage
Steak	$20.00	$10.00	60	$1,200	$600	$600	50.0%
Chicken	12.00	4.80	40	480	192	288	50.0%
Total				1,680	792	888	47.1%

The reversal increases sales by $160, and the food cost increases by a few percentage points, but the gross profit also increases by $56. The latter helps illustrate that one takes dollars, not percentages, to the bank.

Standard-Cost Systems

A standard cost (precost) is the cost of the item determined by using the quantities given in the recipe and the current purchase prices of the ingredients. It does not take into account waste, spoilage, or other losses, so the actual cost is normally higher than the standard cost. A factor may be used to compensate for this. A **standard-cost system** compares the actual cost of all food consumed with the total of the number of each food item served multiplied by its standard cost. The closer the actual figures are to the standard costs, the more efficient the food-cost control. A standard-cost system can be used for a meal, a day, a week, a month, or any other period. It can also be used when management wants to pinpoint discrepancies indicated by other controls.

Let us assume that a banquet with the following raw food cost per item will be served to 100 people:

Appetizer	$0.50
Salad	0.44
Entrée	3.00
Vegetable	0.30
Potato	0.40
Roll and butter	0.10
Dessert	0.70
Total	$5.44

The total cost is $5.44 per person. If it is planned to serve 100, the total food cost should be $544.

After the banquet is served, the following are the actual costs:

Direct purchases	$420
+ Storeroom requisitions	170
= Total actual food cost	590
− Standard cost	544
= Variation or potential savings	$ 46

This means that actual costs were $46 more than the standard cost. This can be called the variation or potential savings.

Generally, the primary objective of a standard-cost system is to determine cost variations on a daily basis and enable management to take corrective measures immediately. For the system to function, the standard costs must be calculated as accurately as possible. This requires adherence to standard portion sizes, standard purchase specifications, and standard recipes. It also requires that market price adjustments be made promptly. The system is only as accurate as the accuracy of the standard costs applied. In addition to the need to revise recipe costs to reflect price changes, other problems in determining standard costs include giving credit for food consumed by employees and the cost of nonproductive items such as condiments and cooking fat. A percentage figure for other food costs is often used to include these indirectly charged items.

An example of calculating standard costs is found in the standard cost for a serving of yellow cake. Ingredients, quantities, and ingredient costs for 100 servings are listed in Table 21.3.

The standard cost for a serving of yellow cake using these recipes, quantities, and costs would be 5.8 cents per serving. These calculations could also be done by a computerized system.

Standard-cost systems are commonly of two general types. One system compares potential and actual costs on the basis of selected commodity groups. The other does not break foods down into commodities but calculates, on the basis of standard costs, the total potential cost of all the food served, which is then compared with actual costs.

Total Estimated Costs Compared with Total Actual Costs

With this system, it is necessary for a manager to know how many portions of each item have been served. Since each item has been costed in advance, multiplying the number of portions served by the calculated (standard) cost will give the estimated food cost for each item listed on the menu, and the sum of the items for the period will give a total standard cost. If the dinner includes an appetizer, vegetables, salad, dessert, and a drink, only the entrée need be counted. A standard-cost sheet can price the side dishes as part of the cost procedure, or a flat amount can be added for these "makeup" items.

Each installation usually devises its own method of costing side dishes. For example, if coffee is a separate charge in a restaurant, it is not necessary to count each coffee sale. Instead, beverage orders over a specified period may be tabulated to determine a fairly reliable average: Perhaps 85 percent of the customers order coffee, 10 percent order milk, and 5 percent order tea. Thus, the coffee count and its resulting cost can be closely approximated from the customer count alone.

Table 21.3
Calculation of Standard Costs

Ingredients	Quantity	Purchase cost
Eggs	1½ dozen	80¢ a dozen
Shortening	1½ pounds	$1.00 a pound
Vanilla	¼ cup	$8.00 a gallon
Salt	1½ teaspoons	32¢ a pound
Sugar	4 pounds	28¢ a pound
Flour	4 pounds	20¢ a pound
Baking powder	3½ ounces	$2.16 a pound
Dry milk	6 ounces	$2.00 a pound

Costing the recipe for a standard cost per serving:

Eggs—80¢ per dozen or 5¢ apiece, 18 × 5¢	.90
Shortening—1.5 lbs. × $1.00	$1.50
Vanilla— $\dfrac{\$8.00 \text{ (cost per gal.)}}{V6 \text{ (cups in a gal.)}}$ = 50.0¢ per cup, 50¢/4 = 12.5¢ per ¼ c.	$ .13
Salt—kitchen item	—
Sugar—4 pounds × 28¢ per pound	1.12
Flour—4 pounds × 20¢ per pound	.80
Baking powder— $\dfrac{2.16¢ \text{ (cost per lb.)}}{16 \text{ (ounces in lb.)}}$ = 13.8¢ per oz., 3.5 oz. × 13.8¢	.57
Dry milk— $\dfrac{\$2.00 \text{ (cost per lb.)}}{16 \text{ (oz. in lb.)}}$ = 12.5¢ per oz., 6 oz. × 12.5	.75
Total	5.67

$5.67 per hundred servings = .567 or .58¢ per individual serving.

By adding the standard costs for all the items served, a manager can determine the total standard cost for the meal or period. Comparing this figure with the cost of the food actually used provides the difference between the standard and actual cost. Normally, this comparison is made on a daily basis. In Table 21.4, the cost of food actually charged to the kitchen for the day through direct purchases and requisitions was $630. Of this amount, $54 was allocated to employee meals, leaving a net actual food cost of $576. The standard cost was $543. (This figure was determined by multiplying the calculated cost of each item by the number served and adding the extended costs of all items.) The difference (variation) was $33, or 2.2 percent of the $1,500 sales. This particular format provides cost-per-dollar sales and sales ratio to total sales, which are helpful for (but not essential to) a standard-cost system.

Table 21.5 shows an application of standard costs for a college dormitory. The budget for food served is $7.50 a day per student, with a daily clientele of 520 students. For the day, the actual cost of food was $3,768. Precalculated standard costs were $3,585, giving a negative variance of $183, but the amount budgeted for food was $3,900 for the day. The result, then, is a favorable budget variance over the actual food cost of $132. In the table, the actual cost exceeded the standard cost by about 4.3 percent, suggesting that the kitchen operation could be improved even though the actual cost remained under that budgeted.

Table 21.4
Standard Food-Cost Report

	Sales	Calculated cost	Cost per dollar sale	Sales ratio to total sales (%)
Date _____				
Breakfast				
Combinations	180	75	41.7	12
A la carte	90	30	33.3	6
Total	270	105	38.9	18
Lunch				
Complete	225	75	33.3	15
A la carte	105	30	28.6	7
Total	330	105	31.8	22
Dinner				
Complete	240	75	31.5	16
A la carte	60	18	30.0	4
Total	300	93	31.0	20
Banquets	600	240	40.0	40
Total sales	1500			
Standard cost		543	36.2	100
Actual cost		630	42%	
Less adjustments		54	3.6%	
Adjusted actual cost		576	38.4%	
Variation (from $543)		33		
Percentage of variation			2.2%	

Precost-Precontrol Accounting Systems

The first **precost-precontrol** accounting system originally was a manual system developed in the 1930s. It was a very sophisticated standard-cost system for its time and provided a number of features, including:

- recording sales data that could be used in merchandising and to determine future sales

- allowing coordination of purchasing and production with projected sales, eliminating overproduction and waste

- providing an anticipated standard-cost food percentage in advance (if the percentage was not acceptable, changes could be made prior to the meal period)

- providing a standard-cost total for food consumed, which could be compared with actual cost and the variance or potential savings determined

Steps in the system include:

1. The number of sales of every menu item is recorded.

Table 21.5
Standard Food-Cost Report for a Dormitory

Date: January 13	Whole-Dollar Accounting		Day of Week: Friday
	Number served	**Day of week calculated cost ($)**	**Total cost ($)**
Breakfast			
Items 1	100	$1.35	$ 135.00
2	150	1.50	225.00
3	100	0.90	90.00
4	110	1.20	132.00
Total	460		$ 582.00
Lunch			
Items 1	170	$2.70	$ 459.00
2	140	2.40	336.00
3	200	2.85	570.00
Total	510		$1,365.00
Dinner			
Items 1	220	$3.60	$ 792.00
2	110	3.30	363.00
3	140	3.45	483.00
Total	470		$1,638.00
Total for day	1440		$3,585.00

	Today	To-date
Actual food cost	$3,768.00	$22,845.00
Standard cost	3,585.00	22,335.00
Variance	183.00	510.00
Budget cost allowance (520 × $7.50)	3,900.00	23,400.00
Budget actual cost variance	132.00	555.00

2. Figures are entered in a sales analysis book. The sales analysis book records data affecting total sales, such as day of the week or weather, and how items sold in relation to each other, especially when the menu changed. The sales analysis book is used to forecast future sales.

3. A menu precost and abstract is prepared using the format in Table 21.6. The forecast is prepared in advance, with forecasted sales amounts. If the 43.7 percent figure was not acceptable, adjustments could be made. The actual side was filled in after the meal or meal period. It showed how accurate the forecasting was and also provided a projected standard food-cost percent.

4. A summary of food cost and potential savings is prepared. This provides actual food sales during the meal or period and calculated costs. The latter could be compared with actual costs to determine potential savings.

5. The system also requires that the cost of every menu item be determined in advance.

Table 21.6
Menu Precost and Abstract

			Forecast					Actual				
Menu item	Selling price	Item cost	Number	Sales	Cost	Cost (%)	Ratio to total	Number sold	Sales	Cost	Cost (%)	Ratio to total
Steak	$12.00	$6.00	40	$480	$240	50%	40%	60	$ 720	$360	50%	60%
Fish	$ 8.00	$3.00	60	$480	$180	37.5%	60%	40	$ 320	$120	37.5%	40%
Total				$960		43.7%			$1040		46.2%	

The original manual precost-precontrol system required a great deal of clerical work. Its steps now can be computerized, and it is the basis for a number of different computerized food-cost accounting systems.

Steps in a Computerized Precost-Precontrol System

There are many different computerized food-cost accounting systems. General steps for many of the systems include:

1. *Costing of all menu items.* The operator must know the current cost of all menu items. The costing can be computerized. The system requires standard recipes and portions.

2. *Forecasting of sales by item count and dollars for the meal or meal period.* The technique illustrated in Chapter 8 may be used. Again, this procedure can involve computerized record keeping of past sales and trend analysis to provide current sales (with provision for management adjustment).

3. *Preparation of a variation of the menu precost and abstract to show anticipated sales and costs in advance of the meal or meal period.* If these are not acceptable, there is opportunity for change.

4. *Maintaining a count of all items served.* This can be done by POS registers or analysis of guest checks. The number sold should be reconciled with the number prepared and leftovers.

5. *Determination of the standard cost of all items served.* This is found by multiplying the number of each item served by its standard cost and adding all the items together. At the same time standard sales may be found by the same procedure, but using selling prices rather than costs.

6. *Comparison of standard costs with actual costs.* This can be done in different ways, such as dollar amounts (and potential savings noted) or standard food-cost percentages compared with actual food-cost percentages. Although the variance will vary with different types of food operations, it should not be greater than 1 to 3 percent.

A format for such a report is shown in Table 21.7.

Table 21.7
Summary of Food Cost and Potential Savings

| Date | Actual cost | | Standard cost | | Actual sales | | Actual cost percentage | | Standard cost percentage | | Variance (potential savings) | | | |
| | | | | | | | | | | | Dollars | | Percentage | |
	Today	To-date	Today	To-date	Today	To-date	Today	To-date	Today	To-date	Today	To-date	Today	To-date
1	$500	$ 500	$480	$ 480	$1500	$1500	33.3%	33.3%	32%	32%	$20	$20	1.3%	1.3%
2	$550	$1050	$540	$1020	$1600	$3100	34.3%	33.9%	33.8%	32.9%	$10	$30	0.5%	1.0%

A STANDARD FOOD-COST ACCOUNTING APPLICATION

An organization with a large foodservice operation uses standard food cost and standard sales concepts. Every item on the menu is costed out on a food-costing card (Table 21.8). If a menu item is made up of different items, such as on a platter, the stock number and cost are used on the main food-costing card.

The next step is a potential food-cost and sales report (Table 21.9). Every separately priced menu item is listed on the sheet. By totaling all the items, the standard-cost and total standard sales figures are provided. The total standard costs for a period are compared to actual costs (direct purchase and storeroom requisitions). The variance or potential savings can then be determined. The total sales figure can be used to compare actual receipts at the cash register. Total standard cost divided by total standard sales provides a standard food-cost percentage. If the figure calculated is not acceptable, management must make menu or pricing adjustments.

Tables 21.10 and 21.11 are examples of reports that can be generated through a computerized system.

Table 21.8
Food-Costing Card

Item _____ Recipe number_____

Yield _____ Yield cost _____ Portion size _____

Menu price _____ Portion cost _____ Food-Cost %_____

Date of cost _____ Costed by _____

Stock Number	Ingredients	Amount	Cost	Comments

Total Cost _____

Table 21.9
Potential Food-Cost and Sales Report

Area _____ Time Covered _____ Date _____

Menu item	Plate cost	Menu price	Number sold	Total cost	Total sales	Cost (%)
Potential cost and sales total				_____	_____	_____

Table 21.10
Theoretical Cost of Sales Report

Theoretical Cost of Sales Report
ReMACS Grill
For All Items
Default Costing Method
Monday, December 01, 1997 thru Monday, December 01, 1997

Sales Item Description	Avg Price	Theoretical Cost Amount	%	Sales Count	Amount	Cost of Sales Amount	%
2PC ML BR/W GET CDRK	$3.89	$0.073	1.88%	3.00	$ 11.670	$ 0.219	0.01%
2PC ML BR/GET CWHT	5.29	0.073	1.38%	1.00	5.290	0.073	0.00%
2PC ML BR/W GMIXDRK	3.89	0.092	2.37%	1.00	3.890	0.092	0.00%
2PC ML BR/W GORALL Breast	4.59	0.053	1.15%	24.00	110.160	1.272	0.05%
2PC ML BR/W GORDRK	3.89	0.073	1.88%	23.00	89.470	1.679	0.07%
2PC ML BR/W GORWHT	5.29	0.073	1.38%	2.00	10.580	0.146	0.01%
2PC ML BR/W GT DRALL Breast	4.59	0.053	1.15%	3.00	13.770	0.159	0.01%
2PC ML BR/W GT DRDRK	3.89	0.073	1.88%	4.00	15.560	0.292	0.01%
Chicken - 2 PC Totals	$4.03	$0.053	1.32%	98.00	$394.520	$5.151	0.20%
Food - Combo Meals - Chicken - 3 PC							
#5 3PC Th/Lg OR	$5.59	$0.0000	0.00%	2.00	$ 11.180	$0.000	0.00%
#5 3PC Th/Lg TDR	5.59	0.000	0.00%	1.00	5.590	0.000	0.00%
#7 3PC Wing ETC	4.04	0.000	0.00%	1.00	4.040	0.000	0.00%
#7 3PC Wing OR	4.04	0.000	0.00%	6.00	24.240	0.000	0.00%
3PC Wing MLMIX	3.44	0.083	2.41%	1.00	3.440	0.083	0.00%
3PC Wing MLOR	3.44	0.064	1.86%	1.00	3.440	0.064	0.00%
3PC Wing OR	2.74	0.064	2.34%	3.00	8.220	0.192	0.01%
3PC BR/W GORALL Breast	4.99	0.092	1.84%	2.00	9.980	0.184	0.01%
3PC BR/W GORDRK	3.59	0.064	1.78%	3.00	10.770	0.192	0.01%
3PC ML BR/W GET CALL Breast	6.39	0.064	1.00%	2.00	12.780	0.128	0.00%
3PC ML BR/W GET CDRK	4.99	0.064	1.28%	1.00	4.990	0.064	0.00%
3PC ML BR/W GORALL Breast	6.39	0.064	1.00%	4.00	25.560	0.256	0.01%
3PC ML BR/W GORDRK	4.99	0.064	1.28%	10.00	49.900	0.640	0.02%
3PC ML BR/W GT DRDRK	4.99	0.064	1.28%	1.00	4.990	0.064	0.00%
Chicken - 3PC Totals	$4.71	$ 0.049	1.04%	38.00	$179.120	$1.867	0.07%
Food - Combo Meals - Chicken - 4PC							
4PC ML ORCOM	$6.84	$0.070	1.02%	2.00	$13.680	$0.140	0.01%
4PC ML ORDRK	6.84	0.070	1.02%	1.00	6.840	0.070	0.00%
4PC ORCOM	5.44	0.070	1.29%	3.00	16.320	0.210	0.01%
Chicken - 4PC Totals	$6.14	$0.070	1.14%	6.00	$36.840	$0.420	0.02%

ReMACS

Table 21.11
Post-Service Cost Detail

Cafe West											Post-Service Cost Detail	
Date: Tuesday, January 21, 1997		Meal: BREAKFAST							Report Period: 3/9/97 - 3/15/97			
									Customer Count:		302	
	Per Portion			Quantity		Totals			Cost	Per Customer		
Item Name	Price	Cost	Margin	Prep	Srvd	Sales	Cost	Margin	(%)	Sales	Cost	Margin
Scrambled eggs & bacon	1.00	0.28	0.72	192	192	192.00	53.76	138.24	28%	0.40	0.11	0.29
Scrambled eggs & ham	1.00	0.37	0.63	111	111	111.00	41.07	69.93	37%	0.23	0.09	0.15
Totals for: 09 - ENTREES						303.00	94.83	208.17	31%	0.63	0.20	0.43
White toast		0.25	0.05	0.20	58	58	14.50	2.68	11.82	18%	0.03	0.01
Wheat toast	0.25	0.07	0.19	24	24	6.00	1.56	4.44	26%	0.01	0.00	0.01
Totals for: 12 - BREADS						20.50	4.24	16.26	21%	0.04	0.01	0.03
Orange sections	0.50	0.35	0.15	68	68	34.00	24.12	9.88	71%	0.07	0.05	0.02
Totals for: 13 - DESSERTS					68	34.00	24.12	9.88	71%	0.07	0.05	0.0
Lowfat milk (8oz pour)(b)	0.35	.015	0.20	72	72	25.20	10.71	14.49	42%	0.05	0.02	0.03
Lowfat milk (crtn 8oz) (b)	0.35	0.17	0.18	269	269	94.15	45.73	48.42	49%	0.20	0.10	0.10
Apple juice (m-maid)	0.50	0.17	0.33	24	24	12.00	4.00	8.00	33%	0.03	0.01	0.02
Grapefruit juice (m-maid)	0.50	0.11	.039	24	24	12.00	2.74	9.26	23%	0.03	0.01	0.02
Orange juice	0.50	0.12	0.38	216	216	108.00	25.73	82.27	24%	0.23	0.05	0.17
Tomato V-8 juice	0.50	0.16	0.34	48	48	24.00	7.56	16.44	31%	0.05	0.02	0.03
Coffee brewed	0.35	0.03	0.32	480	480	168.00	13.21	154.79	8%	0.35	0.03	0.32
Totals for: 15 - BEVERAGES						443.35	109.67	333.68	25%	0.92	0.23	0.70
Totals for: BREAKFAST	302 Customers					800.85	232.86	567.99	29%	1.67	0.49	1.1
Totals for: 3/9/97	302 Customers					800.85	232.86	567.99	29%	1.67	0.49	1.1
Totals for: *Cafe West*	302 Customers					800.85	232.86	567.99	29%	1.67	0.49	1.1

SUMMARY

Food-cost accounting is designed to provide information on what the food costs are for an operation and if they are appropriate for that operation. The information can also be used in menu forecasting and menu pricing and costing.

There are two general food-cost accounting systems. One provides a food-cost percentage figure to analyze and control food costs. The other is standard-cost systems, which provide a standard-cost figure to

which actual costs can be compared. If the variance is too large to be acceptable, further investigation can be made and corrective action taken. A system can provide both standard costs and a food-cost percentage.

Other aspects of food-cost accounting include calculation of the sales mix and the sales analysis, purchase analysis, and inventory records and reconciliations.

KEY TERMS

food-cost percentage
precost-precontrol
sales mix

standard-cost system (food-cost accounting)
stores (food cost)

REVIEW QUESTIONS

21–1 How has the work of the food-cost accountant changed from the past?

21–2 How does food-cost accounting differ from general factory-cost accounting?

21–3 List steps in the development of food-cost accounting.

21–4 Why is determining the cost of food used for employee meals important?

21–5 What is the concept behind a percentage food-cost accounting system?

21–6 What is the concept behind a standard-cost system?

21–7 Provide the format for a simple food-cost percentage system.

21–8 What are advantages of a "summary of food cost and sales" food-cost accounting system (Figure 21.1) over a simple six-column percentage system (Table 21.1)?

21–9 What can be learned by sales analysis performed by the food-cost accountant?

21–10 Show two ways the cost of certain food classifications can be expressed.

21–11 Explain the concept of inventory variance accounting.

21–12 List the steps in a computerized precost-precontrol accounting system.

PROBLEMS

21–1 From the following data for March 14, determine:
a. Food-cost percentage
b. Closing value of the food inventory

Closing food storeroom inventory		
March 13		$2,400
Requisitions from storeroom		350
Receiving report:		
Direct	$650	
Stores	400	
Sundry	40	
Sales		$3,000
Cigarette sales		150

21–2 A restaurant has a closing food inventory of $1,100 on May 14. Receiving report figures for May 15 were direct purchases $200, storeroom purchases $215, sundry purchases $32; storeroom requisitions were $195; food for employee meals was $35; food sales for May 15 were $1,200; and standard costs were $380. Calculate:

a. Value of the closing food inventory for May 15
b. Food-cost percentage for May 15
c. Amount and percentage of potential savings

21–3 The following data are presented:

Food sales	$100,000
Beverage sales	$ 30,000
Food purchases	$ 41,500
Food usage	$ 40,000
Employee meals	10% of food usage
Opening food inventory	$ 1,500
Beverage cost percentage	30%
Closing beverage inventory	$ 1,000

Calculate (showing all calculations):

a. Food-cost percentage
b. Closing food inventory
c. Cost of goods sold—food
d. Beverage inventory turnover

21–4 The following data are presented:

Sales		Receiving report	
Food	$2,000	Direct	$ 400
Beverage	$1,000	Stores	$ 600
Cigarette and other	$ 200	Sundry	$ 100
Total sales	$3,200	Total receipts	$1,100

Opening food inventory value	$1,300
Food requisitions from the storeroom	$ 350
Beverages sent from bars for kitchen use	$ 10
Food sent from food storeroom to bar	$ 20
Employee meals (cost of food)	$ 80
Beverage inventory	$ 900

Calculate:

a. Daily food-cost percentage
b. Closing value of food inventory
c. Cost of food used this day

21–5 The following data are presented for a restaurant:

Direct purchases	$ 220
Standard food costs	$ 300
Employee meals	$ 40
Requisitions from storeroom	$ 180
Sundry purchases	$ 60
Cigarette sales	$ 40
Storeroom purchases	$ 230
Food from storeroom to manager's apartment	$ 10
Food sales	$1,000
Opening storeroom value	$ 800

Determine:

a. Percentage of potential savings
b. Food-cost percentage
c. Closing value of food inventory

21–6 The following data are presented:

Food sales	$1,000
Total sales	$1,200
Receiving report data	
Direct	$ 150
Stores	$ 300
Sundry	$ 50
Storeroom requisitions	$ 200
Transfers to bar from storeroom	$ 10
Transfers to bar from kitchen	$ 10
Opening storeroom balance	$2,000

Determine:

a. Food-cost percentage
b. Closing inventory figure

21–7 The following data are presented:

Sales	$1,000
Receiving report	
Direct	$ 200
Stores	$ 300
Sundry	$ 50
Opening food inventory	$ 900
Food requisition to kitchen from storeroom	$ 250
Beverage from bar to kitchen	$ 5
Food from storeroom to bar	$ 10
Employee meals are 10% of daily food usage and are a personnel expense.	

Calculate:

a. Daily food-cost percentage
b. Closing value of food inventory

21–8 From the following data, calculate:

a. Closing inventory
b. Food-cost percentage
c. Potential savings percentage

Receiving report

Direct purchases	$ 200
Stores	$ 250
Sundry	$ 50
Sales	
Food	$1,100
Other	$ 100
Opening inventory	$1,000
Food storeroom requisitions	$ 300
Employee meals (food)	$ 50
To kitchen from bar	$ 20
To bar from storeroom	$ 20
Standard costs	$ 450

21–9 The following data are presented:

Food sales	$1,000
Food storeroom requisitions	$ 250
Sundry purchases	$ 50
Standard food cost	$ 450
Food storeroom purchases	$ 280
Direct food purchases	$ 240
Wine (for cooking) from bar to kitchen	$ 10
Opening food inventory	$1,200
Cherries from food storeroom to bar	$ 20

Calculate:
a. Closing inventory
b. Daily food-cost percentages
c. Potential savings

21–10 The following data are presented for a standard food-cost control system:

	Sold	Sales	Calculated costs	Cost per $ sale
Dining room	200	$500	$200	40%
Banquet	150	$500	$150	30%
Stores purchases	$225			
Direct purchases	$180			
Requisitions	$240			
Employee meals	$ 40			

Determine:
a. Potential savings (or variation)
b. Percentage of variation

12. Explain the two elements of a foodservice prechecking system.

13. Repeat an outline for the general, seven-step prechecking sequence.

14. List nine elements in restaurant guest check control.

ACCOUNTING DEFINITION

A traditional accounting definition of **internal control** follows:

> Internal control comprises the plan of organization and the coordinate methods and measures adopted within a business to safeguard its assets, check the accuracy and reliability of its accounting data, promote operational efficiency, and encourage adherence to prescribed managerial policies.

This is quite a long definition, so let's break it down into its components.

Plan of Organization

Every organization should have a plan that lists the responsibilities of each employee (there may be a number of employees who perform the same type of job with the same responsibilities), to whom each employee reports, and whom the individual supervises. The plan of organization should show lines of authority and responsibility. You cannot have one without the other. It should specify the requirements for each job and include a job description. These personnel policies are an integral part of the organizational plan.

This organizational plan can increase efficiency by providing goals for each section of the organization, coordinate the activities of the various sections, and integrate the whole system for the accomplishment of specific goals. There is one caveat: Whenever possible, it is desirable to separate jobs between operating, controlling, and management functions in the plan of organization. For example, it may not be desirable for the person who purchases food also to receive it or for a cashier to make up the bank deposits. Although these practices are common, they afford employees a ready means to defraud the organization.

Safeguarding of Assets

Cash is the asset most often stolen, but many other articles, such as food, silver, linen, even time, can attract a thief. Another possible type of fraud is through manipulation of payroll records. Safeguarding these assets requires controls such as cash registers, inventory records, guest checks, and antitheft techniques. A crucial step in safeguarding assets is simply being able to determine when assets are missing so that further action can be taken.

Providing Reliable Financial Records

A large part of internal control is the paperwork, or financial records. More often than not, trouble occurs when financial records are not adequate and management is not aware of what is going on. Foodservice operations should maintain a regular system of accounts with periodic financial statements (financial accounting). They should also develop control reports, budgets, and special studies (management accounting). The financial records should be checked periodically or audited by an outside person. Operations should be broken down into separate profit or cost centers. Thus, there should be separate financial

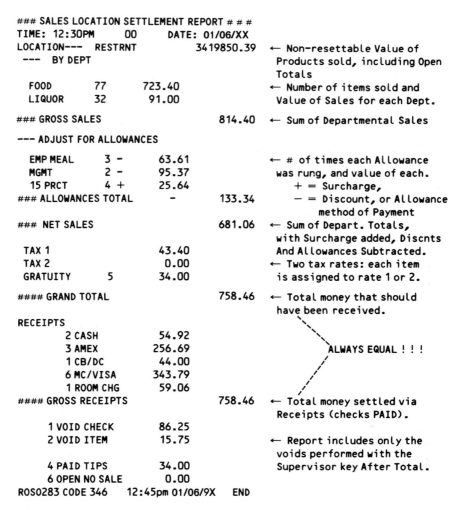

```
### SALES LOCATION SETTLEMENT REPORT # # #
TIME: 12:30PM      00      DATE: 01/06/XX
LOCATION---  RESTRNT            3419850.39    ← Non-resettable Value of
   ---  BY DEPT                                 Products sold, including Open
                                                Totals
   FOOD        77      723.40                 ← Number of items sold and
   LIQUOR      32       91.00                   Value of Sales for each Dept.

### GROSS SALES                     814.40    ← Sum of Departmental Sales

--- ADJUST FOR ALLOWANCES

   EMP MEAL    3 -      63.61                 ← # of times each Allowance
   MGMT        2 -      95.37                   was rung, and value of each.
   15 PRCT     4 +      25.64                     + = Surcharge,
### ALLOWANCES TOTAL    -           133.34         - = Discount, or Allowance
                                                     method of Payment
###  NET SALES                      681.06    ← Sum of Depart. Totals,
                                                with Surcharge added, Discnts
   TAX 1               43.40                    And Allowances Subtracted.
   TAX 2                0.00                   ← Two tax rates: each item
   GRATUITY    5       34.00                    is assigned to rate 1 or 2.

#### GRAND TOTAL                    758.46    ← Total money that should
                                                have been received.
RECEIPTS
        2 CASH         54.92
        3 AMEX        256.69
        1 CB/DC        44.00                   ALWAYS EQUAL ! ! !
        6 MC/VISA     343.79
        1 ROOM CHG     59.06
#### GROSS RECEIPTS                 758.46    ← Total money settled via
                                                Receipts (checks PAID).
        1 VOID CHECK   86.25
        2 VOID ITEM    15.75                   ← Report includes only the
                                                 voids performed with the
        4 PAID TIPS    34.00                    Supervisor key After Total.
        6 OPEN NO SALE  0.00
ROSO283 CODE 346   12:45pm 01/06/9X    END
```

Figure 22.1
Sales Location Settlement Report

records for the dining room, bar, lounge, and banquet facilities, rather than just total figures for the whole food and beverage operation. Through accounting records, the facility's management, even though it is not constantly in one area, can maintain control by noting discrepancies from planned or budgeted figures or unusual increases in costs or decreases in revenues or profits. See, for example, the sales location settlement report in Figure 22.1.

Promoting Operational Efficiency

Most of what we have been studying is designed to promote operational efficiency. Labor-cost analysis or food-cost accounting systems are examples of methods to promote operational efficiency. The more efficient an operation, the lower the costs, the more one can offer patrons, and the greater the profit (or the easier the budget). Increased efficiency can also provide the opportunity to offer more benefits to employees.

Adherence to Management Policies

This phrase assumes a management that has established and publicized policies and standard operating procedures (SOPs) for issues such as overtime, absenteeism, and punctuality. Management has the responsibility to establish such policies and a duty to see that they are uniformly enforced. Trouble arises when policies are enforced at one time but not at another or are enforced for some employees but not for others. There may also be legal or union consequences if policies are enforced against only some: Courts have ruled against management when management used policies to discipline some employees but did not apply them to others in similar circumstances. In today's climate of litigation, employees are prone to sue an employer. Policies may help avert possible lawsuits or help in defending against them.

SECURITY

Security includes the protection of all cash, merchandise, equipment, and supplies. Theft in any form represents a loss of profit and can be a major management concern. Since most theft losses are ultimately attributable to management complacency and carelessness, management's efforts can go far in reducing these losses.

Theft is a major problem both for the foodservice industry and for the general economy. Internal theft losses, which involve billions of dollars annually, have been estimated for the hospitality industry to be around 7 or 16 percent of sales, and the percentage is rising.

In the foodservice industry the three areas of most frequent dishonesty are money thefts, food and beverage pilfering, and collusion between employees and purveyors. Money is, of course, easily concealed and disposed of and thus represents the most attractive target. Money is accessible to cashiers, serving personnel, and bartenders.

Food is vulnerable to the many employees who have access to the kitchen and storage area. Obviously it is consumable on the premises or in any household. The term *grazing* is sometimes used to describe employees' unauthorized snacking while on the job.

The food industry is also particularly susceptible to collusion between purchasing personnel and receiving people on the one side, and purveyors and their delivery personnel on the other. The collusion usually takes the form of falsely inflated prices, with the difference split and part of it "kicked back." Or the delivery might not be made at all, with the value of the merchandise not received shared by the colluding parties.

Unfortunately, petty thievery abounds. Given the chance, many basically honest people will pinch a burger, a soda, or a loose dollar or two. These tendencies cannot be reduced by discussing morals or appealing to consciences. However, vigilance will help. Most authorities blame management ineptitude, complacency, poor executive examples, and failure to adopt preventive security programs for rising business theft. Much of the money and property lost could be saved through tighter control, and the key to theft control is management interest and concern. Why do people steal? Following are several answers:

1. *A desire for material possessions.* Very few of us have the wherewithal to satisfy all of our material wants. Our economy constantly exhorts us to purchase this and con-

sume that, and theft becomes a means to obtain new and different things. For some low-paid employees or for those who squander their income, theft may be almost essential to satisfy the desire for new things.

2. *Temptation.* An old adage suggests that a small part of the population is completely honest, a small part is incorrigibly dishonest, and the remainder is as honest as circumstances permit. If it is difficult to steal, people are less inclined to steal. If it looks easy, they will try. It is management's job to keep the temptations and the prospect of success low. Leaving attractive temptations in place makes management partially responsible for thefts.

3. *Fond memories.* Some stealing is simply the acquisition of souvenirs or mementos taken by people who do not need the item or could readily pay for it.

4. *Social distance.* People who would not steal from an individual have fewer scruples about stealing from large, anonymous, impersonal organizations. In their eyes, taking from a large restaurant chain is less of a crime than taking from a small restaurant owner.

5. *Anger and resentment.* Employees who are unhappy or patrons who have received unsatisfactory meals may feel that the operation owes them something, or they may want to strike back by stealing.

6. *Kleptomania.* Some unfortunate people have an abnormal and persistent impulse to steal.

7. *Thrills.* Stealing presents a challenge to some people. It is an accomplishment for them to remove items, and the risk of apprehension adds zest to the adventure.

8. *Social problems.* A personal need may become so acute that normally honest people resort to thievery. Overpowering expenses such as the maintenance of a drug habit and the bills following a long illness are examples.

EMPLOYEE THEFT

Employee theft is the cause of 7 percent of all bankruptcies, and property lost through "inside jobs" is probably more than twice that lost through burglaries, holdups, and car thefts. One authority claims that 85 percent of all employees have stolen at least something from an employer and 3 out of 10 will regularly try to steal. Many of these employees would never have stolen if they had not been tempted and emboldened by management laxity and poor security policies.

A good internal security program usually begins in the employment office. Good foodservice employees are at a premium, and the industry tends to resort to spot hiring without investigation. One should always try to contact an applicant's past employers to inquire about work habits and any problems with theft. In the preemployment screening, the operation's policy about theft (and drugs and alcohol) should be addressed. This can include what the operation considers theft, such as grazing, overpouring in the bar, or loitering on the job. New employees may be asked to sign a statement attesting to the fact that they have received orientation and are aware of the consequences if they break company policy. Too often employees are fired from one job for stealing, then walk around the corner and take another job somewhere else the same day. Local police can often check their files regarding convictions for names submitted to them by employers. In some areas, local law requires that all employees be checked. One should conduct a complete investigation on all employees who will have responsible positions and have the opportunity to cause considerable loss. Some authorities recommend that outside firms do background checks. Not only can they do a better job but they assume the liability if false information emerges and the prospective employee is not hired and makes a legal complaint. A fidelity bond may also be secured. This is a type of insurance protection against loss, including employee theft. Specific employees or specific types of employees, such as cashiers, may be covered. To recover losses, however, the company must prove through confessions or other evidence that theft occurred. An advantage of bonding includes the prior investigation that the insurance companies may make of covered employees.

Checks should be made occasionally and unexpectedly on all parcels carried out by employees, and each employee should know that any package he or she takes out may be inspected. Some employers require that all packages be checked and held by the security guard. Inspections should also be made of trash and garbage containers, since they have long been used to move merchandise outside the building for a later pickup. Management may even find it wise to rake over its refuse occasionally.

Do not maintain unobserved employee entrances and exits. One operation with heavy theft losses solved its problem by keeping the receiving door locked at all times except when supervised deliveries were made. It is best to have an employee entrance that is observed at all times; mirrors or a closed-circuit TV system may even be used.

The attitudes and activities of other personnel, particularly supervisors, can have a great influence in the area of internal control. If employees see others take merchandise, they may be inclined to try too. If employees know the chef conducts under-the-table dealings with purveyors, they may also be inclined to reward themselves at the operation's expense. Thievery is contagious.

Anger and resentment toward an employer can prompt an employee to steal. It is wise personnel policy and good human relations to try to bring an employee close to the operation and to alleviate causes of friction. This approach also discourages dishonesty.

In general, enlightened personnel policies promote internal control. Try to get employees to identify with the operation as much as possible. If employees feel the operation is "ripping them off," they will be tempted to retaliate. Good personnel policies with fair and equal treatment can go far to alleviate this temptation. The attitude of management itself is very important. If management appears not to care, employees may ask themselves why they should bother. It is even worse if supervisors defraud the operation. One study of general industry suggests that 62 percent of management personnel had stolen from their employers.

It is crucial to maintain good communication between the enterprise and its employees if the employees are to consider themselves vital parts (which they are) of the enterprise. This communication can include keeping employees informed about what is going on, showing appreciation for a job well done, and stressing that dishonest behavior will be punished. Along with communication there should be regular employee evaluations. This allows management to develop realistic performance goals and to reward superior performance. If too much is asked of employees, enough resentment can develop to rationalize theft.

INDUSTRY INSIGHTS   by William Fisher and Michael D. Gehrisch

William Fisher is President and Chief Executive Officer of the American Hotel and Motel Association. He also served as Executive Vice President of the National Restaurant Association.

Michael D. Gehrisch is Senior Vice President and Chief Financial Officer for the American Hotel and Motel Association in Washington, D.C. He previously worked in various financial and management capacities for Marriott Hotels & Resorts and Hilton Hotels.

HOSPITALITY INDUSTRY CHARACTERISTICS

All businesses have areas of weakness and vulnerability to fraud and embezzlement. Hospitality businesses have the same general control weaknesses that affect all enterprises. In addition, the hospitality industry has the following general operating characteristics that render it relatively more vulnerable to theft:

- many cash transactions
- small businesses
- relatively low-skill jobs
- positions with low social status
- items of relatively high value (e.g., wine)
- the use of commodities

Cash   Even as we evolve into a "cash-less" society, hospitality workers continue to handle plenty of currency. With the widespread use of hotel charge accounts, credit cards, debit cards, and in the near future, "smart cards," it is true that far less cash changes hands in many hotel transactions. Most hotels today require guests to present a major credit card for registration and establishment of credit, regardless of how they wish to settle the bill. In spite of that fact, hotels still need to maintain and deal with a great deal of cash. For one thing, guests expect it. They want easy access to cash for tipping, shopping, entertainment and recreation, and foreign exchange. Most hotels also have numerous revenue outlets that are open for long hours, requiring many more cashier shifts and cash banks than businesses that have a single revenue outlet operating only from nine to five.

Size   Even though many properties are large and many hotels are part of a chain, a hotel operates primarily like a small business. Even large hotels are aggregations of many relatively small revenue outlets. In a large, modern, full-service hotel, the rooms department may be a fairly large revenue center, but there will be many bars, restaurants, and other revenue centers that individually are small operations. Thus, the critical mass of economies of scale that helps larger operations with efficiency and control is often lacking.

Job Status   As a service business that operates 24 hours a day, seven days per week, a hotel is comprised of many unskilled, low-paying jobs. Most revenue dollars are brought in by wait staff, food and beverage cashiers, and office clerks. The high turnover and low social status that often come with that type of employment do little to help the internal control environment. Automation is raising the skill levels necessary in many of these jobs, but it will be a long time before growth and economic viability raise the overall standard.

Commodities   The items of inventory used in the hospitality industry are commodities—that is, goods that employees would normally need and buy for their own consumption. The industry is, after all, providing lodging and food, and most people need to provide lodging and food for themselves and their families. At the same time, the inventory items are also of high value relative to their size and weight. Seafood, steak, good wine, and other items can have considerable cost and sales value, yet do not take a good deal of space and are easily concealed or consumed.

A controversial technique for keeping employees honest is encouraging certain employees to spy on other employees and to reward them for doing so. Proponents of the stool pigeon technique say it can reduce theft losses and help keep employees honest. Opponents say it is unethical, undermines morale, and causes suspicion and unproductive tensions among employees.

Coupons, such as "two-for-one-entrees" or "second entree for half price," used in advertising promotions can also be used by unscrupulous servers. They can clip or obtain their own coupons, use them when noncoupon customers pay their bills (in cash), and pocket the value of the coupon.

PATRON THEFT

Patron theft is hard to control, and management must always be alert to possible lawsuits. Souvenir collecting is one cause of stealing. A name, logotype, or monogram is really the thief's target in these cases, and the simple elimination of the monogram often reduces the stealing. Also, offering the most frequently stolen items for sale at the cashier's desk or in a gift shop allows the patron who wants them to buy them, increasing the operation's profit.

A little psychological ingenuity may reduce patron thievery. A card on a room-service table, stating that the waiter is responsible for the service items, shifts the loss from an impersonal organization to a visible individual. Many will take advantage of the former but not the latter. Signs indicating that a protective service agency supervises the operation may discourage a thief. A very obvious closed-circuit TV camera in fire corridors, gift shops, or newsstands may also prevent theft since patrons never know whether or not they are being monitored.

Some operations burden their serving personnel with the responsibility for expensive and desirable items that can be easily removed. Servers who are financially responsible for these items have an increased incentive to see that patrons do not remove them, but they also bear a responsibility that may distract from their main job, or there may be legal issues.

Patrons who pay their checks themselves at the cashier's desk have been known to alter the addition on the checks for their own benefit, and it requires an alert cashier to detect these changes. Printed POS checks can help eliminate this. The cashier should also be situated so that a patron will not be tempted to walk out without paying.

One final, common source of loss occurs when customers use expensive napkins to wrap extra food to take home instead of "doggie bags" for this purpose.

CASH CONTROL

Control of cash within a foodservice operation is most important. Some techniques that can reduce potential losses are:

- Assign a manager or noncashier to read the totals on the register and reconcile with the actual cash turn-in.

- Have a different person from the one who makes up the bank deposits count cash turn-ins by denomination and total the deposit.
- Insist that two people count money. Larger operations may require money handling within view of a video camera.
- Look for telltale signs such as stacks of matches or piles of coins that may indicate a cashier is trying to keep track of transactions not run up.
- Insist the cash drawer be closed after each transaction. Prohibit "batching" transactions.
- If possible, have all "no sale" ring-ups approved by management.
- Keep control of the operation's blank and cancelled checks.

THE CASHIER

In the average foodservice operation, cash control from sales centers on the cashier. The cashier usually performs four duties in handling the operation's money:

1. preparing the change fund for business
2. accepting money
3. making change
4. accounting for and recording receipts and sometimes preparing the bank deposit

Most cashiers operate with a change fund, a definite amount of money used for making change. The fund remains constant, and any surpluses or shortages are reflected in the day's cash receipts. Many operations find it most feasible for each cashier to have a separate fund that (except for management checks and audits) only he or she has access to. The fund may be stored in a locked container in the safe when the cashier is off duty. Preparing the change fund requires predetermined amounts of coins and bills available to make change. Normally, the cashier arranges this before going off duty. Some operations give the cashier a new fund each day; if so, the cashier should immediately count the money.

When a customer presents a guest check for payment, the money should be placed first on the register shelf or on top of the cash drawer. Then the cashier should recite the amount of the check and the amount of money presented aloud: "Eight-forty out of twenty," for example. This procedure helps the cashier keep the transaction clearly in mind, conveys the figures to the patron who may not have been concentrating, and allows any disputes over payment to be resolved before the money merges with the cash fund and other receipts. Only after the customer accepts the change, signifying approval of the transaction, should the cashier place the money in the cash drawer. Large-denomination bills should be kept separate, perhaps under the change tray. If these procedures are not followed, a customer may claim to have presented a larger bill than that for which he or she received change. If this in fact does happen, the cash drawer, if possible, should be counted at that moment or at least at the end of the shift. If there is a commensurate surplus, the money can be returned to the customer. (POS registers record the entry of amount tendered and automatically calculate the change.)

There are three steps in giving change. The first is to audibly count up from the amount of the check to the amount of money tendered. Begin, "eight-forty out of twenty." Tender a dime, calling out "eight-fifty"; then two quarters, calling out "nine"; a dollar, calling out "ten"; and a ten, calling out "twenty." The second step is to give change in the largest denominations. It is better to give one dime than two nickels, one quarter than two dimes and one nickel, or one five-dollar bill than five ones. The more coins or bills involved, the easier it is to make errors. (Sometimes the second principle is modified to supply change for tips.) The third principle in making change is to place the change directly into the patron's hand. It should not be left on the counter for the customer to pick up.

ROBBERY AND BURGLARY

Robbery is defined as stealing or taking anything of value by force or violence or by the use of fear. It has been called the fastest-growing crime in the nation, with the greatest increase occurring in retail stores. Only about one-third of the robberies in this country are solved and result in an arrest. Even when robbers are caught, the cash and property recovery rate is low. Robbery is a violent crime that relies on the use or threat of force. In about 65 percent of store holdups, the robber uses a weapon.

Burglary is any unlawful entry to commit a **felony** (a crime more serious than a misdemeanor) or a theft, even though no force was used to gain entrance. Fast-food operations can be leading candidates for robbery. They may be open at late hours and tend to be located on major highways, which provide for an easy getaway. All operations may be susceptible to burglary.

Two general strategies can help to prevent robberies and burglaries. One is to maximize the risk to the robber, and second is to minimize the dollar return. According to one survey, the five most common factors considered by robbers in evaluating a potential target are amount of money, escape routes, anonymity, interference, and number of personnel on duty. The money factor rates five times higher on the survey than anything else, so to minimize the dollar return, the best strategy is to keep only a limited amount available. Never keep more than a small amount in the register. Large bills and extra cash can be put in a special cash controller that relies on an electronic time-release mechanism to prevent a burglar from getting the money in a hurry.

If feasible, the safe should not be hidden in the back of the store; if possible, it should be visible from the street. It should also be bolted to the building structure. (Two thousand-pound safes have been carried off.) Even with an adequate safe, a minimum amount of cash should be kept on hand.

Other ways to discourage burglaries include adequate lights, burglar alarm systems, and closed-circuit TV systems.

Almost all store break-ins occur at night when darkness can conceal burglars and give them time to work. Some operations do not allow the back door to be opened or garbage taken out after dark. Good lighting inside and outside in the parking lot can frustrate burglars. Also, employees should know what to do when a robbery occurs. Emphasize that the protection of life is more important than money. Employees should not try to be a "hero." Instruct employees when and if they face a robber to (1) reassure the robber of cooperation, (2) stay as calm as possible, and (3) take mental notes of the criminal's build, hair color, complexion, voice, clothing, and anything else that might later help identify the culprit. Employees should not compare descriptions until the police arrive. One foodservice chain keeps marks on the door jamb so that accurate height measurements may be ascertained. Another reason to cooperate is that there have been a number of suits by employees who were injured in robberies. Another chain encourages taxi drivers to park in their lot at night to have people around. Other techniques include keeping the rear door locked, having more than one employee on hand to open and close, and checking that doors and windows are intact before entering the building at opening time.

KEY AND LOCK CONTROL

A lock is an obstacle to burglary or unauthorized entry. In addition, a strong lock requires a burglar to use force to enter, and under standard burglary insurance policies, evidence of forced entry is necessary to collect on the policy. Dead-bolt locks should be used. They cannot be opened by sliding a piece of flexible material between the door edge and door jamb. A **dead-bolt** is a lock bolt that is moved positively by turning the knob or key without the action of a spring.

A double-cylinder dead-bolt lock may be used. This prevents a burglar from entering by breaking a glass or other panel and opening by turning a handle. Also, thieves who conceal themselves after closing cannot break out because the door requires a key on the inside. The security of any locking system depends on two factors. The first is vulnerability to picking, drilling, and forcing. The second and most vital factor is key control, the restricted duplication of keys for that lock or lock system.

To keep keys from falling into the hands of burglars, issue as few keys as possible, and keep a record of the keys issued. Exercise the same care with keys as you would a $1,000 bill by doing the following:

1. Avoid the danger of key duplication. Caution employees not to leave store keys with parking lot attendants, in a topcoat hanging in a restaurant, or lying about the office or stockroom.

2. Keep your key distribution records up-to-date so you know what keys have been issued and to whom.

3. Whenever a key is lost or an employee leaves the firm without turning in the key, re-key your store. (Unfortunately this can be expensive.)

4. Take special care to protect the "master key" used to remove cylinders from locks.

5. Have one key and lock for outside doors and a different key and lock for your office. Have as few master keys as possible because it weakens your security.

6. Have a code for each key so that it does not need to be tagged and only an authorized person knows the specific lock the key fits. Do not use a key chain that carries the store's address.

7. Take a periodic inventory of keys. Have employees show you each key so that you will know it has not been lost, mislaid, or borrowed.

8. Stamp keys with a notation that they cannot be duplicated.

WHITE-COLLAR CRIME

The most common white-collar crime is **embezzlement**, which is the fraudulent appropriation of property by someone to whom it has been entrusted. The embezzler is someone in the organization you trust. The stories of highly regarded and trusted employees who have defrauded their employers for years are legion.

There are, in fact, many ways for an embezzler to defraud an operation. A simple one is to pocket cash without making a record of the transaction. Controls with cash registers and checking systems described in this chapter are designed to prevent this sort of basic theft. Another form of back office embezzlement is called **lapping**. The process involves the temporary withholding of receipts such as payments on accounts receivable. A continuing scheme, lapping usually starts with a small amount but can run into thousands of dollars before it is detected. For example, consider the employee who opens mail or otherwise receives cash and checks as payment on open accounts. The employee retains a $100 cash payment made by customer A on March 1. To avoid arousing suspicion on A's part, the employee then takes $100 from a $200 payment made by customer B on March 5. He or she uses this payment to credit A's account. The embezzler pockets the remaining $100, which increases the shortage to $200.

As this "borrowing" procedure continues, the employee takes increasingly larger amounts of money involving more and different accounts. A fraud of this nature can continue for years. Of course, it requires detailed record keeping by the embezzler to keep track of the shortage and transfer it from one account to another to avoid suspicion. Any indication that an employee is keeping personal records of business transactions outside your regular books of account should be looked into.

Rebate-check theft can also occur. A supplier sends a rebate or refund check to a restaurant. A dishonest employee responsible for bank deposits uses it to replace cash in the deposit and keeps the cash.

Embezzlement can occur through payroll frauds where fictitious individuals are added to the payroll and their checks collected. Another is the recording of unearned overtime pay. The embezzler then can work out an arrangement with the nonworker who receives a payroll check or unearned overtime.

Purchasing agents can accept kickbacks from suppliers who charge inflated prices. Dishonest employees have even been known to set up dummy suppliers and falsify the documentation for completely fictitious purchases. When the bill arrives, they pay it and share the proceeds with the payee.

Expense accounts can be padded. Personal items can be charged to the company. One common embezzlement is charging personal long-distance telephone calls to the company.

A number of behavior quirks can signal embezzlement. An employee may never take a vacation so that no one else can see his or her work or records. Some organizations require that employees take vacations specifically to prevent this. Books of account may always be in perfect balance. This is not realistic and, if it happens, suspicions should be raised. An employee may resent an outside audit calling it "a needless expense" to prevent someone from seeing the books and discovering fraud.

An employee may resist sharing work with another. He or she may appear to be very dedicated and to put in long hours, but does not want another to check the books or deal with purveyors.

An extravagant lifestyle may be a sign of embezzlement. If you find yourself asking, "How can he (or she) afford all this?" embezzlement may be the answer. On the other hand, the lifestyle may be simple but the embezzler may be ensnared by gambling, drugs, or other vices. One can take a number of steps to prevent embezzlement; the key element in many of them is the separation of duties, such as not having the cashier prepare the bank deposit. The more people involved, the harder it is to embezzle.

Other precautions include requiring authorizations to place someone on the payroll, and requiring the manager or a nonbookkeeper to open the mail and record the money received. Some operations even have their mail sent to a post office box rather than the company office.

One can compare bank deposits with a separate record of checks and cash received. The manager may want to reconcile bank statements, which may also be sent to a separate post office box. One should examine all canceled checks and endorsements, occasionally spot check accounting records, retain supporting data for all checks, and cancel all invoices when the checks are signed. Most of all, managers should not sign blank checks.

THEFT INVESTIGATIONS

Sometimes evidences of theft such as cash shortages, inventory variances, costs that are too high, and confidential tips indicate that normal controls are not working. Management knows theft is going on—perhaps even has an idea of the extent—but does not know how it is being committed or who is responsible. In such cases, management might consider the use of an outside investigator whose purpose is to gather ironclad evidence to confront suspects. The evidence may be of two forms: physical witnesses and written documents from the paper flow of cash and goods through the operation.

For the most effective investigation, employees should not be aware an investigation is being pursued. Investigators are hired through normal procedures and pose as employees. Ideally, their job would require mobility to circulate in different areas of the operation. Normally, during the first month, investigators do not ask any questions but pick up a lot of general information and develop a rapport with other employees. In addition to theft, they may also find other problems, such as drug use or unsanitary practices, safety violations, and customer satisfaction or dissatisfaction. One investigatory firm has reports that cover 350 areas of operation. Once the source of theft is discovered, the next step is obtaining documentation. A favorite tool is pinhole cameras and long-play recorders.

The time to conduct the investigation and gather evidence is usually 60 to 120 days. One option at that time is to have a surprise shrinkage review survey. Employees are summoned together without notice. They are told that theft has been going on and they are being given a chance to cooperate voluntarily. Questionnaires with the employees' names on them are given to every employee with questions such as "Have you ever seen anyone high or intoxicated on the job?" "Have you ever seen another employee stealing food or merchandise?" "How is stealing accomplished?" The questionnaires are to be returned within 24 hours.

Obviously, some are concerned about having employees tattle on the activities of other employees, but the questionnaires can elicit a great deal of helpful information. If the information does not come in on the questionnaires, there is still the evidence from the investigator.

When confronted with the evidence against them, about 85 to 90 percent of the perpetrators will confess verbally and then sign a confession. Many experts recommend immediate discharge and prosecution. They contend theft is like a malignant cancer, and perpetrators must be removed and should be used as examples to deter others. However, some operators have found that some employees who have been discovered stealing and have been given a second chance become the most honest of employees. They are grateful for the second chance and know they would be under suspicion.

POINT-OF-SALES SYSTEMS

For a long time the basic cash register, which originally was developed by a restaurateur, was used to record sales, account for cash in or out, and determine the balance in the cash drawer. But this once-familiar register is being rapidly replaced by point-of-sale (POS) stations. A POS register is a minicomputer that can store data through transactional keys and manipulate this data to provide a variety of reports, many of which are shown in this book. One can use the POS register for other functions besides collecting cash. In fact, it may produce all or most of the cost reports an operation needs.

It can track employees' working hours for labor and productivity reports both in the aggregate and for individual workers. Having recorded sales, it can break them down into many categories. It can keep track of food inventory items and prepare appropriate cash reports. It can be used to transmit orders to the kitchen or bar, and as a prechecking device. It can provide the necessary reports for credit card accounting. In fact, some POS register manufacturers claim that the hospitality industry has not yet caught up with all the capabilities of this equipment.

These capabilities have definitely changed foodservice management, especially in the area of control. Management now has a tool that permits the efficient, fast, and economic handling of data to provide for a vastly improved management information system. It enhances internal control in keeping these records and improving operational efficiency.

Input Devices

Input devices collect the data and forward it to the processor. The most common input device is a keyboard. The keys may be alphanumeric (letters and numbers) or more specialized. Specialized keys include preset labeled keys that, when pressed, automatically handle the data for the item. They are very common in fast-food operations. **Open department register keys** break down sales by categories such as appetizers, entrées, and desserts. Tender keys refer to how payment is made: in cash, by credit card, or by check. Price look-up keys (PLUs) break down sales by specific items. Instead of having one preset key per item, each PLU key can track as many as 1,000 items. These keys work best with numbered items; by inputting the number of the item on the keyboard, one can retrieve all the information about it.

Keyboards can also be of different types. Many boards have standard keys. A paged keyboard has pages like a book and a new page can be turned on top of the micro switches. One keyboard page, for example, could be used for breakfast and another for lunch. A micromotion or flat keyboard slips on top of the switches and can readily be changed for different meals or occasions.

An important input device is the key lock, which involves control and specifies various modes. On some models the first mode is sometimes referred to as the **A mode** and allows one to record sales transactions. Each cashier can use a separate key as a personal identification. Managers may use the void key to make corrections. Also, a training mode allows the machine to be used for training purposes but does not affect data in the machine. The management mode allows for changes and report generation. Only management should have the key for access to this information. The management mode (**X mode**) produces reports up to a certain time period without resetting totals (refer to Figure 22.1). The amount of business done until 4 p.m., for example, could be determined with the *X mode*. The **Z mode** produces final reports and clears the information from the machine. Access to this mode is usually limited to management so that data cannot be eliminated prematurely. For control purposes, grand totals are not usually eliminated but are added on to each period.

Output Devices

Output devices provide information to the user. Printers are a type of output device. A printer may be placed at some distance from the POS register, perhaps in the kitchen where orders rung up on the register or some other terminal are reproduced for kitchen fulfillment. Other printers can be a receipt or journal tape, similar to those provided at the supermarket checkout counter. This can also be used as an order slip. The register may have another tape for audit purposes, and there can also be a printer for guest checks. Other output devices include displays such as digital displays, which are part of the register, or cathode ray tubes (CRTs), which are similar to TV screens. Chapter 6, Management Information Systems, has tie ins with POS registers.

PRECHECKING SYSTEMS

A **prechecking system** has two elements:

1. a written or electronic requisition to the kitchen or other unit authorizing release of the food, and
2. an independent record of what was ordered or dispensed.

Its purpose is to help avoid loss through unscrupulous serving personnel. Restaurants have long tried to combat this type of loss. At one time separate food checkers observed what went out of the kitchen into the dining area. They might check to see that every item was on the guest check, or they might keep a running tally of the sales value of the food taken out by each server. This provided a check between sales and receipts. Various duplicate check systems were used where a server had to present a duplicate slip for what was picked up. From these "dupes" could be reconstructed what each server's sales should be and what the total sales were. This could be compared against actual receipts.

In the 1950s, food checking machines began to appear. These machines made out checks (somewhat similar to supermarket tapes) that servers would present to get their food items from the kitchen. They also kept a running total of items and dollar sales for each server. Although effective, these systems presented problems. They added an extra step that slowed down servers and were new to most servers. It was estimated that when such systems were first installed, about 10 percent of the servers left. Their reasons—from added complexity to elimination of an opportunity to defraud the operation—probably varied for different operators.

With the advent of POS registers or prechecking terminals, the delays were eliminated by using remote kitchen-production printers, which printed the orders in the producing areas. Preset keys (each key handles the details of one menu item) and price look-up keys (which expand preset keys by using predesignated numbers to call up menu items and prices) aid in this. With the new systems the server need not leave the dining room to give the order to the producing areas. In some operations bus persons or other personnel bring the food from the producing areas, which further enhances servers' effectiveness.

Although prechecking systems may vary in application and equipment, an outline of the general sequence follows:

1. The server takes an order on an order form or other paper.
2. The server sets up an account at the prechecking terminal, entering his or her ID number, the number in the party, the table number, and a number assigned to the account.
3. The guest check is inserted into the check printer and the menu items and their cost are recorded. Preset keys, PLU keys, and modifier keys (such as "rare" or "well-done" for meats) along with the date and time of the entering are recorded. Data from item 2 may also be recorded.
4. The menu items are printed at the same time on the remote printers, which can also print the account number, server's number, time, table number, and number of people in the party.
5. If additional items are ordered, they can later be added to the check; the check printer can pick up the account number and the previous balance, or they can be entered manually.
6. At the end of the meal, the host receives the check automatically totaled with the sales tax calculated.
7. Payment is recorded before the check account number is closed.

The prechecking system can provide a number of controls. Receipts should equal totals in the register. A record of items ordered can be compared to inventory records or production quantities. (Nothing should be given from the production areas without a printout.) Servers are identified. The record of the number in the party and the table number (which should indicate the capacity of the table) allows a comparison of the number of items on the check and the number in the party.

RESTAURANT GUEST CHECK CONTROL

Guest checks, whether written manually or produced by mechanical or computerized means, have a number of uses. They can provide orders to the kitchen, bar, or other producing unit; be used by servers to match patrons and orders; provide statements to patrons for payment; provide independent records of receipts to check cashiers' turn-in; provide the information to make sales histories; provide information on individual servers' sales; and serve as receipts to patrons for reimbursement or tax purposes.

A foodservice operation could once suffer much loss through guest check manipulation, but a computerized prechecking system includes guest check control in its system. An item cannot be ordered unless it is entered in the register. The menu items are automatically printed, priced, and totaled, and a record is kept of the various check numbers and of servers who recorded them.

Some operations do not use computerized systems, and for them, handling and controlling guest checks still presents some special problems. Most transactions involve rather small amounts, and normally there is no tangible merchandise to be seen and checked (as there is in most retail establishments) when the customer settles the bill. A single entrance and exit and the fact that a number of customers are often covered by one check may tempt some customers to stroll out without settling their bills. A counter-service operation may employ one person to write out the order, pick it up, serve it, present the bill, collect payment, and then put the money in the cash register. Better control is obtained by separating functions and employing a cashier, but there is still ample room for confusion, theft, and negligence. The more items recorded on a check, the greater the chance for error. A server who may be adept at giving good table service may write sloppily, add incorrectly, or remember prices poorly.

There are many ways that both serving personnel and customers can defraud an operation with poor guest check control. For example, unscrupulous servers could collect a check, then keep both the check and the money. They might use their own checks to collect payment and, again, pocket the money if no other record of the sale exists. A server might total the check higher than the figures call for, collect the higher amount, correct the total before turning in the check, and keep the difference.

Customers and serving personnel may work in collusion. Items may be purposely left off the check in exchange for a higher tip from knowing customers. Expensive items may be served, but inexpensive ones listed on the check the patron pays. Customers may connive to get two different checks during their service and pay only one.

To keep personnel and customers from defrauding, an operator must have control over guest checks. Elements of this control include:

1. *Use of guest checks.* If money is collected and sales rung up without any substantiating checks, it is impossible to determine if all sales have been accounted for.

2. *Distinctive identification for all checks.* It is very easy to purchase pads of the common green checks from variety stores. The use of these checks permits easy substitution for fraudulent purposes. The check should be distinctive enough that its substitution will alert other personnel and customers.

3. *Checks printed on erasure-proof paper.* This type of paper shows when changes have been made—for whatever reasons. Mistakes should be crossed out, not erased.

4. *Use of pens or indelible pencils.* This precaution, like the previous one, helps prevent figure finagling.

5. *Prenumbering of all checks.* Accountability is basic to guest check control. Checks should be numbered in such a way that it can be determined precisely who is responsible for specific checks. The common green unnumbered checks make it difficult to determine whether all checks have been turned in.

```
          YOUR RESTAURANT NAME
          WILLIAM        CK# 1002
          06/30/XX  10:02AM 07 TABLE- 20 COVERS- 2
                                                    - 16 character alpha for all
                                                      menu items.
            3 FOOD      11 OZ N.Y. STRIP    9.95  - menu items categorized by
            4              BAKED POTATO      0.00    product group
            5              GARDEN PEAS       0.00  - automatically assigned
            6           MAINE LOBSTER       12.95    check number.
            7             FRENCH FRIES       0.00  - no need for costly 2-part
            8             FRESH BROCCOLI     0.00    checks.
            9          2 COLOMBIAN COFFEE    1.50  - table and cover counts
           14             BWL CLAM CHOWDER   1.75  - time and date
           15             CHEFS SALAD        4.25  - eight character alpha
           ########TOTAL FOOD              30.40    server name
            1 BEVERAGE   DEWARS             2.55  - subtotals by product
            2            EARLY TIMES        2.55    groups.
           12            DEWARS             2.55  - accurate pricing
           13            EARLY TIMES        2.55  - tip add on
           ########TOTAL BEVERAGE          10.20  - no previous balance
           10 WINE       GLASS CHABLIS      1.50    pick ups.
           11            GLASS ROSE         1.50  - no handwriting on check
           ########TOTAL WINE              3.00  - header and trailer message
           43.60 SBTL    1.67 TX      45.27 TTL    printed on every check.
                                                  - easy but controlled void.
```

Figure 22.2
POS-Produced Guest Check

6. *Requirement that all servers sign for their checks (and their duplicates) when they are issued to them.* With numbering, accountability can be obtained. If questions of property arise, it is possible to determine the food server involved. Some operations require food servers to turn in unused checks at the end of the day and to secure new ones at the beginning of the next day.

7. *Including the number of people in the party and their table number on the check.* With this information, it is easier to check the number of items served against the number of customers. Also, meaningful cover and average check statistics can be developed from these two figures.

8. *Periodic audits of checks for pricing and addition errors.* It may not be practical to audit every check, but every food server should know that checks will be audited occasionally. In addition to revealing mistakes, this practice provides the psychological motivation to eliminate errors because there is a greater chance for their discovery. Some operations that do routine audits impose a fine or penalty for each mistake discovered.

9. *Accounting for all used checks.* When a check is paid, it is taken out of circulation, and the possibility of its being used again is thereby eliminated. If used checks remain unaccounted for, it may be a sign that they are being reused to divert the payment.

A check stub receipt, retained by the server and endorsed by the cashier, can show that the cashier has accepted responsibility for the check.

The use of computer-generated guest check systems simplifies the preceding controls considerably. The system automatically supplies the check, and the name or identification of the operation is printed on the check. The check cannot be altered. The sys-

22

Internal Control

The term *internal control* covers a wide field and involves many areas previously discussed. Internal control is concerned particularly with how people can be prevented from defrauding an operation. The larger the operation, the more need for internal control. The owner and operator of a one-man hamburger stand needs no internal control over employees and probably little over customers, but as enterprises get larger, need more employees, and have more customers, their need for internal control grows. The cost to an operation of being defrauded by employees or customers has grown greatly in recent years, making ever more vigilant controls necessary. Since foodservice operations are people intensive, they have a strong and special need for internal controls.

This chapter will first discuss the theoretical concepts of internal control and then consider specific applications such as security, theft control, cost control, embezzlement, and guest checks. The goals of internal control include making the operation as efficient as possible and eliminating loss from various types of fraud.

After completing this chapter, you should be able to:

1. List five general procedures for achieving internal control.
2. State six reasons why a customer or an employee might steal.
3. List 10 commonsense ways to reduce employee theft.
4. Explain four functions of the cashier in a foodservice operation.
5. Define *robbery* and *burglary,* explain how they differ, and state two general strategies for reducing both.
6. State principles of key and lock control.
7. Define and discuss *embezzlement.* Define *lapping* and *kickback.*
8. State seven ways to discourage an embezzler.
9. Briefly explain the functions of ECR and POS systems.
10. Describe components of the typical POS system.
11. List and describe four POS configurations.

tem automatically numbers the checks, eliminating prenumbering. Servers do not have to sign for checks, and most of the auditing can be done automatically by the system.

Figure 22.2 analyzes guest checks produced by a POS register. The POS register would keep track of guest check accountability.

GUEST CHECK HANDLING

There are different systems for pricing meals on the check, totaling these prices, and receiving payment for them. The server may mark the price at the table, or item prices may be printed on the check by a POS register or a food-checking device. The server or the cashier may total the check. Having the cashier do this job increases the element of control but may delay service at the cashier's desk. The server may collect payment for the check, take it to the cashier, and return with the change. Or patrons may pay when they leave the dining area. The server who collects payment usually can see that no one leaves without paying. (He or she can also present the change in such a way as to encourage the patron to tip generously.) Some feel that having the server handle the details of payment is a subtle nicety of table service. However, having the server take the check to the cashier adds still another chore to the server's work. Another approach is to allow servers to carry money and to make their own change. Their responsibility is to turn in the total amount shown on their guest checks and any bank funds that might have been issued to them. Of course, control diminishes when one person takes the order, picks it up, makes up the check, and collects the money. Control increases when other people are involved in the procedure.

SUMMARY

Internal control is vital to a hospitality organization, and the five areas of internal control from the accounting perspective include (1) developing a plan of organization, (2) safeguarding assets, (3) providing reliable financial records, (4) promoting operational efficiency, and (5) adhering to management policy.

A foodservice operation must have the security it needs to protect its cash, merchandise, supplies, and equipment. Employees and customers may steal for a variety of reasons that include a desire for material possessions, temptation, acquiring souvenirs, the operation's apparent impersonality (or "distance"), anger or resentment, kleptomania, thrill seeking, and social problems such as drug or gambling addiction. Separate security programs should be devised for patrons and for employees who might steal.

Robbery and burglary committed by outsiders may be a problem for some operations. Employees should be instructed to keep limited amounts of cash available and not to try to be heroes and capture a robber or burglar themselves. Rather, they should

concentrate enough to be able to describe the criminal for the authorities.

Key and lock control is also important, and this chapter lists a number of procedures for implementing this type of control.

Embezzlement is a form of white-collar crime defined as the fraudulent conversion of property by one to whom it has been entrusted. The most innocent appearing of employees may embezzle, but there are techniques and procedures to help reduce opportunities for embezzlement or help with the detection of an embezzler.

POS registers can also be used in a prechecking system, which has two elements: (1) a written or electronic requisition authorizing the release of food and (2) an independent record of what was ordered or dispensed.

Finally, there are many ways an operation that does not have guest check control can be victimized, but, once again, many techniques and procedures are available to help reduce this threat.

KEY TERMS

A mode	lapping
burglary	open department register keys
dead-bolt lock	prechecking system
embezzlement	robbery
felony	X mode
internal control	Z mode
kleptomania	

REVIEW QUESTIONS

22–1 List the components of the accounting definition of internal control.

22–2 What is included in the "plan of organization" in the accounting definition of internal control?

22–3 List and briefly explain six reasons why people steal.

22–4 Explain how social distance is involved with patron theft.

22–5 List five ways to deter employee theft.

22–6 What procedures should be followed in making change?

22–7 Differentiate between burglary and robbery.

22–8 What did the text suggest as the five most common factors considered by robbers in evaluating a target?

22–9 What are the two main factors regarding the security of a locking system?

22–10 Define embezzling.

22–11 List four signs of embezzlement.

22–12 In general, what can a POS register do when it functions as a computer?

22–13 Briefly explain the components of a POS register.

22–14 Differentiate between the A mode, X mode, and Z mode on a POS register.

22–15 Describe the sequence of a prechecking system.

22–16 How can a foodservice operation with POS guest check control be defrauded?

22–17 How can a foodservice operation with POS guest check control be defrauded?

22–18 In what ways are guest checks audited?

PROBLEMS

22–1 You are involved with a midsized family restaurant that is having problems of absenteeism and punctuality with employees. Prepare appropriate standard operating procedures (SOPs) regarding absenteeism and punctuality for the operation that may help alleviate the problems. Address any legal considerations in the SOPs.

22–2 An operator of a fast-food operation (nonchain) that is located on the outskirts of a medium-sized town off a busy highway has been robbed four times in two years. He asks for your help in preventing more robberies or apprehending the robbers. List steps he might take to accomplish this.

PROJECT

22–1 Analyze a foodservice operation and make recommendations regarding procedures and recommendations it can take to help prevent a burglary.

CASE PROBLEM

This case study provides you with stylized, perhaps oversimplified, but illustrative situations that invite you to consider the ethical considerations involved. The potential ethical issues are numbered.

Cosmo Cuisiner at the Phoenix

Cosmo Cuisiner, manager of the Phoenix, a large suburban restaurant, starts his day with the breakfast special of eggs, sausage, home fries, and coffee. As he eats, he remembers a local "health nut" urging him to stop pushing high-calorie, high-cholesterol, high-sodium foods and to provide some nutritious alternatives.

Cosmo replied that he only served what his customers wanted and that, besides, his high-calorie desserts were far too profitable to abandon. (1)

The glow of a hearty breakfast quickly fades when Cosmo walks into his kitchen to find a Teamsters organizer circulating among his employees. Cosmo orders the organizer to leave and threatens to have him arrested for trespassing if he returns. The organizer angrily replies that the Phoenix employees approached him first, that there will soon be a union representation election, and that the Teamsters are sure to win it. (2) Cosmo makes a mental note to confer with Tillie, the stool pigeon he secretly pays to spy on her co-workers. (3) It would be helpful, Cosmo thinks, to learn who the union instigators are. Even though it is unlawful to discriminate against union activists, Cosmo has ways of dealing with disgruntled workers. (4)

Cosmo realizes that the Phoenix is ripe for unionization. He has awarded no general wage increase in two years despite steady inflation. Food service workers often start with the lowest wages in his town, and only the lack of job opportunities in the area keeps them from leaving. Cosmo once asked the owners of the Phoenix to use some of their profits for wage increases, but they informed him that they felt entitled to a healthy return on their investment first and then they had to channel money into renovations. The law of supply and demand, they said, should control wages. (5)

They also said no restaurant can afford to pay more than its competitors pay, and they deplored those radicals at the state capitol trying to enact a higher state minimum wage. Such a bill might doom those operations that cannot absorb or pass on the extra expense. (6)

One solution to Cosmo's union dilemma might be to arrange a sweetheart contract with a local union, thereafter recognized as a bargaining agent, in preference to the Teamsters, who would no longer then be able to force a representation election. The hospitality union would receive the union dues with little effort on its part and, in return, would make only slight demands on behalf of its members at the Phoenix. This sweetheart arrangement would deprive the workers of a choice of unions and eliminate any chance of their receiving more benefits through the more militant union. (7)

Cosmo also wonders whether he ought to join his trade association in lobbying for right-to-work legislation, which curtails union effectiveness by exempting from unionization those employees opposed to it, even though the majority of their co-workers vote to unionize. "That's the American way," Cosmo thinks. "No one should have to join a union. I can't understand why anyone who accepts the gains won by a union without joining it is called a free-loader, especially when the union uses collective action to win them." (8)

Cosmo's thoughts of unionization are interrupted by a cook who reports that he has almost run out of chicken for the chicken à la king. He wants to extend the chicken with some leftover turkey. Under the sauce, no one will tell the difference, and the Phoenix's menu has already been printed. Cosmo agrees, secretly pleased that there is no truth in menu law in his town. (9) In some localities, zealous enforcers impose stiff fines for such routine substitutions, but Cosmo chuckles to himself remembering the time he used day-old pork for chicken and received several compliments on the unusually tasty chicken salad. (10)

Meanwhile, waiting patiently in Cosmo's office is a visitor from a minority rights group wanting the Phoenix to give minority people some hiring preference in the future. Cosmo bristles at the very suggestion that he has been guilty of discrimination in hiring. The visitor tries to explain that unemployment affects minorities more than others and that social stress could result from disproportionate joblessness. Making no promises, Cosmo asks his visitor to leave. (11)

Soon thereafter, a police officer arrives soliciting ads for the Police Benevolent Association's *Yearbook*. Cosmo knows the ad will be a useless promotion, but he reasons, "It never hurts to stay on the good side of the city's finest." (12) He prefers paying for PBA *Yearbook* space to being shaken down by the building inspector who found several violations at the Phoenix a week ago. Cosmo knew the violations would be thrown out of court, but it would cost him time, legal expenses, and no doubt more harassment. For a $50 bill, the inspector tore up his citation and left the Phoenix saying, "I'll see you again in a year." (13)

Cosmo realizes, of course, that not all inspectors are corrupt. Why only the day before, grateful for suggestions about cleaning up some potential health code violations, Cosmo invited a helpful sanitation inspector and her family for dinner on the house. (14)

Among the papers on his desk, Cosmo finds a notice from the State Milk Control Board announcing a hike in milk prices. "More bureaucratic meddling," he thinks, "but luckily I can get around it." While some less ethical operators might demand under-the-table reimbursements to bring milk prices down to competitive levels, Cosmo keeps himself above such behavior. Instead, the Phoenix pays the legal price for its milk but receives compensatory discounts on the ice cream and cottage cheese the dairy supplies. (15)

An assistant brings Cosmo next week's employee schedule. The Phoenix's business is slightly off, and Cosmo knows he should trim the labor hours. He decides to reduce some full-time waitresses to part-time and chooses those whose husbands have jobs and can afford the reduction. He is glad his employees remain unorganized because a union could force him to reduce hours in strict accordance with seniority. (16) The more he thinks about the part-time idea, the better Cosmo likes it. He can schedule his waitresses only for the four-hour rush period and avoid all the wasted time that occurs over a full eight-hour shift. Also, he need not pay part-timers the expensive health and pension benefits full-time employees receive. (17)

Unlike the labor cost, the food cost at the Phoenix has been steadily rising, and Cosmo suspects some employees of stealing food even though he has yet to find a culprit. He thinks about making a polygraph test a condition of employment, and he also thinks about ordering a polygraph test for all employees whenever he believes someone is stealing. Lie detector tests would, he reasons, reveal the

guilty party and discourage others from taking food. Despite the civil liberty questions they raise, polygraph tests do reduce employee theft. (18)

Although not one hundred percent accurate and illegal in many jurisdictions the polygraph test can reveal some who have theft tendencies. The fact that they can be discovered through the test even though they can successfully remove the food deters some from trying to steal. Congress may limit the use of polygraph tests nationally.

Polygraph testing might have prevented Sally Jones's problem. Sally had been a cashier at the Phoenix for ten years, but Cosmo recently slipped a $20 overage into the register receipts and caught Sally taking it for herself. (19) Sally tearfully assured him it was her first offense, and he believed her. He also knew that Sally, a widow with four children to support, was woefully underpaid. She pleaded that she desperately needed the money to buy shoes for her youngest child, but Cosmo fired her anyway, because he knew that no operation could safely tolerate stealing and that Sally's dismissal would serve to warn the other employees. (20)

Cosmo remembers another personnel matter he may have to take care of soon. Old Jonas has been working in the Phoenix dishroom since it started forty years ago. He is probably in his midseventies (well beyond the age discrimination legislation) and is not producing the way he once did. His only other income source would be social security, and this income would be limited because he was not covered until relatively late. Even after coverage became mandatory, the Phoenix paid Jonas under the table for a while to avoid the deduction. He has no relatives, he has no savings, and he would have a hard time existing on just social security. (21)

Hazel Smith presents another dilemma. Hazel is only sixty, and she still produces when she works. However, she suffers from a chronic disease and is often hospitalized. Her absences cause scheduling problems (22), and her medical bills have raised the Phoenix's medical insurance rates to the point where it now limits the money available for coverage to other employees. (23)

From these nagging personnel problems, Cosmo turns his thoughts to a bright spot in his operation, the renovated bar lounge. He hired a new bar manager six months ago, and the new man has attracted a lot of new trade among out-of-town business executives. The bar manager arranges "dates" for them in a discreet way. There is no open solicitation in the bar, and the bar manager is the only employee involved. Cosmo can't understand why Mrs. Cuisiner became upset when she heard about the bar manager's sideline. Nobody pushes these men; they would probably find female companionship elsewhere anyway. It is better to handle this dating discreetly than to encourage open prostitution on the street. Cosmo rather wishes he could get a commission from the nearby hotels. (24)

The new bar manager, does, however, pose one disturbing problem. Cosmo knows he serves short drinks to some and pockets the difference. He also overcharges tipsy or careless patrons now and then. However, the bar percentage is acceptable, and with the increase in business, the bar operation is more profitable than ever. Cosmo decides this is no time to rock the boat and ruin a good thing. (25)

Cosmo remembers some flak about the new somewhat skimpy uniforms from some waitresses when the bar reopened. They were not skimpy enough to invite discrimination suits but they are sexy. Some waitresses resigned. However they were older and not quite as decorative as the ones who stayed. Some waitresses have also favorably commented on the higher tips they now generate with the outfits. (26)

His morning of decisions and contemplations over, Cosmo orders the Phoenix's luncheon special, which he eats with a blissfully clear conscience.

The following discussion questions, keyed by number to the decision notes, frame the ethical implications of the Cosmo Cuisiner case study:

1. Should restaurants offer healthful foods or only what their customers expect?
2. Is it ethical to keep union organizers from contacting employees?
3. Should a manager ask employees to spy on one another?
4. Should a manager make work uncomfortable for union sympathizers?
5. Should supply and demand alone determine wages, or should other considerations govern an operation's salary structure?
6. What are the ethical implications of a state-mandated minimum wage law?
7. Do you consider sweetheart contracts ethical?
8. What are the ethical implications of right-to-work legislation?
9. Does truth-in-menu legislation encourage fair dealing or corner cutting?
10. Is this extreme example of menu substitution defensible?
11. Is it fair to hire minority people preferentially?
12. Do you like the idea of business people currying favor with the police?
13. Does business necessity ever justify bribery?
14. At what point does a favor given in gratitude become a bribe?
15. Does the circumvention of a milk-pricing law raise ethical problems?
16. What ethical considerations attend the act of reducing full-time employees to part-time?
17. Does an employer ever have a responsibility to provide fringe benefits even when the law does not require them?
18. Do you consider polygraph testing an ethical business practice? (Assume it is legal.)
19. Does the discovery of Sally's dishonesty justify her entrapment?
20. Should a manager extend leniency to an otherwise loyal employee caught stealing?
21. What responsibility does an operation assume for a long-time faithful employee who can no longer support herself?
22. Should an operation retain an employee who cannot work regularly?
23. Is it ethical to dismiss a marginal employee for the high medical costs he or she generates?
24. Should a bar involve itself in pandering, no matter how inevitable or discreet?
25. What are ethical implications in employing someone who is unscrupulous but produces profit?
26. Is it ethical to require bar waitresses to wear suggestive outfits? (Assume they are not suggestive enough to invite discrimination suits.)

Budgetary Control

The primary purpose of any commercial food operation is to earn the largest profit possible, and a nonprofit organization wants to provide for its patrons the best food and service its financial resources allow. Proper financial management is necessary to both goals, and a budget is a basic tool for proper financial management. Without some form of budgeting or financial planning, problems arise quickly: Costs become excessive, the cash drain becomes too heavy for a balanced cash flow, the operation may get caught in a profit squeeze when costs rise without compensatory selling price increases, or major or capital improvements must be deferred. A planned budget is vital to anyone considering the feasibility of a new operation and to anyone interested in maintaining an existing business. In fact, budgeting has been called *profit planning* or *survival planning.*

Nonprofit operations do not seek profits but budgeting is just as important to them. If an operation depends on appropriations, budgets are vital to make sure that the facility operates within its appropriated funding boundary.

This chapter begins by discussing the budgets used in commercial operations and then focuses on budgets in institutional operations. Many of the same principles apply to both.

Particularly helpful in budget preparation are electronic spreadsheets, which correspond to an accountant's worksheet. They consist of a grid of columns and rows with cells of information that can be displayed on a cathode ray tube screen. Not only can the information be readily moved about and new data inserted or removed, but when a figure is changed, the computer will also automatically change all other figures affected by the first change.

After completing this chapter, you should be able to:

1. Define the word **budget.**
2. Describe at least seven types of budgets.
3. Describe at least six advantages and four disadvantages of budgets.
4. Suggest a typical procedure for preparing a foodservice operation's budget.
5. List the eight factors likely to influence a particular budget.

6. Explain the difference between an operating budget and a cash budget.

7. Explain what is meant by "adding flexibility" to a budget.

8. Briefly explain the difference between a fixed cost and a variable cost.

9. Briefly show how capital requests might be prioritized.

10. Develop a typical budget calendar.

11. Explain how one might project food and labor costs for a nonprofit institution's budget.

12. List four typical reasons for making a capital investment.

13. List four methods of ranking investment proposals according to operational needs.

14. Briefly explain how to use an economy study.

15. Calculate an anticipated payback period according to procedures outlined in this chapter.

16. Calculate an anticipated rate of return according to procedures outlined in this chapter.

WHAT IS A BUDGET?

There are many definitions of the term **budget**. A convenient one is "an organized plan of operation for a specified period of time that forecasts activity and income, determines expenses and other disposition of funds, and concludes with an estimate of an overall financial position at the end of the specified period." A budget is a plan, often in chart form, of how one expects to perform during a specified period. It coordinates financial factors, sales, and operating results. It forecasts (for a commercial operation) the amount of money that will be coming in, it determines how much should be disbursed, and it predicts what will be available at the end of the period. For an institution or operation without direct sales, a budget estimates expenses and, therefore, the necessary cash appropriation.

In addition to its role as a plan for business operation, a budget is an important control device. It provides a basis for comparing actual operations with planned or desired results. There are many kinds of budgets. One is the overall financial budget that coordinates every aspect of the operation. Components of this are **operating budgets**, which forecast, for example, sales activity and expense categories such as food and labor. A **cash budget** merely shows the inflow and outgo of funds and the amount on hand. An equipment budget indicates when it is financially feasible to purchase equipment and helps establish the priority of purchases. A renovation, remodeling, and repair budget provides for, surprisingly enough, renovation, remodeling, and repair.

Budgets are not limited to dollar expressions. A sales budget can specify the number of meals an operator expects to serve along with the dollar volume. A labor budget may be expressed in terms of the number of personnel, workdays, or work-hours required, as well as labor dollar costs.

A capital budget differs from other types of budgets in that it has effects that will continue over a long period of time. It usually involves expenditures for major equipment or facilities acquisition.

ADVANTAGES OF BUDGETS

Operating budgets offer many advantages. From a practical standpoint, they do the following:

1. *Provide a goal.* An operation that should do a $1 million volume per year is not achieving its potential if it does only $800,000. In the budget process, a realistic goal is determined to provide incentive for both individuals and departments. If these goals do not exist, there may be little that will cause individuals to go beyond routine performance or enable management to gauge performance.

2. *Provide a control device.* Expenses and needs have been determined in advance. Comparing actual costs with the predetermined ones reveals deviation from the predetermined standards.

3. *Establish a yardstick.* A budget allows you to plan your operation and measure the results. It is much better, for example, to discover through your budget a possible loss situation than to have the loss become apparent later when you are close to bankruptcy.

4. *Coordinate the organization.* To prepare a budget, one must consider all aspects of the operation. Sales, expenses, personnel, and equipment needs must be coordinated. With an effective budget there is direction and less possibility of the interdepartmental confusion that occurs when departments work independently.

5. *Provide responsibility.* In addition to providing goals for individuals and departments, the budget places a responsibility on personnel to generate sales and control costs. Everyone must do his or her part in conforming to the budget if it is to be effective.

6. *Help in planning.* By definition, a budget is a plan for the future. Forecasting the volume of activity helps determine what must be provided to meet this level of activity. Knowing the anticipated financial status of your operation is essential to planning future policies.

7. *Solve problems.* Along with broad considerations, a budget is very helpful in many down-to-earth, pragmatic ways. Problems such as whether an operation can afford a disbursement, what changes to make in staffing, whether selling prices should be changed, and who is responsible for a particular task are all answered in part by a good budget.

DISADVANTAGES OF BUDGETS

Budgets have their price, however. Here are some of their disadvantages:

1. A budget requires time to prepare, and time costs money. The preparation time can also take personnel away from their necessary management functions. Workable budgets are usually not a one-person job but require cooperation and coordination.

2. Budgets are based on forecasting, and the future cannot always be told readily. Factors may occur that were impossible to predict and that affect the budget and plans based on it considerably.

3. To be truly effective, the budget and budgeting process must have the support of the organization. Going through the motions of preparing and working with a budget, without really trying to use it, often results in a false sense of security. Sometimes the allocation

of resources in the budget can cause difficulties within the organization, when, for example, various factions compete against one another for allocations.

4. A budget also requires that management make known its plans and goals, which, for various private reasons, it may not wish to do.

FACTORS TO CONSIDER IN BUDGET PREPARATION

Budgets may be classified in different ways. A **top down budget** is prepared by top management and given to operating units. This is the opposite of a **bottom up budget** where individual units prepare their own budgets, which are then sent to upper management for approval and combining.

A **zero-based budget**, as its name implies, starts with no previous figures then determines outlays, costs, and inflows. An opposite approach is a **baseline budget**, which starts with a previous budget period and adjusts the figures for current conditions. Many budgets do not work well because of poor preparation and planning. Using a previous budget, or operating figures borrowed from the previous period with only casual hopeful adjustments for a new budget, can be more damaging than having no budget at all. Or, if a casual forecast of business volume is made and expenses are determined with preestablished percentages based on the sales, trouble can result. The implication is that these ratios are static, cannot be improved upon, and are not to be changed, but they are often misleading and sometimes overlook facts.

In larger operations, a budget officer, someone from operations research or the controller's office, is familiar with budget preparation and is assigned this responsibility. Although the budget may require work and cooperation from many people, there should be one person assigned the responsibility (and authority) to carry through budget preparation. In some operations a budget committee may work with the budget project officer.

The first step in budget preparation is to ascertain the general level of income or activity—by individual departments, if there is more than one contributing to this activity. Once the level of activity is determined, appropriate costs for this level can be established. Various departments may prepare their own cost estimates in the bottom up approach, and the budget officer may participate in these deliberations. Then the budget officer combines and coordinates the estimates from the various sections. He or she also prepares the cash budget that covers the whole operation and is based on the general budget. The budget officer submits the combined budget to top management or to the owners, and they may demand changes. Their desires must be resolved, and they must approve the completed budget.

A budget timetable indicating when budget work should start and when the deadlines for the various phases occur is very helpful. Otherwise, preparation may be put off until the last minute. A budget developed under the pressure of time may not be well thought out or reflect the desired cooperation and coordination among those affected by it. The results often create disappointment or discontent. It is better for the completion of a yearly budget to occur several months before the beginning of the budgeted year.

Budgets may cover various periods, but the budget prepared for a forthcoming fiscal, or business, year is most common. It is usually preferable to break down the year by weeks or months first, and then add the periods to determine a total budget for the year. In an annual budget, some fixed expenses and some fixed income may be divided by twelve (or whatever the periods of activity) for the breakdown. But other budget categories will vary according to the number of days, weekends, or holidays in the month or seasonal energy costs, and these should be calculated separately for each month.

It is possible to make appropriate changes in the budget once the budget period has begun so as to increase the budget's accuracy over the remainder of the period. A steep rise in food purchase costs, for example, may necessitate higher menu selling prices, and the budgeted sales and food costs would have to be adjusted.

Budgets may be fixed or flexible. The **fixed budget** is based on a definite level of sales or activity, whereas a flexible budget provides cost information for differing levels of sales activity. Cost percentages may differ for different sales volumes. Thus, labor costs might be 28 percent of sales at a monthly sales volume of $15,000 but 26 percent at a $25,000 monthly sales volume.

To provide accurate forecasts of sales and expenses, it is necessary to know the operations of the particular department thoroughly. Some useful knowledge to collect while the budget is being made includes:

- the department's actual operating and budget variance figures from previous years
- the department's goals
- the department's sales experience, sales reports, and sales statistics
- the department's future operating policies
- national and local economic conditions
- sales and expense trends
- menu prices, customer selection, portion sizes, and food cost per portion
- payroll statistics such as the number of employees and their duties, hours, and wage rates

Table 23.1 shows a budget format for a seaside restaurant, owned by two partners, that has considerable seasonal and monthly fluctuations. Monthly food sales range from $13,200 in December to $102,300 in July and August and total $567,500 for the budget year. Beverage sales range from $4,420 in December to $34,255 in July and August and total $190,065 for the year.

Factors that influence the forecasting of beverage sales include past percentages of beverage sales to food sales, the number and dollar value of drinks served per food cover, and seasonal fluctuations in beverage consumption. This operation wants food and beverage costs to be 40 and 30 percent of food and beverage sales, respectively. Both cost and merchandising factors must be considered in determining these percentages. The cost considerations involve how much food the partners can provide for the desired selling price and whether this amount will be commensurate with the quality and quantity their customers want. Merchandising considerations involve determining the highest price patrons will readily pay for the food and service provided. In the expense categories, some items, such as payroll and direct expenses, vary according to sales. To determine the payroll cost,

Table 23.1
Budget Format

Seashore Restaurant Budgeted Profit and (Loss)

	January	February	March	April	May	June	July	August	September	October	November	December	Total
Sales													
Food	16,500	24,750	33,000	41,250	49,500	66,000	102,300	102,300	69,300	33,000	16,500	13,200	567,600
Beverage	5,525	8,290	11,050	13,815	16,575	22,100	34,255	34,255	23,205	11,050	5,525	4,420	190,065
Total sales	22,025	33,040	44,050	55,065	66,075	88,100	136,555	136,555	92,505	44,050	22,025	17,620	757,665
Cost of sales													
Food	6,600	9,900	13,200	16,500	19,800	26,400	40,920	40,920	27,720	13,200	6,600	5,280	227,040
Beverage	1,660	2,485	3,315	4,145	4,975	6,630	10,275	10,275	6,960	3,315	1,660	1,325	57,020
Total cost of sales	8,260	12,385	16,515	20,645	24,775	33,030	51,195	51,195	34,680	16,515	8,260	6,605	384,060
Gross profit	13,765	20,655	27,535	34,420	41,300	55,070	85,360	85,360	57,825	27,535	13,765	11,015	473,605
Controllable expenses													
Salaries and wages	7,050	9,910	13,215	16,520	18,500	24,670	38,235	38,235	25,900	13,215	7,050	5,640	218,140
Direct	1,320	1,980	2,645	3,305	3,965	5,285	8,195	8,195	5,550	2,645	1,320	1,055	45,460
Utilities	1,250	1,250	1,250	1,250	1,250	1,250	1,250	1,250	1,250	1,250	1,250	1,250	15,000
Marketing	500	500	500	500	500	500	500	500	500	500	500	500	6,000
Repairs and maintenance	1,000	1,000	1,000	1,000	1,000	1,000	1,000	1,000	1,000	1,000	1,000	1,000	12,000
Administrative	1,000	1,000	1,000	1,000	1,000	1,000	1,000	1,000	1,000	1,000	1,000	1,000	12,000
Total controllable expenses	12,120	15,640	19,610	23,575	26,215	33,705	50,180	50,180	35,200	19,610	12,120	10,445	308,600
Operating profit	1,645	5,015	7,925	10,845	15,085	21,365	35,180	35,180	22,625	7,925	1,645	570	165,005
Non-controllable expenses													
Occupation expenses	2,500	2,500	2,500	2,500	2,500	2,500	2,500	2,500	2,500	2,500	2,500	2,500	30,000
Interest expenses	160	215	270	270	270	270	270	270	255	245	230	220	2,945
Income before depreciation	(1,015)	2,300	5,155	8,075	12,315	18,595	32,410	32,410	19,870	5,180	(1,085)	(2,150)	132,060
Depreciation	1,800	1,800	2,250	2,250	2,250	2,250	2,250	2,250	2,250	2,250	2,250	2,250	26,100
Amortization	1,000	1,000	1,000	1,000	1,000	1,000	1,000	1,000	1,000	1,000	1,000	1,000	12,000
Income before taxes	(3,815)	(500)	1,905	4,825	9,065	15,345	29,160	29,160	16,620	1,930	(4,335)	(5,400)	93,960

it is necessary to estimate the number of employees needed and their cost for various customer volumes. In Table 23.1, this cost works out, on a percentage basis, this way:

Payroll cost percentage	Sales dollar volume per month
32%	Less than $30,000
30%	$30,000 to $60,000
28%	Over $60,000

Although in practice the percentages may not be exact they can be a guide and control. Expenses such as repairs and maintenance or administration may be spread out equally during the year. Although different amounts for these expenses may have to be paid during different months, it is often impractical to break these costs down to correlate directly with sales.

Table 23.2 shows the cash budget for the Seashore Restaurant. It shows only the amount of money coming in and the amount that must be disbursed (cash flow). The difference between inflow and outflow of funds is usually not the same as the profit figure for the period. Depreciation cost, for example, is an expense item, but it does not require an immediate outlay of cash. The restaurant depicted in the example has suffered from a severe shortage of working capital. It will, however, start its fiscal year with a line of credit that will allow it to borrow necessary funds. The budget was very helpful in obtaining the line of credit, since it demonstrated that loans could easily be repaid with cash generated.

An operation that makes an overall profit may still be short of cash and need additional funds at some period or other. In January, our Seashore Restaurant generated $22,025 in sales and received $32,000 in loan proceeds. These two amounts, with the opening balance of $2,600, made $56,625 in cash available. Applications of $51,580 in cash—including $3000 to each partner—leave a cash balance of $5,045 at the end of the month. Repairs and maintenance expenses of $12,000 for the year, which were divided into 12 equal monthly amounts, are now budgeted to show when the $12,000 will most likely be disbursed. Cash payments are shown when they actually will be paid, not when the obligation was incurred. Thus, if food bills are paid the month after the food purchase, the cash paid will be shown for that following month. In the general budget, the food cost was shown the month it was incurred, rather than when it actually was paid, to provide a true profit-and-loss figure.

Usually, the most difficult problem in preparing a budget is forecasting sales. This estimated sales figure is extremely important, since it is not only the largest figure and the basis for many other budget calculations, but it is also the goal for the period and the motivation for the entire operation. The planned sales figure should be realistic, but it should also provide the incentive to improve on past performance. Therefore, past sales records showing the number of covers and average charge per cover must be examined. One should also discover what might be done within the operation itself to increase volume. For example, would advertising changes, renovations, better merchandising, and different pricings help? Outside influences, such as local population and general prosperity levels, inflation trends, and new competition, can be equally important. All factors that influence volume must be appropriately weighed to estimate how the volume will change. This change is usually expressed as a percentage of the current year's level. However, one

Table 23.2
Cash Budget

Seashore Restaurant Cash Budget

	January	February	March	April	May	June	July	August	September	October	November	December
Opening balance	2,600	5,045	5,145	5,400	8,575	15,990	24,985	63,715	87,925	80,895	65,855	47,470
Sources of cash												
Sales	22,025	33,040	44,050	55,065	66,075	88,100	136,555	136,555	92,505	44,050	22,025	17,620
SBA loan	32,000	11,000	10,500	—	—	—	—	—	—	—	—	—
Total	56,625	49,085	59,695	60,465	74,650	104,090	161,540	200,270	180,430	124,945	87,880	65,090
Applications of cash												
Food	27,640	6,600	9,900	13,200	16,500	24,800	26,400	40,920	40,920	22,720	13,200	6,600
Liquor	1,660	2,485	3,315	4,145	4,975	6,630	10,275	10,275	6,960	3,315	1,660	1,325
Payroll	7,050	9,910	13,215	16,520	18,500	24,670	38,235	38,235	25,900	13,215	7,050	5,640
Direct	1,320	1,980	2,645	3,305	3,965	5,285	8,195	8,195	5,550	2,645	1,320	1,055
Repairs and maintenance	2,500	2,500	700	700	700	700	700	700	700	700	700	700
Other controllable	2,750	2,750	2,750	2,750	2,750	2,750	2,750	2,750	2,750	2,750	2,750	2,750
Other	—	—	—	—	—	—	—	—	—	—	—	—
Mortgage amortization	—	—	3,000	—	—	3,000	—	—	3,000	—	—	3,000
Mortgage interest and taxes	2,500	2,500	2,500	2,500	2,500	2,500	2,500	2,500	2,500	2,500	2,500	2,500
SBA interest	160	215	270	270	270	270	270	270	255	245	230	220
SBA principle	—	—	—	—	—	—	—	—	2,500	2,500	2,500	2,500
Equipment loan	—	9,000	10,000	2,500	2,500	2,500	2,500	2,500	2,500	2,500	2,500	2,500
To partners	6,000	6,000	6,000	2,500	2,500	2,500	2,500	2,500	2,500	2,500	2,500	2,500
Total	51,580	43,940	54,295	51,890	58,660	79,105	97,825	112,345	99,535	59,090	40,410	34,790
Closing balance	5,045	5,145	5,400	8,575	15,990	24,985	63,715	87,925	80,895	65,855	47,470	30,300

Table 23.3
Breakdown of Weekly Sales

Meal	Number of Covers	Average Check	Total
	Week of January 2		
Breakfast	1,200	$ 5.00	$ 6,000
Lunch	2,200	$ 7.00	$15,400
Dinner	1,800	$12.00	$21,600
			$43,000

Table 23.4
Breakdown of Monthly Sales

Month	Covers Last Year	Forecast Covers Budget Year	Food Sales Budget Year	Beverage Sales Budget Year	Total Sales Budget Year
January					
February					
December					

should hesitate to conclude that this volume throughout the new year will increase over the last year by a certain amount—say 5 percent. It would be better to expect the volume to be 7 percent higher in the budgeted year during the winter months and 2 percent higher during the summer months, even though the overall result may be the desired 5 percent.

It is also important to remember that sales dollar volume is composed of two factors: the number of covers and the average price per cover. In forecasting, one must estimate the number of covers that can be expected to be served. These estimates should be broken down according to meal periods (breakfast, lunch, and dinner), and the average check price should be determined for each meal period. Multiply the number of covers per meal period by the average check and add the meal periods together to find the sales volume. This process is demonstrated in Table 23.3.

Sales volume may be calculated on a weekly basis, as in Table 23.3, and then on a monthly basis, as in Table 23.4. Or instead of 12 months, 13 periods of four weeks may be used. The four-week periods allow the use of whole weeks, each with seven equal operating days; monthly calculations require the division of the last week. Four-week periods also permit accurate comparison with the same four weeks from previous periods. Despite theoretical advantages of the four-week period, however, some operations have trouble converting from a monthly period to a four-week period.

ADDING FLEXIBILITY TO THE BUDGET

A budget should be a plan, a guide and a control, but not a rigid program. A budget that becomes unrealistic is quickly ignored. Forecasts may need to be changed despite the fact that they are basic to the plan of operation. It is easier to change your weather forecast

Table 23.5
Projection of Restaurant Sales

	Actual Sales ($)				
	Four years ago	Three years ago	Two years ago	Last year	Budget
January	48,300	48,000	48,700	48,200	48,500
February	50,800	50,900	50,300	50,700	51,000
March	52,700	53,200	52,700	52,800	53,000
April	55,200	54,900	55,600	55,500	56,000
May	57,900	58,100	58,200	57,900	58,500
June	51,300	51,500	51,600	51,400	52,000
July	47,300	47,900	48,100	46,000	48,000
August	42,600	42,900	43,000	45,000	44,000
September	47,700	47,800	47,100	47,600	48,000
October	50,100	50,900	51,100	50,700	51,000
November	52,300	52,600	52,900	53,200	54,000
December	55,400	55,900	55,100	57,100	56,000
Annual sales	611,600	614,600	614,400	616,100	620,000

than it is to change the weather. Supplemental figures may be prepared to show operations at other levels that are related to those forecasted. Sales, for example, can be calculated this way:

	90% of Budget	Budget	110% of Budgets
Sales	$45,000	$50,000	$55,000

Expense categories can then be correlated with the adjusted sales. Because the budget is really a goal, every effort should be made to reach (or surpass) its estimates. An amended budget may be prepared during the budget year that offers realistic goals under current conditions, and a breakeven chart is especially helpful in determining costs at different sales volumes.

Tables 23.5 to 23.8 present a short, simplified method of preparing sales, food cost, and payroll budgets. Budget sales figures, shown in Table 23.5, are determined partially on the basis of sales for the last four years. (Consideration, of course, is given to external and internal factors affecting the operation during the budget year.) Food-cost ratios to sales for the four years are analyzed and potential and budget cost ratios determined in Table 23.6. The basic staff for additional business is predetermined in Table 23.7. Table 23.8 permits actual figures to be compared with budgeted figures.

INSTITUTIONAL BUDGETING

This section focuses primarily on the dietary operations of institutions such as hospitals. But dietary departments are only a part of the institutional facility. It is helpful to consider factors involved in the overall budgeting of the entire institution and then concentrate on

Table 23.6
Analysis of Food-Cost Ratio to Sales

	Food-Cost Ratio to Sales (%)				
	Four years ago	Three years ago	Two years ago	Last year	Budget
January	41.1	40.3	40.0	40.4	40.0
February	39.8	39.8	39.7	40.1	39.5
March	39.3	39.3	39.4	39.7	39.5
April	39.1	39.6	39.1	39.3	39.0
May	38.7	38.8	38.5	38.7	39.0
June	39.5	39.7	39.9	39.4	39.5
July	40.3	41.8	40.2	40.1	40.0
August	42.0	42.8	41.9	41.2	41.0
September	39.1	40.1	41.0	40.0	40.0
October	39.6	39.6	39.1	39.5	39.5
November	39.8	39.4	39.5	39.2	39.5
December	39.2	38.8	39.1	38.7	39.0
Annual ratio	39.3	39.7	39.6	39.7	39.6

budgeting for the dietary department. For our purposes, a hospital will be used as a model of an institutional facility, although the principles of budgeting are equally applicable to all types of businesses and institutions.

A hospital uses different types of budgets. One, the operating budget, forecasts the level of activity and then develops the costs necessary to support this activity. A capital budget considers expenditures whose effects will continue for long periods as compared to expenditures for food and salaries, which involve short periods. Generally speaking, capital expenditures are for major pieces of equipment and facilities. A cash budget is involved with forecasting cash receipts, cash expenditures, and the resulting cash position. It helps a manager determine when funds will be available for major expenditures. It can also show when additional outside funds such as bank loans may be necessary. Cash budgeting is usually handled by the controller or financial people and normally is not a responsibility of dietary personnel.

However, various levels of hospital personnel are involved in budget preparation. At the top, the governing board must establish the policies and goals that the budgets will implement and must also approve the final budget and provide support for it. The hospital administrator or director has the overall responsibility for preparing and implementing the budget, though he or she may delegate much of the actual work.

Department heads should also be actively involved. They must have expertise in their various departmental operations and must make management aware of problems in their areas of responsibility that may affect the budget. Involving them in budget preparation also helps achieve better cooperation.

Financial and accounting personnel are key workers in budget preparation. Titles of the chief people may vary; in some institutions it may be the controller, in others it could be the chief accountant, and in large institutions it could be a vice president for finance.

Table 23.7
Projection of Payroll

Position	Number of Employees	Average Monthly Wage ($)	Total Monthly Payroll ($)
Manager	1	2,800	2,800
Assistant manager	2	1,500	3,000
Total	3		5,800
Preparation			
Chef	1	1,400	1,400
Cooks	3	1,000	3,000
Pantry help	3	640	1,920
Potwasher and porter	2	640	1,280
Total			7,600
Sanitation			
Dishwashers	7	640	4,480
Total			4,480
Service			
Hosts/Hostesses	1.5	800	1,200
Servers	14.0	500	7,000
Bus persons	4.0	500	2,000
Total	19.5		10,200
General			
Storeroom	1.0	850	850
Office clerks	1.0	800	800
Cashiers	1.5	800	900
Total	3.5		2,550
Total monthly payroll			30,930

Sales	Total monthly payroll
Under $90,000	$30,930: Basic staff required Add:
$90,000–$100,000	$32,070: 1 dishwasher at $ 640 1 server at $ 500
$100,000–$110,000	$33,570: 1 cook at $1,000 1 server at $ 500
$110,000–$120,000	$35,210: 1 dishwasher at $ 640 1 server at $ 500 1 bus person at $ 500

Table 23.8
Comparative Sales, Food Cost, and Payroll Budget

			Food Cost				Labor Cost			
	Sales		Budget		Actual		Budget		Actual	
Month	Budget	Actual	Amount	Ratio	Amount	Ratio	Amount	Ratio	Amount	Ratio
January	$ 48,500		$ 19,400	40.0%			$ 16,035	33.06%		
February	51,000		20,145	39.5			16,785	32.91		
March	53,000		20,935	39.5			16,785	31.66		
April	56,000		21,840	39.0			17,605	31.43		
May	58,500		22,815	39.0			17,605	30.09		
June	52,000		20,540	39.5			16,785	32.27		
July	48,000		19,200	40.0			16,035	33.40		
August	44,000		18,140	41.0			15,465	34.36		
September	48,000		19,200	40.0			16,035	33.40		
October	51,000		20,145	39.5			16,785	32.91		
November	54,000		21,330	39.5			16,785	31.08		
December	56,000		21,840	39.0			17,605	31.43		
Total	$620,000		$245,530	39.6%			$200,310	32.3%		

In any case, much of the statistical, historical (in the sense of previous operating records), and forecast data must come from these people.

Often a budget committee may be formed to facilitate budget preparation. This committee may consist of the controller or a top financial person, some department heads, and other personnel who have insight and expertise and who have part of their time delegated for budgetary matters.

Institutions may also maintain a **budget calendar**, which specifies deadlines for completion of the different parts of the budget process. These deadlines should allow reasonable time for the budget preparation to be completed on schedule. Different organizations can have different sequences and time constraints, but a possible budget calendar for a budget year beginning July 1 might be as shown in Table 23.9.

As mentioned, one important part of budget preparation is the development of forecasts by the controllers or accounting section. To determine appropriate costs, these forecasts of activity must be followed by estimates of the costs of handling this level of activity. A hospital would estimate how many outpatients and inpatients it expects during the budget year and how much activity units such as the operating rooms, pharmacy, X ray, and so forth could expect. The various separate units depend, of course, on the number of inpatients and outpatients served by the hospital. Once the level of activity is determined, it can be priced out to determine expected revenue. Other revenue, such as investment income or governmental funds, can be added to determine the total revenue. Once the level of activity for various budgetary units is determined, the amount of supplies and personnel to service this activity can be costed out with appropriate amounts added for general expenses and overhead.

Table 23.9
Budget Calendar

Dates	Involved	Functions
March 15–April 15	Administrator, budget director, budget committee, department head, input from governing body	General projections, assumptions, new services to be introduced, changes to be made
April 18	Governing body	Approval of general assumptions, any policy or goal changes for the year
April 21	Committee, budget director, administrator, department heads	Presentation of general assumptions, projections, goals and guidelines
April 22–May 13	Committee, budget director, administrator meeting department heads individually	Development of specific assumptions for each budgeting unit
	Heads of budgeting units	Draft development of unit budget
May 20	Committee, budget director, department heads (individually)	Review of unit budget draft, suggestions for change
May 27	Committee and/or budget director	Consolidation of unit budgets into master budget
May 30	Administrative management	Review, revise if necessary, and approve for submission to governing body
June 1–14	Budget director Governing body	Preparation of cash and capital budgets; review, revise if necessary and approve
June 15	Budget director, administrative groups, department heads	Presentation of final approved budget
July 1	All personnel	Implementation

In determining costs, it is helpful to consider costs as either fixed or variable. Fixed costs do not change regardless of volume. If a health-care operation has a permanent staff that does not change regardless of volume, their salaries would be a fixed cost.

Variable costs change with the volume. The amount of food consumed should vary directly with the number of meals served, so the food cost would be a variable cost. In determining the budget costs for a specific unit of the organization, one should consider the amount of fixed costs and then add variable costs. If, for example, in a hospital food facility the personnel costs are $200,000, other direct overhead costs are $40,000, the food cost per meal is $3.00 per meal (in practice, breakfast, lunch, and dinner would have different amounts), supply costs per meal are $0.50, and 200,000 meals are expected to be served in the budget period, the budgeted amount would be $940,000.

Fixed personnel costs	$200,000
Other fixed costs (direct overhead)	40,000
Food costs (variable)	600,000
Supply costs (variable)	100,000
Total	$940,000

Capital expenses are those that have an effect beyond one year. Typically, not enough funds are available to supply all the capital requests for equipment and new facilities. Still, there must be constant capital improvement or the physical plant will become obsolete, inefficient, and suddenly expensive to maintain. Department heads usually list their capital requests. These are then costed out and prioritized. One set of priorities could be

1. urgent
2. essential
3. economically desirable
4. generally desirable

One can then decide which of the projects can be achieved with the funding available. Of course, hospital officials must rank the relative desirability of projects from various areas of the hospital. For example, the importance of capital expenditure requests by the dietary unit may need to be compared to those from the medical area. Also, as Table 23.10 shows, a lower cost, "generally desirable" item may be feasible when a higher cost, "economically desirable" one is not.

The dietary department is not usually involved in the cash budget, but the cash budget is of vital concern to the hospital. Cash planning is important: Cash must be available to pay obligations as they become due. Cash planning is also necessary to determine when and if there will be cash available for major expenditures. One major expense is depreciation, but because the actual replacement is delayed, depreciation does not drain immediate out-of-pocket cash as do salaries or supplies. The hospital cash flow will probably be different from revenue from patients and from income statements as there is usually a time lag before the hospital actually receives payments from patients or from third party reimbursers. There may also be other income from fund-raising drives, philanthropy, endowments, and government sources. In some institutional operations with a precarious financial situation or poor cash flow, making sure that funds are available is a difficult task.

It is usually the responsibility of the foodservice director to at least help prepare the dietary department's operating budget. The first step is to determine the activity of the dietary department for the budget year. This activity naturally depends on the overall activity of the whole facility. The number of patient meals served directly reflects the number of patient-days the facility will service. A rule of thumb for some hospital operations is to multiply the number of patient-days by 2.8 to determine the number of patient meals. Thus, if an operation has 50,000 patient days, it could be expected to serve 140,000 patient meals. Estimates of nonpatient meals served to employees or visitors are usually determined by analyzing historical data. If 60,000 nonpatient meals were served during the budget period last year and patients are expected to increase by 10 percent, one might assume that 66,000 meals will be served if the increase in staff and visitors is proportionate. Once the level of

Table 23.10

Ranking of Additions, Improvements, or Replacements

	Additions	Improvements	Replacements	Cost Each	Total	Estimated Date of Payment	Justification
Urgent							
Tray Cart (1)			✓	$1,450	$1,450	Aug.	At present a cart is inoperative and cannot be fixed and a cart must be reloaded, slowing service
Essential							
Fire extinguisher system over range hood	✓			$2,000	$2,000	Sept.	Fire marshal and safety committee strongly recommend
Economically desirable							
Minicomputer system	✓			$5,000	$5,000	Apr.	Estimates are that it could pay for itself in 3 years
Generally desirable							
Four stainless steel shelving units for storeroom	✓			$ 250	$1,000	May	Improved appearance and sanitation

activity is determined, it is then possible to calculate expenses. Dietary expenses are usually divided into food, labor, supplies, and other costs. If food costs per meal were $2.00 and are expected to increase by 12 percent, the new food cost per meal would be $2.24. Multiplying this by the anticipated number of meals would give the anticipated food cost. Different food-cost-per-meal figures may be used for patient and nonpatient meals. The previous cost per meal for the other cost categories can be determined by dividing the previous costs per category by the number of meals served. If supply costs were $28,000 for 140,000 meals served, the cost was $0.20 per meal. If management thinks that costs will be 10 percent higher for the budgeted period, the budget figure would be $0.22.

Labor costs for the health-care food facility can be calculated in several ways. One is to handle them as were food costs. The past labor cost per meal is determined, then an adjustment is made to the current labor cost per meal to reflect salary increases or other factors. Thus, if labor costs per meal last year were $0.60 and labor costs are expected to increase by 10 percent, the new labor cost per meal would be $0.66. Multiplying this by the anticipated number of meals would give the anticipated labor cost.

Another and more exact way is to cost out labor. One method is to cost out every job. This technique may be modified to total income paid to salaried staff first. Then estimate the number of hours in each wage category (and each section of the dietary department) and multiply the anticipated number of hours by the proposed hourly rates.

Salary fluctuations from one year to another can be caused by different factors. There might be an across-the-board wage increase because of inflation. This could be in the form of a percentage increase or by dollar amounts. Merit increases could be given. Also, the number of total employee-hours worked could change from one period to another. This could be caused by changes in the organization's volume of business. This information is projected for each coming year by management and the budget committee and is given to the dietary department. Changes in equipment, menus, levels, and types or level of service all affect labor and labor-cost requirements.

Each organization must also determine how it will handle fringe payroll costs. For instance, it must decide whether expected contributions for retirements should be charged to the dietary department or handled as general costs for the organization. It is often helpful to include a factor for expenses such as overtime, unexpected illness, and vacation relief.

The labor budget should be regarded as flexible. If activity surpasses forecasts, then more money should be available. Decreases in activity may permit personnel cutbacks and a lower budget.

Let us do some budget calculations using the data in Table 23.11. The calculations are provided in Table 23.12.

Using this information, the dietary program head could submit the following figures for inclusion in the proposed budget:

Dietary

Salaries and wages	$189,000
Food cost	226,040
Supplies and expenses	36,000
Total dietary	$451,040

In practice, budgeted figures are often divided on a monthly basis with the totals of the 12 months equaling the yearly total. This is shown for a restaurant earlier in the chapter. The restaurant figures differ from a health-care dietary department in that the latter usually does not have direct sales except for cafeterias and catering. The direct expenses of the cafeteria are included on the supplies and expenses figure of $36,000. We are assuming that any advertising, utilities, repairs and maintenance, and depreciation are included in the general health facility budget.

In trying to determine if the submitted figures are feasible, the administration might further analyze them by calculating ratios such as cost per patient meal, fixed cost per patient meal, and labor cost per patient meal. Labor for patient service would be a separate cost.

We have also assumed that all income from the cafeteria or other sources will be commingled with the organization's funds. A health-care food administrator would probably want more exact operating figures for each cost or profit center (such as the cafeteria). With one kitchen producing food for both patient care and nonpatient care, it is often difficult to divide costs between them. This can be done on a percentage basis with an educated guess as the basis for the division. Thus, a certain percentage of the kitchen labor costs would be allotted to the cafeteria. Any employees working only for the cafeteria would, of course, be charged to the cafeteria.

Table 23.11
Dietary Budget Data

1.	Anticipated patient days	55,000
2.	Anticipated nonpatient meals	25,000
3.	Last year food cost per patient meal	$ 1.20
4.	Number of meals per patient day	2.8
5.	Anticipated food cost increase	5%
6.	Last year nonpatient meal food cost	$ 1.16
7.	Anticipated food cost increase, nonpatient meals	10%
8.	Labor cost last year	$175,000
9.	Anticipated salary increases	8%
10.	Labor cost breakdown	
	Patient care	80%
	Nonpatient care	20%
11.	Last year supply and expense cost	$ 32,000
12.	Budgeted year supply and expense cost this year	$ 36,000
13.	Supply cost breakdown	
	Patient care	90%
	Nonpatient care	10%
14.	Anticipated utility costs	$ 60,000
15.	Utility cost breakdown	
	Patient care	85%
	Nonpatient care	15%
16.	Dietary repairs and maintenance	$ 30,000
17.	Repairs and maintenance breakdown	
	Patient care	85%
	Nonpatient care	15%
18.	Anticipated charge per nonpatient meal	$ 4.00

Table 23.12
Dietary Budget Calculations

Anticipated patient days	55,000		Last year cost per patient meal	$1.20
× Number of meals per patient day	2.8		× Anticipated increase	5%
= Number of patient meals	154,000		= Anticipated cost per patient meal	$1.26
× Food cost per patient meal	$ 1.26			
= Food cost for patient meals	$194,040			
Anticipated nonpatient meals	25,000		Last year food cost per nonpatient meal	$1.16
× Food cost per nonpatient meal	$ 1.28		× Anticipated increase	10%
= Food cost for nonpatient meals	$ 32,000		= Anticipated cost per nonpatient meal	$1.28
Last year dietary labor cost	$175,000			
+ Anticipated increase	8%			
= Dietary labor cost	$189,000			
Food cost for patient meals	$194,040			
Food cost for nonpatient meals	$ 32,000			
Total food cost	$226,040			

Table 23.13
Cafeteria Budget for Year Ending June 30, XXXX

Sales	$400,000
Food cost (cost of sales)	128,000
Gross margin	262,000
Controllable expenses	
Labor	$151,200
Repair and maintenance	18,000
Utilities	36,000
Supplies	14,400
Total controllable expenses	$219,600
Operating gain or loss	$ 42,400

A budget for the cafeteria using previous figures is shown in Table 23.13. In this case the cafeteria shows a profit of $42,400 in an operating sense. If depreciation and other overhead costs were included, the cafeteria operations would probably result in a loss. Some health organizations purposely keep employee meal prices low and are content to run at a loss. The current trend is to try to make such operations at least self-supporting. These figures could also be broken down on a monthly basis.

CAPITAL BUDGETING

A technique used to help plan major expenditures is **capital budgeting**, which is defined as the planning of expenditures whose returns are expected to extend beyond one year. Usually, these expenditures would be in the area of fixed-asset management. Funds for these capital expenditures can come from depreciation, retained earnings, debt, or new equity. Capital budgeting is significant in that it requires financial commitments that extend into the future, cannot be changed, and are usually substantial. If it makes financial commitments that are too large to pay, an operation is in trouble. On the other hand, if it fails to make necessary commitments, the operation suffers from not achieving its profit potential or, perhaps, gradually becoming obsolete.

Capital investment categories can include:

1. replacements of present facilities or equipment
2. expansion to provide additional capacity for present product lines, such as enlarging a restaurant
3. expansion with new product lines, such as providing take-out services
4. other miscellaneous categories, which can include items such as sandblasting the exterior

Usually there are more needs, proposals, or projects than an operation has funds for or is willing to accept. This necessitates the ranking of proposals. To rank the proposals, the estimated benefits must be calculated from each proposal and then the proposals ranked against each other for desirability.

ECONOMY STUDY

An **economy study** is a comparative analysis of the financial factors of two or more alternative programs to determine which would be economically advantageous. An economy study is often used to compare an existing procedure with possible innovations. Some questions involving economy studies follow:

1. Should expensive or inexpensive equipment be purchased?
2. Are extra features worth the cost? Will new equipment pay for itself?
3. Is it financially desirable to replace equipment before it is obsolete?
4. Which of several possible purchases should be made? (For example, should a back-office accounting system or a point-of-sale register be purchased?)

Table 23.14 depicts an economy study for the replacement of dishwashing equipment with newer equipment. Fewer worker hours are needed to operate the new equipment, which has an expected life of 10 years, costs $12,000 installed, and has no expected

Table 23.14
Economy Study

<table>
<tr><th colspan="5">PROPOSED PURCHASE OF FLIGHT-TYPE
DISHWASHING EQUIPMENT</th></tr>
<tr><th></th><th colspan="2">Project A</th><th colspan="2">Project B</th></tr>
<tr><th></th><th colspan="2">Present</th><th colspan="2">Proposed</th></tr>
<tr><td>Fixed Expenses</td><td></td><td></td><td></td><td></td></tr>
<tr><td>Interest, 6% of $2,500
  (average value)</td><td></td><td>$ 150</td><td>6% of $6,000</td><td>$ 360</td></tr>
<tr><td>Depreciation, 20% of $5,000</td><td></td><td>1,000</td><td>10% of $12,000</td><td>1,200</td></tr>
<tr><td>Taxes and Insurance,
  %5 of $2,500</td><td></td><td>125</td><td>5% of $6,000</td><td>300</td></tr>
<tr><td></td><td></td><td>$ 1,275</td><td></td><td>$ 1,860</td></tr>
<tr><td>Operating Expenses</td><td></td><td></td><td></td><td></td></tr>
<tr><td>Direct labor</td><td></td><td>$16,000</td><td></td><td>$12,000</td></tr>
<tr><td>Related labor costs 12%</td><td></td><td>1,920</td><td></td><td>1,440</td></tr>
<tr><td>Power and water</td><td></td><td>1,200</td><td></td><td>1,800</td></tr>
<tr><td>Supplies</td><td></td><td>600</td><td></td><td>600</td></tr>
<tr><td>Repairs and maintenance</td><td></td><td>400</td><td></td><td>100</td></tr>
<tr><td></td><td></td><td>$20,120</td><td></td><td>$15,940</td></tr>
<tr><td>Total cost</td><td></td><td>$21,395</td><td></td><td>$17,800</td></tr>
<tr><td>A. Net annual savings before income taxes</td><td></td><td></td><td></td><td>$ 3,595</td></tr>
<tr><td>B. Net annual savings after taxes (48% + 4.8% = 52.8%)</td><td></td><td></td><td></td><td>1,697</td></tr>
<tr><td>C. Net capital investment ($12,000 cost minus $2,000 salvage)</td><td></td><td></td><td></td><td>10,000</td></tr>
<tr><td>D. Annual return on initial cash investment ($1,697 ÷ $10,000)</td><td></td><td></td><td></td><td>17%</td></tr>
<tr><td>E. Annual return on average investment ($1,697 ÷ $5,000)</td><td></td><td></td><td></td><td>34%</td></tr>
</table>

salvage value at the end of the 10 years. The present equipment is still in good condition, has a net book value of $5,000, and could be expected to last five more years. It could probably be sold now for $2,000. The economy study considers fixed expenses such as interest, depreciation, taxes, and insurance. These total $1,275 for the present machine and $1,860 for the proposed new machine. Operating expenses, which are largely labor, total $20,120 for the present machine and would total $15,940 for the proposed replacement.

Based on these computations, the new machine would save, after income taxes, $1,697 annually. This represents 17.1 percent annual return on the net capital investment of $10,000 ($12,000 − $2,000) in the new machine. Using the average investment figure of $5,000 over 10 years, the annual return would be 34.0 percent.

Management should continually make studies of this nature to remain competitive and maintain annual earnings. In this example, the economy study was used to compare the replacement of equipment with a newer product. However, other factors, such as the ability of the new equipment to handle increased sales, must be evaluated separately. It is necessary to forecast future costs in preparing an economy study. All operating expenses for the various options should be included: payroll and related costs, utilities, interest on equipment, and maintenance and supplies. Depreciation presents a problem because it is always difficult to estimate an actual effective life or the actual salvage value. A conservative approach is to ignore any salvage value and use, instead, straight-line depreciation, which is determined by dividing the value of the equipment by the number of years of useful life to give the depreciation per year. The value of the investment is usually decreasing constantly during its useful life, and in an economy study it is better to use the average value of the investment for interest cost considerations instead of the initial value. One formula for computing the average value of the investment:

$$A = \frac{\text{Initial investment minus salvage value}}{2}$$

The existing rack dishwashing machine has a book value of $5,000 and should have five more years of useful life with no salvage value. Substituting the figures in the formula, the average value of the investment for interest computations becomes

$$A = \frac{\$5,000}{2} = \$2,500$$

Dividing the expected useful life of 5 years into the present value of $5,000 provides the straight-line depreciation figure of $1,000 a year.

The average cost of the new equipment would be

$$A = \frac{\$12,000}{2} = \$6,000$$

The actual cost of the new equipment less any salvage value is used in determining depreciation. The rate of depreciation is one over the anticipated useful life, which in this case is 10 years. On $12,000, this amounts to $1,200 per year.

Properly interpreted and used, the economy study can be very valuable in bringing the economic variables inherent in acquiring new equipment into focus. However, it should be used only as a guide and not as the sole determinant since there may also be noneconomic intangibles.

ANTICIPATED PAYBACK PERIOD

One technique for evaluating capital expenditures is to determine the length of time it will take to recover the expenditure. Generally speaking, the shorter the **payback period**, the better the investment. An operation can set standards for capital expenditures, such as requiring that they pay for themselves within two, three, five, or some other specified number of years. However, larger expenditures often require longer payback periods than smaller ones, and a different standard may need to be applied. It may be reasonable to expect a microwave oven to pay for itself in three years, but a new building will probably take far longer. One formula for determining the payback period is

$$\text{Payback period} = \frac{\text{Cash or cash outlay for project}}{\substack{\text{Annual net income (or savings) for project} \\ \text{before depreciation but after taxes}}}$$

Using the net savings figure of $1,697 from Table 23.14 and adding back net depreciation ($1,200 − $1,000, or $200), one reaches the figure $1,897. Dividing this into the net cash outlay of $10,000, a payback period of 5.27, or about 5 years and 3 months, emerges.

The actual cost of the project is sometimes used, but using only the actual cash required is often a more practical approach. A project may not be feasible if the entire cost must be paid when the equipment is acquired. If the cost can be financed through savings from the project itself and comparatively little cash is required for the initial payment, the installation may then become both feasible and desirable.

Tax considerations also influence the desirability of expenditures. If additional income or profit must, in large part, be given up in taxes, the new equipment may be less desirable and less justifiable than the old.

If the project brings in additional sales, this amount of additional sales would be used to calculate the payback period; if the project cuts costs, the amount saved would be used.

It is often hard to place dollar values on the benefits accrued from improvements. What is redecorating the dining room worth in sales potential? What is a remodeled employee lounge worth in employee satisfaction? Both of these projects may be very desirable—even necessary—but it is difficult to put a quantitative value on such tangibles as these.

Income or savings may vary from year to year, and it is necessary to add up dissimilar amounts to determine the payback figure. The higher the immediate gain, the more desirable the project. A dollar received or saved today is worth more to the operation than a dollar received or saved two years from now. Also, a project may pay for itself in a short period but then produce comparatively little more profit. Another project may take longer to pay for itself, but it may continue, after doing so, to reap profits over a long period. The second project may be more desirable in the long run, but—on a payback-period basis—the first project could be rated higher because of its performance during the first years.

ANTICIPATED RATE OF RETURN

A proposed capital expenditure may be elevated by comparing the savings (or additional income) to the amount expended. One formula for making this comparison, the **anticipated rate of return**, follows.

$$\text{Anticipated rate of turn (or accounting rate of return)} = \frac{\text{Average additional income or savings generated by project (after taxes and depreciation)}}{\text{Average amount invested in project}}$$

Income taxes and depreciation reduce the true return from an investment, and they must be subtracted from the income, or the savings, figure. The value of the acquisition will generally decline during its life, so an average value should be used rather than the initial one. A new piece of equipment costs $10,000 and will last 10 years with no salvage value. Management expects to earn (or save) $1,000 more (after taxes and depreciation) during each year of the useful life of the new equipment than it would have earned (or saved) by operating the old equipment. The rate of return calculated on the initial outlay would be $1,000/$10,000, or 10 percent. The average value of the equipment is $5,000, and the rate of return on the average value of the equipment over its lifetime would be $1,000/$5,000, or 20 percent.

As explained previously, the saving after taxes in our economy study example was $1,697 annually with an average investment of $5,000. This would give an anticipated rate of return (ARR) of 34 percent.

COST CATEGORIES

For management decision making, costs may be categorized differently than in conventional accounting or financial reporting. These different categories help provide a better understanding and evaluation of costs involved in decision making and can provide a broader cost perspective. Some of the categories used to analyze costs follow.

Relevant Costs

Relevant costs are those costs that are relevant to the proposed decision. If a cost is not changed by a possible alternative, it should not be considered in the analysis. If, for example, the labor cost remains the same under different options, it would not need to be considered. However, if an option affects the labor cost, it would then be relevant.

Sunk Costs

Sunk costs denotes costs that have already been incurred and cannot be recouped by a new decision or alternative. Normally, sunk costs should not be considered in decision making. A common example is an installation cost that would have to be duplicated if the equipment, already installed, is subsequently replaced. The original cost of installation would be a sunk cost. You can also think of sunk costs as expenses that will not be changed by a decision; therefore, they are irrelevant.

Opportunity Costs

Opportunity costs are the costs of the profit that is forgone when an opportunity is rejected. For example, a foodservice establishment may need both new kitchen and new dishwashing equipment but may have resources enough to acquire only the kitchen equipment. The savings (or the profit) sacrificed by not securing the dishwashing equipment would be considered an opportunity cost. Often a decision depends on a choice between alternatives. One alternative may be selected over another because the anticipated profit or savings is greater than the opportunity costs of the other alternatives. This difference between chosen profit and the remaining opportunity costs is called the *incremental cost.*

Incremental Cost

Incremental cost, then, is the difference in cost between one alternative and another. Considering two projects, *A* and *B,* the incremental cost would be the difference between profits or savings resulting from Project *A* and the profits or savings that would have been realized by implementing Project *B.* The decision maker may handle this calculation as Project *A* minus Project *B* or Project *B* minus Project *A,* as long as he or she is consistent and handles all cost items in the same manner. Incremental costs may thus be either positive or negative.

Table 23.15
Incremental Approach

PROJECT *B* MINUS PROJECT *A*			
	Project *B*	Project *A*	Incremental
Fixed expenses			
Interest expense	$ 360	$ 150	$ 210
Depreciation	1,200	1,000	200
Taxes and insurance	300	125	175
Total incremental fixed expenses			$585
Operating expenses			
Direct labor	$12,000	$16,000	$(4,000)
Related labor costs	1,440	1,920	(480)
Power and water	1,800	1,200	600
Supplies	600	600	—
Repairs and maintenance	100	400	(300)
Total incremental operating expenses			$(4,180)
Total net incremental expenses			$(3,595)

The ($3,595) indicates a negative value to our incremental costs; in effect Project *B* will cost $3,595 less than Project *A,* which agrees with our net annual savings before income taxes [line (A)] in Table 23.14.

OTHER METHODS OF RANKING PROPOSALS

Two other methods of ranking capital investment proposals are the net present value method and the internal rate of return. They both use the time value of money, the earning power of money over a period of time, the value of a present sum of money in the future, or the value of a future sum in present dollars. If you were asked if you would like $1,000 now or $1,500 in five years, you might want to determine the earning power of the $1,000 over five years to decide if it would be more or less than $1,500. Net present value is defined as the present value of future returns discounted at the appropriate cost of capital minus the cost of the investment. It can be used to determine if a capital investment can provide more returns than the capital could earn in other forms of investment.

The internal rate of return is the compound rate of return (discount rate) that equates the present value of the initial outlay and the future cash benefits from a capital investment project. It provides a rate of return on the initial investment that can be compared to returns on other options.

Internal rates of returns and net present values require the use of tables or formulas for their preparation. For more information, refer to a financial management or accounting textbook. These methods are very effective in capital budgeting.

SUMMARY

Budgeting is extremely helpful for a commercial operation that is attempting to earn the largest profit possible or for a nonprofit operation that wants to provide the best services its resources permit. A number of different types of budgets exist, including general, operating, cash, capital, labor, and sales budgets, among others. Budgets have a number of functions and advantages. For example, they provide basic plans of operation, serve as control devices, provide business goals, help coordinate personnel, provide ongoing progress yardsticks, and specify operational responsibilities. They also have disadvantages, including the time and effort it takes to prepare them and the usual troubles associated with any prediction. The chapter discussed a number of factors involved in budget preparation. Large organizations—for example, city hospitals that must collect data and compel coordination from a number of different sources and departments—may require a budget committee and may adopt a budget calendar with completion deadlines for various segments of the budget.

Capital expenses have an effect beyond one year and often require much larger amounts of money than required by the usual day-to-day operations. Typically, there are not enough funds to cover all capital needs, and it then becomes necessary to cost out these capital requirements and set priorities. This chapter explained how to go about these activities.

KEY TERMS

accounting rate of return (ARR)
anticipated rate of return
baseline budget
bottom up budget
budget

budget calendar
capital budget
cash budget
economy study
fixed budget

incremental cost
operating budget
opportunity costs
payback period

sunk costs
time value of money
top down budget
zero-based budget

REVIEW QUESTIONS

23–1 Define a budget.

23–2 List advantages of using budgets.

23–3 List disadvantages of using budgets.

23–4 What set of priorities was suggested for capital requests?

23–5 What role does the governing board of an institution have concerning the annual budget?

23–6 What is capital budgeting?

23–7 What makes capital budgeting significant?

23–8 List four capital budgeting categories.

23–9 What questions can be answered by an economy study?

23–10 Provide formulas for a payback period and anticipated rate of return.

PROBLEMS

23–1 An acute-care hospital has 150 beds and will open a new 50-bed wing during the next budget period. Using the following data (which includes the new beds), calculate the following for the new budget period:
   a. food cost for patient meals
   b. food cost for nonpatient meals
   c. anticipated dietary labor costs for patient care
   d. anticipated total dietary budget figure

Anticipated patient days	61,000
Anticipated nonpatient meals	30,000
Previous year's food cost per patient meal	$ 1.50
Number of meals per patient-day	2.8
Anticipated food cost increase	10%
Previous year's nonpatient meal food cost	$ 1.20
Previous year's labor cost	$240,000
Anticipated salary increase	8%
Labor cost for three new employees	$ 36,000
Labor cost breakdown—patient care	75%
Labor cost breakdown—nonpatient service	25%
Previous year's supply and expense costs	$ 30,000
Budgeted year supply and expense costs	$ 45,000

Anticipated utility costs	$ 70,000
Dietary repairs and maintenance	$ 25,000

23–2 You are planning to open a new restaurant on January 1. Monthly food sales should start at $60,000 and are expected to increase 10 percent a month for the first six months. Beverage sales are expected to be 25 percent of food sales. The food-cost percentage should be 32 percent, and the beverage-cost percentage should be 25 percent. The basic labor staff cost will be $30,000 a month to start. It is expected that every additional $10,000 monthly increase in sales will require one new employee costing $1,000 a month.

Direct expenses should be 6 percent of sales. Planned marketing costs will be $10,000 a month for the first three months and $2,000 a month for the next three months. With new facilities and equipment, repairs and maintenance expenses are calculable at 1 percent of sales. Administration and general costs should be $6,000 a month, occupation costs $10,000 per month, depreciation $8,000 per month, and interests cost $4,000 a month.

Prepare an operating budget for the first six months showing the monthly profit or loss expected before taxes. (Round all figures to the nearest $100.)

23-3 To finance the opening of the restaurant in problem 19–2, a separate line of credit has been established with a local bank which requires a cash budget for the first six months of operation. For the cash budget assume payroll costs, liquor purchases, and occupancy costs are paid the month incurred and other expenditures are paid the month after being incurred. Expenditures made in December (before opening) that will be paid in January are initial food inventory, $15,000; preopening marketing, $6,000; energy costs, $2,000; and direct expense supplies, $6,000. The restaurant will borrow $10,000 to provide an initial cash balance in January.

The loan agreement stipulates that up to $8,000 a month may be withdrawn by the owners as long as the cash balance remains above $10,000. Any excess over the required balance and withdrawals (total $18,000) must be used to repay the line of credit loan. Prepare a cash budget for the first six months. (Round off figures to the nearest $100.)

23-4 *Ranking Problem*
An operation has space to install either a popcorn machine or a soft ice cream maker. No extra personnel would be required, making labor cost irrelevant. The operation is in the 25 percent tax bracket. With the following data, use the ARR and payback methods to determine which would be most advantageous from a financial standpoint.

Popcorn Machine		Soft Ice Cream Machine	
Cost	$1,500	Cost	$3,000
Interest on purchase money	8%	Interest	8%
Anticipated life	15 years	Anticipated life	6 years
Projected yearly sales	$1,500	Projected yearly sales	$3,000
Supplies	200	Supplies	500
Repairs and maintenance	100	Repairs and maintenance	200
Utility cost	100	Utility cost	200
Salvage	0	Salvage	0

23-5 Calculate the ARR and payback periods for this data:

Purchase price	$20,000
Interest on purchase cost	10%
Estimated savings	$6,000/year
Expected life	10 years
Tax rate	20%

23-6 You are considering the addition of more floor space in your leased restaurant. The cost would be $120,000. The lease lasts 10 years and the leasehold improvements would be depreciated over this period (straight line). Interest costs are 8 percent. Without including the above expenses, anticipated profits on the facilities are estimated at $36,000 a year. You are in the 25 percent tax bracket. Calculate:
a. Anticipated rate of return
b. Payback period

23-7 The following data is given for a proposed new dishwasher:

Purchase price	$18,000 (to be paid in cash)
Salvage value of old machine	$2,000
Expected life	10 years
Depreciation	Straight line
Labor savings per year	$5,000
Tax rate	30%

Calculate:
a. ARR
b. Annual depreciation
c. Average cost
d. Payback period

Cost-Volume-Profit Analysis (Break-Even Analysis)

hapter 2 introduced the importance of appreciating the cost-volume-profit relationship and understanding the contribution margin. In this chapter, the construction of a break-even chart showing these relationships in graphic form is discussed. The figures expressed in a break-even chart can be used in planning control and decision making. The relationships can also be helpful in appreciating how all costs must be covered in menu pricing. Involved in these relationships is the contribution to overhead and profit, or contribution margin.

After completing this chapter, you should be able to:

1. Make break-even calculations.
2. Prepare a break-even chart.
3. Use a break-even chart to answer questions.
4. Explain advantages and disadvantages of using a break-even chart.

BREAK-EVEN ANALYSIS (COST-VOLUME-PROFIT)

Cost-volume-profit analysis, better known as break-even analysis, shows the varying relationships of sales, costs, and profits (or bases) at various volumes. After fixed costs, defined as those that do not change with volume (such as rent or depreciation), are paid or covered, the operation becomes increasingly profitable since only variable costs, such as food and linens, that vary with volume need to be paid.

The contribution margin (CM), contribution rate (CR), and variable rate were discussed in Chapter 2. Using them allows for the solution of such problems as

- sales/revenue necessary for the operation to break even (or where volume covers all costs, both variable and fixed)

- sales volume necessary to produce a desired profit
- the number of meals necessary to break even or produce a desired profit

The contribution margin may be defined as the excess of revenue from a product over the variable costs of producing it, or the contribution to profit and overhead. It is the contribution to the recovery of fixed costs and profit, or sales minus variable costs. The contribution margin, when expressed as a ratio to sales, becomes the **contribution rate**, or

$$CR = \frac{P + FC}{S} \quad or \quad \frac{S - VC}{S}$$

If fixed costs and profit are subtracted from sales, the resulting figure would be the variable costs which, if expressed as a percentage of sales, would be $VC = \dfrac{variable\ costs}{sales}$.
If the variable rate is subtracted from sales $(1.0 - VR)$, the resulting figure would be the contribution rate. If an operation has $500,000 in sales, $275,000 in variable costs, $200,000 in fixed costs, and $25,000 profit, the contribution margin (CM) would be fixed costs (FC) $200,000 + profit (P) $25,000 or $225,000.

The variable rate would be $275,000/$500,000 or 55%. The contribution rate could be found by subtracting the variable rate from 100% or $1.0 - .55 = .45$.

For these calculations it is necessary to discriminate between fixed and variable costs. Some costs such as labor may have a fixed component for permanent full-time employees and a variable component for those who are hired depending on volume or demand. It is necessary to separate such components as exactly as possible.

The formula presented the contribution rate $CR = \dfrac{P + FC}{S}$. This can also be expressed as $S = \dfrac{P + FC}{CR}$ or $FC = (S \times CR) - P$ or $P = (S \times CR) - FC$.

Let us assume the following data

Sales (S)	$500,000	100%
Variable Costs (VC)	$275,000	55%
Fixed Costs (FC)	$200,000	40%
Profit	$ 25,000	5%
Contribution Rate	$225,000	45%
Meals Served	50,000	
Average Meal Price	$ 10	

The **break-even point** (in sales) where there is zero profit can be found using the formula

$$S = P+FC/CR \ or \ S = 0+\$200,000/.45$$

$$Sales\ at\ BE = \$444,444.44$$

This can be verified using the formula

$$P = (S \times CR) - FC \ or \ 0 = (\$444,444.44 \times .45) - \$200,000.00$$

$$or\ Zero\ Profit$$

Since there is no profit or loss, $444,444.00 is the break-even point.

If used to find the Profit (P), the calculations would be

$$P = (S \times CR) - FC$$

$$P = \$225,000 - \$200,000$$

$$P = \$25,000$$

The data at BE would be

Sales (S)	$444,000	100%
Variable Costs (VC)	244,000	55%
Fixed Costs (FC)	200,000	45%
Profit	0	0%
Contribution Rate	200,000	45%

Let us assume management is considering raising menu prices by 10% but expects meal counts to drop by 5%. Is this a good idea? The average meal price is now $11.00 but new meals served are 47,500 which produces a new sales figure of $522,500.
Using the formula

$$P = (S \times CR) - FC$$

$$P = (\$522,500 \times .45) - \$200,000$$

$$P = \$235,125 - \$200,000$$

$$P = \$35,125$$

This is higher than the prior profit of $25,000 and would appear to be a good idea if projections are accurate.

Another strategy might be to lower prices 5% and expect a 5% increase in meals sold. The average selling price is now $9.50 and 52,500 meals are expected to be sold or sales of $498,750 using the formula

$$P = (S \times CR) - FC$$

$$P = (\$498,750 \times .45) - \$200,000$$

$$P = \$24,438$$

This is less than the original profit and would appear not to be feasible.

Assume management would like to target a profit of $50,000 and would like to determine the sales volume to obtain it.

$$S = P + FC/CR, \text{ or } S = \frac{50,000 + \$200,000}{.45}$$

$$S = \$555,555$$

Or at $10 a cover, it would require 55,555 covers.

Breakfast provides 15% of the sales of the operation but consumes 30% of variable costs. Should it be eliminated? Without breakfast, sales would be $425,000. Variable costs would decline to $192,500 and fixed costs are the same. This provides a variable cost rate of $192,500 ÷ $425,000 or .453 or .45. The contribution rate would be 1 − .45 or .55.

Using the formula

$$P = (S \times CR) - FC$$

$$P = (425,000 \times 54.7) - \$200,000$$

$$P = \$33,750$$

This is more than the original profit of \$25,000 and should be considered.

THE BREAK-EVEN CHART

Successful management requires an awareness of those relationships between costs and sales that determine profit or loss. A **break-even chart** can plot these relationships and help answer these and other questions:

- At what sales volume will the operation make money?
- What should the profit (or loss) be at a particular sales volume?
- How much should expenses be at a particular sales volume?
- How will changing menu selling prices (and, thereby, possibly changing the number of covers served) affect profit?
- Is it feasible to incur costs designed to increase sales, such as additional advertising?
- Should the operation expand (or even begin)?

A break-even chart shows in graphic form the relationship between the volume of business produced (that is, the number of meals) and the resulting sales income, expenditures, and profits or losses. In doing so, it shows at what sales volume the operation will cover expenses and begin making a profit. It can portray the anticipated effect of menu price changes. It could help determine whether higher menu prices would more than offset a predicted lower customer volume (or number of sales), or whether lower menu prices could be balanced by a customer increase.

Sales and cost categories are shown in graphic form on a break-even chart. The chart can be a visual and variable budget. It allows managers to see preplanned costs for any volume. By indicating profits along with sales, it encourages concentration on both components. Potential financial troubles may be revealed before they are incurred, allowing action to be taken before the difficulty arises rather than after it has eaten into profits. The portrayal of costs and sales in graphic form makes it easier for some to assimilate the information than if it had been presented in conventional tabular or statistical form. A break-even chart may be used to illustrate past performance, or it may be prepared as a budget or a forecast of future performance.

PREPARING A BREAK-EVEN CHART

The format for a break-even chart is an *L*-shaped graph. Usually, the vertical line on the left is used to indicate dollar amounts, and the horizontal bottom line indicates the number of units or meals. For example, 1,000 meals sold at an average price of \$10.00 would be plotted at the point where lines running perpendicular to the bottom scale mark of 1,000 and perpendicular to the side figure of $10,000 converge (point *B* in Figure 24.1).

In preparing the chart, one must classify costs as either fixed or variable. The fixed costs remain constant regardless of volume. These might include items such as rent and insurance. Variable costs such as food costs or linens vary more or less directly with volume. Some costs may be semivariable since they fluctuate with volume, but not in direct proportion to the volume change. Labor may be a semivariable cost because a certain basic staff is always required and rather resembles a fixed cost. However, as volume increases, more staff is needed, although a 50 percent increase in volume would probably not require a 50 percent increase in personnel. In the break-even chart, fixed personnel costs would be in fixed expenses and the variables plotted as closely as possible with variable costs.

Except in the case of fixed costs where an unchanging dollar amount regardless of volume can be plotted, it is necessary to have two or more points to draw sales and cost lines on the chart. Of course, a straight line may be drawn between two points. But if more points that do not fit on a straight line are included, a line may be drawn that represents the points, even though it does not quite intersect them. If enough points are plotted, curves may be drawn. If changes at specific volumes are unusually sharp, a staggered or plateau-type plot may be used. For illustrative purposes, consider an operation that has an average charge of $10.00 per meal and is presently serving 800 meals at a daily profit of $450. The following information is given for two levels of activity on a daily basis. (The percentages represent percentage of sales.)

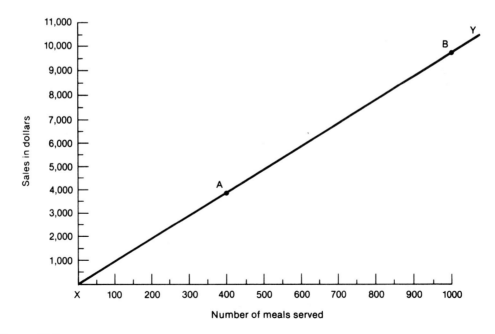

Figure 24.1
Plotting a Sales Line

	Low volume	High volume
Number of meals sold	400	1,000
Income at $10.00 per meal	$ 4,000	$ 10,000
Fixed charges	$ 1,000	$ 1,000
General administrative	$ 800 (20%)	$1,600 (16%)
Food cost	$1,400 (35%)	$3,500 (35%)
Labor cost	$1,400 (35%)	$3,000 (30%)
Profit (or loss)	$ (600)	$ 900

Using these figures, one can easily determine that the operation will lose about $600 at the low volume and will earn about $900 at the higher volume. With a break-even chart, it is possible to determine what the profit or loss would be at any level and what the various expense categories should cost for any level of activity.

The sales figure is found by plotting the low-point sales of 400 meals on the bottom scale and $4,000 on the side scale (point *A* of Figure 24.1). The high-volume point is plotted at 1,000 meals and $10.00 (point *B*). The sales line or curve, then, is line *YX*.

The fixed expense of $1,000 would be a horizontal line at the $1,000 mark, since it does not vary with volume (line *CD* of Figure 24.2). (Daily fixed expenses are found by dividing the total fixed expenses for the year by the number of days of operation.)

General administration expenses of $800 (at 400 meals volume) and $1,600 (at 1,000 meals volume) are added to the fixed cost, making total costs so far $1,800 and $2,600 for

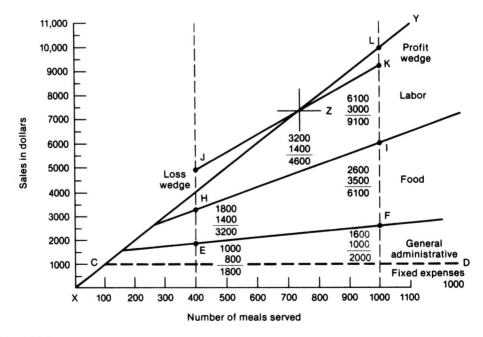

Figure 24.2
Showing Profit or Loss

their respective volumes. These points are plotted, allowing line *EF* to be drawn. Food costs of $1,400 and $3,500 are added to the cost totals accumulated so far, making new totals of $3,200 and $6,100 (line *HI*). Labor costs are then added, making new totals of $4,600 and $9,100 and line *JK*, which is also the total expense line. The point where the line crosses the sales line, at 750 meals and $7,500 sales volume, is the break-even point (point *Z*). The wedge to the left of the point shows the loss at any level of volume, and the profit may be read at any volume to the right of the point. A break-even chart can be prepared on a daily or any other basis to show what volume is necessary to produce a profit and what the costs should be at any volume.

A 10 percent increase in selling prices is being considered. However, it is expected that the number of covers sold will drop by 5 percent as the price increases. Is the proposed increase feasible? A 10 percent menu increase would make the average check $11.00; at 400 covers, sales would be $4,400 (point *A* of Figure 24.3) and $11,000 at 1,000 covers (point *B*), or line *XY*. Total costs, line *JK*, remain the same. If the 800 daily covers are reduced 5 percent because of the price increase, the new average number of covers would be 760. The profit at 760 covers (wedge *Q-R*) is $1,100, a very desirable increase over the former $450 profit.

Assume that the operation is still serving 800 meals with a profit of $450, the horizontal difference between line *XY* and line *JK* read off perpendicularly on the left-hand side on Figure 24.2. What greater sales volume would be required to allow a menu selling price reduction of 5 percent but to still maintain the $450 profit? The average price per cover is now $9.50. Four hundred covers would produce sales of $3,800 (point *A* of Figure 24.4) at

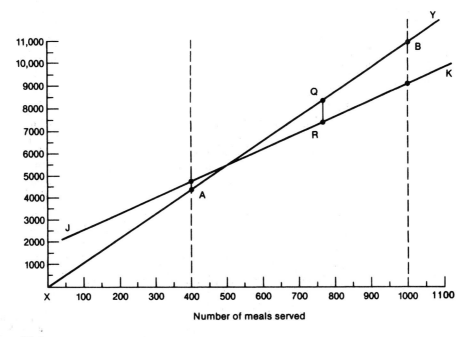

Figure 24.3
Effect of 10 Percent Menu Selling Price Increase

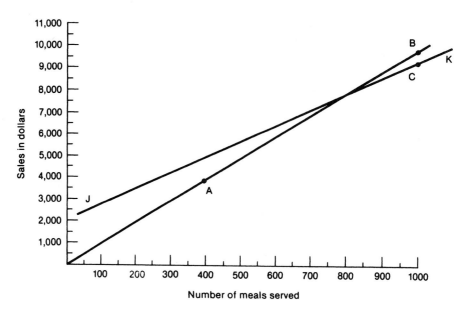

Figure 24.4
Effect of Lower Selling Price

the low volume, and $9,500 at 1,000 covers (point *B*). The chart shows that about 1,000 meals (or a gross of $9,500) instead of 800 meals (a gross of $1,600) would need to be achieved (wedge *B-C*) for a $450 profit (the reading between income and cost lines) with the lower selling price.

The charts may be prepared for a day, a week, a month, a year, or for any other period. A yearly break-even chart may be very helpful in determining the feasibility of expanding the operation, or projected figures may be used in planning the feasibility of a new operation.

DISADVANTAGES OF BREAK-EVEN ANALYSIS

Break-even analysis can be a helpful tool in analyzing the volume-cost-profit relationship. It can also portray the information in a very desirable graphic form. However, foodservice managers should be aware of some complicating factors.

A break-even chart is most effective for one product. The menu of a foodservice establishment usually contains many items or products. The markups and profit percentages of these various items may vary considerably, making it difficult to apply a general price increase or decrease to the whole menu, since the same adjustments would probably not be made for each item. To overcome this, it is possible to consider weighted or average changes in break-even calculations. It is also possible to use a break-even analysis for a major menu item. If a steak selection, for example, is one of your major sales items, break-even analysis could be used to determine the optimum selling price. Of course, managers would need to make assumptions for the proportion of fixed and other expenses that should be allotted to the steak sales.

Another complication in using break-even charts is the relevant range of the data portrayed. Straight lines, if used, extend from the vertical axis to the opposite edge. These may be misleading, especially for variable costs, since the cost line may not have the same unit cost-times-volume relationship over the whole length of the line. At different volumes, the unit costs may change due to different use of resources. Different unit costs at different volumes cannot be reflected in a straight line. Curves or staggered lines may then be used to show this information if supporting data is available.

Because of the nature of its construction, a break-even chart cannot provide exact information. It is helpful as a first step in developing the basic data for pricing or other financial decision making. Before the final decisions are made, however, other analyses should also be employed.

SUMMARY

The relationships between volume, costs, and profits can be expressed graphically on a break-even chart. Such a chart can be used for decision making, for determining what costs or profits should be at various volumes, and to anticipate the effect of menu price changes. Also involved is the contribution to overhead and profit. Once the contribution ratio is determined, it is possible to calculate at what volume of meals or dollar sales an operation will break even or produce a desired profit.

KEY TERMS

break-even chart
break-even point

contribution rate

REVIEW QUESTIONS

24–1 Provide three formulas to find the break-even point.
24–2 What is a break-even chart?
24–3 What questions can a break-even chart answer?

24–4 What are disadvantages of using break-even analysis?
24–5 Define *contribution margin*.

PROBLEMS

24–1 Using the following data, prepare a bar chart.

	Low Volume	High Volume
Number of meals sold	3,000	9,000
Average price per meal	$ 20.00	$ 20.00
Fixed charges	$40,000	$40,000
General and administrative	10%	16%
Labor cost	36%	33%
Food cost	38%	36%

a. What is the profit (or loss) at low and high volumes?
b. What is the profit (or loss) at 8,000 meals?
c. Management is considering a 10 percent increase in menu prices. It estimates a 5 percent drop in volume. Compare the resulting profit and loss with the figure computed for the previous question, b.

24–2 The following data are provided for the Nittany Restaurant:

Sales	$800,000
Fixed Costs	240,000
Fixed Labor Costs	80,000
Variable Labor Costs	170,000
Other Fixed Costs	110,000
Other Variable Costs	120,000
Number of Meals Served	80,000

a. What is the profit?
b. What is the contribution margin?
c. What is the contribution rate?
d. What is the variable rate?
e. What is the average cost per meal?

24–3 Using the data determined from 24–2,
a. Calculate the break-even point.
b. Because of a recession, management expects business covers to drop 10%. What is the estimated profit at this volume?
c. If some other developments in the area occur, business covers could increase by 10%. What would be the estimated profit if fixed costs remain the same?

d. Management is considering raising menu prices by 10% but feels this would decrease the number of meals served by 5%. Calculate if this is desirable.

24–4 Fixed expenses at the Happy Valley Restaurant are estimated to be $300,000. Variable expenses are 48% and a profit of $100,000 is desired. What sales must be generated to provide this profit?

24–5 An operation is increasing sales by $50,000. The CR is 40%. What should the additional profit be as fixed costs remain the same?

24–6 You are consulting with someone about starting a restaurant. A feasibility study estimates 60,000 meals will be served at an average of $5.00 per meal. Fixed costs should be $200,000 and variable costs about 60% of sales.
a. What is the break-even point?
b. How many meals would have to be sold to produce a $50,000 profit?

Glossary

A mode   Mode of a key lock on a POS cash register that allows transactions to be recorded.

Absenteeism ratio

$$\frac{(\text{Number of daily absences during period}) \times 100}{(\text{Average number of employees})}$$
$$\times$$
$$(\text{Number of working days})$$

Access control system   *See* privilege control system.

Accident incidence rate (AIR)

$$\frac{(\text{Number of accidents in period}) \times 200,000}{\text{Number of employee-hours worked in period}}$$

Accounting rate of return (ARR)   Comparing savings or additional income to the amount necessary to achieve these savings or income. Also called *anticipated rate of return* or *rate of return*.

Accounts receivable turnover   Total sales divided by average accounts receivable.

Acid test ratio   *See* quick ratio.

Actual-pricing method   All costs plus a desired profit are included to provide a menu selling price.

Advertising   The purchase of space, time, or printed matter to increase sales.

Á la carte   Each item served in a meal is priced separately.

Annuity   The promise of a definite payment for a specified period.

Anticipated rate of return

$$\frac{\text{Average additional income or savings generated by project (after taxes and depreciation)}}{\text{Average amount invested in project}}$$

Application (computer)   A discrete and identifiable program.

As purchased (AP)   The gross weight of a food item purchased before processing, which will reduce the weight to actual yield (or edible portion).

Balance sheet   A statement that portrays the financial condition of an enterprise at a particular point in time.

Bar charts   A graphic way of showing how employees are scheduled in relation to work loads or how busy they are.

Baseline budget   A budget based on a prior budget and adjusted for current conditions.

Base price method   A method of menu pricing in which optimum menu prices are decided and the amount that can be spent on raw food is then determined.

Basic marketing moves   The four basic moves that an operation can use to increase business volume.

Batching   Adjusting extended recipes for equipment or recipe size constraints.

Behavioral approach to organization   In the study of organized groups, emphasis on the individuals and groups involved rather than the work to be done.

Behavioristic approach to control   Control through workers' desire to perform for the best interests of the organization.

Benchmarking   Comparing an operation's features with the best of its competitors in the industry.

Blast chill system   A cook/chill system for nonpumpable foods that are blast chilled.

Blind receiving   Invoices have no quantities or weights, so the receiver must count or weigh.

Block scheduling   All workers on a shift start and stop at the same time.

Bottom up budget   Lower units prepare this budget and send to upper management for approval and combining.

Break-even chart   A chart that shows in graphic form the relationship between the volume of business produced and the resulting sales income, expenditures, and profits or losses.

Break-even point   Where income and costs are equal and the operation is not making or losing money.

British thermal unit (Btu)   The amount of heat required to raise 1 pound of water 1°F.

Budget   An organized plan of operation for a specified period of time that forecasts activity and income, determines expenses and other disposition of funds, and concludes with an estimate of an overall financial position at the end of the specified period.

Budget calendar   The dates that various phases of a budget should be completed.

Burglary   Unlawful entry to commit a felony.

Business interruption insurance   Insurance that covers specified costs when a business cannot operate as normal.

Business plan   A document that helps define the business concept, clarifies the goals of the operation, evaluates markets and competition, determines costs and capital needs, and enhances chances of success.

Call brand   A brand of liquor required by a customer.

Capacity management   Making optimum use of an operation's resources to serve the greatest number of patrons.

Capital budget   A budget of expenditures whose effects will continue for long periods of time. Usually for major equipment or facilities.

Capital costs   The long-term financing of an enterprise.

Cash budget   The amount of money received, the amount of money disbursed, and the resulting cash position.

Cash flow   Profit plus depreciation allowances.

Cash on delivery (COD)   Merchandise must be paid for on delivery or previous to delivery.

Cathode ray tube (CRT)   An output terminal with a digital display.

Central processing unit (CPU)   The program operating instructions and data storage capacity of a computer.

Chain of command   A principle of traditional organization dictating that every organization should have a top authority together with a clear line of authority from that top to each person in the organization. Also called the *scalar principle.*

Classical administration theory   Concerned with the organizational structure of an enterprise and the basic functions of management within the organization.

Classical principles (or theory) of organization   An approach to the study of organization that focuses on enterprise structure and work allocation.

Classification ranking system   Establishing grades and categories to rank various jobs.

Closed loop system   Data is only communicated internally between network computers.

Coinsurance clause   A requirement in a fire insurance policy that a minimum percentage of the insurable value of a property be covered by insurance purchased to receive full policy reimbursement.

Committed item   A product that is scheduled for production between the time an order is placed and the product is received.

Common size analysis   Analysis of financial statements by dividing each item on two or more statements by the total revenue for the period.

Company-wide quality control (CWQC)   *See* total quality management.

Comparative analysis   Analysis by showing the dollar difference of line items on financial statements for two or more financial periods (income statement) or two or more financial dates (balance sheet) along with the percentage changes.

Concept blueprint   Macro or broad picture of a service system blueprint.

Consumer orientation   Basing management decisions on the needs of consumers.

Contract purchasing   An agreement with a purveyor to supply certain goods for a specified period of time, often at a determined price.

Contribution margin   Contribution to profit and overhead, or the excess of revenue of a product over the variable costs of producing it.

Contribution rate   The contribution margin in dollars divided by sales.

Control   Helping to ensure performance conforming to plans, objectives, and goals.

Controllable expenses   Expenses that are the direct responsibility of management and can be influenced and controlled by competent management and efficiency.

Cook/chill system   Cooking a food item to a "just-done" state, packaging it (above pasteurization temperature), and chilling it rapidly.

Co-op buying A group of similar operations that band together to secure, through mass purchasing, quantity discount prices.

Cost-benefit analysis The cost of producing a unit of effect within a given program expressed in monetary terms.

Cost-effectiveness analysis Identifying the cost of producing a unit of effect within a given program in nonmonetary terms.

Cost-plus buying An agreement is made between a customer and a purveyor that the purveyor will buy certain items for the customer and charge a specified percentage or amount over cost.

Cost of sales The cost of food used in a foodservice operation.

CPA (certified public accountant) An accountant who has fulfilled certain requirements and adheres to rules and regulations prescribed by the American Institute of Certified Public Accountants.

Current asset Cash or an asset capable of being turned into cash, such as accounts receivable or inventory.

Current liability An obligation that will become due within a year.

Current ratio Current assets divided by current liabilities. A measure of liquidity.

Customer queuing Feeding customers into an operation at a rate management desires.

Cyclical menu A menu that is repeated in a regular cycle.

Data Facts or concepts suitable for processing by a computer.

Database A comprehensive file containing information in a format applicable for a user's needs and available when needed.

Data input Obtaining data for a foodservice management information system.

Dead-bolt lock A lock bolt that is moved positively by turning the knob without the action of a spring.

Debit card A card encoded with a cash balance that can be used in a vending or other electronically controlled device.

Decision making Choosing the best course of action between possible alternatives.

Deep-pockets theory Including in a legal suit organizations that may have more resources or deeper pockets.

Defined-benefit plan Employees receive specified benefits from the employer during retirement (as opposed to defined contribution).

Defined-contribution plan The employer agrees to make specified contributions to an employee's pension plan but does not guarantee the amount of the pension.

Degree day The difference between outside temperature and 65° F.

Delegation The distribution of authority and responsibility downward through an organization.

Demand charge The part of an electrical rate that covers the cost of having the capacity to meet peak demands.

Deming, W. Edwards Developer of total quality management (TQM) concept.

Demographics The statistical study of human populations, with particular regard to density and distribution.

Demographic segmentation Segmentation based on human population variables such as age, gender, family size, etc.

Depreciation The systematic and rational means by which the costs associated with the acquisition and installation of an asset are allocated over the estimated useful life of the asset.

Differential (beverage) The difference of the sales value of a particular drink from the standard sales value of beverages used.

Direct costs (food) Costs associated with direct purchases. *See also* direct purchases.

Directing Explaining to others what has to be done and then helping them do it.

Direct method (cash flow) Principal components are operating cash receipts and payments, such as cash received from customers and cash paid to suppliers and employees, the sum of which is net cash flow from operating activities.

Direct operating expenses Costs directly involved in service to the customer, such as laundry and china.

Direct purchases Food that is delivered directly into the kitchen and is charged as a food cost on the day received.

Direct routing (insurance) Insurance sold directly through employees of the insurance company who do not handle other companies.

Dogs In menu engineering, a classification of items that are not profitable or popular.

Double-walled hood A ventilation hood that uses a separate supply of untempered makeup air and introduces this air at the perimeter of the exhaust hood.

Dram shop liability Responsibility of an establishment that serves alcoholic beverages for the actions of patrons after they leave the premises.

Earnings per share Earnings of a company divided by the number of its stock shares outstanding.

Earnings ratio The net profit before taxes divided by net sales. Also called *operating margin, operating ratio,* or *profit ratio.*

Economic order quantity (EOQ) A formula that determines a purchase quantity that has the best mix of minimizing purchase and inventory costs.

Economic person concept A theory that money is the prime motivator.

Economy study Comparative financial analyses of the financial factors of two or more alternative programs.

Edible portions (EP) The actual yield available for processing a food item.

80/20 rule Eighty percent of the value comes from 20 percent of the resources.

Elasticity of demand The rate at which demand for a product can fluctuate in response to other factors.

Electronic cash register (ECR) A cash register with electronic rather than mechanical parts.

Electronic data interchange (EDI) Allowing a foodservice operator to receive a supplier's prices electronically and generate an order form to send back.

Electronic spreadsheet Computerized equivalent of an accountant's worksheet that consists of vertical and horizontal columns that can readily be manipulated.

Embezzlement The fraudulent appropriation of property by someone to whom it has been entrusted.

Employee assistance program (EAP) A program promoted by employers to help employees overcome alcoholism or drug abuse.

Empowerment Allowing lower level employees the responsibility and authority to solve patron problems.

Entropy A lack of useful input that can solidify a system or cause it to run down.

Equifinality No single way to design a system to meet organizational goals.

Equity financing Financing by owners of the organization (as opposed to borrowed funds).

Exception principle An aspect of the principle of delegation. According to this principle, recurring decisions are handled in a routine, specific manner, and only unusual ones are referred upward for appropriate action.

Exploded recipe Changing recipe quantities to produce the number of portions required.

Exponential smoothing A moving average forecasting method that is most efficiently performed by a computer.

Extended coverage Insurance coverage beyond a basic fire policy. *See also* standard fire policy.

External environment Conditions, circumstances, organizations, and individuals with which a system must interact and to which it must react but cannot change.

Extra industry benchmarking Comparing your practices with other industries.

Extranet An intranet partially accessible to outsiders.

Factor-comparison system A ranking system that uses factors to rank employees with benchmark jobs used to rank the factors in other jobs.

Factor system A method of menu pricing where raw food cost is multiplied by a factor to determine a menu selling price.

Feedback The element of a system that signals a need for adjustments or exchanges in input and subsystems.

Felony A crime more serious than a misdemeanor.

FIFO (first in, first out) Used for pricing inventories and using old inventories first.

Firewalls A combination of hardware and software to keep unauthorized people from gaining entrance to a network.

Fixed budget Figures based on a definite level of activity.

Fixed employees Employees who are necessary regardless of the volume of business.

Flexible capacity strategy Handling varying volumes of business without having high overhead costs all the time.

Flex plan A plan giving employees some choice regarding fringe benefits. Also called *cafeteria plan.*

Food-cost percentage Cost of food divided by sales from that food.

Food ingredient data base A file that contains basic information about each food item, such as name, costs, purchase units, inventory units, issue units, vendors, and conversion factors. Also called *inventory file.*

Food item data file (FIDF) number The number under which a food item is filed in a database.

Foodservice delivery system The system employed to provide food to customers after preparation.

Foodservice management information system (FMIS) *See* management information system (MIS).

Forecast method (of food purchasing) Purchasing based on forecast consumption quantities (rather than past usage).

Four Cs of credit The basis on which loans are made: character, capital, collateral, and the capacity to repay.

Fourteen points Fourteen points enumerated by Dr. W. Edwards Deming as necessary for a total quality management program.

Franchise A privilege or right granted to another. In hospitality operations, a franchise grants the right to use a name, methods, product, and so forth, in return for franchise fees.

Franchisee The person or organization acquiring the right to use the franchise obtained from the franchisor.

Franchisor The person or company selling the franchise.

Freezer burn Fat under the surface of a food item becomes rancid and causes a brown deterioration.

Full-time equivalents (FTEs) Translating the number of part-time workers into the number required if all would be working full time.

Fundamental equation Assets = Liabilities + Equity.

Grazing Eating throughout the day rather than having only three meals. Also employees consuming unauthorized food.

Gross cost The cost of food consumed.

Gross profit Profit after deducting the cost of food (for a restaurant) from sales.

Gross-profit method A method of menu pricing where the gross profit per customer is added to the raw food cost to provide a menu selling price.

Hardware The physical components of a computer system.

Hard water Water containing excessive calcium and magnesium salts.

Hawthorne experiments A forerunner of human relations approach. Showed that motivation need not be primarily financial.

Health maintenance organization (HMO) Health providers that provide medical care using their own physicians and facilities.

Homogeneous assignment A form of specialization that either assigns an employee to one job or limits the employee to closely related tasks.

House brand The brand of a liquor normally served by a bar. Also called *well brand*.

Hurdle rate Acceptable ratio of popularity in menu engineering.

HVAC Heating, ventilation, and air conditioning.

Importance/performance analysis (IPA) Plotting on a grid the importance of an attribute of foodservice as well as the performance of the operation in satisfying this attribute.

Inactivity ratio (absenteeism)

$$\frac{\text{Number of hours of absenteeism}}{\text{Number of hours worked in a period}}$$

Incidence ratio (absenteeism)

$$\frac{\text{Number of employees absent}}{\text{Total number of employees}} \times 100$$

Income statement *See* statement of income.

Incremental cost The difference in cost between one alternative and another.

Indirect method (cash flow) Starts with net income and adjusts it for revenue and expense items that were not the result of operating cash transactions in the current period to reconcile to cash flow from operating activities.

Ingredient room A concept where pre-preparation is done by noncooking personnel before the food is sent to cooking personnel.

Input Resources available to a system. These can include men (personnel), machines, methods, money, markets, and materials.

Insurance Trading the possibility of a loss for the certainty of reimbursement for a certain but small cost called a *premium*.

Insurance adjuster An employee or agent of an insurance company who determines the amount of a loss from the insurer's side or determines insurable values.

Insurance broker One who represents the insured rather than the insuring company.

Integrated beverage control system An automatic beverage dispensing system integrated with a computer or point-of-sale register.

Internal control The plan of organization and of the coordinate methods and measures adopted within a business to safeguard its assets, check the accuracy and reliability of its accounting data, promote operational efficiency, and encourage adherence to management policies.

Internal environment   Forces from within an organization (as opposed to external environment) that affect its operation.

Internal rate of return (IRR)   The compound rate of return (discount rate) that equates the present value of the initial outlay and the future cash benefits from a capital investment project.

Internet   A public communications system that allows computers to communicate with each other.

Intranet   A private computer network accessed via the Internet, local area network, or wide area network.

Inventory control method (beverage)   The amount of beverage used is determined from guest checks and reconciled with replacement requisitions.

Inventory file   *See* food ingredient database.

Inventory turnover   The number of times inventory turns over during a period, or dividing a value for the inventory into the cost of food or beverage consumed during the period.

Inventory variance accounting   The number of actual sales of a food item is compared with the number used from inventory records, and the variance is noted.

Job analysis   A job description and job specifications.

Job description   A description of the tasks and duties performed on a job.

Job evaluation   The process of investigating the facts concerning the operation and responsibilities of a job.

Job number control list   A number for each job (and employee) with a job description and specification for each numbered job.

Job specifications   The qualifications one has to have to hold a job, including educational, physical, mental, and age requirements.

Joint and several liability   More than one party having liability for the actions of one such as a bar for the actions of an intoxicated patron.

Kitchenless kitchens   Using foods mainly prepared elsewhere and reconstituting them at the operation.

Kleptomania   An abnormal and persistent impulse to steal.

Lapping   A form of embezzlement in which funds are withdrawn from an account and covered with later receipts.

Latent heat   Heat in the water vapor in the air.

Legitimate power   Power from assigned responsibility.

Leveraging   Using borrowed money to acquire assets to make money.

Line of implementation   Separates planning and organizing activities from "doing" activities.

Line of interaction   Demarcates actions performed by the customer from actions performed by contact personnel in a service blueprint.

Line of visibility   Separates onstage from backstage actions in a service blueprint.

Liquidity ratios   Ratios that show an organization's ability to meet its short-term obligations.

Local area network (LAN)   Series of computers linked together in a closed loop system.

Long-term debt   Obligations not due to be paid within a year. Also called *fixed liabilities*.

Loss control   An attempt at preventing losses.

Management information system (MIS)   A system of regular or irregular data collection, selection, storage, and dissemination processes and applications.

Management proficiency ratio   Net profit after taxes divided by total assets.

Market price index   A market cost index that can be used to show the general change in the cost of raw foods.

Market share   The share of a market that a business has for its product or service.

Marketing   Those business activities involved in the flow of goods and services from producers to customers.

Marketing mix   The combination of activities and elements used to attract customers. These include merchandising strategy, pricing, brand name, channels of distribution, personal selling, advertising, promotion, and service.

Marketing segmentation   Definite customer groups with definable needs and interests. A market segment must be definable, sizeable, and available.

MBWA   Management by walking around.

Meat tag   A tag attached to an individual meat item for control purposes.

Menu engineering   A technique to analyze menu items in terms of popularity (*MM*) and profitability (*CM*).

Menu mix   Consumer demand or popularity in menu engineering.

Menu preference forecasting Predicts how various menu items will sell, especially when in competition with other menu items.

Menu scoring A technique to compare one menu of an organization with other menus of the same organization in terms of profitability and popularity.

Mission statement A statement providing the reason for an organization to exist and what sets it apart from other organizations.

Modern organization theory A behavioral approach to organization.

Module A discrete and identifiable program.

Moving average Dividing the total of demand in previous periods by the number of periods. Used in forecasting.

Municipal solid waste (MSW) Waste products deposited in landfills.

Net present value (NPV) The present value of future returns discounted at the appropriate cost of capital minus the cost of the investment.

Objectives Ideas or statements that help steer the activities of an organization toward the attainment of its goals.

One-stop purchasing A concept involving a purveyor's handling a wide variety of products so that a customer does not have to go elsewhere and the customer's calling orders in rather than having them taken by salespeople.

Open department register keys Cash register keys that break down sales by categories such as appetizers, entrées, and desserts.

Open market buying A method of food purchasing where competitive bids are secured for the various items.

Operating budget Forecasts level of activity and develops the costs necessary to support this level of activity.

Operating margin *See* earnings ratio.

Operating ratio Net profit divided by net sales. Also called *earnings ratio, operating margin,* or *profit ratio.*

Opportunity costs Costs of the profit forgone when an opportunity is rejected.

Optics An inverted beverage bottle dispenser that releases a predetermined measured amount.

Organizational chart A graphic form that shows the relationships of jobs to each other, and lines of authority, responsibility, and communication.

Organizing Determining what tasks and skills are necessary to achieve chosen objectives and allocating resources to achieve the objectives.

Output The end product or goals of a system.

Outsourcing Having other firms help supply your products.

Overhead-contribution method A method of menu pricing where all nonfood-cost percentages are subtracted from 100. The resulting figure is divided into 100, and that figure times the raw food cost equals the menu selling price.

Parkinson's law Workers adjust their pace to the work available to be done.

Par stock A standard inventory quantity is determined and replacement issues maintain this par.

Payback period The time period required to recover an expenditure, or

$$\frac{\text{Cash or cash outlay for project}}{\begin{array}{c}\text{Annual net income (or savings) from project}\\ \text{before depreciation but after taxes}\end{array}}$$

Percentage control system Costs (usually food or beverage) are divided by sales to provide a percentage. The closeness of the actual percentage to a desired one is the control.

Perception of value What a consumer feels a product is worth.

Perpetual inventory A running inventory count is kept of items.

Physical inventory Physically counting inventory items.

Plow horses In menu engineering, a classification of items that are popular but not particularly profitable.

Plug-and-play capability Different hardware and software elements can recognize each other and communicate with each other so a user can "plug" in one application to another.

Point-of-sale (POS) register A minicomputer that in processing sales transactions at the time of sale can store the data received through transactional keys and manipulate this data to provide reports.

Point-of-sale (POS) terminal A data input device close to the customer or where sale is made.

Point ranking system A system that assigns points for significant factors in ranking a job.

Point-to-point tunneling protocol A dedicated internet connection that allows for continued communications.

Popularity index The total sales of an item in numbers or in dollars divided by total number of that type of item sold or total dollar sales of that type of item.

Post-cost analysis   Entering actual customer counts and menu items prepared into a computer that provides detailed consolidation and summaries of daily production results. It also compares forecasted and actual results.

PPBSE   Planning, programming, budgeting, staffing, and evaluating.

Prechecking system   A system where an independent record is maintained of what is ordered from a kitchen.

Precost-precontrol   A food cost accounting system that determines what the food cost should be, compares it with the actual food cost, and includes sales analysis.

Preferred provider organizations (PPOs)   Employers or insurers that make contracts with health providers that agree to charge less in return for access to the group.

Preventive maintenance   Work performed to an operational device or facility to continue its operation at its proper efficiency without interruption.

Price look-up key (PLU)   A cash register key that can track and break down sales of a number of items.

Prime costs   Food and labor costs.

Prime-cost system   A system of menu pricing where the raw food cost and direct labor cost are multiplied by a factor to provide a menu selling price.

Privilege control system   A system that can permit or deny access to restricted areas, verify dining privileges, and provide billing information for foodservice operations. Also called *access control system*.

Procurement planning   Long-range planning in procurement of food products.

Production schedule   What food items and what quantities must be produced for a specific meal, day, or other period.

Profit-and-loss statement   *See* statement of income.

Profit ratio   *See* earnings ratio.

Pro forma   A statement prepared on the basis of anticipated results.

Psychographic segmentation   Market segmentation based on lifestyles.

Puzzles   In menu engineering, a classification of items that are profitable but not popular.

Qualitative forecasting   Forecasts made using non-historical data such as current and industry trends, experience, and intuition.

Quality control   Getting it right the first time, every time.

Quantitative forecasting   Forecasting based on past and present numerical data.

Quantitative methods   Using numbers to help make decisions.

Quick ratio   Current assets less inventory value divided by current liabilities. Also called *acid test ratio*.

Rabble hypothesis   Industrial workers are a disorganized rabble of individuals, each acting in his or her own self interest.

Random walk   Assuming a present period of sales will be the same as a similar past period.

Rate-of-return method   Comparing savings or additional income to the amount necessary to achieve these savings or income. Often called *accounting* or *anticipated rate of return*.

Ratio analysis   Ratios separated into different classifications or formulas, such as liquidity, solvency, activity, operating, and profitability.

Receiving clerk's daily report   A form that shows quantity and value of food items received from various purveyors.

Red lining   Putting a red mark on a guest check so it cannot be used again.

Reengineering   An approach to change an enterprise to be more customer oriented or more efficient.

Regression   A statistical technique used in forecasting that can utilize both historical and non historical data.

Residual income analysis (RIA)   The return on an investment compared to the cost of invested capital.

Return on investment   A ratio found by dividing profit by investment.

RFP   Request for proposal.

Risk avoidance   *See* risk management.

Risk management   Methods to handle possible risk including risk avoidance, risk retention, risk transfer, loss control, and insurance.

Risk retention   *See* risk management.

Robbery   Stealing or taking anything of value by force or violence, or by the use of fear.

Sales mix   Analysis of the number or quantity of the different food items sold.

Scheduling   Assigning workers to work specific hours or days.

Sealed bid buying   Purveyors submit sealed bids, with the lowest one receiving the order.

Semivariable employees Employees whose time requirements vary, but not in direct proportion to changes in business volume.

Sensible heat Heat measured by a thermometer.

Service system blueprint Shows the pattern of service and steps involved.

Severity ratio A ratio measuring the length or severity of the average absence.

Shrinkage (inventory) The difference between what is on hand and what should be on hand based on purchases and issues.

Simple ranking system Ranking jobs in order of difficulty or importance.

Smart card A credit card with a computer chip embedded in it to house data.

Smoothing constant An alpha or dynamic trend predictor used in exponential smoothing.

Smoothing demand strategy Encouraging patrons to come at nonpeak periods.

Social approach to management An approach that considers management's responsibility to employees, customers, and the community in addition to its stockholders.

Software The programming components of a computer system.

Solvency ratios Ratios that show how well an organization can meet its long-term debt obligations.

Span of information The number of people reporting to a supervisor is not as important as the amount of information that must be processed.

Staffing Having an appropriate group of workers available.

Staggered scheduling Employees on a shift do not start and stop at the same time but are scheduled according to the work pattern.

Standard-cost method (beverage) Determines what the cost of beverages should be from the number of each beverage sold and compares it to the cost of beverage requisitions.

Standard-cost system (food-cost accounting) A food-cost accounting system that compares actual food costs with precalculated ones.

Standard fire policy A policy used to insure against loss from fire, lightning, and goods that were temporarily removed from the premises because of the fire.

Standard recipe A definite formula of amounts and procedures to produce a particular food (or drink) item.

Standard-sales method (beverage) The sales value of the beverage issues is compared with actual beverage sales.

Standing order An order for delivery that is automatic and not changed often.

Stars In menu engineering, a classification of items that are both profitable and popular.

Statement of income A statement that shows whether an operation has made or lost money over a certain period. Also called *income statement* or *profit-and-loss statement*.

Static menu A menu that rarely changes.

Steward's market order sheet Printed lists of foods purchased and spaces for different purveyors' quotes. Also called *steward's quotation sheet* or *purchase order sheet*.

Storeroom purchases Food that is put into storage upon receipt rather than sent to the kitchen.

Stores (food cost) The value of food that is obtained from storage.

Strategic benchmarking Compares financial performance in TQM programs.

Subsystems The processes or components in a system necessary to change system resources into system goals or output.

Sundries Nonfood items received in the food receiving unit.

Sunk costs Costs that have already been incurred and cannot be recouped by a new decision or alternative.

System A group of components working together toward a goal in the most efficient way possible.

Table d'hôte A complete meal at one price.

Tender keys Cash register keys that break down sales by method of payment, such as credit card, check, or cash.

Texas Restaurant Association method A menu pricing method that includes all costs and a varying profit markup to determine the menu selling price.

Therm 100,000 Btu.

Time series Quantitative models for predicting the future based on the assumption that the future is related to past data.

Time value of money The earning power of money over a period of time, the value of a present sum of money in the future, or the value of a future sum in present dollars.

Tipping fee Cost of disposing of waste at a landfill.

Top down budget   A budget prepared by upper management and "passed down" to operating units.

Total quality control (TQC)   *See* total quality management.

Total quality management (TQM)   An approach to management that stresses quality rather than objectives, worker involvement, and cutting costs by "getting it right the first time." Also called *total quality control* and *company-wide quality control.*

Total shopping capability   Purveyors supply a complete list of food items and other equipment.

Traditional control theory   A theory that relies on measurement and comparison of performance with goals and the use of direction.

Tumble chill system   Pumpable foods prepared with steam kettles and rapidly chilled.

Turnover rate

$$T\text{ (Separation rate)} = \frac{S\text{ (Number of separations)}}{M\text{ (Mid-month workforce)}} \times 100$$

Uniform product code (UPC)   A computer readable code on a package.

Uniform System of Accounts for Restaurants   A carefully specified system of accounts for various types of restaurants that allows easy comparison with published figures. (There are also uniform systems for hotels, hospitals, and clubs.)

Unity of command   A management principle stating that an employee should take orders from only one supervisor.

Usage method (of food purchasing)   Food is purchased based on past consumption rather than forecast consumption.

Value analysis   Determining the best value in services and features for the price obtained.

Variable employees   Workers whose time requirements change directly with changes in business volume.

Variable rate   Variable costs divided by sales.

Voice recognition technology   Allows a computer to recognize the spoken word, eliminating the need to have a person manually enter data.

Wage and salary administration   Determination of the proper wage for a job or employee in comparison with other jobs or employees.

Warehouse-club buying   A purchasing method whereby a foodservice operator obtains a membership to purchase smaller quantities at prices usually available only for large quantities.

Well brand   *See* house brand.

Wide area network (WAN)   A series of LANs linked to each other and communicating over a private network.

Work production standards   A gauge to measure what is expected from an employee or position, or the desired output (usually in dollar sales or covers served) from a labor impact.

Work simplification   Studying and analyzing a job or task to find the easiest and most productive way to perform it.

Workday   Eight hours of a job category.

Working capital   The difference between current assets and current liabilities.

X mode   This mode allows reports to be produced on the POS register without resetting totals.

Yield conversion factors   A factor that when multiplied by the gross-weight amount of an item purchased shows how much will actually be available.

Z mode   This mode produces final reports and clears information from a POS register.

Zero-based budget   A budget prepared without using previous budget figures.

Index